A NEW HISTORY OF THE ISLE OF MAN

Volume 3

The Medieval Period, 1000–1406

Published volumes:
Volume 1 Evolution of the Natural Landscape
Volume 5 The Modern Period

Forthcoming volumes:
Volume 2 Prehistory
Volume 4 Derby and Atholl Periods, 1405–1830

A NEW HISTORY OF THE ISLE OF MAN

Volume 3

The Medieval Period 1000–1406

Edited by

SEÁN DUFFY AND HAROLD MYTUM

Liverpool University Press

First published 2015 by
LIVERPOOL UNIVERSITY PRESS
Liverpool L69 7ZU

British Library Cataloguing-in-Publication data
A British Library CIP record is available

ISBN 978-0-853236-177 (hardback)
ISBN 978-0-853236-276 (paperback)

Typeset in 10½/12½pt Sabon by XL Publishing Services, Exmouth
Printed and bound by CPI Group (UK) Ltd, Croydon, CR0 4YY

Contents

Preface

The New History of the Isle of Man is an important initiative, placing the Island within modern scholarship through the contribution of a large number of researchers. Some are based on the Island, but many are international experts from across the globe. The task of co-ordinating such a project has fallen on a number of shoulders, and Volume 3, covering the Middle Ages, was largely initiated and initially edited by Seán Duffy. For a number of reasons, however, the final stages of editing and production stalled. After Peter Davey had kindly prepared a draft bibliography, Harold Mytum took up the task of the final editing and steering the book through to publication. The volume was largely competed a number of years ago, and whilst authors have had the opportunity of updating footnotes, the main text largely stands. The editors wish to express their thanks to the authors for their forbearance over the unforeseen interruption in production. Nevertheless, the volume still reflects the current state of knowledge across a wide range of disciplines, and brings together perspectives in social and economic history, archaeology, numismatics, language and literature, and place names. After a hiatus in the production of the New History series, it is anticipated that the appearance of this volume will herald a regular production of the remaining volumes.

This book is designed for popular and academic use, and each author has used the naming conventions appropriate for their discipline and academic setting. This has meant that many individuals and some places appear through the volume with a variety of names, represented in the many languages of the sources and indeed the people who inhabited the Isle of Man during the Middle Ages. Joshua Copeland very kindly compiled the index and names concordance, with advice from Andrew Hamer and staff at the University of Liverpool. The concordance should greatly assist readers in identifying the names in their various linguistic forms. We are grateful to Culture Vannin for a grant towards the production of the index and concordance.

This volume at last allows the character of the Isle of Man during the Middle Ages to be identified, evaluated, and interpreted using the critical approaches to sources required by twenty-first-century scholarship. It will ensure that those on the Island can better appreciate its complex past, and those elsewhere can understand the Island's place in the shifts of political and economic power within the western coastal areas of Europe.

HAROLD MYTUM

Names Concordance

Compiled by JOSHUA COPELAND

English/Old English	*Irish/Old Irish*	*Old Norse*	*Latin*
Alan	Ailean		
Alice			Alicia
Angus	Aengus/Óengus		
Athelred/Æthelraed			
Athelstan/Æthelstan			
Aud		Auðr	
Cnut		Knútr	
Donald	Domhnall/Domnall		Dom(p)naldus
Dougall	Dubhgall/Dubgall	Duggáll	
Duncan	Donnchad		
Edgar/Eadgar	Étgar		
Erik/Eric		Eiríkr	
Ewen	Eógan		
Gerald			Giraldus
Gilchrist	Gilla Críst	Gillikrist	
Godred/Godfred	Gofraid	Guðröðr	
Hakon		Hákon	
Harold	Aralt	Haraldr	
Hugh	Aed		
Ingimund		Ingimundr	
Ironknee	Glún Iairn	Iárnkné	
Ivar	Ímar	Ívarr	
John		Jón	
Kenneth	Cináed		
Lawspeaker	Lagman	Lögmaðr	
MacSorley	Mac Somairle		
Magnus		Magnús	
Malcolm	Máel Coluim		
Mary			Maria
Olaf	Amlaíb	Óláfr	
Phingola	Finnguala		
Reginald/Ragnald	Ragnall	Rögnvaldr	Reginaldus
Roolwer		Rolfr/Hrólfr	
Sigurd		Sigurðr	
Sitric/Sihtric	Sitriuc	Sigtryggr	
Somerled	Somhairle/Somairle	Sumarliði	

English/Old English	*Irish/Old Irish*	*Old Norse*	*Latin*
Sverre		Sverrir	
Sweyn		Sveinn	
Thorkell	Torcall	Þorkell	
	Ascall	Áskell	
	Béthoc	Bjaðok	
	Muirchertach	Mýrkjartak	
	Néill	Njáll	

Contributors

MICHAEL J. BENNETT, Professor, School of Humanities, University of Tasmania, Australia

KRISTIN BORNHOLDT COLLINS, independent researcher

RUTH COSTAIN-RUSSELL, independent researcher

EDWARD J. COWAN, Professor, Department of History, University of Glasgow

BARBARA E. CRAWFORD, Honorary Reader, School of History, University of St. Andrews

P.J. DAVEY, Honorary Research Fellow, Centre for Manx Studies, University of Liverpool

DAVID DITCHBURN, Honorary Research Fellow, School of Divinity, History and Philosophy, University of Aberdeen

SEÁN DUFFY, Associate Professor, Department of History, Trinity College, Dublin

GILLIAN FELLOWS-JENSEN, Professor, Department of Name Research, University of Copenhagen, Denmark

BENJAMIN T. HUDSON, Professor, Department of History, Pennsylvania State University, USA

A.C.C. JOHNSON, Curator, Field Archaeology, Manx National Heritage

ANDREW MCDONALD, Associate Professor, Department of History, Brock University, St Catherine's, Canada

COLM MCNAMEE, independent researcher

CHARLES W. MACQUARRIE, Associate Professor, Department of English, California State University, Bakersfield, USA

HAROLD MYTUM, Professor of Archaeology and Director, Centre for Manx Studies, University of Liverpool

W. MARK ORMROD, Professor, Department of History, University of York

ROSEMARY POWER, independent researcher

R.L. THOMSON, independent researcher

TIM THORNTON, Pro Vice-Chancellor (Teaching and Learning), University of Huddersfield

BERNADETTE WILLIAMS, independent researcher

GARETH WILLIAMS, Numismatist, British Museum

ALEX WOOLF, School of History, University of St Andrews

Introduction – Setting the scene: Man at the turn of the millennium

DAVID M. WILSON

History cannot easily be divided into convenient slices. Even if a cataclysmic event supervenes some sort of survival invariably takes place. While the turn of the first millennium is in many ways a convenient date from which to provide a starting point for a new phase of Manx history, it would be untrue to say that it was in any way immediately meaningful. Certainly the year 1000 was not significant in Manx history in the way that the accession of the Stanleys to the regalities of Man in 1406 was significant. On the other hand there is a certain logic in choosing this date in that the eleventh century is a period when scholars can begin to discuss a new phase in the history of the island, a phase when the historical record can be more securely based on written sources. But the historian must always look over his shoulder. Many of the chapters in this volume of the *New History of the Isle of Man* of necessity look back to roots dealt with in the previous volume. The origins of the Manx language, for example, can only be postulated on the basis of a few casual references in histories and inscriptions which go back at least to the sixth century. Again, the medieval system of land assessment can only be properly understood in the light of putative early Norse and possibly earlier Celtic systems, however dimly discerned. In similar fashion the history recounted in the previous volume spills over into the eleventh century because it deals with the Viking Age, which, by common academic consent, terminates in the middle years of that century. It is essential in this context, for example, to link the silver coin hoards of the tenth century together with those of the eleventh century and to take into consideration in both volumes the extraordinary early Manx coinage.

By the year 1000 Scandinavian adventurers had been settled in the Isle of Man for about 100 years. In the rest of western Europe the Vikings were still a force to be reckoned with. In England the king, Æthelred, was being challenged by increasingly severe Norwegian and Danish raids and invasions and his English followers made a number of incursions into the Irish Sea. One of these, recorded in the Anglo-Saxon Chronicle under the year 1000, is sometimes said to be an attack on Man, but is more likely to refer to Anglesey *(þa geherergodon hi Monige – Mœnige* only appears in the derivative text E). In Ireland the great struggle for the kingship of Ireland had been initiated by Brian Bóruma (Boru), who by 1005 could with some justice claim to be king of all Ireland. The power of the Scandinavians, who controlled the major towns of Dublin, Wexford, Waterford and Cork and the surrounding areas, had by this time been largely broken, although they were a potent economic and cultural force in the country and their leaders (petty kings with Norse names) were to flit across the Manx scene for most of the century. To the north of Man were the people closest in cultural tradition to, and possibly in political contact with, the Norse settlers of Man – the inhabitants of the Western and Northern Isles of Scotland. This contact is particularly demonstrated, for example, in the furnishings of the early tenth-century Viking graves, which show remarkably common traits in both Man and the Isles.

In the island itself the Norse were now firmly settled as the dominant force. Their king seems to have played some part in the political and military structure of the countries surrounding the Irish Sea; sometimes bowing to Dublin, sometimes to England, and possibly sometimes to the powerful Earls of Orkney. The leader described in the Irish annals as *rí Innsi gall* (king of the islands of the foreigners) may refer to the Norse ruler of Man and the Hebrides, as almost certainly, did the entry in Florence of Worcester to a Maccus, king of many islands (*plurimarum rex insularum*), who acknowledged the overlordship of Edgar, King of England, in 974. As to the king himself, nothing is known of his seat, of his wealth or of his power, although the presence of a Manx mint between *c.* 1025 and *c.* 1065 might indicate royal pretension, or merely reflect the suzerainty of Man from Dublin.

The Vikings had first come to Man towards the end of the ninth century and had probably taken over many of the farms of the pre-existing population, perhaps even dividing the land into something approaching the estate structure seen in the later Middle Ages. The incomers retained their language and may even have imposed it on the natives of the island. For much of the tenth century runic inscriptions were written, in Old West Norse, on memorial stones to people with both Norse and Celtic names, indicating that the incomers had married into local families. Their linguistic influence over the Celts is illustrated by the fact that hardly any place-names of the pre-Viking period survived, although just sufficient evidence remains in other areas to postulate the survival of a Celtic (Goidelic) language alongside Norse through the Viking Age and beyond.

The native inhabitants of the island had quickly introduced the incomers to Christianity in the early tenth century – probably in a fairly relaxed fashion. Their conversion is best illustrated by the fact that they buried members of their community in graves furnished in pagan fashion in cemeteries made sacred by the presence of the Christian dead. That the pagan practice of accompanied burial gave way to burial in Christian fashion in pre-existing churchyards, either of keeills (small chapels) or monasteries, is best illustrated on St Patrick's Isle, at Peel, where there is a short intermittent period of pagan burial in an important and ancient Christian cemetery, which was later to become the burial ground of the cathedral of St German. For most of the tenth century the incomers raised Christian memorials decorated in part with Scandinavian ornament to commemorate their kinsmen. The runic inscriptions which occur on some of these stones provide a major source for the social history of the island in the Viking Age.

Of the organisation, structure and land-holding of the Church at the turn of the millennium we know nothing, although there are one or two indicators which would link the Church to Ireland, as, for example, the round tower of Irish form and presumably eleventh-century date on St Patrick's Isle. On the other hand, until the transfer of the see to the metropolitan authority of Nidaros (modern Trondheim) in 1154, the bishopric seems to have been mainly under the authority of York, and at least some of the first recorded medieval bishops have English names. It is assumed that there was a pre-Norse monastery at Maughold; a thesis supported by a number of inscriptions, one of which, of eighth- or ninth-century date, records the bringing of water to the site. Burials continued at Maughold during the Viking period, as is attested by sculptured memorial stones in Scandinavian taste, some with Norse runic inscriptions; but whether the monastic establishment survived the coming of the Scandinavians – and what was its form and tradition – is not known. Even more difficult to analyse are the remains on St Patrick's Isle. Sometimes considered to be a monastic site, it was certainly an important Christian centre and was, in all probability, a seat of political power in the Viking period. Excavation here has provided the only dated keeill-type building on the island; it seems to belong to the beginning of the eleventh century and could be earlier. The presence of the cathedral on the islet from the twelfth century onwards, alongside the later parish church of Kirk Patrick, the round tower mentioned above and the continuous run of burials from before the Norse period into the Middle Ages, suggest that this was an ecclesiastical centre of some importance and antiquity at the beginning of our period.

The English connection is important. At one point in the tenth century – in 974 – there is, as has been mentioned, a glimpse of apparent political control of the island from England. In that year a 'king of many islands' (a title which presumably subsumed the island of Man) had paid homage with other kings to the powerful English king Edgar by symbolically rowing him on the Dee at Chester. This political contact with England, which may even be documented in the seventh century, is underlined in other ways, particularly by the close parallels seen in the ornament of the memorial stones of the Manx Viking Age. These stones, which firmly demonstrate Scandinavian decorative detail, show no trace of Irish influence, but are quite clearly related to similar tenth-century memorials in north-west England, which was for much of the first half of the tenth century under Scandinavian control. It is possible that the Manx 'kingdom' drew closer to Ireland with the weakening of English power in the reigns of Edgar's successors (weakened by attacks of kings and chieftains from Denmark and Norway). The growing power of Dublin, economically at least, towards the end of the tenth century helped this process. Although it is clear that the Irish had contact and even influence in the island from at least the sixth century, this was much hyped by later chroniclers emphasising the importance of the Patrician tradition. Such influence is, however, only dimly discerned in the material culture and the almost invisible historical sources. Only in the eleventh century is there evidence that Ireland really impacted on the polity of Man, when kings with Norwegian names, clearly linked to Irish-Norse dynasties, began to take more substantial form in the history of the island. More concretely, the establishment of a mint in the island *c.*1025, with dies imported from Dublin, emphasises the Irish link.

The mint is one of the few indicators of the presence of a central power in Man in the eleventh century. There can be little doubt that this power was royal and that Man existed from the early tenth century onwards as an independent kingdom or a dependent sub-kingdom, for which the references in the Anglo-Saxon Chronicle and the Irish annals are important indicators. With such power came law and regulation, and it is likely, if not provable, that the Scandinavians introduced Norse law into the island. It is almost certain that the incomers established the annual national assembly, Tynwald. Here the king would settle civil and criminal cases in a manner familiar throughout the Viking world.

Man's links with the Scandinavian north cannot be underestimated. The chief seat of power for Scandinavian settlers in the west of Britain, after the collapse of the Danish polity in England, was located in Norway, either with its great earls or, in the late tenth and eleventh centuries, with the kings of a united Norway. Many settlers in the Northern and Western Isles looked directly back to their homes, families and chieftains in Norway; and the same must be true of Man. Halfway to Norway, the Earldom of Orkney was one of the most powerful political units within the Norwegian kingdom and had ambitions – occasionally fulfilled – in the southern islands. Direct expressions of Norwegian or Orcadian power, however, usually waned in the more southerly settlements as distance allowed the possibility of more independent, more potentially rewarding, action. This had been particularly true in the late ninth and early tenth centuries, when close relationships and enmities bound together or separated the Scandinavian kingdoms of York and Dublin. But it must also be true of the period after the collapse of the Scandiniavian kingdom of York, when Ireland became a vital element in the southern influence of Norway. The rulers of the Isle of Man were caught in the middle, both physically and politically. They could make alliances and break them according to their political power and nerve. Man could form a base for military, political and economic action in what was in reality a Norse sea, and the skilful and powerful rulers of the island (if there were any) could play both ends against the middle. In the eleventh century, as the political power of the Scandinavians waned in Ireland, at the same time their economic power developed. This is symbolised by the establishment of the Dublin mint in the 990s, but is most clearly demonstrated in the eleventh century by the material excavated in Dublin itself, whether it be walrus ivory from Greenland or pottery from France. The nature of the exotica found in the Dublin excavations emphasises the economic significance of Dublin as the most important centre of trade between north and south, on the main sea route between the lands of the north of the North Atlantic and the ports of the Bay of Biscay. This was a route controlled in the eleventh and early twelfth centuries by the Scandinavians. The Norse settlements on the route would have been in a strategic position to protect or pillage traders and even, as is suggested in chapter 17, to combine in trading voyages with Dubliners or Norwegians.

Of such activity by the Scandinavians in the Isle of Man we have no evidence, although the shadowy traces in the annals and sagas of the activities of the rulers of Man in the Irish Sea and beyond would suggest that the island could not have been isolated from them. The most concrete evidence to support such economic and trading contact is provided by the establishment of the mint in Man, already referred to. This allows us to assume the presence of a market, or at least of a royal centre for the control of economic activity, a control which would include the gathering of tolls from merchants. There is, however, no physical or historical evidence of a major market centre in Man during the Viking Age, save for the arm of a merchant's balance of Viking-Age type found in the Ronaldsway excavations. There is no reason why the Ronaldsway site should not be related to a seasonal beach market at Derbyhaven – and there may have been others. This would easily chime with market places in other parts of the

Irish Sea (at Meols in the Wirral and at Whithorn in south-west Scotland, for example). The growth of power of the Hansa and the Norman conquest of Ireland severely curtailed activity along the north/south route through Dublin. The economic potential of the island in this context must have withered in proportion, the economic basis of life returning to a subsistence dependent on agriculture, supported by certain other industries as the export of specialist foods and the product of lead mining.

PART ONE: POLITICS

1 *Man and the Irish Sea World in the Eleventh Century*

SEÁN DUFFY

In the judgment of many, a people's history begins when they start to keep a record of their affairs. If that were the case, Manx history would begin in the eleventh century. It is not that we have contemporary documentation from the island from that point; rather, the Manx chronicle, put together from earlier materials in the mid-thirteenth century, chose the eleventh century as its starting point, for whatever reason, and therefore has left us with little choice. Unfortunately, however, since the chronicle is so much later in date, it is not a very reliable source for this early period. Not only that, but although the chronicler begins with a flourish at the start of the new millennium (in fact, 1016, as his dating system is very confused), Man itself does not feature until 1066. Prior to that point his subject matter relates exclusively (in descending order of detail) to England, Denmark, Norway, Scotland, Rome, Wales, and Normandy. We are not, therefore, dealing with a Manx source at all for this information: these are just summaries of major events lifted from other assorted sources.[1] Only when we get to the account of the battle of Stamford Bridge do we find information of Manx origin, however dubious. This is to the effect that among those on the losing Norwegian side who fled from the battle was 'a certain Godred nicknamed Crovan son of Harald the Black of *Ysland*, and he came to Godred son of Sitric who was then ruling in Man'. Under what appear to be the events of the year 1070 we are told that Godred son of Sitric, king of Man (*Rex Mannie*), died and was succeeded by his son Fingal.[2]

This is obviously important information: we have the name of the king of Man in 1066, and the name of his son and successor; we also hear of another individual who later went on to play a central role in Manx affairs. But there is not much detail to it all. Let us start with this first recorded king of Man. All we know about him is that he had the Norse name Guðröðr (Latinised Godred in the chronicle; to the Irish, Gofraid) and his son what is presumably a Gaelic name, Fingal. Guðröðr's father is said to be Sigtryggr (Ir. Sitriuc) but on the two occasions on which the latter is mentioned in the manuscript the scribe has crossed out Sigtryggr and replaced it with Fingal: so, the three generations are either Fingal son of Guðröðr son of Fingal or Fingal son of Guðröðr son of Sigtryggr. Frankly,

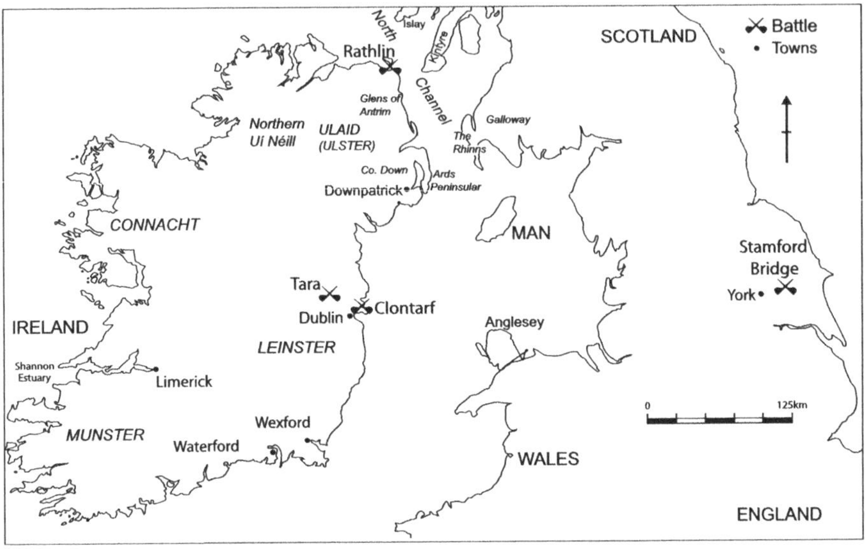

Fig. 1.1 *Man and the Irish Sea world.*

in the absence of further evidence, we have no idea which is correct but, at a push, the latter looks slightly more plausible.[3] The chronicle does not even tell us that Guðröðr was Manx, merely that he ruled Man. If his father's name was something like 'Fingal', the latter has left no trace in the historical record: in fact, the name has no very close equivalent in Gaelic,[4] although existing as a modern forename adapted from the famous Fionn of Ossianic lore.

If, on the other hand, Guðröðr's father was Sigtryggr, two contemporaries of that name may fit the bill. A Sigtryggr son of Ívarr (Ir Sitriuc mac Ímair) died as king of the Irish Viking town of Waterford in 1022.[5] This family certainly had strong Manx connections: Sigtryggr's nephew Echmarcach mac Ragnaill (ON Rögnvaldr) was king of Man in the 1050s, as we shall see, and members of the next generation of the family turn up in the island in 1075 and again in 1087.[6] The problem is that we have no evidence that the Waterford Sigtryggr had a son Guðröðr. The other contender is the better-known Sigtryggr *silkiskegg* (Sitriuc 'Silkbeard'), the long-reigning king of Dublin who died in 1042, and who did have a son of this name. Unfortunately, this Guðröðr is reported to have been killed in Wales in 1036, which does rather rule him out, unless, that is, the information is faulty or Sigtryggr had two sons of that name, doubtless by different mothers – he seems, for instance, to have had two sons called Óláfr (Ir Amlaíb), one of whom is reported as dying in 1013, the other in 1034.[7]

That Guðröðr son of Sigtryggr, if indeed he is a historical figure, might have belonged to the related dynasties that ruled Dublin and Waterford should not surprise us. The Vikings who established these bases probably did so from a position in the Isles.[8] As the newly founded kingdom of Dublin in particular grew in power, ruling York for much of the tenth century, Man had immense strategic significance, and control of it must have been of vital concern.[9] In the early to mid-tenth century the Isles appear to have provided a refuge for the family of one Haraldr son of Sigtryggr *Gale* or *Cáech* (king of Dublin, d.927), who died as king of Limerick in 940.[10] Haraldr's son Magnús, along with what the Irish annals call the 'lagmanns' (ON lögmaðr, 'lawspeaker') of the Isles, was raiding the Viking base on Scattery island in the Shannon estuary in 974, when they captured the rival Viking ruler of Limerick.[11] Haraldr's sons were in Waterford a decade later, apparently plotting with the celebrated king of Munster, Brian Bóruma (Boru), to attack Dublin.[12] As enemies of the Dubliners, it is unlikely that Haraldr's sons were among the 'foreigners of the islands' who fought without success alongside the Dublin Vikings at the famous battle of Tara in 980.[13] Instead these 'foreigners' may well have formed the opposition to Haraldr's sons at a battle fought in the Isle of Man in 987. It is difficult to know what importance to attach to this battle, but the fact that the Irish annals report it, and add that 1,000 people lost their lives, suggests it was a major event.[14] It seems to have secured Haraldr's sons in power, because when one of them, Guðröðr, died two years later, the annals call him *rí Innsi Gall*, literally 'king of the islands of the foreigners', a term that included the Hebrides and almost certainly also Man.[15] That Man was within his domain is suggested by the fact that he was killed by the men of Dál Riata, past whose territory in the Glens of Antrim he would have had to navigate in order to come and go from Man.[16] He was succeeded by his son Rögnvaldr (Ir Ragnall) who, from what we can tell, reigned relatively securely as 'king of the islands (*rí na nInnsi*)' until his death in 1005.[17] It is possible that he faced opposition from Sigurðr Hlöðversson *digri* ('the Stout'), earl of Orkney from *c.* 985 until his death at the battle of Clontarf in 1014, for whose authority in western Scotland and the Isles great claims have traditionally been made, although hard evidence is slight.[18]

Certainly, the Dublin dynasty does not seem to have had control of Man at this point. For instance, it is notable that when Brian Bóruma (Boru) invested Dublin in the early days of the year 1000, Sigtryggr Silkbeard fled by sea and vainly sought refuge in Ulaid, east Ulster;[19] if Man had been in friendly hands he would surely have disembarked there. It was a different story 14 years later when Brian returned to reclaim his overlordship of

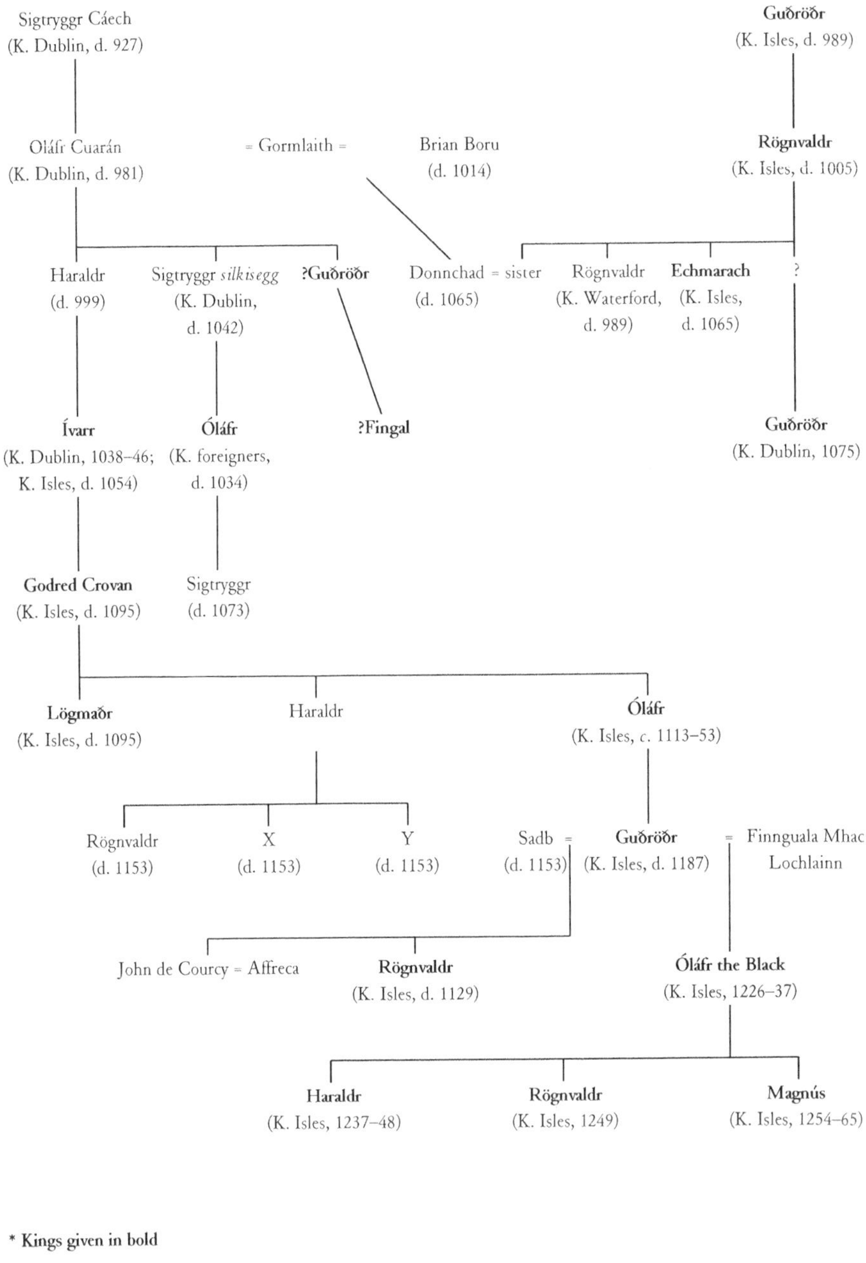

Fig. 1.2 *Genealogy of the Kings of Dublin and Man.*

Dublin. The coalition of forces Sigtryggr managed to assemble, and which faced the highking at the battle of Clontarf, included the Manxmen.[20] They were again defeated in this momentous encounter, and the Dublin fleet was also solidly routed in a sea battle against the men of Ulaid in 1022.[21] This probably took place somewhere off the coast of what is now County Down, and it seems likely that ships from Dublin were in the area because of its proximity to Man, and that the latter was under their rule. A year later, when the Dublin Norse captured a local Irish lord, the annals report that he 'was taken overseas'.[22] Man would be an obvious destination, although it should be mentioned that there seems to have been a Dublin presence in North Wales, probably Anglesey, at this point: Sigtryggr's son Óláfr (Amlaíb) is said in a later Welsh source to have had a castle there (in 1029 he proffered 120 Welsh horses in part-payment of a ransom to secure his release) and another son, Guðröðr, is understood to have been killed in Wales in 1036 by his nephew, the son of Guðröðr's brother Iárnkné ('Iron-knee', Glún Iairn to the Irish).[23]

By now this family was facing something of a crisis. Sigtryggr had lost three sons in the previous five years – Glún Iairn (1031), Óláfr (1034) and Guðröðr (1036) – and was himself an old man having been king of Dublin since 989 (he eventually died in 1042). He had even gone on a pilgrimage to Rome in 1028, to mark his retirement as much as anything else – his son Óláfr was called 'king of the foreigners' in 1029–but was forced to re-enter public life following the succession of tragic deaths that struck the family soon afterwards.[24] It is no surprise, therefore, that in 1036 Sigtryggr was ousted from power. His overthrow seems to have been an act of revenge for his murder in Dublin in the previous year of the king of Waterford, Ragnall mac Ragnaill (Rögnvaldr Rögnvaldarson), since the man who replaced him was the latter's brother, who bore the Gaelic forename Echmarcach (literally, 'horse-rider').[25] The annals say that Sigtryggr then went 'over the sea', which may mean Wales since that is where his son Guðröðr was killed in that same year, but Man cannot be ruled out. This is suggested by the following: two years later Echmarcach mac Ragnaill was himself ousted from the kingship of Dublin by a man whom the Irish annals call Ímar mac Arailt, probably a son of Sigtryggr's brother Haraldr who died in 999.[26] In 1045, this man Ívarr, at the head of the Dublin army, slaughtered 300 nobles of the Ulaid dynasty on Rathlin,[27] suggesting a contest between the two sides for possession of the island, and it is unlikely that Dublin could have put up much of a challenge for Rathlin without a base such as Man could supply.

Be that as it may, a year later, in 1046, Haraldr's son was expelled as king of Dublin and Echmarcach mac Ragnaill returned, and ruled for a further six years until overthrown in 1052 by the king of Leinster, Diarmait mac Maíl na mBó.[28] The annals state that Echmarcach 'went overseas' without specifying where, but it seems certain that he fled to the Isle of Man: Diarmait installed his own son Murchad as governor of Dublin and in 1061 the latter invaded Man, did battle with and defeated a man whom the annals call merely 'mac Ragnaill', presumably Echmarcach, and exacted tribute from the Manx.[29] This is one of the landmark events in Manx history in this age. To begin with, if Echmarcach mac Ragnaill was able to flee Dublin in 1052 and routinely take up rule of Man, it must be assumed that it was his to begin with, and that he had control of it while king of Dublin. This would explain why Murchad of Leinster descended on the island in 1061 to take tribute (*cáin* in Gaelic) from the inhabitants: the right to exact *cáin* has been described as 'a definitive right of kingship' in medieval Ireland, and in asserting such a right Murchad was proclaiming that as ruler of Dublin he was *ipso facto* overlord of Man.[30] The significance of this cannot be overstated. Of course, Ireland and Man had always enjoyed a close link, and there had been perennial if sporadic Irish intrusion in Manx affairs for centuries. But we have to go back half a millennium, to the reign of the Ulster king Báetán mac Cairill (572–81), to find the last time that an Irish king had successfully claimed overlordship of Man.[31] What is more, one can well understand how a ruler like Báetán, based in east Down, who could almost see the Isle of Man from the battlements of his fortress in Downpatrick, might have contemplated conquering it; but the meddling in Manx affairs of an Irish prince who hailed from south-east Leinster is an altogether more unlikely development.

The Irish annals do not tell us what happened to Echmarcach after his defeat in 1061, apart from recording his death three years later. However, in the latter notice, two unrelated sets of annals, the Annals of Inisfallen and the Annals of Ulster, give him the same title, '*rí gall* (king of the foreigners)', indicating that he was still a powerful figure, and was probably still regarded as ruler of Man. Curiously, they fail to tell us the unusual circumstances of his death. For this we are dependent on another Irish source, the chronicler Marianus Scotus, then based in the German monastery of Fulda and later Mainz. Because he had studied in the monastery of Movilla in the Ards peninsula in County Down, he would have known of Echmarcach, and under the year 1065 he records the arrival and subsequent death in Rome of Brian Bóruma (Boru)'s son, Donnchad, whom he calls *rex de Hibernia*, and of Echmarcach, *rex Innarenn*.[32] That Donnchad and Echmarcach should have travelled together is no surprise, as they had been allies for many years: Donnchad married Echmarcach's sister in 1032,[33] and they had a mutual enemy in the Leinster king, Diarmait mac Maíl na mBó, who ejected Echmarcach from Dublin in 1052 and was the main opposition in the way of Donnchad's claim to be high king of Ireland.[34] The title *rex Innarenn* is something of a puzzle. One possibility, suggested many years ago by A.O. Anderson, is that it should be read *rex inna renn*, 'king in the Rinns', the hammer-head peninsula at the tip of Galloway.[35] This suggestion has the merit that the Rinns had links with the Hiberno-Norse: the men of the Rinns aided Sigtryggr Silkbeard at the battle of Clontarf and his son Óláfr is said by a Welsh source to have held sway there.[36] The difficulty lies in proposing '-*inna*-' as the Gaelic preposition *in na* ('in the [plural]') since a Latin form should follow *rex*, as in *rex de Hibernia*. It may therefore be more sensible to view it as a corruption or misreading of *rex insularum*, 'king of the Isles', not unlike the title given Echmarcach in the Irish annals.[37]

Fig. 1.3 *The Hiberno-Norse coin hoard from Glenfaba was discovered in 2003. The photograph shows a few of the 464 silver coins, four of the 25 ingots and the broken silver armlet.* Photo: courtesy Manx National Heritage.

If we believe the Manx chronicle, Echmarcach mac Ragnaill was succeeded by a certain Guðröðr son of Sigtryggr, who was king in 1066 and died, apparently, in 1070.[38] Giving the chronicle the benefit of the doubt, and allowing for the fact that chronology is not its strong point, it is worth noting that the king of Dublin in 1072 was a certain Guðröðr son of mac Ragnaill.[39] He could be Guðröðr son of Echmarcach or a nephew, possibly Guðröðr son of a Sigtryggr mac Ragnaill. We have no record of this Sigtryggr, but then even the Irish annals were confused about Guðröðr's father: when he died in 1075, the annals of Ulster call him 'Gofraid son of Amlaíb [Óláfr] *or son of Ragnall*, king of Dublin'. Whatever the precise link, we are probably not too far off the mark in suggesting that when Echmarcach went off to Rome, where he died in 1064-5, he was succeeded in Dublin and Man by a member of his family, perhaps a nephew, called Guðröðr. The latter was in Man at the time of the battle of Stamford Bridge in 1066, as the chronicle has it, to provide a refuge for Guðröðr (better known as Godred) Crovan. But in 1072 he was in Dublin when Brian Bóruma (Boru)'s grandson, Toirrdelbach Ua Briain, marched to the city and claimed overlordship of it, at which point Guðröðr dutifully submitted.

In asserting lordship over Dublin, Ua Briain knew that this gave him a claim to the Isle of Man and, sure enough, the annals report that two grandsons of Brian Bóruma (Boru) (in other words, brothers or first cousins of Toirrdelbach) were killed in Man in 1073.[40] This cannot be coincidence and is proof that the family were seeking to replicate the position of power over Man that Leinster had obtained a decade or more earlier. If anything, in fact, Toirrdelbach had a better claim to Man than the king of Leinster, because his family had long since made Limerick their capital, and, as we have seen, the Vikings of Limerick had a record of supremacy over Man. In the company of these two members of Toirrdelbach's family was a certain Sigtryggr son of Óláfr, who was also killed. As ever, his identity is a matter of conjecture, but it is not a matter of inconsequence and is worth pursuing. Sigtryggr was in Man along with the two grandsons of Brian, and, presumably, a substantial army, in order to gain power there. The resident ruler appears to have been a member of the Mac Ragnaill family, originally from Waterford, so Sigtryggr was probably an enemy of this family. Their bitterest foes throughout the previous half-century or more had been the family of Sigtryggr Silkbeard of Dublin. The latter had a son Óláfr (d. 1034) and this later Sigtryggr was perhaps his son.

By the defeat of this expedition to Man in 1073, Toirrdelbach Ua Briain failed to get control of Man and to oust Guðröðr. But this would not deter him for long. Two years later, therefore, the annals inform us that the king of Dublin, Guðröðr grandson of Rögnvaldr (Gofraid Ua Ragnaill), was 'banished over the sea' by Toirrdelbach, 'and he died beyond the sea, having assembled a great fleet [to come] to Ireland'.[41] Again, we can reasonably surmise that Guðröðr fled to Man, and that it was a Manx and perhaps Hebridean fleet he had assembled, but that fate intervened. At this point, Ua Briain followed the precedent set by the Leinstermen and appointed his own son Muirchertach to govern Dublin.[42] The Manx chronicle would have us believe that Guðröðr was now succeeded by his son Fingal, but, as earlier stated, there is no trace of this individual in any other source. The chronicle itself does not appear to have much confidence in him, because it immediately proceeds to describe the conquest of the island by the famous Godred Crovan, and has a lengthy account of the spirited, if unsuccessful, resistance given to him by the islanders,[43] but never once mentions Fingal, who seems to have vanished without trace.

The arrival of Godred Crovan in Man tends to be regarded as a major turning point, but this is to read too much into it.[44] Godred is significant because, after a brief hiatus following his death, all future kings of Man were his direct descendants, including at least one son, one grandson, two great-grandsons, and three great-great-grandsons, after which point the kingdom of Man and the Isles ceased to exist. Godred is therefore given an elevated position because, when these latter kings of Man sought to legitimise and celebrate their kingship, they looked back to Godred Crovan as an apical figure in their ancestry and had their court historians record his deeds, in so far as they were recoverable in the popular memory. Hence, the first detailed Manx entry in their chronicle is a (no doubt highly fictionalised) description of Godred's conquest of the island, and this has tended to be used by historians as a logical starting point for Manx history, since after this juncture we are dealing with the history of a dynasty, ever more firmly established, in contrast to what appears as the chaos that preceded it. The problem with giving Godred this superior status is twofold. First, we are falling into the trap set for us by those who commissioned the chronicle and reproducing as 'history' what is in fact dynastic propaganda,[45] or, worse still, allowing the King Gorree/Orry of much later legend influence our interpretation of fact. And second, it gives rise to a great and artificial discontinuity in the narrative of Manx history: it encourages us to see Godred as dissimilar to and, to say the least, a cut above his predecessors, and it discourages us from tracing his links with, and placing him in the context of, all that went before.

In fact, there does not appear to be a great deal that is novel about Godred. When he first appears in the chronicle he is called 'a certain Godred nicknamed *Crouan* son of Harald the Black *de ysland*'.[46] If we look first at his nickname, there seems little doubt that it is Gaelic *crob bhán*, 'Godred of the White Hand'.[47] It was not unheard of for people in the Gaelic-speaking world to have such nicknames, *crob dearg* ('red hand') occurring, for instance, in the case of Cathal Crobderg Ua Conchobair, king of Connacht from 1198 to 1224, where the possession of a red mark on the hand was said to be an indication of great promise. Oddly, though, the Irish annals give Godred what is at first sight an unrelated nickname, *meranach*, which can mean one of two very different things depending on whether there is a length accent on the *e*: *meránach* means mad, confused, giddy, and such like, whereas *méránach* (or more usually *mérach*) is an adjective that qualifies the noun *mér*, meaning finger (or toe), and could be translated as something like 'Godred of the Fingers', implying perhaps that he had some kind of deformity or other noticeable feature to do with his hand. The latter, therefore, could make it merely a variation on *crob bhán*, but before such a link can be made it is vital to establish whether we are, in fact, dealing with *mér*-ánach rather than *mer*-ánach. This is where poetry can come to the rescue because the necessity for rhyme does not allow for any confusion. And, indeed, we have a Gaelic poem written in honour of Godred's great-grandson, Rögnvaldr (d. 1229) in which, in lauding his distinguished ancestors, the poet clearly refers to Godred as *mérach*, 'of the fingers', which would seem to clinch the case:[48] Gaelic-speaking inhabitants of the Isle of Man referred to their king as *crob bhán*, while the Irish, also aware that there was something peculiar about one or both of his hands, called him *méránach*.

The chronicle also refers to Godred's father as being *de ysland*. This has caused even greater confusion. It has sometimes been taken to refer to Islay,[49] partly because the chronicle later tells us that Godred died there.[50] But when the Manx chronicle refers to the latter it spells it *yle*, a very apposite spelling since the *s* in Islay serves no function and is a modern affectation.[51] If the chronicler did not intend Islay by *ysland*, the obvious alternative is Iceland, from Old Norse *Ísland* (although it would usually be rendered *Islandia* in a Latin source such as the chronicle). Most scholars would favour such an interpretation, but again we are left with a problem. We have no other evidence of a link between Godred, or his alleged father Harald the Black, and Iceland. What little evidence we have, including the Gaelic nicknames *crob bhán* and *méránach*, points to Ireland. The Manx chronicle claims that Godred 'subjected to his rule Dublin and a great part of Leinster'.[52] We seem to have confirmation of this from the Irish annals which record that in 1091 the king of Dublin was a certain *Gofraid mac mic Arailt*, literally 'Guðröðr son of Haraldr's son' or 'Guðröðr son of Mac Arailt'.[53] Although this conflicts with the Manx chronicle which has

Haraldr as his father rather than grandfather, the Irish annals are probably to be preferred on this point, and it allows for an obvious identification of Godred Crovan. He is presumably a son of the Ímar mac Arailt (Ívarr Haraldsson), apparently Sigtryggr Silkbeard's nephew, who became king of Dublin in 1038, sought to conquer Rathlin some years later, was driven from Dublin in 1046, and died as '*rí gall* (king of the foreigners)' in 1054.

If this were accepted Godred would fit very neatly into the pattern of kingship in Man in the eleventh century, where its kings are drawn from one of three families, the descendants of Haraldr of Limerick (until 1005), the Mac Ragnaill dynasty from Waterford (intermittently from 1046 until 1075) or Sigtryggr Silkbeard's Dublin family (intermittently from 1005 onwards, and virtually without interruption until 1266 if Godred can be identified as a member of this family). The only obstacle is the chronicle's reference to *ysland*, but there may be an explanation for this. Although the chronicle was written in Latin in the mid-thirteenth century – and therefore uses the word *Hibernia* (in fact, *Ybernia*) for Ireland – it draws on earlier materials not all of which were necessarily Latin. In the earlier part of the chronicle there is so much detail of events in England that it must have come from an English source, perhaps a version of the Anglo-Saxon chronicle, and it is very sympathetic to the Anglo-Saxons, describing William the Conqueror, for instance, as having 'subjected the English to perpetual slavery'.[54] In the English of this period, Ireland was rendered *Yrland*. The letters *r* and *s* are easily misread. This, one suggests, is what happened here: the Latin chronicler, reading an English text, saw something like *Yrland* and mistook it for *Ysland*, and hence gave his hero a more exotic Icelandic background instead of a Dublin one.[55]

The fact is that there seems little doubt that Godred did indeed hail from Ireland. Even when the Irish annals record his death, it is as an Irish person. They tell us that the year 1095 was one of plague throughout Europe and that 'some say that a fourth part of the men of Ireland died of the malady'; they then provide a list of 'some of the distinguished persons; ecclesiastical and lay' who died, including Gofraid Méránach, 'lord of the foreigners of Dublin and the islands'.[56] Godred, of course, was by no means devoid of contacts with Man prior to its conquest. His father, if he can be identified with Ímar mac Arailt (d. 1054), probably ruled the island, which may account for the statement of the Manx chronicler that Godred took pity on the inhabitants when he defeated them, apparently in 1079, and spared their lives because he was 'moved with compassion... since he had been reared among them for some time'.[57] The chronicle, as we have seen, also states that he fled to Man after the defeat of the Norse at Stamford Bridge and was given refuge by the then king, Guðröðr son of Sigtryggr, who, if his father was Silkbeard, was Godred Crovan's first cousin once removed.

That he should have participated in Haraldr *harðráði*'s attempted conquest of England is not entirely a revelation. Eight years earlier, in 1058, King Haraldr had assembled a fleet for a similar purpose, under his son's leadership. The Irish annals report this great naval expedition and say that it attracted to its cause the fleets of Orkney and the Western Isles and Dublin.[58] Some years earlier, in 1052, Echmarcach mac Ragnaill had been banished by the Leinstermen from Dublin, and although Godred's putative father, Ímar mac Arailt, had died in 1054, we can assume that his family, including Godred Crovan, were ensconced in Dublin in 1058 when its fleet joined the failed Norwegian expedition. By the time of the second great Norse expedition in 1066, Echmarcach had been removed from Man, and it is because of this that the island now provided a refuge for Godred. On the other hand, he could not go to Dublin because it was no longer safe: its Irish overlord, Diarmait mac Maíl na mBó, king of Leinster, was a staunch ally of the new English king, Harold Godwinneson, opponent of the Norse and Godred at Stamford Bridge, and in fact, within weeks, King Harold's sons were in refuge in Dublin themselves, following defeat at Hastings.[59]

The circumstances in which Godred Crovan seized Man by force are obscure. The Manx chronicle says that he ruled for 16 years, which would date his conquest to about 1079, but this is by no means certain. We know that the last Mac Ragnaill king of Dublin and Man died in 1075. When, as the chronicle says, Godred 'mustered a great number of ships and came to Man', he was forced to do battle, not with a king, but 'with the people of the land (*cum populo terre*)'; when this failed, he came again and 'fought with the Manxmen (*cum Mannensibus*)'; returning for a third time, again 'the Manxmen (*Mannenses*) formed up in battle order and after a massive charge joined battle with'.[60] The context of this assault seems to be one in which the Manx were without a king, which would fit the circumstances after 1075. The chronicle states that following Godred's victory at the third attempt, he offered his troops the choice of booty or land, and most opted for the former, 'plundering the land entirely and returning home'. 'Home' was the Western Isles, and we are told that Godred then 'granted the southern part of the island to the few islanders (*paucis... insulanis*) who had stayed with him', while giving the northern part to 'the remainder of the Manxmen (*reliquiis Mannensium*)' who had survived the battle.[61]

This was therefore a conquest of Man by an individual whose background lay in Ireland, but whose support-base at that point was in the Western Isles. It would have taken him several years to consolidate his position in Man, but he was certainly well in control by 1087 when the Mac Ragnaill family launched their last bid for power. The Irish annals report that in that year 'a sea expedition' was led to Man by 'the grandsons of Ragnall and by the son of the king of Ulaid'.[62] The latter, from east Ulster, was presumably trying yet again to extend his dynasty's influence over the island, while the Mac Ragnaill scions were no doubt continuing to press their claim to kingship of Man. But it proved a disaster and the latter did not even escape with their lives. Godred would have felt a lot more secure having repulsed this assault and it was in its aftermath that he set about staking his claim to Dublin, one based on very solid foundations if, indeed, he was an heir of Sigtryggr Silkbeard. The first we hear of his presence there is the bare statement in just one set of annals under the year 1091: 'Gofraid son of mac Arailt king of Dublin'.[63] There is no verb, so we do not know for certain that he became king in that year, although that seems the most likely explanation. Occasionally, the Irish annals use that construction to record a person's death, but there seems little reason to doubt that this is the same Godred whose death as 'king of the foreigners' the Irish annals note some four years later.

In the interval he seems to have been a force to reckon with. The Manx chronicle claims that he 'subjected to his rule Dublin and a great part of Leinster'.[64] One would normally take the latter part of this statement with a pinch of salt, but a glance at the Irish political landscape at this particular juncture is instructive. Two years before Godred is first mentioned in the annals, they record the death, in 1089, of the Leinster king but give him the title 'king of Leinster and of the foreigners', by which Dublin is meant (as well perhaps as the other Viking-founded enclaves in the province, particularly Wexford).[65] A different set of annals says that at that point the Munster king, Muirchertach Ua Briain, 'took the kingship of Leinster and Dublin'.[66] In the former case, therefore, we have the ruler of Leinster claiming Dublin, and in the latter we have Ua Briain getting his hands on Dublin and then trying to claim influence further afield, in Leinster. In the aftermath of this, Godred Crovan arrives on the scene and takes control of Dublin, and it seems perfectly consistent with recent practice that he should, as the Manx chronicle asserts, try to subject part of Leinster to his authority. Of course, Ua Briain was having none of it, and the annals report that in 1094 he gathered together a coalition of the armies of Munster, Osraige, and Leinster, under his command, and marched on Dublin. His enemies from the northern part of the country assembled against him, in support of Godred, who had a fleet of 90 ships, and Muirchertach's army was heavily defeated, but when Godred's allies returned home, Muirchertach unexpectedly returned, and expelled him from Dublin.[67] He died in the following year, the Irish annals say of plague, the Manx chronicle adding that his death occurred in Islay.

At this point, the chronology of the Manx chronicle takes a plunge into confusion that is impossible to reconcile with known events. It tells us that Godred left three sons, Lögmaðr (Lagman in the chronicle), Haraldr, and Óláfr. Lögmaðr ruled for seven years after 1095 (i.e., till 1102), then, having mutilated Haraldr for rebellion, abdicated out of remorse and died on pilgrimage to Jerusalem. Since Óláfr was too young, the Islesmen sent to Muirchertach Ua Briain asking for a regent. He sent his nephew Domnall, who ruled as a tyrant for three years (i.e., till 1105) before being banished. Only at this point in the chronicle does King Magnus Barelegs (ON Magnús *berfœttr* or *berbeinn*) of Norway arrive, although we know that he made two expeditions to the west, the first in 1098, the second in 1102-3. Something, therefore, has to give. At first sight the most remarkable of the episodes in this account is the invitation to Ua Briain, and yet this is something for which we do in fact have corroboration. Godred Crovan died in 1095, having been ejected from Dublin by King Muirchertach in the previous year. If we ignore for a moment the reign of Lögmaðr, for which there is no supporting evidence, the Islesmen would have found themselves in 1095 without a king. Let us suppose it was at this point that, to quote from the chronicle, 'all the noblemen of the Isles (*omnes proceres insularum*)' sent an embassy 'to Muirchertach Ua Briain, king of Ireland (*ad murecardum obrien regem ybernie*)' requesting that he send a man of royal blood to rule them until Godred Crovan's son Óláfr came of age, and that he agreed, as the chronicle says, and sent a certain Domnall son of Tadc (*quendam dompnaldum filium tadc*), who ruled as a despot for three years until forced to flee.[68] That would take us to 1098, at which point Magnus Barelegs enters the scene, and the chronology is back on track.

The attractions of this reconstruction of events are several. First, when Muirchertach Ua Briain drove Godred Crovan from Dublin in 1094, it would be perfectly consistent with earlier practice for the Munster king to interfere in the Isles soon afterwards, especially after Godred's death in the following year. That is what the Leinster king Diarmait mac Maíl na mBó did after the events of 1052 and what Muirchertach's father, Toirrdelbach Ua Briain, did after 1072. Second, it is certain that the chronicler had some quite accurate written source for this episode, which accounts for the precision of his spelling of the names of the Irishmen involved. This is especially noticeable in the case of the name Tadc; it is pronounced *Tyeg*, and would surely have been spelt along those lines if his source was a vague oral recol-

Fig. 1.4 *Later Norse/eleventh-century defences revealed during the archaeological excavations at St Patrick's Isle during the 1980s.*

lection, rather than written. The third argument is more substantial. The Dompnaldus filius Tadc of the chronicle is none other than Muirchertach Ua Briain's nephew, Domnall son of Tadc. The latter had a history of involvement in the Irish Sea region, seized the kingship of the Isles much later in the year 1111, and is credited in Irish genealogical sources with having also conquered Galloway.[69] In 1096, at precisely the time into which it is here suggested these events fit, the Irish annals record that his brother Amlaíb (ON Óláfr) was killed fighting in the Isle of Man.[70] Undoubtedly he was there in pursuance of Domnall's attempt to conquer the island.

The only fly in the ointment is Lögmaðr, and the most logical explanation for his lost seven years is that he was in power somewhere in the Isles, but acting as a subordinate ruler under Irish and Norse overlordship. He does seem to have been a historical figure and is recorded in Norse sources.[71] His two brothers also feature on record. The youngest Óláfr eventually succeeded to the kingship, apparently in or around 1113.[72] A year later Muirchertach Ua Briain fell from power after a reign of nearly 30 years; his nephew, Domnall son of Tadc, who had reappeared in the Isles, as we have seen, in 1111, returned to Munster to contest the succession, leaving the way clear for Óláfr who, the chronicle tells us, had been raised at the court of Henry I of England.[73] This English involvement in Manx affairs was a sign of things to come, but it was not the end of the Dublin link. The third of Godred's sons, Haraldr, may have been castrated by Lögmaðr, as the chronicle says, but not before he begat at least three sons. As befitted descendants of Sigtryggr Silkbeard, the chronicle reports that 'they were reared in Dublin (*nutriti fuerant apud Dubliniam*)', and in 1152 they 'collected together a huge throng of men and all the exiles of the king' and came to Man demanding half the kingdom. When Óláfr prevaricated, one of them, Rögnvaldr, beheaded him with his axe, and they proceeded to take over the island. They even made an assault on Galloway, but, having been repulsed there, soon lost Man too when Óláfr's son Guðröðr returned from Norway and exacted vengeance for his father's murder.[74] Before long, the chronicle tells us, Guðröðr assembled 'a large fleet and a substantial army and came to Dublin and was received graciously by its citizens with much dancing; a few days later by common decision and agreement they elevated him into the kingship'.[75] His rule may not have lasted long and may not have amounted to a great deal, but it was significant. If his descent is as suggested above Guðröðr son of Óláfr represented at least the eighth generation of his family to have held power in Dublin and Man, and he was also the last, ending a convention that had endured more than 300 years. With it, Ireland's relationship with Man may not have ended, but it had certainly entered a new and less intimate phase.

Notes

1 See chapter 14 below.

2 Broderick, *CKMI*, fol. 32v.

3 See the genealogical table at p. 12.

4 Donnchadh Ó Corráin and Fidelma Maguire, *Gaelic Personal Names* (Dublin, 1984), *passim*.

5 AFM; AT; AU; CS.

6 AI; AU.

7 For 1013, see AFM; AU; CS; for 1034, see AFM; AT; AU; CS; for 1036, see AT.

8 See Donnchadh Ó Corráin, 'Viking Ireland–afterthoughts', in *Ireland and Scandinavia in the Early Viking Age*, ed. H.B. Clarke, Máire Ní Mhaonaigh, Raghnall Ó Floinn (Dublin, 1998), 421–52.

9 See, for example, N.K. Chadwick, 'The Vikings and the western world', in *Proceedings of the International Congress of Celtic Studies... 1959*, ed. Brian Ó Cuív (Dublin, 1962), 13–42, at p.25; A.P. Smyth, *Scandinavian York and Dublin: the History and Archaeology of Two Related Viking Kingdoms* (Dublin, 1975–9); Barbara E. Crawford, *Scandinavian Scotland* (Leicester, 1987), 50.

10 AFM; AI; AU.

11 AFM; AI.

12 AI.

13 AFM; AU.

14 AU.

15 AT; AU.

16 The Irish annals are here most likely using the term Dál Riata to refer to the latter's Irish homeland, rather their kingdom in Argyll and the Western Isles.

17 CS.

18 Crawford, *Scandinavian Scotland*, 63–8.

19 AI.

20 ALC; *Cogadh Gaedhel re Gallaibh*, ed. J.H. Todd (Rolls Series, London, 1867).

21 AFM; AT; AU.

22 AFM; AT; AU.

23 *Historia Gruffud vab Kenan*, ed. D. Simon Evans; for 1029, see AFM; AU; CS; for 1036, see AT.

24 For 1028, see AI; AT, AU; CS; for 1029, see AFM; AT; CS.

25 For 1035, see AFM; AT; for 1036, see AT.

26 AT.

27 AFM; AI.

28 For 1046, see AFM; AT; for 1052, see AFM; AT; AU; CS.

29 AFM; AU; CS.

30 Katharine Simms, *From Kings to Warlords. The Changing Political Structure of Gaelic Ireland in the Later Middle Ages* (Woodbridge, 1987), 132.

31 F.J. Byrne, *Irish Kings and High-Kings* (London, 1973), 109–10.

32 G.H. Pertz (ed.), *Monumenta Germaniae Historica: Scriptores* (Hanover, 1844), v, 559.

33 AI.

34 For Diarmait, see Donnchadh Ó Corráin, 'The career of Diarmait mac Máel na mBó, king of Leinster', *Journal of the Old Wexford Society*, 3 (1971), 27–35; 4 (1972–3), 17–24.

35 Anderson, *Early Sources*, i, 592. Anderson in fact suggests another location called the Rinns, in County Roscommon, Ireland; whatever about the Rinns of Galloway the Roscommon identification carries no conviction.

36 See Duffy, 'Irishmen and Islesmen', 99.
37 *Pace* Duffy, 'Irishmen and Islesmen', 99.
38 Broderick, *CKMI*, fol. 32v.
39 AI.
40 AU.
41 AI; AT; AU; CS.
42 AI.
43 Broderick, *CKMI*, fols 32v.–33r.
44 A.W. Moore, for instance, states: 'The history of the Isle of Man during the Scandinavian domination naturally divides itself into two main epochs–one before its conquest by Godred Crovan in 1079, and the other after it' (*Isle of Man*, i, 82).
45 See Bernadette Williams below, chapter 14, 305–28.
46 Broderick, *CKMI*, fol. 32v.
47 See the discussion in Ó Cuív, 'A poem in praise of Raghnall', 284. Basil Megaw, in 'Norseman and native', is cautious in accepting the interpretation, but offers no alternative (at p.16).
48 Ó Cuív, 'A poem in praise of Raghnall', 284.
49 George Broderick offers Islay in parentheses in his translation: Broderick, *CKMI*, fol. 32v.
50 Broderick, *CKMI*, fol. 33v. See, for instance, Crawford below, chapter 10, 223.
51 See William J. Watson, *The History of the Celtic Place-Names of Scotland* (Edinburgh, 1926), s.n.
52 Broderick, *CKMI*, fol. 33r.
53 AT.
54 Broderick, *CKMI*, fol. 32v.
55 I owe this rather ingenious suggestion to the very ingenious Mr Alex Woolf. See the comments of Bernadette Williams below, 327, n.40.
56 AFM; AT; AU.
57 Broderick, *CKMI*, fol. 33r.
58 AT.
59 See Ben Hudson, 'The family of Harold Godwinson and the Irish Sea province', *Journal of the Royal Society of Antiquaries of Ireland*, 109 (1979), 92–100.
60 Broderick, *CKMI*, fols 32v.–33r.
61 Broderick, *CKMI*, fol. 33r.
62 AU.
63 AT.
64 Broderick, *CKMI*, fol. 33r.
65 AT; CS.
66 AI.
67 AFM; AI; AT; AU.
68 Broderick, *CKMI*, fol. 33v.
69 See Duffy, 'Irishmen and Islesmen', 108–10, 114.
70 AFM.
71 See p. 24 below, n.18.
72 Broderick, *CKMI*, fol. 35v. The chronicle says he ruled for 40 years and died in 1153.
73 Broderick, *CKMI*, fol. 35r.
74 Broderick, *CKMI*, fols 36r.–v.
75 Broderick, *CKMI*, fol. 37r.

2 *The Isle of Man and the Kings of Norway: Magnús Barelegs and After*

ROSEMARY POWER

Scandinavian writers of the thirteenth century found that the kingdom of Man and the Isles and its relations with Norway were subjects of sufficient interest to ensure that sporadic but invaluable accounts of events in the kingdom were recorded. Their interest is understandable, for the kingdom had been conquered and made subject to Norwegian rule at least in name by King Haraldr Finehair (*hárfagri*) in the late ninth century. However, a regular Norse interest in Man and the Isles began only with the expedition of the Norwegian king Magnús Barelegs (Magnús *berfættr*) in 1098, an expedition that resulted in a formal, and at times actual, recognition of the sovereignty of Norway. The purpose here is to consider the sources for the period when the kingdom was subject to Norway and when Norse influence in Man and the Isles was extensive.

Information on Man and the Isles in this period is relatively scarce. Only one source, the thirteenth-century *Chronicles of the Kings of Man and the Isles*,[1] is native. Written Gaelic sources other than those of Irish origin were compiled from oral tradition centuries later, and the Isles figure relatively rarely and in passing in the Scottish *Chronicle*s and official records of the time. There are relatively few official Norwegian records concerning dealings with the kingdom or bishopric,[2] and little has survived from any source on ecclesiastical matters in general. Irish annals and genealogical tracts provide a chronological backbone and some valuable information, but there is not enough to provide a general picture.[3] The fullest sources are Norse, and include Icelandic sagas and other Icelandic and Norwegian works. There are also a few relevant entries in Scandinavian annals.

The Norse sources record matters in Man and the Isles only when they provide details so colourful that the authors found them irresistible; or when they impinge in some way on affairs in the Scandinavian world. They seldom give the background information that would assist an understanding of events in the kingdom in their own right. Moreover, the Norse works were composed as *literary* works, following prevailing fashions in taste, structure, and literary device, among which may be included the appearance of objectivity. The majority of Norse sources for the period, though they may concern Norway, were written not by Norwegians but by Icelanders. The evidence, such as it is, indicates little direct contact between Man and the Isles on the one hand and Iceland on the other, and though people from both must have met from time to time in Norway, there is little to suggest that Icelanders had a direct knowledge of Man and the Isles. It is possible that much of what was reported was at best second hand.[4]

Some of the Norse accounts were written long after the events in question. The sources for Man and the Isles in the twelfth century nearly all date from the thirteenth, and some are from the fourteenth century. While the *Orkneyinga saga*,[5] written in Iceland in about 1200, is an invaluable source for events in the Northern Isles, and carries references to matters affecting the Hebrides and Man, there are very few extant works from before 1200 and none contemporary to the excursions of Magnús Barelegs at the start, or to the activities of Somerled in the middle, of the twelfth century. In the case of Magnús, every surviving prose source was composed over 100 years after his death. Some of the authors used verses said to be contemporary with the events in question, as well as accounts transmitted orally, and, in the case of the later authors, the written accounts of others. There may be a bias in Icelandic accounts in favour of Magnús, as one of his daughters married into the powerful patrons of saga-writing, the Oddaverjar family of southern Iceland.

An advantage rare to those who use Norse material is that a fair amount of biographical detail is known about the writers of the main sources for the twelfth century and for the period from 1217–63. The authors in question were the Icelandic uncle and nephew Snorri Sturluson (1179?–1241) and Sturla Þórðarson (1214–84). The latter wrote a saga of Norway's king Hákon Hákonarson which includes an almost contemporary account of the Norwegian expedition to the Isles in 1263. A few years later he wrote a similar life of Hákon's son and successor Magnús.[6]

The bulk of the Norse sources, thirteenth-century sagas, most of them anonymous, concern the deeds of the Icelanders' Viking ancestors in the ninth and tenth centuries. References in these sagas – the *Islendingasögur* – and to a lesser extent in the legendary sagas of earlier heroes – *Fornaldarsögur* – to the lands west of the sea, are frequent and uninformative. To go *í vesturvíking* – 'in western Viking' – was a common activity, but little information is given about western lands, and there are no references to monasteries or anything else identifiable and regularly mentioned in insular sources as the subject of Norse attention.

Sometimes the sagas give the names of aristocrats in the Gaelic world. However, identification of them with known personages is rare and doubtful. There are also numerous Gaelic names, mostly male, in the two medieval accounts of the Viking-Age settlement of Iceland, the *Book of Icelanders* and the *Book of Settlements*,[7] but practically nothing is known of the majority of those named, and any identifications are at best tentative.

While Scotland is usually geographically recognisable in the sagas, Ireland is by and large peripheral and mysterious. Occasionally Ireland, or Ireland the Great beyond the western ocean, is the setting for fabulous adventures. The Isle of Man, when mentioned at all in the sources for the Viking period, falls into the position of being at the extremity of the known world.

There are indications from Irish sources that as early as the beginning of the eleventh century, Man and the Isles were regarded as a single unit, notwithstanding the difficulties and dangers of travel through the North Channel; and that the Isle of Man was included in the term *Innse Gaill*, 'the islands of the foreigners'; whose governing class was of mixed *Gaill-Gaedhil* descent. The Norse term *Suðreyjar*, the Southern Isles (as opposed to the 'Northern Isles' of Orkney and Shetland), is sometimes used as the equivalent. As discussed in Chapter One, there is evidence of an Irish interest in the area for much of the century. The rulers of Man at times ruled Dublin too; and in 1094 when the king of Man, Godred (in Norse Guðröðr) Crovan, was expelled from the city by Muirchertach Ua Briain of Munster, he may have fled to the Hebrides, for he died in Islay in 1095.[8] This island, so significant in the medieval lordship, may already have held a particular standing in the region, and its position looking towards the north coast of Ireland and south to the North Channel gave it strategic advantage in a maritime culture. While Irish attraction to nearby Man is obvious, given its position to help or hinder entry to Dublin, it is less immediately apparent what the attraction, other than a historical affinity, was for the Norse-dominated Hebrides, unless it was that they were in any case closely linked to Man politically; or because it was deemed essential to control their fleets and prevent them from raiding or acting as mercenaries.

Indications of some of the links can be seen from accounts of the arrival of Magnús Barelegs at the turn of the twelfth century. The Norwegian king's activities are recorded not only in the north but in sources from Ireland, Scotland, Wales, England and the Isle of Man. While the insular hints at a Norwegian royal expedition in 1058 have no Norse correlation and run counter to what is known from a Scandinavian perspective,[9] in this case, where so many records are available, there is no difficulty in recognising that the Norse accounts correspond with what is known from the variety of other, independent sources; and that they provide valuable additional information.

The Norwegian sources include, firstly, a brief history of Norway, written in Latin in about 1180,[10] and a slightly fuller account in Norse, *Ágrip af Nóregs konungasögum*,[11] from the end of the twelfth century. There are two closely related works, apparently derived from an Icelandic original of the1220s, the Norwegian *Fagrskinna*,[12] and the Icelandic *Morkinskinna*,[13] which has been expanded and includes new detail. Closely related and best known is Snorri's *Heimskringla*,[14] also composed in the 1220s. In the case of Magnús, Snorri's account is the fullest and most artistic. There are also references to the events in the late twelfth-century *Orkneyinga saga*, but the *Danish History* of Saxo Grammaticus,[15] written in about 1200, contains no reference to Magnús's activities in the west.

Magnús was born in about 1073, the illegitimate but recognised son of King Óláfr *kyrri* (Olaf the Peaceful). He came to power at the death of his father in 1093; and for the first six months Norway was divided while an uneasy peace held between him and his cousin Hákon, who had also been proclaimed king. Hákon died early in 1094, and Magnús spent the next few years consolidating his power and quelling opposition within Norway. He seems to have displayed no interest in the islands to the west during this period . While the *Chronicle* of Man treats Magnús's expeditions as a single event, giving the impression that Magnús spent some years in Man and its environs, the Norse sources make it clear that there were two separate expeditions, on both of which Magnús asserted authority in Man and the Isles.

While Magnús's expeditions have been discussed elsewhere,[16] there are some elements that have a specifically Manx context. King Godred Crovan's rule of Man, and apparently the Hebrides too, coincided with the rise of interest in the west by the Norwegian king. Godred also controlled Dublin until 1094, when the Irish king Muirchertach Ua Briain (r.1086–1119) captured the city and expelled him. His death in 1095 seems to have caused an upheaval on Man, which the Ua Briain dynasty used to its advantage. In 1096 a nephew of Muirchertach's, who bore the Norse name Óláfr (Amlaíb mac Taidc), was killed on the island.[17] According to the *Chronicle*, it was after the death of Godred and as a result of strife between his sons Lagman (Lögmaðr) and Haraldr that the Manx requested Muirchertach to send them a ruler. He sent Domnall mac Taidc, almost certainly Muirchertach's nephew of that name. Domnall, the *Chronicle* continues, ruled as a monster for three years and was then thrown out, never to return.[18] In fact, if this occurred during the 1090s, he did return later, at least to the Hebrides, for he took them by force in 1111, perhaps in an attempt to raise a fleet with which to return to Man.[19] He probably went back to Ireland in 1114 when Muirchertach, among whose heirs he then was, became seriously ill. Domnall was killed in 1115.[20] If Domnall ruled after 1095, Godred's son Lagman was at least partially in control by 1098, for the Norse sources speak of his being captured that year in the Hebrides by King Magnús.[21] It may have been turmoil in Man and the Isles in 1098 that encouraged Magnús to assert an overlordship of the kingdom. Other factors may include a degree of peace in his own country and the need to employ his forces elsewhere. A desire for more land and for plunder is the suggestion put forward in *Orkneyinga saga*, and control of the *Suðreyjar* would certainly have extended his opportunities throughout the Irish Sea area. Ireland is included in the lands suggested for his attention; as is England, in revenge for the death of his grandfather, Haraldr *harðráði*, in England in 1066, though all these suggestions are made by writers over 100 years after the events in question took place. Another reason could be that Magnús, who had had personal experience of a divided kingdom, may have wished to provide land elsewhere for one of his sons. He took the second of them, the eight-year-old Sigurðr, with him.[22]

In 1098 Magnús descended on the Orkneys, and then Hebrides. Verses said to be contemporary tell how fire leaped to the heavens over Lewis, Uist was put to the flames, the sater of carrion birds warred on Skye, the wolf's tooth was reddened on Tiree, the folk of Mull fled mad with fear.[23] Leaving only Iona in peace, Magnús continued on his way, raiding and burning. He passed on into the Irish Sea, where that year the crews of three ships, 120 'foreigners of the Isles', were slain by the Ulaid, the men of east Ulster.[24] These may have been Hebrideans fleeing from Magnús (whose first expedition as such is not mentioned in Irish annals) or even members of his band, though a loss of such a huge number of his men is unlikely to have gone unrecorded by the saga writers. Magnús then arrived on Man. The *Chronicle* says that, finding it laid waste as a consequence of fighting between the men of the north and south of the island (a reference perhaps to Irish settlement on the island's northern plain), he set about restoring it, compelling the men of Galloway to assist by sending timber. Magnús then set out from his base on Man with a fleet of only six ships, either in search of more timber or to involve himself in Norman politics. This led to a skirmish off Anglesey with the Norman invaders of Gwynedd. Here Magnús slew Hugh, Earl of Shrewsbury, an event widely recorded in writings from Wales and England as well as in Norse sources.[25] He considered raiding in Ireland but left it for the time being and returned north. It appears that he made a treaty with the Scots King Edgar by which the islands off the western seaboard were to be recognised as Norse. A much retold popular theme is Magnús's attempt to claim Kintyre, 'the best of the Suðreyjar, except for Man', by having his ship drawn over the isthmus at Tarbert.[26]

Norse claims, repeated by Hákon Hákonarson in the early 1260s, were never recognised by Scotland and the boundaries of the kingdom, and later of the bishopric, initially followed the pattern of the offshore islands.

Events in his own country and a border dispute with Sweden kept Magnús away from the west for a few years. A curious story in *Morkinskinna* tells of a Norman called Giffarðr, possibly one of the Giffard family, to whom Hugh of Shrewsbury had belonged, who came to Magnús's court during those years.[27] This may relate to the statement by Orderic Vitalis that Magnús had regretted his slaying of Hugh of

Fig. 2.1 *Peel Castle and harbour: aerial view of St Patrick's Isle from the west. The causeway to the islet was not built until the mid-eighteenth-century* (Photo: Dennis Read, courtesy Manx National Heritage, reproduced by permission of the executors of Manx Technical Publications).

Shrewsbury in 1098. If this is correct, it may be that he was to some extent interested in English affairs, and the financial gains this would bring, and if so, his influence on the Isle of Man, with its fleets and good harbours, takes on extra significance.

When he set out again in 1102 Magnús turned his attention to Ireland. He may have sent a preliminary excursion in 1101 to test the situation, for in that year a raid took place near Muirchertach's city of Limerick.[28] Magnús himself set out the following year, returning to his base on Man, and presumably intent on reinstating the Manx link with Dublin. This meant a confrontation with Muirchertach, the great-grandson of Brian Bóruma who had initiated the family's rise to power. Muirchertach at this stage ruled Munster, and Dublin, controlled Leinster and had acted as king-maker in Connacht. To the Norse writers, Muirchertach, known as Mýrkjartak,[29] was merely one king in an island that had many, and the connection with Brian Bóruma, who was well-known in Icelandic sources, is not made.[30] The Norse sources give no indication of the ambitions of Muirchertach and his family in the Gaelic-Norse region of the Isles.

Magnús may have already been aware that it was more advantageous to join with Muirchertach than to confront him; and a formal 'peace of a year' was made between them. The peace was strengthened by a marriage between Magnús's son Sigurðr, now 12 and again accompanying his father, and Muirchertach's five-year-old daughter.[31] At about the same time, Muirchertach married another daughter to Arnulf de Montgomery, brother of the Hugh of Shrewsbury whom Magnús had slain in 1098. Arnulf was at this time in rebellion against Henry I of England, and it seems possible, in view of Magnús's control of Man, that the two allies may have intended to assist the rebel Normans.[32] It also seems likely that Muirchertach intended to use the alliance to strengthen his hold over Man and the Hebrides, possibly extending it to the Northern Isles, acting through the nominal ruler in the west, his young son-in-law Sigurðr, once Magnús returned to Norway.[33] While the sagas recount an initial period of raiding, followed by wintering of the Norse fleet in Connacht, or more probably either at Dublin or Limerick, Muirchertach's intention seems to have been to use Magnús and his ships in an attempt to achieve personal sovereignty of the entire island. This required the defeat of his prime opponent, Domnall Mac Lochlainn, king of the Cenél nEógain, whose heartland lay in what was later to become the diocese of Derry. Muirchertach was, however, defeated by him in battle on 4 August 1103, and a few weeks later Magnús died in a fight with the Ulaid, the dynasty inhabiting the north-east of the island.[34] This may have been an accident, for the Ulaid were allies of Muirchertach and therefore also of Magnús. According to the *Chronicle*, Magnús was buried in Downpatrick. The memory of him survived into the twentieth century in two Gaelic ballads, in one of which he returns home and in one of which he is slain.[35]

The Icelandic writer Snorri provides a few descriptions of the Gaelic world, which, as they were not recorded by earlier writers or were recorded differently, indicates that he was receiving information in his own time of events that had occurred more than 100 years previously. Snorri uses, among other things, earlier, allegedly contemporary, verses on Magnús's depredations of the Hebridean islands, taking the verses from his source and rearranging them. It seems likely that he had informants from the kingdom, and could easily have met them during his sojourn in Norway. It is possible that he had at least one Manx informant, for his work contains a long passage on Magnús's death, which is more detailed than the sources from which he drew and contains a description of low hills, bogs and drainage systems. These correspond to the Downpatrick area of Ireland with its brushwood-covered clay drumlins interspersed by bog and by salty marshes, which have since been reclaimed.[36] Land reclamation could have been in progress at the time of Magnús's death in 1103, but is more naturally associated with the arrival of the Cistercians at nearby Inch abbey in the 1180s, and the description is likely to refer to the landscape as it was in the lifetime of Snorri and his contemporaries. A Cistercian source may have provided the description, perhaps by way of Rushen on Man, which like Inch was a daughter-house of Furness in Lancashire.

Information may have passed more sporadically but more directly by fighting men. The Anglo-Norman invaders of the north of Ireland used existing alliances between the Ulaid and the more powerful Cenél nEógain and forged new ones with the Manx.[37] It is not at all unlikely that fighting men who knew Ulaid went with their leaders to Norway and may have met Snorri and his contemporaries. Curiously, and independently of any of the major sources, a saga of an Icelandic bishop, *Jóns saga helga*, contains an account of Magnús's hostages arriving at Muirchertach's court. One of them, a Norwegian, offers to greet the king, saying that he can speak Irish. It is one of the oldest ploys, for the words he says mean 'Damned be you'. The extant saga dates from the early fourteenth century, and there is no reason to suppose that the words survived in Iceland since the time of Magnús. They may have come later, perhaps again through contact with people from the kingdom and Icelanders in Norway.[38]

After Magnús's death, England's King Henry I confiscated property held in Lincoln, which it has been suggested were payments made for Magnús's engagement in the Earls' rebellion.[39] They give an indication that he was motivated by the need for finance hard to obtain at home, for as

Snorri tells us, he was popular with his followers but the farmers thought him demanding. His son Sigurðr returned to Norway and the country was divided in three between him and his brothers. One of these, Óláfr, a small child in 1103, died a few years later, and the eldest, Eysteinn, died in 1122. In about 1128 a man named Gillikrist (Gaelic *Gille Críst*, 'servant of Christ'), who also bore the name Haraldr, came to Norway, accompanied by his mother. He claimed to be a posthumous son of Magnús, and, according to *Orkneyinga saga*, alleged that his mother's family were based in both the 'Suðreyjar' and Ireland.[40] Sigurðr may have remembered Haraldr's mother from his own childhood, and in all events the story they told was sufficiently convincing for Sigurðr to allow Haraldr to undertake trial by ordeal as corroboration, and when this was completed successfully, to recognise him as a half-brother. Of the many men who claimed in twelfth- and thirteenth-century Norway to be unrecognised sons of previous monarchs, Haraldr *gilli*, as he was known, was one of only three who succeeded to the kingship. Writing a century later about the king of Saxo Grammaticus terms *Haraldus Hiberniensis*, Snorri describes Gaelic dress worn on one occasion and says that Haraldr *gilli* spoke Norse haltingly, both features perhaps encountered by Snorri in Norway in his own day by visitors from Man and the Isles. Snorri is the only author to give

Fig. 2.2 Ivory chesspiece of a knight found in a stone cist on the west coast of Lewis, mid-twelfth-century.

the well-known description of Magnús Barelegs adopting Gaelic dress while in the west and going barelegged. Both these descriptions are presumably also based on observation of Hebrideans or Manxmen in the streets of thirteenth-century Bergen.[41]

It can hardly have escaped the notice of the author of the mid-thirteenth-century Norwegian work, *The King's Mirror*, when he described the Irish as bloodthirsty but as never killing any of their holy men,[42] that Haraldr *gilli*'s one claim to international attention was his execution in 1135, of Reinald, the English-born bishop of Stavanger. Haraldr *gilli* was himself assassinated in 1136, and was succeeded by three of his young sons by different mothers, each of whom had been proclaimed king at different assemblies. One of them died while still a small child, and this perhaps motivated the arrival 'from the west' six years later of Haraldr's eldest son, Eysteinn, who also claimed a portion. Eysteinn, who had kinsfolk both in Ireland and the Suðreyjar, was probably born about 1123 and named after Eysteinn, son of Magnús Barelegs, who died at that time. Like Haraldr *gilli*, he arrived with his mother, who, according to Snorri, was named Bjaðok, which may be the Gaelic name Bethoc. Haraldr *gilli* had acknowledged him in advance, but it seems likely that his acceptance as king of Norway was dependent on powerful relatives from Man and the Isles. His family were 'partly from *Suðreyjar*, and partly from Ireland', and while his paternal grandmother was Irish, and possibly from Dublin, it may be that he was also related to the family from which Somerled of Argyll came.[43]

Nothing is known about the situation in the Hebrides during the brief reign of Haraldr *gilli* (1130–36), and there is almost total silence in the sources during the reign of Eysteinn (1142–57). After the death of Magnús Barelegs, Man and the Isles were ruled by Óláfr, son of Godred Crovan, for nearly 40 years. In 1152 or 1153, Óláfr's son, also Godred (Guðröðr), went to Norway. The Orkney earls had submitted to King Eysteinn in about 1150,[44] and Godred did homage to King Ingi, the dominant king who shared the realm with Eysteinn and another brother, Sigurðr, probably in the hope that this would ensure a clear succession after the death of his elderly father. He may have paid the tribute of ten marks in gold that Robert of Torigni says was due on the accession of each new king of Norway.[45] While he was away, his cousins, who had been raised in Dublin, invaded Man and King Óláfr was killed. This may have been an attempt to reverse the situation in the 1140s, as from 1142 to 1148 a lord of the Suðreyjar, Óttarr, had managed to seize and hold on to Dublin.[46] Godred's return to Man, apparently in 1154, led him to gather a fleet, and apparently take Dublin some time later. According to the *Chronicle*, this was done with the support of its citizens.[47] If this occurred, and it is not referred to in Irish sources, the Manx rule did not last. Another attempt may have been made by the Manx to invade Dublin in 1162.[48]

It may be significant that Godred did not go to Eysteinn, who would undoubtedly have had a first-hand knowledge of the situation and of the powerful personalities within the kingdom, through his own kinsfolk and where descent through the female line may have carried more weight as it did in the Norse world. It is possible that as well as approaching the most popular of the three Norwegian kings, Godred was deliberately avoiding one with Hebridean relatives.[49] It is also possible that Eysteinn was not in Norway when Godred arrived, as he engaged that summer in raiding the east coasts of Scotland and England.[50]

If Godred was in Norway in 1152, his visit may have occurred at the same time as that of the papal legate, Nicholas Breakspeare, who was there from July until about September. He was engaged in establishing the new metropolitan see of Nidaros, which was to include under its jurisdiction, after its formal ratification in 1154, the bishopric of Man and the Isles, the anglicised name of which, Sodor, comes from *Suðreyjar*. Its inclusion may be the consequence of special pleading, or at least a strong secular presence representing the kingdom, in Norway at the right moment. Nicholas Breakspeare, who forced the brothers Eysteinn and Sigurðr to make their peace with him, favoured Godred's patron Ingi, who was, according to *Orkneyinga saga*, the most peaceable and popular of the brothers, and also legitimate.[51] Breakspeare, who had come to Norway by way of his native England, was not favourably disposed to Eysteinn, and indeed the destruction of monasteries, in which the king had engaged at Whitby and the Farne islands, carried the penalty of excommunication.[52] It seems possible that Godred either arrived in Norway to plead for the inclusion of Man and the Isles in the Norwegian church province, or was there at a time when to do so would be judicious. It would counter the risk to his kingdom of a possible extension of the see of Dublin, established the previous year, a risk made the greater because of long-standing and often uneasy links between Man and Dublin founded on conquest. The town currently harboured his opponents, and distant Nidaros (Trondheim) must have seemed a more satisfactory choice.[53] At about this time he gave various estates to the Cistercians.[54] This monastery, in Man, and therefore in the proposed diocese, may have encouraged the Cistercian pope Eugenius III and the four Cistercian cardinals of the Curia to favour the inclusion of this bishopric in the new Norwegian archdiocese.[55] Rushen may also have been seen as a potential counterbalance to Iona, which still followed the ancient Columban rule. It was perhaps partly for this reason that Furness, the mother-house of Rushen, had held rights to the election of the bishop from the incipience of the diocese in about 1135.

Norway was still a relatively new convert to Christianity, which had become widely accepted in the early eleventh century under King Óláfr Haraldsson. A desire for local saints and places of pilgrimage led to the popular acclaim of Óláfr Haraldsson, who died in battle in 1030, and Magnús of Orkney, who was executed in about 1117. Their cults lasted, but there were others whose cults did not, including that of Eysteinn, the son of Haraldr *gilli*, who was executed by his brother Ingi's followers in 1157. Cornered while attempting to flee, either he himself or his later biographers modelled his death on accounts of that of Magnús of Orkney. An apparent attempt to claim sanctity for Haraldr *gilli* had also failed.[56]

Godred's secular activities, including his seeming involvement in Dublin, were unsuccessful, as were his attempts to hold on to his existing kingdom. In 1156 his brother-in-law Somerled (Gaelic Somairle, ON Sumarliði) met him in a naval battle and ensured the partition of the kingdom, an event that the Norse kings were unable or unwilling to prevent and which is only referred to in the Norse world, and then in passing, by Sturla Þórðarson while recording the demise of the Norse kingdom in the following century.[57] Somerled took for his family the central part of the kingdom, leaving the Isle of Man in the south and Lewis in the north. While his heartland Man was a prized possession, Lewis is described as barren, and while his descendants may have come into possession of Skye, the kingdom was not only geographically divided, but had lost control of the North Channel. In 1158 Somerled again attacked Man, and Godred left to seek aid. He went first to Scotland, for Somerled was in revolt against the Scots king over his mainland possessions, and was there until at least the spring of 1159.[58] On failing to raise support there, he went to seek assistance in Norway, but found there civil conflict that left no help available. He remained for a time, for in 1161 Godred withdrew his forces during a crucial battle, in an action which led to the death of his patron King Ingi.[59]

The loss to Somerled's family of most of the Hebridean islands did not necessarily mean loss of influence by the Manx royal house on the monastery of Iona. There is no indication of Manx involvement in Somerled's attempt in 1164 to reinstate Iona as the leading house of the Columban federation.[60] This occurred when the Norwegian archbishopric was embroiled in political troubles at home; and at a time when it is unclear who was bishop of the diocese. The move was opposed by the secular powers in Scotland and Ireland at the time; and it may have ceased to be feasible when Somerled met his death later that year. The Manx line retained sufficient influence on the island for Godred to be buried there in 1188, a right once held until by the Scots kings but taken over by the rulers

Fig. 2.3 *Aerial view of Iona showing remains of vallum in the foreground and middle distance; the Reilg Oran chapel (twelfth-century mortuary chapel for the Kings of Man and the Isles?); the "little church of Colmcille" (Magnúss saga berfaetts) just north of the abbey's west door.*

of the kingdom, some of whom at about this time built the mortuary chapel that lies just outside the central monastic enclosure.[61]

In 1203, a Benedictine monastery was built within the enclosure at Iona, apparently in consequence of a decision of the existing community on the death that year of their elderly abbot, Domnall, a member of the Ua Brolcháin monastic family of Derry. There survives a papal letter of protection, dated 9 December 1203, which puts the Benedictine house under the immediate authority of the pope rather than the bishop.[62] The new monastery, whose church was begun on the central sacred site of the Columban foundation, was razed in the following year by the clergy of Derry, who replaced the prior with one of their own choice.[63] The Benedictine monastery survived, causing the demise of the Columban one; and a few years later an Augustinian nunnery was established. These new foundations are associated with Reginald (Ragnall, ON Rögnvaldr) son of Somerled, and his sister Bethoc, the first prioress. The position of the church establishment is unclear, for the bishop of the Isles, a Manxman Michael, had died earlier in 1203 and the bishopric appears to have remained vacant for some time. While the archbishopric failed to prevent the opposition to a change of which they must have approved, the mutilation of the bishop of Caithness in 1202 had caused grave scandal and may have led to the metropolitan taking active steps in the Isles. It is also possible that the rapidity with which the charter was granted after the death of the elderly abbot Domnall may have been influenced by the presence in Rome of an excellent informant on matters in the northern world, the bishop of Greenland, Jón Árnason *smyrill*, who had arrived there that year by way of Iceland and his native Norway.[64] A mainstream European house on Iona, to balance Rushen on Man, may have been seen as highly desirable, and the women's foundation was the first within the kingdom. The province was led during this period by two prominent archbishops, Eiríkr Ívarsson (1189–1205) and Þórir Guðmundarson (1206–14), both Victorine Augustinians, and both of whom may have been instrumental in the change.

The latter archbishop was however unable to prevent violence. In 1210 those members of the Norwegian factions, the Baglar and Birkibeinar, who wished to seal their reconciliation by a pilgrimage to Jerusalem, first raised the finance by plundering the Hebrides, including Iona.

This may be associated with other events within the kingdom of Man and the Isles. In 1188 Guðröðr had been succeeded as king of Man not by his ten-year-old legitimate son Óláfr (nicknamed *Dubh*, 'Black[-haired]'), but by his adult son Rögnvaldr, a warrior of consequence. In the course of his long reign Rögnvaldr became known not only for activities within the kingdom, but for his actions on behalf of the king of Scotland, and his holding open the passage to Dublin on behalf of the English crown for an annual fee, an arrangement which took him several times to the English court. He is the subject of a praise poem in Irish, which attributes to him

Fig. 2.4 (a) and (b) *The harbour at Sandy, off Canna.*

possession not only Man but also Dublin and several islands belonging to the Somerled family.[65] At this relatively early stage of Rögnvaldr's career, according to the *Chronicle*, Óláfr Dubh was given on coming to adulthood possession of Lewis. He may also have had control of Skye and had influence in other islands, for he is named in an Icelandic saga, which recounts how in 1202 a party of storm-driven Icelanders reached harbour in a Hebridean island, Sandey, probably Sanday off Canna.[66] In about 1208 Rögnvaldr arranged for Óláfr to be imprisoned in Scotland where he remained until released in 1214. The sons of Ragnall son of Somerled fought a battle in Skye in 1209, while in the following year Áengus son of Somerled and his three sons were slain, events which may have been in some way associated with Óláfr Dubh's removal.[67] Rögnvaldr and his nobles were absent from Man in 1210, perhaps engaged in the battles in the Hebrides, giving part of King John's army the opportunity to lay waste to Man as part of John's campaign in Ireland.[68] The Norwegian expedition of 1210 included a Hebridean named Óspákr, and the expedition, which had been fitted out the previous year, may have had royal sanction and been a punitive raid on the local petty kings, both Manx and Hebridean, for failing to pay tribute. While there may indeed have been family interests in the plundering of Iona in particular, raiding a monastery was an act punishable by excommunication and the lack of sanction other than ill-repute is noteworthy. It is also possible that in 1210 Óspákr, who is in all probability the Óspákr, a descendant of Somerled, who was again active in 1230, intended to bring support either for the imprisoned Óláfr Dubh, or to engage with others of the Somerled line in extending their possessions to include Skye. The Small Isles were certainly a part of the Somerled possessions soon after this date. It seems that as a result of the expedition, whatever motivations lay behind it, a joint delegation of Manx and Hebridean kings went to Norway and paid tribute or protection dues.[69]

Manx violence on Iona in 1223, which involved Óláfr Dubh and the governor of Skye,[70] indicates a continuing interest in the monastic island and coincided with the extension of the new abbey church. The killing of the followers of Óláfr's nephew and rival, and the mutilation of the nephew in these circumstances prompted a visit to Norway in 1224 of Manx or Hebrideans concerned for the kingdom. A second delegation in 1226 included the bishop-elect Simon on route to his consecration, the abbot of Iona and others pleading for help for their land.[71] A further request two years later and the subsequent outbreak of civil war finally led to a Norwegian response.

The bishopric, which remained formally under Nidaros until 1472, seems to have been a trouble to the Norwegians from the start. They had difficulty filling the see, and only once, just after the establishment of the church province, had a Norwegian bishop. Complaints about the long and dangerous journey seem weak excuses as Nidaros had to provide bishops for other dioceses, reached over wider and rougher seas, including those of the Northern Isles, Faroes, the two sees of Iceland, and Greenland. While provision for Greenland in particular proved increasingly difficult after the climatic changes of the late twelfth century, and the remoteness and smallness of the settlement, it may be that the Norwegians merely found the Isles alien. In 1244, it was agreed that the archbishop of York might, with the agreement of the archbishop of Nidaros, consecrate a bishop of the Isles.[72] The bishopric of the Isles was also given responsibility for the impoverished bishopric of Lismore in western Scotland. Simon, bishop of the Isles, requested in 1236 that he be freed of this additional burden.[73]

While occasional provision was made for shipwrecked mariners,[74] Norse accounts are silent on trade with the kingdom, and there are few sources of any kind from the north for the end of the twelfth century. The first part of King Rögnvaldr's long and forceful reign coincided with that of the formidable Norwegian monarch Sverrir (1177–1202), who after 1184 was the sole king in Norway. Sverrir, who also claimed to be the posthumous son of a previous king, had considered going to the Orkneys and Suðreyjar during his bid for kingship, though in the event, this never happened.[75] His saga had been composed in Iceland and was well known at the time Snorri Sturluson was writing his history of the kings of Norway. Snorri's nephew, Sturla Þórðarson, composed a long and complex history of his own day, of Iceland's dissolution into civil war and the handing over of power to the Norwegian crown. He found it necessary in 1263 to go in person to the Norwegian court, and arrived just after Hákon had left for the Hebrides. Sturla remained for a time in Norway and at the behest of the reigning monarch Magnús, wrote a saga of Hákon, which he completed in 1265. He had access to those who had been on Hákon's expedition west, to the dowager queen, and others who had known Hákon well. On this, and on a subsequent visit to Norway in 1278, he gathered material for a saga of Magnús himself, of which only two fragments survive. Sturla thus provides almost contemporary accounts of the events leading up to the expedition of Hákon to the west and the loss of the Isles.

Hebridean and Manx kings in the twelfth century were appointed locally. In the Hebrides the title seemingly passed in Norwegian fashion to all in the male line who claimed it, could hold it, and could force a division of lands rather than in the Gaelic fashion to the single strongest claimant. However, on the Isle of Man the norm was as in Ireland for a single heir to succeed, a procedure which frequently led to the removal of other contenders. A division of the Manx lands occurred only in the case of Rögnvaldr and his brother Óláfr, and in 1223 Óláfr's faction ensured that this would not be repeated and he would be the sole heir, by the capture and mutilation of Rögnvaldr's son. The title these leaders gave themselves was *rex*, and this title is used by others of the kings of Man, but rulers of the Somerled line are usually referred to as *regulus* or *dominus*, both before and after their acquisition of the Isles. In Gaelic, the title, *rí*, long survived the treaty of Perth in 1265. In Norse texts the word used, accompanied by a sense of *regalitas*, is *konungr*, up to the loss of the kingdom to Scotland.

Magnús Barelegs's death had been followed on the Isle of Man by the long reign of Óláfr over the entire kingdom until his death in 1153. He may never have gone to Norway to be confirmed king by any of the monarchs little more powerful than he was. A change in situation in Norway was to result in a gradual enforcing of Norwegian power. When in 1217 the 13-year-old Hákon IV began his reign as king of Norway, there was little evidence of the changes that would be made. Hákon was the posthumous, illegitimate son of a short-lived king, and was accepted in the succession after it was agreed that his mother undertake trial by ordeal. Once Hákon had established himself, and internal war ended in 1228, he was able to change Norway into a recognisable power, ruled by a single monarch under a more European concept of kingship. He immeasurably strengthened his kingdom by introducing succession based on legitimacy and male primogeniture, ending the divisions and disruptions caused by multiple kingships which had often been held by the very young sons of previous monarchs. Once Hákon was able to give attention to the western kingdom, Manx and Hebridean kings found themselves required to go to Norway and be appointed as kings. While there is no record of Rögnvaldr being confirmed in his kingship by King Sverrir, this may have been the intent of his younger half-brother and successor, Óláfr Dubh, who arrived in Norway in 1230, in urgent need of assistance.

Hákon had already imposed his own king on the Hebrides, though without attempting to take that title from those already holding it. No action had followed directly from the delegations from the Suðreyjar which had come to Norway seeking assistance in 1224, 1226 and 1228, but in 1229 a battle on Man between Rögnvaldr, supported with a Galloway fleet, and his brother Óláfr Dubh, had led to Rögnvaldr's death. Óláfr immediately found himself under pressure of attack from Alan of Galloway, who had been in league with Rögnvaldr.[76] *Hákonar saga* says that Óláfr, appointed co-king two years before his brother's death, was faithful to Hákon while the Somerled line of kings was often treacherous. As Sturla goes on to name the latter as the sons of Dubgall son of Somerled, this may refer to their preferring the patronage of the Scots king.[77] Another Hebridean king not mentioned in the saga, Ruaidrí, was otherwise engaged that year, supporting insurrection in Badenoch on the mainland.[78] Hákon appointed king another Hebridean, Óspákr, who presumably may be identified with the leader of the raid on the Hebrides in 1210, and a band of followers was gathered for him. As he was about to set out, Óláfr of Man arrived, seeking aid against Alan of Galloway, and the expedition became a joint one. The Manx and Hebridean alliance appears to have been strained, and on arrival in the Hebrides Óspákr assisted to safety those of his kinsmen whom he could. Family feeling was clearly strong, and Sturla differentiates between *Norðmenn* and *Suðreyingjar*, Norsemen and Hebrideans, though without saying whether this distinction is territorial, linguistic or cultural. An unsuccessful attack was made on the Scots garrison on Bute, after which Óspákr died. Óláfr of Man took control of the entire fleet, which sheltered that winter under the *Kaupmanna eyjar*, the merchants' islands, most probably the Copeland Islands off the Ards peninsula, on the Irish side of the North Channel, a choice made possible by the long-standing Manx alliances with this region.[79]

Óláfr Dubh was summoned back to Norway in 1236 and appears to have returned to Man only just before his death in the spring of 1237.[80] Norwegian attempts to control the kingdom come to the fore immediately on the succession of Óláfr's 14-year-old son, Haraldr. He had to struggle with dissension, but even so, the following year Hákon sent a force to depose him on the grounds that he had failed to have the title and succession conferred on him in Norway by King Hákon. In 1239 Haraldr succumbed and made the journey, staying until 1242. He won Hákon's approval and confirmation of the title, and then returned home, and, even though he arrived with followers from the Isles, he was accepted by the Manx, which may indicate that those described as Islesmen were from his own territories of Lewis and Skye. In 1246–7 he was at the English court, where he was dubbed a knight by Henry III. Hákon summoned him back for the occasion of his own coronation in 1247, and he travelled by way of England, and then stayed in Norway for two years.[81] In 1248, he was joined by two kinsmen who had claims to kingship in the Somerled family's part of the Isles. Jón, Eógan Mac Dubgaill (Ewan Macdougall) of Lorn and his second cousin, Dubgall Mac Ruaidrí of Garmoran, arrived in Norway, seeking to have kingship conferred on them. Hákon, who had increased the number of kings in 1230, appears to have been reluctant to have more than one at this time, and was slow to accept Dubgall. His father Ruaidrí may have been the 'mac Somurli' king of Argyll, who, old age notwithstanding, was killed in battle at Ballyshannon in Ireland in 1247.[82]

Haraldr, king of Man, married King Hákon's daughter, Cecilia, but the bridal ship was lost off Sumburgh Head in Shetland on its way to Man that autumn. When the news reached Norway, Eógan Mac Dubgaill, head of the Lorn branch of the Somerled family, was sent home to assert authority in the kingdom. He may have been accompanied by Dubgall Mac Ruaidrí, who assumed the kingship at this time.[83] Eógan's immediate problem when he reached the kingdom was not Man, but Scots' incursion in the Isles and his own difficult situation in holding lands from both Norwegian and Scots kings, a situation which led him to flee for safety from Alexander, out to the westernmost, and Manx, territory of Lewis.[84] Alexander II's representations to Hákon over his claim to the Isles had been unsuccessful, and in 1249 he attempted to invade. Matters were suspended by the sudden death of Alexander, and Eógan then gave his attention to Man. There, Haraldr's brother had succeeded him, but was slain the same month. Then a kinsman, Haraldr son of Godred *Donn* ('brown[-haired]'), son of King Rögnvaldr, succeeded. In spite of the demands of practical politics, he too was summoned to Norway in 1250, which provided an opportunity for his opponents to attempt to seize Man. Magnús, son of Óláfr Dubh, the rightful heir by the standards of male primogeniture, arrived championed by Eógan Mac Dubgaill of Lorn, who was presumably acting on the orders of King Hákon. His intervention was resisted by the Manx, although later, in 1252, they accepted Magnús.[85] The initial opposition may have been to excessive influence from the Somerled line for Magnús son of Óláfr Dubh was, or came to be, married to Eógan's daughter. Magnús followed the now customary pattern and went to Norway in 1253. He was treated with distinction and remained for a year, after which he was sent home as king. In the case of both Haraldr and Magnús, Hákon not only confirmed a king in his status but also chose between two claimants, both of whom he had at his court. He was also able to recall the two Hebrideans, Eógan and Dubgall, in 1253.[86]

Hákon was in some ways too successful for the warriors and mercenaries of the Hebrides, for by this stage he had no real use for them. The submissions of the Greenlanders to Norway in 1261 or 1262, and of the majority of Icelanders in 1262, were achieved without bloodshed. The Hebrideans, like the Manx, looked in other directions. While the latter continued to benefit from alliances with the English crown and the Anglo-Norman conquerors of Ireland, the former found new outlets with the resurgence in Ireland of Gaelic power.

When in 1261 Alexander III of Scotland sent ambassadors to Hákon concerning Man and the Isles, Hákon claimed the Suðreyjar as his right through the treaty made by Magnus Barelegs. There were small-scale Scots military activities in the Isles in the following year, and when Alexander showed himself prepared to invade, Hákon decided to sail west in person to combat this attempt.[87] Hákon's views of his rights in the Hebrides and Man are made explicit in the near-contemporary saga, and his undertaking an expedition in his declining years, bears substantial echoes of the activities of his predecessor Magnús Barelegs. He declined the offer of his heir, another Magnús, to lead the expedition and set sail with a large fleet in July. This was rather late to start on a major expedition and indicates an expectation of wintering in the west, as had the much smaller fleet in 1230, and also of the intention to assert control forcibly throughout the region as Magnús Barelegs had done. Even before the fleet had set sail, Duggáll Mac Ruaidhrí had proved an enthusiastic supporter in the Hebrides. Magnús of Man also provided early support, but his father-in-law Eógan, from whom Hákon had expected much, declined to take action on the grounds of divided lands and loyalties. The leaders of the Islay branch of the Somerled family were forced to submit to Hákon, but the lack of overall support for the expedition must have made it necessary to reconsider the extent to which action could be taken, in particular after two storms and the inconclusive engagement at Largs had weakened the fleet.

Hákon, at the height of his powers, confident of asserting Norwegian supremacy in Man and the Isles, may have seen Ireland as yet another country to add to his possessions, and a means of surpassing the success of Magnús Barelegs. Such action would have required him to set aside his long friendship with Henry III of England, who had tried to mediate between Hákon and his son-in-law Alexander III. Henry's ability to resist was at the time particularly weak due the dispute that was shortly afterwards to become war with the baronial party led by Simon de Montfort. Given the situation in Ireland and the information Hákon would have received through Manx and Hebridean members of his court, such as Duggáll Mac Ruadhrí's son Eiríkr, he is unlikely to have been unprepared when on his expedition west Hákon received an Irish delegation requesting him to assume kingship in Ireland. There is even a slight possibility that he had long-standing ambitions in the area, for nearly 40 years previously, a rumour had been around to that effect.[88] The request that Hákon would free the Irish from the Anglo-Normans, must have come not through the kingdom of Man, which had allied itself with the latter and the English crown, but from Connacht, where Áed Ua Conchobair, who was married to Duggáll Mac Ruaidrí's daughter, was leading a full-scale attack upon the Anglo-Normans.[89] However, Hákon's counsellors were not convinced of the wisdom of taking the fleet to Ireland, a journey the evidence suggests would be around the dangerous north coast rather than through the North

Channel, and the fleet retired to the safety of Orkney, where in the course of the winter Hákon sickened and died.

Sturla, loyally rather than realistically, treated the events of the summer of 1263 as a victory, a final success of Hákon's before his death that winter. From the viewpoint of the Manx *Chronicle* Hákon achieved nothing. The Annals of Ulster and Connacht ignore the final battle of Largs and the Hebrides in general, and in an echo of the annalistic reports of the expeditions of Magnús Barelegs, which note only that he was killed by the Ulaid, these annals state merely that Hákon died on his way to Ireland.

While the concept of kingship in Man and the Isles differed considerably from Hákon's own, increasingly Europeanised, concept, there was no attempt until the very end to remove the title from the petty kings of the western lands. The Norwegian concept of *regalitas* prior to Hákon's time was much less clear than it became, and this seems also to be the case in Man and the Isles, where in Gaelic the title survived.[90] While there had been several kings and an over-king in Viking times, by the twelfth century the land was regularly shared out between several kings of roughly equal status. Only one king, Magnús (1130–5), was deposed by his rival, the half-Irish Haraldr *gilli*, and was mutilated rather than killed outright, a pattern of events common in the Gaelic world, but otherwise unknown in Norway. Others who aspired to be king, or were proclaimed king by a *ðing* died, naturally or violently, still holding that state. Hákon's intent on consolidating power was to retain a unified Norway. He was himself crowned in 1247, and his eldest legitimate son was crowned in his father's lifetime. After the latter's death in 1257, his younger brother, Magnús, was crowned in turn. In Sturla's account of an event in 1253, Hákon is described when accompanied by three other kings, his son Hákon the young and the two Hebridean kings Eógan and Dubgall. Only then are named the chief magnate of Norway, Earl Knútr, and Hákon's younger son Magnús, who at the time of writing was Norway's monarch and Sturla's patron.

In 1265 the problem of the *regalitas* of the kings in Man and the Isles was largely solved for Hákon's successor, Magnús, who was keen to come to terms, by the time of the sale of the kingdom under the Treaty of Perth. Hákon's main supporter in the kingdom, Magnús son of Óláfr Dubh of Man had pragmatically submitted to Scotland, and matters were further eased by his death and the consequent termination of the royal title in 1265. Of the three main Hebridean leaders, Eógan seems to have relinquished his kingly title as he temporarily lost his Norwegian-held lands. Áengus of Islay, who apparently never went to Norway, is not regarded as a king in the saga.[91] Dubgall Mac Ruaidrí escaped to safety and seems never to have submitted or accepted the Treaty of Perth, but he can have posed little threat. His death in 1268 is recorded in Irish and Icelandic annals, which retain his title of king unlike Sturla's *Magnús saga lagabætis* (the saga of Magnús 'lawmender'), where he is referred to as *Herra* (Lord) Duggáll.[92] His brother Alan accepted the treaty, and Dubgall's son Eiríkr left for Norway.[93]

The other Hebridean leaders were to prove loyal to Alexander III in 1275 when an attempt to re-establish the kingdom of Man failed. It may be partly due to the lack of sources, for no new kings' sagas were composed, but also because Man and the Isles dropped out of Norwegian reckoning, that there are few references to it in Norse sources after this date. In King Magnús's new laws of 1276, the list of lands with which Norway traded included neither Ireland nor Man and the Isles. In church terms, Norwegian sources provide little more on the bishopric, nor are there accounts of Hebrideans travelling to the Scandinvian shrines, though it appears that Hebrideans assisted with the cost of the cathedral at Skálaholt, now Skálholt, in southern Iceland. There is no indication of how long it took for the Norse language to die out in Man and the Isles.[94]

The relationship between Man and the Isles and Ireland was originally brought about by proximity rather than a sense of common identity. In spite of Irish attempts to control the kingdom in the eleventh and early twelfth centuries, events were determined largely on a local basis, and a living was made not only by farming and fishing but also by control of trade routes, piracy and the hiring out of mercenaries. It is possible to see the emergence of the kingdom, a formal unit by the 1090s, in which Norway asserted authority, but failed until much later to maintain it in any substantial sense. For much of the twelfth century Norway was in strife, and there was no leader strong enough to give attention to Man and the Isles. From a church perspective, the creation of the metropolitan see in 1152–4 may be seen as an attempt to increase Norwegian authority, though the political reasons for including the bishopric of Man and the Isles relate to other issues, including the establishment of the see of Dublin and relations between the bishopric and the see of York.

Within four years of the bishopric's establishment, the kingdom had been divided, apparently without any reference to the Norwegian kings. The bishopric itself was challenged by the actions of the monastic community on Iona in 1164 and 1203. Somerled's activities in the middle of the twelfth century drew his share of the Isles more closely into Scottish affairs, a feature that was inevitable when his family held lands on both the mainland and the islands. After the Anglo-Norman invasion of Ireland in 1169 the Isle of Man became of greater interest to the English, ideally situated as it was for guarding routes to Dublin as well as to Bristol and Chester.

Successive kings of England attempted to get Dublin to pay for this protection. While it is impossible to know much about activities in those parts of the Hebrides controlled by Man, by the middle of the century Somerled's descendants were engaged with the struggling Gaelic dynasties of Ireland, forming patterns of involvement there that were to outlive the kingdom of the Isles. Meanwhile, the church had moved from Gaelic involvement to accepting the technical domination of Norway and the actual involvement of Scotland. Hákon's attempts to re-establish Norwegian authority in the kingdom were increasingly successful during his long reign until the denouement of 1263, when Hákon was faced with a concentrated effort by a strong Scottish crown, and the attractions to the inhabitants of closer links with their cultural and geographical neighbours. Norwegian authority could stretch to far more distant lands where there was no alternative source of external power, but was insufficient to maintain control where alternative kingdoms held attraction and were ultimately in a position to enforce their authority. Hákon's son Magnús saw a more effective and durable arrangement in recognising the realities of Irish Sea politics. He settled for the sale of the kingdom and new relations with the kingdom of Scotland and with its centre of power on the east coast, nearer to Norway.

Research for this chapter was made possible by a grant from the Catherine MacKickan Trust.

Notes

1 Broderick, *CKMI*. See also, D. Goss (ed.), *Chronicon Regum Manniae et Insularum: The Chronicle of Man and the Sudreys*. With historical notes by P.A. Munch. The Manx Society, xxii (Douglas, 1874). An earlier edition still is Peder Andreas Munch (ed.), *Chronica Regum Manniae et Insularum* (Christiania [Oslo], 1860).

2 These are to be found in a number of places, including English records. See C.A. Lange *et al.* (ed.), *Diplomatarium Norvegicum* (22 vols, Christiania [Oslo], 1849–1995). Volume xix, edited by Alexander Bugge (1910), contains many of the records of Norway's relations with Britain and Ireland. Another useful source of reference (in Norwegian) is *Regesta Norvegica*, Norsk Historisk Kjeldeskrift-Institutt (Oslo, 1978–), which summarises the contents of letters and refers to their place of publication. Vol. i (ed. Erik Gunnes, 1989) contains a 'Regesta Sodorensia' (312–30) of sources for relations between Norway and Man and the Isles. Vol ii (ed. Narve Bjargø and Sverre Bagge, 1978) also contains references to Man and the Isles.

3 The most important in this context are AI; AU; AC; ALC; AFM. Excerpts of these and other relevant sources are translated in volume two of Anderson, *Early Sources*.

4 The literary background and the sources for the Hebrides in the twelfth and thirteenth centuries are discussed in a sister paper by the present author, 'Meeting in

Norway: Norse-Gaelic relations through the kingdom of Man and the Isles, 1098–1270', *Saga-book* xxix (2005), forthcoming. For references to the debate see Gísli Sigurðsson, *Gaelic Influence in Iceland*, Studia Islandica 46 (Reykjavik, 1988).

5 Finnbogi Guðmundsson (ed.), *Orkneyinga saga*, Íslenzk Fornrit xxxiv (Reykjavik, 1965). English translations are: Alexander Burt Taylor, *The Orkneyinga Saga* (Edinburgh, 1938); and Hermann Pálsson and Paul Edwards (trans.), *Orkneyinga Saga: The History of the Earls of Orkney* (London, 1978).

6 Five medieval codices contain *Hákonar saga*. Two are Norwegian: Finnur Jónsson (ed.), *Eirspennill: AM 47 fol.* (Christiania [Oslo], 1918); and C.R. Unger (ed.), *Codex Frisianus* (known as *Fríssbók*), (Christiania [Oslo], 1871). Both are dated to the early fourteenth century. The somewhat condensed *Eirspennill* now ends in 1261 with the crowning of Hákon's son Magnús. Anderson, *Early Sources*, uses *Eirspennill* as his main source this far and then the more condensed *Fríssbók*. He gives copious references to the other texts. The Icelandic compilation, *Flateyjarbók* (ed. Guðbrandur Vigfússon and Carl Unger, 3 vols, Copenhagen, 1860–8), contains in its late fourteenth-century section all of *Hákonar saga*, but the end is again somewhat condensed. Another incomplete Icelandic text is in print: A. Kjær and L. Holm-Olsen (eds), *Det Arnamagnæanske Håndskrift 81A fol.* (*Skálholtsbók yngsta* (5 vols, Christiania, Oslo, 1910–86)). The relevant saga is also printed in Guðbrandr Vigfússon (ed.), *Hákonar Saga and a Fragment of Magnús Saga with Appendices*, Icelandic Sagas, vol ii, Rolls Series, 88ii (London, 1887); George Dasent (trans.), *The Saga of Hacon and a Fragment of the Saga of Magnús with Appendices*, Icelandic Sagas, vol iv, Rolls Series, 88iv (London, 1894). *Skálholtsbók yngsta* is dated to about 1450–75, and in its current form ends with the period 1258–9. The remainder of the Rolls Series text is taken mainly from the final medieval codex, which has been published since Anderson's time: Marina Mundt (ed.), *Hákonar saga Hákonarsonar etter Sth. 8 fol., AM 325 viii 4° og AM 304 4°*, Norsk Historisk Kjeldeskrift-Institutt, Norrøne tekster 2 (Oslo, 1977); and James Knirk, *Rettelser til Hákonar saga Hákonarsonar etter Sth. 8 fol., AM325 viii 4° og AM 304 4°* [Corrections], Norsk-Historisk Kjeldeskrift-Institutt, Norrøne tekster 2 (Oslo, 1980). This text is also Icelandic, part of it from the mid-fourteenth century and the remainder from about 1500 (Mundt edn, xi). The end of the saga is more detailed than the other two surviving versions on the battle at Largs and its preceding storm.

Only two fragments of Sturla's *Magnúss saga lagabœtis* have survived. They are printed and translated in the Icelandic Sagas volumes above.

7 Jakob Benediktsson (ed.), *Islendingabók, Landnámabók*, Íslenzk Fornrit i (2 vols, Reykjavik, 1968).

8 Broderick, *CKMI*, fol. 33v.; AI; AU. See ALC; AFM.

9 Thomas Jones (trans.), *Brut og Tywysogion or the Chronicle of the Princes: Peniarth MS 20 Version*, (trans.), Board of Celtic Studies (Cardiff 1952); and William Stubbs (ed.), *Willelmi Malmesburiensis monachi de Gestis Regum Anglorum*, 2 vols, Rolls Series 90, London 1887–94, ii 376. Other English sources note that Magnús Barelegs' uncle Magnús Haraldsson attempted action in the Irish Sea area. However, English *Chronicles* name the Magnús in question the son of Harald *hárfagri*, not *harðráði*, and it is not always clear whether they are referring to the expeditions of Magnús, the grandson of Harald *harðráði* rather than to an expedition by his uncle, Magnús Haraldsson, who was then about eight. He died in 1069. For an authoritative account see Kari Gade, 'Norse attacks on England and Arnórr Jarlaskald's Þórfinnsdrápa', in *Scandinavia and Christian*

Europe in the Middle Ages: Papers of the 12th International Saga Conference, Bonn/Germany, 28th July–2nd August 2003. Ed. Rudolf Simek and Judith Meurer, 155–64. For insular sources see too Colmán Etchingham, 'North Wales, Ireland and the Isles', *Peritia* 15 (2001), 145–87.

10 Gustav Storm (ed.), 'Theodrici monachi Historia de antiquitate regum Norwagiensium', in *Monumenta Historia Norvegiæ* (Christiania [Oslo], 1880), 59–64. The arrival of Haraldr *Hiberniensis* is referred to (66), but the work ends with the death of King Sigurðr Magnússon in 1130.

11 Bjarni Einarsson (ed.), *Ágrip af Nóregskonunga sögum, Fagrskinna – Nóregs konunga tal*, Íslenzk Fornrit xxix (Reykjavik, 1985), 42, 46–7. *Ágrip* now ends during the reigns of the sons of Haraldr *gilli*. See also, Matthew J. Driscoll (ed. and trans.), *Ágrip af Nóregs konungasögum: A Twelfth-Century Synoptic History of the Kings of Norway* (London, 1995), 60, 68–71.

12 *Fagrskinna*, Bjarni Einarsson (ed.), 301–2, 307–10, 312–15. A recent annotated translation is Alison Finlay (trans.), *Fagrskinna: a catalogue of the Kings of Norway. A translation with Introduction and Notes* (Leiden/Boston, 2004).

13 Finnur Jónsson (ed.), *Morkinskinna*, Samfund til udgivelse af gammel nordisk litteratur 53 (Copenhagen, 1932), 316–22, 331–7. The original ending of *Morkinskinna* has been lost and it now ends with the capture of Eysteinn Haraldsson in 1157. See too Theodore M. Andersson and Kari Ellen Gade (trans.), *Morkinskinna: the Earliest Icelandic Chronicle of the Norwegian Kings (1030–1157)*,with Introduction and Notes, *Islandica* li, (Ithaca/London, 2000), and Ármann Jakobsson, *Staður í nýjum heimi: Konungasagan Morkinskinna* (Reykjavík, 2002), which has a summary in English.

14 Snorri Sturluson, *Heimskringla*, Íslenzk Fornrit xxvi–xxviii, ed. Bjarni Aðalbjarnarson (3 vols, Reykjavik, 1941–51), vol. 3, pp 210, 219–25, 229–30, 233–7. English translations are Snorri Sturluson, *Heimskringla* (trans. Samuel Laing, 2 vols, Everyman, revised edn, London, 1961–4), i (revised by Peter Foote); and Snorre Sturluson, *Heimskringla: The Lives of the Norse Kings* (ed. Erling Monson, trans. with A.H. Smith, Cambridge, 1932, repr. New York, 1990).

15 J. Olrik, H. Ræder and Franz Blatt (eds), *Saxonis Gesta Danorum* (2 vols, Copenhagen 1931–57), i, 342^{10}, 363^{8-14}; *Saxo Grammaticus, Danorum Regum Heroumque Historia, Books x–xvi*, trans. Eric Christiansen, 3 vols, BAR Int. Series 84 (London, 1980–1), i, 108, 139.

16 Rosemary Power, 'Magnús Barelegs' expeditions to the West', *SHR*, lxv (1986), 107–32, and 'The Death of Magnus Barelegs'. *Scottish Historical Review* 73 (1994), 216–22; Seán Duffy, 'Irishmen and Islesmen in the Kingdoms of Dublin and Man, 1052–1171'. *Ériu* XLIII (1992), 93–133; and *Ireland in the Middle ages* (Dublin, 1997); Judith Jesch, 'Norse Historical Traditions and *Historia Gruffud vab Kenan*: Magnús berfættr and Haraldr hárfagri', in *Gruffudd ap Cynan: a Collaborative Biography*, K.L. Maund (ed.), 1996, 117–48. A suggestion that there was an earlier expedition was first made in the seventeenth century by the Icelandic historian Torfaeus (Þormóðr Torfason), and this was popularised by Peter Munch in his notes to the Manx *Chronicle*. The evidence indicates that such an expedition is highly unlikely.

17 AFM. See chapter 1 above, p. 24.

18 Broderick, *CKMI*, fol. 33v., incorrectly dated to 1075.

19 AI. See Anderson, *Early Sources*, ii, 143.

20 AI; AU; ALC.

21 *Orkneyinga saga*, 95; *Heimskringla*, iii, 221.

22 *Orkneyinga saga*, 93–4. In *Heimskringla* (iii, 221), Sigurðr is set up as nominal

ruler of the Orkneys. See also, Thomas Jones (ed. and trans.), *Brut y Tywysogyon; or, The Chronicle of the Princes. Peniarth MS. 20 version*, Board of Celtic Studies, University of Wales History and Law Series, xi (Cardiff, 1952) on Magnús 'thinking to conquer all the island of Britain' (1096=1098).

23 *Heimskringla*, iii, 219–20.

24 AU; ALC; AFM.

25 John Williams ab Ithel (ed.), *Annales Cambriae*, Rolls Series 20 (London, 1860); *Brut, Peniarth MS.*; Thomas Jones (ed. and trans.), *Brut y Tywysogyon; or, The Chronicle of the Princes, Red Book of Hergest Version*, Board of Celtic Studies, University of Wales History and Law Series, xvi (Cardiff, 1955); Thomas Jones (ed. and trans.), *Brenhinedd y Saesson, or the Kings of the Saxons*, Board of Celtic Studies, University of Wales History and Law Series, (Cardiff, 1971); D. Simon Evans (ed. and trans.), *A Mediaeval Prince of Wales: the Life of Gruffydd ap Cynan* (Lampeter, 1990); Cecily Clark (ed.), *The Peterborough Chronicle 1070–1154* (Oxford, 1958); Marjorie Chibnall (ed.), *The Ecclesiastical History of Ordercius Vitalis* (6 vols, Oxford, 1969–80), iii, 149; v, 219–25; vi, 49–51; J.S. Brewer *et al.* (eds), *Giraldi Cambrensis Opera Omnia*, Rolls Series 21 (8 vols, London, 1861–91), James Dimock (ed.), vol vi (1868), 129. There are accounts in other *Chronicles*.

26 *Orkneyinga saga*, 98–9; *Heimskringla*, iii, 224; *Fagrskinna*, 308–9; *Morkinskinna*, 321. A legendary precedent is in *Orkneyinga saga*, 6–7; see ix–x, xiii. See Anderson, *Early Sources* ii, 113–14. Snorri wrongly names the Scots king as Malcolm (d. 1093). See Duncan and Brown, 'Argyll and the Isles', 194.

27 *Morkinskinna*, 323–6. The suggestion was first made by E.A. Freeman, *The Reign of William Rufus* (2 vols, revised edn, London, 1882), ii, 451. Hans Toll, 'Konung Magnús Barfots välske riddare', *[Norsk] Historisk Tidsskrift*, Series 6, Part 5 (1927), 174–81, suggested the identification. The episode has been examined recently by Kari Gade, 'Morkinskinna's Giffarðsýáttr: Literary fiction or historical fact?' *Gripla* XI (2000), 181–97, who suggests an alternative identification.

28 AI; AU.

29 The name is found as Mýr(k)jartak or Mýr(k)jartan, the latter form influenced by the name of the hero of *Laxdæla saga*, Kjartan (Irish Ceartainn); or else reflecting an Irish diminutive of the name.

30 The battle of Clontarf is recounted in *Njáls saga*. See Einar Ólafur Sveinsson (ed.), *Brennu-Njals saga* (Reykjavik, 1954), xlvi–xlix, 440–53, 460. The saga was composed in the later thirteenth century but this section is thought to be derived from an earlier work on Brian Bóruma.

31 *Heimskringla*, iii, 224–5 places the wedding wrongly in 1098; *Fagrskinna*, 309, and *Morkinskinna*, 323, also do so, and call her the daughter of Malcolm of Scotland.

32 *Brut, Peniarth MS.*, 1100=1102. William of Malmesbury speaks of difficulties between the two (Muirchertach and Henry); and that Henry stopped trade for a time. William Stubbs (ed.), *Willelmi Malmesbiriensis Monachi De Gestis Regum Anglorum Libri Quinque*, Rolls Series 90 (2 vols, London, 1887–9), ii, 484–5. See too Orderic Vitalis, vi, 50–51 on Henry's relief at hearing of Magnús's death. Irish annals record the marriage at this point of Arnulf de Montgomery to a daughter of Ua Briain.

33 *Fagrskinna*, 309, states that Sigurðr was set up as ruler of both the Northern Isles and the 'Sudreyjar'; and *Morkinskinna*, 323, that Magnús set up Sigurðr as leader over all the islands to the west of the sea. *Heimskringla*, iii, 219, and *Orkneyinga saga*, 95, refer to him as ruler of the Northern Isles, but name no other as ruling

Man and the Hebrides. For an Irish viewpoint, see Duffy, 'Irishmen and Islesmen', 112.

34 AI; AU; AFM. *Heimskingla* and *Morkinskinna* date Magnús's death to St Bartholomew's Day (24 August), and *Ágrip* to the previous day.

35 Reidar T. Christansen, *The Vikings and Viking Wars in Irish and Gaelic Tradition* (Oslo, 1931), 131–71, 401–6.

36 *Heimskringla*, iii, 234–6. Discussed in Power (1994).

37 The marriage of Guðröðr of Man and Finnguala, daughter of Mac Lochlainn, king of Cenél nEógain, was regularised in 1177. See Broderick, *CKMI*, fol. 40r.; it is discussed in Marie Therese Flanagan, 'Hiberno-Papal Relations in the late twelfth century', *Archivum Hibernicum*, xxxiv (1976–7), 55–70, esp. 59. In *c.* 1180 the Anglo-Norman John de Courcy, having gained control of Ulaid, married Affreca, daughter of Guðröðr. De Courcy was assisted by a Manx fleet in 1205 (ALC). In 1212 King John of England granted Rögnvaldr, king of Man, a fief in the Carlingford area: *CDI*, i, 428, 898; also printed in *Dip. Norv.*, xix, no 93, 83–4. De Courcy's successors, the de Lacys, were assisted by Manx fleets, particularly in the 1220s. There was even a rumour that King Hákon was coming to aid the de Lacy rebellion: Walter W. Shirley (ed.), *Royal and other Historical Letters illustrative of the Reign of Henry III*, Rolls Series 27 (2 vols, London, 1882–6), i, 219–20 (no. 195); also printed in *Dip. Norv.*, xix, no 157, 120. The rumour may refer to Rögnvaldr, rather than Hákon; or it may relate to Hákon's response to Rögnvaldr, doing homage to John for Man: see *Dip. Norv.*, xix, no 132, 105–6. The attempts by the English kings to make the Irish government pay for Rögnvaldr's services are well recorded. See ibid., nos 124–6, 99; 101; 129, 103; 178–9, 130; 219–20, 148–50; 224, 152. For this, see chapter 4 below.

38 Sigurgeir Steingrímsson, Ólafur Halldórsson and Peter Foote (eds), *Biskupa sögur I*, Íslenzk fornrit XV, 2003, 333; *Jóns saga helga*, in Jón Sigurðsson and others (ed.), *Biskupa Sögur* (2 vols, Copenhagen, 1858–78), i, 227. See W.A. Craigie, 'Gaelic words and names in the Icelandic sagas', *Zeitschrift für Celtische Philologie*, i (1897), 439–54, esp. 443; also Rosemary Power, 'Cursing the king: an Irish conversation in *Jóns saga helga*', *Saga-Book*, xxv (2000), 310–13. For the dating of *Jóns saga*, see Peter Foote, 'Jóns saga ens helga', in Phillip Pulsiano *et al.* (ed.), *Medieval Scandinavia: An Encyclopedia* (New York and London, 1993), 345.

39 Orderic Vitalis vi, 49–51; Gade (2000).

40 *Orkneyinga saga*, 130–1. Haraldr had a brother, Kristrøðr, who died fighting with him: *Heimskringla*, iii, 280–1.

41 *Heimskringla*, iii, 229. The Danish Saxo Grammaticus has a different description of the way in which Magnus got his cognomen. Saxo, 342^{10-16}, Christiansen, *Saxo*, i, 108, note 291. Saxo was hostile to Haraldr *gilli* and his claim, blaming him for the wars that racked Norway: Saxo, i, 363^{7-15}; Christiansen, *Saxo*, i, 138.

42 Ludvig Holm-Olsen (ed.), *Konungs Skuggsjá*, Norsk-Historisk Kjeldeskrift-Institutt, Norrøne tekster 1 (Oslo, 1983), 22. L.M. Larson (trans.), *The King's Mirror* (New York, 1917), 106.

43 David Sellar, 'The origins and ancestry of Somerled', *SHR*, 45 (1966), 123–42, drew attention to both the later Highland tradition that a woman of the medieval Somerled family married a King Harald of Norway, and a late suggestion that Bjaðok was the aunt of the *regulus* of Argyll (129). The latter was made by the eighteenth-century antiquarian James Johnstone in *Antiquitates Celto-Normannicæ* (Copenhagen, 1786), 152. Johnstone, the English chaplain in Copenhagen, published in the same year relevant parts of *Heimskringla*, with

translations into Latin (in *Antiquitates Celto-Scandicæ*, Copenhagen, 1786). In the absence of any older references, he may have created the relationship himself. Craigie, 'Gaelic Words and Names...' suggested that Bjaðok was Irish *Blathmach* (444). Somerled's daughter was named Bethoc. While it seems unlikely, if the relationship is correct, Eysteinn would have been first cousin to Somerled (himself married to a daughter of Godred Crovan's son and successor, King Óláfr of Man), and thus possessed of relations that make his lack of involvement in the affairs of the kingdom the more remarkable.

44 *Orkneyinga saga*, 193–5, records the visit, though not homage as such. The Manx *Chronicle* (Broderick, *CKMI*, fol. 36r.) speaks of Guðröðr doing homage (incorrectly dating it to 1142).

45 Richard Howlett (ed.), *Chronicles of the Reigns of Stephen, Henry II, and Richard I*, Rolls Series 82 (4 vols, London, 1884–9), iv, 228–9. Translated in Anderson, *Scottish Annals*, 245. See Johnsen, 'Payments from the Hebrides'.

46 AFM. For the family relationships of the Manx kings, see the genealogical table on p. 12.

47 Broderick, *CKMI*, fol. 37r. See Ian Beuermann, *Man amongst Kings and Bishops* (Oslo, 2002), 182–91.

48 AU. See Duffy, 'Irishmen and Islesmen', 121–7. See too Seán Duffy, 'The Bruce brothers and the Irish Sea world, 1306–29', *Cambridge Medieval Celtic Studies*, 21 (1991), 55–86, 67.

49 See Beuermann, *Man among kings and bishops* for a discussion of the journey of the Manx king to Norway, and the secular and ecclesiastical motivations. For the situation with Eysteinn esp. 52–63.

50 *Heimskringla*, iii, 327–9. The effects on the Farne Islands off Lindisfarne were described by the monk Reginald of Durham. See *Reginaldi Monachi Dunelmensis Libellus de Admirandis Beati Cuthberti*, Publications of the Surtees Society, i (1834), 65–6.

51 *Orkneyinga saga*, 193.

52 See Arne Odd Johnsen, *Er Einar Skulesons fyrstedikt '. . . lutter historiske og historiske nøjagtige . . .'?* Det Kgl Norske Videnskabers Selskabs skrifter nr 2. (Oslo, 1965), 8, and the reference to Hefle-Leclerq, *Histoire des conciles*, v, I, Paris 1812, 826.

53 Beuermann argues convincingly for this interpretation. See esp. 202–32.

54 Recorded in a papal bull of 1152–3. J.C. Atkinson (ed.), *The Coucher Book of Furness Abbey*, Chetham Society (new ser., vols 9, 11,14, Manchester, 1886–8), vol. 14 (1888), 591–5, 594. See Johnson, *On the Background*, 9.

55 Arne Odd Johnsen, *Studier vedrørende Kardinal Nicolaus Brekespears legasjon til Norden* (Oslo, 1945), 328–30; *idem.*, *On the Background for the Establishment of the Norwegian Church Province. Some new Viewpoints* (Oslo, 1967), 9. See the discussion by Alex Woolf below, chapter 15.

56 Margaret Cormack, 'Saints and sinners: reflections on death in some Icelandic sagas', *Gripla*, viii, Rit Stofnunar Årna Magnússonar á Islandi (1994), 187–218, esp. 192–3 (note), 199–200.

57 *Hákonar saga*, *Eirspennill* text, 555; Dasent trans., 150. Broderick, *CKMI*, fol. 37v. In *Orkneyinga saga* (274) the family is known as Dalverjaætt.

58 As king of Man, Godred witnessed the Great Charter to Kelso Abbey in April or May 1159. G.W.S. Barrow (ed.), *Regesta Regum Scottorum, I. The Acts of Malcolm IV, King of Scots 1153–1165* (Edinburgh, 1960), 8, 192–5 (no. 131), 194.

59 *Heimskringla*, iii, 367.

60 AU. See Máire Herbert, *Iona, Kells and Derry. The History and Hagiography of the Monastic Familia of Columba* (Oxford, 1988), 120.

61 Broderick, *CKMI*, fol. 40r. For the buildings on Iona, see *Royal Commission for the Ancient Historical Monuments of Scotland (RCAHMS). Argyll. An Inventory of the Ancient Monuments. 4: Iona.* (Edinburgh,1982). The chapel in the cemetery is the oldest surviving building on the island and shows evidence on mid-twelfth-century Irish work.

62 *Dip. Norv.*, vii, no. 4, 4–5. Also printed in Munch, *Chronica Regum Manniae*, 152–3. See Ian B. Cowan and D.E. Easson, *Medieval Religious Houses. Scotland* (2nd edn, London, 1976), 59, see also 49; D.E.R Watt, 'Bishops in the Isles before 1203: bibliography and biographical lists', *The Innes Review*, xlv, no. 2, (Autumn 1994), 99–119, esp. 113 n.7, 119.

63 AU.

64 Steinar Imsen, 'Nidarosprovinsen', in Steinar Imsen (ed.), *Ecclesia Nidrosiensis 1153–1527* (Bergen, 2003), 15.

65 Ó Cuív, B. (ed.), 1957.'A poem in praise of Raghnall king of Man'. Baile Suthach Sídh nEamhna. *Éigse* VII: 4, 283–301. Rögnvaldr's career can be traced through *Orkneyinga saga* and through English diplomatic records, in particular those collected in *Dip. Norv* xix and *Regesta Norvegica* vol.i.

66 Guðrún P.Helgadóttir (ed.), *Hrafns saga Sveinbjarnarsonar* (Oxford, 1987), 22. The editor dates the saga to *c.* 1230–60 (lxxxviii). In this account, Óláfr Dubh demands landing-tax from the Icelanders, but, seeing that the Icelanders are prepared to resist, settles for much less than originally required. There is no evidence that Óláfr had rights in Sanday, which was shortly afterwards in the control of the Garmoran branch of Somerled's family.

67 AU. They also raided Derry with Thomas of Galloway in 1212 and one of the brothers, Ruaidrí, with Thomas again in 1214 (AU, ALC s.a. 1211, 1213).

68 Broderick, *CKMI*, fols 41r–v.

69 *Böglunga sögur* in *Eirspennill*, 468; Gustav Storm (ed.), *Islandske Annaler indtil 1578* (Christiania [Oslo], 1888), 123, s.a. 1209, 1210; both cited in Anderson, *Early Sources*, ii, 378–9, 381–2. The text is condensed in *Eirspennill* (and incomplete in the other medieval codices). The journey from the kingdom to pay tribute is found in the longer text, which survives only in complete form in a Danish translation from about 1600. Hallvard Magerøy (ed.), *Soga om Birkebeinar og Baglar. Böglunga sögur* (1988).

70 Broderick, *CKMI*, fol. 42v.

71 *Eirspennill*, 522, 546; Anderson, *Early Sources*, 455, 461.

72 *Dip. Norv.*, i, no. 28, 22–3. Also printed in Munch, *Chronica Regum Manniae*, 156–7. The excuse of the dangerous seas was used again in 1349: see *Regesta Norvegica*, v (ed. Erik Gunnes, 1979), no. 1171, 410. The situation in Greenland was far worse. In 1242, Nicholas was consecrated to a see already vacant for ten years. He died in 1242, never having gone to Greenland. In 1246 his successor, Óláfr, was consecrated: he went to Greenland the following year, and, notwithstanding a journey to Iceland in 1262–4, he survived until 1280. The see was then vacant for another eight years. See Ólafur Halldórsson, *Grœnland í miðaldaritum* (Reykjavik, 1978), 67.

73 *Dip. Norv.*, vii, no. 12, 12–3.

74 See *Dip. Norv.*, xix, no. 51, 57–9 and no. 52, 59–64 for Icelandic laws (before *c.* 1170) on those who died abroad. See no. 63, 68 on shipwrecks; no. 65, 69 for the 1180s; no. 82 (1204–14), 76; all three lost, also listed in *APS*, i, 3; see too for trade reference *Dip. Norv.*, xix, no. 91 (1208), 82–3.

75 Gustav Indrebø (ed.), *Sverris saga*, Den Norske Historisk Kildeskriftkommission (Christiania [Oslo], 1920), 81.
76 Broderick, *CKMI*, fols 43v.–44r. See chapter 4 below, pp. 93–4.
77 *Hákonar saga*, *Eirspennill*, 555; Dasent trans., 150.
78 See G.W.S. Barrow, 'Badenoch and Strathspey, 1130–1312: 1. secular and political', *Northern Scotland*, 8 (1988), 1–15, 5–6.
79 *Eirspennill*, 555–8, Anderson, *Early Sources*, ii, 472–8. See note 37 above.
80 *Dip. Norv.*, xix, no. 223, 151 (24 May 1236); 228, 153 (8 April 1237).
81 Broderick, *CKMI*, fols 46r.–v.; *Dip. Norv.*, xix, no. 238, 158; *Hákonar saga*, *Eirspennill*, 626, *Frissbók*, 534–5, Anderson, *Early Sources*, ii, 547–8.
82 AFM. It is also possible that this refers to the death of Ruaidrí's brother Domnall. Neither could have been younger than 60, and were probably of an age with the third grandson of Somerled Dungaðr (Donnchad, fl. 1177–1237), and nearer 80. Ruaidrí and after him, Dubgall, held Garmoran, but had a claim on Kintyre. Dubgall is named lord of 'Machumel' in Kintyre in a letter of 17 April 1247, printed in Munch, *Chronica Regum Manniae*, 157; and is later named as king of Argyll (AC; ALC). Hákon gave Dubgall a castle on Kintyre in 1263, perhaps in recognition of this claim. *Hákonar saga*, *Flateyjarbók*, iii, 222, 227; Dasent trans., 363. See Duncan and Brown, 'Argyll and the Isles', 200.
83 Storm, *Islandske Annaler*, 132, s.a. 1249.
84 Eógan's difficulties with holding land from both Scotland and Norway are dealt with in the saga. Matthew Paris was also aware of them: H.R. Luard (ed.), *Matthœi Parisiensis, Monachi Sancti Albani, Chronica Majora*, Rolls Series 57 (7 vols, London, 1872–83), v (1880), 88–9.
85 Broderick, *CKMI*, .fols 48r, 49r.
86 As Magnús son of Óláfr Dubh was in Norway in that year, and as Eógan was increasingly involved with Scotland, Munch suggested that the reference should be to Magnús rather than Eógan (*Chronica Regum Manniae*, notes, 206–7).
87 He set out on 5 July, and may have waited to hear whether the remaining Icelandic chieftains had submitted at the Alðing, held in the last week of June.
88 There is the partial text which Queen Joanna of Scotland wrote to her brother Henry at about this time. Shirley (ed.), *Royal and other Historical Letters*... i, 219–20 (no. 195); also printed in *Dip. Norv.*, xix, no. 157, 120.
89 *Hákonar saga*, *Frissbók*, 574–5, 578; Anderson, *Early Sources*, ii, 622, 634.
90 See R.W. Munro, Monro's Western Isles of Scotland and Genealogies of the Clans, 1549 (Edinbugh and London, 1961), 56.
91 In one of the verses he and his supposed brother, Margað, are termed 'jöfrar', a poetic word most often used of kings: *Hákonar saga*, *Frissbók*, 573.
92 AC; ALC. Storm, *Islandske Annaler*, 137, s.a. 1268; also *Flateyjarbók*, Annals, iii, 537. AFM calls Dubgall 'lord'.
93 Eiríkr died in Norway in 1287 (Storm, *Islandske Annaler*, 196). The two Norwegian texts of *Hákonar saga* preserve Dubgall's patronymic, Ruðrason, while this is lost in two of the three Icelandic texts. *Flateyjarbók* mistakenly refers to Eiríkr as Dubgall's father (iii, 219).
94 See chapter 11, below.

3 *Man, Somerled, and the Isles: the Rise of a New Dynasty, c. 1100–64*

R. ANDREW McDONALD

By the eleventh century, the Irish Sea and the Hebrides comprised a single maritime sphere of influence linked by the highway of the western seas and the fleets of galleys commanded by those who aspired to greatness there. Within the ambit of this Irish Sea world, competition for hegemony was intense, encompassing Irish, Scandinavian, Manx, Hiberno-Norse, Hebridean, and later, English and Scottish elements. This is demonstrated clearly enough by the events of the late eleventh century, as discussed in greater detail above. For 20 years after the death of Guðröðr Crovan in 1095, dominance in the Isles was a glittering prize sought by, among others, Lögmaðr (Lagman), a son of Guðröðr Crovan; Ingimundr, a Norseman appointed by King Magnús III 'Barelegs' of Norway; and Domnall son of Tadc Ua Briain, a nephew of Muirchertach, the powerful king of Munster. It was not until *c.*1113 that Óláfr, another son of Guðröðr Crovan, began to reign in Man and an element of stability was restored, but by then the discord of the preceding decades had sown the seeds for further strife as a new power came of age to compete for supremacy in the Isles.

One of the key features in the history of the Hebrides is the Scandinavian invasions and settlements of the ninth and tenth centuries. The impact of the Vikings on Scotland's western islands is best seen in the distribution of Scandinavian place-names,[1] and in the nomenclature of the islands themselves: to the Gael they became known as *Innse Gall*, the islands of the foreigners. The Scandinavian settlement in the Hebrides (mostly Norwegian in nature) effectively wrested control of the islands, as well as parts of the adjacent mainland territory of Argyll, away from the Scots, a fact formally acknowledged in the 1098 agreement between King Magnús Barelegs of Norway and King Edgar of Scotland (1097–1107, wrongly called Malcolm in the *Orkneyinga saga*), whereby 'King Malcolm [*sic*] would let him [Magnús] have the islands off the west coast which were separated by water navigable by a ship with the rudder set'.[2] But in making this agreement the two kings were partitioning territory that they did not in fact effectively govern. Control in the Isles required the presence of a powerful stabilising force, which neither the Scottish nor Norwegian monarchies were able to provide. The successors of Magnus proved unable to follow up on his achievements, thanks in large measure to disturbed civil conditions in Norway until 1208.[3] Thus, no king of Norway visited the Isles personally between the time of Magnús Barelegs and the formidable Hákon Hákonarson a century and a half later, in 1263. This void might have opened the way for a waxing of Scottish influence in the Isles, but there was to be no such resurgence; the descendants of Malcolm III 'Canmore' (1058–93) and Queen Margaret (d.1093) diverted their attentions and ambitions southwards. The result was a power vacuum or no-man's-land in the Isles into which an aggressive new dynasty could flex its muscles and carve out a sphere of influence for itself. From about 1100 the kings of Man and the Isles began to lose the race to fill this power vacuum to chieftains of mixed Scandinavian and Gaelic descent, whose position was based upon an impressive control of the seas.[4] The most prominent of these leaders in the twelfth century was Somerled mac Gilla Brigde, and from *c.*1150 to the end of the kingdom of the Isles in 1266 the history of the islands was dominated by competition between Somerled's kin and the descendants of Guðröðr Crovan for mastery of the western seas.

THE SOURCES

The sources that record the career of Somerled are diverse, and are the subject of considerable debate among historians. In assessing the source material, three interrelated problems present themselves: first, how reliable are the medieval and post-medieval sources, especially the Gaelic pedigrees and clan histories? Second, what is the proper balance between these two types of source material? And third, what is the perspective from which the sources were composed?

There are four major contemporary sources upon which much of our knowledge of Somerled rests: the two Scottish chronicles of Holyrood and Melrose; the *Chronicles of the Kings of Man and the Isles*; and the Latin poem known as the *Carmen de Morte Sumerledi.* To these may be added the Irish annals, but their entries relating to Somerled are so sparse that they do little more than corroborate the other sources. Nevertheless, their value should not be underestimated: not only do they fill in crucial details that are missing from other accounts (such as the name of the son of Somerled slain at Renfrew in 1164) but they also provide important information on the status of Somerled. Yet, for all their value as contemporary documents, the four major sources just mentioned are not without their difficulties. They are jejune. They take no notice of Somerled before 1153, when he was carving out territories for himself in Argyll and the Hebrides.

And, most significantly, they are uniformly hostile in their attitude to the Hebridean chieftain. It is worthwhile exploring in greater detail the nature of this hostility, since it has significantly affected Somerledian historiography through the centuries.[5]

Although the two Scottish chronicles of Holyrood and Melrose are of the first importance to the historian of medieval Scotland, they also have serious limitations. The most significant is simply that, as Bruce Webster has so aptly stated: 'Both were compiled by members of new monastic orders which were introduced from outside Scotland by kings who were anxious to modernise their kingdom'.[6] In short, then, these chronicles were composed by writers who had many interests outside of Scotland and who represented alien elements in Scottish society; consequently, they can hardly be expected to understand fully the structure and hierarchy of native Scottish society, much less the even more fluid situation in the Isles. Moreover, the connection between the kings of Scots and the monastic centres at which these chronicles were produced is not insignificant: it meant that the chroniclers were very sympathetic to the cause of the kings descended from Malcolm III and Queen Margaret. The bias in the Scottish sources can be clearly seen in the 1164 entry for the Melrose chronicle: Somerled is said to have been 'wickedly rebelling' against King Malcolm IV, whom the chronicler regarded as his lord, and his death is attributed to divine vengeance.[7]

At first glance the Manx chronicle known as *Cronica Regum Mannie & Insularum* might appear to be less biased than either of the Scottish chronicles, since it was compiled on the Isle of Man in the thirteenth century and narrates the activities of the kings of Man and the Isles from *c.*1066 to 1266.[8] It therefore notes the doings of Somerled and his descendants in an insular context, and is of particular significance for the present study. It is, however, known to be unreliable and is often confused in its chronology; moreover, because Somerled had wrested power from the Manx king in 1156, and expelled him entirely in 1158 as he expanded his dominion over the Isles, the Manx chronicle is hardly objective and tends, like the chronicles of Holyrood and Melrose, to be unfriendly to Somerled and his descendants. Thus, when it discusses the partitioning of the kingdom between Somerled and Guðröðr, the Manx king, in 1156, it notes that, 'the reason for the collapse of the kingdom emanated from the time the sons of Somerled got possession of it'.[9]

Finally, there is the Latin poem entitled *Carmen de Morte Sumerledi.* Although it is of more value to the study of Somerled in a Scottish rather than an insular context, in many ways this is a remarkable document, composed by an eye-witness, describing the assault of Somerled on the

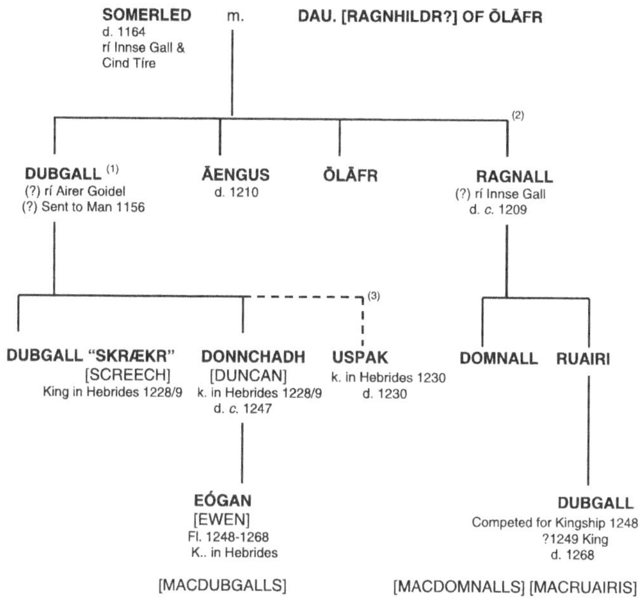

Notes:
(1) It is uncertain whether Dubgall or Ragnall was the eldest son of Somerled
(2) Somerled had other children about whom little is known
(3) Speculative

Fig. 3.1 *The family of Somerled (simplified) and the kingship of the Isles.*

Scottish mainland in 1164 and the fate of the attacking army as it was defeated by a local force. But the Glasgow provenance of the document ensures that it takes a profoundly hostile tone in treating of the Hebrideans, who plundered the area around the city and cathedral. Thus, Somerled can be described as 'foul with treachery, the cruellest of foes', while his army is similarly described as treacherous and barbaric.[10]

These more or less contemporary accounts possess two major shortcomings. In the first instance, they are uniformly hostile to Somerled and his cause, a fact, as noted above, that has had serious repercussions for Somerledian historiography. Second, there is their sparse nature: they lack specific details about Somerled's origins, ancestry, and rise to power – precisely the sorts of things about which we need to know more in the present context. In order to assess these problems it is necessary to turn to the late medieval and post-medieval genealogies and clan histories. The traditional genealogy of Somerled is preserved in at least 15 accounts in Latin and Gaelic, ranging in date from the late fourteenth to the eighteenth

Fig. 3.2 *Monastery at Maughold that was surrounded by Somerled's chieftains and his men, in a failed attempt to attack and steal booty from the church, which Somerled had reluctantly agreed to, as graphically described in the Manx Chronicle. Viewed here from the east with North Barrule in the background. Photo: Peter Davey.*

century, while the Clan Donald traditions about Somerled and his descendants are preserved in the book of Clanranald and by the *seanchaidh* Hugh MacDonald, both of seventeenth-century date.[11] The attraction of these sources is that they provide considerable detail on the early life of Somerled; the drawback is the debate over whether they possess any validity at all because of their late date and the nature of their transmission. Yet recent research has demonstrated that, when utilised with caution, these sources can be made to divulge significant information. David Sellar, who has explored in great detail the Gaelic genealogies of Somerled, has shown that they correspond remarkably well with one another and with other extant sources like the annals, and that, 'there is a strong case for believing the pedigree from Somerled back to Fergus [ninth century] to be authentic in detail'.[12] As for the accounts of the clan historians, they are only beginning to be explored as fossilized oral histories, passed down for centuries by generations of *seanchaidhe*, but here again the work of Sellar has been instrumental in revealing their significance. By carefully corroborating these sources with the genealogies and the chronicles, he has stressed that

> in their narration of the general trend of events they are usually correct...Their account of the origins of Somerled is verifiable inasmuch as he does appear to have risen from obscurity and to have carved out for himself a principality in Argyll and the Isles.[13]

SOMERLEDIAN HISTORIOGRAPHY

As a ruler on what historians have come to term the periphery of the Scottish kingdom, Somerled has tended to fall between two stools in modern historiography. On the one hand, most recent Scottish historical writing, taking as its central theme the 'making of the kingdom' – the development of the Scottish monarchy and the territorial consolidation of the kingdom – has paid relatively little attention to the peripheral regions. Where these regions are discussed, it is most often in the context of the 'winning of the west' – of the integration of Argyll and the Isles, Galloway, and the far north into the feudal kingdom of Scotland.[14] Indeed, it seems safe to say that modern historians, like their medieval counterparts, have been both frightened and fascinated with the unruly frontier regions on the periphery of the Scottish kingdom, although a considerable corpus of material dealing with these regions has appeared since the 1990s.[15] On the other hand, despite the Irish connections of Somerled in both genealogical and political terms (his descendants claimed descent from one Gofraid mac Fergusa, lord of Airgialla; and we know that in 1164 he was able to call upon warriors from Dublin for his ill-fated invasion of the Scottish main land), the fact that his main sphere of activity was the Isles and the Irish Sea means that he does not enjoy a place in the sun in modern Irish historical writing.

It has been said that the writing of national history as a genre 'has had the unfortunate result of obscuring entities once important in their right that have not survived as nation states or even as geographical units'.[16] This is particularly apropos of the kingdom of Man and the Isles, which has tended to slip through the cracks of national historiography, so to speak: a 1994 study on King John, for example, has nothing to say of John's relations with the Manx rulers in a discussion of his interactions with the native kings in Wales, Ireland, and Scotland.[17] One of the unfortunate results of this development is that, in company with the Manx kings, Somerled is seldom, if ever, viewed primarily in a maritime context.[18] I began with the assertion that the culture of the Irish sea and the western islands was a maritime one, and that, as such, the Hebrides were intimately connected with Ireland, the Isle of Man, the Northern Isles and Norway. It is well to remember that, from the Isles, the Scottish court at Edinburgh, Perth, or Stirling was less accessible than Norway was by sea. We must therefore set aside the tendency, partly inherited from the chronicles of Holyrood and Melrose, to study Somerled from a purely Scottish perspective. Viewed only from the standpoint of Scottish national historical writing, Somerled becomes at best an over-mighty subject or a vassal of the Scottish king, at worst a rebel and a traitor. Yet much depends on perspective; only when Somerled is placed within a broader maritime context, outwith the usual strait-jacket of traditional historiography, does his true standing and significance as a sea-king and a dominant force in the history of the Isles become apparent. In short, the traditional perspectives need to be set on their heads: the periphery becomes the core; the core becomes the margins. To Somerled and the Manx kings, as well as to others who plied the western seas, the seaways defined their own core, with Scotland, England and Ireland representing the periphery – a concept that has been effectively developed in recent writing on the subject.[19]

SOMERLED'S ORIGINS AND ANCESTRY

The date and place of Somerled's birth are lost to history, and the topic of his ancestry has provoked some lively debate. Nineteenth- and early twentieth-century historians and antiquarians were divided over whether his heritage should be regarded as Norse or Gaelic. His name, Sumarliði, is Norse, meaning 'Summer Warrior', and is rendered Somurli and later Somhairle (hence, Sorley) in Gaelic. Although it originally seems to have denoted not a personal name, but rather an epithet for Viking, by the end of the tenth century it had begun to appear as a given name. Some historians, arguing on the basis of this evidence and a distrust of the traditional genealogies, viewed Somerled's background as primarily Norse. Others, regarding the pedigrees with less scepticism, pointed to the Gaelic names of his father, Gilla Brigde, 'devotee of St Brigit', and grandfather, Gilla Adomnáin, 'devotee of Adomnán' (abbot of Iona, biographer of St Columba), and stressed his predominantly Gaelic nature.[20] In fact, Somerled's heritage was neither purely Norse nor purely Gaelic but mixed Gaelic-Norse, a legacy of the Scandinavian settlement in the Hebrides and the subsequent intermarriage between Gael and Norse. The traditional genealogies of Somerled, as already noted, have asserted that his descent can be traced back to the mid-ninth-century Hebridean chieftain Gofraid mac Fergusa, lord of Airgialla in the north of Ireland. This is without doubt the same individual who is said to have assisted Kenneth mac Alpin in 836 and who, in his obit in Irish annals, was styled *toisech Innsi Gall* (lord of the Hebrides). From Gofraid the genealogies continue back to the mythical Colla Uais, many generations too short, but here they probably represent merely a pointer to the tribe or people of Airgialla from whom Gofraid and Somerled were purportedly sprung. Somerled's supposed ancestry thus contains not only Irish but also Scandinavian threads; it places him firmly in a Hebridean context; and it may well have given him an ancestral claim to the Isles which he asserted with vigour in the early part of the twelfth century.[21]

Somerled's family connections also reinforce his mixed Gaelic-Norse heritage and his place within an insular context. Through marriage, he was able to establish ties with the leading figures of the western seaboard of Scotland and the Irish Sea world in the early twelfth century. Perhaps the most important of these matrimonial connections was that which linked Somerled to the Manx king, Óláfr son of Guðröðr Crovan, and which, ironically, helped to bring about the downfall of Óláfr's own descendants. The *Orkneyinga saga*, an otherwise confused source for Somerled's activities, records that he married a daughter of Óláfr of Man named Ragnhildr. However garbled it may be in its account of Somerled's death, the *Orkneyinga saga* accurately records both the fact that Somerled was ruling in Argyll, as well as the names of three of his sons by Ragnhildr: Dubgall, Ragnall (ON Rögnvaldr), and Áengus; the Manx chronicle adds a son named Óláfr.[22] The date of the marriage remains unknown. The year 1140 has been cited and is commonly repeated, but on the basis of no good evidence; perhaps the most that can be said is that it had been contracted by *c.*1150. On the other hand, it can hardly have taken place before Somerled's rise to prominence on mainland Argyll and in the Isles, and as is argued below, there is good evidence that this did not occur until the 1130s. Thus, Somerled's marriage to a daughter of King Óláfr of Man is likely to have taken place between about 1135 and 1150. It is instructive to note, however, that this was not Somerled's first marriage. Later, and therefore less reliable sources, indicate that he had several children from other unions, perhaps in the Gaelic tradition of handfasting, or else perhaps simply from what contemporary reformers regarded as barbarous marriage customs. It is worthwhile here drawing parallels with Ireland, where kings married early and often, where concepts of illegitimacy were vague, and where divorce was easy for both parties. Moreover, polygamy appears to have been practised in the Irish Sea in the twelfth century; the Manx chronicle noted with disapproval that Óláfr, the son of Guðröðr Crovan, 'over-indulged in the domestic vice of kings', presumably a reference to its earlier comment that he 'had many concubines'.[23] Whatever the case may have been, the marriages of Somerled are significant because they produced many offspring, making Somerled the founder of a vigorous race of sea-kings who were in constant competition with the Manx kings for hegemony in the Isles until the 1260s.[24]

Although the marriage of Somerled to Ragnhildr is the most significant of his matrimonial connections in the present context, it is instructive to note one other. Somerled's sister married Malcolm mac Heth (d. 1168), a figure prominent in the history of the Scottish highlands in the early twelfth century but whose identity and ancestry form one of the important unsolved mysteries of twelfth-century Scottish history.[25] This marriage must have been contracted before 1134, since in that year mac Heth was captured by the Scots and confined in Roxburgh Castle, where he was to spend the next 23 years in captivity. A daughter of this match was eventually to marry Haraldr Maddadsson (1139–1206), the last of the great Orkney earls.[26]

The patterns of matrimony demonstrated by Somerled and his kin are significant. Medieval marriage was, of course, a political tool – it cemented alliances, secured status, honour, and power, and provided important resources. Tracing the matrimonial politics of prominent figures in the Isles reveals a network of marriage alliances that criss-cross the Irish Sea like war-galleys and take as their nexus the Scandinavian dynasty of Man. Somerled was by no means unique in securing an alliance with this powerful and important dynasty. Fergus of Galloway, a contemporary of Somerled and like him the progenitor of a family with interests in the Irish Sea in the twelfth and thirteenth centuries, gave his daughter Affreca in marriage to King Óláfr of Man. The marriage of Fergus's daughter to Óláfr and of Óláfr's daughter to Somerled are enlightening in a Scottish context, since we see these powerful rulers on the periphery of the Scottish kingdom making no attempt to forge links with the Francophile Scottish monarchs or with the Anglo-Norman settlers. Indeed, it is tempting to suppose that the matrimonial politics of Fergus and Somerled represent a conscious policy of separation from the Canmore dynasty and its attendants at court; an interpretation reinforced strongly by the marriage of Somerled's sister to Malcolm mac Heth since both mac Heth and Somerled were involved in conflict with the Scottish kings.[27]

This web of matrimonial connections was not restricted to a Manx-Hebridean axis; it is also possible to extend it westward towards Ireland. Later in the twelfth century, the warrior-adventurer John de Courcy, who had carved out a territory for himself in Ulster, would marry the sister of the Manx king Rögnvaldr – an alliance which proved expedient when, in

1204, de Courcy was driven from Ulster and sought assistance from his brother-in-law. Rögnvaldr responded with 100 war-galleys and assisted de Courcy in an abortive attempt to regain his foothold in Ulster in 1205, thus illustrating the potency of an alliance with the Manx kings.[28] Even as late as the middle of the thirteenth century there were still alliances between the descendants of Somerled and the Manx dynasty: Somerled's great-grandson, Eógan son of Donnchad mac Dubgaill (Ewen Macdougall), gave a daughter in marriage to Magnús son of Óláfr Dubh, the last of the Manx kings, and on his death she was wed, *c.*1268, to the earl of Strathearn, a vivid example of how marriage alliances reflect political outlook, since in 1266 the Hebrides and Man were ceded to Scotland.[29] Tracing the marriage alliances of some of the key figures of the Irish Sea in the twelfth century reveals further the difficulties inherent in traditional approaches, and reinforces the trans-national nature of the Irish Sea world in the period in question. It was only natural, as well as a reflection on his prominence and status, that Somerled should have allied himself with the Manx kings. That the alliance would disintegrate in the lifetime of Óláfr's son, Guðröðr, and turn to rivalry between the descendants of Somerled and Óláfr is one of the prominent themes in the history of the Isles – but before addressing it, we need to explore briefly the rise to prominence of Somerled in the west.

THE WHEEL OF FORTUNE: SOMERLED'S RISE TO POWER

The rise of Somerled to prominence first in Argyll and then in the Isles is a process largely obscured by the fragmentary nature of the historical evidence. Somerled appears in the light of history in the first half of the twelfth century already mature and already in control of both mainland Argyll and some, at least, of the adjacent islands. The evidence for his rise to power in the west rests largely upon the seventeenth-century clan historians and upon the circumstantial evidence provided by the marriage alliances just discussed. According to the seventeenth-century sources, Somerled's ancestors held a position of prominence in Argyll before being either forfeited or dispossessed by MacBeth (king of Scots 1040–57), Domnall Bán (1093–7), and the Scandinavians; since little is known of these ancestors other than their names, their status cannot be corroborated, and these traditions remain unverified. It is possible that the rise to power of Guðröðr Crovan in the Isles or the expedition of Magnus Barelegs to the west in 1098 had been responsible for the displacement of some local chieftains, but so much remains speculation. We are on firmer ground in stating that the process of Somerled's re-establishment began on mainland

Argyll: the Chronicle of Melrose styled him *regulus* of Argyll, the Latin equivalent of *rí Airer Goidel*, and Somerled's descendants, the Mac Dubgaill dynasty of Lorn, took the territorial designation *de Ergadia*, so there is good evidence for regarding Argyll as the ancestral territory of Somerled. Whether this is so or not, Somerled's activities on the mainland were certainly eclipsed by those in the Isles, and with this expansion the title of *rí Airer Goidel* gave way to that of *rí Innsi Gall*, the more important of the two.[30]

The rise of Somerled must have taken place in the decades between about 1120 and 1140. Between the death of Henry I in 1135 and the second treaty of Durham in 1139, the Scottish king, David I, had diverted his attention southward as a major player in the civil war between King Stephen and the Empress Matilda, and was attempting to make territorial gains in the north of England.[31] During the decade of the 1130s the Scottish king was therefore in little or no position to oppose Somerledian expansion on the west coast. Moreover, the marriage alliances made by Somerled can only have been contracted after his rise to prominence; no Manx king would allow his daughter to marry an unknown upstart, and although the date of this marriage is not known, that of Somerled's sister to Malcolm mac Heth must have taken place before 1134, when Malcolm was captured and imprisoned in Roxburgh Castle. That Somerled's rise occurred before his marriage might be supported by the largely untrustworthy details provided in the seventeenth-century sources, where he had already made himself master of Argyll, Morvern, Kintyre, Lorn, Knapdale, and Mull before his marriage to Ragnhildr.[32] In summary then, Somerled, a chieftain of mixed Gaelic-Norse heritage from an insular milieu, began his rise to prominence in Argyll in the first half of the twelfth century and subsequently expanded his activity into the Isles. It is to this expansion that we must now turn.

SOMERLED AND THE ISLES

The deaths of both David I of Scotland in 1152 and Óláfr of Man in 1152 or 1153 destabilised the political situation in both Scotland and the Isles. The two powerful rulers who had, at least in part, held Somerled in check were removed from the scene, and, as has been poignantly stated, 'in these troubled waters Somerled fished assiduously'.[33] Between 1153 and 1157 he was involved in an uprising on the Scottish mainland against the young king of Scots, Malcolm IV, but it is clear from his subsequent activities that his primary interest and sphere of influence lay in the western seas. This is demonstrated by the fact that, when he was invited to intervene in the Isles in 1155 or 1156, Somerled seems to have abandoned his efforts on the Scottish mainland – which led to the capture of Domnall mac Heth, one of the leaders of the uprising.[34]

The Manx chronicle recorded of King Óláfr that 'he was a peaceable man and had all the kings of Ireland and Scotland as confederates in such a way that no-one dared disturb the kingdom of the Isles during his lifetime'.[35] But if this was so, then his death and the accession of his son Guðröðr paved the way for the expansion of the new dynasty of Somerled into the Isles. Guðröðr was in Norway at the time of his father's death, doing homage to the king of Norway for Man and the Isles. He returned to deal with the killers of his father and, after undertaking an expedition to Dublin, returned to Man. The Manx chronicle records that:

> When he saw that he was firmly established on the throne, and that no-one was able to oppose him, he began exercising tyranny against his chieftains, for some of them he disinherited, while others he deprived of their positions'.[36]

One of the disinherited chiefs, Þorfinnr, son of Óttarr, sent word to Somerled of Guðröðr's behaviour and invited him to send his son Dubgall, 'that he should make him king over the Isles'. Somerled, the chronicle relates, 'was very much pleased to hear this request and handed his son Dubgall over to him [Þorfinnr], who took and conducted him through all the Isles'.[37] Hostages to secure the good behaviour of the Islesmen were taken, but one disconcerted chieftain escaped to warn Guðröðr, who, hearing the news of Somerled's attempted coup, collected a fleet with which to challenge him. On the night of the Epiphany (5-6 January) in 1156, Somerled's fleet of eighty vessels met and defeated Guðröðr's galleys. According to the Manx chronicle there was a great slaughter on both sides, but when the day dawned,

> they made peace and divided the kingdom of the Isles between them. The kingdom has existed in two parts from that day up until the present time, and the reason for the collapse of the kingdom emanated from the time the sons of Somerled got possession of it.[38]

The invitation by Þorfinnr the son of Óttarr to Somerled to send Dubgall to assume the kingship of the Isles raises important questions. Who was Þorfinnr son of Óttarr, and why did he seek out Somerled? Why did he request Somerled's son and not Somerled himself?

The problem of Somerled's expansion into the Isles is intimately connected with the politics of the Irish Sea since the mid-eleventh century. One of the major themes in the history of the region between *c.*1050 and the late twelfth century is the close connection between Dublin and Man, and it is difficult to escape the conclusion that it was this axis that drew Somerled into Manx affairs in the mid 1150s. Although Dublin and Man had probably been ruled by separate kings since *c.*1112, in the mid-twelfth century, 'they continued to be dominated by a clique of aristocrats with a foot in both camps'.[39] In 1152, Man had been invaded by the men of Dublin, and in 1157 (according to the Manx chronicle) Guðröðr the son of Óláfr was invited to assume the overlordship of Dublin by the populace, in what has been regarded as a preference for non-Irish domination. According to the chronicle, Guðröðr fought a fierce battle with Muirchertach Mac Lochlainn, the king of Cenél nEógain in Ulster and overlord of Dublin, although Irish sources seem to know nothing of such a conflict.[40] Þorfinnr, son of Óttarr, described by the Manx chronicle as a chieftain of the Isles, 'more powerful than the rest', has been identified as a relative of that Óttarr, an Islesman, who seized power in Dublin in 1142 and held on until his assassination in 1148. In 1154 the Ulster king Muirchertach Mac Lochlainn assumed the kingship of Dublin, and an incident of that same year reveals connections between Dublin and Argyll and the Isles. The Annals of the Four Masters record a naval conflict between Mac Lochlainn and Toirrdelbach Ua Conchobair of Connacht, and Mac Lochlainn's fleet is said to have included ships from Galloway, Arran, Kintyre, Man, and the 'shores of Scotland also' – presumably a reference to Argyll and the Hebrides.[41] Further connections between Dublin and the Hebrides are demonstrated by the composition of the fleet with which Somerled invaded the Scottish mainland in 1164: it included a contingent of ships and warriors from Dublin.[42]

Somerled's expansion into the Isles must be regarded in the light of these intrigues, counter-intrigues, and conflicts, however obscure they may be. The Manx chronicle has Guðröðr's Dublin expedition followed by his so-called tyranny, which in turn led to the overtures of Þorfinnr to Somerled. These events are dated to 1157 by the chronicle. The naval battle of the Epiphany, however, is subsequently dated to 1156, but unless its sequence of events is hopelessly garbled at this juncture, the chronicle cannot be correct here. But what the politics of the Irish Sea in the 1140s and 1150s appear to indicate is the following: first, mac Ottair, an Islesman, had a Dublin connection; second, Somerled had a Dublin connection from at least 1154 and may have been an ally of Muirchertach Mac Lochlainn; and third, in the 1150s, the rulers of Man and Dublin were at odds over the overlordship of both kingdoms in a tradition going back at least a century, so that Guðröðr of Man may therefore have been a rival of Muirchertach Mac Lochlainn. The Arab proverb that the enemy of my enemy is my friend seems appropriate here: the connections between Dublin and the Isles and the animosity between Dublin and Man make it difficult to avoid the conclusion that Somerled had been sucked into the swirling vortex of Irish Sea politics in the 1150s. Whether mac Ottair was acting as an emissary of Muirchertach Mac Lochlainn, or was acting on his own initiative and was scheming to restore his family's fortunes, or was pursuing some sort of a private vendetta against Guðröðr, one thing seems clear: the story given in the chronicle of Man that Þorfinnr and the other chieftains were simply reacting against the 'tyranny' of Guðröðr cannot be taken at face value. The ongoing competition between the rulers of Dublin and Man had expanded to engulf a Hebridean element, and the result was probably more than any of the players would have bargained for.

A better understanding of Irish Sea politics in the twelfth century should also dispel a recurring bugbear with regard to Somerled's activities in the Isles. The seventeenth-century clan historians saw the Somerledian expansion and the ousting of the Norse as something akin to racial hostility, and praised Somerled as a great Gaelic lord heading a Celtic revival; the glorious progenitor of the Clan Donald. Such a view has often been favoured by more recent historians, who believed that Somerled's aim was the establishment of an independent Gaelic kingdom.[43] There is in fact little evidence for either theory, and both can be dispensed with quickly. As has been noted, Somerled's ancestry was mixed Gaelic-Norse and his family connections brought him into close contact with the Scandinavian dynasty of the Isles. It makes little sense to suppose that Somerled entertained racial hostility towards his neighbours and kinsmen. The answer to Somerled's activities in the Isles is found in sheer opportunism and the disturbed politics of the region through the early twelfth century: he had been invited to Man, after all, and took full advantage of the opportunities this presented. As it has been so aptly put, 'this was...the time for men with sharp swords and ruthless ambition to carve out spheres of profit and power for themselves'.[44] Such opportunism is a recurring theme in the history of the Isles: a century later, Somerled's great-grandson, Eógan Mac Dubgaill (fl. 1248–66), would demonstrate similar qualities when he benefited from the unexpected death of the Manx king in 1248 and received kingship over the Isles.[45]

Another important question is why the Islesmen had asked for Somerled's son to rule over them, and not Somerled himself. It has been suggested that Somerled was, for some reason, not acceptable to the Islesmen,[46] and it may be that the descent of Dubgall from Ragnhildr, the daughter of King Óláfr of Man, lent credibility to the son which Somerled may have lacked, perhaps because of his relatively recent rise to power on the western seaboard. On the other hand, it may be that in this episode we are simply witnessing the Irish type of kingship which had been transferred to the Isles by the Scandinavians upon their arrival there: the practice of setting up a son as a king under the overlordship of the father was nothing novel in societies which recognised grades of kingship. As recently as 1098–9, in the wake of his expedition to the Isles, Magnús Barelegs married his nine-year-old son to the five-year-old daughter of the king of Munster and set him up as ruler over the Hebrides and Orkneys with the title of king.[47] Perhaps Somerled nursed similar aspirations, although once again the sources raise more questions than they answer. However, two facts are perhaps noteworthy in this context: no source mentions Dubgall in the context of holding kingship in the Isles (indeed, nothing more is known of him until 1175, when he appears in the *Liber Vitae* of Durham cathedral), and Irish sources, which noted Somerled's demise in 1164, styled him *rí Innsi Gall & Cind Tíre*, king of the Hebrides and Kintyre.[48] In the perception of Irish writers, at least, it was Somerled, and not his son, who was the king of the Isles, a perception that was probably reinforced by the events of 1158 when Somerled expelled Guðröðr from the Isles entirely.

THE CRUCIAL YEARS: 1156–64

The result of the battle of the Epiphany was that Somerled and Guðröðr divided the kingdom between them. The division thus created was to form an important feature in the history of the Isles until they were annexed by Scotland in 1266. As the Manx chronicle put it, 'the kingdom has existed in two parts from that day until the present time'.[49] But the peace that followed the battle of the Epiphany did not endure. The chronicle relates that, in 1158, Somerled came to Man with fifty-three ships and joined battle with King Guðröðr, putting him to flight and then ravaging the island. The circumstances that led up to this conflict are unknown, but the chronicle, perhaps naturally enough given its bias, portrayed Somerled as the aggressor. At this point the chronicle neatly inserts a story about the vengeance wreaked by St Machutus on one of the members of Somerled's army who wished to plunder that saint's church: he was struck down by the saint in a dream and awoke only in time to seek forgiveness (unsuccessfully) before perishing horribly. Somerled and the rest of the army were so terror-stricken by this episode that they immediately departed the island.[50]

Two key issues emerge from the events of 1156 to 1158. First, what was the nature of the division between Somerled and Guðröðr? And second, what befell Guðröðr between his defeat in 1158 and the death of

Somerled in 1164? The exact nature of the 1156 division is obscured by the fragmentary and incomplete nature of the historical record. The Isle of Man itself was clearly retained by Guðröðr, but the extent of his authority in the rest of the Isles was probably limited. It would seem, based upon the division of the Isles between Somerled's descendants, on the one hand, and Guðröðr and his descendants, on the other, later in the twelfth and thirteenth centuries, that the Manx king retained control of Lewis and Harris as well as Skye, while Somerled took control of the Islay and Mull groups of islands. As one scholar has remarked: 'By this curious arrangement an independent sovereignty was interposed between the two parts of Godred's kingdom'.[51] But the more conclusive defeat of Guðröðr in 1158 means that Somerled almost certainly assumed control over all of the Isles, including Man itself, and held on until his death in 1164. Such a conclusion is reinforced by the composition of the army Somerled gathered for the 1164 invasion: various sources confirm that it contained men from the Hebrides and Argyll, Kintyre, and also Dublin.[52] Moreover, when he attempted the revival of the abbey on Iona in 1164, Somerled did so with the counsel of the men of Argyll and the Hebrides.[53] Thus, in 1158, Somerled made himself master of most of the western seas. A new power had come of age in the west, a power with which Manx, Scottish, English, and Norwegian kings would have to contend in the next century.[54]

The activities of Guðröðr following his defeat in 1158 can be traced clearly enough from English, Scottish, and Scandinavian sources. He appears in both England and Scotland in 1158–9. The sheriffs of Worcester and Gloucester, in accounts for the year ending 29 September 1158, received allowances to make payments to the king of the Isles for arms and equipment.[55] In 1159, Guðröðr was in Scotland, where he witnessed Malcolm IV's great charter to Kelso abbey, probably given between the end of March and the middle of May.[56] But if Guðröðr had gone to England and Scotland to seek aid in restoring himself to his kingdom – a Manx Diarmait Mac Murchada – he appears to have enjoyed little success; certainly Malcolm IV of Scotland was, at that time, preoccupied with preparations for his expedition to France with Henry II, in the course of which he hoped to attain knighthood at the English king's hands.[57] Failing to obtain assistance from the two British superpowers of the day, Guðröðr seems to have gone to Norway. The Icelandic annals record that in 1160 Guðröðr, Óláfr's son, 'took kingship in the Hebrides', but in 1161 the *Saga of Hákon Broad-Shoulder* has him participating in a battle between King Ingi and Hákon son of Sigurðr.[58] According to the Manx chronicle, Guðröðr came from Norway with a large force of men following the death of Somerled in 1164, and his rapid re-establishment as king of the Isles is implied.[59] But if Somerled's period of domination of the kingdom of the Isles had been brief, the partition that was arranged in 1156 was more enduring. From 1164 until 1266 Somerled's descendants continued to rule their part of the kingdom independently of the king of Man. As late as 1231 the kingdom of Man and the Isles was said to have excluded 'those [islands] that Somerled's sons held',[60] and in 1248 two of Somerled's great-grandsons, Eógan Mac Dubgaill and Dubgall Mac Ruaidrí, journeyed to the Norwegian court, competing for kingship over the 'northern part of the Hebrides', roughly the Inner Hebrides.[61]

CONCLUSION

Somerled, a chieftain of mixed Gaelic-Norse ancestry and insular context whose pedigree is traceable, however suspect, back to the time of Gofraid mac Fergusa in the mid-ninth century, rose to power in the early twelfth century as a result of the power vacuum created by a lack of strong Norwegian or Scottish royal authority in the Isles. His rise to power seems to have taken place initially in mainland Argyll, which involved him in the politics of the Scottish kingdom, and he is most often treated in a Scottish context. His main sphere of activity was in fact the western seas: in 1156 he apparently abandoned his operations on the Scottish mainland, where he was involved in a conflict with the king of Scots, in order to intervene in the Isles. But the significance of Somerled in the history of the kingdom of Man and the Isles is less personal than dynastic. Although it is true that between 1158 and his death in 1164 he was master of the western seaways and he expelled Guðröðr son of Óláfr from the Isles entirely, his own achievement was relatively limited. It was in the longer term that the rise of Somerled had serious implications for the kingdom of the Isles. He was the progenitor of a vigorous race of sea-kings, and his descendants would compete with the Scandinavian kings of Man descended from Guðröðr Crovan for hegemony in the Isles until the events of 1263–66 overtook both kindreds and the Isles fell under Scottish authority. Somerled's significance is therefore not restricted to the confines of Scottish national historiography, but lies equally in the trans-national and multi-ethnic milieu of the Isles in the first half of the twelfth century.

Notes

1 See chapter 12 below.

2 *Orkneyinga Saga*, ed. F. Guðmundsson, Íslenzk Fornrit, vol. 34 (Reykjavík, 1965); a good translation is *Orkneyinga Saga. The History of the Earls of Orkney*, trans. H. Palsson and P. Edwards (Harmondsworth, 1978), chapter 41.

3 See chapter 2 above.

4 A good study of the vessels that plied the western seaways is D. Rixson, *The West Highland Galley* (Edinburgh, 1998).

5 See now R.A. McDonald, *The Kingdom of the Isles: Scotland's Western Seaboard c. 1100–c.1336* (East Linton, 1997), chapter 2.

6 Bruce Webster, *Scotland From the Eleventh Century to 1603* (Ithaca, New York, 1975), 38.

7 *The Chronicle of Melrose from the Cottonian Manuscript, Faustina B.IX in the British Museum.* A complete and full size facsimile in collotype, with an introduction by A.O. Anderson and M.O. Anderson and an index by W.C. Dickinson (London, 1936), 36–7; trans. Anderson, *Early Sources*, ii, 254–5.

8 See chapter 14 below.

9 Broderick, *CKMI*, fol. 37v. For Somerled's family, see the genealogical table on p. 61, and for the Manx kings that on p. 12.

10 *Carmen de Morte Sumerledi* in T. Arnold (ed.), *Symeonis Monachi Opera Omnia* (London 1882–5), ii, 386–7, trans. Anderson, *Early Sources*, ii, 256–8.

11 *History of the MacDonalds*, in J.R.N. MacPhail (ed.), *Highland Papers* 4 vols, Scottish History Society (Edinburgh, 1914–34) i, 5–12; see also *Book of Clanranald*, in Alexander Cameron, *Reliquiae Celticae: Texts, Papers and Studies in Gaelic Literature and Philology*, eds A. MacBain and J. Kennedy, 2 vols (Inverness, 1894), ii, 153–7.

12 W.D.H. Sellar, 'The origins and ancestry of Somerled', *SHR*, 45 (1965), 137. Mr Alex Woolf has challenged the historicity of Somerled's descent from a ninth-century Gofraid mac Fergusa, A. Woolf, 'The origins and ancestry of Somerled: Gofraid mac Fergusa and "The Annals of the Four Masters"', *Medieval Scandinavia*, 15 (2005), 199–213.

13 Sellar, 'Origins and ancestry of Somerled', 124. On these narratives see also the comments of E.J. Cowan, 'Norwegian Sunset–Scottish Dawn: Hakon IV and Alexander III', in Norman Reid (ed.), *Scotland in the Reign of Alexander III 1249–1286* (Edinburgh, 1990), 112, n. 40, and J. MacInnes, 'Clan sagas and historical legends', *Transactions of the Gaelic Society of Inverness*, 57 (1990–2), 377–94. A negative view of their value is expressed in Duncan and Brown, 'Argyll and the Isles', 195.

14 See, for example, G.W.S. Barrow, *Kingship and Unity: Scotland 1000–1306*, New History of Scotland, vol. 2 (London, 1981), or A.A.M. Duncan, *Scotland: The Making of the Kingdom*, Edinburgh History of Scotland, vol. 1 (Edinburgh, 1975).

15 See for example McDonald, *Kingdom*; R. Oram, *The Lordship of Galloway* (Edinburgh, 2000); A. Grant, 'The Province of Ross and the Kingdom of Alba,' in E.J. Cowan and R.A. McDonald (eds), *Alba: Celtic Scotland in the Middle Ages* (East Linton 2000), 88–126; and K.J. Stringer, 'Periphery and Core in Thirteenth-Century Scotland: Alan son of Roland, Lord of Galloway and Constable of Scotland', in A. Grant and K.J. Stringer (eds), *Medieval Scotland: Crown, Lordship and Community. Essays Presented to G.W.S. Barrow* (Edinburgh, 1993), 82–112.

16 F.J. Byrne, 'The trembling sod: Ireland in 1169', in Art Cosgrove (ed.), *A New History of Ireland II: Medieval Ireland 1169–1534* (Oxford, 1987), 18. See also Susan Reynolds, *Kingdoms and Communities in Western Europe 900–1300* (Oxford, 1984), 250–3.

17 R.V. Turner, *King John* (London and New York, 1994), 135–46.

18 Even Kinvig, *Isle of Man*, 54–5, has disappointingly little to say of Somerled.

19 E.g. McDonald, *Kingdom*, *passim*; S. Duffy, 'The Bruce Brothers and the Irish

Sea World, 1306–29', *Cambridge Medieval Celtic Studies* 21 (1991), 55–86; and the stimulating work by B. Cunliffe, *Facing the Ocean: The Atlantic and Its Peoples* (Oxford, 2001).

20 See Eoin MacNeill, 'Chapters of Hebridean history I: The Norse kingdom of the Hebrides', *The Scottish Review*, 39 (1916), 254–76; compare C. MacDonald, *History of Argyll* (Glasgow, 1950), 73.

21 Sellar, 'Origins and ancestry of Somerled', *passim*.

22 *Orkneyinga saga*, chapter 100. Broderick, *CKMI*, fol. 35v., notes the marriage without recording Ragnhildr's name.

23 Broderick, *CKMI*, fol. 35v.; see also Byrne, 'The trembling sod', in Cosgrove (ed.), *A New History of Ireland*, 41–2 on Irish marriage customs.

24 McDonald, *Kingdom*, chapters 3–4.

25 The marriage is known from the Chronicle of Holyrood: *A Scottish Chronicle Known as the Chronicle of Holyrood*, M.O. Anderson (ed.) with some additional notes by A.O. Anderson (Edinburgh, 1938),124–5, 187. Mac Heth's pedigree is contentious. He has sometimes been identified as an illegitimate son of King Alexander I of Scotland (1107–24), but this is unlikely. His patronymic suggests a connection with the *Beth comes* (probably a confused Latinisation of Aodh or Heth) who appears in several early twelfth-century Scottish royal charters and who may have been earl of Moray. If this is so, then Malcolm mac Heth may have been a brother or son of the Angus of Moray who was killed at Stracathro in 1130 and who was a representative of the Moray dynasty of Lulach (1057–8) and MacBeth (1040–57), which claimed descent from the Dalriadic Cenél Loairn. See B.T. Hudson, *Kings of Celtic Scotland* (Westport, Conn. and London, 1994), chapter 6; and R.A. McDonald, *Outlaws of Medieval Scotland: Challenges to the Canmore Kings, 1058–1266* (East Linton, 2003), 75–81.

26 *Orkneyinga saga*, chapter 109.

27 See R.A. McDonald, 'Matrimonial politics and core-periphery interactions in twelfth- and early thirteenth-century Scotland', *Journal of Medieval History*, 21 (1995), 227–47.

28 Broderick, *CKMI*, fol. 41r. See chapter 4, p. 91.

29 *Scotichronicon*, v. 345.

30 On these titles see: K. Steer and J. Bannerman, *Late Medieval Monumental Sculpture in the West Highlands* (Edinburgh, 1977), Appendix II, 201–2; MacDonald, *History of Argyll*, 89–90.

31 K.J. Stringer, *The Reign of Stephen. Kingship, Warfare and Government in Twelfth-Century England*, Lancaster Pamphlets (London and New York, 1993), 28–37.

32 *History of the MacDonalds*, 6.

33 Duncan & Brown, 'Argyll and the Isles', 196.

34 See McDonald, *Kingdom of the Isles*, chapter 2.

35 Broderick, *CKMI*, fol. 35v.

36 Broderick, *CKMI*, fol. 37v.

37 Broderick, *CKMI*, fol. 37v.

38 Broderick, *CKMI*, fol. 37v.

39 Duffy, 'Irishmen and Islesmen', 126.

40 Broderick, *CKMI*, fol. 37r.; see also Duffy, 'Irishmen and Islesmen', 126.

41 *Annals of the Kingdom of Ireland by the Four Masters* (ed./trans.) J. O'Donovan (Dublin 1856), ii, 1110–12; see also Anderson, *Early Sources*, ii, 226–7. On the Dublin-Manx axis see Duffy, 'Irishmen and Islesmen', *passim*, and *Ireland in the Middle Ages* (Dublin, 1997), 42–3 .

42 *Annals of Ulster* (ed./trans.) W.M. Hennessy and B. McCarthy (Dublin, 1887–1901), ii, 144; sources conveniently collected in Anderson, *Early Sources*, ii, 253–6.
43 For example, W.F. Skene, *Celtic Scotland* (2nd ed., Edinburgh, 1886–90), i, 468–9; see also R. Williams, *The Lords of the Isles: The Clan Donald and the Early Kingdom of the Scots* (London, 1984), 111–24.
44 J. MacInnes, 'West Highland sea power in the Middle Ages', *Transactions of the Gaelic Society of Inverness*, 48 (1972–4), 522.
45 *Icelandic Sagas and other historical documents relating to the settlements and descents of the Northmen on the British Isles. Volume II: Hakonar Saga, and a fragment of Magnus Saga*, G. Vigfusson (ed.), (London 1887), 259; conveniently trans. Anderson, *Early Sources*, ii, 549–50, 554–5.
46 Duncan & Brown, 'Argyll and the Isles', 196.
47 Snorri Sturluson, *Heimskringla*, B. Adalbjarnarson (ed.). Íslenzk Fornrit v. 28 (Reykjavík 1941–51), iii, 224–5; trans. Anderson, *Early Sources*, ii, 116–18; Duffy, 'Irishmen and Islesmen', 112.
48 Somerled's title: *Tigernach's Continuator* (ed.) W. Stokes in *Revue Celtique* 18 (1898), 195; on Dubgall see McDonald, *Kingdom*, ch. 3.
49 Broderick, *CKMI*, fol. 37v.
50 Broderick, *CKMI*, fol. 38r.–fol. 39r.
51 A.W. Moore, 'The connexion between Scotland and Man', *SHR*, 3 (1906), 393–409.
52 *AU* ii, 144; Anderson, *Early Sources*, ii, 254–6.
53 *AU* ii, 144; Anderson, *Early Sources*, ii, 253–4.
54 McDonald, *Kingdom*, chapters 3–4.
55 Cited in Duncan & Brown, 'Argyll and the Isles', 196, n. 5.
56 G.W.S. Barrow (ed.), *The Acts of Malcolm IV King of Scots 1153–1165*, Regesta Regum Scottorum I (Edinburgh, 1961), no. 131.
57 *Acts of Malcolm IV*, 11, 113.
58 *Íslenzkir Annálar* in *Sturlunga Saga including the Islendinga Saga of Lawman Sturla Thordsson and other works*, G. Vigfusson (ed.), (Oxford 1878), ii, 360; *Heimskringla*, Adalbjarnarson (ed.), iii, 367; both trans. Anderson, *Early Sources*, ii, 246, 248.
59 Broderick, *CKMI*, fol. 39r.–fol. 39v.
60 J. Stevenson (ed.), *Chronicon de Lanercost* (Edinburgh 1839), 40–1; trans. Anderson, *Early Sources*, ii, 471–2.
61 *Hakonar Saga*, Vigfusson (ed.), 254–5; trans. Anderson, *Early Sources*, ii, 548; see also Duncan & Brown, 'Argyll and the Isles', 207; Power, in chapter 2 above, p. 45.

4 *The Reigns of Guðröðr and Rögnvaldr, 1153–1229*

RUTH COSTAIN-RUSSELL

The loss of half of his kingdom in 1156 to Somerled of Argyll may have seemed a personal humiliation to Guðröðr (Godred) II but in retrospect it had a certain inevitability. The long-term integrity and cohesion of the kingdom of Man and the Isles had perhaps always been a fragile, even illusory, notion since the late 1070s when Godred Crovan seized the opportunity of power vacuums in Dublin and Orkney to fashion an independent kingdom with himself at its head. In a world in which personal ambition was the almost invariable driving force, there would always have been a tendency for its components to spring apart, despite Godred Crovan's efforts to oversee the creation of an enduring identity and structure for his kingdom. We may sense that he was well aware of the importance of providing for a continuing measure of autonomous expression for the island leaders and their followers: though the evidence is far from conclusive, it is he who is credited with having set up a consultative process which included representatives ('Keys') sent from the Western Isles to join their peers on Man at Tynwald (ON *þing-völlr*, 'assembly place') and he clearly recognised the importance of allowing warbands to continue to maintain their separate identities during military campaigns as a means of expressing and sublimating potential rivalry between inter-island and intra-Man factions.

Although Godred Crovan's kingdom was given formal political status by Magnus Barelegs shortly after Godred's death, geographical realities too militated against internal cohesion. Man was both part and yet not part of the chains of islands lying to the west of Britain: it lay alone, considerably apart from the other islands and south of the narrow channel between north-east Ireland and Galloway, and was more fertile and populous. Culturally and linguistically, it had much in common with the Hebrides, yet its position to the south had brought subtly different cultural influences to its shores. As for the Western Isles, some of the islands were only a part of wider possessions extending onto the mainland and so their loyalties could not lie entirely with the kingdom of Man and the Isles, while the chieftains of the islands, powerful men in their own right, would only subsume their ambitions to the needs of the Manx kingdom so long as it seemed in their interest to do so. In the interests of cohesion, it would therefore always have been important for a Manx king to travel energetically about the islands, meeting local chieftains and their concerns, entertaining foreign emissaries or visiting them, presiding over Tynwald, and leading the war-fleets when peace was threatened. Such evidence as exists suggests that Godred Crovan's son Óláfr was 'peaceable',[1] a man of deep spiritual concerns rather than a dynamic leader, and given the seemingly freelance activities of Óttarr of the Isles in Dublin and Wales,[2] of which we read between 1142 and 1148, and the clear and growing power of Somerled, it seems likely that in the latter years of his reign the aging king lacked the energy and inclination to patrol his far-flung territory as he ought and to challenge and discipline his restless Hebridean chieftains.

In such a context, Guðröðr II's attempts shortly after his succession to impose his authority by depriving some of his chieftains of their lands or titles must have appeared heavy-handed and deeply unwelcome to islanders who had become used to considerable freedom of action. The account of his behaviour in the Manx chronicle seems likely to be accurate, as one of Guðröðr's first actions on succession had been to confirm his father's gifts to the Cistercians, and the Rushen-based author of the chronicle would not lightly speak ill of him. Attempts to assess Guðröðr's immediate state of mind illustrate well the difficulties historians of this period face: it is necessary as so often to juxtapose meagre and conflicting accounts, and to consider their particular viewpoints and justifications, and their uncertain dating, which can confuse symptom and cause. 'Non sequiturs' abound, and we must often accept that vital evidence is missing and may never be recoverable. Above all, in trying to assess probabilities in this unstable Norse-Gaelic world, we may veer between over-facile assumptions and a failure of imagination about the fluid rules and expectations which governed relationships between groups of people.

Two episodes occurred in the early years of Guðröðr's reign which in their telling show how potentially significant evidence can be vitiated for us by enigmatic omission and muddled dating. In the first, perhaps in 1154 according to the Four Masters, fleets 'of Manann' were among a number hired by the Irish highking Muirchertach Mac Lochlainn to meet an internal threat, and successfully deployed. In the second incident the outcome is less clear: depending on which of three sources one accepts,[3] a putative invitation to King Guðröðr by the Hiberno-Norse of Dublin to become their king resulted in temporary success, or in an inconclusive truce, or in outright failure in face of the opposition of the Irish highking. Thus, when the Manx chronicle tells us of Guðröðr's 'tyranny' against his chieftains, it is very difficult to state with certainty that this was, for instance, an act of arrogance on his part, or an indication of frustration at their unwillingness to accept his overlordship, or an attempt to recover ground lost to Somerled.[4] What we can be sure of is that this mid-point in the twelfth century, when not only the reigning Manx but the English and Scottish kings died and were replaced, saw the beginnings of great political change for the kingdom of Man and the Isles. Increasingly from the time of Guðröðr's accession, these seaways, the centre of a world which they had long dominated, were gradually to become of peripheral importance to the real centres of power, and the leaders of the kingdom would be forced to engage with the world beyond on terms set by others.

The break-up of the Manx kingdom in 1156 was of significance because it came at a time when size of territory and political unity were increasingly important to counteract the growing power of England and Scotland: little protection during these years could be expected from Man's overlord, Norway, deeply divided within itself at this time. The personal, even parochial, ambitions of men such as Guðröðr, Somerled and Mac Lochlainn (then highking of Ireland) also made them susceptible to exploitation by kings of more powerful polities in their pursuit of affairs of state. Medieval rulers were often forced by an unstable environment and slow communications to react to events rather than to develop and pursue policies in a planned way.[5] But when King Stephen's troubled reign was over and Henry II came to power in England, it is possible to see him pursuing general goals to secure his northern and western boundaries. A prime aim would have been to recover the territory which had been ceded to King David of Scotland in the preceding years. Gerald of Wales has spoken of Henry's 'immense shrewdness [which] led him to contrive many schemes'.[6] Henry's possible informal alliances with Gaelic rulers,[7] including Somerled, Muirchertach Mac Lochlainn, and, more demonstrably, Diarmait Mac Murchada of Leinster, were no doubt designed to discomfort and put pressure on Malcolm IV, the boy-king of the Scots, and (if in fact they existed) did indeed bear fruit as by 1157 Henry had regained Northumberland, Lancaster and Cumberland. Such a high-level connection may well have emboldened Somerled when the opportunity arose to confront Guðröðr in 1156, and have encouraged him to launch his attack in 1164 to halt the threat to his lands on the Scottish mainland and customary rights presented by Malcolm's increasingly slavish pursuit of Anglo-Norman favour. The failure of this campaign was to have dire and far-reaching consequences for the Gaelic world, for it has been suggested that Somerled's death in his abortive invasion of Scotland produced a kind of domino effect:[8] Mac Lochlainn's position in the northern Irish Sea was thereby weakened, and his defeat and death followed by the transfer of the highkingship in 1165 eclipsed the power of Diarmait Mac Murchada, whose fortunes had been closely linked to theirs, and set in motion the events which brought the Anglo-Normans to Ireland and thence to a closer scrutiny of an involvement with Man.

The detail of these events illustrates the impact upon the fortunes of Celtic countries, and upon the political ecology of the whole area, of the increasing dominance and power of the English. Such impact may come about by direct policy decisions; often it resulted from English kings' ad hoc or equivocal reaction to events as they unfolded, distracted as they were so often by the demands of their far-flung territories. Such was the situation as Diarmait sought Henry II's help, having run him to ground in Aquitaine in the southernmost reaches of his 'empire'. There had been a resurgence of native power in Wales, and after an abortive campaign Henry had given up his military attempts to reassert English domination there. Henry was not interested in becoming personally involved with Mac Murchada in Ireland – that country had become less important now that his policy in Wales was in abeyance, and he was fully occupied with his Continental possessions. Diarmait's request, however, seems to have presented him with an excellent opportunity to 'siphon the discontented and bellicose Anglo-Norman knights away from Wales' and redirect their territorial ambitions, and so he gave Diarmait some kind of approval to approach them.[9] In short, 'far from being the object of a Henrician Irish policy, Ireland became more the offshoot of Henrician Welsh strategy'.[10]

After Somerled's death at Renfrew in 1164, Guðröðr had returned to his permanently depleted kingdom from Norway with a large force of men evidently provided by the Norwegian king, despite the demands and distractions of the latter's own civil war.[11] While Guðröðr's personal rule appears to have been largely unchallenged in the remaining 22 years of his reign, developments in Ireland increasingly impinged on Manx activities and consciousness. As Seán Duffy has pointed out: 'the principal targets of the [Anglo-Norman] assault [on Ireland] were the seaports of the east coast, Wexford, Waterford and Dublin, and these were for all intents and purposes the Islesmen's only remaining footholds in Ireland'.[12] The Ostman king of Dublin Ascall Mac Turcaill (Áskell Þorkelsson) was expelled by Diarmait and his new supporters. Late in 1170, he mustered a hosting that included ships from Man, the Hebrides, the Orkneys and (perhaps) Norway, in an effort to reinstate himself in Dublin, although, surprisingly, the Manx chronicle makes no mention of the fact of Manx participation in the expedition. The attempt failed and Ascall was captured and executed, but it was evident that the English (if such we can call them, though they were of very mixed origin) were now short of both men and supplies. So

Guðröðr and other men of the Isles were recalled by the new highking, Ruaidrí Ua Conchobair of Connacht, and by the archbishop of Dublin, to participate in an encirclement of Dublin by 'almost all the princes of Ireland'. The source for this, Gerald of Wales, tells us that Guðröðr was sent letters in which a 'generous promise of financial reward accompanied persuasive arguments'.[13] Gerald continues: 'Their fear of the threat of English domination, inspired by the successes of the English, made the men of the Isles act all the more quickly'.[14] Even if we discount his prejudices, Gerald may well have been right: no doubt there were some among the island ships in Dublin in 1170 who had been with Somerled at Renfrew in 1164 trying vainly to hold back the tide of Norman and Angevin influence. Now, in Ireland, they had once again been routed. As 'the greater part of [the Dublin Ostmen] went on board ship, taking their most precious belongings, and sailed off' to settle in Man and the Hebridean Isles,[15] one senses the beginnings of a chill throughout the Isles, a recognition that there might be no escaping new forces – and not only military forces – of which they could not get the measure.

Just a year later, in 1171, Dublin, the city with which Man had such long historical links, was ceded to King Henry. At Christmas that year, all the kinglets of Ireland who had submitted to Henry were invited to a banquet. 'Throughout the great hall', as Gerald observes wryly, 'in obedience to the king's wishes they began to eat the flesh of the crane, which they had hitherto loathed'.[16] The process of domination, as the Welsh historian R.R. Davies has so feelingly written,[17] is a complex and subtle one, one which worked for the most part between Anglo-Normans and native Celts because it was presented and seen by many as ultimately attractive and rewarding. The Normans' military superiority, however brutal in practice, could be admired, and techniques were, where possible, copied; submission to it, given provisionally and without shame, was often seen as preferable to surrender to Celtic peers – and it brought protection. But domination through the demonstration of social and cultural superiority could be equally compelling and could bring about long-term change through the internalisation of new ideas, values and lifestyles. The twelfth century has long been acknowledged as a period of 'renaissance' and 'renewal' in the spiritual and secular spheres of European life. To what extent might such tendencies and influences have reached the Isle of Man and its leading men during Guðröðr's reign?

Social historians such as Georges Duby have seen the process of cultural development as linked to the prolonged movement of material progress from the late eleventh century onwards,[18] and in particular greatly increased prosperity on the part of secular aristocracy. Aristocratic courts became centres of cultural creativity: intellectual as well as physical entertainments led to the development of the concept of chivalry and the encouragement of intellectuals. There was increased religious observance, the renewal of religious art and music, a new optimism and awareness of the possibility of progress, the growth of self-awareness and new, more positive views of the power of human reason. At the current state of our knowledge, it is difficult to assess the level of cultural and material sophistication that had been attained at Guðröðr's court by the 1170s, and the quality and degree of behavioural change that might have been attributable to the spread of influence from England and beyond. The lavishing of gifts, attention and flattery, the splendour, manners and style of the Anglo-Norman and Angevin royal courts, seems likely to have dazzled visiting Celtic leaders with the exception of those few, like Diarmait Mac Murchada, who had had prolonged contact with the English. Guðröðr could claim kinship with the English royal family through his mother's ancestry, but such a connection was hardly distinctive given the proliferation of marriages contracted by Henry I's many illegitimate offspring and may well not have resulted in frequent presence at the English or Scottish courts, while some visits that we know of, notably those in search of support against Somerled in 1158, seem more likely to have alienated Guðröðr, stressing as they did client status *vis-à-vis* the Angevins.

The excavations of St Patrick's Isle off the west of the Isle of Man, carried out in the 1980s, revealed its use over about 1,000 years, and in the medieval period the military, ecclesiastical, and political administration were all housed on this small rocky island to the south-west of Peel Bay. Buildings changed their use over the centuries with much remodelling, the blurring of areas of use, the over-laying of buildings, and shoring up due to erosion.[19] We know that Guðröðr lived and died here in 1187, as did his son Óláfr Dubh ('the Black') in 1237; but not a great deal can be deduced of their material lifestyle or that of the bishop who is thought also to have lived there at this period.[20] Though individual chiefs may well have lived in material comfort on the island, there seems no architectural or archaeological evidence to suggest the existence of extensive 'baronial' households there prior to the late thirteenth or early fourteenth century. Elsewhere in the British Isles such aristocratic courts, particularly as they perambulated around territorial possessions that might straddle England, Scotland, Wales and Ireland, introduced new European ideas and tastes throughout these areas. Such men were becoming increasingly powerful: England had, with Henry II's accession, become part of a wider realm than ever before, and the constant itineration of the king and his government around his dominions on the Continent and in England led of necessity to a much more structured government at the second level: judicial, fiscal and administrative frameworks were developed or refined, and greater autonomy by local aristocracies was required and exercised. The kingdom of Man and the Isles, its territory of course at this time beyond the gift of the English king, may well, perhaps until the late 1170s and the de Courcy connection, have been largely isolated from the influence of the cultural and administrative practices of this baronial sector.

Of course other important conduits of secular influence existed: commerce and trade, merchants and their goods would have had their effect on the economy and lifestyles of island residents and are discussed fully elsewhere in this volume.[21] In the sphere of religious influence, long-standing links between Furness in England and Rushen abbey, one of its daughter-houses, established on the island by Guðröðr's father in 1134, may have ensured a continuing exchange of ideas and spiritual nourishment between the two houses. In theory, too, the requirement on abbots of the Cistercian order to attend the annual General Chapter at Cîteaux would present Manx kings with an opportunity for keeping up-to-date with papal and monastic politics and legal developments, though in practice it has been estimated that on average no more than one-third of all abbots attended, due to 'the dangers, expenses and time of travel'.[22] Giles Constable has written of the 1160s as having been the culmination in Europe of a period of intense concern with the nature of religious life, and the interiorisation for many of a set of values previously reserved for monks.[23] In 1176, Guðröðr agreed to be lawfully married to Finnguala, daughter of Mac Lochlainn of Cenél nEógain in Ulster, and mother of his son Óláfr, now three years old. The papal legate, Cardinal Vivian, came to witness the ceremony, which was performed by the abbot of Rievaulx, who was rewarded with land for a monastery at Myroscough.[24] We cannot know whether it was personal piety which motivated Guðröðr – a feeling that he was improving his relationship with God – or whether his willingness to cast aside 'barbarous' Celtic customs in order to conform to the sexual norms of the Anglo-Norman church should be interpreted in a quasi-political light.

It was perhaps at some time between 1177 and 1180 that a marriage was arranged between Guðröðr's daughter, Affreca, and John de Courcy, the dashing freelance conqueror of the east Ulster kingdom of Ulaid, an event which was to tie the Manx kingdom more closely, politically and religiously, for better and for worse, to the rest of Britain. Such marriages between Anglo-Normans and native Celts had, as R.R. Davies observes, been a feature of Anglo-Norman penetration of the British Isles from earliest days, and 'were crucially important...in beginning the process of cultural integration'.[25] More to the immediate point for the ambitious de Courcy, he would not only secure the use of Guðröðr's fleet to reinforce his territorial acquisitions to the east and the Isle of Man itself for mustering and provisioning, but would be likely by this alliance to neutralise the Mac Lochlainn kings of Cenél nEógain – who might otherwise have intervened on behalf of the Ulaid – the reigning Mac Lochlainn, probably Niall, having so recently become Guðröðr's father-in-law.[26] That the marriage between de Courcy and Affreca took place at all would seem to indicate that despite living in an apparently quiet backwater Guðröðr and his daughter were at the very least not intimidated by the prospect of the union, and that Guðröðr was subsequently able to accommodate and entertain suitably either de Courcy himself and his retinue, on perhaps rare visits to Man, or those of his officials and agents.[27] De Courcy was a man in a hurry: 'he soon gave himself the trappings of a monarch – court officials and feudal officers, such as marshal, constable, seneschal and chamberlain; he created barons, distributed lands, authorised coinage and allowed himself to be described as *princeps Ulidiae*'.[28] If Guðröðr visited him there, which is scarcely beyond doubt, the experience is likely to have been instructive.

Of great significance too in the long term was the way the marriage had the effect of putting Man at the geographical centre of an extensive personal network which linked de Courcy's land-holdings and family monastic connections in Cumbria (and to a lesser degree in Somerset) with new monastic foundations and Cumbrian settler families in Ulster. This network was further elaborated as time went on. It is thought that the de Courcy instigated grants of land on Man to the abbots of Bangor and Saul in Ulster,[29] Guðröðr granted land near Douglas, and de Courcy gave land at Nendrum in Down, to the Prior of St Bees in Copeland,[30] which had been founded by John de Courcy's grandfather, William Meschin; Guðröðr granted privileges to enter and trade freely to the monks of Holm Cultram, a favoured abbey of de Courcy;[31] monks from Rushen's mother-house, Furness, were sent to people de Courcy's new monastery at Inch; and Jocelin, a member of the Furness community, was commissioned to write a new Life of St Patrick.[32] It was Affreca who in 1193 made her own foundation, Grey Abbey, which she gave as a cell to Holm Cultram, and where she was eventually buried.[33] Excavations of the Rushen abbey site suggest that the abbey church can be dated to *c.*1190, given the similarity of its plan and proportions to those of Grey Abbey, and we might therefore imagine Affreca sharing her new expertise with her brother Rögnvaldr (Gaelic Ragnall, Latin Reginaldus), the new king of Man, and exchanging ideas, and perhaps designers, stonemasons and other craftsmen from England, for their respective projects in Ulster and on Man.[34]

Fig. 4.1 *Grey Abbey, County Down, founded in 1193 by Gudrud's daughter, Affrica.*

These developments must have had a considerable impact on Man and its remaining Western Isles, not only in forging wider ecclesiastical links with Cumbria and implicating them in the colonisation of the Ulaid under John de Courcy, but in more subtle and pervasive ways. Like Ireland with the Anglo-Norman invasion, Man would gradually be drawn, in Katharine Simms's words, into 'a world of shared ideology, custom, law and culture which gave most of western Europe in the high Middle Ages a sense of community'.[35] Acceptance of, and acceptance into, that western European community was for Man a long and uncertain process, a time of weighing past and future, profit and loss, of alternating doubt and affirmation, of living in parallel worlds.

The tensions of the early years of this process were exacerbated by the combative nature of Guðröðr's son and successor, Rögnvaldr. Guðröðr had not intended Rögnvaldr to succeed to the Manx throne: before his death in 1187, he had designated Óláfr Dubh, his only legitimate son, as his heir. The Manx chronicle goes to some lengths to explain why this instruction was not followed. Óláfr was still a tender little boy (*tenellus adhuc puer*) and the Manx felt that he was too young to look after himself let alone govern a people subject to him. So his half-brother, Rögnvaldr, an energetic man of maturer years, was summoned from the Isles to be king. The chronicle, under that same year (1188), contains a hint of a threat to the Manx throne when it notes that 'Murcard, a man of power and energy in the entire kingdom of the Isles, was killed'.[36] The preferment of Rögnvaldr may at the time therefore have been well founded, but it sowed the seeds of bitter rivalry. It is in Rögnvaldr that we have a sense of a man living simultaneously in two cultures, a man at home in a quasi-heroic past and fighting to retain his place in it, while coexisting, even learning to exploit, the growing pervasiveness of English power. Our impression of him and his reign reflects an increase in the breadth, quantity and authoritativeness of our sources for the first decades of his reign: secular and monastic chronicles had their 'golden age' from 1180 to 1200,[37] Anglo-Irish administrative records proliferated, and from the start of King John's reign (1199) we have available to us the informative close and patent rolls of the English chancery. Such records and others (for example the Irish annals) serve to illuminate the varied nature of King Rögnvaldr's activities and relationships as he sought to gain best advantage for himself and his kingdom through his pragmatic and ad hoc responses to the developing political scene.

As the provider of fleets for hire, the kingdom of Man and the Isles and its like had long operated in an environment of political manoeuvrability, indeed almost neutrality, in which temporary alliances – and hostilities – were contracted for cash or kind and might cease once their purposes were accomplished. In the earlier days of the Conquest, the Normans had seemed just another faction and hirer of mercenary fleets who sometimes outbid, or were themselves outbid by others in need of military assistance, for example in Ireland. As Anglo-Norman and Angevin power grew and the technical superiority of their armies and fleets increased, it might be assumed that Celtic leaders would band together against a mutual threat. But the idea of invariable 'solidarity' based on common ethnicity between Celts is an anachronism: collusion was rare and any appearance of it likely to be simply a response, as Seán Duffy has said, to the same set of stimuli, for example taking advantage of occasions when the Anglo-Normans were distracted elsewhere.[38] Loyalties were generally much closer to home, and the protection and promotion of leaders' personal power, their families and close matrimonial connections all took priority. King Rögnvaldr, like most of his contemporaries, seems to have been a man of action rather than a visionary, and in the immediate term his kingdom needed to earn its keep by hiring out its naval services, and so the exchange of such services for cash or kind continued. The evidence is in fact that the provision of military and naval help to the English from the early thirteenth century, and the rewards offered to the providers, involved the Manx deeply in English hegemony. As for the growing English and European cultural influence, it may be unrealistic to expect medieval leaders to have been alive to the stealthy connection between this and gradual political overlordship, while ambivalence towards that culture and the insidiousness of its spread would in any case have hindered effective confrontation.

The arrival of the English in Ireland, as has been observed, had 'signalled the beginning of the end of the maritime free zone in the west',[39] as Man's watery environs became increasingly crowded with English ships plying to and from Ireland. The need to respond to such presence in this arena and elsewhere about the islands would have been met with relish by Rögnvaldr if we are to believe a bardic praise poem composed in Irish lauding his exploits and supposed illustrious antecedents;[40] the *Orkneyinga saga* too writes: 'King Rögnvaldr was then the greatest viking in the western lands. It was three winters that he had lain out in his warships without coming under a smoky rafter.'[41] Indeed Rögnvaldr's reign seems to have been a

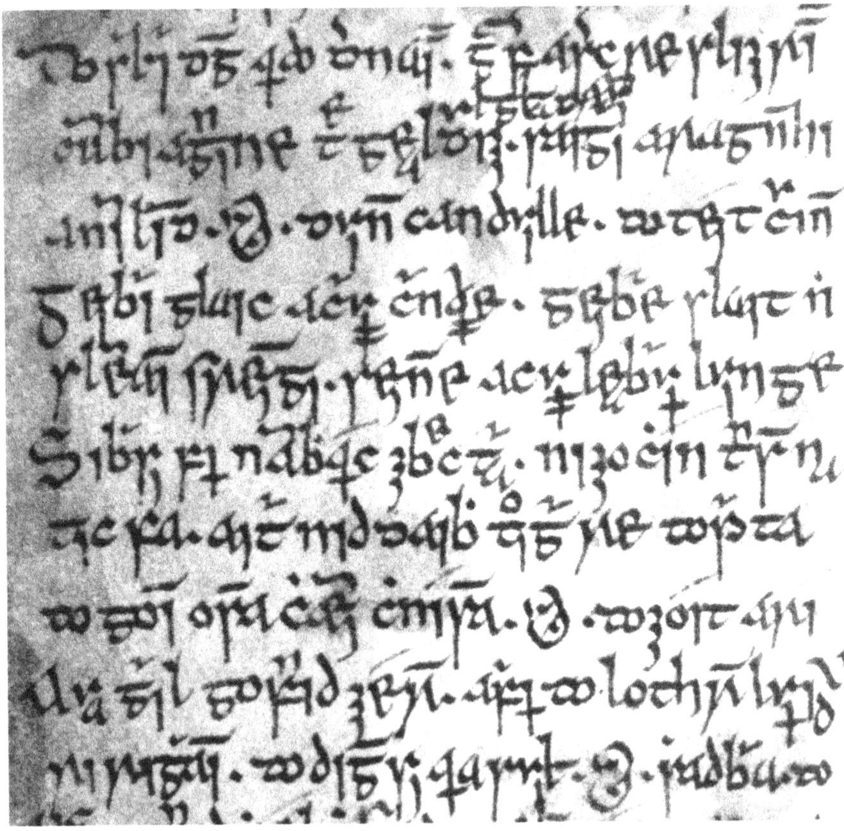

Fig. 4.2 *Verses 22–25 from the Praise poem of Rhagnall describing his great prowess with spears and ships including 'thou knowest how to step on a thwart to wound the fair bosom of a knight ... O fair descendant of Gofraidh Mear ach'.*

time of increased maritime activity, pursued with the sort of enthusiasm, even recklessness, which has come down to us as having a 'Viking' cast which had not been apparent to us during his father's and grandfather's reigns, and this at a time of minimal actual Norwegian presence.

While Rögnvaldr might have enjoyed his depiction as a Viking and have been aware of its propaganda value, recalling as it did the traditions of independence from England and Scotland enjoyed by the Manx kingdom, the word itself has an anachronistic ring to it as the twelfth century turns into the thirteenth, by which time the Manx could by no means claim a monopoly of seafaring expertise and daring. The first Manx royal seal of which we have a description was one attached to a charter of the 1190s – that is in Rögnvaldr's time – held in the duchy of Lancaster's office: 'in the

Fig. 4.3 *There is now only a description of the Royal seal of Rögnvaldr, showing effigies on horseback and, on the reverse, a ship with furled sail, but an illustration of a similar ship seal of Angus Moar of Islay, 1292, is shown here. He was grandson of Reginald, son of Somerled.*

foreside it exhibits his Effigies on Horseback and on the reverse the Ship under Sail'.[42] Camden, in the 1607 edition of his *Britannia*, also refers to seals of the king of Man and the Isles before the 1260s as having a ship with furled sail. The seal of Guðröðr II's kinsman by marriage, Ragnall son of Somerled, also bore a ship full of armed men, as did those of Somerled's descendants in the Isles.[43] It has to be admitted though that this emblem of a Viking-type ship was hardly unique to Man and the Isles, for it was used by maritime trading communities all over western and northern Europe at this time; though few would have had more right to its use than the Manx, Basil Megaw thought that the fact that the seal combined the ship emblem with a depiction of the mounted knight, typical of twelfth-century Anglo-Norman court circles, makes it very likely that it was, ironically, commissioned from English seal engravers.[44] In real life, too, the invasion of Ireland had been accomplished by ships of much the same type as those used by men of Gaelic-Norse descent.[45]

There is a reference in the praise-poem mentioned earlier of a conquering visit by Rögnvaldr to Dublin, but this may have been exhortation rather than fact and there is little other evidence to support such activity by him. Seán Duffy believes, however, that the ancient links between the Manx and that city and its environs survived the Anglo-Norman capture of Dublin and were further bolstered by grants by John de Courcy and Affreca to religious institutions in and around the city.[46] The de Courcy connection may also explain one source of Irish arms which Rögnvaldr seems to have had at his disposal in 1193, when he campaigned in Anglesey in support of the successful re-instatement of his son-in-law, Rhodri ab Owain Gwynedd, who had been driven from Anglesey by his nephews during a succession struggle which followed Owain's death. The Gwynedd family too had retained their long-standing connection in and around Dublin, and Rhodri may, like many of his antecedents, have been taking refuge there.

Irish arms, perhaps supplied by de Courcy, supplemented Rögnvaldr's Hebridean troops when he responded to a call from King William the Lion of Scotland to help him curb the powerful Earl Haraldr Maddadson who 'had been attacking feudal representatives of the new Scottish order' and was married to a daughter of the elusive Malcolm mac Heth. According to the *Orkneyinga saga*, Rögnvaldr was a collateral descendant in the earldom,[47] entitled to claim it according to Norse custom, and William's grant of authority to Rögnvaldr was a device to elicit Haraldr's submission. This it did in 1202 when Haraldr bought back William's goodwill and his former status for £2,000 of silver. On the face of it, this campaign appears to show how Rögnvaldr was willing to support the Scottish king's efforts against a fellow Norse-Gaelic ruler, and it must be assumed that the financial rewards for his mercenary help, the personal prestige of exercising his right to the earldom if only temporarily, and the prospect of acquiring a powerful ally who might be (and in the event was) useful in his own dynastic struggle, all helped to assuage any reservations he may have had over the action.

Rögnvaldr's stance *vis-à-vis* the English king was tested when he became caught up in the fortunes of his brother-in-law, John de Courcy, in 1204. De Courcy had been deprived of Ulster by his former allies, the de Lacy brothers, and came to Man seeking refuge. The following year de Courcy struck back, his own troops supplemented by a fleet of 100 ships supplied and led by Rögnvaldr, but the attempt to besiege Dundrum Castle on the County Down coast failed.[48] We do not know the precise date of the engagement, and it is unclear whether the letters patent issued on 8 February 1205 – by which King John announces he has taken his 'beloved kingsman', Reginald, king of Man, under his 'keeping, protection and defence'[49] – and a grant of land in Lancashire together with various gifts,[50] should be viewed as 'carrot' or 'stick' for this occasion or the future. Whichever they were, they seem to be the first official intimation of Manx kings coming under pressure in this way to behave in conformity with an English king's wishes.

King John's loss of Normandy in 1204 had made him more determined to consolidate his position in Ireland, and from 1207 he carried on a game of harassment, bluff and counter-bluff against his barons there, notably William Marshall, William de Braose and the de Lacys.[51] In 1210 when he mounted a massive and largely successful campaign to elicit the submission both of his magnates and the Irish kings, John de Courcy, no longer a threat and now reconciled to him, accompanied him and gave him virtuous service. Not so King Rögnvaldr who, in his usual independent way and pursuing a 'professional' mercenary role, supplied war-parties on this occasion to de Lacy and what is more gave the fleeing de Braose and de Lacy families safe passage through Man. King John's patience snapped: he then 'sent part of his army...to Man where in a fortnight they laid waste almost the whole island [and] took hostages from there'.[52] This time, Rögnvaldr heeded the message and two years later became John's liegeman. He received one knight's fee at Carlingford on the frontier of Ulster in County Louth, with an annual payment of 100 seams of wheat, though as Duffy observes, it may not be coincidental that Rögnvaldr's land was located 'within arm's length of the new and imposing royal fortress overlooking Carlingford Lough'.[53]

A continuous preoccupation for Rögnvaldr during the last 20 years of his reign was the challenge for the throne made by his half-brother, Óláfr Dubh. This bitter dispute between the brothers epitomised the continuing power of Gaelic succession practices in the face of a growing acceptance of primogeniture among legitimate sons in more Normanised areas, a practice which of course conferred moral advantage on Óláfr. As the Manx kingdom was riven, destabilised and neglected by the dispute, other 'powers' were drawn into the conflict, either invited in as proctors or allies, or seizing the opportunity to offer their services with a view to acquiring strategic and political advance. It seems that after Rögnvaldr took up the kingship Óláfr had been sent from Man to Lewis, safely out of the way at the other end of the kingdom. It may be that as he grew up he was given the duty of guarding the Manx Hebrides (Lewis, Skye and perhaps the Uists), for there is mention of an army,[54] and a chance encounter – by ships blown south from their route between Iceland and Norway in 1202 – of Óláfr and the bishop on 'Sandey', who exacted a toll.[55] Lewis was 'mountainous and rocky, and...almost completely untilled',[56] but when Óláfr appealed to his brother for some more suitable land to support himself and his followers he was seized, taken to King William the Lion, Rögnvaldr's ally, and held in 'safe-keeping' for almost seven years until William's death in 1214, when he was released by the new Scottish king.

There are signs that before this Rögnvaldr felt under threat. It seems unlikely that Óláfr's supporters were inactive during these years, and saga literature recounts that a party of Norwegians sailed south during a lull in their civil war, possibly to punish Rögnvaldr or if possible to free Óláfr.[57] These are thought by A.A.M. Duncan to have been responsible for the deaths of Áengus, son of Somerled, and his three sons,[58] but lack of evidence makes it difficult to say whether they were targeted or the victims of opportunistic violence. However, an alarmed Rögnvaldr went to Bergen to do homage and belatedly pay the tribute due since his accession. Norway had been virtual non-players in the international arena for many years. Another five years were to pass before the descendants of the Faroese usurper, Sverrir Sigurðarson, triumphed and his grandson, Hákon IV, took the throne in 1217. For now, Rögnvaldr may have had an ambivalent reception for he is found shortly after at the court of King John, perhaps in search of more practical help against the raiders. In addition to the grant of land at Carlingford, John now issued letters patent commanding officials in Ireland to assist Rögnvaldr against 'Wikini' offending in his territory – with Rögnvaldr to give John reciprocal service in John's lands. The 'territory' here referred to is not thought to be Rögnvaldr's new acquisition in Carlingford but rather the whole of his kingdom of the Isles, a significant development, to the detriment too of the Scots king.[59]

The author of the Manx chronicle favours Óláfr Dubh, presumably because of his legitimacy, and we are sadly deprived of evidence of the extent of Óláfr's own machinations to secure the throne. He is depicted, amusingly, as a saintly and forebearing man whose first action on release from prison was to go on pilgrimage to Compostela, and thereafter return quietly to Lewis with Lauon, a new wife chosen by Rögnvaldr, whose sister-in-law she was. This marriage was annulled shortly after as canonically illicit. Óláfr's apparently swift remarriage to the daughter of the earl of Ross led to the hatching of an unsuccessful assassination plot – by Rögnvaldr's bitter and resentful wife, according to the chronicle – followed by several years of outright conflict between the brothers, with Óláfr based on his new father-in-law's territory. There are further indications that Rögnvaldr felt under stress, for he over-reacted recklessly in 1217 to aggressive behaviour by visiting Norse-Gaelic mariners from Ireland not only by executing those concerned but by mounting a retaliatory action into Ireland. In response during 1218 he was summoned twice by the new English king, Henry III, as latters patent show, to do homage and 'make amends for excesses to men of [Henry's] realm in England and in Ireland'; in 1219, further acts of homage were required before protection was commanded for him from the justiciar and other men of Ireland '*quamdiu fideliter se habet erga nos*'. Henry's reservations about the slippery Manx king were well founded: only 27 days later, Rögnvaldr was issuing his own letters patent, probably at Furness, giving to Pope Honorius III 'his island of Man...to hold it in fee from the Roman Church, and to pay homage and fealty for it, paying yearly 12 marks in England at...Furnis'.[60]

Rögnvaldr's homage to Henry III produced a reaction from the king of Norway, and in 1220 Rögnvaldr was telling Henry that the king of Norway 'lays snares for him and threatens his land with evil': once again, the English king ordered support for him from the Irish justiciar should an invasion materialise.[61] At much the same time, Rögnvaldr sought more practical help from his – now rather remote – kin in Galloway.[62] Both Alan, lord of Galloway, and his younger brother, Thomas, had been reared as members of a wealthy, powerful and Normanised élite and had gained further lands and social distinction by their marriages in 1209 to Margaret of Huntingdon and Isabel of Athol respectively. They had been close to King John, supporting many of his campaigns, and enjoying nothing better than to cruise the western waters in their war-galleys. Alan, however, seems to have had a stronger motive for responding positively to the aging Rögnvaldr's need than the mere indulgence of his addiction to seafaring.[63] He had three daughters but as yet no legitimate male heir, and under feudal law – and particularly under the new Scottish king, Alexander II – his illegitimate son Thomas could not inherit. He was therefore in search of a patrimony for Thomas – and the kingdom of Man and its remaining western isles looked a feasible and attractive prospect.

Advantage passed from one side to the other over the years: Óláfr Dubh enjoyed considerable support in the Isles and among many of those living in Man itself. His cause was furthered by the people's fury when, having raised a large sum ostensibly for Rögnvaldr's trip to the English court, they found that Rögnvaldr had gone to Alan of Galloway's court to marry his daughter to young Thomas, who was now in line for the Manx throne if Rögnvaldr were to prevail. Óláfr secured the throne and reigned for two years from 1226 but was deprived of Man by Alan of Galloway during an absence in the Isles. Henry III was quick to offer to mediate but Óláfr seems to have regained his throne without Henry's help. Though the island had been 'practically reduced to a desert' by the Gallovidians, the Manx chronicle records poignantly that now 'the Manxmen who had before been scattered all over began to come together and to live in safety'.[64]

Rögnvaldr made a final attempt, with Gallovidian help, in 1229 to elicit a share of the kingdom, but was killed by over-zealous supporters of his brother: Alan of Galloway was at the time away in Ireland arranging his marriage to Hugh de Lacy's daugher in his continuing – and ultimately vain – search for an heir. Victor for now in the rivalry with his brother, Óláfr Dubh inherited nevertheless not only the hostility of Rögnvaldr's ally, Alan, but the opportunistic eye of the English king and the determined interest of a Norwegian king now established on his throne and more than ready to re-assert a Norwegian presence in the western seas. Troubled times were to continue for Godred Crovan's descendants, as they struggled to exploit the pattern of competition established between the kings of England, Norway and later Scotland in order to secure their own precarious hold on the throne and to preserve the integrity of their kingdom.

Notes

1 Broderick, *CKMI*, fol. 35v.
2 Duffy, 'Irishmen and Islesmen', 121–2.
3 Broderick, *CKMI*, fol. 37r.; AU, s.a. 1162; AFM, ii, 1147.
4 See the remarks by McDonald above, pp. 69–71.
5 L. Hayes and E.D. Jones, 'Policy on the run: Henry II and Irish Sea diplomacy', *Journal of British Studies*, 29 (1990), 295.
6 Giraldus Cambrensis, *Expugnatio Hibernica: The Conquest of Ireland*, eds A.B. Scott and F.X. Martin (Dublin, 1978), 131.
7 Hays and Jones, 'Policy', 295.
8 F.X. Martin, in Cosgrove (ed.), *A New History of Ireland*, 62.
9 Hays and Jones, 'Policy', 297.
10 Hays and Jones, 'Policy', 298.
11 Broderick, *CKMI*, fol. 39v. See the genealogical table of the Manx kings (p. 12),

and the family of Somerled (p. 61).

12 Seán Duffy, 'Ireland and the Irish Sea Region, 1014–1318', (unpublished PhD thesis, University of Dublin, 1993), 59.

13 Giraldus, *Expugnatio*, 79.

14 Giraldus, *Expugnatio*, 79.

15 Giraldus, *Expugnatio*, 69.

16 Giraldus, *Expugnatio*, 97.

17 The process is the subject of R.R. Davies, *Domination and Conquest: the Experience of Ireland, Scotland and Wales 1100–1300* (Cambridge, 1990).

18 Georges Duby, 'The culture of the knightly class, audience and patronage' in R.L. Benson and Giles Constable (eds), *Renaissance and Renewal in the Twelfth Century* (Harvard, 1982, repr. Toronto, 1991), 248.

19 D.J. Freke, *Excavations on St Patrick's Isle, Isle of Man, Prehistoric, Viking, Medieval, and Later, 1982–88* (Liverpool, 2002).

20 By the 1240s, the bishop had his own court and residence seven miles away at Kirk Michael, a more convenient and accessible place, as Anne Ashley says (*The Church in the Isle of Man* (York, 1958), 18), for diocesan business. A medieval tower still forms part of the complex which has been much rebuilt.

21 See chapter 17 below.

22 L.J. Lekai, *The Cistercians, Ideals and Reality* (Kent, Ohio, 1977), 69.

23 Giles Constable, *The Reformation of the Twelfth Century* (Cambridge, 1996), 4.

24 Broderick, *CKMI*, fol. 40r. Óláfr was said at the time to be three years old though the chronicle describes him as still a little boy in 1187 at his father's death (fol. 40r.). Legitimacy was normally conferred if the child was one or two years old.

25 Davies, *Domination and Conquest*, 52.

26 Seán Duffy, 'The first Ulster plantation: John de Courcy and the men of Cumbria', in T. Barry *et al.* (eds), *Colony and Frontier in Medieval Ireland* (London, 1995), 26; Martin, in Cosgrove (ed.), *A New History of Ireland*, 135.

27 One disincentive was the difficulty of sea-travel especially against the prevailing west wind; T. O'Neill in 'Trade and shipping on the Irish Sea in the later Middle Ages' in M. McCaughran and J. Appleby (eds), *The Irish Sea* (Belfast, 1989), 27, quotes the Laud Annals for 1204: 'John Curcie…attempted fifteen times to sail over to Ireland but was always in danger and the wind ever more against him wherefore he waited awhile among the monks of Chester. At length he returned to France and there rested in the Lord.'

28 Martin, in Cosgrove (ed.), *A New History of Ireland*, 135.

29 Basil Megaw, 'The barony of Bangor and Sabal in Kirk Patrick: an account of its origin', *JMM*, IV, 60 and 61 (1939), 160.

30 Wilson (ed.), *Register of St Bees*, 43, 72–3; Duffy, 'First Ulster plantation', 6.

31 W.T. McIntire, 'A Note on Grey Abbey and other religious foundations on Strangford Lough affiliated to the abbeys of Cumberland', *Cumberland and Westmorland Antiquarian and Archaeological Society*, new ser. 41 (1941), 171.

32 Duffy, 'First Ulster plantation', 8–9 and 'Ireland and the Irish Sea Region', 63 n.84.

33 McIntire, 'Grey Abbey', 171.

34 Lawrence Butler, 'The Cistercian abbey of St Mary of Rushen: Excavations 1978–79', *Journal of the British Archaeological Association*, 141 (1988), 84; P.J. Davey (ed.), *Rushen Abbey, Ballasalla, Isle of Man: First Archaeological Report*, Centre for Manx Studies, Research Report 7 (Douglas, 1999); *idem*, chapter 16 below; Roger Stalley, quoted in Davies, *Domination and Conquest*, n.55, speaks of 'an almost constant flow…across the Irish Sea' from 1200.

35 Katharine Simms, 'The Norman invasion and the Gaelic recovery' in R.F. Foster

(ed.), *Oxford Illustrated History of Ireland* (Oxford, 1989), 53.
36 Broderick, *CKMI*, fols 40r.–v. Rögnvaldr is described as *strenuus*, an adjective of some resonance, see Robert Bartlett, *The Making of Europe: Conquest, Colonization and Cultural Change*, 950–1350 (London, 1994), 85.
37 Antonia Gransden, *Historical Writing in England c.550–c.1307* (London, 1974), 219.
38 Duffy, 'Ireland and the Irish Sea Region', 85.
39 Frame, *Political Development of the British Isles*, 37.
40 See Ó Cuív, 'A poem in praise of Raghnall'; Megaw, 'Norsemen and native', 278; and the discussion by McQuarrie below, chapter 13, pp. 297–300.
41 Quoted in Moore, *Isle of Man*, i, 115.
42 Basil Megaw, 'The ship seals of the Isle of Man', *JMM*, VI, 76 (1959), 79, quoting Clarencieux, King of Arms, *c.*1735.
43 *Ibid.*, 79–80, drawing on thirteenth- and fifteenth-century sources. See the important discussion in R.A. McDonald, 'Images of Hebridean lordship in the twelfth and thirteenth centuries: the seal of Raonall Mac Sorley', *SHR*, 74 (1995), 129–43.
44 Megaw, 'Ship seals of the Isle of Man', 80.
45 A.E. Christensen, 'The Vikings in the Irish Sea', in McCaughan and Appleby (eds), *The Irish Sea*, 17.
46 Duffy, 'Ireland and the Irish Sea Region', 60.
47 *Ibid.*, 63, n.80–1.
48 B.E. Crawford, 'The earldom of Caithness and the kingdom of Scotland, 1150–1266', in Keith Stringer (ed.), *Essays on the Nobility of Medieval Scotland* (Edinburgh, 1985), 30–2 and 41, n.60–1; Duffy, 'Ireland and the Irish Sea Region', 63 n.82.
49 Duffy, 'Ireland and the Irish Sea Region', 64 n.89.
50 *Ibid.*, 64 n.90.
51 Seán Duffy, 'John and Ireland: the origins of England's Irish problem', in S.D. Church (ed.), *King John: New Interpretations* (Woodbridge, 1999), 241–5.
52 Broderick, *CKMI*, fol. 41r.–v.
53 Duffy, 'Ireland and the Irish Sea Region', 65.
54 Broderick, *CKMI*, fol. 41v.
55 Guðrún P. Helgadóttir (ed.), *Hrafns saga Sveinbjarnarsonar* (Oxford, 1987), 22; see Power, chapter 2 above, at n.56.
56 Broderick, *CKMI*, fol. 41v.: interestingly, Ian Armit, *The Archaeology of Skye and the Western Isles* (Edinburgh, 1996), 227ff, has traced a picture of gradual environmental degradation of the area from the first millennium: 'by the post-medieval period the interior [of North Uist] was regarded as unfit for human settlement, its uses restricted largely to the provision of fuel and rough pasture'.
57 Moore, *Isle of Man*, 117.
58 Duncan & Brown, 'Argyll and the Isles', 197.
59 Duffy, 'Ireland and the Irish Sea Region', 65.
60 W.H. Bliss (ed.), *Calendar of Entries in the Papal Registers relating to Great Britain and Ireland, Papal Letters, Vol. 1, A.D. 1198–1304* (London 1893, repr.1971), 4 Honorius III, 69.
61 Duffy, 'Ireland and the Irish Sea Region', 104, quoting *CDI*, the source of much of our information insofar as Ireland was involved.
62 Daphne Brooke, *Wild Men and Holy Places: St Ninian, Whithorn and the Medieval Realm of Galloway* (Edinburgh, 1994), 132.
63 *Ibid.*, 131.
64 Broderick, *CKMI*, fol. 44r.

5 *The Last Kings of Man, 1229–65*

EDWARD J. COWAN

> Magnus died in 1265 the ninth and last of the race of Godred Crovan who for two hundred years enjoyed the name of Kings but were in truth little better than lieutenants to the crown of Norway and their inheritance became an insensible addition to the kingdom of Scotland and rather took away an evil than conferred a good.[1]

The slaughter of King Rögnvaldr (Ragnall in Gaelic, sometimes rendered Reginald) at Tynwald on St Valentine's day 1229, by the supporters of his brother Óláfr *Dubh* ('the black[-haired]'),[2] provides a neat vignette of the bloody internecine strife which consumed not only the kings of Man, but the Scandinavian inhabitants of the whole Atlantic world, in the middle years of the thirteenth century. In Norway Hákon Hákonarson was to emerge from a prolonged power struggle with his father-in-law, Duke Skúli, as one of the strongest and most aggressive of Norwegian kings, and one who was determined to re-assert his authority over the kingdom of Man and the Isles, as well as over the Icelandic Commonwealth and the ice-bound shores of distant Greenland. In 1230 Alexander II, king of Scots, suppressed one of the last native pockets of resistance led by the MacWilliam family.[3] A year later the last of the Norwegian earls of Orkney, Jón, was hacked to death in his house at Thurso, in Caithness, by a bunch of inebriated assailants, his own kinsmen among them.[4] His successor was a Scot, ominously for the Orcadians whose fertile islands had long been coveted by Scottish kings. The latter were becoming ever more aggressive towards the kingdom of the Isles riven as it was by the rival factions of the descendants of Godred Crovan and those of Somerled (the Meic Somurli or MacSorleys), their hostilities manipulated to their own mutual advantage by the kings of Scotland and Norway. The kings of Man not only had their problems with the Scottish monarchs, Alexander II (1214–49) and Alexander III (1249–86), but also with Henry III of England who regarded the island as an important part of his strategy for Ireland. Baronial factions in Scotland, England, Ireland and Wales could also impact upon the Manx rulers from time to time.

It may well be the case that Óláfr Dubh regretted Rögnvaldr's death for the rest of his life but both, as were their successors, were small pieces of a mosaic which was designed elsewhere, the victims of powerful political forces they did not always comprehend but which ground them as relentlessly as did winter seas the shores of their beloved Man. The point was well made by the contemporary author of the *King's Mirror*, *Konungs skuggsjá*, an absorbing tract produced in Norway:

> The petty kings, having rent the realm asunder will quickly divide the loyalty of the people who inhabit the land, both of the rich and of the poor, and each of these lords will then try to draw friends about him as many as he can... Soon immorality begins to multiply, for God shows his wrath in this way, that where the boundaries of the territories of the chiefs touch, he places a moving wheel on a restless axle. After that each one forgets all brotherly love and kinship is wrecked.[5]

Manx kings as well as Icelanders, Hebrideans and Norwegians would prove the fatal victims of that inexorably spinning wheel.

There are two major narrative sources for the history of Man between 1230 and 1266, the familiar *Cronica Regum Mannie & Insularum* and the great *Hákon's saga*. It is appropriate that the former should preserve the plural, *Chronicles of the Kings of Man and the Isles*, in its title for there is an exact analogue in the older name for *Orkneyinga saga* which was *Jarla saga*, the *sagas* of the earls of Orkney, whose history closely parallels that of the kings of Man. It is quite likely that the rather cryptic and often chaotic entries in the Manx chronicles preserve echoes of sagas about the Manx rulers. Some of the information is remarkably detailed, the monks of Rushen preserving first-hand or near eyewitness accounts, but on other matters, of which some notice might have been expected, the chronicles are bafflingly silent. *Hákon's saga* was written by the Icelander Sturla Þórðarson, a lifelong opponent of King Hákon and of his imperialist ambitions for Iceland. Ironically when he was banished to Norway in 1263 Sturla was commissioned by King Magnús Hákonarson to compose the saga of his father who was at that time absent on his celebrated expedition to the Hebrides. Sturla was an experienced saga-man with other memorable compositions to his credit in comparison with which *Hákon's saga* appears somewhat lifeless and tedious, a circumstance that may have been occasioned by Sturla's general disdain for his subject. Certain it is that as a man who lamented the demise of the old Icelandic Commonwealth, in defence of which he had so assiduously striven, Sturla was highly sympathetic to the plight of the kings of the Isles and their people who were clearly in the process of falling victim to the inexorable forces of History and the ambitions of powerful competing monarchies.[6]

Rögnvaldr's death did not diminish Óláfr Dubh's problems. Alan of

Galloway, 'the greatest warrior in that time', doubtless with the backing of Alexander II, was reportedly still intent upon harrying Man and the Isles.[7] Furthermore the Mac Somurli kindred, notably the grandsons of Somerled, Dubgall *Screech* and Donnchad, took the opportunity to prove 'unfaithful to Hákon' thus presumably adding to Óláfr's woes. The latter was forced to seek solace at Hákon's court where he reported Alan's proud boast that it was as easy to cross from Scotland to Norway as in the opposite direction and that Norwegian harbours were just as attractive to would-be plunderers as Scottish ones, though as the saga noted, 'that was said not done'.[8] In Norway the Manx king learned, much to his chagrin, that a third Mac Somurli brother, Óspakr, whom Hákon favoured by conferring his own name upon him as well as the kingship of the Isles, had been charged with an expedition to the Hebrides. Óláfr Dubh spent only four nights at Bergen before he was once again bound for the west in the company of Páll Bálkison, with whom he had earlier conspired, willingly or otherwise, in the mutilation of his nephew Guðröðr.[9] The expedition, made up largely of Norwegians and 12 ships strong, was commanded by Óspakr-Hákon.

The earl of Orkney contributed a further 20 ships, including the 'Ox' which was presented to Óláfr Dubh. In the Sound of Islay the invaders encountered Dubgall and Donnchad and another relative (perhaps a brother) named Somerled. The three MacSorleys, displaying true Hebridean hospitality, invited the newcomers to a feast, 'because they had strong wine', potentially lethal conviviality which Óspakr sensibly declined.[10] The Norwegians then attacked the Hebrideans, killing Somerled and capturing Dubgall who was taken into Óspakr's protection while Donnchad was allowed to escape. Some collusion between the Meic Somurli may be legitimately suspected; although Somerled was killed, the other two were spared through Óspakr's connivance. The Norwegian force allegedly recruited a further 45 ships from the islands and, thus reinforced, they sailed around the long peninsula of Kintyre to attack Rothesay Castle in Bute which, in a fierce fight lasting three days, they captured, though not without suffering significant casualties. Alarming reports that Alan of Galloway with 150 ships was preparing to attack them led to a discreet retreat and raids upon Kintyre. When Óspakr died suddenly, having been hit by a large stone according to the Manx chronicle, Óláfr Dubh took over as leader and the expedition advanced on Man. His presence resulted in the evaporation of Manx resistance and the capture of their leader, Þorkell Njálsson – or, as he might have been known to some of his supporters, Torcall Mac Néill – an adherent of the late King Rögnvaldr. Members of Þorkell's family had earlier come to grief in an encounter with some

Norwegians in Skye but his antecedents are otherwise a mystery. His later release, through the complicity of two Norwegians, which ' some liked ill', may suggest that he was yet another of King Hákon's agents in the Hebrides and perhaps one who exceeded his authority by usurping power in Man. Óláfr Dubh and his nephew Guðröðr Donn 'divided the kingdom of Man and the Isles between them'. Óláfr held Man itself but, since the Meic Somurli controlled the Inner Hebrides, Guðröðr's share seems to have centred on Lewis to which destination he was accompanied by the Norwegian force, which sailed through the Minch on its way home to Bergen. Both saga and chronicle are somewhat confused as to the sequence of events in 1231, though the Manxmen had to pay a fine of three pennies for each cow on the island to provide for the over-wintering of the invasion force. Páll Bálkison fell at Guðröðr's hands, probably in Skye, which was still considered to be part of the Manx kingdom of the Isles. Shortly thereafter, however, Guðröðr Donn was himself killed in Lewis, leaving Óláfr as sole ruler.[11]

Óláfr Dubh was to enjoy a further six years as king of Man and the Isles though on his career the sources are completely silent. An absence of contact with Norway implies an absence of noteworthy activity. What is known is that Henry III issued letters of protection to Óláfr while he was in England to consult with him in April 1235. Identical letters were sent to Maurice fitz Gerald, the baron of Offaly and justiciar of Ireland who spearheaded English expansion in that country and who manipulated the native kings of Ireland in exactly the same way that the monarchs of Norway, Scotland and England interfered, for their own ends, in the affairs of the Hebrides. In July that same year Henry informed Maurice that he had granted to the king of Man and the Isles forty marks, 'one hundred crannocks of corn and five doles of wine' to be annually received at Easter from the hands of the Irish justiciar in return

> for his homage and service in guarding, at his own cost, the coast of the sea of England towards Ireland, and towards the Isle of Man, and likewise the coast of the sea of Ireland towards England, and towards the aforesaid Isle of Man, lest injury might happen to the aforesaid our lands of England and Ireland, upon these coasts'.[12]

In May 1236 Henry placed under his protection the people, lands and possessions of Óláfr Dubh who was about to depart for Norway at the command of that country's king. He set out a year later but ill health forced his return and he died at Peel Island on 21 May and was buried in St Mary's abbey, Rushen,[13] 'lamented by the people, in a just old age; a prince worthy of better times, a better kingdom and better subjects', or so, at least thought

William Sacheverell, though on what basis, is not revealed.[14]

Óláfr Dubh was succeeded by his 14-year-old son, Haraldr, who commenced his rule by mounting an expedition to the Hebrides leaving his kinsman, Lochlainn, in charge of affairs in Man. He presumably made for Lewis, the poorer caput of the Isles kingship ever since it had been granted to his father by King Rögnvaldr, 'cultivated by few inhabitants because it is mountainous and rocky and almost wholly inarable',[15] yet comfortably outside the sway of the Meic Somurli and a suitable point of embarkation for Orkney and Norway, while conveniently remote from Henry III and the piratical barons of the Irish Sea littoral. Whatever the destination of Haraldr son of Óláfr Dubh, he was welcomed by the Islesmen and from his base he despatched three Njálssons – Dubgall, Þorkell and Máel Muire, as well as a friend of his named Joseph – back to Man. An assembly was called at Tynwald where the Njálssons and Lochlainn, with their respective supporters, uneasily confronted one another. As had been known to happen at the Icelandic Althing on other occasions, 'after much abuse and vilification against each other, and as no reconciliation seemed possible, the two factions leapt out of the meeting and attacked one another with hostile intent'.[16] Of King Haraldr's delegates only Þorkell survived the carnage. Next spring Haraldr landed with a force at Ronaldsway and this time Lochlainn fled, taking with him another of Óláfr Dubh's sons, Haraldr's brother Guðröðr. In depicting the 14-year-old King Haraldr as taking charge of his own destiny the Manx chronicle may have obscured the possibility that Lochlainn was a usurper rather than a guardian, Haraldr a refugee rather than a king on royal progress. If so Lochlainn redeemed himself when the ship in which he and his young charge were sailing to Wales was wrecked in a savage storm. He scrambled ashore to hear Guðröðr calling to him and responded by leaping back into the doomed ship in which the pair died in one another's arms: 'the entire ship was so full of water to its upper decks', says the chronicle, 'that the sea seemed to be in the ship and not the ship in the sea'.

In 1238 Haraldr son of Óláfr Dubh was driven out of Man by Gospatrick and Gilchrist (Gaelic *Gilla Críst*), sent by the Norwegian king because the Manx ruler had refused to present himself at his court. We know that both of these men were kinsmen of a man called Ferchar, which makes them landowners in the Knapdale and Glassary districts of Argyll; and they were soon to find favour with Alexander II.[17] Haraldr was thus banished to the islands making several unsuccessful attempts to return to Man, the revenues of which were forwarded to Hákon. He eventually relented and betook himself to Norway where after two or three years he found favour with Hákon who made him king of the Isles. Haraldr is said

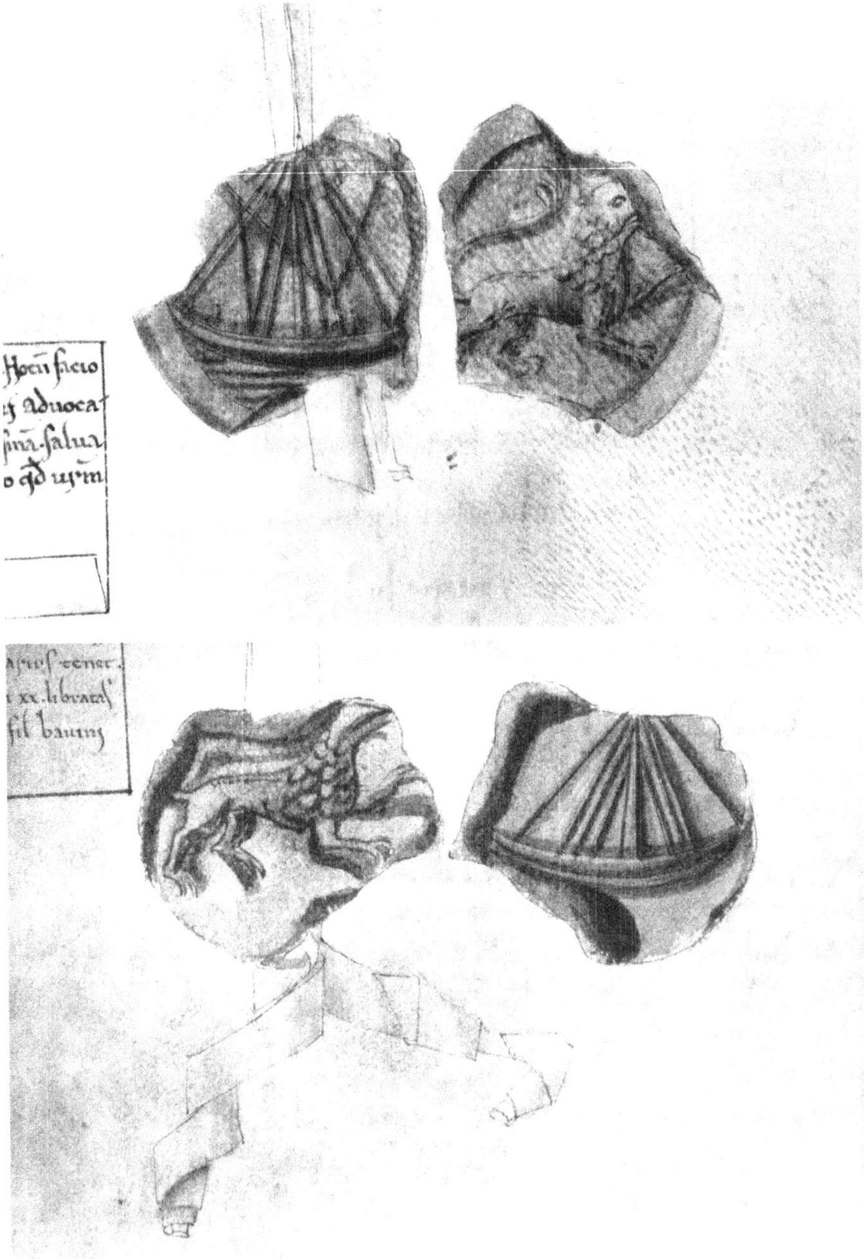

Fig. 5.1 *The lost and fragmentary seals of King Haraldr, c.1242–48, depicting a lion and a ship with a furled sail, both presumably surrounded by a circular border (cf Scrope's seal, Fig 8.1). The ships had high stem and stern-posts and one perhaps depicts figures of crew or warriors. From the Hatton Book of Seals in Northamptonshire Record Office.*

to have assembled a large fleet with which he descended upon St Patrick's Isle to be greeted by the joyful Manx folk: 'And so from that time on he began ruling quietly and peacefully in Man, and held a very stable peace with the king of England and the king of Scotland, and was an ally of theirs in friendship'.[18] So friendly was he that the English king made him a knight in 1246 but a suspicious Hákon summoned him to Norway to which he travelled via England, a well-established route, which also afforded the prospect of diplomatic communication between England and Norway. Haraldr arrived too late for Hákon's coronation but he accompanied the king to Oslo where he soon achieved unimaginable favour which, almost unthinkably, might have been jeopardised had he failed to heed Hákon's summons. That winter Haraldr son of Óláfr Dubh courted the widow Cecilia, Hákon's daughter, and they were married at Bergen in the summer of 1248. These months found two other visitors in Bergen who were to play a notable role in Hebridean affairs. Both Eógan son of Donnchad Mac Dubgaill (otherwise known as Ewan or John of Lorn) and his cousin Dubgall Mac Ruaidrí were prominent members of the Mac Somurli kindred and they were in Norway to request nothing less than the kingship of the Isles. Hákon had clearly signified much closer links between himself and the Isles in the Haraldr-Cecilia alliance, but now disaster struck. Hákon had actually appointed Eógan Mac Dubgaill of Lorn as some kind of acting king of the Isles and he expected that he and his cousin Dubgall would accompany the happy couple on the return voyage. For some reason the Meic Somurli did not sail but Haraldr and his wife did, and they, together with other dignitaries, were drowned when their ship was wrecked in Sumburgh Roost at the south tip of Shetland: 'It was the greatest harm and ill-luck to the islanders that they lost so suddenly such a prince, when his voyage to Norway had been so lucky, for the marriage which he had made, and for other honours'.[19] The disaster was also, it must be said, a remarkably fortunate development for Clann Somurli.

Haraldr son of Óláfr Dubh was succeeded by his brother Rögnvaldr who 'began reigning in Man on 6 May 1249'. Much has been made of the delay in Rögnvaldr assuming the kingship which has been attributed to the lapse of time before Haraldr's fate became known in Man. Rögnvaldr probably underwent some sort of inauguration, although, on that subject as on so much the sources do not comment. At any rate he ruled for precisely 24 days before being killed near the church of the Holy Trinity at Rushen by 'the knight Ívarr and his men'. At this point the kingship of Man was temporarily seized from the line of Óláfr Dubh by a representative of the line of the famous half-brother, the late King Rögnvaldr (d.1229). The new king was Haraldr son of Guðröðr Donn, but King Hákon summoned him to Norway, where he remained a virtual prisoner.

It was the Scottish belief that when Alexander II died, unexpectedly, at Kerrera in July 1249 he was engaged upon an expedition to 'pacify the Argyll region', while at the same time attempting to subdue its ruler, Eógan of Lorn, who refused to compromise his allegiance to Hákon.[20] The latter's saga describes Alexander's dream on the eve of his death. He was visited by St Óláfr of Norway, St Magnús of Orkney and, lastly, by none other than St Columba himself, who warned him against plundering in the Hebrides.[21] The Manx chronicle stated quite baldly that the Scottish king 'gathered a large fleet as he wanted to subject to his sway the kingdom of all the Isles'.[22] The 1249 campaign undoubtedly marked renewed aggression on the part of the king of Scots who had led his first foray into the Hebrides back in 1221-2. Alan of Galloway, whose tempestuous career ended in 1234, may have undertaken his adventures of the 1220s and 1230s, in part at least, at the bidding of his king, thus maintaining pressure on the islanders. Alexander seems to have planned another Hebridean adventure in 1238, but in the 1240s he relied in the main upon diplomatic overtures, while not totally rejecting the military option. Two Scottish bishops were delegated to ask King Hákon if he would hand back the islands that Magnus Barelegs 'had won with some unfairness'. He pointed out that Magnus and the Scottish king had drawn up a legal agreement, adding that, in any case, the Scots at the end of the eleventh century had no authority over the Hebrides whereas Magnus was simply claiming his ancestral rights, a reference to the ninth-century Viking settlement of the area. Thus rebuffed, the ambassadors further incurred the wrath of Hákon when they asked if they could purchase the islands. According to the saga King Alexander sent several embassies to similar purpose and effect.[23] Although his approaches came to nothing it is clear that throughout his reign the Scottish frontier was moving ever closer to the shores of Man.

The Manx chronicle preserves a story, 'just as we learned it from the man himself', of one Domnall, an adherent of Haraldr son of Óláfr Dubh, who miraculously escaped the tyrannous treatment of his cousin Haraldr son of Guðröðr Donn when the shackles which confined him dropped from his legs and he was able to flee to the shelter afforded by the credulous monks of Rushen abbey. Domnall's tormentor having been safely placed out of trouble's way in Norway, Magnús son of Óláfr Dubh (Magnús Óláfsson to the Norse, Magnus Mac Amlaíb Duibh in Gaelic) and Eógan Mac Dubgaill of Lorn, with a party of Norwegians, descended upon Ronaldsway in 1250. The account of what followed is related in some detail in the chronicle and may represent the testimony of a witness. Eógan, *rex Insularum*, attempted to exert his recently conferred authority by ordering the Manxmen 'to do this and this'. The islanders, who regarded Magnús as their rightful king, were unimpressed and refused to comply. Eógan responded by invading St Michael's Isle where he prepared for battle, a challenge which his opponents, led by Ívarr, did not shirk as they too placed themselves in battle formation. The men of Man challenged Eógan's claims by demanding sight of any letters with which King Hákon may have furnished him, undertaking, for their part, 'to execute any order the king has mercifully enjoined upon us'. Such missives Eógan could not, or would not, produce. His response was to withdraw part of his force to their ships, leaving some of his men to die at the hands of their attackers; others were killed as they tried to swim out to the ships. Eógan of Lorn had achieved precisely nothing and to compound his miseries further he suffered additional casualties when one of his galleys was wrecked in a storm.

William Sacheverell perceptively observed that in Man, 'three qualifications seemed requisite for descent of government – a male successor, consent of the people, approbation of the king of Norway, and when either of these was wanting it generally proved fatal to the prince and people'.[24] His point receives corroboration from the surviving evidence: when Magnús returned the following year, unaccompanied by Eógan of Lorn, 'all the Manxmen received him gladly and made him their king'. Thus acclaimed, Magnús son of Óláfr Dubh spent a year at the Norwegian court, at the end of which Hákon 'established [him] over all the Isles which his predecessors possessed by right of inheritance and he confirmed them to him, and to his heirs and successors by the protection of his seal forever'.[25]

Henry III, ever anxious to exploit the misfortunes of the Manxmen to his own advantage, had issued a safe conduct to Haraldr son of Guðröðr Donn in 1250, presumably when he was en route to Norway, and he performed a similar service for Magnús son of Óláfr Dubh in 1253.[26] In April that same year he sent letters to the Welsh lords Llywelyn ap Gruffudd and Owain ap Gruffudd, King Hákon of Norway, and King Alexander of Scotland, commanding them to prevent their men from hostile invasion of the lands of Magnús, heir of Man and the Isles, so long as he remained in Norway by the king's licence.[27] Three years later Henry conferred a knighthood on Magnús and letters of protection, which were to remain in force as long as the Manx king remained loyal to the English crown, while Henry's subjects were expressly forbidden to receive Haraldr, Ívarr or their accomplices. Magnús, in turn, celebrated his good fortune by freeing from tribute the ships and goods of the prior and convent of Coningshead in the palatinate of Lancaster; his charter was dated at Furness Abbey, motherhouse of Rushen.[28] The Manx chronicle records that opposition to Magnús son of Óláfr Dubh gradually faded away after Hákon's recognition of his title but it has little more to note about his career save his death at Castle Rushen and burial at St Mary's in 1265. The picture presented is of a king living happily among his adoring subjects, husband of Mary, the daughter of Eógan Mac Dubgaill of Lorn (an alliance designed to provide some respite from his long-time rival), a patron of the church, a man at peace with his world and on good terms with such powerful figures as King Hákon and Henry III. It was to prove the last bright flash before the flame went out.

Such contentment was sadly short-lived for, when Alexander III took full charge of the kingdom of Scotland, and his own destiny, in 1260, he immediately resurrected his father's policies in the Hebrides. When diplomatic overtures once again failed he sent a force, commanded by the earl of Ross, to attack Skye, a direct challenge not only to Norway but also, in view of what has been suggested above, to the king of Man, in whose domain the island lay. King Hákon responded by summoning levies, fully provisioned, for the summer of 1263 'to avenge the warfare that the Scots made in his dominions'.[29]

In 1251 King Alexander had married Margaret, eldest daughter of Henry III;[30] the English king thus had considerable potential influence over his son-in-law, which he was content to wield to his own advantage. In 1262 Henry accepted Hákon's protestations of peaceful intentions; he recommended amity between Scotland and Norway and urged Alexander to make amends for any injuries recently inflicted upon Hákon's Hebridean subjects. As late as 1263 Henry was attempting to dissuade the Scottish king from undertaking an expedition to the west, and even when an advance Norwegian force arrived in the Outer Isles English reports maintained the fiction that its ultimate destination was uncertain.[31] Henry had his own distractions in 1263, but he was doubtless also prepared to seek advantage from any setback Alexander might suffer at the hands of the invader. Alexander was young, inexperienced and untried, whereas Hákon was a seasoned campaigner who was clearly intent upon restoring Norwegian sovereignty over the archipelago which Magnus Barelegs had seized so long ago.

Alexander clearly had the king of Man in mind when he ordered the fortification of Wigtown on the Solway coast. King Magnús son of Óláfr Dubh, for his part, had no doubt about where his allegiance lay, unlike Eógan of Lorn, who tried to play off Hákon and Alexander against one another; the Manx king joined up with the first ships to reach Scottish waters, probably in Lewis or Skye. In the Sound of Skye he rendezvoused with Hákon who also received the support of King Dubgall Mac Ruaidrí of the Isles, seeking to benefit from his knowledge that Eógan Mac Dubgaill of Lorn had rejected Norwegian suzerainty to throw in his lot with the king of Scots. The combined force advanced to Kerrera whence Hákon despatched 50 ships under the leadership of Magnús and Dubgall, supported by some Norwegian veterans, to harry Tarbert in Kintyre. The number of vessels seems excessive since Hákon was said to have controlled a total of 120 ships 'all in good trim both as to men and weapons',[32] and a further 15 were sent to Bute. It was obviously essential to dominate the important portage at Tarbert and to subdue Áengus Mac Domnaill of Clann Somurli (the MacSorleys), who held that part of the Kintyre peninsula. There was also a symbolism about the place for it was there that Magnus Barelegs had ordered his galley drawn across the isthmus thus giving rise to the tradition that whoever sailed across Kintyre would rule the Hebrides. The saga suggests that through Dubgall Mac Ruaidrí's intervention, Áengus Mac Domnaill and Murchad (?Mac Suibne, McSween) submitted to Hákon. Meanwhile the Tarbert force attacked their lands, burning farms, seizing plunder and slaughtering some of the inhabitants, though not without stubborn resistance. They were about to intensify their activities when Hákon sent word that their depredations were to cease, orders which 'they did not like', though they obeyed and linked up once more with the king at Gigha. Magnús had thus been blooded, an experience commemorated with some poetic exaggeration in Sturla's fairly conventional verse:

> Brave warriors of the treasure-keeper
> Marched from the south across Kintyre;
> The lovers of the sword-storm, sated
> On Scotland's soil the birds of Odin,
> Black-clad ravens fiercely swooping
> Upon the corpses of the slain.[33]

At Gigha Irish envoys visited to request Hákon's aid in freeing their country from the yoke of slavery imposed by the English who 'held all the best towns along the [Irish] coast'. Later, after the encounter at Largs, Irish representatives offered to maintain the Norwegian force over the winter in return for assistance against the English. 'King Hákon was much inclined to sail to Ireland' but his men objected. Dubgall Mac Ruaidrí may be presumed to have played a role in all of this since he was the father-in-law of Áed Ua Conchobair who was intent upon expelling the English out of his native Connacht,[34] a fascinating example of how the tangle of Atlantic politics could extend its long strands from the west of Ireland, via the Inner Hebrides, to western Norway where another King Magnús (Hákonarson) was anxiously and vainly, awaiting his father's return.

From Gigha Hákon sailed to Arran in the Firth of Clyde. Based at Ayr, Alexander initiated a series of ambassadorial exchanges, which came to nothing. The Scots were rightly suspected of deliberately spinning out 'matters more and more, having set their faces against the making of peace at all; for the summer was passing away and the weather was taking a turn for the worse'.[35] A frustrated Hákon finally demanded serious negotiation or the option of battle at the prospect of which Alexander declared himself undaunted. Hákon then sent 60 ships up the narrow fjord of Loch Long under King Magnús of Man, King Dubgall of the Isles and his brother Alan, along with Áengus and Murchad all of whom were important players in the Hebrides; they also enjoyed a hefty contingent of Norwegian support. When they reached the head of the loch at modern Arrochar:

> they took their ships and drew them over the land to a great lake which is called Loch Lomond. Round the lake lay an earl's domain which is called Lennox. There were also very many well cultivated islands on that lake; and those the Northmen wasted with fire and sword. They burned too the whole district around the lake and created the greatest havoc.
>
> Sturla celebrated their great deeds in verse as they:
>
> Drew ships over dry land
> For many a length;
> Those warriors undaunted
> They wasted with war-gales
> The islands thick-peopled
> On Lomond's broad loch.

Alan, brother of Dubgall Mac Ruaidrí went further and attacked overland towards Stirling Castle.[36]

The kings of the Isles were performing the perfectly sensible and laudable function of attempting to divert the attention of the Stewarts – who at that moment were charged with the defence of the Clyde and who would lead the Scottish army at Largs – towards the defence of the Stewart earldom of Menteith and its ally the earldom of Lennox. But there was a further purpose, for the island kings had long recognised, ever since the time of Somerled, that the main threat to their power base was represented by the powerful house of Stewart, guardians of the Clyde estuary and bridgehead against the Isles. As it transpired the future belonged to the Stewarts who were also closely allied to the Strathearn family whose earldom neighboured Menteith. Eógan Mac Dubgaill of Lorn was simply recognising the inevitable when, about 1268, he married his daughter to the earl of Strathearn. The significance of the liaison is highlighted when it is recalled that this lady's first husband had been King Magnús of Man; when she did homage to Edward I in Galloway in 1291 she was still known as 'the noble Lady Maria Queen of Man'.[37] Nothing more neatly captured the worst fears of the great Somerled; Stewart control spelled ultimate doom for the people of the Isles.

The Loch Lomond expedition lost ten ships when a storm hit during the first days of October, almost certainly the same which drove five of Hákon's ships on to the Ayrshire coast. The true victor at Largs was the weather:

> a most severe gale arose on the sea. It smashed the ships together, tore up anchors and hurled sails into the waves, and the separate bits of rigging were seen to be torn away completely from every joint in turn by the huge waves and the fury of the winds and smashed to bits. The ships being thus driven out of position relative to each other, hurtling about and being crushed together, and also smashed against the land and rocks, and dashed into thousands of pieces, the sea rendered shapeless the bodies of the people who had been drowned close to the shore when thrown out of the boats.[38]

So fierce was the tempest that the Norwegians attributed it to witchcraft. *Hákon's saga* also preserves accounts of fouled anchors and shredded sails, adding the detail that when the Scots attacked the stranded ships further gales prevented Norwegian reinforcements from landing. The saga shares with the Scottish sources a penchant for exaggeration and the magnification of its own side's achievements; like them it unconvincingly makes a case for victory. In truth the battle was indecisive. Hákon withdrew to the Cumbraes where he was rejoined by King Magnús and the daughters of Lennox. There in the Firth of Clyde the two men parted for the last time. The last king of Man said his farewells to the last great king of medieval Norway and headed his ships southwards. Hákon enjoyed a leisurely progress back through the Hebrides, more reminiscent, it must be said, of victory than of defeat, until in Orkney he suddenly became ill. He died in the bishop's palace at Kirkwall on 15 December 1263, the words of the sagas ringing in his ears.

Although Sturla valiantly maintained that Hákon had 'won back those realms which Magnus Barelegs had won from Scotland and the Hebrides', the campaign was obviously seen in Norway as a failure. At the very least it had demonstrated the futility of trying to retain effective control of lands and people so distant from Norway yet proximate to the aggressive kingdom of Scotland. Hákon's son Magnús decided upon a pragmatic solution to the problem. According to surviving fragments of his saga he sent his chancellor, Askatin, and Henry, bishop of Orkney, at the prompting of the Orcadians and the remnants of Hákon's force, to negotiate with the Scots who gave them a hostile reception. In the summer of 1264 Bishop Henry and two friars were sent on a further diplomatic mission, receiving more favourable treatment on this occasion. Alexander reciprocated towards the end of the year and such exchanges became fairly regular until they culminated in the treaty of Perth, 2 July 1266, by which Magnús Hákonarson ceded Man and the Hebrides 'and all other islands on the west and south of the great sea, with all rights which he and his predecessors had of old therein' to the King of Scots.[39] The treaty constituted the 'settlement and final agreement for terminating the disagreements, complaints, losses, damage and disputes concerning the islands of Man and the Hebrides and of the rights thereof'. The islands would henceforward be subject to Scottish rule and law but their inhabitants were to be safeguarded by Alexander's lordship; those who wished to remove themselves were permitted to 'do so with their goods, lawfully, freely and in full peace'. No one was to be punished for 'misdeeds, or injuries or damage committed while they adhered to the king of Norway'. The rights of shipwrecked sailors were also protected. The Scottish king was to pay 4,000 marks over four years and 100 marks a year in perpetuity.[40]

Throughout 1264 King Alexander had maintained the military pressure. Walter Bower, drawing upon Fordun's chronicle, was convinced that Hákon had been invited to lead his fleet to the west by certain treacherous Scottish noblemen, namely those Hebrideans who could have been accused of double-dealing in recent months and years, even though they had not always specifically recognised the kingship of Alexander. Revenge seems to have inspired the punitive raids on the Hebrides, ordered by the king, under the leadership of the earls of Mar and Buchan with Alan Durward, once the most powerful noble in Scotland though his star was, by this point, somewhat on the wane.[41] Further conflict occurred when Alexander despatched a party to Caithness whose inhabitants were to be punished for their reluctant support of Hákon. Dubgall Mac Ruaidrí, adhering to his Norwegian allegiance, descended upon the Scots in Caithness, allegedly recovering the fines exacted from the Caithnessians and killing 'the lawman of the Scots'. This last reference may reflect wishful thinking, for the justiciarship of Scotia, the most powerful political office in the country, was held by Alexander Comyn, earl of Buchan, who at that moment was allegedly carrying out plunderings and hangings in the Western Isles. Meanwhile the Norwegians prepared to defend Orkney against a Scottish attack, the task of defence being entrusted to Eiríkr son of Dubgall Mac Ruaidrí.[42]

If *Magnus saga* is alluding to the same events as Bower's *Scotichronicon* Áengus of Islay and several others who had supported Hákon the previous year, entered the peace of the king of Scots, rather than face the ravages of the highland triumvirate. Part of the Scottish force then attacked Man 'and forced Magnús their lord to swear oaths to them'.[43] The wording implies that renegade Hebrideans (i.e., those who were now subject to the Scots) took part in the action against Magnús of Man. Dubgall Mac Ruaidrí, on the other hand, eluded them and sought refuge with his son, Eiríkr, in Orkney. It is a further possibility that the saga was confusing reports of a much more formidable opponent who confronted Magnús and his Manxmen – none other than Alexander himself. The later chroniclers Fordun and Bower borrow from the Chronicle of Melrose the notable coincidence that on 21 January 1264 Alexander III had double cause for joy since he received news both of his son's birth and of Hákon's death. In their version of events Alexander collected a large army and prepared to launch a fleet against the Isle of Man, an action which sits ill with his assurances to Bishop Richard of Sodor that he would not move against Man for the time being, but which is worthy of the misleading missives of Henry III and Hákon IV. When the *regulus* ('kinglet') of Man allegedly learned of this development 'he was more terrified than can be imagined'; he sued for a truce and offered to submit anywhere in Scotland. Alexander responded with a safe conduct, which brought Magnús to Dumfries where he became the king's man and did homage for his *regniculum*, or under-kingdom, on condition that if the Norwegian king should attack him he would be granted safe refuge in Scotland.[44] The Manx king also undertook to provide Alexander, when needed, with ten 'pirate type galleys', *galeae piraticae*, five of 24 oars and five of 12. The odd terminology was simply an attempt to render 'viking ships'. The chronicles were clearly drawing upon an agreement between Magnús and Alexander that has since been lost.[45] Hostages were also taken to guarantee Magnús's good behaviour and Scottish baillies were placed in the island.[46] Alexander had neatly outflanked Henry III who had long schemed to become superior of Man and whose protection Magnús supposedly enjoyed, but the English king, at that time a prisoner of his own barons, was in no position to block a Scottish presence in the Irish Sea.[47] Scotland's victory was not only Man's defeat, but England's also.

External royal interference in the affairs of the Isles was accompanied, as elsewhere in the Scandinavian world, by the inroads of an ever-assertive church that ultimately operated to the disadvantage of the inhabitants and of such independence as they may have craved. To judge from the admittedly scanty evidence Man had been cursed by rapacious bishops ever since the reorganisation of the diocese and the recognition of Trondheim as metropolitan, 'remote' as it was and 'separated by a dangerous sea'.[48] King Rögnvaldr, in 1219, in an effort, no doubt, to maintain his secular independence, had resigned Man to the pope to be held as a papal fief. He was rewarded by His Holiness with a demand that he provide land to support the island's priests.[49] A papal bull dated to 1231, but actually a later forgery, may preserve some historical fragment when it states that the bishop of Sodor was entitled to one third of the tithes of the churches in the Western Isles, which islands the document proceeds to list although identifications become more blurred in due proportion to their distance from Man.[50] King Haraldr son of Óláfr Dubh was a generous patron of the church in the 1240s. The regal rhetoric of his charter perfectly symbolises the partnership into which the kings of Man had entered with the muscular church of such popes as Honorius III and Innocent IV, so bolstering, as they thought, their title and position but ultimately succumbing, as in Iceland and Norway, to the authority from which they confidently anticipated support. The treaty of Perth was subject to papal sanction, which meant that anyone who infringed its terms – such as a future king of Man – was liable to be excommunicated.

In taking Rushen abbey with its monks and possessions under his protection Haraldr had piously proclaimed:

> It is just and consentient with every law that kingly authority should yield an easy assent to the pious vows and honest petitions of suppliants, and more especially to assure our holy religion that it will not part from the paths of justice.

He reassured the faithful that whatever should be done to the monks and their property 'either for good or evil, we will consider as done to ourself, and that if any injury should be inflicted upon them, which God forbid, we will duly punish it as our own'. A further charter granted to Rushen the mineral rights of the whole island 'since, as Solomon witnesses, mirth shall be mingled with lamentation, and grief shall seize upon the extremes of gladness [and] that I may provide for the safety of my soul and may receive the favour of the Lord'.[51] In 1257 King Magnús granted to Bishop Richard the right to hold 'a court of life and limb' and freed the church from any secular exactions. His charter also conveyed to the bishop 'the Island of St Patrick entire, with its appurtenances, fisheries, breweries, customs, anchorages and wharfage of all kinds of goods, coming from all sides and everywhere through Man to the territory of the bishop'.[52]

Magnús's generosity most likely coincided with the rededication of St Mary's, Rushen by Bishop Richard. His predecessor, Simon (consecrated 1226), 'a native of Argyll, a man of great discretion and an expert in the holy scriptures', was entrusted, as befitted his birth, with the care of the diocese of Argyll, based on the island of Lismore in the Firth of Lorn which, 'on account of the evils of the times had fallen into great poverty'. From this honour he sought release 'owing to his many infirmities',[53] which must have been compounded by the perennial hostilities between the Mac Somurli dynasty and the Manx kings. He died in St Michael's church on 29 February 1248 and he was buried in the cathedral of St German's on Peel, which he had begun to rebuild.

If it is possible, from the scanty materials available, to construct a fragmentary account of the kings of Man between 1230 and 1266 the same cannot be said of the people of Man at large for their history is largely forgotten. The synodal statutes of Bishop Simon (1229) give some insights into the lives of the Manx folk, albeit the bishop's legislation was designed to wring as much as possible, at the point of death, from the very people who supposedly enjoyed the church's care and protection. The demonstration of ecclesiastical greed recalls the situation in Caithness in 1222 when episcopal rapaciousness inspired a local revolt.[54] The statutes involved the requisite payments for the proving of wills and of those dying

Fig. 5.2 *The Cathedral of St German, St Patrick's Isle, Peel. Viewed from the south-west. Photo: Peter Davey.*

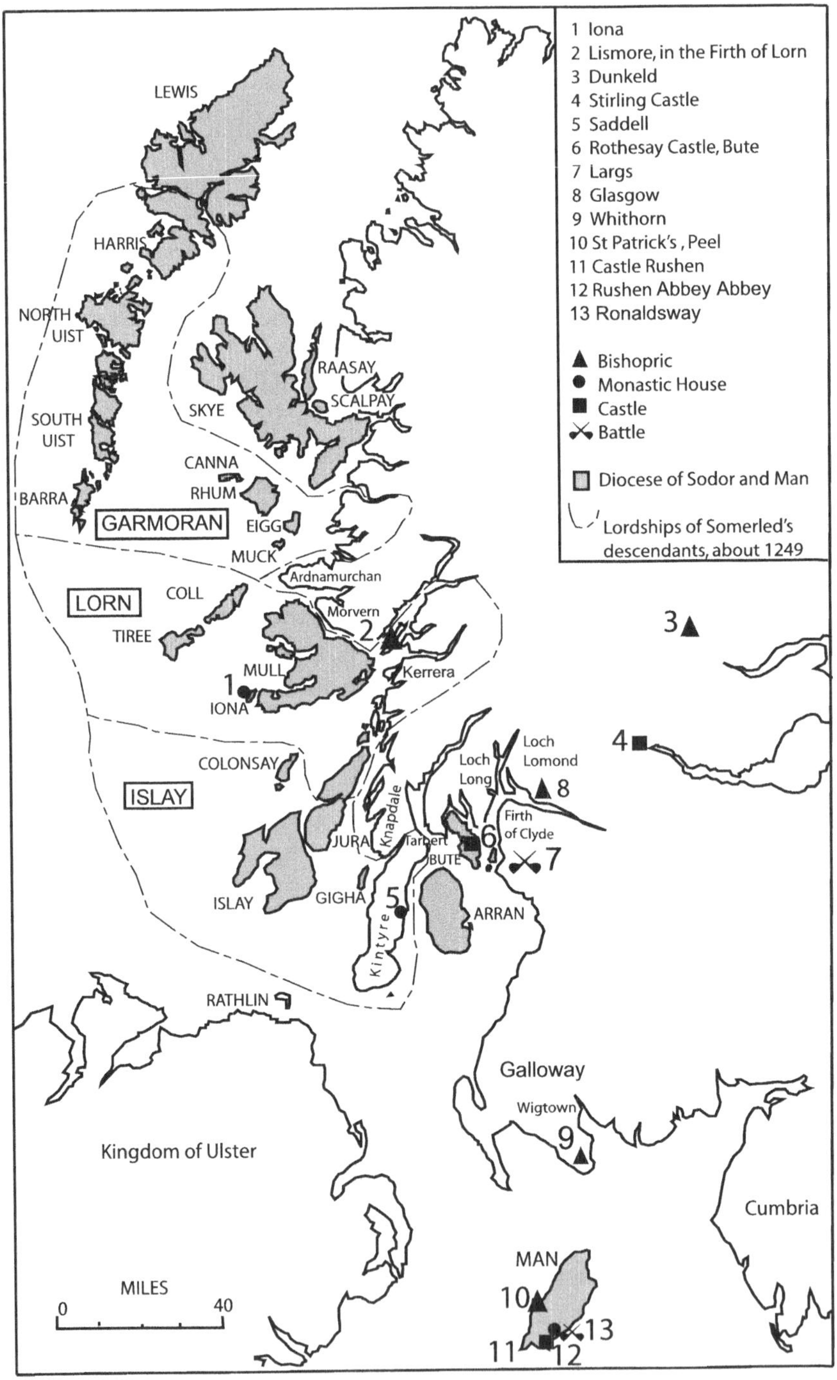
1 Iona
2 Lismore, in the Firth of Lorn
3 Dunkeld
4 Stirling Castle
5 Saddell
6 Rothesay Castle, Bute
7 Largs
8 Glasgow
9 Whithorn
10 St Patrick's , Peel
11 Castle Rushen
12 Rushen Abbey Abbey
13 Ronaldsway
Bishopric
Monastic House
Castle
Battle
Diocese of Sodor and Man
Lordships of Somerled's descendants, about 1249
LEWIS
HARRIS
NORTH UIST
SOUTH UIST
BARRA
SKYE
RAASAY
SCALPAY
CANNA
RHUM
EIGG
MUCK
GARMORAN
Ardnamurchan
Morvern
LORN
COLL
TIREE
MULL
IONA
Kerrera
COLONSAY
ISLAY
JURA
Knapdale
Tarbert
BUTE
GIGHA
Kintyre
ARRAN
Loch Long
Loch Lomond
Firth of Clyde
RATHLIN
Galloway
Wigtown
Kingdom of Ulster
Cumbria
MAN
MILES
0
40

intestate, which latter were, ominously perhaps, 'subject to the will of the bishop'. Mort-dues were payable by the heir or *Gilbogus*, in the form of the best beast such as a cow, ox or horse to the value of 6s. or less, as well as the deceased's clothing to the value of 3s. 6d. There was a carefully described sliding scale of payments due from poorer people, detailing the times of the year at which such items as geese, pigs, bullocks, calves and chickens could be claimed. In the case of persons dying without anything their relatives had to satisfy the church's requirements. People moving from one parish to another had to pay the maximum amounts even if 'the greater portion of their effects should have been left in another parish'. There were regulations about the payment of the tithes, be they of grain, beer (every tenth flagon) or cloth made by male or female weavers.[55] It would appear that the people of Man were subject to plunder, not only from external aggressors, but at the hands of their own priests.

It is of note that the last surviving charter of a Manx king should contain a witness list almost wholly made up of Manx names such as Dompnald the archdeacon, Gormand and Magro parsons, Fogal McHascatt steward and Fogal son of Ivar. A name such as McHascatt offers strong support for Basil Megaw's persuasive argument that Manx Gaelic continued to be spoken, alongside West Norse, throughout the Scandinavian period.[56] To refer to the king who ruled Man in the 1230s as Óláfr Guðröðsson is to highlight his Scandinavian affiliation but it should be remembered that to others of his subjects Óláfr the Black (ON *svarti*) was Amlaíb Dubh or Amlaíb Mac Gofraid.[57] Two worlds met in Man but the inhabitants of each seem to have lived comfortably in that of the other. One of these worlds effectively ended at Dumfries in 1264 when Magnús paid homage to Alexander III, to die shortly thereafter. After that, says a chronicler, *cessaveruntque reges regnare in Mannia*, 'kings ceased to reign in Man'.

Notes

1 William Sachevrell, *An Account of the Isle of Man* (London, 1702), 62–3.
2 Broderick, *CKMI*, fol. 44v. See the genealogical table of the Manx kings (p. 12) and the family of Somerled (p. 61).
3 R. Andrew McDonald, '"Treachery in the remotest territories of Scotland": northern resistance to the Canmore dynasty, 1130–1230', *Canadian Journal of History*, 33 (1999), 161–92.
4 Edward J. Cowan, 'Caithness in the Sagas', in *Caithness. A Cultural Crossroads*, ed. John R. Baldwin, Scottish Society for Northern Studies (Edinburgh, 1982), 27.

Fig. 5.3 *Map of Man in relation to the Kingdom of the Isles with places mentioned in the text.*

5 *The King's Mirror*, trans. L.M. Larson (New York, 1917), 199; text *Konge Speilet*, ed. R. Keyser, P.A. Munch and C.R. Unger (Christiania [Oslo], 1848). See too Sverre Bagge, *The Political Thought of the King's Mirror*. Medieval Scandinavia Supplements 3 (Odense, 1987).
6 Cowan, 'Norwegian Sunset – Scottish Dawn', 103–31.
7 K.J. Stringer, 'Periphery and core in thirteenth-century Scotland: Alan Son of Roland, lord of Galloway and constable of Scotland', in *Medieval Scotland: Crown, Lordship, and Community*, ed. Alexander Grant and K.J. Stringer (Edinburgh, 1993).
8 *Icelandic Sagas*, 4 vols, Rolls Series (London, 1887–94), vol. ii (Icelandic Text) *Hákonar Saga and a Fragment of Magnus Saga with appendices*, ed. Gudbrand Vigfusson (London, 1887), vol. iv (translation). *The Saga of Hacon and a Fragment of the Saga of Magnus with appendices*, trans. G.W. Dasent (London, 1894) cap. 166. Dasent's translation leaves much to be desired and I have modified it in many places. Anderson, *Early Sources*, ii, 474.
9 King Rögnvaldr seems to have had two sons called Guðröðr (probably by different mothers), the one blinded and castrated by Óláfr Dubh and Páll in 1223 (Broderick, *CKMI*, fol. 43r.) and another nicknamed *Donn* ('brown-haired') who became joint-king with his uncle Óláfr Dubh in 1230, but was killed shortly afterwards (*ibid.*, fol. 44v.).
10 On the MacSorleys, see Duncan & Brown, 'Argyll and the Isles'.
11 *Hákonar Saga*, 167; Broderick, *CKMI*, fol. 44v.
12 Oliver, *Monumenta*, i, 72–5.
13 Moore, *Isle of Man*, i, 121.
14 Sacheverell, *Man*, 56–7.
15 Broderick, *CKMI*, fol. 41v.
16 Broderick, *CKMI*, fol. 45r.
17 W.D.H. Sellar 'Family Origins in Cowal and Knapdale', *Scottish Studies*, 15 (1971) 29. The Manx chronicle erroneously has 'Murkerthac' instead of Ferchar.
18 Broderick, *CKMI*, fol. 46r.
19 *Hákonar Saga*, caps. 259–61.
20 Anderson, *ES*, ii, 558; *Scotichronicon*, 5, 191–3.
21 *Hákonar Saga*, 271; Anderson, *Early Sources*, ii, 556–7; Cowan, 'Norwegian Sunset – Scottish Dawn', 116.
22 Broderick, *CKMI*, fol. 47r.
23 *Hákonar Saga*, cap. 245.
24 Sacheverell, *Man*, 60.
25 Broderick, *CKMI*, fol. 49r.
26 Oliver, *Monumenta*, i, 85–6.
27 *CDS*, i, no. 1917.
28 Oliver, *Monumenta*, i, 87–8.
29 *Hákonar Saga*, cap. 342.
30 Anderson, *Early Sources*, ii, 569–71.
31 Cowan, 'Norwegian Sunset – Scottish Dawn', 117–18.
32 *Heimskringla History of the Kings of Norway by Snorri Sturluson*, ed. and trans. Lee M. Hollander (Austin, 1964), 677; Richard I. Lustig, 'The Treaty of Perth: a re-examination', *SHR*, lviii (1979), 52.
33 *Hákonar Saga*, cap. 321.
34 Seán Duffy, *Ireland in the Middle Ages* (London, 1997), 121–4.
35 *Hákonar Saga*, cap. 323.
36 Cowan, 'Norwegian Sunset – Scottish Dawn', 121–2.

37 Oliver, *Monumenta*, i, 116.
38 *Scotichronicon*, v, 341.
39 For a full discussion of the negotiations and outcome see Lustig, 'Treaty of Perth', 35–57.
40 *APS*, i, 420.
41 Alan Young, 'Noble families and political factions in the reign of Alexander III' in Reid (ed.), *Scotland in the Reign of Alexander III*, 1–30.
42 *Scotichronicon*, v, 349; *ERS*, i,11.
43 *Hákonar Saga, Saga of Magnus,* cap. 4.
44 *APS*, i, 112.
45 *Scotichronicon*, v, 347–9, 466.
46 *ERS*, i, 17.
47 Duncan, *Scotland. The Making of the Kingdom*, 581.
48 A. Ashley, *The Church in the Isle of Man* (York, 1958), 14.
49 Oliver, *Monumenta*, i, 53–5, 62–3.
50 Moore, *Isle of Man*, i, 171n.; R.L. Poole 'The Scottish islands in the diocese of Sodor', *SHR*, vii (1911), 258–63; Megaw, 'Norseman and native', 29–34. For surveys of the church in the Isles, see McDonald, *The Kingdom of the Isles*, 200–33, and chapter 15 below.
51 Oliver, *Monumenta*, i, 179–81.
52 Oliver, *Monumenta*, i, 89–92.
53 Broderick, *CKMI*, fol. 51r.; Munch, *Chronicle of Man*, App. 8.; *Fasti Ecclesiae Scoticanae Medii Aevi ad annum 1638*, ed. D.E.R. Watt (St Andrews, 1969), 200–1.
54 Cowan, 'Caithness in the Sagas', 41–2.
55 Oliver, *Monumenta*, iii, App., 176–83.
56 Megaw, 'Norseman and native', 16–17.
57 Oliver, *Monumenta*, i, 70.

6 *The Isle of Man under Scottish Rule, 1266–1333*

DR COLM MCNAMEE

It is beyond dispute that from 1266 events on the Isle of Man, once intimately connected with affairs in the Hebrides, Orkney and Norway, were increasingly dominated by developments in the British kingdoms.[1] By the treaty of Perth between Scotland and Norway, the Scottish monarchy stepped nimbly into the vacuum created by Norwegian defeat and withdrawal from the Western Isles, seizing the overlordship of both the Isle of Man and the Hebrides. For Scotland this was a *coup* of enormous significance. For England, however, the Scottish takeover of Man was a peripheral matter and not of such importance as to jeopardise her long-standing peace with Scotland. Therefore as long as relations between the British monarchies remained harmonious, Man would remain Scottish. However from 1286 two related crises convulsed the British monarchies. These were the Scottish succession crisis and Wars of Independence (1286–1314) and the struggles between Edward II of England and his baronial opposition (1308–22). Running concurrently, they created conditions in which the Isle of Man changed hands repeatedly between the two kingdoms. The Scots actually controlled the island for only 45 of the 67 years from 1266 to 1333; during the other third of the time, the English had possession.

These rapid changes in lordship make this period of Manx history fascinating and challenging. It is difficult in places to piece together even the bare succession of events, despite the availability of a greater volume of source material than for any previous period. The nature and quality of the sources varies considerably. Norwegian sources no longer contribute significantly to the history of Man, but the Manx chronicle contains entries until 1316. Records of monastic houses with possessions on the island continue to be invaluable.[2] However it is the increasing frequency of allusions to Manx affairs in the records of the British kingdoms that adds most to our knowledge. References to the Isle of Man now appear with some regularity in the vast royal archive of England,[3] in the chronicles, exchequer rolls and royal *acta* of Scotland,[4] and in the chronicles and justiciary records of Ireland.[5]

The submission of Magnús, the last king of Man, to Alexander III of

Scotland in 1264 was a necessary prelude to the absorption of the island into the Scottish kingdom by the treaty of Perth in 1266. Magnús's capitulation took place at Dumfries, to which place he had travelled in order to forestall Alexander's approaching invasion force. The terms, discussed in the previous chapter, were not harsh. Homage was to be performed for Man as a sub-kingdom (*regniculum*); hostages were to be surrendered; and ship service of ten galleys was specified.[6] The hostages were definitely taken, for in 1266 seven hostages of Man appear in the account of the sheriff of Dumfries.[7] For his part, Alexander guaranteed Magnús against retribution by the Norwegian king. In this way Alexander took advantage of simultaneous weakness in two other monarchies, namely the death of Hákon IV of Norway (which appears to have occasioned the expedition), and the imprisonment by his baronial opponents of Henry III of England. Henry had been keen to prevent a Scottish seizure of Man and had previously written to the Scottish council to dissuade Alexander from undertaking such a campaign while his heir was so young.[8] Alexander disregarded this self-interested advice, and in 1264 and 1265 he continued to campaign against his enemies on the western seaboard of Scotland. Though he maintained a menacing posture towards the sub-kingdom of Man, Alexander did not intervene there. The records of the Scottish exchequer show that the archdeacon of Man and friars preachers went twice to the island as messengers of the king of Scotland, and canons of Whithorn and 16 men were subsequently sent to the archdeacon, presumably as Alexander's emissaries.[9] Alexander wrote to the bishop of Sodor promising that he would not go against Man 'for the time being'.[10]

For two years therefore Alexander waited for the sub-kingdom of Man to drop into his hands. But when Magnús died without heir on 24 November 1265 the Scottish king took direct possession of the Isle of Man, and it seems that there was a danger of armed opposition from the inhabitants of Man to the transfer of sovereignty:

> Alexander caused his army to be summoned for an expedition to the Isle of Man, so that he might build a fortification there against the assaults of rebels. Then, after taking further advice, he sent some of his own men over there along with some men of Galloway, and the army went home.[11]

The threat of rebellion by the islanders had therefore been avoided for the present. However, there was still a need to reconcile the Norwegians to the Scottish takeover of Man, and the Melrose chronicle proudly relates that in 1265 Alexander sent Reginald of Roxburgh, a monk of Melrose abbey, 'to acquire the land of Man which was formerly called a kingdom, together with the lesser islands lying around the broad kingdom of Scotland'. Reginald returned in the following year having accomplished his mission.[12]

To recap, by the treaty of Perth, concluded on 2 July 1266, King Magnús IV of Norway acquiesced in the Scottish annexation of Man.[13] Magnús ceded to Alexander III of Scotland all his right in the territory of 'Man with the rest of Suðreyjar and all other islands on the west and south of the great sea'. In return, Alexander undertook to pay Magnús 1,000 marks per year for four years, and in addition Alexander and his successors were to pay 100 marks per year to the kings of Norway in perpetuity. Although the Scottish king was to have the right of patronage of the archbishopric of Man, the bishop of Nidaros (or Trondheim) in Norway was to remain metropolitan. Orkney and Shetland were to remain Norwegian territories. Neither king would provide sanctuary for traitors to the other. It was agreed that Norwegian sailors shipwrecked on Scottish territories were to be allowed to sell their goods and ships, rather than be deprived of them by royal right of wreck. For Manx history however the most significant term of this treaty is that the men of Man and the Isles were to be 'subject to the laws and customs of the realm of Scotland'. By this it is clear that by two strokes of remarkably successful diplomacy Alexander had brought to an end the kingdom of Man, the existence of which he had recognised in 1264 and the Isle now became annexed to the kingdom of Scotland.

The position of the treaty of Perth as a watershed in Manx history and in the history of the whole region of the Western Isles has been clearly established.[14] From this time onwards for the rest of the Middle Ages the Isle of Man was regarded as a Scottish territory, a fact acknowledged even by English kings.[15] Yet it is important that continuities, less well documented but undoubtedly present in the life of late thirteenth-century Man, are not ignored. For that reason it is worthwhile to pause to consider Man's connections with neighbouring territories in the mid-thirteenth century.[16] It is apparent that the treaty of Perth did not violate the island's ecclesiastical connections with the Hebrides and Norway. Religious associations with Ireland, too, went back a long way. Of Man's 17 parish churches, 12 are under the protection of Irish saints.[17] But events in the recent past indicate that political links with Ireland were equally strong. Magnús, the last king of Man, had won his kingdom with an army raised in Ireland as recently as 1252. Other sources suggest powerful associations with Wales, in particular with the island of Anglesey. Historically, that island seems to have provided a convenient refuge for Manx exiles. Lochlainn, keeper of Man, had drowned off the Welsh coast in 1238; and in 1253 Llywelyn ap Gruffudd and his brother Owain were ordered by Henry III of England to prevent their men from meddling in the affairs of Man. This association between Man and Wales appears to have been recognised by the Scots during this period, since the lordship of both was united in the person of the earl of Moray.[18] Finally, there were powerful English influences at work on the island. Both the English monasteries of St Bees in Copeland in Cumbria and Furness in Lancashire held lands on the island; and indeed Furness abbey claimed the right to elect the bishop of Sodor and Man.[19]

The Scottish kingdom then could not hope to exert an exclusive influence on the Isle of Man, but Scottish rule was firm. On the death of Richard bishop of Sodor in 1275, the abbot of Furness claimed the right of electing Richard's successor by gift of the pope. He travelled to King Alexander's court to protest his claim, but the Furness chronicle claims that Alexander intimidated the islanders into rejecting the Furness candidate. The islanders then elected a candidate of their own, Gilbert, abbot of Rushen, whereupon Alexander imposed his own candidate on the see. This was Mark, a relative (*germanus*) of the bailie in charge of Man, and Alexander sent him off to Nidaros for consecration with credentials extorted from the clergy and people of the Isle.[20]

In at least one document dated between 1266 and 1282 Alexander the son of Alexander III is referred to as 'lord of Man'. From this it would seem that Man had become the appanage of the heir to the Scottish throne, Lord Alexander, the elder son of the Scottish king.[21] This is unlikely to have implied any degree of autonomy for Man; rather, because the lord was a minor, the island was committed to a series of royal bailies. The names of these are listed in the Lanercost chronicle as follows: Godred MacMares, Alan fitz Count, Maurice Okarefair (or Akarsan), and lastly Reginald the king's chaplain. McDonald remarks that the first of these surnames 'suggests a Hebridean context', though he could well be Manx. The second appears to have arrived on the island with the invasion force of 1275; the third appears in a document preserved in the *Register of St Bees* as royal justiciar.[22]

There is no evidence by which to evaluate the government of Man by these officials, but Scottish rule was evidently resented and bitterness continued. A rebellion broke out in September 1275 that is recorded in three chronicle sources.[23] It was inspired by the arrival on the island of Gu[d]rö[d]r (or Godred), an illegitimate son of Magnús, the last king of Man. The Furness chronicler describes Gu[d]rö[d]r's reception:

> Some of the people rejoiced at his arrival and received him, and some turned round and were grieved; but in a short time he subdued all to himself in fear and affection, and finally they universally and unanimously appointed him their prince.

Gu[d]rö[d]r took possession of the fortress on the island (presumably the castle at Rushen), the Scottish garrison having fled, and 'disposed of the kingdom at his pleasure'. He may have been responsible for the exile of Mark, the bishop appointed by King Alexander, who caused an interdict to be imposed on the rebellious inhabitants of the Isle.[24] The rebellion provoked a punitive expedition by the Scots of more than 90 ships, which put in at Ronaldsway. The army landed on 7 October on St Michael's Island according to the Lanercost account. The Furness chronicler lists the leaders of the expedition. First mentioned is John de Vesci, a 'cross-border baron' who was lord of both Alnwick in England and Sprouston in Scotland. The other nobles involved show that the expedition was predominantly Gallovidian in composition: John Comyn of Badenoch (the justiciar of Galloway); Alan fitz Count (the son of Thomas of Galloway, the earl of Atholl); Alexander son of Eógan Mac Dubgaill (or MacDougall, lord of Lorn) and Alan Mac Ruaidrí (lord of Garmoran).[25]

According to the Lanercost account an offer of peace was made to Gu[d]rö[d]r, but that was rejected, and so the Scots attacked in the early morning 'while still the shades of darkness were upon the land and the minds of the foolish men were darkened'. The Furness writer shows more sympathy with the Manx and gives greater detail:

> So a battle was fought, and the Manxmen, unarmed and naked, could not resist the slingers, ballistaries [crossbowmen], archers and armed men, and fled with Godfrey their king. And the others pursuing them cut down and slew man and beast, as many as they could catch, sparing not for sex or place. But Godfrey [i.e., Gu[d]rö[d]r] with his wife and some of his followers escaped, fleeing to Wales.

The Manx chronicle states that in the conflict the Manx lost 537 and adds the following rhyme about the slaughter: 'Ten fifties and three tens plus five and two did fall. O Manxmen, do beware, lest more horrors ye shall befall!'. From all accounts it seems that King Alexander had brought to bear on the unarmoured islanders all the refinements of late thirteenth-century warfare, including crossbowmen, archers and quite possibly cavalry as well. The Scottish army went on to plunder the abbey of Rushen and rob the monks; and, allowing for the Furness chronicler's pious exaggeration, it seems that reprisals were severe: 'At that time too perished miserably all the nobles and the captains, and also the rest of the people, whose exact number no-one knows'. King Alexander III was later remembered by an abbot of Rushen as 'the conqueror of Man by the sword'.[26]

Since Gu[d]rö[d]r fled to Wales, it seems most likely that he had come from that direction in the first place. Quite probably Anglesey was

Fig. 6.1 *St Michael's Isle where John de Vesci and his largely Gallovidian expedition routed the Manx on 7 October 1275. An aerial view from the north: at the far end of the islet lies St Michael's Chapel, surrounded by a small rectangular burial ground defined by a bank. Indications that the cemetery was once more extensive have been discovered. In the foreground lie more recent defences, including a round battery and the slight earthwork remains of a seventeenth-century fort. St Michael's Isle and the peninsula of Langness beyond together provided essential shelter to the anchorage of Derbyhaven.*

providing safe haven for Manx political refugees once again. It is possible too that the Manx provided some assistance to the Welsh when they too were ground under the heel of an overweening neighbour. Writing in 1282 Edward I's commander in Wales, Roger Mortimer, requested from his government an order 'that no iron, salt or food be sent to [the king's] enemies in Wales from Scotland, Norway or Man'.[27] Thereafter until 1290 the Isle of Man appears to have submitted meekly to Scottish rule. It is possible that the crushing of the rebellion of 1275 had the effect of strengthening the Gallovidian element in Manx society. Three bishops of the period – Mark, Alan and Gilbert – are all said to have been from Galloway, and the Gallovidian influence remained strong under the English and Bruce regimes that followed.[28]

In view of the severity with which the rebellion was crushed however, other Manxmen may have derived satisfaction from the catastrophes that befell the Scots thereafter. Alexander, the young lord of Man, had died in 1284; and two years later there began the succession crisis that was to threaten the very existence of the Scottish monarchy. King Alexander himself died without heir in that year, and the next in line to the Scottish throne was Margaret, his granddaughter, living in Norway. In the autumn of 1290, Margaret also died. Over the next few years Scottish politics became polarised as two camps of hostile noble factions emerged, each aspiring to the vacant throne. On the one hand were the Bruces of Annandale, who numbered among their allies the Stewarts, the Mac Ruaidrí family in the Hebrides and Clann Domnaill (Mac Donalds) of Islay. On the other hand were the Comyns, the Balliols and Clann Dubgaill (MacDougalls) of Argyll. Edward I of England, meanwhile, began gradually to manoeuvre for control of Scotland; and Man, Scotland's latest acquisition, was the first part of that kingdom to be taken over by him.

From the death of Alexander III in 1286 to the intervention of Edward I in 1290, the sequence of events on the island is unclear. The death of the king of Scotland threw open the way to claims to the Scottish throne, as is well known. But it also opened the way for dynastic claims to the lordship of Man. Two claimants to Man approached Edward I at this time. The first was John Waldeboef, who claimed the lordship of the Isle in right of his wife Maria, widow of Magnús the last king of Man, and formerly Countess of Strathearn. John was eventually told to bring his case to the court of the king of Scotland.[29] The second claimant to Man was Affreca 'de Connaught'. The precise identity of this Affreca is unknown but she claimed to be cousin and heiress (*consanguinea et haerede*) to Magnús the last king. It has been suggested, though hard evidence is lacking, that she may have been a granddaughter of Affreca the wife of John de Courcy, and therefore a great-granddaughter of the famous twelfth-century King Gu[d]rö[d]r (d.1187). She later appears to have married into the Montacute family of Somerset, bringing her claim to that family.[30]

While lawyers argued, magnates took action. It is known that at some time during this period from 1286 to 1290 the earl of Ulster, Richard de Burgh, took control of the Isle of Man.[31] By what authority he acted is not known. He may have acted on the orders of Edward I. He may equally have been striving on his own initiative to protect the interests of his Scottish allies, the Bruces and Stewarts, to prevent the island from falling into the hands of the Comyns or Clann Dubgaill. An item in the account of James the Steward, as sheriff of Ayr, might support either of these possibilities. In 1289, the Steward paid 4s. 2d. towards the 'expenses of two friars preachers, going to Ireland with letters of the king of England concerning the Isle of Man'.[32] But it is possible also that Earl Richard was acting on behalf of Affreca of Connacht, whose name suggests a connection with the de Burgh earls of Ulster, since they were also lords of Connacht.

The next occurrence was an assembly of the islanders (or at least of notables) at Rushen abbey, at which they bound themselves under their common seal to obey the king of England as their lord.[33] The instrument of this surrender, which is dated by year only, states that the island is 'abandoned and afflicted by many woes, lacking protection and defence' (*desolata et multis miseriis occupata, defectu protectionis et defensionis*). In this document the inhabitants promise, under pain of a 2,000 mark fine, not to rise up against Edward's lordship or otherwise to grieve him. The cause of the island's woes is not identified. It is interesting that the islanders possessed a common seal, though this is not altogether surprising as by this stage in their history there had been several instances of communal action. Edward – whose servants had clearly orchestrated the assembly – granted his protection to the inhabitants on 4 June 1290 and appointed Walter de Huntercombe to the custody of the Isle of Man 'which Richard de Burgh earl of Ulster has surrendered into the king's hands'.[34] He then commissioned his powerful servant Antony Bek, bishop of Durham, to receive to his peace the men of the Scottish Isles, 'threatened by war and dissension'.[35] This grant of protection and imposition of a keeper on the island amounted to a flagrant violation of Scottish rights. Edward's biographer states: 'However justified this was by conditions there, this was a surprising intervention in the affairs of another realm'.[36] In taking possession of Man, Edward's concern was probably less to relieve the woes of the people than to secure convenient supplies of lead for the construction of his chain of Welsh castles. Safe conducts were issued on 6 February 1290 to tenants from Chester and the Welsh March, and to merchants of Cahors going with merchandise to the Isle of Man, which appear to have served this purpose. These letters were issued to keepers, who, it must be assumed, were appointed by the earl of Ulster.[37] From documents issued on 2 June 1290 it appears that they were trading in the Isle of Man, for lead for the castles in Wales.[38]

Given their history of resistance to Scottish rule, it might be expected that the Manx people welcomed Edward's intervention. But by now a pro-Scottish party had apparently developed for there was at least some opposition to the English intervention. On 19 February 1291 letters were ordered for despatch to the bishop of Sodor

> to lead his subjects to cherish tranquillity and quiet and to abolish scandals and dissensions, as the king understands that certain priests of the Isle of Man by conspiracy and false suggestion have made diverse complaints against the king's ministers and others and so stir the whirlpool of suggestion that disturbances are feared.[39]

It could be that this letter is unrelated to the lordship of the island and represents a purely clerical reaction to three presentations to churches on the island that Edward had made in June 1291;[40] but the mention of 'disturbances' suggests a more widespread dissatisfaction. The priests referred to were probably led by Bishop Mark who owed his appointment to the Scottish king and later sided with the Scottish opposition to Edward I.

This first episode of English interference in Man was short lived. Edward I was asked by the Scots to adjudicate as to who should succeed to the throne of Scotland, and having extracted recognition of himself as overlord of Scotland, he pronounced in favour of John Balliol in 1292. Edward then formally recognised the rights of King John I of Scotland over the Isle of Man and on 5 January 1293 handed over the island to Scottish control.[41] Just before he did so, he arranged for a sum of about £800 to be collected from various debts and paid to the king of Norway, apparently to satisfy arrears of the annual fee of 100 marks required by the treaty of Perth.[42] It seems likely then that the bailies of the king of Scotland returned to administer the island. But in 1296 Scotland rebelled against Edward, whom she had earlier acknowledged as overlord. The causes of the Anglo-Scottish war were many and complex, but appeals by Scots to the English king's court were a factor in goading the Scottish monarchy into rebellion. One such appellant was Affreca of Connacht, who declared that she had been denied justice at the court of the Scottish king in the matter of her claim to the Isle of Man.[43] Edward invaded Scotland, defeated the Scots in battle and distributed their English lands to his servants. On 29 August 1296 the bailiff of Dumfries was commanded to bring Mark, bishop of

Sodor, to attend King Edward at Dumfries, presumably to do him homage, a duty being required of magnates of Scotland at this time.[44] Mark had already sworn fealty to Edward I as 'superior and great lord of the kingdom of Scotland' in 1291 while the Scottish throne was vacant. He may now have refused to do fealty or otherwise offended Edward, for in 1299 both he and Bishop Robert Wishart of Glasgow were believed by Pope Boniface VIII to be imprisoned by the English king. On 27 June 1299 the pope wrote to Edward commanding the release of both bishops.[45]

Between 1296 and 1301 the isle may have changed hands several times. During the long imprisonment of Bishop Mark, control of the island probably returned to Antony Bek;[46] it is inconceivable that Edward I would have left the island in 'rebel' hands. But at some stage thereafter – possibly during the Scottish resurgence under William Wallace – Bek must have lost control of Man, for according to Camden the isle was recovered from the Scots by the Somerset adventurers Simon Montacute and his son William. Bek reappears from about 1301, not only in control of the isle, but as lord of Man.[47] We have seen that Bek was involved in the Irish Sea region from as early as 1290, but exactly how he acquired this legal title to the lordship of the isle is uncertain.[48] Later Edward I demanded to know by what warrant Bek held the isle, which implies that he had not acquired the island from the English king.[49] It is possible that Bek received the island from one who had been granted it by a king of Scotland; but it seems most likely that he derived it from Montacutes.[50]

Only one explanation of how Antony Bek came by the lordship of Man has been advanced. It is found in the pages of Camden's *Britannia*:

> But what he [John Waldeboef] could not effect by right, William Montacute, his kinsman descended from the kings of Man, did by arms. For, with a body of English troops hastily collected, he drove all the Scots out of the island; but having contracted a considerable debt for this war, and being unable to discharge it, he mortgaged the island and its revenues for seven years to Anthony Bec, bishop of Durham and patriarch of Jerusalem, to whom the king afterwards gave it for life.[51]

Camden appears to have had access to sources of which we know nothing. While it is necessary to treat his version with caution, there is a lot that rings true here. William Montacute (d.1319), Simon's son, was militarily active from about 1301; and in that year Simon provided two substantial ships, a galley and a barge manned by 100 men between them, for the naval war around the western isles.[52] This naval activity appears to have included the seizure of Man from the Scots, broke the Montacutes financially and forced them to mortgage their prize to Antony Bek. Mortgage is exactly the sort of arrangement in which Bek involved himself; he participated in other large-scale private financial transactions while in royal service.[53] The seven-year mortgage arrangement with Bek was probably made in 1301 when Bek began to style himself Lord of Man. Meanwhile, both claims by inheritance were still being pursued. John Waldeboef, grandson of Maria, pursued his claim to Man by petitioning parliament in 1304.[54] In March 1305 however Affreca of Connacht quitclaimed to Simon Montacute all her rights in the Isle of Man, and notified all her tenants on the island to give obedience to him.[55] This quitclaim may be interpreted as marking the occasion of Affreca's marriage to Simon Montacute. It buttressed the Montacute claim by right of conquest with a claim by right of inheritance.[57]

Antony Bek uses the style 'Lord of the land of Man' (*dominus terre Manniae*) when confirming gifts to the prior and monks of St Bees in June 1301.[58] His control of the isle was beyond dispute. On 19 June 1301 he once more he installed Walter de Huntercombe as his justiciar. In a record of pleas held at the church of St Lupus in Rushen between the prior of St Bees (in Copeland) and the abbot of Rushen on 16 January 1302 Huntercombe and Brother William de Malton are described as justiciars of 'Antony, Lord of the said Isle'.[59] The presence of his bailiffs is referred to; and at least one document made on the island is dated by Bek's pontificial year.[60] But towards the end of the reign Edward I turned on his eminent servant. Three times he confiscated Bek's palatinate franchise of Durham, and he also contemplated depriving Bek of the Isle of Man. On 28 June 1307 the sheriff of Northumberland was ordered to summon Bek to appear before the king within a fortnight 'to give reason why the Isle should not be taken into the king's hand'.[61] But by this time Edward I had then less than a fortnight to live, and it seems unlikely that any action was taken. In Bek's obituary in the Durham chronicle it is said that he was given the Isle of Man for life by gift of the king, an assertion which, as we have seen, is repeated by Camden.[62] While there is no trace of this grant in the chancery rolls such a gift was made, probably by Edward II of England using the Scottish great seal (1307–27). After Bek's death Edward II charged Bek's steward Gilbert MacAskil with arrears of rent and MacAskil's account reveals the terms of the grant. Bek was due to pay 1,000 marks per annum in moieties due at Michaelmas and Easter as rent for the isle. At sometime between 1307 and 1311 therefore, Edward II had disregarded the claims of Waldeboef and Montacute alike, and granted the island to Bek.[63] In view of Bek's well-established control of the territory the Montacutes might have decided to endure this situation for the old bishop's few remaining years, but their resentment was to become manifest on his death.

At this time the various lordships bordering on the Irish Sea had begun to realign themselves in reaction to developments in Scotland.[64] Since 1296 Edward I had tried to absorb that kingdom into his realms. He had defeated in battle the supporters of King John Balliol, occupied Scottish castles, and, in person, led three great invasions of Scotland in 1300, 1301 and 1303. Yet Edward's advanced age and deteriorating health invited rebellion. In a daring but bungled *coup* in 1306, the Bruce faction resurrected its claim to the throne. Robert Bruce, earl of Carrick, killed a rival for the Scottish throne, John Comyn, and had himself enthroned as Robert I, King of Scotland. Robert was swiftly defeated and exiled with his brothers to the Western Isles and to Rathlin, off the northern coast of Ireland. The occasion of the Bruces' western exile sees further involvement in the region of the Montacute family. In February 1307 Simon Montacute was in Edward I's service against them, commanding a fleet of 15 vessels based at Ayr and including his son William. His commission was 'to keep the seas in the parts of Galloway', effectively patrolling the North Channel to prevent the Bruces and their allies from slipping back into Scotland.[65] Man is such a convenient base for shipping that it is certain to have been involved in these naval operations, which provided the Montacutes with a welcome pretext for remaining in and around the territory which they still had high hopes of acquiring. William Montacute also travelled to Ulster to arrest supporters of Robert. He and three others were paid £10 for capturing them and sending them to Dublin Castle.[66] The aim of these activities was to prevent the Bruces from returning to Scotland to raise rebellion with Hebridean and Irish support.

As is well known, however, the Bruces did indeed cross back into Scotland.[67] Robert's force landed safely; but 18 ships led by his brothers Thomas and Alexander were met on landing by the Galloway lord Dungal MacDowell and heavily defeated. Thomas and Alexander Bruce were captured and beheaded and only two of their ships escaped.[68] There is no evidence surviving of how the Isle of Man was affected by the ensuing conflict, but all the indications are that sympathies on the island were divided. Gallovidian elements in Manx society will have been opposed to the Bruces. Dungal MacDowell himself may have been among those holding estates on the island; it is said that an element of the name MacDowell is preserved in the place-name Balladoole.[69] For these reasons the islanders must closely have followed the war in the surrounding waters and territories.[70] In Scotland Robert's tactics typically involved the terrorising of isolated communities; the destruction of castles, to prevent shelter being given to the occupation; and the taking of truces in return for money or kind. These activities he extended into the Irish Sea region, where the war acquired a distinctively bitter and tribal aspect. Robert received solid support from many quarters, notably from the Stewarts, the Mac Ruaidrí kings of the Hebrides and the Clann Domnaill of Islay. On the other hand, fierce opposition to the Bruce claim and support for the English was forthcoming from the Balliols, the Comyns, the Clann Dubgaill of Argyll and the chiefs of Galloway. But the death of Edward I on 7 July 1307 sapped the morale of these 'Anglo-Scots' and Robert was now assisted by significant numbers of mercenaries from the Isles. Edward Bruce (now Robert's sole surviving brother) launched a devastating attack on Galloway in 1308. For this success Robert granted him the title of lord of Galloway, which may have implied a claim to the Isle of Man.[71] Furthermore in 1309 Robert attacked Mac Dubgaill of Argyll with a large army and galley fleet, sending Eógan of Argyll into exile in Ireland. Both campaigns were to have serious consequences for the Isle of Man.

The keen interest that Robert I took in the Irish Sea region has been emphasised by Professor Barrow.[72] However it is also quite clear that Edward II showed an anxiety over this region. Every land-based, east-coast campaign that Edward planned against the Scots, from 1309 to 1317, was intended to be assisted by a simultaneous diversion in the Irish Sea. These diversions were directed at encouraging the sullen and resentful population of Argyll to revolt against Robert. The Bruces' return to Scotland in 1307 had been assisted by an unnamed Irish king, and they hoped for further assistance from that country. Man was the base for Montacute's fleet, and the easy access it provided to the Solway Firth, the Galloway coast and Kintyre had thus far ensured that supply vessels from Ireland, Wales and England could safely reach Edward II's increasingly threatened garrisons of Ayr, Dumfries and Carlisle. Edward Bruce may also have considered that Man was a part of his lordship of Galloway; however there is no certain evidence that this is so.

This guaranteed that the Isle of Man would continue to be involved in the war; and the first evidence of a threat to the isle comes in 1310. At midsummer in that year a fleet from Dublin was to land Irish magnates led by the earl of Ulster at Ayr on the Scottish coast. The earl was to supply 500 men, wearing chain mail hauberks. This was part of an Irish force of 300 light cavalry and 2,000 foot intended to support Mac Dubgaill resistance to Robert in Argyll, and to coincide with an invasion of Scotland by way of the eastern march.[73] However on 2 August the expedition from Ireland was called off on account of deteriorating weather. The earl's 500 hauberked men and ships from the ports of the English West Country were ordered instead to join Simon Montacute's fleet on the Isle of Man. Montacute had been promoted to admiral.[74] Perhaps an attack on the island was anticipated. In December two letters reached Edward II from Bek's steward on the island, Gilbert MacAskil, revealing a clear threat of invasion. Edward's response was to issue MacAskil on 15 December 1310 with a commission to collect ships and crews in Cheshire, Lancashire, Cumberland and Westmorland to go with him to the defence of the isle at his own expense. The commission opens with the following words:

> We understand from several sources that Robert Bruce, our enemy and traitor, is exerting pressure with his forces and intends to send his whole galley fleet from the Western Isles against the Isle of Man this winter to destroy that island and to seize for himself and his abettors, our enemies and rebels, all victuals and necessaries in the said Isle of Man and to use them for his own ends and to sustain his accomplices.[75]

The surviving fragments of Gilbert MacAskil's letters suggest that Robert had allies on Man, for they include a reference to persons 'who are in the said land and who victual him and his ships and maintain the enemies'.[76] There is further evidence that the Manx population was divided in the revelation that MacAskil would provide details of Manxmen who sympathised with the Bruces, who stayed in England, Ireland and Wales and whose arrest the king now ordered.[77] While Edward II was apprecia-tive of his services, MacAskil no doubt seized the opportunity to 'finger' his local rivals. This servant of Antony Bek and Edward II, who governed the isle in these turbulent years, was almost certainly a native. Though described in the chancery rolls as Bishop Bek's steward on the Isle of Man, MacAskil does not appear as a servant of the bishop in any other capacity; and his name suggests that he was of Manx origin (perhaps Gilla Brigde Mac Ascaill). He first appears attesting a charter in 1301, and then as coroner, together with Sir Nicholas de Moriceby and Reginald MacStephan, in January 1302.[78]

The first serious threat to MacAskil's control of the isle occurred in February 1311. On 18 February, a fortnight before the death of Bishop Antony Bek, MacAskil was appointed constable of the castle and keeper of the Isle of Man.[79] The seizure of a bishop's temporalities before his death was an extraordinary step. Despite Bek's enormous debts to the crown, the royal treasurer in England had been expressly instructed to delay until the bishop's death before seizing his money and moveable property.[80] An immediate threat to Man must have been perceived; but the threat seems to have come not from the Scots, but from the Montacutes who had seized the isle from the Scots a decade previously, mortgaged it to Bek for seven years, and which they had seen granted, irrespective of their claims, to Bek for life. Simon seems to have planned to take over the isle just before the bishop died and his temporalities were seized by royal officials. In this way he hoped to acquire a strong position for subsequent negotiations with the Crown. We know nothing of what transpired; but by 20 October 1311 Dungal MacDowell had brought charges against Simon Montacute before the king at Berwick 'concerning felonies in the Isle of Man'. On that date Edward II demanded that the record and process of the appeal be brought before the king and council without delay. In 1311 Simon was imprisoned for a time in Windsor. From the subsequent acquitance issued in 1313 it appears that these felonies involved an 'attempt to occupy the land of Man to the king's disinheritance'. [81]

Bek died on 3 March 1311, and the Annals of London describe him as bishop of Durham, Patriarch of Jerusalem and *rex Mannorum* ('king of the Manx').[82] Gilbert MacAskil's appointment as royal keeper was made under Edward II's seal for Scotland, recognition by the English king that Man was a part of the kingdom of Scotland.[83] MacAskil's first duty was to collect the issues of the island that were outstanding and to forward them to the executors of Bek's will, since the bishop had indeed died heavily in debt to the crown.

A number of chronicles record that Piers Gaveston, Edward II's much hated favourite, was next given the isle.[85] Again the gift is not recorded in the English chancery records. At this time Edward II must certainly have been casting around for somewhere in which his adoptive brother would be safe from the vengeance of the English magnates. Gaveston had earlier been dispatched to Ireland in 1308 as lord lieutenant; and the vacant lordship of Man might in 1311 have seemed an equally attractive haven. But by 1311 Edward II's chancery was under the control of the lords ordainers, a committee of magnates set up to oversee reform of the royal household and finances and whose precepts Edward II was bitterly opposed. Certain royal orders were at this time subjected to obstruction or outright contradiction in the chancery,[86] and a favour granted to Gaveston in the spring of 1311 would have stood little chance of being processed.

Henry Beaumont, another disliked but less notorious foreign *curialis* was granted the island for life on 1 May 1311, rendering for it the same services that previous lords had given the kings of Scotland.[87] This royal grant of the Isle to Henry Beaumont was specifically revoked by the ordainers. The 22nd ordinance laid down that because

> Sir Henry Beaumont has received from our lord the king, to the loss and dishonour of the king... the kingdom of Man and because he has badly advised the king contrary to his oath, we ordain that he be removed from the king's council forever and that he come no more near the king anywhere.[88]

The ordainers further proposed that 'the land of Man should be in the keeping of a good Englishman', which neither Henry Beaumont nor Piers Gaveston could claim to be.[89] Henry Beaumont was duly deprived of Man on 9 October 1311 by order of the ordainer-controlled chancery. But as soon as Edward II regained control of his household, many of the precepts of the ordainers were overturned. On 20 January 1312 Robert Leyburne and Gilbert MacAskil were ordered to restore the land of Man to Henry Beaumont.[90] The regrant was made exactly one year after the original grant, on 1 May 1312, and in particularly grand terms. Beaumont was to have Man

> with all its dominion and royal right, together with knights' fees, advowsons of churches and religious houses, liberties, free customs, escheats and all other of its appurtenances to hold by the service which the lords of Man were accustomed to render to the kings of Scotland.[93]

From 18 February until 1 May 1311 and again from 9 October 1311 to 20 January 1312 Gilbert MacAskil was managing the government of Man on Edward II's behalf. His accounts for the period were audited in 1316. He was credited with paying £308 7s. 61/2d. outstanding from the time of Bek, and the 500 marks due for the Easter term.[93] All the money was spent in the Irish Sea region. The £308, raised from MacAskil's own resources, was paid to Gilbert de Bromley, receiver of the king's victuals at Carlisle, for defence of the town and castle of Carlisle and surrounding districts. Robert I was now firmly in control of all but a few enclaves of Scotland. Cumberland and Northumberland were being subjected by the Scots to devastating raids, and Carlisle was under serious threat. Much of the £308 sent by MacAskil might have been handed over to the Scots in August 1312 in return for the temporary truce or *suffrance de guerre* taken at that time.[94] The 500 marks were handed over to the Scottish exile and inveterate foe of the Bruces, Eógan Mac Dubgaill of Argyll, for purposes unspecified.[95] It also appears that MacAskil paid a daily rate of 2s. to certain men at arms and to foot 3d., whereas the going rate was respectively 1s. and 2d. per day.[96] This might suggest that the garrison on Man was in serious danger, or perhaps that MacAskil's stewardship was unpopular.[97]

Edward II's attempt to settle the island under the undisputed lordship of Beaumont betrays the great uncertainty about the English position in the Irish Sea. The king's withdrawal from Berwick in the summer of 1312 marks a withdrawal of English royal power and interest in the whole of northern Britain that played into the hands of the Scots. In June 1312 Edward II gave protection until Christmas throughout the realm for the men of the Isle of Man, 'on account of their loyalty to the king'.[98] Manxmen on the English mainland needed protection from the arbitrary seizures by royal purveyors that went on everywhere in England at this time. It is possible too that they were occasionally mistaken for Scots.

Beaumont, for his part, seems to have attempted to use ecclesiastical sanctions to pacify the inhabitants of the Hebrides. On 26 June 1312 Edward II, at the request of Henry Beaumont, gave leave to Alan, bishop 'of Inchegall', to make a visitation of the Outer Isles of his see, 'enjoining him to use all means to secure the obedience of their inhabitants to himself'. Alan had been elected while Man was under the influence of Antony Bek, and so, unlike his predecessor, he was co-operative with the English regime.[99] The Hebrides were clearly hostile to the English; and Beaumont's involvement suggests that their inhabitants may have harassed the Isle of Man through seaborne raids. Campaigning in Argyll allowed Robert to extend his control over the Irish Sea littoral. This ushered in a period of chronic instability for the Isle of Man as for the next few years the English government effectively left the island to fend for itself.

Two significant events preceded Robert's attack on the Isle of Man. The first was the renewal of the treaty of Perth between Scotland and Norway in October 1312,[100] which confirmed Robert's power in the north and along the western seaboard, and facilitated the accumulation of a galley fleet for assault on Man. Robert may also have had help from the Norwegian territories of Orkney or Shetland. The second has a more personal aspect. On 7 February 1313 Dungal MacDowell surrendered the castle of Dumfries, which he had been defending on Beaumont's behalf against assault by Robert.[101] MacDowell in 1307 had captured and handed over for execution Robert's brothers Alexander and Thomas, and is in one source described as 'hated by the enemy'.[102] On leaving Dumfries he crossed to what may have been his family estates on Man and assumed responsibility for the garrison of the island. Ordinarily such a veteran commander might have been an accession of strength. In fact it looks very much as though MacDowell attracted the personal enmity of the king of Scots. In a move that resembles blood feud, Robert pursued him to Man:

> In 1313 Lord Robert, king of Scotland, landed with a large navy at Ramsey on 18 May, and on the following Sunday he went to the monastery at Douglas, where he spent the night. On the Monday following he laid siege to Castle Rushen, which was held by Lord Duncan MacDowyl against the king, until the Tuesday after the festival of St Barnabas the apostle [12 June], when Lord Robert took the castle.[103]

Fig. 6.2 *Castle Rushen: its siege by Robert the Bruce lasted one month until it fell on 12 June 1313.*

The siege of Rushen, then, lasted a month, and the garrison's resistance must therefore have been fierce. Robert was forced to send ships to Ulster to forage for supplies for his own forces during the siege. The Dublin chronicle records that

> on the last day of May Robert de Brus sent certain galleys to parts of Ulster with his pirates to despoil them. The Ulstermen resisted them and manfully drove them off. It was said nevertheless that Robert landed by licence of the earl to levy tribute.[104]

Both castle and island fell to the Scots. Once again MacDowell managed to escape the vengeance of the Bruces, fleeing this time to Ireland. The Dublin chronicle reports that on taking the castle Robert demolished it.[105] This is entirely consistent with Robert's strategy on the Scottish mainland, where every castle taken up to this time was destroyed to prevent the English from recovering control of the countryside.[106] That the castle was demolished is confirmed by the fact that subsequent captures of Man by Eógan Mac Dubgaill of Argyll, the earl of Moray and Edward III appear to have been effected swiftly and easily.

The attack on Man by the Scots was an obvious threat to the supply lines of Carlisle, now the forward garrison of the western march. It also coincided with an increase of Scottish pressure on the English marches. In August 1312 the northern counties had agreed to pay exorbitant sums in return for *suffrance* to midsummer 1313; but the Scots continued to threaten them. The bishop of Durham excused himself from attending parliament because of the dangerous situation; the Scots had recently burnt his vill of Norham as a reprisal for the depredations of the garrison.[107] In these circumstances the invasion of Man not only gave outlet for the Scots' lust for action and booty during time of truce; it also provided a salutary demonstration of Scottish power to the English borderers and a warning of what would happen if they did not pay up.

Professor Duncan suggests that Edward Bruce (now also earl of Carrick) assumed control of the isle as a part of his lordship of Galloway, since when the island was recaptured by the English in 1315, they seized at the same time 'Moryauch Makennedy' and 22 comrades. This was probably Muiredach Mac Cennétig, a member of the Kennedy family of Dunure in Edward Bruce's earldom of Carrick.[108] Makennedy may have been Edward Bruce's bailie on the island; but since Robert destroyed the castle it seems unlikely that the Scots would leave a garrison or attempt to occupy Man. Probably impoverished by the month-long siege, the isle can have had little value to the warring parties but for its harbours. The Clann Dubgaill and other Scottish exiles whose squadrons plied the North Channel may have raided it at will. Their leader, Eógan of Argyll, was made admiral of Edward II's Irish Sea fleet in March 1314 and he was to lead the western arm of the attack on Scotland planned for the coming summer. In September after the campaign had failed, Eógan was still coursing the Irish Sea with 12 ships probably raiding Man and Argyll.[109] On 18 October 1313, Edward II granted three protections, one for MacAskil without specifying the place, a second for MacAskil in Man and third for the bishop of Sodor in Ireland. This last document might well indicate the place of refuge of the Isle's pro-English faction.[110]

For Edward II the loss of Man was only a foretaste of the disasters to come. Carlisle's maritime supply lines were now exposed to attack; the Scots were able to mount impressive raids on the English west march at Christmas 1313 and April 1314; and then real catastrophe befell the English in June 1314, when Edward II's great invasion force was defeated on the field of Bannockburn. On 28 September 1314 Edward granted a safe conduct until Christmas for Walter Galloway and Adam le Mareshal, whom Henry Beaumont was sending to the Isle of Man on his business.[111] Beaumont may then have been attempting through these emissaries to negotiate for the recovery of his lordship.[112]

The 20 months of Scottish control (if such it can be called) had come to an end by 15 February 1315, when Edward II became aware that Eógan Mac Dubgaill had recaptured Man, expelled Bruce's supporters from it, and left a garrison to defend it.[113] This implies that Eógan took steps to rebuild the fortifications at Rushen. It was not an isolated action; rather, an attempt by Eógan to forestall the expected Scottish invasion of Ireland. The Scots in early 1315 were expecting a great shipment of arms and supplies from Flanders probably intended to equip the expedition to Ireland.[114] Robert I appears to have advertised Scottish intentions to invade Ireland: by 16 February 1315 a messenger of the Scottish king by the name of Henry had been imprisoned in Dublin.[115] Edward Bruce's projected invasion of Ireland may then have been common knowledge in the Irish Sea region, and Eógan Mac Dubgaill determined to strike first by taking Man. His forces were composed of other Scottish exiles, including his own vassal 'Duncan Makoury' or 'MacGoffrey' (probably Donnchad Mac Gofraid) and ships and men at arms from the east-coast Irish port of Drogheda.[116]

It was at roughly the same time that Moryauch Makennedy and 22 accomplices were taken prisoner. These are not described as the Scottish garrison, or even as having been captured on the island, but rather as 'Scottish rebels... and mariners on the sea coast of Scotland, at present secured in the Isle of Man'. Eógan of Argyll, who as an exile was always strapped for cash, reminded the English king that he might have received a large sum for their release. But Edward II was determined to keep them locked up, 'since they had inflicted much damage upon the king and his subjects'. They were then more likely to have been Scottish privateers, perhaps based on Man, rather than Edward Bruce's garrison. Makennedy and the 22 were therefore brought at the king's expense to Dublin Castle.[117] Fourteen of the captured men are named in the records of the Irish government; the rest were presumably taken to Beaumaris in North Wales, and elsewhere. The earl of Ulster interceded on behalf of two of them, Henry le Welbe and John le Masoun of Carlingford, that they might find sureties for bail. Why he should do this can only be guessed at; these two are not described as Scots, but as being 'in the company of Scotch enemies of the king' and likelihood is that they were Irish. The others are described as Scots. John McKerysi, John McMartyn, Michael Plantefolie, and John McCorlete were taken first to Dublin and thence to Kildare; Macoline McCoffok, Sandre son of Thomas, Gilbert son of Peter, and Robert son of Thomas were taken to Carlow; and McIertagh McKenedy, Thomas de Estholine, Patrick of Manne and Diconn of Estholine to Kilkenny.[118] The prisoners may have been dispersed in order to provide hostages for garrisons now perceived to be under potential threat. We may be confident that Patrick of Manne was Manx, evidence perhaps that some inhabitants of the island continued to support the Scots. Other Scottish prisoners, referred to as 'hostages of the Isle of Man' were held in Beaumaris Castle in January 1322, when the chamberlain of North Wales was ordered to pay the arrears of their keep.[119]

The recapture of the Isle of Man was the beginning of a new English offensive in the Irish Sea. Edward II was determined to retain Man and to use it as a forward base from which to attack Scotland. To this end he secured the links between Man and North Wales. He gave orders that armour for 100 crossbowmen and 20 foot should be bought in London and taken to Beaumaris. Provisions were to be sent from Ireland for the use of the chamberlain at Caernarvon.[120] Orders were also issued to the justiciar of Ireland, to find out how many men Eógan had left on the island and what expenses he had incurred, and to pay him a sum for maintenance of the garrison.[121] This is an indication that the English government had determined to leave the burden of defending Man to its Irish counterpart. The rationale for such a transfer appears to have been that the 'Anglo-Scottish' forces who controlled the island were based in Ireland, but the Irish government was impoverished and beleaguered and fighting a Scottish invasion of its own territory until 1318.[122] Henry Beaumont was still the lord of the isle, yet his lordship continued to be interfered with by officials on the ground that it was contrary to the ordinances. As late as 22 May 1315 the king was still issuing orders to his escheator to desist from such harassment.[123]

Three days after they became aware that Man had been regained, the English government dispatched orders to launch an attack on Scotland by way of the western approaches. The justiciar, treasurer and chancellor of Ireland were commanded to raise 10,000 men in Ireland and a fleet of 60 ships manned at double strength to be ready by 6 April 1315. The expedition was to be led by Eógan Mac Dubgaill. Presumably his newly recovered base on Man was fairly central to operations. Eógan was commanded to receive to the king's peace magnates and communities of the Isles, including Edward Bruce's vassal, Domnall of Islay.[124] From the Scottish perspective, of course, these preparations made it imperative that the invasion of Ireland should proceed with all haste. Edward Bruce's invasion took place in May 1315,[125] averting Eógan of Argyll's planned invasion of western Scotland. In spite of the Scottish invasion of Ireland the English government saw no reason to abandon either its planned attack on eastern Scotland with a land army by way of Berwick, or its amphibious attack on the west from Ireland.[126] The co-operation of the Cinque Ports, which had traditionally provided the bulk of the English navy, was obtained. Probably as a condition of such assistance William de Creye and

Thomas de Hewys were appointed joint admirals, and Eógan Mac Dubgaill relegated to captain. Royal debts in Ireland were to be collected and applied to the costs of the fleet. Irish officials John of Athy and Alexander le Convers were at work in Bristol and Gloucestershire, pressing crews into service. There was at least one raid on Scotland, for le Convers accounted for £466 received in 1315–16 for the wages of the Cinque Ports fleet, 'which came from Ireland in the company of Alexander and went from there to Scotland in the king's service'. But in the autumn of 1315, 17 ships of Winchelsea rode at anchor, trapped in the harbour at Portsmouth by contrary winds. In October the expedition was called off. Attempts at gathering men and victuals for a land-based campaign had been abandoned, due to the famine that then prevailed throughout Britain.

The Isle of Man cannot have provided a very comfortable base for Eógan of Argyll's men. The Irish government can have ill afforded to maintain the garrison. Some supplies did arrive from Ireland; the Dublin purveyors delivered to Eógan of Argyll, to his knights Dungal MacDowell and Duncan MacGoffrey, and their men at arms in the fleet, 18 crannocks of wheat, 7 casks of wine and 12 1/2 quarters of flour between May 1315 and the following March.[127] A petition survives from one of the exiled 'Anglo-Scots' of the Man garrison, holding on grimly despite lack of pay and provisions. Duncan Makoury, bachelor of Eógan of Argyll, relates how his faithful service to Edward II had cost him his father, his kindred and his lands 'and he himself has lived the whole of this year in Man in great distress, in service of the king against the enemy'. He begged recompense: a grant of the ward of Nicholas de Ledewyche's lands in Ireland, 20 marks yearly and the marriage of his widow, so that Duncan could maintain his wife and children.[128]

Another difficulty facing the garrison on Man was the threat from Scottish privateers. Operating at this time in the Irish Sea was a band of strikingly successful privateers, probably of diverse origins but working exclusively for the Scots. The leader of this squadron was Thomas Dun or 'of Downe'. The first that is heard of him is when his four ships appeared to rescue the army of Edward Bruce, trapped on the coast of Ireland by the banks of the River Bann, shortly before 1 September 1315.[129] Next he carried out an audacious raid on the harbour of Holyhead on Anglesey on 12 September, when he captured a laden cargo ship, the *James* of Caernarvon.[130] Although on this occasion he is said to have commanded 'a great navy' he is in other sources described as leading only four ships. He also brokered negotiations between Edward Bruce and the beleaguered garrison at Carrickfergus Castle which Bruce was besieging.[131] It seems likely that Dun was a vassal of Thomas Randolph, earl of Moray; for within days of raiding Anglesey, he was ferrying the earl, his hostages and the spoils of the Irish campaign back to Scotland.[132] This hostile and rapacious presence on the Irish Sea cannot have failed to impact upon life in the Isle of Man; and one must assume that the island was subjected to raiding. Eógan Mac Dubgaill himself retired from the war in 1315 or 1316, 'impotent in body', wounded perhaps, in the fighting (although his nickname, Eógan Bacach ('the lame') indicates he had a longstanding disability).[133] On 3 July 1315 command of his squadron of 11 ships of Bristol passed to John of Athy. A further difficulty that the garrison may have faced in these years was the invasion of Man by Anglo-Irish marauders under the leadership of Richard de Mandeville of Ulster: however, although the Manx chronicle ascribes that episode to the year 1316, its historicity is open to doubt as it does not appear in record sources at this point, whereas a very similar raid is recorded under the year 1337.[134]

When the fall of Carrickfergus Castle to the Scots became imminent in the late summer of 1316 the three Scottish lords with the greatest invest-

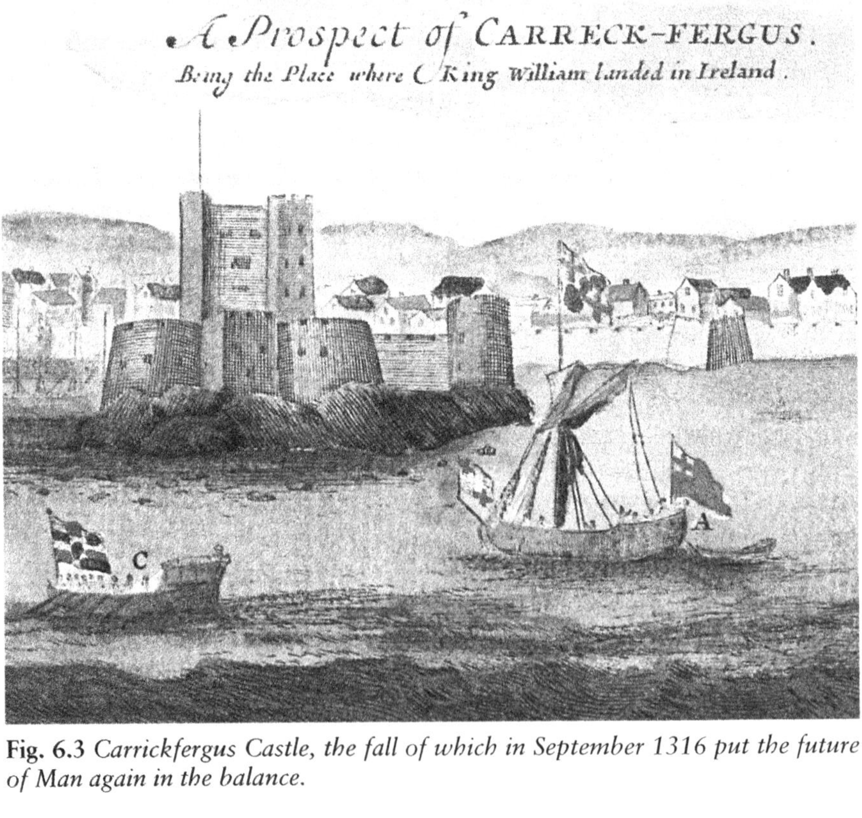

Fig. 6.3 *Carrickfergus Castle, the fall of which in September 1316 put the future of Man again in the balance.*

ment in the western venture – Robert I, Edward Bruce and Thomas Randolph, earl of Moray – began to negotiate among themselves over the Isle of Man. It may then be that the survival of the English outpost on Man was considered contingent upon that of Carrickfergus, and that with the collapse of that stronghold, the fall of Man was considered a foregone conclusion. At some time around then Robert I granted the Isle of Man to the earl of Moray. On 30 September 1316 Robert I sealed a confirmation of this grant, with the specific consent of Edward 'King of Ireland', that is, Edward Bruce.[135] Duncan considers that this confirmation may have been necessary because the earlier grant to Moray (which is now lost) did not contain Edward Bruce's consent. In return for the isle, Moray seems to have agreed to further participation in Ireland, and in particular to serve in the campaign planned for 1317 alongside both Robert and Edward. Moray was therefore titular lord of Man for some months before he actually recovered the island from the English, and he witnessed charters as lord of Annandale and Man during that period.[136] This is one of several examples of Robert I granting lordships as an incentive for the grantee to reconquer them.[137] But, before they recovered the island, the Scots suffered a serious setback in the Irish Sea war. In a great sea battle in July, Thomas Dun's privateer squadron was destroyed and 40 of his men slain by John of Athy. Geoffrey de Coigners captured Thomas Dun alive and the privateer chief was made to reveal that Moray was planning attacks on both Man and Anglesey with the help of English traitors.[138]

Gilbert MacAskil, Antony Bek and Edward II's long-standing and able keeper of Man, retired at around this crucial juncture in July 1317. In his account he claimed that he had spent £565 in wages of knights, esquires and other warriors for the repulse of the Scottish enemies then attacking the said land. He had enormous difficulty in getting credit for the £308 he had sent to Carlisle in 1312; apparently warrants for this sum had been 'lost in Scotland by the attacks of the enemy'. The exchequer demurred over the 500 marks he had paid to Eógan of Argyll. Remarkably, the exchequer quibbled over his account on the ground that at that critical time he had paid over the odds for military service.[139] Given the desperate conditions in the Irish Sea war and the divided loyalties of the Manx people, this penny-pinching attitude seems extraordinary. To his credit Edward II recognised MacAskil's outstanding service and twice commanded the treasury to assist him in recovering what was due to him, writing that the king 'wishes to show him especial grace, because he learns that Gilbert served him in a praiseworthy manner in defending the land of Man, in Scotland and in the Marches, and for this purpose exposed himself and his goods'.[140] MacAskil died in 1319, before his account was settled.

Custody of the Isle of Man had already passed to John of Athy by 6 July 1317.[141] Athy was the hero of the hour, having triumphed over Thomas Dun, but his appointment as keeper continued the trend towards making the Isle of Man an Irish responsibility. By the terms of his appointment Athy was to provide, out of the issues of the isle, three ships victualled and armed to protect the island from hostile Scottish raids.[142] But Moray's attack was now imminent. Edward II still believed that he controlled Man in October 1317,[143] but even at that date it may already have been retaken by Moray for the Scots. The planned invasion divulged by Thomas Dun was executed successfully some time in the autumn of 1317.[144] It is worth noting that after Moray's invasion a Manxman of standing remained loyal to Edward II and presumably was forced into exile, since on 25 October 1319 Edward granted protection for a year to one Abel MacToryn of Man.[145] But from that time until 1328 the only notice of the island in English or Irish records is a licence granted by the Irish government to the abbot of Newry in Ulster to visit the abbot of Rushen in obedience to the wishes of their superior, the abbot of Furness.[146]

Under Thomas Randolph, earl of Moray, the Isle of Man clearly enjoyed a long respite from hostilities. The 13-year truce of Bishopsthorpe with the English in 1323 held out the prospect of stable Scottish lordship; and, since Moray's control of Man was to be unchallenged for the foreseeable future, Robert I decided to adjust the terms of the earl's tenure. On 20 December 1324 the king granted the earl a new charter, which elevated his lordship of the island to the status of a regality. Though we do not know the terms under which Moray previously held the island, this new document clearly broadened his powers as lord and enhanced the terms of his tenure.[148] The earl was to hold Man by ship service of six galleys, each of 26 oars, with men and victuals for six weeks. In addition, 100s. was to be paid annually at Inverness, intended no doubt for the king of Norway as the annual fee for the island. He was required to attend the Scottish parliament personally on 40 days' notice, an unusual provision that Duncan interprets as an assertion of the island's links with the Scottish crown. However the earl was granted 'exceptionally wide powers of regality' including 'patronage of all kirks, all pleas of the crown, all pertinents, royal administration and justice'. The fact that the charter grants Moray rights of administering royal justice over the men of the bishop's estates probably indicates that hitherto those estates had constituted a liberty on the island. Patronage of the bishopric was reserved to the king; this was almost the only reservation on the earl's power in the island. Finally King Robert guarantees the grant against all mortals. This was to allay any fears Moray might have that Robert, or his newly born son and heir, David, would use the island as a bargaining chip to gain a permanent peace settlement with England. Altogether this charter is one of the most comprehensive alienations of royal rights in the whole corpus of Robert I's *acta*, 'Such creations', writes Duncan, 'came only for the earl of Moray. No others received grants on such generous terms, however close their relationship to the king.'[149] It is testimony to the closeness of the relationship between the king and the earl, and it is also evidence of Robert's vision for the island of Man: complete autonomy, yet inseparably linked to Scotland through the personal loyalty of the lord. The Isle of Man was mentioned in the peace treaty of Edinburgh-Northampton in 1328, in terms that suggest that Robert did not take its security for granted:

> And likewise it is settled and agreed that if anyone wage war on the king of Scotland, or his heirs or successors, in the island of Man, or the other isles of Scotland, that the king of England, or his heirs or successors will not help the said enemies.[150]

There were apparently too many harbouring dynastic claims to the island for Robert's taste, chief among them Henry Beaumont and William the son and heir of William Montacute (d.1344).

Moray's own deeds as lord of Man are interesting. At some time before 1325 Moray granted the parish of Kirk Bride to Whithorn priory. This is confirmed by Robert I's charter to Whithorn in 1325.[151] In a deed recorded in the *Register of St Bees* the style 'earl of Moray, Lord of Wales, Annandale and Man' is used.[152] This style calls to mind the assertion that Moray intended to capture Anglesey in 1317 and demonstrates that, like Edward Bruce, Moray too had pretensions to pan-Celtic lordship. The deed confirms to the monastery at St Bees in Cumberland a gift of Rögnvaldr, king of Man, and adds one half of the port of Corna, Tolloney and the right to wreck of the sea. The possessions on Man held by St Bees and its motherhouse at St Mary's, York, were fully restored. It is not known whether those of Furness abbey were also restored. This deed is also proof that Moray actually visited the island; it was given on 2 May 1329 at Rushen abbey, and interestingly the witness list includes some other important Scottish magnates: Walter the hereditary Steward of Scotland, Eustace Maxwell and John Fraser. Presumably the occasion for this assembly was the death of the illustrious Bernard, bishop of Sodor. Though promoted to the see only the previous year, this Bernard had been Robert's long-standing chancellor and the author of the Declaration of Arbroath.[153]

Little can be said about the economy of the island in this period. One cannot fail to observe that among a people dependent upon subsistence farming, fishing and seaborne trade, livelihoods must have been devastated by almost a decade of warfare. This involved invasion and counter-invasion, quartering of garrisons, looting and exactions by hostile and 'friendly' armies alike, and coastal raiding by fleets and privateer squadrons, to say nothing of the devastation of trading hinterlands on adjacent coasts. The ship service due from the lord is unlikely to have been any genuine reflection of the island's capacity to fit out ships, but known variations seem broadly to fit expected trends. Ten galleys had been stipulated by the settlement of 1263; John of Athy was to provide only three from the issues of the island in 1317, one of the worst years of war; and in 1324, in peacetime once more, Moray was to provide six. The provost of Galloway accounts for Manx revenues in August 1329, and according to his record the island was keeping up with some tax demands but not with others. For the tithe granted in 1327 the island was assessed at £60 per annum payable at two terms. As a tenth of the island's wealth, this figure broadly agrees with (and indeed may well have been based upon) the service of 1,000 marks (£666) which had been due from Antony Bek to Edward II.[154] The £150 due to date for the five terms of this tenth had come in as expected. However nothing was forthcoming from the further tenth to finance the payment of £20,000 promised to the English as part of the 'final peace'. Nor was there any income from the temporalities of the bishopric, then vacant. The earl was to be consulted about these matters.[155]

Just as in the period before 1290, the peace that Man now enjoyed under Moray was dependent upon continued harmony between the kingdoms. But the treaty of Edinburgh-Northampton was deeply unpopular in England and Robert I had concluded it with the unstable regime of Edward II's queen Isabella and her lover, Roger Mortimer. The first pillar of this settlement collapsed when Robert I died on 7 June 1329. The second gave way in October 1330, when the young Edward III seized control of his own government, ousting his mother and Mortimer who had made the peace on his behalf. Edward III was now free to harbour and encourage those who had been deprived of lands and titles by the peace between the kingdoms. Among these 'disinherited' were Henry Beaumont and William Montacute, both of whom still held dynastic claims to the island. The third and final pillar of the settlement was Moray himself, who died in July 1332 while marching to defend the kingdom of Scotland against anticipated attack.

Edward III appears to have been determined to recover the island of Man after war had started in earnest, and while he was advancing to besiege Berwick in April 1333. In that month Roger Turtle fitted out three large warships in Bristol, probably with the intention of taking the island. By 30 May this was accomplished, for on that date Edward III proclaimed that

Man had been taken into his own hands. On 8 June he gave custody of the isle to William Montacute, and from that time the Scottish claim to Man passed from reality into legal theory.[156] It was not of course allowed to expire. The claim to the island passed first to Moray's heir, Thomas, but he was killed at Dupplin Moor in August 1332, unmarried and leaving no issue. John, Moray's second son, used the style 'lord of Annandale and Man' but seems to have allowed the claim to Wales to drop. He too died without heir in 1346. The title lord of Annandale and Man had passed to the earls of March by 1372 and to Alexander, duke of Albany, in the late fifteenth century. By a curious irony, possession of the island returned to a Scot in 1736, when it passed to James Murray, second duke of Atholl, who held it until the purchase of the Isle in 1765.[157]

For the inhabitants of Man a large part of the period 1266 to 1333 was unsettled and violent, beginning as it did with the loss of independence, the rebellion against Scottish rule, and the island's being fought over by the warring British kingdoms. In the years 1275 and 1311 to 1317 the Isle of Man must have witnessed scenes of terrible violence. Yet these were also years rich with possibilities. Alexander III intended Man as an appanage for the heir of the Scottish kingdom. Robert I envisaged the island bound firmly to Scotland by the unquestioning loyalty of his closest adherent, yet enjoying complete autonomy. Moray, who styled himself lord of Man and Wales, may even have intended Man as the centre of 'a middle lordship', between Scotland, England and Ireland. It is ironic that the memory of Scottish overlordship, so bitterly resisted at first by the inhabitants, should be perpetuated by English administrators, who continued to refer to the island as 'Man in Scotland' for long after it had passed into English hands.

Notes

1 The relationship between Man and Scotland has been the subject of a number of articles, notably A.W. Moore, 'The connexion between Scotland and Man' *SHR*, 3 (1906), 393–409; A.I. Macinnes, 'Scotland and the Manx connection: relationships of intermittent violence, 1266–1603' *Proceedings*, VIII, 362–77; Tim Thornton, 'Scotland and the Isle of Man, *c*.1400–1625: noble power and royal presumption in the northern Irish Sea province' *SHR*, 77 (1998), 1–30.

2 J. Wilson (ed.), *Register of St Bees*, 1915. The 'Annals of Furness abbey' are contained in full in R. Howlett (ed.), *Chronicles of the Reigns of Stephen, Henry II and Richard*, 2 vols, Rolls Series (London, 1885), vol. ii, and relevant passages are translated in Anderson, *Scottish Annals*, 380–83.

3 *CCR*; *CCW*; *CPR*; *CDS*; D. Macpherson (ed.), *Rotuli Scotiae*, 2 vols, Record Commission (London, 1814–19); J. Strachey *et al.* (eds), *Rotuli Parliamentorum 1272–1326*, 7 vols (London, 1767–1832).

4 *Scotichronicon*; A.A.M. Duncan (ed.), *Regesta Regum Scotorum. V. The Acts of Robert I* (Edinburgh, 1988); *ERS*.

5 J.T. Gilbert (ed.), *Chartularies of St Mary's Abbey, Dublin*, 2 vols, Rolls Series

(London, 1882–3), ii; [E. Tresham (ed.)], *Rotulorum Patentium et Clausorum Cancellarie Hiberniae Calendarium*, 2 vols (Dublin, 1828), vol. i.

6 *Scotichronicon*, v, 347–9.

7 *ERS*, i, 17.

8 Duncan, *Scotland. The Making of the Kingdom*, 577.

9 *ERS*, i, 22.

10 *APS*, i, 112.

11 *Scotichronicon*, v, 369.

12 A.O. Anderson, M.O. Anderson and W.C. Dickinson (eds), *Chronicle of Melrose* (London, 1936), 128–9.

13 Gordon Donaldson, *Scottish Historical Documents* (Edinburgh, 1970), 34–36.

14 McDonald, *Kingdom of the Isles*, 120–1.

15 Thornton, 'Scotland and the Isle of Man', 4, 9–12; Ranald Nicholson, *Edward III and the Scots* (Oxford, 1965), 123.

16 The connections referred to in this paragraph are succinctly summarised in Duffy, 'The Bruce Brothers'.

17 Michael Dolley, *Some Irish Dimensions to Manx History* (Queen's University Belfast, New Lecture Series, No. 92, 1976), 11–12.

18 See note 155 below.

19 *Coucher Book of Furness*, iii, 594. Furness claimed ownership of the following lands by the gift of 'Olaf king of the Isles': Carneclet; the vill of Thore son of Asser; Melon Magna; the vill of Saint Melius; the vill of Narwe Stainredale with appendices; and the vill of Saint Carebrec and Fagerul.

20 Howlett, *Chronicles of the Reigns of Stephen, Henry II and Richard*, ii, 569, translated in Anderson, *Scottish Annals*, 381–2. See chapter 15 below, p. 343.

21 Duncan, *Scotland. The Making of the Kingdom*, 582; McDonald, *Kingdom of the Isles*, 137, citing G.G. Simpson (ed.), *Handlist of the Acts of Alexander III, The Guardians, John, 1249–1296*, (Edinburgh, 1960), no. 171.

22 J. Stevenson (ed.), *Chronicon de Lanercost* (Maitland Club, Edinburgh, 1839), 64, translated in Anderson, *Early Sources*, ii, 657; McDonald, *Kingdom of the Isles*, 137; *Register of St Bees*, no. 497, 489.

23 *Chronicon de Lanercost*, 97–8 (translated in Anderson, *Early Sources*, ii, 672–3); Broderick, *CKMI*, fol. 50r.; and the Annals of Furness, in *Chronicles of the Reigns of Stephen, Henry II and Richard*, ii, 570–1 (translated in Anderson, *Scottish Annals*, 382–3. *Lanercost* and *CKMI* draw on the same source, but Furness adds detail independently.

24 Broderick, *CKMI*, fol. 50r. The interdict is said to have lasted three years, but the chronicle accounts seem to imply that Gu[d]rö[d]r reigned for less than a year.

25 Identified in Duncan, *Scotland. The Making of the Kingdom*, 582.

26 *Register of St Bees*, no. 497, 489.

27 *CDS*, v, no. 46, 141.

28 Broderick, *CKMI*, fol. 50r. For Gallovidian influence on Man in the past, see Seán Duffy, 'Ireland and the Irish Sea Region, 1014–1318' (University of Dublin PhD thesis, 1993), 97. In 1329 the revenues of Man were accounted for by the provisor of Galloway.

29 *Rotuli Parliamentorum*, i, 168; Oliver, *Monumenta*, ii, 135–6. Maria Queen of Man did homage to Edward I in 1291 and 1296 along with other magnates of Scotland, *CDS*, ii, 124, 212.

30 *Rotuli Scotiae*, i, 18. A. Kelly, 'Echoes of Manx history in Somerset records', *Proceedings*, 4 (1945 for 1940–2), 527–40. See also, Seán Duffy, 'The "Continuation" of Nicholas Trevet: a new source for the Bruce invasion',

Proceedings of the Royal Irish Academy, 91 (1991), 303–15.
31 This is clear from *CPR, 1281–92*, 359.
32 *ERS*, i, 47.
33 *Foedera*, i, II, 739; Oliver, *Monumenta*, ii, 110–11.
34 *CPR, 1281–1292*, 359.
35 *CDS*, ii, no. 437, 104; J. Stevenson (ed.), *Documents Illustrative of the History of Scotland*, 2 vols (Edinburgh, 1870), i, 161–62.
36 Michael Prestwich, *Edward I* (London, 1988), 362.
37 *CPR, 1281–92*, 341.
38 *CPR, 1281–92*, 358.
39 *CCW 1244–1326*, 31; Oliver, *Monumenta*, ii, 133–4.
40 *CPR, 1281–92*, 433; Oliver, *Monumenta*, ii, 113 (incorrectly dated).
41 *Rotuli Scotiae*, i, 16; Oliver, *Monumenta*, ii, 125–6.
42 *Rotuli Scotiae*, i, 14–15 (28 December 1292).
43 *Rotuli Scotiae*, i, 18; Oliver, *Monumenta*, ii, 127–9; G.W.S. Barrow, *Robert Bruce and the Community of the Realm of Scotland*, 3rd edn (Edinburgh, 1988), 58.
44 *Rotuli Scotiae*, i, 24; Oliver, *Monumenta*, ii, 132.
45 *Calendar of Papal Letters 1198–1304*, 11 vols (London, 1895–1921), i, 584–5. Mark had been released by 7 February 1302, *Register of St Bees*, no. 46, 75–7.
46 Bek obtained protections for one of his men, Robert le Venur going to the Isle of Man in April and October 1298, *CPR, 1292–1301*, 340, 366.
47 C.M. Fraser, *A History of Antony Bek Bishop of Durham 1283–1311* (Oxford, 1957), 76.
48 Fraser, *A History of Antony Bek*, 76.
49 *CCR, 1302–7*, 540.
50 G.E. Cokayne, *The Complete Peerage*, revised by V. Gibbs *et al.*, 12 vols (London, 1910–59), ix, 79; Oliver, *Monumenta*, ii, 127.
51 *Rotuli Parliamentorum*, i, 168.
52 William Camden, *Britannia*, ed. R. Gough, 4 vols (London, 1806), iv, 516.
53 M. Prestwich's biography of Simon de Montagu in *Oxford Dictionary of the National Biography*.
54 Fraser, *A History of Antony Bek*, 108–9, 220–1; J.M.W. Bean 'The Percys' acquisition of Alnwick', *Archaeologia Aeliana* (4th series) XXXII, 309–19.
55 *Rotuli Parliamentorum*, i, 168.
56 G.E. Cokayne, *The Complete Peerage*, revised by V. Gibbs *et al.*, 12 vols (London, 1910–59), ix, 79; Oliver, *Monumenta*, ii, 127.
57 Kelly, 'Echoes of Manx history in Somerset records', 533 posits a different chronology, placing the Montacute seizure of the isle and mortgage arrangement in 1297 or 1298, seven years before the quitclaim.
58 Fraser, *A History of Antony Bek*, 108–9, 220–1; J.M.W. Bean 'The Percys' acquisition of Alnwick', *Archaeologia Aeliana* (4th series) XXXII, 309–319.
59 *Register of St Bees*, no. 48, 78–80.
60 *CPR, 1292–1301*, 340; *CCR, 1296–1302*, 490; *Register of St Bees*, no. 46, 75–7.
61 *Register of St Bees*, no. 48, 78–80.
62 *CPR, 1292–1301*, 340; *CCR, 1296–1302*, 490; *Register of St Bees*, no. 46, 75–7.
63 *CCR, 1302–7*, 540; Oliver, *Monumenta*, ii, 139–40.
64 J. Raine (ed.), *Historiae Dunelmensis Scriptores Tres*, (Surtees Society, no. 8, 1839), 91; Camden, *Britannia*, iv, 516.
65 PRO E352/107, m. 29. Kelly, 'Echoes of Manx history in Somerset records', 534 dates this grant to 1309. I have not found her source.

66 Barrow, *Robert Bruce*, 145–202.
67 *CDS*, v, no. 492 (ix, xi, xiv, xvi), 211, 214, 215.
68 Duffy, 'The Continuation of Nicholas Trevet', 306.
69 Colm McNamee, *The Wars of the Bruces: Scotland, England and Ireland 1306–1328* (East Linton, 1997), 36–40.
70 Barrow, *Robert Bruce*, 169.
71 J.J. Kneen, 'Manx personal names and their romance' *Proceedings*, IV (1936), 83.
72 For what follows, see Barrow, *Robert Bruce*, 169–82.
73 Barrow, *Robert Bruce*, 181–2; Duncan, *Regesta*, v, no. 101, 379.
74 Barrow, *Robert Bruce*, 289–92, 314–17, 321.
75 *Rotuli Scotiae*, i, 78, 93; *CDS*, iii, no. 156, 29.
76 *Rotuli Scotiae*, i, 92.
77 *Rotuli Scotiae*, i, 96.
78 These fragments are printed in *CCW 1244–1326*, 332.
79 *Rotuli Scotiae*, i, 96; Oliver, *Monumenta*, ii, 152–3.
80 *Register of St Bees*, nos. 46, 497.
81 *CCR, 1318–23*, 63–4.
82 Fraser, *History of Antony Bek*, 227.
83 *CCW*, 1284–1326, 379; *CPR*, 1307–13, 565; *CDS*, iii, no. 307, 60; see M. Prestwich's biography of Simon de Montagu in *Oxford Dictionary of the National Biography*.
84 W. Stubbs (ed.), *Chronicles of Edward I and Edward II*, 2 vols, Rolls Series (London, 1882–3), i, 176 (*Annales Londonienses*).
85 *CCR, 1318–23*, 63–4.
86 W. Stubbs (ed.), *Chronicles of Edward I and Edward II*, 2 vols, Rolls Series (London, 1882–3), i, 176 (*Annales Londonienses*).
87 Duffy, 'The Continuation of Nicholas Trevet', 306; H. Maxwell (ed.), *The Chronicle of Lanercost* (Glasgow, 1913), 184; H.T. Riley (ed.), *Thomas Walsingham, Historia Anglicana,* 2 vols, Rolls Series (London, 1863–4), i, 120. Neither recent work on Gaveston mentions the alleged grant: J.S. Hamilton, *Piers Gaveston, Earl of Cornwall, 1307–1312* (Wayne State University Press, 1988), Pierre Chaplais, *Edward II's Adoptive Brother* (Oxford, 1994).
88 As early as 1308 baronial opposition was interfering in Gaveston's comital title, Chaplais, *Piers Gaveston*, 45–9. In 1311 the ordainers were issuing flat contradictions of royal orders. Compare, for example, orders on the keeping of Carlisle Castle: *CFR, 1307–19*, 120 and *CPR, 1307–13*, 450.
89 *CPR, 1307–13*, 300.
90 *Rotuli Parliamentorum*, i, 284.
91 Stubbs, *Chronicles of the Reigns of Edward I and Edward II*, i, 201.
92 *CPR, 1307–13*, 411.
93 *CPR, 1307–13*, 461.
94 *CCW 1244–1326*, 379; *CPR, 1307–13*, 565; *CDS*, iii, no. 307, 60. Kelly takes the view that Simon made an attempt to seize Man in 1311, 'Echoes of Manx history in Somerset records', 536.
95 *CDS*, iii, nos. 397, 400.
96 PRO E352/107, m. 29.
97 McNamee, *Wars of the Bruces*, 56, 133.
98 *CCR, 1318–23*, 41–2; Oliver, *Monumenta*, ii, 154–5; PRO E352/107, m. 29.
99 *CDS*, iii, no. 637, 121.
100 McNamee, *Wars of the Bruces*, 56, 133.

101 *CPR, 1307–13*, 465.
102 *CDS*, iii, no. 277, 55; see Watt, *Fasti Ecclesiae Scoticanae*, 201.
103 Duncan, *Regesta*, v, no. 24, 307–12.
104 Barrow, *Robert Bruce*, 191; *CDS* iii, no. 304, 60.
105 *CDS*, iii, no. 84, 17.
106 Broderick *CKMI*, fol. 50r.; *Scotichronicon*, vi, 351.
107 *Chartularies of St Mary's Abbey, Dublin*, ii, 342.
108 *Chartularies of St Mary's Abbey, Dublin*, ii, 343.
109 John Barbour, *The Bruce* ed. A.A.M. Duncan (Edinburgh, 1997), 366–408.
110 McNamee, *Wars of the Bruces*, 56.
111 Duncan, *Regesta*, v, 379.
112 *Rotuli Scotiae*, i, 121, 132.
113 *CPR, 1313–17*, 30. See also Oliver, *Monumenta*, ii, 168 where 'John' appears to be a mistake for Alan.
114 *CPR, 1313–17*, 181; *CDS*, iii, no. 391, 74.
115 *CDS*, iii, no. 474, 91.
116 *CCR, 1313–18*, 153.
117 *CCR, 1313–18*, 218–19; McNamee, *Wars of the Bruces*, 169.
118 NAI RC 8/10, 760.
119 *CDS*, v, no. 682, 252; *CCR, 1318–23*, 613.
120 *CCR, 1313–18*, 153.
121 NAI KB2/7, 31–2.
122 *CCR, 1318–23*, 415.
123 *CCR, 1313–18*, 147–8, 148.
124 *CCR, 1313–18*, 153.
125 See James Lydon, in Cosgrove (ed.), *A New History of Ireland*, 275–302.
126 *CCR, 1313–18*, 180.
127 *Rotuli Scotiae*, i, 138–9, 143–4.
128 *Chartularies of St Mary's Abbey, Dublin*, ii, 344.
129 For this, see McNamee, *Wars of the Bruces*, 175–6.
130 *CDS*, iii, no. 479, 92.
131 Oliver, *Monumenta*, ii, 166–7; *Rotuli Parliamentorum*, i, 310; *CDS*, iii, no. 521, 99
132 Barbour, *The Bruce*, ed. Duncan, 538–40 (Book 14).
133 *CDS*, iii, no. 451, 84; *CPR, 1313–17*, 421.
134 G.O. Sayles, 'The siege of Carrickfergus Castle, 1315–16' *Irish Historical Studies*, 10 (1956–7), 94–100.
135 *Chartularies of St Mary's Abbey, Dublin*, ii, 346.
136 *CDS*, iii, no.912, 166.
137 Broderick, *CKMI*, fol. 50r.; *Rotulorum Patentium et Clausarum Cancellariae Hiberniae*, 42. The matter is likely to remain in doubt.
138 Duncan, *Regesta*, v, no. 101, 378–9.
139 Duncan, *Regesta*, v, nos. 106 and 113.
140 Duncan, *Regesta*, v, 110.
141 *CDS*, iii, no. 562, 108.
142 *CDS*, iii, nos. 637, 121.
143 *CCR, 1318–23*, 41–2, 63–4; *CDS*, iii, nos. 637, 120–1.
144 *Rotulorum Patentium et Clausarum Cancellariae Hiberniae*, 21.
145 *Rotuli Scotiae*, i, 173.
146 *CPR, 1317–21*, 38.
147 Barrow, *Robert Bruce*, 193.

148 *CPR, 1317–21*, 398. He was perhaps a relative of that Duncan MacToryn who was outlawed and imprisoned in the Tower of London, but reinstated in 1293, *CCR, 1288–96*, 290.
149 *Rotulorum Patentium et Clausarum Cancellariae Hiberniae*, 27.
150 Barrow, *Robert Bruce*, 193.
151 J.M. Thompson (ed.), *Registrum Magni Sigilli Regum Scottorum 1306–1424*, new edn (Edinburgh, 1912), Appendix I, no. 32, 446–7; discussed in Duncan, *Regesta*, v, 40, 75.
152 Duncan, *Regesta*, v, 41.
153 E.L.G. Stones (ed.), *Anglo-Scottish Relations 1174–1328: Some Selected Documents* (London, 1965), 167; Duncan, *Regesta*, v, no. 342, 593.
154 Duncan, *Regesta*, v, no. 275, 535.
155 *Register of St Bees*, no. 47, 77–8.
156 Watt, *Fasti Ecclesiae Scoticanae*, 201–2. Bernard is often incorrectly referred to as 'de Linton', see Duncan, *RRS* v, 201–3
157 See note 57 above.
158 *ERS*, i, 151; Barrow, *Robert Bruce*, 301.
159 Nicholson, *Edward III and the Scots*, 122–3.
160 J. Balfour Paul (ed.), *The Scots Peerage*, 9 vols (Edinburgh, 1904–14), i, 488, 490, 151; iii, 270; Cokayne, *Complete Peerage*, i, 81 note (a); Stephen Boardman, *The Early Stewart Kings: Robert II and Robert III 1371–1406* (East Linton, 1996), 52.

7 *Man under the Montacutes, 1333–92*

W.M. ORMROD

On 9 August 1333, by letters patent under the great seal of England, King Edward III renounced all his personal and dynastic claims to the Isle of Man and announced that his close friend and political ally, William, Lord Montacute, was the rightful lord of the island.[1] Although both Edward I and Edward II had claimed some form of suzerainty over Man and set up their own rulers there, this action of Edward III's is conventionally taken as the formal starting point of English rule on the island, not least because it marked the beginning of a period during which the lordship of Man was more or less consistently in the hands of, or at least claimed by, a single aristocratic dynasty. The Montacutes were to assert their rights as lords of Man for the following 60 years, until the island was sold by William's son to Sir William Scrope of Bolton in 1392. It is to these 60 years that this chapter is principally devoted.

To understand the significance of the Montacute regime, however, it is necessary to look back in time to the period of the Scottish succession crisis in the early 1290s and, as discussed at length in the previous chapter, to the claims to the vacant throne of Man lodged at that time with the king of England by Mary, countess of Strathearn, and Affreca 'de Connacht'. Edward I's decision to support the candidacy of John Balliol for the Scottish crown in 1292 and his formal acknowledgement of Balliol's resulting rights to the Isle of Man in 1293 meant that Mary and Affreca were referred to Balliol, and nothing more was heard of the matter. In 1304, however, Affreca effectively reopened the dispute by quitclaiming her rights in Man to Simon Montacute, a Somerset baron: although there is no direct evidence, it seems most likely that the occasion of this transfer of titles was a marriage between the two parties.[2] In the following year Simon Montacute may have tried to assert his claim, for Affreca wrote to her former tenants on the island ordering them to show loyalty to their new lord, while John Waldeboef, grandson of the countess of Strathearn, reasserted his own claim to Man in the English parliament.[3] Waldeboef's petition was referred to the court of king's bench, where protracted litigation seems to have ensued: in 1313, Simon Montacute, no doubt taking advantage of his son William's new position in the king's household, secured a release from suits brought against him in king's bench as a result of his attempts to occupy the island.[4] Nevertheless, in the confusion that resulted first from Edward II's efforts to set up Henry Beaumont as lord of Man and then from Robert Bruce's grant of the island to Thomas Randolph, earl of Moray, the Montacute claim to the island effectively went into abeyance until the 1330s.

The resurrection of that claim by Simon Montacute's grandson, William, in 1333, is to be explained primarily in the context of Anglo-Scottish relations and the revival of English ambitions, and fortunes, in the northern kingdom during the early 1330s. The English victories at Dupplin Moor in 1332 and Halidon Hill in 1333 did much to vindicate the domestic regime of the young Edward III by avenging the defeat of Bannockburn and the disastrous consequences of Edward II's rule and linking the new king's military enterprises with those of his esteemed grandfather. However, Edward III chose not to revive the official English standpoint held from 1296 to 1328 – namely, that Scotland was no longer a separate kingdom but a mere 'land' subject to direct English control – but instead to adopt the stance originally taken by his grandfather between 1292 and 1296 by recognising Edward Balliol, son of the original claimant to the Scottish throne, as king of Scots, and placing the latter in a subordinate position by asserting the rights of the English king to act as feudal suzerain of the northern kingdom. At the same time, Edward III also sought to take full advantage of Balliol's weakness by securing the surrender of Scotland's eight Lowland counties into direct English rule. Because Edward adopted this policy, proceeding by negotiation rather than conquest, it was not until the agreement made with Balliol at Roxburgh in November 1332 had been confirmed in both the Scottish and English parliaments in 1333, and Balliol had formally ceded sovereignty over the Lowlands in 1334, that the English king was able to make domestic political capital out of the new arrangements and begin to distribute lands and rights in his new territories to the English nobility – particularly to the group of 'disinherited' lords whose desire to regain lands lost to Robert Bruce and his infant successor, David II, had provided the initial momentum for the reopening of hostilities in the north.

However, it is very important to notice that the re-establishment of English claims to Man preceded these agreements. On 30 May 1333 Edward III first announced that Man had been taken into his hands, claiming that his grandfather had been legitimately seized of the island and, by inference, that the Scottish suzerainty exercised both by John Balliol and latterly by the Bruce monarchy had not been lawful.[5] It is possible that this initial assertion of authority was backed up by a small naval force dispatched to Man from Bristol in April.[6] Then, on 8 June the island was committed to the custody of the king's friend, William Montacute, for the period until Michaelmas and thereafter for another year: at this stage, Man was still deemed to be under the direct control of the king, and Montacute would be required to render account for his custody at the English exchequer.[7] Finally, on 9 August, Edward III issued the letters patent renouncing all claim to the island and recognising Montacute's hereditary and absolute rights to ownership of Man. Edward had therefore proceeded unilaterally, acting in advance of and independently of the Anglo-Scottish settlement in a move that at once implied the separation of Man from the Scottish crown and gave English recognition to its special and quasi-autonomous status within the political structure of the British Isles.

Three further aspects of this new dispensation call for particular comment. First of all, there is the question of Montacute's legal status as ruler of Man. Technically speaking, Edward III's quitclaim was not a formal transfer of property and rights but a renunciation of Plantagenet claims: the inference was that the Montacutes had a better right to the island than had the king of England. It has often been assumed that the absence of any reference to residual English suzerainty in this document and the apparent revival of the title of king of Man by the end of the fourteenth century signified the re-establishment of a fully independent regality recognising no temporal superior.[8] Certainly, the fact that Montacute was present in both the Scottish and the English parliaments that ratified the Roxburgh settlement, clearly acting at least in the former assembly as ruler of Man, may indeed suggest that the island and its new lord had emerged from Edward III's strategy with renewed status and importance. On the other hand, it seems highly improbable that Montacute considered his newly confirmed rights to be unconditional. The tradition whereby the rulers of Man, whether kings or lords, had acknowledged the suzerainty of a superior crown – be it Norwegian, Scottish or English – made it unlikely that either Edward III or William Montacute intended the island to revert to total autonomy in 1333. In a period when definitions of both absolute property and territorial sovereignty were still in the process of formation, it seems much more reasonable to assume that Man after 1333 was perceived as having the same status as the Welsh marcher lordships (or, another interesting parallel, the lordship of Ireland under Robert de Vere in 1385-8), where regalian rights were exercised directly by members of the aristocracy but the king of England retained the position of ultimate overlord.

Such a parallel would certainly have had resonance for Montacute, who had himself come into possession of the valuable marcher lordship of Denbigh after the fall of Roger Mortimer, earl of March, in 1331.[9] Furthermore, if Montacute and his son ever exercised the title of king of

Man, it was clearly only within the island: after his elevation to an English earldom in 1337, Montacute's formal style, as used in public documents and in the legend on his seal, was 'earl of Salisbury and lord of Denbigh and Man'.[10] To have actively exercised the title of king and thus displaced the honours he had received from the English crown – as Edward III's third son, John of Gaunt, was later to do on claiming the throne of Castile – was obviously quite inappropriate in this case. Finally, although there is certainly no evidence that either Montacute or his son performed homage specifically for the lordship of Man, any suggestion that the transfer of rights should jeopardise the interests of the English monarchy was clearly unthinkable, not only because of the legal ramifications bound up in Montacute's existing oath of fealty as a member of the English aristocracy, but also (and this was an area where Edward III placed a good deal of emphasis) as a result of the very strong personal friendship that existed between the original parties to the quitclaim of 1333.

The recognition of the Montacute lordship of Man also carried great significance in contemporary English politics. William Montacute was not only Edward III's closest friend, having acted as his secret agent during the minority regime and actively assisted him in overthrowing Roger Mortimer at Nottingham in 1330; he was also the son of one of Edward II's controversial courtiers and favourites. In singling Montacute out for particularly generous patronage, Edward III had therefore to be careful to avoid the accusations of political and personal preference that had dogged his father's regime. His answer was not so much to restrict his acts of favour (Montacute was not only given extremely valuable estates and rights in England, Wales, Scotland and Ireland but was also singled out for special honour by being granted the extraordinary privilege of bearing the king's personal crest of an eagle),[11] as to ensure that major patronage had the real or assumed support of the established nobility. In some ways, it is perhaps surprising that Edward III did not choose to support the claim of Henry Beaumont to the Isle of Man under the terms of Edward II's grants of 1311 and 1312; Beaumont was, after all, a conspicuous supporter of the young king and as a prominent participant in – if not the chief instigator of – the English invasion of Scotland in 1332-3, after which he received generous settlements both from the English crown and from Edward Balliol.

But Beaumont's claim to Man was probably too much tarnished by association: Edward II's grant had been very much an assertion of his personal right to control patronage and had been challenged directly by the lords ordainers in 1311. It is therefore very interesting that Edward III's quitclaim to Montacute in August 1333 was evidently approved by discussion in council: the letters patent were issued explicitly 'with the assent of the prelates, earls, barons and other nobles present with us' during the round of tournaments and pilgrimages that followed the fall of Berwick to the English.[12] By recognising Montacute's prior dynastic claims to Man, Edward III was not only effectively negating the claims of Henry Beaumont but also dissociating himself from his father's political mistakes. Beaumont's reaction is unknown: although he is recorded as having styled himself earl of Moray in 1334 and thus supposedly sought Scottish support for his cause by appropriating the title of the deceased Thomas Randolph to the Isle of Man, there is no evidence that he made any further efforts to pursue this strategy or, indeed, that he was any the less committed to Edward III's political regime down to his own death in 1340.[13] The establishment of the Montacute lordship of Man in 1333 therefore begins to emerge as a striking example both of Edward III's successful assertion of dominion in the British Isles and of his considerable capacity for domestic political management.

The third and final aspect of the 1333 settlement that requires attention may also have been the one that was most immediately apparent to Edward III: namely, the important strategic role played by the Isle of Man. The need for a secure and reliable English presence in the Irish Sea was a matter of considerable urgency in the early 1330s. Even after the establishment of Edward Balliol as king, Scotland was by no means quelled: Balliol himself was unable to attend the English parliament held at York in February 1334 because of the problem of Scots 'lurking in the Isles', and there were powerful displays of resistance not only in the Highlands but even in Galloway, which under normal circumstances could usually be regarded as a Balliol stronghold. The situation in Ireland was also grave: from late 1331 to mid-1332 Edward III's government had given considerable attention to the state of the lordship and, before the Scottish question intervened, had been planning a major expedition there. The murder of the young earl of Ulster in June 1333 created a particularly serious power vacuum in the north of Ireland and opened up the possibility of a repetition of the Bruce rebellion of 1315 and the associated threat of co-ordinated resistance to English domination in Ireland and Scotland. Even though that threat failed to materialise, it was still vital to ensure control of the seas and maintain communications across the North Channel in order that the supplies of Irish manpower on which the English forces in Scotland continued periodically to depend could be transported speedily and safely.[14]

The Isle of Man was obviously acknowledged both in government policy and in the more general public perception as the very key to such a strategy: 'Man stands in the middle between the Irish Ulster and the Scottish

Galloway, as it were the navel of the sea'.[15] It is surely no coincidence, then, that the Montacute family, chosen to take charge of the island in 1333, had a particularly strong maritime tradition. Early in Edward II's reign, Simon Montacute had charge of a fleet operating in the Irish Sea and the Western Isles and was keeper of Beaumaris Castle. In 1310 he was appointed admiral and dispatched to Man with a force of ships from Bristol and the southern English ports. Simon's son William also took an active part in Scottish and Irish affairs and was involved in his father's naval enterprises.[16] His son William, the beneficiary of Edward III's patronage in 1333, went on to be joint-keeper of the Channel Islands in 1334-7 and served briefly as admiral of the western fleet in 1337.

The family tradition was sufficiently strong that William appears to have kept his own personal fleet: during the opening stages of Edward III's French war in 1338-40, the new earl of Salisbury received payments from the crown for four ships – the *Margaret*, the *Christopher Montacute*, the *Magdalene Montacute* and the *Katherine Montacute* – used in the king's service.[17] Indeed, it is tempting to suggest that as a result of such experiences and capabilities, the Montacutes developed something of a reputation for the defence of England's island dependencies: William Montacute acquired Lundy Island the year before he was recognised as lord of Man and had landed interests on the Isle of Wight, while his son, the second earl of Salisbury, was appointed custodian of Carisbrooke Castle and keeper of the Isle of Wight for a year in 1382 and for life in 1385, on the latter occasion also being recognised by Richard II as lord of Wight.[18] There were thus sound strategic reasons alongside the diplomatic and political considerations that led Edward III to recognise his closest friend as lord of Man.

* * *

All this, of course, was by way of aspiration. What of the achievement? The written evidence for the history of Man between the 1330s and the 1390s is very sparse, and many intriguing and important questions about the English regime of the fourteenth century remain not only unanswered but regrettably unanswerable. The assumption of the regalities into private hands meant the withdrawal of royal interest and the consequent absence of all but a handful of references to Man in the English state archive; and if the Montacutes kept any organised records of their regime on the island, they have long since disappeared. Nor do the chronicles substitute for this shortage of documentary evidence. The Manx chronicle, which is such an important source for an earlier period, is restricted after 1316 to brief biographical sketches of the bishops of Man, and finishes altogether in 1377. Perhaps more striking still is the indifference demonstrated by contemporary English chroniclers either to the island or to its lords. Regardless of its political affiliation, Man continued to be regarded as geographically and ethnically Scottish, an island associated schematically with northern Britain in just the way that Anglesey was part of Wales and the Isle of Wight part of England. Despite the links maintained by merchants, churchmen and others between the island and the mainland, Man was perceived as a culture apart: the *Polychronicon*, written by the Chester monk Ranulph Higden in the early fourteenth century and subsequently popularised through English translations, preserves the contemporary beliefs that the women of the island practised witchcraft by selling the wind to sailors, while visitors who stood on the feet of native men could witness the dead communicating with the living.[19] The fact that Man was generally mentioned only in such contexts strongly suggests that the switch from Scottish to English rule had barely impinged on the consciousnesses of those outside royal and aristocratic circles and inevitably raises questions as to whether the declared position of an Edward III or a William Montacute had any real bearing on the harsher realities of governance in the Irish Sea world of the fourteenth century.

It seems obvious that if Edward III did indeed see the acquisition of Man by Montacute as a lasting solution to the search for English domination of the British Isles, then the marked shift in his own diplomatic and military priorities during the late 1330s – away from Scotland and towards France – meant an immediate and substantial reduction in the level of commitment demonstrated either by the new lord or by the crown to the establishment of effective English control on the island. Montacute's creation as earl of Salisbury in the March parliament of 1337 itself symbolises this shift of emphasis, for it was part of a conscious attempt by Edward III to build up the ranks of the English aristocracy, and thus of the English military high command, in preparation for a major conflict with the French. Within a month of his elevation, Montacute was dispatched to the Low Countries with the bishop of Lincoln and the earl of Huntingdon to negotiate alliances with Flanders and the princes of the Empire; in July 1338 he accompanied Edward and his household to the continent and thereafter was almost wholly preoccupied with the French war. The result, not surprisingly, was that Man slipped further and further down the English order of priorities and shifted from what at times had seemed the very centre of the crown's military concerns and aspirations in the 1310s and early 1330s to the peripheral position it occupied for most of the period of the Hundred Years War.

This is not to say that the Montacute family were altogether neglectful of their new acquisition. Continued disturbance in the Irish Sea and, in particular, an attack on Man from Ireland, led by Richard de Mandeville in 1337, made it clear that William Montacute's claim to the island, let alone any desire to establish his rule and collect his revenues there, would have to be backed up with considerable force.[20] The well-informed English chronicler, Geoffrey le Baker, believed that Montacute secured control of the island by conquest and was crowned king there in the early 1340s. If such an expedition did take place, it is most likely to have occurred between Montacute's release from captivity in Paris at the end of 1340 and his departure on campaign in Brittany in 1342, though there is no corroborative documentary evidence to support the chronicles on this point.[21] In any case, by 1342 Montacute himself was publicly acknowledging the uncertainty of his rule on the island and the disturbed state of affairs in the North Channel by permitting the Manxmen to establish a one-year truce with the Scots and pay them an indemnity of 300 marks. When news of this arrangement reached the English royal government, the crown itself officially sanctioned private truces arranged between the islanders and the Scots.[22]

It has become a convention to say that English rule on Man was established more firmly and permanently after the defeat and capture of David II of Scotland at the battle of Neville's Cross in October 1346, presumably because the truces that obtained during the long negotiations for David's release put an end to Scottish raids across the northern border and into the Irish Sea. It is also worth noting that John Randolph, earl of Moray, who had inherited his father's rights to the Isle of Man, died in this battle without an heir and the Moray claim, such as it was, went into temporary abeyance. All of this, however, is to neglect the fact that William Montacute himself had died two years earlier from wounds received in the Windsor tournament of 1344. The new earl of Salisbury was only 16 years old at his accession and, unlike his father, had neither the military credentials nor, apparently, the political commitment needed either to win Man for himself or to secure the assistance of the king of England in the process. Indeed, the middle decades of the fourteenth century witnessed some serious reversals in the fortunes of the family: most dramatically, in 1354, Montacute was deprived of the lordship of Denbigh by a king anxious to ensure that the fruits of patronage were enjoyed only by those individuals and families actively and consistently committed to his regime. Under these circumstances, it was highly unlikely that the Montacute regime on Man would receive any more than the token support of the king of England.

This is not to say that the regime was without its achievements. Just because the Montacutes were not resident on Man does not in itself mean that either the rights of its lord or the material or spiritual needs of the islanders were totally neglected. The second earl of Salisbury at least is known to have appointed a receiver for the Isle of Man in 1371, a post that obviously implies that a regular and not unsuccessful administrative machinery had been established on the island.[23] A decade later, Montacute is found granting rents on Man to the value of £40 to his retainer, Sir William Faringdon.[24] There is no evidence that the new regime minted coins on the island, though when the English crown attempted to fix an exchange rate between the Scottish and English currencies in 1375 it made the ordinance applicable also in Ireland and Man.[25] In 1367 the first and only mendicant convent on the Isle of Man, the Franciscan priory of Bemaken, was founded under the patronage of the second earl of Salisbury.[26] In more

Fig. 7.1 *Bymacan Friary, Ballabeg. The east gable of the friary chapel, with the original window visible above the door. The chapel was founded in 1367 under the patronage of the second Earl of Salisbury. It now stands in a working farmyard.*

practical terms, the principal fortress on the island, Castle Rushen, shows signs of considerable building work during the period of English control in the fourteenth century: although the French attack on Man in 1377 is now regarded as historically suspect, the comments made by the English chronicler John Capgrave in his account of this putative incident still provide some kind of evidence of the strength of the defences established at Castle Rushen in this period.[27] Salisbury's successor, William Scrope, certainly took active steps to ensure adequate provisions for the garrison at Castle Rushen.[28] And in 1392 Scrope also expressed his intention to repair and maintain the cathedral church of St German and to build a fortress nearby to provide it with added protection.[29] The periodic references to the parlous state of the Isle of Man are therefore probably as much a general commentary on the dismal effects of war, famine and plague encountered in many parts of the British Isles during the fourteenth century as a particular indictment of the English regime on the island.[30]

A similar sense of proportion needs to be established when estimating the extent and consequences of the political manipulation of ecclesiastical

Fig. 7.2 *Castle Rushen. An historical artist's reconstruction of how the castle may have appeared from the north-west during the fourteenth century.*

Fig. 7.3 *St German's Cathedral, Peel Castle. During the fourteenth century, St German's Cathedral, having suffered war damage, was altered and fortified with defensible battlements.*

jurisdiction on the island. After 1266, patronage of the bishopric of Sodor and Man had fallen to the kings of Scotland, though metropolitan jurisdiction was still exercised by the archbishop of Trondheim. But the disputes surrounding control of Man during the Scottish wars of independence encouraged both the English crown and the papacy to challenge this situation. After 1349, rights of consecration passed effectively from Trondheim to the papal curia, while under Edward III the English crown clearly demanded the full allegiance of the bishop of Man in the same way that it expected the loyalty of all the people of the island.[31] As a result, after the Great Schism of 1378 there was an effective split within the diocese, with Man following the Roman obedience favoured by the English crown and church and a separate episcopal line directed from Avignon being appointed in the Western Isles as bishops of Sodor. This successful assertion of English influence, if not direct jurisdiction, over the bishops of Man represents a remarkable and neglected example of the subjection of ecclesiastical to secular jurisdiction and the resulting extension of the English crown's effective control over the church throughout its dominions.

* * *

The gradual evolution of the English regime on the Isle of Man during the fourteenth century therefore took a number of different forms and directions. Underlying and conditioning most of the attitudes of the Plantagenet dynasty towards the island, however, was the larger question of Anglo-Scottish relations. On two previous occasions – in 1293 and 1328 – the English crown had recognised Scottish control of Man in order to secure diplomatic settlements with the Scots. The capture of David II at Neville's Cross in 1346 necessitated another negotiated settlement. Was it possible that Edward III himself might be prepared – or able – to consider a further volte face on the question of Man if presented with otherwise favourable terms? The first round of negotiations for David's release, which proceeded to 1352, is particularly poorly documented; but although it is clear that the settlement envisioned during these talks involved English withdrawal from the Lowlands, it is noticeable that there is no mention in the extant material of the renunciation of Man.[32] Indeed, it seems most unlikely that such a position was discussed, given that the later and less ambitious ransom settlement contained in the treaty of Berwick of 1357 classified Man as a dominion of the English crown in very much the way that the treaty of Edinburgh of 1328 had earlier deemed it integral to the Scottish crown: it is particularly striking that whereas both Edward Balliol and John of Islay, Lord of the Isles, were named as separate parties to the Anglo-Scottish truce established under the terms of 1357, the earl of Salisbury was accorded no special status as lord of Man and his subjects there were treated as the 'people' of the king of England.[33] Under these circumstances, it would appear that Edward III had determined to maintain the English regime on Man and, unlike his grandfather in 1293 and his mother in 1328, was not prepared to countenance the loss of Man even as the price of a lasting peace with Scotland.

The other major impediment to the use of Man as a bargaining counter in Anglo-Scottish relations was, of course, the constitutional status it held as a result of Edward III's decision to renounce all claims to the island in 1333. Man, quite simply, was not his to give away. Much the same problem faced the Scottish crown as a result of the revival of the earldom of Moray and its associated claims to the regalities of Man. In 1357-8, Patrick Dunbar, earl of March, was recognised as earl of Moray by right of his wife, Agnes, the sister of John Randolph. Technically, the resulting claim to Man then passed to Henry of Grosmont, duke of Lancaster, who was created earl of Moray by David II in 1359, and passed after Lancaster's death in 1361 to the latter's son-in-law, John of Gaunt, son of Edward III.[34] It is therefore interesting that during the renewed Anglo-Scottish negotiations of the early 1360s, when Edward proposed that Gaunt be nominated as heir to the childless David II, a great council meeting at Perth in January 1365 actually set conditions on the proposal and indicated that Gaunt would be required to provide a large landed endowment, including not only 1,000 librates of land formerly held by Edward Balliol in Galloway but also the Isle of Man itself.[35]

However, the fact that this proposal included recognition of the earl of Salisbury's right to the island and actually suggested that Edward III compensate the earl with 1,000 marks a year for the resulting loss of lands and rights very much suggests that the Scottish political community placed more emphasis on the reality of the English occupation of Man than on the theoretical descent of the Moray claim to John of Gaunt. Given that Edward III had already deprived Salisbury of the lordship of Denbigh in a highly arbitrary manner, it is by no means impossible that he considered buying up the latter's lordship of Man and using it as a means of securing a highly desirable diplomatic settlement that would set up one of his own sons in time as king of Scots.[36] In the end, however, the proposal was still-born. The Scots preferred to resume payments of David II's ransom rather than entertain the prospect of an English ruler. The lordship of Man therefore remained inviolate and Montacute and his successors, although not immune from confiscation in the event of treason, were in the normal course of events considered the sovereign rulers of the island.

The consequence of these rather hesitant diplomatic manoeuvres of the 1360s appears to have been a gradual move back towards a fuller recognition of the quasi-independent status of Man in relation both to England and to Scotland. Whereas Man had been assumed to be a parcel of the Scottish crown in 1328 and of the English crown in 1357, the diplomatic relations between the governments of Richard II on the one hand and Robert II and III on the other formally acknowledged the independence of the lords of Man and the resulting need to secure their consent to Anglo-Scottish truces and treaties. To some extent this was a consequence of a further resurgence of Scottish interest in the island. George Dunbar, who succeeded to the earldom of March in 1368, was descended through his mother from Thomas Randolph and claimed to be rightful heir to the latter's rights on Man. This stance may account for Dunbar's refusal to bind himself to the Anglo-Scottish truce in *c.* 1390; it certainly explains why he had to be included, as lord of Man and ally of the Valois monarchy, in the Anglo-French truces of the period.[37] From the English point of view, it was therefore necessary to neutralise the Scottish claim by specifically asserting the earl of Salisbury's own rights to the island: accordingly, Salisbury was acknowledged as taking a separate and independent role in the preservation of the Anglo-Scottish truce after 1389.[38] From the perspectives of both the English and the Scottish crowns, much of this was mere diplomatic form and political posturing, akin to the way in which the Plantagenet and the new Stewart monarchies tried to play each other off by pandering to the separatist tendencies of the Lords of the Isles from the1370s onwards. The net result, however, was an informal recognition of Man's very special and privileged status within the political configuration of the British Isles. Whether or not the Montacutes actively asserted the title of king of Man, it was clearly acknowledged in England by the end of the fourteenth century that they had the right to do so.[39]

* * *

Under these circumstances, it is interesting to ask why the second earl of Salisbury should have given up his claims to Man by selling the lordship of the island to Sir William Scrope. This transaction was evidently negotiated as early as 22 November 1389, when Scrope undertook to pay Montacute the considerable sum of 10,000 marks; although the Isle of Man is not mentioned in the record of the completion of payment, dated 25 April 1392, it seems clear that the money represented compensation for Montacute's renunciation of claims to the island.[40] It was in this same record that Montacute first dropped the title of lord of Man, while Scrope himself began formally to exercise the title between 20 September and 24 October 1392.[41] The correct date for the completion of the sale is therefore 1392; although Montacute's will, made in 1397, styled him lord of Man, he had dropped the title in other public instruments issued after 1392 and there is no real foundation for the tradition that he maintained an interest in the lordship of Man until his death.[42] The most obvious consideration behind this transaction was, then, financial: Montacute was undoubtedly handsomely rewarded for his loss of status and revenue. It may also be that since he had no direct heir (his only son died in 1382 and he was succeeded as earl of Salisbury in 1397 by his nephew, John Montacute) he felt less constrained to preserve the title for succeeding generations. There are hints, however, that other factors were also at work and that Montacute's decision to give up the Isle of Man was not taken altogether freely. Since the English had lost command at sea in the 1370s, Man had once more become vulnerable to attack: in 1388 it was attacked by a Scottish raiding party returning from the north of Ireland.[43] By 1392 at least, a major English expedition into the troubled lordship of Ireland was being organised, and Man seemed about to resume the strategic importance it had held in the early 1330s. Under these circumstances, Montacute may well have been relieved to pass on responsibility for the island to a man who by experience and inclination was much more fitted to major military command.

The most important explanation for the transfer of the lordship of Man, however, was probably the political ambition of William Scrope. During the final decade of Richard II's reign, Scrope emerged as one of the major, and, towards the end, one of the most controversial and detested of Richard's inner circle of friends and advisers. If the original agreement for the purchase of the lordship of Man is to be dated to 1389, it seems unlikely that the king involved himself directly or brought any undue influence to bear on Montacute to effect the transaction: at this stage, Scrope was not the influential figure he was to become after his appointment as vice-chamberlain of the king's household and member of the royal council in 1393. Instead, it may be more accurate to say that the Isle of Man provided Scrope with the initial title and landed interest that was to grow, under his own careful management of royal patronage, into a major regional power base during the 1390s. Beginning in 1394, he systematically accumulated offices, titles and lands for himself on both sides of the Irish Sea, becoming chamberlain (1394) and justiciar (1395) of Ireland, lord of Anglesey (1397), justice of Chester, North Wales and Flint (1398) and keeper of the lordship of Denbigh (1398). In the latter case, it is particularly interesting to notice that although Richard II had initially supported the dynastic claim of another of his close friends, John Montacute, to Denbigh when the latter succeeded as earl of Salisbury, it was Scrope who took control of the lordship on the death of the earl of March in 1398: the shift of power in the region, away from Montacute and towards Scrope, had apparently become virtually inexorable. Since Richard himself had a strong personal and political interest in his own county of Chester, which he raised to the status of a principality in 1397 and employed as his personal power base during the last years of the reign, it seems evident that Scrope's own aggrandisement followed a coherent and parallel pattern: it has been suggested that Richard was trying to do for Scrope what he had earlier done for Robert de Vere in Ireland and raise him to a uniquely privileged status in the governance of the king's dominions.[44] In that case, the very special constitutional status that the Isle of Man had gradually assumed over the previous 60 years obviously had a particularly powerful symbolism.

In the end these plans, like so much else in Richard II's personal agenda, came to little, and Scrope himself fell victim to the violent reaction that accompanied the deposition of 1399. His great Irish Sea empire was dismantled and the lordship of Man fell into the gift of the new king, Henry IV. Two years earlier, however, Man had taken on an altogether different role that illustrated perhaps more typically the prevailing attitude of the

English monarchy towards the island, when it had been selected as the place of imprisonment and exile for Richard's declared enemy, the discredited lord appellant Thomas Beauchamp, earl of Warwick. Having been stripped of his titles and estates in parliament on 28 September 1397, Beauchamp was initially taken into custody at Queenborough Castle in Kent by Scrope's brother, Stephen, and then set out on 12 October under an escort of 60 men-at-arms and 100 archers, led by the Scrope brothers, and crossed from Chester to Man on 3 November: it took five ships to transport the 40 men-at-arms and 60 archers recruited from Lancashire and Cheshire to accompany the former earl across the Irish Sea.[45] Scrope was subsequently advised to provide 'moderate and honourable custody' for Beauchamp, who was allowed six servants while detained on the island and promised an annuity of 500 marks; the chroniclers, however, had no doubt that the distasteful Scrope treated his prisoner vindictively and harshly.[46]

This new phase in the history of the Isle of Man was no accident: Man was clearly chosen as Warwick's prison in 1397 not simply because of its isolation from the mainland but also because it was controlled by Scrope, a royal favourite who himself benefited directly from the fall of Warwick and was granted a proportion of the Beauchamp estates to support his new title of earl of Wiltshire. Nevertheless, the sense of political and cultural exile implicit in these arrangements was also undeniable. From the point of view of the English crown, the Isle of Man may have carried a certain significance at the end of the fourteenth century as one of the few remaining elements of the new Plantagenet dominion built up in the British Isles under Edward I and III. But precisely because it remained outside direct royal control, being immune from English justice and English taxes, the island offered the English crown virtually no quantifiable measure of real authority. The brief emphasis on the recovery of royal rights in Ireland during the 1390s did little in the long term to deflect the focus of English military policy and dynastic ambition away from France, and the defence of Man and the Irish Sea was inevitably subordinated to the altogether greater – and more glamorous – challenge of occupying northern France when Henry V chose to revive the continental war in the1410s.

In another respect, however, the continuity of English control of Man under the Montacutes and their successors stands as testimony to the vital and continuing role played not by the English crown but by the aristocracy in creating and maintaining the Norman, Angevin and Plantagenet empires. The example of the Isle of Man in the fourteenth century suggests that the very notion of medieval empire-building was based not on the modern model of a centralised state apparatus imposing uniform systems of government through systematic conquest and colonisation, but on the actions of an élite caste, including (in different combinations) the king, the royal family, the high nobility and knightly society, co-operating in the less structured process of opportunistic expansionism. There, perhaps, lies an important clue not only to the history of the Isle of Man, but also indeed to the fate of the English regimes in Ireland, Scotland and France during the late Middle Ages.

Notes

1 *CPR, 1330–4,* 64; *Foedera,* ii, 868; Oliver, *Munimenta*, ii, 182–4 (incorrectly dated).
2 PRO, E326/11477; G.E. Cokayne, *The Complete Peerage*, rev. edn by V. Gibbs *et al.*, 12 vols (London, 1910–59), ix, 79.
3 BL, Cotton Ch. v, 73, printed in Oliver, *Munimenta,* ii, 137–8; *Rotuli Parliamentorum,* 6 vols (London, 1783), i, 168; *Memoranda de Parliamento,* ed. F.W. Maitland, Rolls Series 98 (London, 1893), 131; Oliver, *Munimenta,* ii, 135–6.
4 *CPR, 1307–13,* 565; J.R.S. Phillips, *Aymer de Valence, Earl of Pembroke 1307–24* (Oxford, 1972), 131.
5 *CFR, 1327–37,* 362; Oliver, *Munimenta,* ii, 180–1 (incorrectly dated).
6 Nicholson, *Edward III and the Scots*, 122–3.
7 *CPR, 1330–4,* 464; Oliver, *Munimenta,* ii, 182 (incorrectly dated).
8 For this position, and a criticism of it, see *Handbook of British Chronology,* ed. E.B. Fryde, D.E. Greenway, S. Porter and I. Roy, 3rd edn (London, 1986), 65.
9 *CChR, 1327–41,* 199, 210.
10 *CPR, 1338–40,* 110. His son exercised the title to Denbigh only briefly in 1353–4; his usual style was 'earl of Salisbury and lord of Man': *CPR, 1358–61,* 539; *CPR, 1367–70,* 364; *CPR, 1370–4,* 48; *CPR, 1377–81,* 596; *CCR, 1349–54,* 4523, 626; *CCR, 1354–60,* 58, 73; *CCR, 1364–8,* 205–6, 489; *CCR, 1374–7,* 80, 87, 203, 255, 291; *CCR, 1381–5,* 234; *CCR, 1385–9,* 208, 273, 320, 367, 586, 623.
11 *CChR, 1327–41,* 348–9; George Holmes, *Estates of the Higher Nobility in Fourteenth-Century England* (Cambridge, 1957), 26–8.
12 *CPR, 1330–4,* 64; Nicholson, *Edward III and the Scots,* 146 and the references at n. 7. The letters patent are dated from Topcliffe, near Thirsk (Yorkshire) on 9 August: the king's household had itself been at Topcliffe on 7 August, though it was at Knaresborough between 8 and 14 August (PRO, EI01/386/8). In the absence of detailed wardrobe accounts, it is impossible to say which magnates were actually present with the king when the grant was made.
13 Nicholson, *Edward III and the Scots,* 160; *Handbook of British Chronology,* 516.
14 Robin Frame, *English Lordship in Ireland, 1318–1361* (Oxford, 1982), 132, 142–8, 196–202; Nicholson, *Edward III and the Scots,* 196–7, 219–20.
15 Ranulph Higden, *Polychronicon,* ed. C. Babington and J.R.Lumby, 9 vols, Rolls Series 41 (London, 1865–86), ii, 41. The description of the British Isles of which this is part was also used in the *Eulogium Historiarum,* ed. F.S. Haydon, 3 vols, Rolls Series 9 (London, 1858–63), ii, 143–5.
16 Duffy, 'The "Continuation" of Nicholas Trevet', 305–6; *Handbook of British Chronology,* 136; *Rotuli Scotiae,* 2 vols (London, 1814–19), i, 92, 93; Oliver, *Munimenta,* ii, 145–7.
17 R. Douch, 'The career, lands and family of William Montague, earl of Salisbury,

1330–1344', University of London MA thesis (1950), 55, 56, 70; *Handbook of British Chronology*, 137.

18 Douch, 'William Montague', 125, 136. For the second earl's inclusion of 'lord of Wight' in his official style, see Oliver, *Munimenta*, ii, 208–9; *CPR, 1391–6*, 516.

19 Higden, *Polychronicon*, ii, 40–3.

20 A.J. Otway-Ruthven, *A History of Medieval Ireland* (London, 1968), 257.

21 *Chronicon Galfridi le Baker de Swynebroke*, ed. E.M. Thompson (Oxford, 1889), 75, 247; Douch, 'William Montague', 63–4.

22 *CCR, 1341–3*, 654–5; *Foedera*, ii, 1211; Oliver, *Munimenta*, ii, 192–7 (incorrectly dated); *CDS*, iii, no.1396.

23 PRO, E326/4298; Holmes, *Estates of the Higher Nobility*, 65.

24 Oliver, *Munimenta*, ii, 205–7; Holmes, *Estates of the Higher Nobility*, 65.

25 J.A. MacKay, *The Pobjoy Encyclopaedia of Isle of Man Coins and Tokens*, 2nd edn (Sutton, 1978), 11; *CCR, 1374–7*, 202–3. See Bornholdt, in chapter ZZ below.

26 I.B. Cowan and D.E. Easson, *Medieval Religious Houses, Scotland*, 2nd edn (London, 1976), 238. See the account by Davey, in chapter ZZ below.

27 B.H. St J. O'Neil, 'Castle Rushen, Isle of Man', *Archaeologia*, xciv (1951), 1–26, esp. 10–11; John Capgrave, *The Chronicle of England*, ed. F.C. Hingeston, Rolls Series 1 (London, 1858), 232–3; T. Thornton, 'The Alleged French Raid on the Isle of Man, 1377', *Northern History*, xxxv (1999), 208–13.

28 *CPR, 1391–6*, 562.

29 Cowan and Easson, *Medieval Religious Houses, Scotland*, 239.

30 For such references, and the conventional historical tradition that resulted, Moore, *Isle of Man*, i, 198–9.

31 Watt, *Fasti Ecclesiae Scotianae*, 200–1; C.R. Cheney, 'Manx synodal statutes, A.D. 1230(?)–1351. Part I: introduction and Latin texts', *Cambridge Medieval Celtic Studies*, vii (Summer, 1984), 65–6; *CCR, 1339–41*, 594; *CDS*, iii, no. 1344; Oliver, *Munimenta*, ii, 190–1. For the impact of the transfer of rights of consecration, see Munch (ed.), *Chronica Regum Manniae*, i, 118–21.

32 A.A.M. Duncan, '*Honi soit qui mal y pense:* David II and Edward III, 1346–52', *SHR*, lxvii (1988), 113–41.

33 *Rotuli Scotiae*, i, 812; Oliver, *Munimenta*, ii, 199–202

34 *Handbook of British Chronology*, 516; K. Fowler, *The King's Lieutenant* (London, 1969), 175.

35 *APS*, i, 137; *ERS*, i, lxvi; Edward Balliol had already ceded his lands in Galloway and the Isles to Edward III in 1356: PRO, E39/87, printed in *Foedera*, iii, 318 and *CDS*, v, no.818.

36 For the transfer of rights to Denbigh, see Holmes, *Estates of the Higher Nobility*, 16.

37 *The Diplomatic Correspondence of Richard II*, ed. E. Perroy, Camden Society, 3rd series, xlviii (1933), no.125; Alexander Grant, 'The Otterburn war from the Scottish point of view', in *War and Border Societies in the Middle Ages*, ed. A. Goodman and A. Tuck (London, 1992), 38; Oliver, *Munimenta*, ii, 203–4.

38 PRO, SC1/63/279, printed in *CDS*, v, no. 868.

39 'Annales Ricardi Secundi', in *Johannis de Trokelowe et Henrici de Blaneforde Chronica et Annales*, ed. H.T. Riley, Rolls Series 28 (3) (London, 1866), 157; Capgrave, *Chronicle*, 257; Thomas Walsingham, *Historia Anglicana*, ed. H.T. Riley, 2 vols, Rolls Series 28 (1) (London, 1863–4), ii, 213; Thomas Walsingham, *Ypodigma Neustriae*, ed. H.T. Riley, Rolls Series 28 (7) (London, 1876), 365.

40 *CCR, 1389–92*, 559; Douch, 'William Montague', 147, n.2.

41 *CPR, 1391–6*, 516; *Calendar of Papal Letters*, 14 vols (1894–1961), iv, 432. For an instance of Scrope adopting the style *rex Manniae* (in 1396), see Michael J. Bennett, 'Richard II and the wider realm', in *Richard II: The Art of Kingship*, eds Anthony Goodman and James Gillespie (Oxford, 1999), 196 n.39.

42 William Dugdale, *The Baronage of England* (London, 1675), 648; Cokayne, *Complete Peerage*, ix, 390 n. (d). For chronicle references to the sale, variously dated 1392/3, see the references cited in n. 39.

43 Grant, 'Otterburn war', 49.

44 Chris Given-Wilson, *The Royal Household and the King's Affinity: Service, Politics and Finance in England 1360–1413* (London, 1986), 166, 168, 186; R.R. Davies, 'Richard II and the principality of Chester, 1397–9', in *The Reign of Richard II*, eds F.R.H. Du Boulay and C.M. Barron (London, 1971), 273–5 and nn; Bennett, 'Richard II and the wider realm', 197–8.

45 *Chronicles of the Revolution, 1397–1400*, trans. Chris Given-Wilson (Manchester, 1993), 2, 16, 61–2, 67, 96; *Chronicon Adae de Usk*, ed. E.M. Thompson (London, 1904), 17; *Chronique de la Traison et Mort de Richart Deux Roy Dengleterre*, ed. B. Williams (London, 1846), 10; *Rotuli Parliamentorum*, iii, 380; *Select Cases in the Court of King's Bench*, ed. G.O. Sayles, 7 vols, Selden Society 55, 57, 58, 74, 76, 82, 88 (London, 1936–71), vii, 100–1; *CPR, 1396–9*, 211; PRO, E364/32, m. 8d; *Issues of the Exchequer, Henry III–Henry VI*, ed. F. Devon (London, 1847), 271; Oliver, *Munimenta*, ii, 212–14; Michael Bennett, *Richard II and the Revolution of 1399* (Stroud, 1999), 111.

46 *CCR, 1396–9*, 346; 'Annales Ricardi Secundi', 220, 252.

8 *English Rule Confirmed: The Isle of Man 1389–1406*

MICHAEL J. BENNETT

At the end of the fourteenth century the Isle of Man lay on the margins of the European imagination. In his epic poem *Méliador* Jean Froissart had his hero visit the island. He landed on a beach eerily deserted until the arrival of fishermen from Scotland searching for herring. He observed that the island was previously ruled by a king with 100 knights.[1] In 1397 a real-life hero of chivalry, Ramon de Perellós, allegedly visited the island in the course of a pilgrimage to St Patrick's Purgatory. He too noted the tradition of a king with 100 knights, dating it to the time of King Arthur, and added that the island was now well populated.[2] It is unclear whether his knowledge was based on prior reading, perhaps of Froissart's *Méliador*, or derived from his guides or hosts. In the European mind the Isle of Man, often confused with Anglesey, belonged with other islands on the continent's Atlantic rim. They were sites of mystery and legend, and focuses for adventure and ambition. In the course of the fifteenth century the European imagination would overleap the Isle of Man as the Atlantic world was increasingly opened up by the conquest of the Canaries and the opening up of large-scale fisheries off the coast of Iceland. In the mean time the political destiny of the island and its people would be more firmly yoked to England with the acquisition of the kingdom of Man by English lords with the means to exploit the connection.

The period between 1389 and 1406, though somewhat obscure in terms of Manx history, represents a critical phase in the redefinition of the Isle of Man's relations with England. The period began with the transfer of the lordship of Man from William Montacute, earl of Salisbury, to Sir William Scrope, a process underway in 1389 though not complete until 1392. The Scrope *regnum* came to an abrupt end a decade later with the overthrow of Richard II and the execution of Scrope, one of the regime's most unpopular ministers, by Henry of Lancaster in August 1399. After his usurpation of the throne, Henry IV granted the lordship to Henry Percy, earl of Northumberland, at that stage his principal ally. The involvement of the Percys in rebellions in 1403 and 1405, however, led to their loss of the lordship. The period ends in 1406 with the grant of the Isle of Man to Sir John Stanley of Lathom in Lancashire, Henry's main agent in the north-west. His descendants, barons from 1455 and earls of Derby from 1485, were to rule Man until the eighteenth century.

This short but tumultuous period thus has some unity in the manner in which Man was caught up, at least through its lords, in the turbulent politics of the reigns of Richard II and Henry IV. Behind the vicissitudes of the lordship, though, there are some discernible trends. There was a continuing awareness at the English court of the strategic significance of the island and a growing association with the island of English lords who had the vision and means to secure, if not its integration into the kingdom, its articulation with English interests.

* * *

In the late 1380s the fate of the lordship of Man was largely determined by the exigencies and ambitions of English noble families. William Montacute, earl of Salisbury, who inherited the lordship of Man from his father, found himself in an unenviable position. In 1382 he lost his only son in a tragic accident, and in the mid-1380s became embroiled in a costly legal wrangle with his brother and heir. Personal factors may have made him less inhibited about selling off his patrimony, but financial pressure must have played the major role. In 1389 he entered into an agreement with Sir William Scrope that seems to have involved the mortgage or outright sale of the lordship of Man. On 22 November Sir William and his brother Stephen entered into a bond of 10,000 marks, the condition of which was to pay Salisbury 5,000 marks over three years. It can be assumed that the sum was the purchase price of the lordship of Man or some part of it. The final instalment was delivered on or before 25 April 1392.[3] It is possible that the Manx acknowledged the Scrope lordship some time previously.[4] Sir William Scrope was certainly acting and styling himself as lord of Man in autumn 1392 when he petitioned the pope for support in repairing St German's cathedral on St Patrick's Isle.[5] Thomas Walsingham made mention of the sale of the lordship of Man in his chronicle under the year 1393.[6] Scrope himself probably had to borrow capital in order to complete the purchase. On 29 August 1394, styling himself lord of Man and the Isles, he entered a bond to pay Richard Whittington, mercer of London, 250 marks.[7] The acquisition was a coup for Scrope, not least because, as the chroniclers observed, the lordship came with a crown.

Sir William Scrope was a man of ambition and imagination. He was the eldest son of Sir Richard Scrope of Bolton, a Yorkshire baron, and Blanche, daughter of Sir William de la Pole, financier and friend of Edward III. Like his father, he made his name as a soldier, advancing in the service of John of Gaunt, duke of Lancaster. Following his maternal uncle, Michael de la Pole, earl and duke of Suffolk and chancellor of England, he also had good contacts with the court of Richard II. By 1383 he was sufficiently well-regarded to be appointed as steward of Guienne. He held this office, involving a wide range of civil and military duties, for almost a decade. On 28 January 1393 the king ordered Scope's immediate return from Gascony to take on an even more crucial role.[8] On 22 February he was appointed vice-chamberlain of the royal household.[9] Thenceforward he was at the centre of the Ricardian regime, and the recipient of generous royal patronage.[10] In September 1397 he was raised to the peerage as earl of Wiltshire and in autumn 1398 appointed treasurer of the exchequer.

William was an able man schooled in the ways of the world. It seems likely, too, that he was well-educated. Given the background of the Scropes and de la Poles some aptitude for and instruction in law and finance may be hypothesised. Scrope was clearly numerate and a successful financial administrator. Some of the duties with which he was charged suggest some familiarity with the principles of Roman law. In 1391, for example, he was appointed to commissions to treat with the king of Castile and to examine the testament of the king of Navarre with regard to the cession of Cherbourg.[11] As steward of Guienne in the early 1390s, he was necessarily involved with issues relating to the juridical status of the duchy, and the nature of its relations with the English crown and with France.[12] Few noblemen of the time would have been in a better position than Scrope to relish the peculiar status of the lordship of Man. He adopted the style of lord of Man and the Isles, and commissioned a new seal incorporating the three legs of Man. His petition to the papal curia in autumn 1392 gave him an early opportunity to present himself as a sovereign prince. His use of the title of king of Man is even attested in the records of the English chancery. On 14 June 1396 William Scrope *rex Manniae* was recorded as a witness to the homage of John, bishop of Llandaff, to Richard II at Havering atte Bower.[13] It is hard to know what to make of this reference. In September 1397 Scrope was raised to the peerage as earl of Wiltshire, and thenceforward the comital title was preferred, at least in England. Yet Scrope's use of the royal title in 1396 was clearly authorised by Richard II. Such authorisation was not inconsistent with the ideological temper of Ricardian absolutism. Indeed it is of a piece with a series of Richard's initiatives in the late 1380s and 1390s that suggest some awareness of recent Romanist thinking on princely and imperial power. The power to create new titles and lordships was seen as a quintessential expression of *imperium*. The creation of the duchy of Milan by Rudolf, king of the Romans in 1395 was a celebrated case in point. Richard was profligate in the creation of

Fig. 8.1 *Seal of William Scrope, c.1395, perhaps the oldest surviving royal seal of Man, with a circular inscription reading (Sig)illum Will(ielmi L)escropp d(omini de) Manne et Insurlaru(m). The legs are clad in plate armour, which by this period had virtually ousted chain mail. Drawn from a cast in the Manx Museum. Courtesy: Manx National Heritage.*

new titles and even principalities. He sought to exalt his crown by the magnificence of the titles of the men subject to him. In 1394–5 he delighted in receiving the submission of the Gaelic kings of Ireland.[14] The kingdom of Man was another jewel, albeit a minor one, in his imperial crown.

There is no firm evidence that Sir William Scrope ever visited his island kingdom. He was in Guienne for much of the time between 1389 and 1393. His brother, Stephen Scrope, was party to the initial agreement with the earl of Salisbury, and was largely responsible for organising the transfer of

Fig. 8.2 *Sir William Scrope's interest in the northern Irish Sea and beyond.*

the lordship. Stephen Scrope later claimed that the Manx had accepted him as his brother's heir at a meeting of the Tynwald in 1391–2.[15] Although John bishop of Sodor, Richard abbot of Rushen, Patrick archdeacon of Man, Christina prioress of Douglas, and other clerical and lay dignitaries, denied this construction of events, it is likely that Stephen was present at some acknowledgment of the Scrope lordship around the time alleged.[16] Of course, it is possible that Sir William took leave from his post in Bordeaux to receive the homage of his Manx lieges. It may have been his personal inspection of the church and defences on St Patrick's Isle that led to his petition to the pope. Still, the likelihood is that, if he visited the island at all, it was after his final return from Guienne in the spring of 1393. He was appointed keeper of Beaumaris Castle in 1394, and a visit to inspect the fortifications may have been combined with a visit to Man. His involvement in the administration of Ireland, where he served a term as chancellor and justiciar during Richard's expedition of 1394–5, provided other opportunities. For example, while Richard crossed St George's Channel to Ireland in October 1394, it may be that Scrope, who was in York as late as 29 August, crossed by way of the Isle of Man.[17]

Scrope's interests in and around the Irish Sea continued to expand. He was appointed constable of Dublin Castle as well as Beaumaris in 1394. He was granted the custody of Anglesey in 1397, and was given the custody of the lordship of Denbigh after the death of the earl of March in 1398. On 23 January 1398 he was appointed justiciar of Chester, North Wales and Flintshire for life, and likewise secured appointment as constable of Conwy Castle. For a time Castle Rushen had the makings of an important pivot of the Scrope maritime empire. The only real monument to the Scrope *regnum*, however, is the rectangular tower at Peel Castle that overlooks the causeway linking St Patrick's Isle to the mainland.[18] In truth, notwithstanding his concern for the fabric of St German's cathedral,[19] Sir William Scrope had little time to make much of his island kingdom. Shortly after his return from Ireland in 1395 he was dispatched on a succession of embassies to France which culminated in the king's remarriage to Isabelle of France in autumn 1396.[20] In 1397 he was appointed treasurer of England and he was increasingly caught up with the frenetic politics of 1397–9.[21] His main residence appears to have been Queensborough Castle in Kent.[22] His interests and responsibilities in Man and around the Irish Sea continued to be largely left in his brother's capable hands.

Through the Scrope connection, the Isle of Man played a cameo role in the drama of Richard II's last years. In July 1397 the king ordered the arrest of the duke of Gloucester and the earls of Arundel and Warwick, the leaders of the baronial opposition in 1387–8. In September Scrope was one of the six lords who laid the appeal of treason, and was rewarded for his loyalty by elevation to the peerage and grants of land. The earl of Warwick, the only member of the triumvirate not put to death, was condemned to banishment to the Isle of Man and was committed to Scrope's custody. From the expenses subsequently awarded to Scrope, Warwick was in his custody at Queensborough Castle from 28 September until 12 October, when Scrope and his brother took him to Chester with an escort of 60 men-at-arms and 100 archers. While William returned to London, Stephen took Warwick on the final stage of the journey to Man, commissioning five ships to carry the prisoners along with about two-thirds of the original escort. Stephen did not tarry on the island, and was back in Chester on 1 December and in London by the middle of the month.[23]

The Scrope brothers must have crossed the path of Ramon de Perellós,

Fig. 8.3 *The rectangular barbican gate tower at Peel Castle, a monument to the Scrope regnum. Photo: Peter Davey.*

the Catalan knight pilgrim, who likewise braved the Irish Sea late in 1397. He arrived in England with a large retinue at the end of October, and made his way to the court of Richard II at Woodstock. His mission was St Patrick's Purgatory in Ireland. Richard gave him passports, letters of introduction, and an escort as far as Chester, where he chartered a ship for Ireland. According to his account, he followed the Welsh coast until he reached Holyhead, and then set course for Dublin. He then states that he landed on the Isle of Man. After noting that it formerly belonged to the king of the 100 knights, he observed that it was now 'well populated' and belonged to the king of England. Given the oddness of his route, and the derivative nature of his knowledge of the island, it may be doubted that Perellós ever made landfall on Man.[24]

For the earl of Warwick, the Isle of Man was all too real. Though initially denied all creature comforts, he was allowed six attendants and a substantial wardrobe.[25] Further insight into his condition comes from William Paris, a loyal retainer, who accompanied him in exile. In a poem, *The Legend of St Christina,* he recorded that he was writing his verse 'in prisone of stone' in 'the Ile of Mane, that stronge cuntre'. He bemoaned the fate of his lord deserted in his misfortune by the men whom he had patronised. Since Paris clearly had the materials as well as the leisure to write, the conditions of captivity cannot have been so harsh. His one surviving poem suggests that there was reading matter available. If, as one commentator has suggested, Paris was inspired by Chaucer's rendition of the life of St Cecilia, it may be that a copy of *The Canterbury Tales* had been brought to the island.[26] More certain is the fact that the poem could not have been written without access to the *Legenda Aurea.* Such a work was probably available in one of the religious houses on the Isle of Man. Since the prioress of Douglas was named Christina it is likely that the work owed something to her good offices.

While Warwick settled into his life of exile on the windswept island, the centre of gravity in the realm of England was shifting decidedly towards the Irish Sea. The king spent Christmas 1397 and New Year 1398 at Lichfield. The parliament that had condemned Warwick and ennobled Scrope had been prorogued to reconvene in Shrewsbury in February. When Ramon de Perellós returned from St Patrick's Purgatory at the end of January he found the court at Lilleshall abbey in Shropshire.[27] For much of 1398 Richard remained in the Midlands and the West Marches. In the north-west, in particular, he was building up a bastion of royalist power, centring on his new principality of Chester, but with bulwarks in the form of the marcher lordships confiscated from the earl of Arundel, the Lancastrian lands in Staffordshire and Lancashire, and the principality of

Wales.[28] There was a definite Irish Sea orientation to his geo-political thinking, and Richard was actively planning a second expedition to Ireland, a move which he saw in some way as central to his revival of royal power. Richard's larger concern with Britain and Ireland was seen as ominous in England. It was rumoured that the king would never view England again with favour, but would rule from outside the kingdom, from Wales or Ireland.[29]

Sir William Scrope was a key figure in this policy shift, a shift which added to the potential strategic importance of the Isle of Man. By the late 1390s Scrope was justiciar of Chester and had in his custody a ring of castles around the Irish Sea littoral: Denbigh, Conwy, Beaumaris, Dublin and Rushen. Early in January 1399 he was paid £832 16s. 7d. for 100 men-at-arms and 400 archers going in his retinue to Ireland.[30] If he crossed over to Ireland briefly at this time, however, he did not take part in the king's expedition of May 1399. As treasurer of England and one of the king's closest confidants, he was too useful at home. During the king's absence in Ireland he was a leading member of the junta that ruled England, and, along with the notorious Bushy, Bagot and Green, was one of the most hated men in the realm.[31] With the arrival of Henry of Lancaster and the large-scale mobilisation on his behalf, Scrope and his associates withdrew to Bristol Castle, desperately seeking to make contact with Richard II. They were the first casualties of the Lancastrian coup. In August 1399 Scrope was summarily executed at Bristol. In the first parliament of the new king, Henry IV, his lands were declared forfeit to the crown.

The lordship of Man, though, was treated separately. It was deemed to be conquered territory rather than a forfeiture. While Henry of Lancaster played down any implication that his title to the English crown was based on conquest, he had no such inhibition with respect to the lordship of Man. On 19 October 1399 he granted the island, castle, peel and lordship of Man by way of reward to his chief ally in the usurpation, Henry Percy, earl of Northumberland.[32] The grant was of all the islands and lordships pertaining to the Isle of Man

> which belonged to Sir William Scrope, deceased, whom when in life we lately conquered, and so decreed conquered, and which by reason of that conquest, as well as the conquest we took into our hands, which decree and conquest in our parliament, by the assent of the lords temporal, in the same parliament assembled, as respects the person of the aforesaid William, and all his lands and tenements, goods and chattels, both within our said kingdom and without it, at the supplication of our said kingdom were confirmed.

The grant was made by Henry and his heirs to Percy and his heirs for the service of carrying the 'Lancaster Sword' at the king's left shoulder during the coronation. This sword was the sword with which Henry had been girded at his arrival at Ravenspur.[33]

The lordship of Man's immediate value to Henry IV was as a means of rewarding a leading magnate who had championed his cause. It must be assumed, too, though, that Henry acknowledged the strategic importance of the island. He had every reason to be concerned about the loyalty of Cheshire and North Wales and the neighbouring regions, and about the security of the Irish Sea, especially given the likelihood that the Scots would take the opportunity of the political crisis in England to assert their interests in the region. In addition to owing Percy a debt of gratitude, the king must have recognised the value of having the lordship in the hands of a loyal magnate who, as a greater northern magnate, had the means to defend the island. In practice Northumberland left this responsibility to his eldest son, Sir Henry Percy junior, better known as 'Harry Hotspur'. Appropriately enough, the latter was granted the justiciarship of Chester and a bundle of other offices in Chester and North Wales, including the custody of Anglesey and Beaumaris Castle, which made him Scrope's successor in the Irish Sea.[34]

The tenure of the Isle of Man by the Percys was short. It is unlikely that Northumberland visited the island, and there is no clear evidence that his son did so. Still, Hotspur spent at least some time in Chester and environs, and sought to build up a following in the north-west. In May 1402 he retained Sir William Stanley and another Cheshire knight to lead companies of men-at-arms and archers in an expedition *sur la meer*.[35] It is conceivable that their mission was the defence of the Isle of Man because in July they had a number of Scots in their custody.[36] In the event, Hotspur used his position to reconstruct Richard II's retinue in the palatinate of Chester, and in alliance with Owain Glyndwr to raise a rebellion against the Lancastrian regime. Sir William Stanley was among the rebels.[37] Hotspur's defeat and death at the battle of Shrewsbury in 1403 opened up a power-vacuum in the north-west, all the more serious in that the rebellion continued in North Wales. For a time the fiction was maintained that Northumberland was loyal, and it was not until the summer of 1405 that his lands were declared confiscate. As Henry IV headed north after the collapse of Northumberland's rebellion, he took steps to secure Man. At Pontefract Castle on 3 June he instructed Sir John Stanley to take the island into the king's hands and keep it until further orders.[38] Stanley put the operation in the hands of his nephew and a number of gentlemen from Cheshire and Lancashire. The nephew was none other than the Sir William Stanley who had served Hotspur in the Irish Sea and in the rising of 1403. Letters of protection in respect of the chief expeditioners were issued at Ripon on 11 June.[39] It cannot be supposed that they met too much resistance in Man.

It was natural that Henry IV should look to Sir John Stanley and his growing affinity in the north-west to secure the island. A native of Wirral in Cheshire, Stanley made his fortune as a soldier in the French wars and by 1378 had re-established himself in the region through his marriage to Isabel Lathom, the heiress of the manors of Lathom and Knowsley in south-west Lancashire. In 1386 he began a long association with the lordship of Ireland, where he served as justiciar from 1386–7, 1389–91, 1399–1401 and 1413–14. A king's knight from 1389 and controller of the wardrobe from 1397 to 1399, he helped to organise Richard II's Irish expedition of 1394–5 and played a key role in the transformation of the palatinate of Chester into a bastion of prerogative power. His submission to Henry of Lancaster in August 1399 was a signal event in the collapse of the Ricardian regime. Stanley rapidly won and soon showed himself worthy of the new king's trust. After a brief turn as lieutenant of Ireland, he proved a pillar of the regime during the rebellion of 1403 when so many Cheshire men, including his nephew, took the field under Hotspur's leadership. Probably Stanley resented Hotspur's aggrandisement in the north-west, and saw the opportunity that would emerge from his defeat. On 10 August he was given a commission to pardon all rebels who sought the king's grace, and on 16 September he was appointed governor of the city and county of Chester.[40] From this time onwards the Stanleys ruled the roost in Cheshire and south Lancashire. Their influence was spreading westwards into North Wales and northwards across the Ribble. The lordship of Man would give them a crown.[41]

Henry IV moved with some circumspection. On 27 June 1405 he settled on his third son the bulk of the earl of Northumberland's lands, but left open the future of the lordship of Man.[42] Sir John Stanley moved to take control on the ground, obtaining a licence early in 1406 to purvey wheat and malt for export to the island.[43] Eventually the king gave him his reward, though his generosity was not unbounded. The grant of the Isle of Man to Stanley and his heirs on 6 April 1406 was linked to the surrender of a royal grant of 100 marks for life. The grant was more detailed than that to the earl of Northumberland, perhaps reflecting Stanley's greater knowledge of the assets of the lordship, and the service required of the Stanleys was the performance of homage and the provision of two falcons at the king's coronation.[44] By this stage Stanley was much involved with affairs of state, and he, like his predecessors, cannot have found much time for his island kingdom. Appointed steward of the household of the prince of Wales in

1403, he became steward of the king's household in 1408. The accession of Henry V brought him another term as lieutenant of Ireland. Prior to his departure he declared his will in London on 20 July 1413.[45] If his reputation among the Gaels in Ireland is any guide, the Manx would have found him a harsh lord. He died in Louth, allegedly a victim of the curse of an Irish bard.[46]

Fig. 8.4 *The Tower at Liverpool was built by Sir John Stanley, c.1406. Nineteenth-century drawing by W.G. Herdman. Courtesy: Liverpool Record Office.*

* * *

Thus began the long association of the Stanleys and the Isle of Man. The Scropes sought to reassert their rights in 1408, and continued to do so throughout the fifteenth century. The Stanleys, however, were well connected at court, and in a uniquely strong position both to exploit the lordship and, perhaps, to bind the Manx to English rule. The lands around the Irish Sea had a natural unity, and there had been long-standing connections between the peoples along its coasts. With the coming of Stanley rule to the Isle of Man, there was established an overarching political nexus which embraced, from time to time, the entire littoral from Cumbria to Anglesey and across to Dublin. Though vulnerable to Scots attack from the north, the Isle of Man anchored this archipelago of interest. Since Sir John Stanley built the Tower at Liverpool around the time of the acquisition of Man, it may be supposed that his was the vision. Nonetheless the consolidation of Stanley rule and indeed English rule on the Isle of Man was very largely the work of his son and namesake, the second Sir John Stanley.

Notes

1 Jean Froissart, *Méliador*, ed. A. Longnon, 3 vols, Paris, Société des Anciens Textes Français (1895, 1899), ii, esp. lines 11,674–715; A.H. Diverres, 'The geography of Britain in Froissart's *Méliador*', in *Medieval Miscellany presented to Eugène Vinaver by Pupils, Colleagues and Friends,* eds F. Whitehead, A.H. Diverres and F.E. Sutcliffe (Manchester, 1965), 99.

2 '...la yla d'Arman, que soc del rey de C. cavalhiers en lo temps del rey Artus, e al jora de huey es be poblada e es del rey de Englaterra': *Voyage au Purgatoire de Saint Patrice. Texts Languedociens du Quinzième Siècle,* eds A. Jeanroy and A. Vignaux, Toulouse: Bibliothèque Méridionale, 1re série, t. viii (1903), 12–13; see also D.M. Carpenter, 'The pilgrim from Catalonia/Aragon: Ramon de Perellós, 1397' in M. Haren and Y. de Pontfarcy (eds), *The Medieval Pilgrimage to St Patrick's Purgatory, Lough Derg and the European Tradition* (Enniskillen, 1988), 99–119.

3 The first 1,000 marks was to be paid by Easter 1390, a further 500 marks at midsummer, another 1,000 marks by Easter 1391, a further 500 marks by midsummer, a further 1,000 marks at Easter 1392, and the remaining 1,000 marks by Michaelmas 1392: *CCR, 1389–92*, 559. For the background, see the discussion in Ormrod in chapter 7 above.

4 The evidence is from a subsequent petition in which Stephen Scrope claimed that the Manxmen had acknowledged him as his brother's heir at a meeting of the Tynwald in the 15th year of the reign of Richard II, that is before 21 June 1392. While the Manx disputed his claim, there is no reason to suppose that Scrope would jeopardise his claim by antedating the Scrope lordship: B.L., Additional Charter 8, 482; Oliver, *Monumenta*, ii, 247–50.

5 Since the relevant papal indults are dated 24 October 1392, the petitions to which they are responses must date from some time in September at the latest: *Cal. Papal*

Letters, iv, 432–3. It is true that William earl of Salisbury styled himself as lord of Man on 20 September 1392, but it should not be assumed that the transfer must have taken place between the two dates: *CPR, 1391–6*, 516. Salisbury used the title in his will.

6 Thomas Walsingham, *Historia Anglicana*, ed. H.T. Riley, 2 vols, Rolls Series (London, 1863–4), ii, 213.

7 The bond was dated at York: B.L. Harley Charters 56 A 22.

8 N.A. [P.R.O.], SC 1/63/294.

9 T.F. Tout, *Chapters in the Administrative History of Medieval England*, 6 vols (Manchester, 1923–35), iii, 463; vi, 50. Since Scrope did not receive the king's letter until 17 March, he could scarcely have returned to England before April: N.A. [P.R.O.] SC 1/63/294v.

10 On 22 May he was granted licence to hunt, shoot and fish in England and Wales as often as he chose. On 30 May he was granted an annuity of 200 marks, which he surrendered on 2 July in return for a grant of the castle and town of Marlborough: *CPR, 1391–6*, 276, 270, 309.

11 *Foedera*, vii, 692.

12 J.J.N. Palmer, *England, France and Christendom 1377–99* (London, 1972), chapter 9.

13 P.R.O., C 270/25/27.

14 M.J. Bennett, 'Richard II and the wider realm' in A. Goodman and J.L. Gillespie (eds), *Richard II. Power and Prerogative* (Oxford, 1999); N.E. Saul, 'Richard II and the vocabulary of kingship', *EHR*, cx (1995), N. Saul, *Richard II* (London, 1997), 291–2; M.J. Bennett, *Richard II and the Revolution of 1399* (Stroud, 1999), 22, 73–5.

15 See note 4 above.

16 B.L. Additional Charter 8,482; Oliver, *Monumenta*, ii, 247–50.

17 B.L. Harley Charters 56 A 22.

18 *Cal. Papal Letters*, iv, 432. Kinvig, *Isle of Man*, 95.

19 *Cal. Papal Letters*, iv, 432–3.

20 He was a member of the original embassy appointed to negotiate the marriage alliance in July 1395, and he spent most of the summer in Paris: *Foedera*, vii, 802; E. Perroy (ed.), *The Diplomatic Correspondence of Richard II* (Camden Society, 3rd ser., XLV111, 1933), no. 223 n. Scrope went on further missions relating to the marriage in the new year, receiving instructions from Richard II in January, and probably attending the ratification of the treaty in Paris in March: *Foedera*, vii, 811–20. On 14 June 1396 Scrope was in attendance on the king at Havering atte Bower, but the very next day he was instructed to return to Paris to arrange Richard II's meeting with Charles VI and the delivery of the bride: P.R.O., C270/25/27: *Foedera*, vii, 834. He undertook further foreign missions in February and March 1397, including demanding and receiving from the duke of Brittany 120,000 francs in gold: *Foedera*, vii, 850–1.

21 He attended parliament at Westminster in September 1397, and was probably in close attendance on the court over Christmas and New Year. He was with the king at Lichfield on 18 January 1398: P.R.O., C270/25/33. He was at Shrewsbury for parliament in February. Along with the duke of Lancaster, he was commissioned to meet with deputies of king of Scotland in April 1398: P.R.O., E403/559, m.1.

22 *CPR, 1388–92*, 25; *CPR, 1391–6*, 206, 715; *CPR, 1396–99*, 578.

23 P.R.O., E364/32, m.8d.

24 *Voyage au Purgatoire de Saint Patrice*, 12–13; Carpenter, 'The pilgrim from

Catalonia/Aragon: Ramon de Perellós, 1397' in Haren and de Pontfarcy, *The Medieval Pilgrimage to St Patrick's Purgatory*, 107.

25 P.R.O., E 364/32, m.8d.

26 G.H. Gerould, 'The legend of St Christina, by William Paris', *Modern Language Notes*, 29 (1914), 129–33.

27 M.J. Bennett, 'The historical background', in D. Brewer and J. Gibson (eds), *The Gawain-Poet. A Companion* (Woodbridge, 1997), 88.

28 R.R. Davies, 'Richard II and the principality of Chester, 1397–9' in F.R.H. Du Boulay and C.M. Barron (eds), *The Reign of Richard II. Essays in Honour of May McKisack* (London, 1971), 56–79.

29 'Annales Ricardi Secundi et Henrici Quarti', in *Chronica Monasterii Sancti Albani*, vol. 3, ed. H.T. Riley, Roll Series (London, 1866), 239.

30 Issue, 8 January 1399. P.R.O., E 403/561, m. 11.

31 Walsingham, *Historia Anglicana*, ii, 213. Richard appointed Scrope as executor of his will, and entrusted him to settle delicate matters in the queen's household: Bennett, *Richard II and the Revolution of 1399*, 147.

32 In general see J.M.W. Bean, 'Henry IV and the Percies', *History*, 44 (1959), 212–27.

33 *CPR, 1399–1401*, 27, 171; Oliver, *Monumenta*, ii, 215–19.

34 *CPR, 1399–1401*, 28, 37, 155, 158.

35 'Calendar of recognizance rolls of the palatinate of Chester', part I, appendix to the *Thirty-Sixth Report of the Deputy Keeper of Public Records* (London, 1875), 380.

36 'Cal. recognizance rolls of palatinate of Chester', 326.

37 He was pardoned in November 1403: 'Calendar of deeds, inquisitions and writs of dower enrolled on the plea rolls of the palatinate of Chester', part II, appendix to *Twenty-Ninth Report of the Deputy Keeper of Public Records* (London, 1868), 63.

38 *CFR, 1399–1405*, 310.

39 *CPR, 1405–8*, 25; Oliver, *Monumenta*, ii, 230–1.

40 'Cal. recognizance rolls of palatinate of Chester', 502, 446.

41 M.J. Bennett, *Community, Class and Careerism. Cheshire and Lancashire Society in the Age of Sir Gawain and the Green Knight* (Cambridge, 1983), 216–19; M.J. Bennett, 'Sir John Stanley of Lathom, c. 1351–1414', *The Oxford Dictionary of National Biography*, 52, 226–7.

42 *CPR, 1405–8*, 40.

43 *CPR, 1405–8*, 145.

44 Oliver, *Monumenta*, ii, 235–46.

45 Lancashire Record Office, DDK 1/8.

46 Otway-Ruthven, *History of Medieval Ireland*, 347.

PART TWO: SOCIETY

9 *The Isle of Man in a European Context*

BENJAMIN T. HUDSON

The 'Chronicles of the Kings of Man and the Isles' begin not with information about the Isle of Man, or even the Irish Sea region, but with the conquest of England by the Danish prince Knútr 'the Great' in 1016.[1] For the next 50 years (1016–66) the Manx chronicle has Danish, English, German, Norwegian, papal, Scottish and Welsh events, but nothing for Man. Setting aside the textual reasons for this beginning, the chronicle serves notice that the Isle of Man needs to be considered not in glorious isolation, but rather within the context of the history of Europe. The period from 1000 to 1400 was one which saw the growth of the states that would dominate European affairs to the present day, and the Isle of Man occupied an important position – geographically, politically and culturally – in the plans of several of those powerful kingdoms. Even though it was located on what has been generally considered the periphery of European affairs, the history of the Isle of Man is sensible only within the wider context of northern Atlantic Europe. In common with so many of the smaller states of western Europe, the Isle of Man, either on its own or as part of the kingdom of the Isles, had a difficult course to follow through the high Middle Ages and into the late medieval period as it participated in the greater European community on which so much of its own prosperity depended. The Manx had to keep at bay larger and more expansionist neighbours while satisfying an overlord who had his own plans for the region. In placing the Isle of Man within a European context, history together with literature and art can provide an estimation of fact and perception.

Literature provides examples of one prevalent perception of the Isle of Man in European tradition, the association of the kingdom of the Isles with the mysterious, the outsider, the outlaw. Throughout the medieval period the Isle of Man was considered a border region, where legendary figures roamed, bandits lived and royal pretenders emerged from the mists of the Irish Sea. Before, as well as during, the Viking Age the Isle of Man is found in Gaelic literature of both a secular and an ecclesiastical nature. The mythological sea-god Manannán mac Lir was traditionally associated with the Isle of Man, although Cormac mac Cuilennáin demoted him to a skilful navigator who lived on the island, and the poem *Estid a eolchu cen on* attributed to the eleventh-century Irish historian Flann of Monasterboice, preserved in the twelfth-century pseudo-historical compilation known as *Lebor Gabála*, places the slaughter of three gods of the Túatha De Danann on Man.[2] In Christian traditions the Isle of Man retained its attributes of mystery, and according to the seventh-century Life of St Patrick composed by Muirchú, after the saint's tormentor Mac Cuill converted to Christianity, as penance for his previous behaviour he was set adrift in a small boat with his hands and feet bound; he landed on the Isle of Man where he served as a missionary and bishop after being rescued by the two men named Conindri and Rumili who had converted the Manx to Christianity.[3] The Patrician connection with the Isle of Man is made more direct in the twelfth century when the *vita* of St Patrick composed by the celebrated hagiographer Jocelin of Furness (written under the patronage of the adventurer John de Courcy whose wife Affrica was the daughter of King Guðröðr II (reigned 1153–87)) has the saint himself travelling to the Isle of Man to convert the Manx.[4]

By the high Middle Ages the greatest of the outlaws were the Vikings. Their victims viewed the Vikings as devils, and occasionally they were considered similarly by their own people. In *Landnámabók*, a twelfth-century account of the settlers of Iceland, the formation of an independent kingdom in the Isles was credited to a Viking named Ketil 'Flat-nose', whose daughter was the famous settler in Iceland named Auðr 'the Deep-minded', widow of the shadowy Viking prince Óláfr the White of Dublin.[5] Ketil, according to *Landnámabók*, was sent to the Isles by the Norse king Haraldr Fairhair, but he turned pirate and his raids on the Norse provoked retaliation in the form of a naval expedition led by Haraldr in order to break his power and bring the region under his control. The appearance of this story in a twelfth-century composition, when the kingdom of Man and the Isles was part of the Norwegian empire, could be a piece of historical revision intended to give a suitable antiquity to that subordination, although there might be a genuine historical basis to the claims of its former status as a pirate base. By the tenth century the Irish annals show Man as a base for freebooters in the Irish Sea, under the leadership of Magnús and Guðröðr son of Haraldr; the raid on Man by the English king Æthelraed in 1000 might have been in retaliation for raids on England.[6]

The image of the diabolical Viking merges with that of the Isle of Man as the haunt of the outsider in the thirteenth-century Icelandic masterpiece *Njáls saga*. *Njáls saga* illustrates how well history combines with fiction to create a compelling story, as the events prior to the famous battle of Clontarf (fought on Good Friday in 1014), for which the writer used a now-lost 'Brian's Saga', are used to illustrate the opposition of paganism to Christianity.[7] In the saga, the Isle of Man is a base for Viking fleets whose services are sought by the king of Dublin named Sigtryggr *silkiskegg* ('Silkenbeard') (*c.*989–1036), one of the historical protagonists at Clontarf, for his fight against the Irish high king Brian Bóruma. Sigtryggr's offer of employment was accepted by a Viking named Bróðir, a lapsed Christian turned sorcerer. Before Bróðir sailed for Dublin, he and his crew are tormented for three nights by apparitions and each morning a crewmember is found dead. Those deadly events foretell the slaughter at the battle of Clontarf and Bróðir's own death. Such apparitions were not unknown elsewhere in the Irish Sea region, although they were not so murderous. Accounts of the earliest English mercenaries in Ireland claim that a force of knights led by the Leinster king Diarmait Mac Murchada on an expedition into Osraige *c.*1169 were visited in the middle of the night by an apparition of attacking warriors.[8] In *Njál's saga* the writer's view of the Isle of Man as a place of otherworldliness is deliberate. Bróðir, like Sigtryggr, was a historical person who did fight at the battle of Clontarf, but according to the contemporary records his home was York, not the Isle of Man.

Njáls saga provides merely one aspect of the perception of the Isle of Man by those outside it. The religious tension of Christianity versus paganism would form an underlying stratum in historical reports about the island. Historians of the twelfth and thirteenth centuries were fascinated by the tales of the Isle of Man, with bishops who became bandit-princes and a nobility that practised grisly rituals. Such a view was not always unjustified or contrived; the career of the famous, or infamous, Bishop Wimund (*c.*1134–*c.*48) seems to bear a great deal of responsibility for it.[9] That Wimund's career is known mainly from the work of an English monk named William of Newburgh says much about the international view of the Isle of Man.[10] According to William, Wimund was a monk of Furness who had gone to the Isle of Man as part of the colony established at Rushen abbey. At that time Furness was a monastery of the order of Savigny (later absorbed into the Cistercian order) and King Óláfr (*c.*1113–53) had granted it the right of selecting the bishop of Man and the Isles.Wimund so impressed the Manx that they asked for him as their bishop, which request was duly granted. After his election and consecration he claimed that he was a descendant of Óengus of Moray, the Cenél Loairn dynast who was slain in 1130 at the battle of Stracathro, a claim that William argues was fiction, adding that Wimund was English. After the Scots took control of north-western England in 1138, Wimund led a force to the district around Furness. His raids were so successful that he was given some lands by King David I. Travelling around the neighbourhood with his warband, he was finally captured, blinded and castrated, then placed in the recently established Byland abbey. The very young William of Newburgh knew the very old Wimund, and he recorded how the pretender boasted that if he had but the eye of a sparrow his enemies would have no cause for joy. One man's bandit could be another's champion, and, before Wimund is dismissed as a mere brigand, the manner in which he was dealt with shows that his genealogical claims appeared genuine to contemporaries, for blinding and castration were the customary way of dealing with dynastic opponents. A charter note survives which shows that Wimund held lands in Westmorland as an apparently accepted member of local aristocratic society.[11] The fifteenth-century historian Walter Bower hints in his *Scotichronicon*, which contains some unique historical materials, that Wimund was merely the agent of the Manx king Óláfr (*c.*1113–53) in a struggle against David I of Scotland.[12]

The image of the Isle of Man as the haunt of the freebooter or pirate was a partial reflection of fact. In 1218 the Manx king Rögnvaldr (*c.*1187–1228) journeyed to the court of the English king Henry III to render homage and he was accompanied by some of his subjects who wished to make amends for their 'excesses' (that is, pirate raids) in England and Ireland.[13] During the Anglo-Scottish wars of the fourteenth century, ships from Ireland carrying supplies for the English forces in Scotland were ordered not to put to sea because of the pirates infesting the waters around Man.[14] Even the Manx nobility was credited with unusual behaviour. Matthew Paris's account of Hugh de Lacy's uprising in Galloway in 1236 claims that the leaders of the troops, drawn from Ireland and the Isle of Man, sealed their bond with sorcery. Looking back to the ancient customs of their ancestors, they filled a bowl with their blood and then drank it to make fast the alliance.[15] These ancient customs appear to be similar to a ritual among the Irish nobility described by Gerald of Wales, in which treaties were sealed by the participants each drinking the blood of the other.[16] The fourteenth-century historian Ranulph Higden claims that women on the Isle of Man practised witchcraft by selling to sailors ropes with knots tied in them in which the loosening of a knot would cause a breeze to blow.[17]

During the earlier Middle Ages the settlement of Vikings on Man placed the island in a cultural and linguistic region that extended from Ireland, across the Irish Sea and Northumbria to Scandinavia. When the glories of the Viking past were being committed to writing in the twelfth century the Isle of Man was part of the Norwegian colonial empire, and the Manx were included in those records. To writers of the twelfth century any human settlement on the Isle of Man was the result of actions of the great princes of the north. The twelfth-century Anglo-Norman historian Orderic Vitalis wrote in his *Ecclesiastical History* that the Isle of Man had been uninhabited until settlers were imported in the late eleventh century at the direction of the Norwegian king Magnús Barelegs.[18] Orderic's naïve speculation would find an attentive audience, although the Icelandic historian Snorri Sturluson, writing in the early thirteenth century, gave a slightly different view of the settlement. Snorri's saga of Haraldr Fairhair in *Heimskringla* claims that Man was inhabited until the expedition there of Haraldr, whose arrival in the Irish Sea so terrified the inhabitants that they abandoned the island.[19] A variation on this story is found in *Orkneyinga saga*, which might be a source of Snorri's account, where Haraldr merely destroys the settlements in order to end assaults on Norway by Vikings from the west.[20]

Literature is complemented by art, and it illustrates the geographical range of the cultural world to which the Isle of Man belonged, one that spanned the northern half of Europe and extended westwards to North America with the famous Vinland and Markland colonies. The designs of the famous Manx crosses fit precisely within the chronological development of those styles in Scandinavia and areas of Scandinavian settlement.[21] Stylistic influence from northern England, from York, has been seen in the designs on contemporary Manx crosses together with, after 1020, influences from the Viking settlements in Ireland, especially Dublin.[22] Moving south, artistic parallels suggest contact between Man and Normandy; especially striking is the similarity in the design of sculptures found at Evercy with tenth- and eleventh-century designs found on Man and in the Orkneys.[23] The Manx chronicle begins with the triumph of a Danish prince in England, and the Danish royal family enjoyed good and close relations with the dukes of Normandy in the early eleventh century, who of course traced their own lineage back to Scandinavia. Artistic parallels between the Orkneys and Man could provide a basis in fact for the claims in Icelandic sagas that in the late tenth and early eleventh centuries the kingdom of the Isles was under the control of the Orcadian lord Sigurðr Hloðvison (d.1014).[24] *Orkneyinga saga* claims that Orcadian influence on the Manx extended to the mid-eleventh century, part of the empire of Sigurðr's son Þorfinnr.[25]

The early eleventh-century historian Adémar of Chabannes noted the distinction between the inhabitants of the Irish Sea and the Scandinavians, but saw them intertwined when he recorded that the fleet of Vikings who raided Saint-Michel-en-l'Herm, on the Bay of Biscay, in the second decade of the eleventh century was composed of troops from Denmark and the Irish Sea.[26] He describes how their tactic of digging trenches around their encampment foiled a retaliatory raid by the local inhabitants. Unlike later commentators, Adémar saw the Irish Sea region as being as sophisticated as any in Europe, and its inhabitants as ferocious as any in Scandinavia.

a

b

c

Fig. 9.1 *(opposite) Artistic parallels, including 'spiral hip' pattern, between the ornament on: a) relief on a stone from d'Evrecy, Normandy; b) a cross slab in the parish church. Kirk Michael, Isle of Man and c) bosses of penannular brooches from Skaill, Orkney. (cf* Anglo-Norman Studies *13, 1900, 35–40 and Wilson D and Klindt-Jensen O* Viking Art *London 1980) [b) and (c), © Eva Wilson].*

The Isles seem to have been part of the Danish empire of Knútr, which is why the king of the Isles named Echmarcach Mac Ragnaill was in attendance on Knútr in 1031.[27] But this Echmarcach travelled in the retinue of the Scots king Malcolm (Máel Coluim) II, suggesting a Scottish interest in the fortunes of the Isles. By the beginning of the eleventh century, the kingdom of the Isles appears to be benefiting from the ascendancy of the Scandinavians in northern Atlantic Europe. Not only would England be conquered by the Danes in 1013 and ruled by them from 1016 to 1042, but on the continent the Scandinavian settlements around the river Seine had formed into the duchy of Normandy which was becoming a major political influence in the western Frankish lands; the formidable Norman dukes traced their ancestry from the Vikings, as already noted, and main-

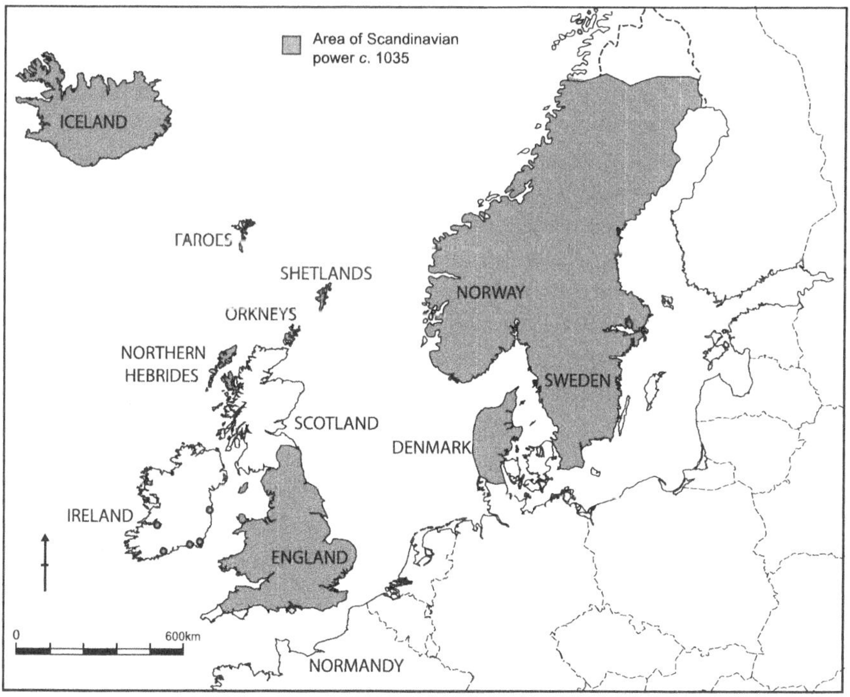

Fig. 9.2 *Man and Scandinavian power in northern Europe, c.1035.*

tained good relations with the Danes and Norwegians.

The apparent general Scandinavian supremacy must be seen in the context of the continuing decline in political and military influence of the Viking colonists on the western shores of the Irish Sea. The defeats of the men of Dublin at the battles of Tara (980) and Clontarf (1014) would lead to the Irish control of all the Viking towns by the mid-eleventh century.[28] The men of the Isles had allied with the men of Dublin for the battle of Tara and a Manx contingent was present at the battle of Clontarf under the leadership of Sigurðr of the Orkneys. A premature collapse of Scandinavian power in the Irish Sea region was prevented by Knútr the Great, king of Denmark and England, who may well have lent support to the Dublin king Sigtryggr Silkbeard and thereby postponed the town's domination by the Irish princes.[29] The kingdom of Man and the Isles seems to have shared in Knútr's protection, and by 1036 its rulers were strong enough to contest in Ireland. The target was the town of Dublin, which was conquered by the men of Man and the Isles under the leadership of the afore-mentioned Echmarcach Rögnvaldsson, who was a grandson of the late tenth-century freebooter Guðröðr (d. 989) Haraldsson who was styled 'king of the Isles' by the Annals of Ulster on his death.[30]

During this period there is every indication that a mint was operating on Man (*c.*1025–*c.*1065), which suggests a degree of economic prosperity on the island.[31] Throughout Europe there was a great surge in the minting of coins during the eleventh century, and Man seems to have benefited from the general economic upturn. The Manx coins of the period were imitations of Dublin issues, which were themselves imitations of the English coinage of Æthelraed (and, to a lesser extent his successor, Knútr), providing yet another illustration of the ties of Man with its neighbours.[32] Other groups of imitations believed to have been minted somewhere in the Irish Sea region in the 1020s and 1030s are also known, such as those copying Knútr's *Quatrefoil* and *Short Cross* types.[33] These coins undoubtedly reached and circulated in Man, for examples are known from several Manx finds, but the mint (or mints) of origin remain uncertain until a larger sample is known.[34] This wealth could have financed the second conquest of Dublin by Echmarcach, which happened to coincide with a change of fortunes in Scandinavia, as Knútr's nephew the Danish king Sveinn Estridsson begged the English king Edward the Confessor for aid against the Norwegians, aid that was refused. It is tempting to suggest, without any real evidence, that the success in Ireland of the Islemen was due, in part, to a newly resurgent Norwegian monarchy. A direct connection of the Isles with Norway becomes visible in 1058, when an invasion of England by Magnús, the son of the Norwegian king Haraldr Hardrada

Fig. 9.3 Coins of Knútr, Dublin and Man:

A Coins of the Long Cross type from Anglo-Saxon England, Dublin and Man.
1. Penny of Æthelred II, Long Cross type, c.997–1003 (Huntingdon Mint, moneyer Osgut, 1.44 g) ex Glenfaba 2003 hoard [11]; imitations of Long Cross pennies of Æthelred II;
2. Hiberno-Scandinavian, Phase II, from the Dublin mint, c.1020–c.1035 (1.11g), ex Glenfaba 2003 hoard [375];
3. Hiberno-Manx, Middle Style, from the Manx mint, c.1025–c.1065 (0.87g) ex Kirk Michael 1972–5 hoard, Manx Museum acc. No. *76–84/20. Images by Richard Hodges.*

B Coins of the Quatrefoil and Short Cross types from Anglo-Saxon England, Dublin and the Irish Sea region.
1. Penny of Cnut, Quatrefoil type, c.1017–23 (Dover mint, moneyer Eadwine (1.41g) ex Glenfaba 2003 hoard [76]);
2. Penny of Cnut, Short Cross type, c.1029–35/36 (Lincoln mint, moneyer Godric (0.93g);
3. Hiberno-Scandinavian, Phase 1 Quatrefoil imitation from the Dublin mint, c.995–c.1020 (0.99g) ex Glenfaba 2003 hoard [105];
4. Irish Sea Quatrefoil imitation, possibly from Wirral?, c1020s (1.07g) ex Glenfaba 2003 hoard [121];
5. Irish Sea Short Cross imitation, 'Winchester' mint (actual mint uncertain), c.1030s (0.86g), ex Andreas parish Churchyard 1874 hoard, Manx Museum acc. no. 1523/4. Images by Richard Hodges.

(ON *harðráðr*), employed troops from the kingdom of Man and the Isles.[35] The international aspect to the expedition increased when Magnús unexpectedly joined a parallel invasion led by the exiled English noble Ælfgar of Mercia, and his son-in-law Gruffudd ap Llywelyn. The outcome of the invasion is unknown, for the Irish chronicler notes that God had not willed its success and the account in the Anglo-Saxon Chronicle states merely that the full story was wearisome to tell. The failure of the invasion of England was followed, in 1061, by the invasion of Man by Murchad son of Diarmait mac Máel na mbó. Diarmait had conquered Dublin in 1052, expelling Echmarcach from the town; by this point he was one of the most powerful, if not the most powerful, king in Ireland with the Isles tributary to him. Echoes of Murchad's conquest of Man might be found in the hagiography of St Óláfr.[36] The Manx mint seems to have ended during this period. Diarmait's friendship with Harold Godwinsson, the earl of Wessex, brother-in-law of King Edward and his successor, whom he had sheltered in 1051–2, and whose sons he would receive after Hastings, suggests that efforts to control the Isles from Leinster might have had English support, and it will be remembered that the final efforts to end the reign of Gruffudd ap Llywelyn by Earl Harold included an English flotilla in the Irish Sea.[37]

For all this, it was the Norman conquest of England, barely noticed in the Manx chronicle, which would tie the Isle of Man more tightly in the embrace of continental Europe. The Manx chronicle does record the Norwegian defeat at Stamford Bridge rather than the battle of Hastings, an eccentricity shared with those contemporary Irish chronicles that mention events in England in that year. Part of the reason might be the participation of the future Manx king Godred Crovan (*c.*1079–95) in the battle on the side of the Norwegian king Haraldr harðráðr; his pause on Man in the flight from England is the first native notice found in the Manx chronicle.[38] Did he fight in the troop of the *rex Hibernensis* whose death at Stamford Bridge was recorded by the contemporary chronicler Adam of Bremen (who apparently had an informant supplying him with interesting material about the Irish Sea region)?[39] The establishment of the dynasty of Godred Crovan in the fourth quarter of the century led to renewed interest outside the Isles. At some point in the early 1090s, Godred captured Dublin from the king of Munster, and claimant to the highkingship, Muirchertach Ua Briain and held it for some time prior to his death in the plague of 1095–6. True to his pan-Irish Sea outlook Godred also sent aid to Wales, to Gruffudd ap Cynan for his assault on the Isle of Anglesey.[40] The newly re-emergent Isles would be submerged once again, this time by the Norwegian king Magnús Barelegs, whose expedition to the west in 1098 solidified Norwegian control of the Isles.[41]

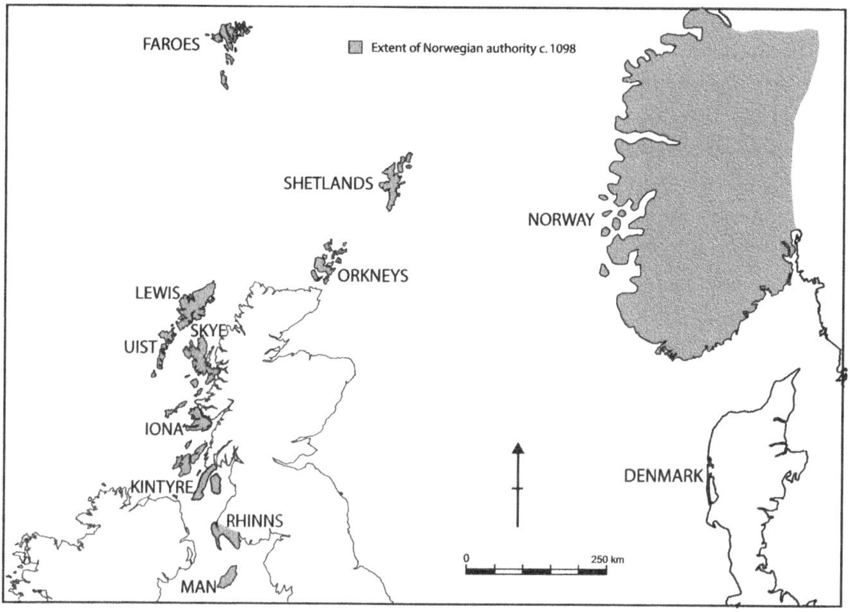

Fig. 9.4 *The extent of Norwegian authority, c.1098.*

Magnús brought the Isle of Man directly under the sovereignty of the Norwegian kings, and made plain the importance of the island for Irish, Scandinavian and English affairs. As far away as Normandy were Magnús's expeditions watched, and the young Orderic Vitalis, beginning his *Ecclesiastical History* at St Évroul, was in no doubt about the threat he posed to the second generation of Norman rulers of England. Magnús had the leisure for his expedition because his reign was a comparatively rare experience among the Norwegians, that of a single king ruling without a powerful royal rival. If his saga by Snorri Sturluson is correct in claiming that Magnús was inspired by the tales of Viking adventures, we would like very much to know if the Isle of Man featured prominently in the stories circulating around the Norwegian court. Magnús contributed to his own legend, and that of the Irish Sea, with his verses, including his declaration of love for an Irish or Hiberno-Norse girl. More likely he was driven less by romantic considerations and more by financial necessity. The kingdom of Man and the Isles was the most southerly part of the Norwegian economic orb, which extended west past Iceland and Greenland to Vinland, somewhere in North America. Its location in the Irish Sea meant that the Isle of Man provided access to one of the main trading zones in

Atlantic Europe. Magnús needed wealth for his contests with his neighbours such as the Danish princes who remained formidable despite the virtual civil war that had prevailed since the death of King Sveinn Estridsson. Moreover, the financial demands on royal government were increasing throughout Europe in the eleventh century. The Irish Sea was an area where the energetic and discontented among the Norse could put their energies to trade rather than treason.

The connection with Norway provided the avenue for Manx participation in the major pan-European military venture of the Middle Ages, the Crusades. The Crusades led, in turn, to the beginnings of the 'Normanisation' of the Isle of Man as the outlook of the Manx began to turn, ever so slowly, to the south towards the Francophone lands. Norwegian lordship allowed the Manx to participate in the Crusades under the leadership of King Sigurðr 'the Jerusalem-Traveller', the son of Magnús. The capture of the city of Jerusalem in 1099 had sent a wave of euphoria throughout Europe, and the capture of Antioch by the crusading army the previous year was recorded in the Manx chronicle. When King Sigurðrof Norway made his celebrated crusade of 1108–10, he spent the winter in Britain where he recruited troops. Among those who joined his crusade appears to have been Lögmaðr (Lagman), the son of Godred Crovan.The Manx chronicle claims that he abdicated after the murder of his brother Haraldr and journeyed to Jerusalem, but died before reaching the city. His departure is placed in the chronicle before the arrival of Magnús, but it has been demonstrated that he was alive after the death of the king in Ulster.[42] The approximate date of Lögmaðr's pilgrimage coincides with the arrival in Britain of Sigurðr's crusading fleet, and it seems that the king of Man and the Isles accompanied his overlord on a crusade.

The expedition of Sigurðr to the Holy Land was recorded by Adalbert of Aachen (who consistently refers to Sigurðr by his father's name Magnús), and by Snorri Sturluson in *Heimskringla*.[43] Snorri describes the fleet's voyage from Britain along the Atlantic coast with stops along the way. The crusaders seem to have fought the Muslim princes in the Iberian peninsula as well as North Africa; there was also a stop in Sicily. Adalbert's account notices this fleet when it landed at Ascolin and then sailed on to Joppa, the main port for the crusading army in Jerusalem. Sigurðr led his men to Jerusalem, he washed in the river Jordan and assisted in the assault on Sidon late in the year 1110. The Manx chronicle, as we have seen, claims that Lögmaðr died before reaching Jersualem, and there is no notice of him in Adalbert of Aachen's history which suggests that he was killed in the fighting before reaching the Holy Land. The unexpected death of Lögmaðr during the Crusade probably was not announced in the Isles until the late summer of 1111, when Sigurðr returned to northern Europe.

The decision by Lögmaðr to accompany Sigurðr was, perhaps not entirely unwittingly, responsible for the introduction of the Norman element on Man. For Lögmaðr entrusted his younger brother Óláfr to King Henry I of England. The choice of the English rather than Norwegian court for the heir-apparent was less odd than would first seem. The Isles required not just a strong prince, but one in the immediate area who could guard a young prince's rights. Óláfr's guardian could ensure the good behaviour of not just the local nobles but, more importantly, the other powerful noble in the Irish Sea region, the Irish king Muirchertach Ua Briain, who had his own plans for the Isles, but not at the price of poor relations with Henry. At the English court Óláfr mingled with other *émigrés* such as Henry's queen Matilda and another heir-in-waiting, her brother the future King David I of Scotland. Óláfr was exposed to new fashions, ideas and institutions from the continent and, like his fellow royal boarder David, he would be responsible for the introduction of many new men and customs into his kingdom. Óláfr was not alone in his appreciation of the new order, and within the Irish Sea province he was part of a wider group of native magnates influenced by the Normans and those who followed in their wake.[44] Ties of friendship were important, and when Óláfr's son Guðröðr was forced to flee his kingdom by Somerled of Argyll he sought help from the Scots King Malcolm IV, the grandson of his father's old school-friend; during his residence at the Scots court at Roxburgh Guðröðr was a witness to the confirmation charter for Kelso abbey.

Admiration for continental styles was buttressed by marriage, and Óláfr's wife Affrica was the daughter of the mysterious Fergus of Galloway and Elizabeth, the sister of the Scots Queen Sibylla, an illegitimate daughter of the English king Henry I.[45] Information about the connection of the Isles' royal family with the English royal house is provided by a writer on the continent named Robert of Torigni who was the abbot of Mont St Michel; he had interviewed the bishop of the Isles, and describes Óláfr's son Guðröðr as the cousin of Henry II.[46] The charters of Henry's son John describe Guðröðr's son Rögnvaldr as the English king's kinsman (*consanguineous*).[47] That kinship helps to explain why the kings of Man and the Isles after Guðröðr were not unhappy with recognizing the lordship of an English king who was, after all, one of the family. By the thirteenth century the kings of Man were becoming more involved with their English cousins, as shown by the safe conducts issued by King John of England for Rögnvaldr, as well as gifts of land in Lancaster and Ulster, and gifts of money.[48] A direct benefit of those ties to his people is seen when Rögnvaldr approached John in order to secure the release of some of his subjects held in custody in England.[49] At the same time that Man and the Isles were subject to the king of Norway, Rögnvaldr formally became the vassal of John in 1205.[50]

The homage offered by Rögnvaldr to John had a tangible benefit in wealth and security, but good relations with the English court also allowed the kings of the Isles admission to the continental sophistication that they wanted very much, especially the cult of knighthood. By the twelfth century the idea of the knight as more than merely a hired ruffian had developed under influences as diverse as Arthurian romances, the idea of courtly love, the sacral aspect contributed by the crusading orders, and the vast landholdings necessary to support a knight. The enthusiasm with which the great men of the lands around the Irish Sea sought knighthood is demonstrated by the Scots king Malcolm IV when, in opposition to the wishes of his nobles, he joined Henry II of England at the siege of Toulouse in order to receive the knighthood he had been denied the previous year.[51] So it is hardly surprising that Rögnvaldr's brother and successor Óláfr Dubh (*c.*1228–37) and his son Haraldr (1237–48) both requested and received knighthood from Henry II's grandson Henry III. This was not idle posturing on the part of the princes of the Isle of Man, for after his release from a Scottish prison Óláfr made a pilgrimage to Santiago de Compostela, one of the most famous pilgrim sites in western Europe; the journey was the thirteenth-century equivalent of the Grand Tour. Efforts at cultural assimilation as well as ties of kinship help explain why the English kings, especially Henry III, appear to have had some sympathy for the multiplicity of ties of the Manx king. Henry issued a letter of protection for Óláfr to visit Norway in 1237, and used his good offices to send the Manx heir-apparent to Norway in 1253.[52] The main duty of a knight was to fight, and the Manx lords used their location in the midst of the Irish Sea to render (well-paid) military service. By 1235 Óláfr was guarding the seas around the Isle of Man, from the Irish to English coasts, on behalf of the English king; Óláfr supplied and personally commanded 50 galleys on naval expeditions.[53]

The family ties and military alliance between the kings of Man and the Isles and the kings of England go some way to explaining the appearance of the kingdom of the Isles in the Arthurian tales. The tales of Arthur and his knights of the Round Table enjoyed a circulation throughout Western Europe. There is no direct mention of the kingdom of Man and the Isles in the work that started the enthusiasm for things Arthurian, Geoffrey of Monmouth's *History of the Kings of Britain*, composed in the second quarter of the twelfth century. Early in the thirteenth century in Lazamon's *Brut*, a vernacular reworking of the *History of the Kings of Britain*, the men of the Isles make an appearance when they ally with the men of Galloway and the Orkneys in order to fight for King Arthur.[54] Lazamon could be reflecting the ties of the kings of Man and the Isles with the Norman aristocracy. In later Arthurian literature, when the Isle of Man was under English control, the alliterative *Morte Arthur* (*c*.1400) has Arthur recapturing the Isles as one of the first events in the poem.[55] In the fifteenth century Thomas Malory's *Le Morte d'Arthur* tells of a king of the Isles named Brian, who features in an adventure with King Pellinor.[56] An interesting aspect to this episode is that a Brian also appears in Geoffrey of Monmouth's history, but there he is a kinsman of Cadwallo of the Britons who delivers a recitation of the wrongs done to the Britons by the Anglo-Saxons.[57] The popularity of the Arthurian stories meant that characters and places from them were used in other tales, one of which was the early thirteenth-century adventure *cum* romance known as the Romance of Fergus, which takes as its hero the historical Fergus of Galloway.[58] The mother of the Manx King Guðröðr (1153–87) was the daughter of Fergus, which might explain, in part, why the Irish Sea region features prominently in the story. The Romance of Fergus is a rather commonplace story in which there are some conventional literary episodes such as the hero's initial obscurity and the recognition of his valour through various quests which are part of the wooing, and winning, of a lovely princess. A point of interest in the story comes when a maiden approaches Arthur's court at Carlisle to seek a champion, but she learns that the knights have dispersed to seek him, with Kay going to the Isles.

Kinship also helps to explain the appearance of the Isle of Man in some Latin and Gaelic literature of Irish origin after the eleventh century. The marriage of Guðröðr's daughter Affrica to the adventurer John de Courcy might explain why the saint, as already noted, makes a journey to the Isle of Man in Jocelin of Furness's *vita* of St Patrick. The geographically important position of the Isle of Man for political affairs is also true for kinship; as the Isle of Man was on the border between the Scandinavian and Celtic worlds, it was also on the boundary between the French and Gaelic literary spheres and, at the time the Arthurian tales were being composed, the Irish literati were placing the lords of Man in a Gaelic context. There is a late-twelfth-century poem in praise of Rögnvaldr written in early modern Irish.[59] The poet traces Rögnvaldr's lineage through the great heroes of Irish mythology and describes his reign in terms more familiar for the great Gaelic lords. Again kinship seems to have a role to play in literary composition, for Rögnvaldr's mother was, according to the poet, an Irish princess named Sadb, apparently a member of the Mac Lochlainn dynasty of mid-Ulster.[60]

The different cultural settings for the Isle of Man reflect the extent of the kinship and political importance of the kings of Man in the thirteenth century; they also show something of the complexities of loyalty. In common with the princes of other European states, the Manx lords needed to maintain cordial relations with larger and more powerful neighbours, which often led to the pledging of fealty to a variety of individuals. In less than 15 years Rögnvaldr became the man of King John of England (in 1205), renewed his loyalty to the Norwegian monarch (*c.*1210), surrendered his kingdom to the papacy (in 1218, apparently in imitation of John's submission to Pope Innocent III), and did homage to John's son Henry III (in 1219). Although Rögnvaldr seems to have been casual about his pledges, his brother Óláfr Dubh renewed the submissions to both Norway and England. Not everyone was willing to accept these multiple loyalties. In 1220 Rögnvaldr complained to Henry III that the Norwegian king set 'snares' for him and wanted to invade his lands because he had rendered homage to the English king; Henry ordered the justiciar of Ireland to give aid to Rögnvaldr in the event of a Norwegian attack.[61] Sometimes the menace was nearer, such as in 1214 when King John ordered his Irish subjects not to enter Rögnvaldr's kingdom.[62] When Henry III learned that an invasion of Man planned in 1251 by Magnús son of Óláfr Dubh was to be launched from Ireland, he ordered his justiciar John fitz Geoffrey to prevent any such force from sailing.[63]

The cultural milieu and political orientation of the Isle of Man are not all that should be placed within the context of general European development. Like Britain and Ireland, the church administration and religious life of the Isle of Man was influenced by the ecclesiastical reform which transformed Europe after the late eleventh century as the so-called Gregorian reform programme swept all before it. In the twelfth century, after the sojourn of Óláfr I at the court of Henry I, Man was part of the province of York, but by 1152 it was placed under the jurisdiction of the archbishopric of Nidaros (Trondheim) in Norway. This shifting responsibility shows how the Isle of Man became caught up in papal plans for northern Europe. Papal efforts to lessen the influence of the Holy Roman emperor by taking Scandinavia from the control of the archbishops of Hamburg-Bremen led to the creation of the archbishopric of Lund in 1104. This had no immediate effect on Man, unlike the division of ecclesiastical influence in Scandinavia in the mid-twelfth century by Pope Adrian IV, who created a metropolitan for Norway at Nidaros. A part of the reorganisation was the formal establishment of the diocese of Sodor (ON Suðreyjar) under the jurisdiction of the archbishop in Norway, which effectively gave papal approval to Norwegian claims of lordship over the Isles. The severing of ties between York and Man, and the subjection of Man to a Norwegian metropolitan by an English pope reinforces the European rather than insular context within which the island must be placed. An English aspect remained, for the Norwegian church had long looked to England as its mentor and close ties between the two endured into the twelfth century.

Óláfr's residency at the court of Henry I had introduced him to the reformed continental monastic orders. So when Óláfr encouraged ecclesiastical reform, instead of patronising the older Norse or English community, he established monks of the order of Savigny at Rushen. The order had been established by Vitalis of Savigny, one of the most famous preachers of the day, and the Savigniacs were part of the famous continental monastic reform movement which included the Cistercians, Carthusians and the Tironians.[64] This French order at Rushen was colonised not from the continent, but from the community at Furness in Lancashire, which was given the right to elect the bishop for the Isles.[65] The Savigniac community at Rushen placed Man in an ecclesiastical federation that extended from Ireland to the continent. The important patron of the Savigniac houses in England was the future King Stephen of England in whose ancestral lands Savigny was located. This might indicate a mingling of religious piety and political preference if Óláfr were preparing to take sides in the coming confrontation between Stephen and Henry I's daughter Matilda over the succession to the English throne. The religious enthusiasms of Óláfr I led to his patronage of English religious houses such as Holm Cultram and St Bees (see map chapter 16). In 1148 the Savigniac houses merged with the Cistercians, and suddenly the Manx had a religious community that was part of the rapidly expanding network of the white monks. The Cistercians dominated Man, with a second house founded at Myroscough by Óláfr's son Guðröðr in 1176, and a house of Cistercian nuns was established at Douglas by Guðröðr's son Rögnvaldr *c.*1226.[66] Not until the fourteenth century would another religious order have a house on Man, when the Franciscans were established at Bemaken by William Montague, the earl of Salisbury. The whole-hearted participation in ecclesiastical reform and innovation by the Manx princes was recognised by the papacy; Vivian, cardinal prefect of St Stephen in Monte Coelio and papal legate, spent the Christmas of 1176 with Guðröðr on the Isle of Man before sailing to Down early the next year and then convening a synod at Dublin.[67]

Regardless of enthusiasm for things French, the king of Norway remained the overlord of the kingdom of Man and the Isles until the later thirteenth century. Within the Norwegian sphere of influence, the men of the Isles enjoyed a special place because so many of the monarchs had ancestral connections with them. Robert of Torigni in his account of the visit of the bishop of the Isles to Henry II noted that the king of the Isles owed ten gold marks to the king of Norway upon his king-making, and no other dues.[68] When Lucian wrote his poem in praise of Chester in the late twelfth century, he noted that the city's northern gate looked to Norway, but it actually looks toward the Hebrides, the extension of Scandinavia.[69] The special relationship of the kings of Man and the Isles with Norway reflects the origins of the Norse monarchs; since the second quarter of the twelfth century, one of the kingly lines among the Norse came from the Isles. Thanks largely to the romantic proclivities of Magnús Barelegs, rarely in medieval Europe was one kingdom so dominated by kings tracing their lineage to a dependency as was Norway by the kingdom of Man and the Isles. King Haraldr 'Gille' (Haraldr Gillecrist) of Norway, the offspring of a casual liaison between Magnus and a Gaelic-speaking woman from the Isles (possibly the Irish girl whose praises he committed to verse), had his claims to the Norwegian succession recognised and briefly reigned. After his murder the claims of all his sons to the throne were recognised, as much the claims of his son named Eysteinn, who came from the Isles and was the offspring of a liaison Haraldr had contracted before his departure for Norway, as those of his son named Ingi, the child of a regular union with the Swedish princess Ingríðr, granddaughter of King Ingi Steinkelsson. While the sons of Haraldr contested with one another, the lord of the Isles played the role of king-maker. King Ingi was defeated and slain at the battle of Oslo (3 February 1161) largely because of the defection at a crucial stage in the fight by his supposed supporter Guðröðr of Man to the side of his rival Hákon 'the Broad-shouldered', son of a third son of Haraldr Gille named Sigurðr Munn. The Sverresson dynasty, that eventually would cede the kingdom of the Isles to the Scots, traced its (possibly fictitious) origin to a third son of Haraldr named Sigurðr. The rather casual attitude of the rulers of the Isles to Norway after the mid-twelfth century reflects the chaotic state of Norwegian political life, as rivals fought for control and pretenders appeared and vanished with rapidity.[70] Even the triumph of Sverre, the Faroese priest who claimed to be the son of Sigurðr Munn, did not bring complete peace because of ecclesiastical opposition to him. Although modern scholars would be concerned that the apparent lack of royal tax collection in the Isles implied a casual political union, it should be noted that for many decades what royal authority there was in Norway had all it could do to collect taxes within that land.[71] The expeditions of Hákon Hákonarson show that, by the mid-thirteenth century, the Norwegian monarch had recognised that if he wanted to gain from Man and the Isles he would have to collect his dues in person.

Political turmoil in Norway, approaches by the lords of Man to English kings or popes and ties between the island and the continent through church and story all indicate the European dimension to Manx affairs by the late twelfth century. The chronicle attributed to Benedict of Peterborough (but in fact the work of the well-known Roger of Howden) notes that in 1174 the papal legate Peter of St Agatha was sent north to summon the clergy of Scotland, Ireland, Galloway and the Isle of Man to the third Lateran council (1179).[72] One would have expected the summons for Man to have come by way of Norway, but the Norwegians seem to have been unworried and this is particularly interesting because one of the chronicler's informants was Archbishop Eysteinn Erlendsson of Nidaros who resided at Bury St Edmunds from 1181–2. Writing slightly later Gerald of Wales, in his *History and Topography of Ireland*, claimed that the Isle of Man properly belonged to Britain rather than Ireland because of the presence of poisonous reptiles.[73]

The surrender of the kingdom of Man and the Isles by the Norwegians to the Scots began the transition of the Isle of Man from active participant in European affairs to poorly regarded appendage. Afterwards the freedom of action enjoyed by the Manx was limited, and the island's affairs were seen merely within the context of Scots, and later English, affairs. When the Isles were formally ceded to the Scots in the treaty of Perth in 1266, the new masters of the land found an openly hostile populace. In hindsight the disposition of smaller powers such as Man and the Isles by their larger neighbours assumes a placid people accepting the inevitable. This was demonstrably not true on Man and within ten years of the Scottish annexation there had been two rebellions on Man. In 1267, the Scots king Alexander III put down a rebellion and in 1275 he was forced to return and completely defeat the Manx at the battle of Ronaldsway. So great was the dislike of a Scottish regime that Alexander's father-in-law Henry III, no stranger to rebellious subjects, had advised him to stay away from the island.[74] Its position on a frontier between Scottish and English interests ensured that the Isle of Man would furnish its battleground for the Anglo-Scottish difficulties of the late thirteenth and fourteenth centuries, and it went from Scots to English lordship for two generations before coming, permanently as it turned out, under English lordship. The establishment of English agents on the island with extraordinary powers in the fourteenth century showed how pivotal the position of Man was in the calculations of invaders. The Isle of Man did not completely disappear from a general European view. The ties extending from the Isle of Man to the continent continued after the island came under English control; the English king Edward II rewarded his friend and kinsman (on his mother's side) Henry de Beaumont with land on the island.[75] The island was important in the Bruce invasion of Ireland. The prestige of Man also continued to be recognised, and not just in Arthurian literature. The new masters of the land did not regard the island itself highly, however. In 1397 when King Richard II was destroying his opponents, Thomas de Beauchamp, the earl of Warwick, was condemned to death, but his sentence was commuted to perpetual exile on the Isle of Man.

In art, literature and politics, the Isle of Man occupied a significant place in Atlantic Europe until its loss of independence, after which it became submerged in the machinations of its masters. A location in an important economic area, and its proximity to the shores of Ireland and Britain ensured that Man exerted an influence far greater than its physical extent would suggest. The variety of contexts – Norse, Gaelic and French – within which the Isle of Man must be considered provides a remarkable insight into the changing influences in the region.

Notes

1 Broderick, *CKMI*, fol. 31r.

2 Thomas F. O'Rahilly, *Early Irish History and Mythology* (Dublin, 1976), 261; Flann Mainistrech, *Estid a eolchu cen on*, in *The Book of Leinster*, ed. R.I. Best *et al.* 6 vols (Dublin, 1954–83), i, 41–46 (43). For a full discussion, see McQuarrie in chapter 13 below.

3 Whitley Stokes and John Strachan, *Thesaurus Palaeohibernicus*, 2 vols (Cambridge, 1901–3; repr. Dublin, 1975), ii, 260; and Ludwig Bieler, *Patrician Texts in the Book of Armagh* (Dublin, 1979), 102–6. See also chapter 15, below.

4 Jocelin of Furness, *Vita Patricii* in *Acta Sanctorum*, 17 March, 540–80 (574). For the family relationships in question, see the genealogical table on p. 12 above.

5 *Íslendingabók. Landnámabók*, ed. Jakob Benediktsson, 2 vols (Reykjavik, Íslenzk fornrit no. 1, 1968), i, 51 and 136.

6 M.K. Lawson, *Cnut* (London, 1993), 107.

7 *Brennu-Njáls saga*, ed. Einar Ól. Sveinsson (Reykjavik, Íslenzk fornrit no.12, 1954), 440–1. B. Hudson, 'Brjáns Saga,' *Medium Ævum* 72 (2002), 241–68 (at 244–5).

8 Giraldus Cambrensis (Gerald of Wales), *Expugnatio Hibernica*, eds A.B. Scott and F.X. Martin (Dublin, 1978), 38; *The Song of Dermot and the Earl*, ed. G.H. Orpen (Oxford, 1892), 72–5 (lines 970–1000).

9 The chronology of Wimund's career is very uncertain, see Watt, *Fasti Ecclesiae Scoticanae*, 198; and Woolf, below pp. 334–6. See also R.A. McDonald, *Outlaws of Medieval Scotland* (East Linton, 2003), 26–7.

10 William of Newburgh, *Historia Regum Anglicanum* in R. Howlett (ed.), *Chronicles of the Reigns of Stephen, Henry II and Richard I*, 4 vols, Rolls Series, 82 (London, 1884–9), i, 73–6.

11 Reference to Wimund's landowning is made in the grant by William de Lancaster of Borrowdale to St Mary's, Byland, to settle a complaint of the former bishop against William's father; see *Report of the Historical Manuscripts Commission*, 10, Appendix, pt 4 (London, 1885), 323.

12 *Scotichronicon*, iii, 154.

13 *CDI*, i, 123 (1 May 1218).
14 *CPR, 1321–25* (19 May 1322).
15 Matthew Paris, *Chronica Majora (to 1259)*, ed. H.R. Luard, 7 vols, Rolls Series 57 (London, 1872–83), iii, 364–6.
16 Gerald of Wales, *History and Topography of Ireland*, ed. J.J. O'Meara (London, 1985), 108 (III, 101).
17 *Polychronicon Randulphi Higden Monachi Cestrensis (from the creation to 1352)*, eds. C.J. Babington and J.R. Lumby, 9 vols , Rolls Series 41 (London, 1865–86), ii, 42.
18 Orderic Vitalis, *Ecclesiastical History*, ed. Marjorie Chibnall, 6 vols (Oxford, 1969–80), book 10, chapter 6.
19 Snorri Sturluson, *Heimskringla*, ed. Bjarni Aðalbjarnarson, 3 vols (Reykjavik, Íslenzk fornrit nos. 26–28, 1941–51), i, 121.
20 *Orkneyinga saga*, ed. Finnbogi Guðmundsson (Reykjavik, Íslenzk fornrit no. 34, 1965), 8.
21 David Wilson, 'Manx Memorial Stones of the Viking Period', *Saga-Book of the Viking Society*, 18:1–2 (1970–1), 1–18, and 'Art of the Manx Crosses', in C. Fell *et al.* (eds), *The Viking Age in the Isle of Man* (London, 1983), 175–87.
22 James Graham-Campbell, 'From Scandinavia to the Irish Sea: Viking art reviewed', in Michael Ryan (ed.), *Ireland and Insular Art, A.D.500–1200* (Dublin, 1987), 144–53 (149).
23 Maylis Baylé, 'Reminiscences Anglo-Scandinaves dans la sculpture romaine de Normandie', *Anglo-Norman Studies*, 13 (1990), 35–40 (36).
24 *Eyrbyggja saga*, ed. Einar Ól. Sveinsson and Matthías Þórðarson (Reykjavik, Íslenzk fornrit, 1935), 76, and *Njáls saga*, 208.
25 *Orkneyinga saga*, 61.
26 Adémar de Chabannes, *Chronique*, ed. Jules Chavanon (Paris, 1897), 176.Those seamen might have been the source for Adémar's interesting summary of the battle of Clontarf, 177–8.
27 Benjamin Hudson, 'Cnut and the Scottish Kings', *EHR*, 107 (1992), 350–60. For the career of Echmarcach Rögnaldsson, see chapter 1 above, pp. 13–15; and B. Hudson, *Viking Pirates and Christian Princes* (Oxford, 2005).
28 Duffy, 'Irishmen and Islesmen', 94–8 and chapter 1 above.
29 B.T. Hudson, 'Knútr and Viking Dublin', *Scandinavian Studies*, 66 (1994), 319–35.
30 Arguments for the association of Echmarcach with the Isles dynasty are offered in Hudson, 'Cnut and the Scottish Kings', 355–6. An alternative identification for Echmarcach is that he belonged to the Viking dynasty of Waterford, see Duffy, 'Irishmen and Islesmen', 96, and p. 13 above.
31 See chapter 18 below, pp. 423–31. Michael Dolley, 'A Hiberno-Manx Coinage of the Eleventh Century', *Numismatic Circular* 7th Ser. 16 (1976), 75–84; Kristin Bornholdt, 'Myth or Mint? The Evidence for a Viking-age Coinage from the Isle of Man' (1999), in Davey (ed.), BAR 278, 199–220; B. Hudson, 'The changing economy of the Irish Sea Province', in B. Smith, ed., *Britain and Ireland, 900–1300* (Cambridge, 1999), 39–66 (at pp. 43–47).
32 See chapter 18 below,
33 Michael Dolley, 'Some insular(?) imitations from the 1030s of contemporary English pence of Cnut', *Spinks and Sons Numismatic Circular*, 38 (1980), 88; Mark Blackburn, 'Hiberno-Norse and Irish Sea Imitations of Cnut's Quatrefoil Type', *BNJ* 66 (1996), 1–20; Kristin Bornholdt Collins, *Viking-Age Coins Finds from the Isle of Man: A Study of Coin Circulation, Production and Concepts of*

Wealth (2003), unpublished PhD dissertation, University of Cambridge, 316–20.

34 The *Quatrefoil* imitations are heavily influenced by the Chester mint, and Blackburn has suggested that one possible location for their mint of origin may have been nearby, within the Scandinavian community in the Wirral, (1996), 14

35 A discussion of that year from a Welsh perspective is given in B.T. Hudson, 'The destruction of Gruffydd ap Cynan', *Welsh History Review*, 15 (1991), 331–50 (332).

36 B.T. Hudson, 'The Viking and the Irishman', *Medium Ævum*, 60 (1991), 257–67 (263).

37 B.T. Hudson, 'William the Conqueror and Ireland', *Irish Historical Studies*, 29 (1994), 145–58 (146).

38 See chapter One above, p. z.

39 Adam of Bremen, *Gesta Hammaburgensis ecclesiae Pontificum*, ed. Bernard Schmeidler (Hanover, 1917), 196.

40 *History of Gruffydd ap Cynan*, ed. Arthur Jones (Manchester, 1910), 136.

41 There are many studies of Magnus's expeditions, but a good survey is Rosemary Power, 'Magnus Barelegs' expeditions to the West', *SHR*, 65 (1985), 107–32, and chapter Two above; see also Duffy, 'Irishmen and Islesmen', 110–13.

42 Power, 'Magnus Barelegs' expeditions', 116.

43 Albertus Aquensis, *Historia Hiersolymitana*, in *Recueil des Historiens des Croisades* (Paris, 1879), iv, 675–8; *Heimskringla*, iii, 239–54.

44 The broad implications are discussed by R.R. Davies, *Domination and Conquest* (Cambridge, 1990).

45 R.L.G. Ritchie, *The Normans in Scotland* (Edinburgh, 1954), 350.

46 Robert of Torigni, *Chronica*, in *Chronicles of the Reigns of Stephen, Henry II and Richard I*, iv, 228–9.

47 Oliver, *Monumenta*, ii, 25.

48 Oliver, *Monumenta*, ii, 26–9.

49 Oliver, *Monumenta*, ii, 33.

50 The charter is printed by in Oliver, *Monumenta*, ii, 25.

51 Ritchie, *The Normans in Scotland*, 350.

52 *CDI*, i, 355.

53 *CDI*, i, 337. For his career, see chapter 5 above, pp. 97–100.

54 G.L. Brook, *Selections from Lagamon's Brut* (Oxford, 1963), 81 (line 2788).

55 *King Arthur's Death: Morte Arthure, Le Morte Arthur*, ed. Brian Stone (London, 1988), 34 (line 30).

56 Sir Thomas Malory, *Le Morte d'Arthur*, ed. John Lawlor and Janet Cowen (London, 1960), i, 112 (Bk. III, chapter 13).

57 Geoffrey of Monmouth, *History of the Kings of Britain*, ed. Lewis Thorpe (London, 1966), 269 (Bk. XII, chapter 2).

58 *Fergus*, ed. Ernst Martin (Halle, 1872). For discussion of the poem and identifications of the places named there see: E. Brugger, '"Pellande", "Galvoie", and "Arragoce" in the Romance of *Fergus*', in *A Miscellany of Studies in Romance Languages and Literatures presented to Leon E. Kastner*, eds Mary Williams and James A. de Rothschild (Cambridge, 1925), 94–107; and M.D. Legge, 'Some Notes on the Roman de Fergus', *Transactions and Journal of Proceedings of the Dumfries and Galloway Natural History and Antiquarian Society*, 3rd ser., 27, 163–71.

59 Ó Cuív, 'A Poem in Praise of Raghnall, King of Man', *Éigse* 8 (1955–7), 283–301.

60 Ó Cuív, 'Poem in Praise of Raghnall', p. 284 makes this suggestion.

61 *CDI*, i, 149 (4 November 1220).

62 *CDI*, i, 80 (3 January 1214).
63 *CDI*, i, 479 (14 November 1251).
64 The standard history of the Savigniacs is Claude Auvry, *L'histoire de la congrégation de Savigny*, ed. A. Laveille, 3 vols (Paris, 1896–8); see also Léon Guilloreau, 'Les fondations anglaises de l'abbaye de Savigny', *Revue Mabillon*, 5 (1909), 290–335, and J. Buhot, 'Le Abbaye Normande de Savigny', *Le Moyen Age*, 46 (1936), 1–19.
65 *The Coucher Book of Furness Abbey*, eds J.C. Atkinson and John Brownbill (2 vols in 6 parts, Chetham Soc., n.s., vols 9, 11, 14, 74, 76 and 78, 1886–1919), ii, 708–9.
66 This information is supplied by D.E. Easson, *Medieval Religious Houses: Scotland* (London, 1957), 196–8. For a detailed discussion on medieval monasticism on Man, see chapter 16 below.
67 William of Newburgh, *Historia*, i, 238.
68 This problem is discussed by Johnsen, 'Payments from the Hebrides'.
69 *Liber Luciani de laude Cestrie*, ed. M.V. Taylor (Lancashire-Cheshire Rec. Soc., 1912), 45.
70 A good English-language guide (though occasionally controversial in its opinions) to the period is by G.M. Gathorne-Hardy, *A Royal Impostor* (Oslo, 1956), 1–74.
71 Johnsen, 'Payments from the Hebrides', 18–34.
72 Benedict of Peterborough, *Gesta Regis Henrici Secundi*, ed. William Stubbs, 2 vols, Rolls Series no.49 (London, 1867) i, 210.
73 Gerald of Wales, *History and Topography of Ireland*, 67.
74 *CDS*, v, 139, no. 32.
75 *CPR, 1307–13*, 1 May 1311.

10 *Man in the Norse World*

BARBARA E. CRAWFORD

1. INTRODUCTION

The ability of the Viking colonists to settle in very different parts of Northern Europe and to adapt their culture to the circumstances of each locality is becoming better understood.[1] There is a growing understanding that Norwegian and Danish settlers were not intent on imposing their own culture to the extent of obliterating what already existed in their new colony. The actual mix of social structures which thereafter developed in the different ethnic and cultural situations is usually, however, a matter of some debate. The complex interplay of social forces involved – such as the ratio of incomer to native, of genetic mingling, of religious influence – will primarily be the concern of the archaeologist. The development of political structures, the extent of language change, the establishment of laws and governing methods, are what the historians are interested in. Each Norwegian or Danish polity is one ecotype in the wider Viking spectrum. We have to understand it against the cultural background of the host country, and in contrast to the varying experiments embarked on in the other Norwegian and Danish settlements of northern Europe and in the North Atlantic world. It is the intention of this chapter to study certain aspects of the kingdom of Man in light of what we know about the other Scandinavian political settlement in the northern British Isles, the earldom of Orkney, in an attempt to refine our understanding of its place in the wider Norse world.

Naturally enough the type of polity which developed arose from the peculiar circumstances of each locality – ethnic, political, geographical. The Icelandic Commonwealth was un-paralleled in any other Viking settlement (or in any other part of the medieval world). Although some of the reasons for this are understandable – such as the absence of any internal or external threat to the settlers – the growth of that particular form of social experiment will never cease to be a cause of wonder to students of Viking history[2]. One fact which can be learned from our knowledge of the settlement of Iceland is that the Norse had the intellectual resources to develop their own very distinctive political mechanisms in an environment free of other influences or pressures. Similarly in the Faeroes, where there was no native population with which the settlers had to come to terms, they established a society which appears to have been relatively democratic and free of hierarchical structures.[3] At least, there was no single dominant family which imposed its authority over the remainder, or gathered the bulk of the islands' resources into its own hands. The personal nature of lordship in these north Atlantic societies may be a surviving feature of the political structures in Scandinavia before kingdoms were established.[4]

1.1 Kings and Earls

The Viking settlements around the British Isles are notable for producing two long-lasting warrior dynasties. The Northern Isles (Orkney and Shetland), along with the north Scottish mainland, came under the control of a dynasty of earls in the late ninth century. This was an ON title *(jarl)* which was the preserve of certain families in Norway as a family dignity (= 'chief'). The Hebrides, including the Isle of Man, came under the sway of a dynasty which took the title of 'king' (ON *konungr)*. This title was used from the beginning of Norse settlement in the west, and Þorstein *hinn rauði* ('the Red'), son of Ketil *flatnefr* ('Flatnose'), who conquered north Scotland with Earl Sigurðr I of Orkney, is said in the Icelandic *Book of Settlements* (*Landnámabók)* to have been king over his dominions on the Scottish mainland.[5] Both titles were current in Norway, where the Viken was ruled by petty kings (ON *konungr)*, possibly under the influence of Danish custom (Danish kings exercised authority in the Oslo region from time to time). The Møre dynasty from western Norway were always earls, and it was members of this latter family which conquered the Orkney islands, and which retained the family title in their new island possession. But there was not any significant distinction between *konungr* and *jarl* at this time. Also, *rí* was used by several ranks of territorial lords in Ireland.[6] Norse rulers in the Western Isles and in Dublin continued to call themselves king, and the use of the OI *rí* in the Celtic world *may* be a relevant consideration here.[7]

Later in the medieval period (second half of the twelfth century), the author of *Historia Norvegia* comments (when discussing the islands which were by that time tributory to the kings of Norway):

> These [islands], occupied by different inhabitants, are now divided into two dominions; the southern islands are elevated to [being ruled by] kinglets, while the northern are adorned by the protection of earls: and both [kinglets and earls] pay large tribute to the kings of Norway (*quae quidem diversis incolis accultae nunc in duo regna sunt divisae: sunt enim meridianae insulae regulis sublimatae, brumales vero comitum*

> *praesidio decoratae, qui utrique regibus Norwegiae nonmodica persolvunt tributa*).[8]

By that date the rulers in the Western Isles seem to have been down-graded to *reguli* (kinglets).

2. GENERAL COMPARISONS WITH THE EARLDOM OF ORKNEY

In terms of the power and influence exercised by the kings of Man (X-ref to genealogy Figures in chap. 1) and the earls of Orkney both rulers governed island empires. These are remarkable political features which survived the demise of the Viking age. They were rather different in terms of their maritime geography. Located in the northern part of the Irish Sea, Man was detached from the Hebridean islands which constituted the major maritime part of the kingdom: this can never have been the basis for a simple political situation, particularly after the mid-twelfth century when the southern Hebrides came under the control of the sons of Somerled.[9] The Orkneys were a much more accessible collection of islands to control and administer, and although both Shetland and Caithness were detached portions of the earl's empire – both separated from Orkney by particularly turbulent stretches of water – nonetheless this situation must have presented few problems from the point of view of a maritime dynasty's controlling capabilities. Nor were the Northern Isles so vulnerable to attack or domination by neighbouring powers, which was the situation presented by Man's position in the Irish Sea, surrounded as it is by Irish, Scottish, Galwegian, Welsh and English coastal territories. However, in one significant respect Man was better protected than the Orkneys, remoter from the exercise of authority by its overlords, the kings of Norway. It was significantly further away than the Northern Isles; Shetland and Orkney were never beyond the reach of the officials of the king of Norway. The difference is exemplified in the manner in which the kings of Norway attempted to exercise control, as will be seen later.

2.1. Power bases and sources of wealth

Wealth and authority are difficult things to measure with the sparse source material available. A comparison of the income from land, from judicial rights, from economic factors – all the things which made up the wealth of earl and king, is impossible to assess. The comment in *Orkneyinga saga* that Kintyre was 'thought to be more valuable than the best of the

Hebridean islands, though not as good as the Isle of Man' (chapter 41) gives us a hint of the value which was accorded to the island in the twelfth century. The fertility of the Orkney Islands was perhaps even more remarkable considering their location at 59° N and in contrast to much of northern Scotland. Moreover, the wealth of the Orkney islands was easily controlled by the earls because of the way they are clustered together. The kings of Man had a much more difficult job to access the wealth of the Hebridean part of their island dominion, scattered as it is along the west coast of Scotland from 54° N to 58.30° N.

For a period of time in the late tenth century and again in the first half of the eleventh, the Hebrides came under the sway of the earls of Orkney, (according to the descriptions of battles in the west won by Earls Sigurðr II and Þorfinnr 'the Mighty').[10] There are many references in the *Orkneyinga saga* to several of the earls raiding in the west or looking to the west to supply them with support.[11] This was their main area of expansion and source of booty, with their sights set to access some of the wealth of the kingdom of Dublin, if the opportunity presented itself. There are no recorded occasions in this period when, conversely, the kings of Man or the Isles looked north to the Orkneys for raiding potential.[12] In the tenth and eleventh centuries opportunities for gain probably kept the kings of Man occupied within the Irish Sea zone, and, as has been shown, the island was brought within the sphere of Dublin's rulers in the mid-eleventh century.[13] In the twelfth century a close family relationship would have been established between the two dynasties when King Olaf married Ingebjorg, daughter of Earl Hakon Paulsson of Orkney (according to the *Orkneyinga saga*, although the Chronicle of Man does not refer to her by name).[14] This family link may explain why Earl Haraldr Maddadson (Ingebjorg's nephew) sought refuge in Man during his struggle with Haraldr Ungi towards the end of the century.[15]

The nodal position of the Isle of Man in the middle of the Irish Sea and with easy access to many centres of early medieval power made it an important entrepôt centre for trade and exchange of goods, (as well, possibly, of the provision of fighting men to the ambitious warlords on every side). The wealth that did flow in is dramatically demonstrated by the numbers of Viking Age silver hoards which have been found in the island.[16] The presence of hoards are however a sign of instability as much as of wealth, given that they are likely to have been buried because of fear of attack, and certainly remained buried because those who knew their whereabouts did not survive to recover their wealth. This is a phenomenon of the Hebrides also – where a similar number of hoards are recorded – as well as of the Northern Isles.[17a] Certainly the number of hoards found in Orkney and

Shetland is fewer but amongst them are included some of the largest hoards ever found in the British Isles. As a crude indicator of wealth Viking hoards tell us much about the commercial activities of the Scandinavian settlers around the coasts of Scotland and in the Irish Sea. This success may however have been achieved by individual warrior-traders and cannot give us proof of the strength of the rulers of the island groups, even though we can be quite sure that these rulers themselves were participating in the process whereby the silver artefacts and coins were acquired.

2.2. Sources of information

Evidence for the strength of the ruling dynasties comes from historical sources. Our knowledge rests therefore on the survival of such sources, and in the Northern Isles we are fortunate to have the *Orkneyinga saga* (or 'Jarls' saga'), written in Iceland *c.*1200.[18] This gives the traditional account of how it was later remembered that the dynasty of earls had established itself over the islands in the late ninth century (*O s*, chapter 4), and the descent of that dynasty up to 1231. It is a piece of saga literature, purporting to give an account of their military endeavours, and the struggles for power among the different segments of the earldom family. The most reliable information is concerned with genealogy and those sections based on the strophes of skaldic poetry which are quoted. The second half of the saga concerns the events of the twelfth century and is therefore fuller and more of a contemporary account of events, being nearer in time to the date of its composition.

It was two centuries after the appearance of the earldom of Orkney that the medieval dynasty of the kings of Man was established by Godred Crovan; although *rí Innsi Gall* ('Kings of the Isles of Foreigners') had been ruling in Man since the tenth century.[19] Unfortunately no continuous narrative has survived from that earlier period to give us a basis on which to draw conclusions about the strength of the first rulers of Man, or of their national origin.[20] From the year 1079 and the successful invasion and conquest of Man by Godred Crovan the *Chronica Regum Mannie et Insularum*[21] provides a historical basis for the succession of kings and information about their struggles to retain control of both Man and the Hebrides. It is a latin text, written by a literate cleric, probably at the behest of the one of the kings, and is a very different production from the vernacular *Orkneyinga saga*. Traditional material is used, interspersed with ecclesiastical information culled from other chronicles. Where the author is giving political history it seems that he can be relied on.[22] Other documentary source material for the deeds of the kings, especially in relation to the church is probably fuller than what has survived from Orkney in the twelfth and thirteenth centuries.[23]

3. POWER OF KINGS OF MAN COMPARED WITH EARLS OF ORKNEY

It is an interesting historical comparison to see how these Norse warlords established their authority and developed their power base; to see how the different forms of medieval polities adapted to the circumstances of the time and location. The tenth to thirteenth century was a period when many new political structures were being established in western Europe, particularly in the British Isles and in Scandinavia. The earldom of Orkney and kingdom of Man are two exceptional examples of such medieval political experiments, created by Viking adventurers and flourishing in the maritime entrepreneurial climate of the age. Their eventual demise was due to the growth and territorial expansion of the Scottish dynasty. The extension of the Norwegian kings' political authority to the maritime fringes of their colonial territories was also an important factor in the subjugation and down-grading of these petty rulers. They held sway in islands and peninsulas remote from the power centres of national kingdoms, but the arm of the medieval kings eventually reached out and brought them to heel.

At the heart of this development was the ability of dynasties to build up their power base, whether in Orkney, on Man, in Bergen or in Edinburgh, and to *maintain* their authority – usually by violence, for it was never unrivalled. The support mechanism offered by the Christian Church was also extremely important. Rulers learned that it was never to their advantage to quarrel with the Church, and ecclesiastical structures were a role model for secular authority. The Church also provided sanction for power, and the legitimisation of authority, vitally important support mechanisms for rulers. The history of the dynasties' relationship with the Church in their dominions is fundamental to our appreciation of the achievements of both earls and kings and will be looked at first.

3.1. Christian polities

As already noted the government of medieval petty principalities – and major ones – rested on ecclesiasatical structures as much as on secular ones. The pre-existing situation of some sort of Celtic church structure can be assumed in both localities, and sculptured stones provide the best evidence for the pre-existence of such structures. In both areas it was however the Roman, mainstream European forms and personnel which dominated – even in Man, where the Celtic imprint was so much stronger.

Any church structures already in existence in the islands in the pre-Norse period were severely disrupted – if not destroyed – in the ninth and tenth centuries when the Vikings dominated the seas around the British Isles and targeted monastic communities. Although there is no historical evidence of the impact of the raiders on any monastic communities in Man or in Orkney we have plenty of evidence of attacks on Iona.[24] The actual Norse settlement in both Man and Orkney is rather difficult to date, although appearing to be rather later in Man (*c.*900) than in Orkney – for by that date the earls were in power over an already established Norse population in the Northern Isles. Certainly there was a settlement of pagan warriors in Man c.900, as is known from the rich mound burials.[25] So we can assume that there was a period of pagan disruption to the established Christian society. But that the Norse newcomers absorbed local beliefs during the tenth century is clear from the magnificent cross slabs which provide evidence of Christian communities all over the island who retained their Norse language and runic script along with their northern legends.[26] Those cross slabs are of course themselves evidence for the retention of Celtic craftsmen and their art styles, and are far superior to anything of the kind surviving in the Northern Isles.

Not until the eleventh century can we be sure about the establishment of a church structure. Archaeological evidence of chapel sites is usually impossible to date closely, but the multiplicity of these small, localised places of worship in both Orkney and Man tells us that beliefs were widespread among the population at the level of farm and family. An unstructured situation eventually developed into the medieval pattern of parish and priestly hierarchy which we know well from later evidence.

3.1.1. Bishops At the top of the Roman church's hierarchy were the bishops, keyed into the European network and important players in the game of power politics. The establishment and ordering of the church structure was headed by them, and they were responsible for maintaining the due form of liturgy and standard of priesthood. They were unable to implement any of this in local societies without the support and co-operation of the secular leaders. Bishops are heard of in the Hebrides and in Orkney in the tenth and early eleventh centuries, but without any fixed power base or much authority. From a multiplicity of different bishops based at various places in the Hebrides as part of the wider Celtic ecclesiastical world, there eventually developed a single see with its cathedral in Man.[27] The earlier situation had disappeared into the mists of antiquity by the time that the chronicler started his list of bishops with Roolwer (= ON *Rolfr*) (mid-eleventh century) and admitted that he was 'ignorant of who or what sort of bishops there were before him'.[28]

The various burial places of the bishops from then until St German's cathedral was founded signify the many different links which the bishops had: Maughold on the east side of Man, Peterborough abbey, Bangor abbey, Fountains abbey, Rushen abbey in Man, and Jervaulx abbey. They may indeed reflect the superiority of different archbishops at different times,[29] and the episcopal appointments themselves indicate divergent political connections: if Roolwer can be identified with Bishop Þorolf of the Orkneys this points to the period of Earl Þorfinnr's power in the west in the 1040s–50s;[30] Gamaliel (c.1154) was an Englishman, perhaps a York appointment; Ragnald, a Norwegian, was appointed in the period after the erection of the archdiocese of Nidaros (Trondheim) in 1152–3; Cristinus of Argyll's appointment *c.*1170 most likely reflects influence from Somerled or his sons; and in the mid-thirteenth century Richard, a canon of St Andrews priory in Scotland, indicates the importance of the Scottish connections at that time. [31]

The links with Furness abbey in north-west England were particularly close, because of the special arrangement made by King Olaf I in 1134 whereby he granted the right of episcopal election to the monks, and authorised them to elect one of their own number on that occasion, asking the archbishop of York to consecrate.[32] This remarkable piece of statesmanship was clearly driven by considerations of creating a more ordered episcopal structure throughout his kingdom, as he complains that episcopal authority had been divided among 'foreigners of mercenary outlook'.[33] The situation was soon altered however by the creation of the diocese of Argyll later in the century, probably as a result of the establishment of Somerled and his dynasty in the southern Hebrides in the 1150s.[34] Before that was to happen, the diocese of the Isles was taken into the newly-erected Norwegian archdiocese of Trondheim in 1152–3, which must have strengthened the political attachment to the Norwegian kingdom, although this momentous change did not even merit a mention in the *Chronicle*.[35] The complexities of ecclesiastical politics in the Irish Sea zone at this time have been fully discussed recently, and the analysis proposed that King Olaf acquiesced in Norway's political and ecclesiastical plans in order to avoid having his bishopric absorbed into the newly-created Dublin archbishopric.[36]

In many respects the situation in Orkney is much simpler, for there were not the same number of divergent political authorities all seeking some influence: although the mainland part of the Orkney bishops' sphere of authority was drawn within the Scottish church in the twelfth century when the diocese of Caithness was created by David I.[37] The earls appear to have exercised more control over the bishops' appointments, and we know from the saga that Earl Þorfinnr was directly responsible for the establishment of a bishop's church dedicated to Christ near to his own residence at Birsay in the 1050s and the installation there of the first bishop. His descendant, Earl Rögnvald Kali Kolsson, was the initiator of the movement of the bishop's see to Kirkwall and the building of the cathedral dedicated to St Magnus in the 1130s.[38] There is no such certain evidence about the earliest episcopal churches in Man, although we can assume that some would have been founded not too far from the residence of the kings. Maughold certainly was a church of status as is clearly apparent from the early sculpture and the burial of Bishop Roolwer there in the mid-eleventh century. The cathedral was eventually built on the Holm of Peel, and it is likely that when Olaf I established one bishop for all his dominions in 1134 he attempted to settle him in that location.[39] It is said in the list of the bishops of Sodor that Bishop Simon (d.1248) was buried in St German's church 'which he himself had begun to build'.[40] The dating of the earliest parts of the cathedral is thought nonetheless to be twelfth century,[41] and it most

Fig. 10.1 *St Patrick's Church, Peel Castle. Various types of masonry are visible in the north wall of the church, indicating the complicated construction history of the building. The herringbone coursing is particularly unusual and is thought to represent a twelfth-century rebuild. (see also the plan at Fig. 20.2).*

probably replaced a previous episcopal church. That one dedicated to St Patrick, which is located on the most central and highest part of the Holm, suggests that it was an important and early ecclesiastical structure.[42] The Cathedral's position on the lower eastern slope seems to have been located so as not to encroach on the existing St Patrick's church, with its remarkable round tower.[43]

3.1.2. Off-shore Cathedrals The location of the cathedral churches of the early bishops of Orkney and of the bishops of Man in rather similar locations, on off-shore islands, can be paralleled at Selja, an island lying off the coast of Stadland, a prominent peninsula along the Norwegian west coast (X-ref map Fig. 9.4). The seat of the first bishops of western Norway was established there, before being moved to Bergen in the late eleventh century.[44] The circumstances are rather significant: the sea-route along the coast was the main means by which missionary bishops could access the heathen population of western Norway in the eleventh century. Selja was also chosen because of the legend of the holy virgin Sunniva and her followers of hand-maidens who were incarcerated in a cave on the island, and whose bones were found by King Olaf Tryggvesson in 996.[45] Here we seem to have the desired supernatural element for the new believers, to give them a holy place at a geographically significant location where the bishops established their power base,[46] at a date before towns existed in Norway. Once Bergen had developed into an economic and political centre the bishops moved their see into the urban community.The rationale behind the founding of bishops' sees on islands in Orkney[47] and Man has particularly to do with political power bases in strategic locations, and the desire to have bishops closely associated with those power bases. Indeed, the first bishops in Norse colonies needed the protection of their secular lord in circumstances in which they were trying to establish a church in a pagan or half-pagan society. The sea power which was the basis of the earls' and kings' success required fully defensible maritime locations for the power centres which they established. As far as Birsay is concerned it is likely – although not proven – that a previous Pictish power centre was taken over by the Norse earls. Once the cathedral had been moved to Kirkwall in the 1130s Birsay's significance as an earldom centre seems to have waned. On St Patrick's Isle (Peel), the church had had a presence since the early days of Christianity, probably of a Celtic monastic type.[48] There is therefore a strong sense of ecclesiastical continuity with the later establishment of the main episcopal church here.

The Holm was certainly valued by the Norse rulers for its strategic and defensive capabilities, and excavations in the 1980s found the remains of

Fig. 10.2 *Location map of the three Norse Episcopal seats on offshore islands: Peel, Birsay and Selja.*

a Norse defensive rampart which could date to the establishment of 'castles' by Magnus Barelegs in the late eleventh century.[49] It can be inferred that the kings of Man had a residence on the Holm of Peel, for two of them certainly died there,[50] and archaeological evidence of a former wooden structure may be the vestigial remains of a timber hall,[51] although the castle at Rushen became their main power centre in the thirteenth century. The last king of Man gave St Patrick's Isle to the Church probably in 1257, while in Orkney the Brough of Birsay was taken over by what is likely to have been a monastic community (from the evidence of the surviving buildings), doubtless similarly gifted by the earls.

3.1.3. Ecclesiastical Structures Matters of church organisation below the level of lord and bishop are very obscure before fuller historical evidence emerges in the later Middle Ages. The institution of a parish structure, ecclesiastical income, and appointments of clerical personnel in Orkney and Man are all evidenced from documentary sources. The Gaelic culture of the Hebrides, and the imprint of the pre-Norse Celtic church made the situation there especially distinctive. The close link between administration for secular purposes – tax and naval organisation – and church divisions makes it likely that these arrangements were distinctively developed along new lines and according to Norse initiative, although pre-existing elements may of course have been useful in establishing them.

In some respects the ecclesiastical achievements of earldom and kingdom are remarkably different. The dramatic success of the Orkney earls in promoting the cult of Magnus Erlendsson, murdered by his cousin Hakon Paulsson in 1116 in a dynastic quarrel over the sharing of power and lands is unprecedented in the Norse colonies and marks the earldom dynasty as exceptional. To have a member of a ruling dynasty enter the ranks of the saints was not only a source of prestige for the saint's successors, but also a source of wealth for the places associated with his martyrdom. The cult of the martyred prince was a phenomenon of the newly-Christianised Scandinavian north, where all three countries looked to murdered members of the royal dynasties as national saints.[52] The martyred earl of Orkney can be regarded as a similar phenomenon, symbolising the island dominion and giving its ruling family a 'national' status. Moreover he was not the only member of the earldom family who was considered to be a saint, for there was a more unofficial cult of Earl Rögnvald Kali Kolsson (Earl Magnus' nephew), in the late twelfth century.[53] It does not appear that any attempts were ever made to get murdered members of the royal house of Man recognised as saints; just as it was not a phenomenon of Irish society either, (perhaps a relevant factor as far as Man is concerned).

However, the kings of Man demonstrated their piety by founding and patronising monastic houses, above all the Cistercian monastery of Rushen, daughter-house of Furness abbey.[54] In contrast, the earls of Orkney do not appear to have been active as founders of religious houses, for there is only slight evidence for monastic foundations in Orkney, barely documented. In contrast they had demonstrated their piety by the founding and building of bishops' churches, first at Birsay, and (after the growing evidence for Earl Magnus' sanctity) at Kirkwall, where the magnificent Romanesque cathedral clearly stretched their resources (as told in the *Orkneyinga saga*), and which took several centuries to be completed. It apparently remained a private possession of the earldom family. St German's cathedral was certainly not a private foundation in the same manner, and it is likely that the funding of its construction was primarily covered by the bishops. Both these magnificent churches provided princely burial places for the members of the ruling families as well as for the bishops.

King Olaf's endowment of the Savigniac (later Cistercian) house of Furness with land at Rushen in south Man to found a daughter house there is in the tradition of all the royal and noble families of England, Scotland and Ireland in this period, and has been seen, rightly, as an event of great significance.[55] The building of Rushen abbey, close by what was to become the kings' main residence during the thirteenth century at Castletown, was the fulfilment of the kings' religious and secular aspirations according to the medieval model. It is likely that the Chronicle of Man was written by the monks at Rushen abbey to record the history of the ruling dynasty and their benefactors.

3.2. Dynastic Survival and Ruling Methods

As examples of medieval dynasties both earls and kings can be ranked as highly successful in maintaining their power and the succession of their families. Indeed the earldom of Orkney must be one of the longest continuous surviving earldoms in Europe, from its founding in the late ninth century until the resignation of the title to the kings of Scotland in 1470.[56] The kingdom of Man was in existence only so long as the Hebrides and Man were part of the Norwegian kingdom, although the Lordship of the Isles survived for some centuries longer.[57]

3.2.1. Succession The nature of the dynastic succession differed slightly, in that the kingdom of Man was indivisible (at least from the conquest of Guðröðr Crovan), but the earldom of Orkney was on various occasions in the tenth, eleventh and twelfth centuries divided between heirs, either two or three. There is no doubt that this was a weakness. The freer method of inheritance deriving from Norse custom allowed any male heir of a previous earl to claim power, even if his descent was through the female line. This led to frequent power struggles, and the opportunity for the king of Norway to exercise influence over the division of power. Dividing up the islands, including Shetland and Caithness, among claimants, meant a much reduced power base for those earls who shared the earldoms.

The kingdom of Man was also weakened by power struggles and internecine rivalries (see genealogical tree). Despite the decisive nature of Guðröðr Crovan's conquest, the principle of single rule does not seem to have been established, and his son Haraldr rebelled against Lögmaðr (his brother) for many years. Then Haraldr's three sons demanded half the kingdom from their uncle, Olaf Guðröðsson in 1152, and after having murdered the king at a meeting at Ramsey, they divided the 'island' between themselves.[58] In these circumstances it is not too surprising that the southern Hebrides were divorced from the kingdom with the rise of Somerled (son-in-law of King Olaf) and ruled independently thereafter. The murderous rivalries of the ruling dynasties in both Man and Orkney gave the kings of Norway their prime opportunity for exercising power by supporting one of the candidates from among the claimants.

3.2.2. Government of the Land In the late eleventh century those who took power in Man were a mixed breed of Norse-Celtic adventurers, whose experience of political authority had been gained in Ireland, the Hebrides, probably Scotland and Galloway and sometimes England. It would not be surprising if governmental practices showed influence from any or all of these regions. Guðröðr himself was said in the Chronicle of Man to be the son of Harold the Black of 'Ysland' (probably Islay in the southern Hebrides), but he is called 'son of mac Arailt king of Dublin' in one of the Irish Chronicles.[59] The language of the court and its culture include both Norse and Irish elements,[60] while as rulers the kings might be expected to have aspired in some respects to emulate the power and dignity of the Anglo-Saxon dynasty and its Norman successors. Olaf, son of Guðröðr Crovan, was resident at the court of Henry I of England before he returned to Man on the death of Magnus Barelegs in 1103. The experience of Anglo-Norman government may have influenced him sufficiently later to regularise the bishopric in his kingdom, grant lands and privileges to the Churches in the Isles, and endow the monastery of Rushen.

It is in the light of that Anglo-Norman influence that we can best understand the explicit statement in the Chronicle that Olaf's father, Guðröðr Crovan, granted the southern and northern parts of Man out to his followers 'on such terms that none of them should at any time dare to usurp any part of the land for himself by right of inheritance' (*tali pacto concessi ut nemo eorum aliquando auderet iure hereditario sibi aliquam Partem terre usurpare*).[61] This far one could say that Guðröðr was doing exactly what all feudal overlords attempted to ensure (and none more so than the Anglo-Norman kings of England): to retain the right of ultimate control over grants of land and to prevent their vassals from treating their fiefs as hereditary possessions. The Chronicler goes on to say 'Whence it has come to pass that up until the present day the entire island is the property of the king alone, and that all its dues belong to him' (*Unde accidit ut usque in hodiernum diem tota insula solius reqis sit et omnes redditus eius ad ipsum pertineant*). This comment must have been made in the middle of the thirteenth century (see introduction to *Cronica Regum*) and would suggest that the dynasty had been remarkably successful in retaining control over lands which may have been granted out in Man itself. This is very unlikely to have been the case with regard to the Hebridean islands further north where control must have been much more difficult to maintain.

Such a situation, of complete authority established by a warlord's conquest is modelled on the 'feudal' prototype of Anglo-Norman England. There was a later belief that Haraldr Finehair, unifying king in Norway, achieved something rather similar when he confiscated all the 'odal' (ON *oðal)* possessions of the farmers after bringing large stretches of western Norway under his sole authority.[62] The 'odal' rights of the farmers continued to be a legal reality in medieval Norwegian society however: one dynasty could not easily establish overriding authority throughout the huge country of Norway. The kings of Man were operating on a far smaller scale, and are better compared with the earls of Orkney. The rulers of the Northern Isles also had their aspirations to control all the lands of their island earldom and would probably have liked to establish firmly the tradition of their own unaided conquest of Orkney.[63] But they had to counter the determined attempts of the kings of Norway to establish superior rights, which are frequently stressed, and they also had their struggles with the Orkney 'bonder' (ON *boendr* = farmers) who insisted that they held their lands by 'odal' right[64]. These struggles manifested themselves in bargaining over some sort of inheritance tax which the earls relaxed when they needed the farmers' support.[65]

Whatever the tenurial situation had been in Man prior to Guðröðr Crovan's conquest of 1079 there seems little doubt that his conquest wiped the slate clean and saw the establishment of a strong personal control over land grants within Man itself. There is simply no evidence about the methods of landholding from the Hebrides in this period (and any Norse customs were unlikely to survive the disruption of the transfer to Scotland in the 1260s).

From the point of view of landholding therefore, the tenurial situation in Man developed within its own particular political framework and under influence from Anglo-Norman England. If we turn to other aspects of the ruler's power structure such as economic and military rights we are in a rather different situation. This is an area about which much has been written, particularly by Norwegian historians early last century who were eager to fit the evidence they found into the familiar mould of their own Norwegian history and custom.

3.2.3. *Ouncelands* (see chapter 19 below) Much work has been done recently on the ounceland and pennyland land divisions which occur all over Scandinavian Scotland, and which are peculiar to these settlements, having no equivalent in other parts of the Norse world.[66] These were valuation units for the purpose of raising land taxes of different kinds. As far as Man itself is concerned only ouncelands are relevant, for the pennylands do not appear to have existed there (perhaps because Peter's Pence was not imposed in Man).[67] The Manx term 'treen' is usually believed to derive from Gaelic *tir-unga* (= 'land-ounce'), which is the term used in the Hebrides. This land-unit is recorded no earlier than sources from the late medieval period, although it is assumed that it must have been imposed in a period of Norse dominance. The similarity of the name of the unit on which the system was based in both Orkney and the Hebrides suggests that the structure was established at the same period throughout Scandinavian Scotland, perhaps by a single overlord. But recent research suggests – as far as pennylands are concerned – that a successful economic and fiscal measure could be adopted by different overlords looking to the example of powerful neighbours.[68] It has also been argued that sophisticated assessment systems are unlikely to have been implemented anywhere before the thirteenth century.[69]

Ouncelands were probably the first of the units to be developed, and the most likely occasion in recorded history when the situation would have allowed for a single assessment system based on ounces to be imposed throughout the Northern and Western Isles was when the earls of Orkney exercised control in the west. It never happened the other way round, that kings of Man controlled the northern earldom. Therefore historians have looked to the reigns of Earl Sigurðr II 'the Stout' (*c.*980–1014) and Earl Þorfinnr 'the Mighty' (1030–*c.*1065) who are known from the sagas to have conquered and controlled the Hebrides, including Man, as being the only period in which a common taxation system could have been imposed.[70] It is unlikely that the kings of Man could have devised their own system of land assessment based on the ounce in the tenth century, a time when there does not appear to have been a strong dynasty in power in the island. Whenever it was, and by whom, these units were imposed, they fulfilled a fiscal function, and fulfilled it well enough for linguistic elements to have survived in the landscape in a remarkably persistent way. This surely tells us that the system was firmly established, and controlled by powerful rulers, whoever they were. It is certainly evidence for an efficient administration by the rulers of these island empires, the kings of Man and the earls of Orkney.

3.2.4. *Justice*

In the realm of justice there are fewer reservations about seeing the system as having its origin in a Norse model. It has sometimes been thought that there were two few reservations, for as was said many years ago, 'there is... a great temptation to reconstruct the Norse constitution of the Isles by comparison with the known practice in other places, especially Iceland'.[71] All early medieval societies had their assemblies and one might expect influences from different sources, particularly Irish, to be evident in Man's judicial arrangements. But the incontrovertible Norse character of the name for the main assembly, Tynwald, from ON *þingvöllr* (= 'assembly field') and probably also of the six divisions (sheadings), firmly indicates the Scandinavian imprint on this aspect of the Manx constitution. Much has been written on this score,[72] and more recent studies of the Vikings and their legacy certainly reinforces a recognition of their remarkable judicial arrangements which have been traced in many areas.[73]

Fig. 10.3 *Continuing the traditional use and function of Tynwald Hill: the 2003 ceremony presided over by Her Majesty Queen Elizabeth who is traditionally entitled 'Lord of Man' but might more accurately be described as 'titular owner'. On the four tiers of the hill are assembled members of Tynwald Court together with the Island's senior public office-holders. During the ceremony, Acts of Tynwald are promulgated, petitions for redress of grievance are presented and the Island's four Coroners are sworn-in. Photo: Island Photographics.*

The location of Tynwald, at the heart of the island and on a through route north– south, has a centrality and accesssibility, as Tingwall in Shetland and Finlaggan in Islay: the latter being where the Council of the Isles met in the later Middle Ages. Tynwald's main function was as the lawcourt of the kingdom (Alþing, = 'general annual assembly'), which served to maintain unity of power over the scattered Hebridean part of the kingdom, as well as to maintain the social cohesion of this very mixed society. This was similarly the function of þingvellir in Iceland, to which the farmers trekked on their sturdy ponies from all quarters of that island at midsummer each year. The Hebridean islands were also grouped into four, each of which sent eight representatives to Tynwald.[74]

There were inevitably differences in the way these assemblies functioned in practice, according to the greatly different political circumstances in the polity, and Tynwald served as an inauguration assembly, in a way which was quite irrelevant to the Icelandic þingvellir. From accounts in the Chronicle it appears that the site also became a battleground, when meetings between rival contenders for the kingship broke down in violence.[75] The situation may have been the same in Orkney although there is no reference to any inauguration ceremony for the earls. It is recorded that the two rival earls Hakon Paulsson and Magnus Erlendsson met at an assembly in 1116/17, where they both drew up their forces and got ready for battle.[76] More usually the Orkney þing was used as a meeting place of earls with the farmers (*bonder*) who wanted to curb the military and fiscal demands of the earls, and at times forced a hard bargain.

It is usually thought that the importance of the role of the assembly in Orcadian society was lessened because of the dominating position of the earls, although this was not the way it worked out in Man, where Tynwald flourished despite the power of the kings. Certainly the one known Orkney Tingwall site seems not to have been used in the later Middle Ages, and what assemblies were held were associated with the earls' *hirð* (= retinue/following) in Kirkwall.[77] The Shetland þing retained its vitality as a meeting place for all the farmers, and this no doubt was a result of the fact that Shetland was taken away from the earls of Orkney in the late twelfth century and brought directly under the rule of the Norwegian crown. The site near the archdeacon's church at Tingwall on the Shetland mainland remains an evocative memorial of the Norse past just as Tynwald on Man (see Fig. 10.3).

4. RELATIONSHIP WITH THE KING OF NORWAY

All the north Atlantic colonies established by the Vikings were claimed by the kings of Norway as part of their realm, once the kingdom of Norway itself had been established in the post-Viking area. It was not impossible for a maritime power to exercise some authority over far-flung islands; Norway managed to implement its authority in both Iceland and Greenland for a century before the union of the three Scandinavian kingdoms. Denmark thereafter became the most powerful element in the union and maintained its north Atlantic Empire until the present century; for much of that period communication between the home country and far-flung islands was scarcely more sophisticated than in the Viking age.

4.1. Royal policies towards the Norwegian colonies

If the kings of Norway were ambitious enough, and if they had peaceful conditions at home then they attempted to exercise authority in the Northern and Western Isles – and indeed did so from time to time. The most effective way of achieving this was for a king himself to launch an expedition which was large enough to impress the natives and compel them and their leaders to submit to his authority. Those heroes who loom larger than life in the sagas, such as Haraldr Finehair, Erik Blood-Axe, Olaf Tryggvesson, Magnus Barelegs and Hakon Hakonarson are the kings whose expeditions to the west were successful. Sometimes they used the islands as springboards to further their own political ambitions in the British Isles, and sometimes they launched expeditions westwards from Norway in order to strengthen their authority and enhance their esteem at home. We may have lingering doubts – and some have more than lingering doubts – about the extent to which we can use the statements in the sagas to establish exactly what these kings achieved in their campaigns west-over-sea. However all of these kings were remembered in skaldic poetry as successful war leaders, and if Man is also mentioned in the poetry as the furthest point on the war route south we can have some confidence in believing that they made use of the island's resources in their campaigns in the Irish Sea.

The most dubious is, not surprisingly, the first, and Haraldr Finehair's campaigns as recorded in his saga are not generally considered to be entirely historically acceptable. As he was the first king to establish some sort of authority in both eastern and western Norway at the end of the ninth century it is thought unlikely that he would have been able to exercise control in the islands round the British Isles as well. Nonetheless skaldic poetry refers to his success against the Scots and there was a later belief that he granted the Orkney earldom out to the first earl, Rognvald of Møre.[78] Whether we can accept the story about his conquest of the Isle of

Man, which he found 'bare both of people and goods' because the inhabitants had fled for fear of his coming, is more doubtful.

Olaf Tryggvesson is a historically-authenticated king of Norway, whose participation in the raids on Aethelred's England in the second Viking Age of the late tenth century is confirmed by Anglo-Saxon sources. There is no doubt about the wide-ranging nature of his raiding, lauded by his court poet Hallfreðr Vandraedaskald who lists the scenes of his activity around the British Isles, including Man.[79] He made his way back home in 996 to claim power in Norway – which was when he stopped off in the Orkneys and is said to have forced Earl Sigurðr to accept Christianity and acknowledge his overlordship.[80] It was the period when successful kings were still winning wealth and military followings through Viking activity abroad, and were trying to impose their authority over far-flung maritime networks. Olaf may have exacted tribute in acknowledgement of his military superiority, but he did not possess the resources to impose a permanent network of administrators and tax collectors or to create a political structure. When did that happen?

It could only happen once the kings of Norway had created a kingdom at home with the requisite administration manned by clerical personnel who had the learning and skill to run a bureaucracy. This slowly developed during the eleventh century with completion of the conversion process and establishment of a church hierarchy. Along with this went the aspiration to create an empire, on the model of the famous Christian emperors such as Constantine and Charlemagne, and to extend practical authority over those lands west-over-sea which had been settled by Norwegian vikings and which the kings considered to be their 'skattlands'.

4.1.1. Man a 'skattland' of Norway The 'skattlands' were those parts of the Norwegian realm which lay outside the frontier of the kingdom but which paid 'skatt' (ON *skattr* = tax/tribute) in acknowledgement of the Norwegian kings' overlordship. The nature of this 'skatt' and the amount demanded must have varied markedly according to the circumstances of each locality, and there is very little hard evidence to be certain about it. The province on the frontiers with Sweden, Ævre Telemark, paid only a calfskin in render.[81] The skatts from Orkney and Shetland were much heavier and well-documented in late medieval rentals,[82] when the kings' official (ON *sysselmaðr*, anglicised to 'sysselman') and his earl had full control over the collection, and probably usage, of the corn, malt, butter, cloth and fish-oil renders from the Northern Isles. But how these were divided up between earl and king is not very clear, and no doubt there were different conditions imposed when different earls came to terms with the kings, starting with Earl Haraldr's loss of income in 1195. Before this happened the earls had paid personal tribute to the kings whose overlordship they acknowledged, as is stated clearly in the *Historia Norvegiae* (see above).

When did a king of Man enter into a formal relationship with his Norwegian overlord and of necessity have to promise to pay some sort of tributary render? Historians have said this happened when Guðröðr Óláfsson went to Norway in the middle of the twelfth century, because of his problems with the claims of Somerled.[83] It seems likely, however, that a formal treaty defining the position of the king of Man under the Norwegian crown would have been established during the expeditions of Magnus Barelegs at the end of the previous century, when he spent some time (six years according to the Chronicle) in the kingdom. Orderic Vitalis' comment that he lived for a time on the Isle of Man, which was deserted, 'and replenished with inhabitants, and fully supplied it with houses and other necessaries for human use'[84] indicates policies going somewhat beyond the raiding and tribute-taking of his predecessors. Moreover, the treaties which Magnus made – with Muircheartach, king of Ireland and with the king of Scotland – suggest that there was some intention to establish a permanent political relationship with those neighbouring kingdoms around Man and the Isles. The 'offer', said to have been made by the king of Scots, Malcolm Canmore (or more probably his successor Edgar who ruled from 1094), to allow Magnus to have all the islands off the west coast of Scotland which could be sailed around with rudder set created an artificial break between the islands and any settlements established by Norse colonists on the mainland coast of Scotland.[85]

Such an arrangement reflects a growing concept of 'terrestrial empire' which became the norm in medieval Europe, and signals the eventual demise of any Viking sea kingdom. For the next one and a half centuries however Man and the Isles remained politically part of the Norse world, as one of the 'skattlands' of the Norwegian king.

4.2. A 'tributary' or 'feudal' relationship?

What this meant in practice clearly depended on the political situation in Norway and the inclination of individual kings to exercise their authority in the west. Between the well-known expeditions by powerful Vikings and kings were long periods of time when weak kings ruled, or when power was divided among two or even three claimants, punctuated by outbreaks of civil war. It was however expected that the kings of Man would make a tributary payment to each new king in Norway. The clearest statement about this comes from the account of Robert of Torigni, abbot of Mont St Michel, of a meeting which took place in 1166 at his abbey, between Henry II of England, William the Lion of Scotland and the bishop of Sodor and Man. The abbot describes the position of the kings of Man in relation to the king of Norway, from whom they held their islands:

> These thirty-two islands the king of the Isles holds of the king of Norway in such tribute (*tali tributo*) that, when a new king succeeds, the king of the Isles gives to him ten marks of gold, and does naught else for him in his whole life, unless again another king is appointed in Norway.[86]

The fact that Robert of Torigni took the trouble to describe this payment suggests that he found it of interest, and thought it signified a rather different relationship between the kings of Man and Norway than that with which he was familiar in the feudalised world of the Anglo-Norman kings. However, A.O. Johnsen argued strongly that this form of *tributum* was in reality a feudal due and signified that the king of Man 'held his kingdom (as a fief) of the crown of Norway against the payment of ten gold marks rendered to every Norwegian king on his accession'.[87]

That is perhaps how the situation may appear from non-feudalised Norway, but in the feudal world of Robert of Torigni it was probably considered rather peculiar (which would explain why he is commenting on it). For a start he calls the payment *tributum*, and not *relevium*; he takes care to explain that it was paid on the accession of each new king of Norway (and not on the death of the vassal, for the renewal of the heir's claim on the family estate); and he states that nothing else was done for the rest of his life by the king of Man. This implies that there were none of the normal duties incumbent on a feudal vassal such as the military obligation to serve his overlord when required, to attend his court on demand, or to pay other casualties on the knighting of the lord's heir, or the marriage of his daughter. Nor apparently did the king of Man have to consult about the marriages of *his* sons and daughters, which would be customary in the 'real' feudal world.

It seems to be stretching the meaning of 'feudal' and 'relief' too far to contend that these terms can describe the nature of the relationship between the kings of Man and their overlords, the kings of Norway. It was rather a personal payment that was made to each Norwegian king, and if previous Norwegian historians were a little ambitious in translating this into 'taxes', implying a regular imposition, it does not help to suggest that the relationship was instead exactly on the lines of feudal relationships as known in western Europe. Inevitably it was far looser, and a more personal relationship, cemented by some form of submission, or doing of homage which would be performed, probably in person, when the ten gold marks were handed over to each new king of Norway. Even this would rest on the circumstances of the day in both Norway and the Hebrides.

It was rather different in the Orkney earldom: the saga-writer suggests that the kings of Norway took some care and trouble to incorporate the earls into their 'hird' (military following) and bind them into a personal relationship with oaths. The eleventh-century earls are said to have visited the kings in Norway for this purpose, and it became customary for each new claimant to the earldom to do so, in order to receive confirmation of his claim. When there were disturbed conditions in Norway and no one king had full power, this arrangement lapsed. Re-assertion of superiority would be made by the next king who had ensured his position sufficiently to be able to go west himself (as Eystein Haraldsson did in 1152), and confront the earl in his own territory (indeed on that occasion he confronted the earl in Thurso in his Scottish earldom which shows how ineffective the power of the kings of Scots was in the northern part of their kingdom). Earl Haraldr Maddason paid three gold marks to ransom himself 'and handed over authority to King Eystein, agreeing to be his liegeman for the remainder of his life; so the Earl became the King's subject under sworn oath' (*iarl leysti sik út # rimr morkum gulls, en hann gaf ríki sitt í hendr E.konungi, svá at hann skyldi at honum halda iafnan sídan. Gerdisk iarl þá maðr E. konungs ok batt þat svardogum*).[88]

At the same date Guðröðr Olafsson, son of the ruling king of Man, took the unusual step of going to Norway in order to submit to Eystein's co-king, Inge Haraldsson. The Chronicle of Man says specifically that he did homage (*hominium suum ei fecit.* f.36r). This visit coincided with the creation of the archdiocese of Trondheim, which included the diocese of Sodor and Man.[89] It must have been the situation created by Guðröðr's relationship with his Norwegian overlord which was reported to Robert of Torigni in 1166.

4.2.1. The Submissions of 1195 and 1210 Guðröðr's successors wisely kept clear of the factions which formed in Norway and which turned into civil war during the whole of the latter decades of the twelfth century. Earl Haraldr Maddadson of Orkney was not so wise and allowed himself to become implicated in the rising of the *Eyiaskjeggar*, the 'Island beardies' who attempted to replace the imposter Sverre on the throne with Magnus Erlingsson's son. This failed and was the reason for the confiscation of Shetland which was brought directly under the Norwegian crown in 1195. Earl Haraldr paid dearly, losing Shetland, and having to divide the judicial fines from his earldom with the king, who put 'sysselmen' in the islands alongside the earl.[90] This marked the beginning of a decline in the earls' independence and the extent of their authority, and the development of the honour into something approaching an official appointment.

When the civil wars finally drew to a close in Norway in 1208, the kings of Man and the earls of Orkney at the time paid visits to Norway to renew their relationship with King Inge Bárðsson; the account of their treatment indicates that a significant difference had developed in their status. Of course the two earls, David and John, were paying for their father's intransigent behaviour after the death of Sverre when Earl Haraldr had murdered the 'sysselman' and seized all the rights which had been taken over by the crown; his two sons therefore prepared the ground by dispatching Bishop Bjarni to Norway as their envoy in 1209 and taking him with them when they submitted their case to King Inge and Earl Hakon the next year. They had to pay a large fine, and give security and hostages; they had to swear loyalty and obedience: 'But in the end, King Ingi made them his earls over Orkney and Shetland, upon such terms as were adhered to until their death-day'.[91] We do not know exactly what these conditions (ON *vilkör*) were, but the clear implication is that the earls were tied down with very specific terms of appointment which must have reduced their freedom of control over the islands and changed the character of their authority.

Nothing of the sort is said about the kings of Man. They were frightened into becoming reconciled with Inge as a result of a plundering raid in 1209,[92] and they also went to Norway to renew their relationship. The saga says that they paid the outstanding taxes (*skatta*) which were due, swore an oath of allegiance (*trúnaðareiða)*, (translated as 'fealty and allegiance' by Johnsen),[93] received their lands in fief (*tóku síðan löndin í lèn)*, and went home again. There is no mention of them being made kings. The 'skatt' was clearly the tribute which had never been paid to Sverre or his son Hakon, as well as that due to Inge, in return for which they were granted their lands in 'len'.

The 'len' was a grant of royal estate or emolument made to a close follower (*håndgangnemann)* of the Norwegian king, and it is generally translated as 'fief'; but the system was not as prevalent or as structured as the word 'fief' implies. Such 'len' could be made as personal favours or as more official grants. Its use in the early thirteenth century possibly indicates that the kings wished to regard the kingdom of the Isles as on a par with grants of royal estate to their 'hirdmenn'. This was hardly the case, and the kings of Man are most unlikely to have regarded their kingdom in this light. Indeed not many years later King Rögnvaldr expressly stated, when promising to pay a yearly tribute of 12 marks stirling to the papacy, that the Isle of Man belonged to him by hereditary right, and without any obligation of service to anyone (*quae ad nos iure hereditario pertinet, et de qua nulli tenemur aliquod servitium facere*).[94] Although Johnsen may say that this was in open contradiction to his obligations to Norway,[95] in actual fact Rögnvaldr did hold his kingdom by hereditary right, for he inherited his title without having to go to Norway for confirmation, as the earls of Orkney had to do. Nor does it seem that he or his predecessors were tied down by feudal obligations of service.

By agreeing to hand his kingdom over to the papal see in 1219 Ragnvald was trying to play the same game as King John of England had done some years earlier, in order to gain a march over his ecclesiastical enemies. He would have seen no reason to desist from doing so by reason of having previously sworn a general oath of loyalty to a secular overlord. So one cannot really castigate him for being 'a somewhat self-centred and faithless man of the viking type who did not take his agreements and oaths seriously'.[96] By swearing fealty to the English king in return for a grant of land in Ulster, he was doing no more than the earls of Orkney always did by holding two earldoms from two different overlords for most of the Middle Ages. This was not a contemptible situation, and the concept of 'liege' loyalty was supposed to help prioritise multiple relationships with different feudal overlords. It merely indicates that we are dealing with ambitious men who were striving to survive in a dangerous world and maintain their influence on the political stage. The kings of Man must always have had to juggle their priorities with regard to the powerful neighbours who surrounded them on every side of their maritime dominion – and with their ecclesiastical overlords.

4. 3. Events of 1263

However, this could of course lead to a very difficult situation if the political circumstances were such that the vassal had to choose between overlords to whom he had sworn fealty, and who would expect him to support their interests in the event of war. The development of strained relations between Scotland and Norway leading to the events of 1263 provides the classic example of such a situation for both the earl of Orkney and the king of Man. In Hakon Hakonarson (IV) they had a Norwegian overlord who had a sustained policy of strengthening and extending his overseas empire. He built up closer contacts with the kings of Man than had existed at any previous time in the history of the Hebridean kingdom, culminating in him bestowing his daughter in marriage to Haraldr Óláfsson in 1248.

However, the naval expedition of 1263 showed up the insuperable difficulties of maintaining any permanent authority in the Hebrides, despite this linking of King Haraldr into the royal household The more determined the Norwegian king was to exercise authority over the Hebrides, the more he attempted to firm up his relationship with the kings, the more doomed was his policy. The Norse world was no longer the maritime diaspora that it had once been. Terrestrial polities were now the forces to be reckoned with, and the kingdom of Scotland was a strong and growing entity which would not tolerate the exercise of power by a foreign king in the island domain off its western seaboard. The 'Norseness' of the islands had become thinned by centuries of cultural mingling with the societies around the Irish Sea.

Even in the Orkneys, which remained part of the Norwegian kingdom for another two centuries, the earl's Scottish bonds seem to have been stronger: for although Earl Magnus III was in his earldom to welcome the Norwegian fleet in August 1263, he disappeared from the scene thereafter and took no further part in the expedition or even in the sad events of the following winter when King Hakon stayed in the Orkneys and died there.[97] In the medieval world of hard political realities Earl Magnus's non-presence in his Norwegian earldom at this time would appear to tell us something about his priorities.

The tenuous connection of Man with Norway was finally broken by the Treaty of Perth in 1266. It had survived for as long as it did because it suited the Hebridean kings' desire for independence to be nominally subject to a remoter overlord, to whom irregular payments of tribute were due, than to be monitored by feudal kings who were closer to hand. Norwegian naval power could be a useful asset for these petty kings who had internal strife to contend with as well as the constant struggle to maintain their independence from Scottish, English or Irish depredations. One can but admire their success in balancing adroitly in a sea of uncertainty for so long.[98]

CONCLUSION

This attempt to define the kingdom of Man's place in the Norse world is inevitably partial and superficial. It should be complemented by attempts to define Man's place in the Irish, or Anglo-Norman world.[99] The conclusions drawn are influenced by the perceptions one has from a basis of particular knowledge of other societies. Manx historiography has been influenced by the viewpoints of English, Norwegian and Irish historians and philologists who interpret the evidence according to their own expertise in other cultural and linguistic situations.

As with most island societies the influences came in from all directions, and the Isle of Man was subject to a greater diversity of cultural influences than the Orkney Islands. The mix of cultures which can be perceived in the sources used above relate to the level of ruler and court.[100] For the whole of the medieval period few other sources have survived which can tell us anything about the general population, except perhaps the place-names which require expertise of a different kind (see chapter 12). Further archaeological excavation will be able to expand and deepen our knowledge of the cultural mix of medieval society in Man and the Isles.[101]

Notes

1 See P. Sawyer, ed., *The Oxford Illustrated History of the Vikings* (Oxford, 1997); D.Hadley and J. Richards (eds), *Cultures in Contact. Scandinavian Settlement in England in the Ninth and Tenth Centuries* (Turnhout, 2000); C. Batey and J. Graham-Campbell, *Vikings in Scotland. An Archaeological Survey* (Edinburgh, 1998); J.H. Barrett (ed.), *Contact, Continuity and Collapse. The Norse Colonization of the North Atlantic* (Turnhout, 2003) for recent publications concerning the Viking settlements in the British Isles.

2 See or example J. Byock, *Medieval Iceland. Society, Sagas and Power (*1988).

3 S. Arge, 'On the Landnam of the Faroe Islands' and H.J. Debes, 'Problems concerning the earliest Settlement in the Faroe Islands', in *The Viking Age in Caithness, Orkney and the North Atlantic*, C. Batey *et al.* (eds), (1993).

4 T. Lindqvist in *The Cambridge History of Scandinavia,* I, K. Helle (ed.), (2003), 162.

5 *Landnámabók. Book of Settlements,* trans. H. Palsson and P. Edwards (Winnipeg, 1972): this is not, however, mentioned in the *Orkneyinga saga.*

6 R.A. MacDonald, *The Kingdom of the Isles* (Edinburgh, 1997), 59.

7 B.E. Crawford, *Scandinavian Scotland* (1987), (hereafter referred to as *Scand. Scot.*) 92. Perhaps too much has been made of the Irish use of *rí* and MacDonald's comments (*Kingdom of the Isles* p.31) are not strictly accurate, for the use of *konungr* is well-established in south Norway at this time.

8 G. Storm, ed., *Monumenta Historica Norvegiae* (1880), 88; english translation from A.O. Anderson, *Early Sources of Scottish History* (hereafter referred to as *Early Sources*) 1, 330. New English translations of *Historia Norvegiae* have appeared since this chapter was written: see *A History of Norway...* trans. D. Kunin, ed. C. Phelpstead (Viking Society for Northern Research Text Series vol.XIII, London, 2001); *Historia Norvegiae*, I. Ekrem and L.B. Mortensen (eds), trans. P. Fisher (Museum Tusculanum Press, University of Copenhagen, 2003).

9 MacDonald, *Kingdom of the Isles*, chapter 3.

10 See recent article discussing the situation at the end of the tenth century by Colman Etchingham, 'North Wales, Ireland and the Isles: the Insular Viking Zone', *Peritia,* 14 (2001), 145–87 and B. Crawford, 'The earls of Orkney and the Hebrides' in *Gall-Ghaidheil: the Western Isles in the Viking World*, M.MacLeod and C. Batey (eds) (forthcoming).

11 Crawford, *Scand. Scot*, 68, 74.

12 Later in the Middle Ages such raids are recorded (*Records of the Earldom of Orkney*, ed. J.S. Clouston, SHS second series 7, 1914, no.XXIII, s.a.1461) when 'caterans and men of Sodor and Ireland' raided and devastated the fertile lands

of the Orkney islands.

13 S. Duffy, 'Irishmen and Islesmen in the kingdoms of Dublin and Man, 1052–1171', *Eriu*, xliii (1992), (hereafter referred to as Duffy, 'Irishmen and Islesmen').

14 See note by P.A. Munch to his edition of the Chronicle, p.167 (full reference in note 20 below).

15 *Ibid.* 182. King William of Scotland then granted Ragnvald (Reginald) of Man Earl Harald's Scottish earldom of Caithness which cannot have helped good relations between the two.

16 J. Graham-Campbell , 'The Viking-Age Silver Hoards of the Isle of Man' in *The Viking Age in the Isle of Man*, ed. C. Fell *et al.* (1983); K. Bornholdt, 'Myth or Mint? The evidence for a Viking-Age coinage from the Isle of Man', in P. Davey, (ed.), *Recent Archaeological Research on the Isel of Man (*BAR British Series 278, 1999), 199–218.

17 J. Graham-Campbell, 'The Viking-age silver and gold hoards of Scandinavian character from Scotland', *PSAS*, (1975–6), 114–35; *Ibid.*, *The Viking-Age Gold and Silver of Scotland*,1994.

18 Hereafter cited as OS. The authoritative Icelandic edition by F. Guðmundsson is published by Íslenzka Fornritafélag, vol. XXXIV (1965). The most convenient English translation is by H. Palsson and P. Edwards, *Orkneyinga Saga. The History of the Earls of Orkney* (Penguin, 1981).

19 MacDonald, *Kingdom of the Isles*, 31.

20 The Irish evidence tells of links with Dublin and shows how struggles to control Dublin could involve assertion of authority over Man also (Duffy,'Irishmen and Islesmen', 9)

21 *The Chronicle of Man and the Sudreys*, trans. and eds P.A. Munch and Dr R. Goss (Manx Society, Isle of Man, 1874); *Cronica Regum Mannie et Insularum, Chronicles of the Kings of Man and the Isles*, transcribed and translated by George Broderick, 1996 (hereafter cited as *Cron. Regum*)

22 A. Harrison, 'Sources for the Documentary History of Peel Castle' in *Excavations on St. Patrick's Isle, Peel, Isle of Man 1982–88*, David Freke (Liverpool, 2002), 15–16.

23 See list of documentary material relating to Man catalogued as Regesta Sodorensia in *Regesta Norvegica I 822–1263*, ed. E. Gunnes (Kjeldeskriftfondet 1989) 312–30.

24 Crawford, *Scand. Scot.*, 44–6; D.N. Dumville, '*The Churches of North Britain in the First Viking Age*' (Whithorn, 1997), 19.

25 J. Graham-Campbell, 'The Early Viking Age in the Irish Sea area' in *Ireland and Scandinavia in the Early Viking Age*, H.B. Clarke *et al.* (eds), (Dublin, 1998), 116–20.

26 S. Margeson, 'On the iconography of the Manx crosses', *The Viking Age in the Isle of Man*, C.Fell *et al.* (eds), (London, 1983), 95–106.

27 D.E.R. Watt and A.L. Murray (eds), *Fasti Ecclesiae Scoticanae Medii Aevi Ad Annum 1638* (rev. edn Edinburgh, 2003); D.E.R. Watt, 'Bishops in the Isles before 1203: Bibliography and Biographical Lists', *The Innes Review*, XLV, (1994), 99–119; A. Ashley, *The Church in the Isle of Man*, 1948.

28 *Cron. Regum* f.50v; see recent analysis of the succession to the see of Man by A. Woolf, 'The Diocese of the Sudreyar' in S. Imsen, (ed.) *Ecclesia Nidrosiensis 1153–1537. Søkelys på Nidaroskirkens og Nidarosprovinsens historie.* Senter for Middelalderstudier. NTNU Skrifter nr.15 (Trondheim, 2003),171–82.

29 *Early Sources*, ii, 382n.

30 Barbara E. Crawford, 'Bishops of Orkney in the eleventh and twelfth centuries: Bibliography and Biographical Lists', *Innes Review*, XLVII (1996), 7.
31 Watt and Murray, *Fasti*, 259–60.
32 *The Coucher Book of Furness Abbey* (Chetham Society, Manchester, 1886–7, 1915–19), ii, 708–9; *Monumenta de Insula Manniae*, ed. J.R. Oliver (Manx Society, Isle of Man, 1860–2), ii, 1–3; MacDonald, *Kingdom of the Isles*, 207–8; I. Beuermann, *Man amongst kings and bishops – What was the reason for Godred Olafsson's journey to Norway in 1152/53?* Centre for Viking and Medieval Studies, University of Oslo, Occasional Papers 4/2002, 205.
33 Watt, 'Bishops in the Isles', 111.
34 D.E.R. Watt, 'Argyll', in *Series Episcoporum Ecclesiae Catholicae Occidentalis*, series VI, Tomus I, Ecclesia Scoticana, 11 (1994); MacDonald, *Kingdom of the Isles*, 212.
35 Beuermann, *Man amongst kings and bishops*, 221.
36 *Ibid*. 230–2.
37 B.E. Crawford, 'Caithness' in *Series Episcoporum* (as in note 31), 30; *ibid*., 'Bishops of Orkney in the eleventh and twelfth centuries', *Innes Review*, xlvii (1996), 1–13.
38 W.P.L. Thomson, *The New History of Orkney* (2nd. edn 2001),104–5.
39 B.E. Crawford, 'Birsay-Peel-Selja. Three Norse Bishops' seats on off-shore islands. A Comparative Study' in *Kirkearkeologi og Kirkekunst. Studier tilegnet Sigrid og Håkon Christie* (Øvre Ervik, 1993), 25.
40 *Cron. Regum*., fol.51r.
41 D.S. Dugdale, *Manx Church Origins* (1998), 172; see *Excavations on St. Patrick's Isle*, 141–2 for evidence of a possible earlier structure below the present Cathedral.
42 D. Freke, 'The Setting and Background to the Site' in Freke, *Excavations on St. Patrick's Isle*, 13.
43 Crawford, 'Birsay-Peel-Selja', 29.
44 K. Helle, *Camb. Med. His. Scand*., 155.
45 *Saga Ólafs Tryggvasonar af Oddr Snorrason munk*, extracts in *Selja-heilag stad I 1000år*, ed. M. Rindal (Oslo, 1997), 299–310.
46 *Idem*., 26; also see B.E. Crawford, 'Holy Places in the British Isles. Some Parallels to Selja', in *Two Studies on the Middle Ages*, ed. M. Rindal, KULT's Skrifterie, no.66 (1996), 22.
47 It should noted that the question of whether the bishop's seat was on the Brough of Birsay or on the coast opposite is a matter of dispute (see Crawford, *Scand. Scot*., 184–90 for a discussion of the evidence).
48 D.Freke,*The Peel Castle Dig* (Douglas, 1995), 13.
49 *Ibid*, 28.
50 Freke, 'The Setting', 14.
51 Freke, *Peel Castle Dig*, 30–2.
52 K. Helle, 'Introductory Survey' to 'The High Medieval Kingdoms' in K. Helle (ed.), *Cam. His. Scand*., 247. The Scottish dynasty had also acquired a saintly member (Queen Margaret) in the the 11th century, although she was not canonised until the 13th century.
53 B.E. Crawford, 'St. Magnus and St. Rognvald, the Two Orkney Saints', *Records of the Scottish Church History Society*, 28 (1998), 23–38.
54 MacDonald, *Kingdom of the Isles*, 218.
55 A.W. Moore, *A History of the Isle of Man*, i (1977), 164–5; MacDonald, *Kingdom of the Isles*, 218.

56 B.E. Crawford, 'Orkney in the Middle Ages' in *The Orkney Book*, ed. D. Omand (2003), 64.
57 MacDonald, *Kingdom of the Isles*, chapters 3 and 4.
58 *Cron. Regum.*, fol.36r–36v.
59 Duffy, 'Irish men and Islesmen', 14–15.
60 See B. Megaw 'Norseman and Native in the Kingdom of the Isles', *Scottish Studies*, (1975–6); 19–20: M. Gelling 'Norse and Gaelic in Medieval Man; the place-name evidence' in *The Vikings* eds, T. Andersson and K. Sandred (1978), 107–18; and most recent assessment by A. MacDonald, *The Kingdom of the Isles*, 1996, 33, where the dominance of the Norse element is assumed in the 10th and 11th centuries.
61 *Cron. Regum.*, f.33r.
62 See discussion of the meaning of the term oðal *in* Crawford, *Scand. Scot.*, 199; and a more recent analysis of Harald's supposed confiscation in C. Krag, 'The Early Unification of Norway' in *Camb. Med. His. Scand.*, ed. K. Helle, 188.
63 Crawford, *Scand. Scot.*, 53.
64 *Idem.*, 200–1.
65 *OS* chapters 11 and 76.
66 See fig. 24 in Crawford, *Scand. Scot.*; L. Macgregor and B.E. Crawford (eds), *Ouncelands and Pennylands* (1987); W.P. Thomson, 'Ouncelands and Pennylands in the West Highlands and Islands', *Northern Scotland*, 22 (2002), 27–43; D. Rixson, *The West Highland Galley* (1998), 55–60
67 B.E. Crawford, 'Norse Earls and Scottish bishops in Caithness' in *The Viking Age in Caithness, Orkney and the North Atlantic*, C. Batey, J. Jesch and C.D. Morris (eds), 1994, 137–43, (particularly 142–3).
68 Thomson, 'Ouncelands and pennylands', 41.
69 P.S. Andersen, 'When was Regular, Annual Taxation Introduced in the Norse islands of Britain? A Comparative Study of Assessment Systems in North-Western Europe', *Scandinavian Journal of History*, xvi (1991); see discussion by Crawford in 'The Earls of Orkney and the Hebrides' (forthcoming).
70 Crawford, *Scand. Scot.*, 86–8; Thomson, *New History of Orkney*, chapter 15.
71 B.R.S. and E.M. Megaw, 'The Norse Heritage in the Isle of Man', in *The Early Christian Cultures of North-West Europe*, ed. B. Dickens and C. Fox (1956), 168.
72 C.J.S. Marstrander, 'Om Tingsteder på Man', *Norsk Tidsskrift for Sprogvidenskap* x (), 384–93 ; R.A. Curphey, *Ancient Centres of Government of the Isle of Man* (no date); G.V.C. Young, *The History of the Isle of Man under the Norse* (Peel, 1980), chapter 9.
73 Crawford, *Scand. Scot.*, 204–10; B.E. Crawford, *Scandinavian Settlement in Northern Britain* (1995), 17–20; G. Fellows-Jensen, 'Tingwall: the Significance of the Name' in *Shetland's Northern Links. Language and History*, ed. D.J. Waugh (1996), 16–29.
74 Megaw, 'Norse Heritage', 167.
75 *Cron. Regum.*, fols 44 and 45.
76 *O S* chapter 47.
77 Crawford, *Scand. Scot.*, 204.
78 *Heimskringla. The Saga of Harald the Fairhaired*, chapter xxii; *OS*, chapter 4; Crawford, *Scand. Scot.*, 52–3.
79 *Heimskringla. King Olaf Trygvesson's Saga*, chapter xxxi.
80 *OS*, chapter 12.
81 *Kulturhistorisk Leksikon for Nordisk Middelalder* (Copenhagen, 1956–78),

(hereafter cited as *KL*) sub *skattland*.

82 W.P.L. Thomson, *Lord Henry Sinclair's 1492 Rental of Orkney* (1996).

83 A.O. Johnsen, 'The Payments from the Hebrides and the Isle of Man to the Crown of Norway 1153–1263. Annual ferme or feudal casualty?'*SHR*. xlviii, 1969, 18–19 and where previous historians' opinions are conveniently summarised (hereafter referred to as Johnsen, 'Payments from the Hebrides').

84 Quoted in A.O. Anderson, *Scottish Annals from English Chroniclers (*1908), 120, n.3.

85 *OS*, chapter 41; Anderson, *Early Sources*, II, 102–18 for all the sources connected with Magnus Barelegs' expeditions; Crawford, Scand. Scot., 25. Also see Power, chapter 2, this volume.

86 A.O. Anderson, *Scottish Annals from English Chroniclers A.D.500 to 1286* (1908, 1991), 245.

87 Johnsen, 'Payments to the Crown of Norway', 18–34.

88 *OS*, chapter 91; trans. Palsson and Edwards, 164; Guthmundsson, *ÍF*, 240.

89 See recent study of this event in Beuermann, *Man amongst kings and bishops*.

90 *OS* chapter 112; B.E. Crawford, 'Harald Maddadson' in the *New Dictionary of National Biography* (2004).

91 Ingi Bardsson's Saga, trans. in *Early Sources*, ii, 380–1.

92 R. Power, 'Scotland in the Norse Sagas' in *Scotland and Scandinavia*, ed. G. Simpson (Edinburgh 1990), 17; the kings are named as Ragnvald (Godredsson) and Godred (his son) in the saga.

93 'Payments from the Hebrides', 23, where the Old Norse text is quoted (n.3).

94 *Diplomatarium Norvegicum*, xix, no. 123.

95 'Payments from the Hebrides', 25.

96 *Ibid*., 24.

97 Thomson, *New History of Orkney*, 2001, 87; B.E. Crawford, 'The earldom of Caithness and the Kingdom of Scotland 1150–1266', in *Essays on the Nobility of Medieval Scotland*, ed. K.J. Stringer (1985), 38.

98 K. Helle (1971), 9.

99 As now in Beuermann, *Man amongst kings and bishops*.

100 See Megaw's classic assessment in 'Norse and Native'.

101 As, for example, recent discoveries at the excavations of Norse sites in South Uist; see M. Parker Pearson *et al*., *Archaeology and History of a Hebridean Island* (Tempus, 2004).

11 *Language in Man: Prehistory to Literacy*

R.L. THOMSON

We do not know the identity of the language spoken in Man in the early centuries of the Christian era, much less those of earlier times. Even as late as the (Latin) Synodal Statutes of 1291 and 1350,[1] the earliest references to the vernacular, the language is not named but referred to as *suum idioma* and *lingua materna,* and while ordering that the formula of baptism and the articles of faith are to be taught to the people, the statutes do not quote a word of them. Celtic scholars generally assume that the language belonged to the Celtic family, either the Brythonic branch from Wales or Cumbria, or Goidelic from Ireland. The first is supported by geography, the second by the fact that when Manx appears in writing, at the beginning of the seventeenth century, it is certainly a form of Goidelic, closer in most respects to Scottish Gaelic than to Irish, though in some it takes a middle position between them. We are reduced, therefore, to relying on the scanty evidence of inscriptions, place-names, and legends, and the inferences we can draw from them. Accordingly there is a considerable variety of opinion.

The Knock-y-Doonee (*Cnoc a' Domhnaich*) inscription (*c.*600) is a bilingual, Brythonic and Goidelic, and in two scripts, Latin and Ogam, bearing the names of a father and son, in the forms appropriate to the two languages '(the stone) of A the son of R'. These would have appeared later as *Imchadh* and *Rochadh,* or *Amgad* and *Rhygad,* according to language. Jackson recognised this inscription as 'a valuable linguistic proof of the existence of a British-speaking population in the Isle of Man in the Dark Ages', and thought it likely that Gaelic 'had been brought to Man in or about the fourth century by settlers from Ireland, exactly as it was brought, about the same time, to Scotland and to parts of Wales and Cornwall'.[2] Jackson no doubt regarded this inscription as a 'valuable linguistic proof' precisely because such clear indications of a Brythonic presence (other than in political connection with Wales later in the first millennium) are so strikingly lacking. On the other hand, this is exactly what we should expect if a small Brythonic-speaking population had subsequently been outnumbered by an Irish settlement. In Wales and Cornwall it was the Irish settlers who were outnumbered, but Man may have followed the Scottish pattern of Goidelic success.

Fig. 11.1 *The bilingual Knock y Dhoonee stone, Andreas, inscription in Latin and Ogham, (a) and (b).*

In a passing comment in a lecture on a quite different subject Professor David Dumville gives as his opinion that 'Mann had been a British-speaking island in the early middle ages (and presumably since time immemorial) despite occasional Gaelic attempts at settlement and at least one Northumbrian English expedition to exercise lordship'.[3] If this is true, the dearth of Brythonic place-names is hard to account for. A Brythonic presence in Man in the time of St Patrick (first half of the fifth century) is hinted at in an incident recounted in the notes on the saint's life collected by Muirchú about AD 700.[4] An Irish brigand named Mac Cuill (later identified with St Maughold despite phonological difficulties) was condemned by Patrick to be set adrift in a boat without food or oars, and was carried by wind and tide to Man, where he found two bishops engaged in converting the inhabitants. These two he first assisted and later succeeded. Their names are given as Conindrus and Romulus, the first apparently the Welsh Cynidr (there is a Llangynidr in Powys), the second a good Latin name such as Christian Britons often bore (as did Patrick's family). It is a reasonable conjecture that the two were Britons, and a possible one that they may have taken Man as their mission-field because the island was wholly or partly Brythonic in speech, which would ease communication with the inhabitants.

The Northumbrian English expedition to which Dumville refers took place in the reign of Edwin of Northumbria (616–33), and is mentioned by Bede as involving Man and Anglesey, which he lumps together as the Mevanian Isles, and describes as 'islands of the Britons', which may have been true politically without being true linguistically.[5] The CRUX GURIAT inscription at Maughold is taken to refer to Gwriad the father of Merfyn Frych, king of Gwynedd (825–44), but the same caveat applies. The language of a king, still less the language of the name of a king, need imply nothing as to the language of his subjects. The early Norman kings of England were all French in name and speech, but England never became a French-speaking country. On the other side we have the reference in *Cormac's Glossary* to the visit to Man by the poet Senchán Torpéist (died 647), paralleled in the story *Tromdámh Guaire*,[6] of visitors who claimed to be poets being required to prove their story by extemporising verses to match those of their challenger. The story takes it for granted that Man was Gaelic-speaking, though this is not a proof that it was so, either when the visit occurred, or when Cormac related it, or when the story about Guaire was written down.

Since the Celtic of Man is eventually revealed as Goidelic it must have reached the island at the latest either shortly before or soon after the Norse period. Watson favoured the earlier date,[7] and this would agree with the presence of Gaelic names in the *Limites terrarum monachorum* ('Boundaries of the monks' lands') probably extracted from the original charters which conveyed them in the twelfth century. He suggested two possibilities: a migration into Galloway from Dalriada, the original Gaelic settlement in Scotland, in the second half of the eighth century, when the power of the Northumbrians was weakened, from which it was an easy step to Man, visible from the Solway coast; or alternatively a similar ninth-century migration by the *Gall-ghaoidhil* (from whom Galloway took its name), people of Norse ancestry who had previously settled and intermarried in the Western Isles and were Gaelic in speech but Norse in culture.

This brings us to the vexed question of the part played by Norse in the linguistic history of the island. The effective introduction of the language is likely to be associated with the beginnings of Norse settlement from 900 onwards. The end of the Norse period, i.e., the time when the political and ecclesiastical connection was with Norway, and the kings bore Norse names, came with the battle of Largs in 1263, followed by the cession of Man and the Isles to Alexander III of Scotland. As regards language, Dr Margaret Gelling,[8] on the basis of the medieval place-name evidence, agreed with Marstrander's opinion of 40 years earlier, that Old Norse was the predominant language of Man from *c.*900 to *c.*1300, that it continued in use and died out in the fifteenth century. Professor Jackson, on the other hand, wrote of Man and the Hebrides as being 'united under Norse rule in a single Gaelic-speaking Kingdom of the Isles until 1266'.[9] It may well be that we are on a wild goose chase if we suppose that at any time in this period there was only one language current in Man. Jackson considered the parallel Ogam-Roman inscription as proof that Brythonic and Goidelic speakers existed side-by-side in the sixth century, apparently not on hostile terms. Gelling describes Norse as the 'dominant language' in Man in the Viking Age, a description which makes no sense unless some other tongue was also in use. There is insufficient evidence to support the view that this was Brythonic, and the place-name evidence favours Goidelic. Manx patronymic surnames, already fixed by the fourteenth century, show that a number of Norse forenames remained current in a Gaelic environment, but also that a far larger number of Gaelic forenames than are found in the fifteenth and sixteenth centuries survived fossilised in this way, and must therefore have been current at an earlier time.

As regards the date at which Manx became distinct from Common Gaelic, i.e., the language common to Ireland, Gaelic Scotland and Man, Professor Jackson considered that by the thirteenth century Common Gaelic was splitting into West Gaelic (= Irish) and East Gaelic (= Scottish Gaelic and Manx), that East Gaelic continued as a unity with common innovations during the thirteenth and fourteenth centuries, but by the fifteenth they too had parted company. The most likely cause of such a split is a diminution or cessation of communication between two areas, and in the case of Manx the beginning of the fifteenth century coincides near enough with the confirmation of the English connection in an enduring form by the grant of the island to the Stanley family in 1406, following a series of other short-lived tenures granted to others in the preceding century. That the orthography of Manx is based on (Middle) English conventions, and not on the Gaelic tradition, is a natural consequence.

It would probably be vain to seek evidence in the language itself for the date of its coming to Man. The material time in dispute between the advocates of a heavy Norse settlement and those of a numerically predominant Gaelic-speaking population in the Viking Age, is included within the Common Gaelic period, so that whether Gaelic existed in Man already or was introduced after a Norse occupation had run its course, the language would be at the same stage of development.

There is, therefore, no certainty about the language of Man until the sixteenth century, but probability seems to favour a Gaelic origin. There may have been a prolonged struggle between Brythonic and Goidelic from the fifth century onwards, but the dearth of surviving Brythonic names gives no support to the idea. If the place-names in the monastic boundaries date from the foundation charters of the twelfth century, they are evidence for a Gaelic-speaking population under a Norse aristocracy. In the Appyn land grant of 1376 Sir Gilbert mac Askill's forename is an Anglo-Norman or Middle English (ultimately Frankish) personal name (though it may be a conventional equivalent of Gaelic Gilla Brigde); his surname is a patronymic formed in the Gaelic fashion with *mac;* and his father's or remoter ancestor's name is Norse, but clearly he himself lives in a Gaelic-speaking milieu. The deed also mentions Henry Botelor, Constable of Holm Patrick, Holmr being old Norse for 'flat land island'; later meaning town; in English, Home Town – town of the island – being the older name for Peel which translates into Gaelic as Balley ny Hinshey – Island Town; Dominus Gilbert McCristyn, rector of the Church of St Brigid in Layr; Dominus Gilbert, vicar of Holm Patrick and John McLavarent to Lord Brian of Stapleton, knight.

At the points where there is definite linguistic evidence, as distinct from statements of uncertain authority and import, that evidence points to a form of Gaelic as the language of Man, though we have to wait for the beginning of the seventeenth century for ocular proof.[10]

Proceeding on this assumption, that Gaelic became the language of the

Fig. 11.2 *Deed of grant of manor of Appin in Glenfaba, 19 February 1376–7.*

inhabitants of the Isle of Man during the second half of the first millennium, and was firmly established as such by the time that it was met by the challenge of Norse on its own ground, perhaps about the beginning of the tenth century, we may go on to trace its development during the long period from which no continuous text has come down to us. In this period Manx is in much the same position as the Gaelic of Scotland, which also has little evidence to show. What little there is begins with the notes in the Book of Deer,[11] contemporary with the late Middle Irish period (mid-twelfth century), and in orthography and language is virtually indistinguishable from Irish Gaelic of the same date, a clear demonstration that relations across the North Channel were, and had been for centuries, sufficiently close to preserve the unity of the language on both sides of the sea, though there may well have been differences of pronunciation perceptible to contemporaries.[12] Although we have no similar document from Man to show that Manx remained equally close to its Irish source, there is no reason to doubt that it too maintained contact with Ireland. This unity of 'the sea-divided Gael' is underlined by the fact that unlike Welsh, Cornish and Breton, where a single language was divided into three geographical areas with three names, Gaelic remained united and retains the one name for all its three modern varieties.

This uniformity of language, moreover, is not simply the result of inertia, of standing still. A great deal of change occurred during the Middle Irish period, and during it Old Irish underwent extensive simplification. The dates of the periods into which the history of a language is divided are dictated by the extent of change observed in the surviving records: Old Irish is the name given to the language from the earliest records down to about 950; Middle Irish from then until about 1350; the long Modern Irish period is divided, with Early Modern Irish extending to about 1650. The much shorter history of Manx has correspondingly shorter periods: Early Manx is essentially Phillips's seventeenth-century translation of the *Book of Common Prayer*; Classical Manx is the product of the eighteenth century and perhaps the first quarter of the nineteenth; Late Manx is the language of the later nineteenth century and the twentieth.

It will be convenient to illustrate the degree of simplification by contrasting the inflections of the Old Irish period with those of Early Manx, indicating whenever possible the date at which the stages of simplification occurred, whether in Common Gaelic (and therefore in all the Gaelic languages), in East Gaelic (and therefore appearing in Scottish Gaelic and Manx, but not in Irish), or in Manx alone after it has parted company with Scottish Gaelic.

The nouns of Old Irish showed four or five cases, nominative, (vocative), accusative, genitive, and dative; they had three numbers, singular, dual, and plural; and three genders, masculine, feminine, and neuter. They followed one of several declensional patterns, of which the most important numerically were the o-stems, ā-stems, i-stems, u-stems, and consonant-stems. (For comparison, the i-stems and consonant-stems were lumped together in the third Latin declension; the o-stems form the second; the ā-stems the first; and the u-stems the fourth.) The stems are named from the vowel preceding the inflectional ending in proto-Celtic, the stage before Old Irish; both vowel and case-ending have disappeared before the Old Irish period, but the vowels often leave traces in their influence on the preceding consonant, so that all consonants had some colouring imparted to them by existing or lost vowels. The major contrast was between palatal and non-palatal ('slender' and 'broad') according as the following vowel was e/i or a/o, with a third, velar quality, imparted by a following u. The

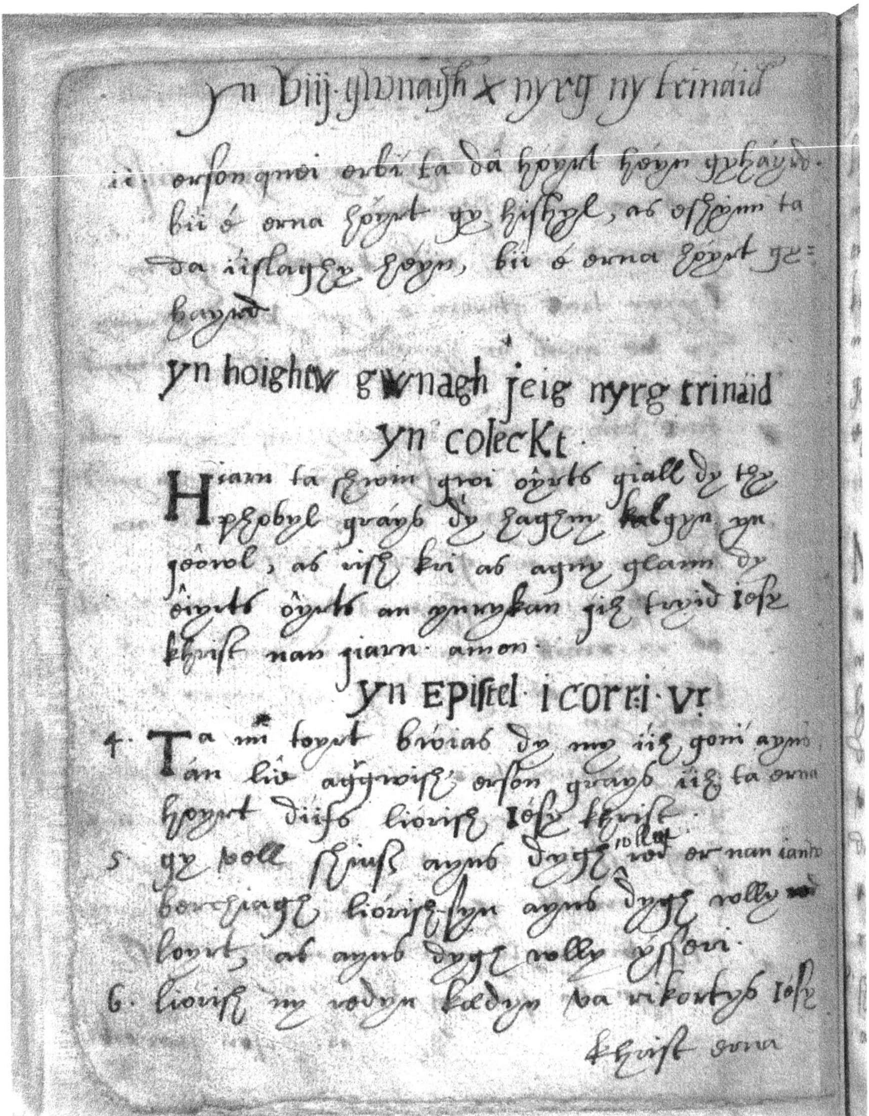
yn viij gluanagh x nyrg ny trinaid

yn hoighew gwnagh jeig nyrg trinaid

yn coleckt

yn Epistel i corri. v

medial and final consonants had already undergone the process called lenition ('aspiration') before the Old Irish period, though the spelling system does not always make this apparent. This lenition also occurred in initial consonants when the preceding word in the phrase had ended in a vowel in the pre-Old Irish period, and similarly with nasalisation ('eclipsis') when the preceding word had ended in a nasal, usually -n. Lenition produced a relaxed articulation, the general effect of which was to convert the stops /t, k, b, d, g/ (/p/ was lacking at this stage) into the corresponding spirants /q, x, b, [d], g/. The consonants /l, n, r/ are also capable of lenition, but no regular change of spelling was ever devised to distinguish the lenited forms. /s/ became /h/, and /f/ (cognate with Latin /v/ and English /w/) became silent. The lenition of /s/ and /f/ was written with a dot above the letter to show that it was not to be sounded, and in time this became the general sign for lenition in the Hiberno-Saxon script, represented by a following *h* when the Roman alphabet was employed. Nasalisation produced a voicing of the voiceless consonants /t, k, f/ becoming /d, g, v/, and converted the voiced ones to the corresponding nasals, i.e., /b, d, g/ become /m, n, _)/.

The features of this system that remain in Manx are

(i) some o-stems retain the nom.pl. formation in -ā, as *fer, fir; boayl, buill; mac, mec; peccagh, peccee;* but most adopt the plural suffix *-yn,* which appears in the East Gaelic period. Some nouns, particularly verb-nouns in *-ey,* though originally u-stems, are treated as o-stems, with gen.sg. and nom.pl. alike, e.g., *caggee, coonee, moyllee, scrieuee,* corresponding to Gaelic -**idh**. The voc.sg. had the same form as the gen.sg and nom.pl. , and in EM the vocatives *veck, yr,* (and *Olbynee* in the Traditionary Ballad) occur;

Fig. 11.3 Bishop Phillip's *Book of Common Prayer in Manx Gaelic c.*1611 was translated from the English 1604 Prayer Book. The only copy, now in the care of Manx National Heritage, was rebound in 1915 by Nelson Cairbrie Cubbon. The manuscript seems to have been written between 1625 and 1630. The original text for the Collect and the Epistle for the eighteenth Sunday after Trinity is is as follows:

> The Collect: 'Lord, we beseech thee, grant thy people grace to withstand the temptation of the world, the flesh, and the devil, and with pure hearts and minds to follow thee the only God; through Jesus Christ our Lord. *Amen*'

> The Epistle (1 Corinthians i 4): 'I thank my God always on your behalf, for the grace of God which is given you by Jesus Christ; that in every thing ye are enriched by him, in all utterance, and in all knowledge; even as the testimony of Christ was confirmed in you; so that ye come behind in no gift; waiting for the coming of our Lord Jesus Christ, who shall also confirm you unto the end, that ye may be blameless in the day of our Lord Jesus Christ.'

(ii) some ā-stems (feminine) retain a gen.sg. as *keeayl, keilley; cloan, clienney; grian, greiney;* and even an accusative-dative as *cass, coshey, cosh; laue* (EM *law,* d. *leyf)* but these occur only in fixed phrases;

(iii) similarly with i-stems, *sooill, sooilley* (though this is a re-formation for **sooylley* with non-palatal *l,* OIr **súlo, súla**, cf. *mooir, marrey,* OIr **muir, mora**);

(iv) and similarly with u-stems, *stroo, yn troa,* OIr **sruth, int srotha**, and *goo,* pl. *goan,* OIr **guth, gotha**;

(v) in consonant stems the accusative and dative sg. are generally alike and this case, presumably from its greater frequency of occurrence, tends to replace the nominative, e.g., *feed,* OIr **fiche, fichit**, *geaylin,* OIr **guala, gualainn**, *Mannin, Nherin* Ir. **i n-Éirinn**, *Nolbin* Ir. **i n-Albain**, nominatives **Manu, Ériu, Albu.** EM has *gharid* as voc. (= acc.) of *karry*;

(vi) in other consonant stems the original nom.sg. is preserved and the consonant appears in the pl. as *briw, briwnyn* OIr **brithem**, acc.pl. **brithemna**; *carrey, caarjyn* OIr **carae**, acc.pl. **cairtea**; *chenney, chentyn* OIr **tene, teintea**; *gaaue, gaauenyn,* OIr **gobae, goibnea**; *thalloo* exceptionally has gen.sg. *thallooin* (formally acc. **talmain**, not gen. **talman**);

(vii) other nouns insert unhistorically before the pl. suffix *-yn* a variety of consonants patterned on the consonant-stems, e.g., (very commonly in nouns ending in an unstressed vowel) from the guttural stems *-agh-yn,* OIr acc.pl. **-acha**, as *aigney, breearrey, caggey, cowrey, garey, peccah, sarey, soilshey, ushtey;* from the dental stems *-ch-yn,* OIr acc.pl. **-tea**, as *balley, billey, cooill, foill,* and *slieau* (**sliab**, gen. **slébe**) makes EM pl. *slœchyn*; and more rarely from the nasal stems, giving *-n-yn,* as *jalloo, naboo, shelloo, greie.* Some of these additions are recorded in MIr also;

(viii) The most distinctive of the plural cases was the dative in **-ib**, which yielded *-w* in Manx, but this survives only in a very few cases, usually in fixed phrases, e.g., EM *er dthy ghwlþ* = **air do chùlaibh** (but also *er my ghwlyn), er my vialw* = **air mo bheulaibh**, *er chew an mealw* = **air taoibh am beulaibh**, *na ghiyrtw* (later ny cheayrtyn), *er aghtw, rish my irerw.*

The use of the dual number gradually declined; by EM the only trace of it is the use of the singular after *daa.* The use of the singular after some other numerals is a vestige of the gen.pl. having the same form as the nom.sg. in some declensions.

The neuter gender likewise lost ground, and nouns of this class were redistributed between masc. and fem., those which belonged to the first declension generally becoming masc. while those belonging to declensions having an additional syllable in the gen.sg. were perceived as belonging to the fem. pattern. So *niart, eeast, skeeal, faiyr, kiaull* became masc., as did *bher, dorrys, ennym* by transferring to the first declension, while *mooir, dreeym, glion, cheer* were drawn by the form of their gen.sg. to the fem. gender.

Adjectives were declined in a way similar to nouns, except for having no dual forms; and except for the o-/ā-stems there was no distinction of genders in the plural. Adjectives used as nouns retained the nominal declension. In the early MIr period the fem. and neut. nom.pl. replaced the masc., and later in the same period the distinctive dat.pl. ending was abandoned. Only the gen.pl. held out till the early ModIr period. The plural adjective thus reached the position of an added open syllable for all cases, and this survived in the case of common monosyllabic adjectives into EM. (Predicative adjectives remained uninflected from the twelfth century.) The only other case with an additional syllable is the gen.sg.fem. and of this only one example *bigy* (beside *beg)* occurs in EM, though a few more are preserved in place-names. The adjective also had three compared forms, equative, comparative, and superlative. The equative in -**ithir** was the first to disappear; the comparative in -(**i**)**u**, and the superlative in -**em/am**, probably became indistinguishable for phonetic reasons, and only a single form remained which, by the weakening of the distinction between final open syllables, fell in with the gen.sg.fem. of the adjective, except where an irregular comparative already existed.

The major seat of complication was in the inflection of the verb, and here the simplification is at its most radical. The OIr verbs might be active or deponent, but the deponent system did not outlive the OIr period. The passive voice is part of the ordinary paradigm, genuinely passive in the third person sg. and pl. but impersonal in the first and second. The tenses were the present, future, imperfect, secondary future or conditional, preterite and perfect in the indicative; the imperative; and the present and imperfect in the subjunctive. The formation of some tenses is achieved by a variety of means, e.g., the s-future, the f-future, the (reduplicated) ā-future, the s-preterite, the t-preterite, the reduplicated preterite, and the ablaut preterite, the ā-subjunctive and the s-subjunctive. In all verbs, and in all tenses except the imperfect, there is a distinction between the absolute and the conjunct inflection: the conjunct is used after any conjunction and when any particle (negative, interrogative, etc.) precedes the verb, the absolute when the verb is affirmative and no particle precedes. In simple verbs, i.e., those without a prepositional prefix or prefixes, the stress falls on the first syllable; in verbs with prefixes the stress, in the absolute form, falls on the root if there is only one prefix, and on the second prefix if there is more than one (deuterotonic stress), while in the conjunct form the stress falls on the first preverb (prototonic stress). In the imperative and the verbnoun the stress always falls on the first syllable, whether it is root or prefix.

As early as the tenth century the distinction between preterite and perfect was breaking down, and by the twelfth in simple verbs the distinction between absolute and conjunct was dying out, and in deuterotonic verbs the tendency was to reconstruct on the basis of the imperative, so converting them into simple verbs; only a few common 'irregular' verbs escaped this trend. In the following century perfective ***ro*** was being replaced by ***do*** in the preterite-perfect, and an analytic form of the verb with personal pronouns replacing some or all the inflections was beginning to appear in the north of Ireland, from which it spread to Scotland and Man.

The most striking change in the verbal system occurs in the East Gaelic area in the fourteenth century; the future tense of Old and Middle Irish disappears and the future sense is conveyed by the old (inflected) present, and the present tense (actual, durative and iterative) is conveyed by the use of 'be' as an auxiliary with the prep. *ag,* OIr **oc**, with the verbnoun, a construction which goes back to OIr but which has only a limited use at that period. The shift of present to future sense is paralleled in Welsh and the pattern of the new present is similar, so that this change has been interpreted by some as a resurgent Brythonic feature in areas which were Brythonic-speaking before they adopted Gaelic.

The EM verb has as its inflected forms the imperative (2nd pers. only; the rest are modelled on English 'let him, let us, let them' with *lhig da;* a very few examples of the 1pl.fut. occur which can be interpreted as imperative), the future, the conditional, the preterite only. The conjunct future serves also as present subjunctive, the conditional as past subjunctive, but already in EM the use of the verb *foddym* 'I can' as an auxiliary of the subjunctive, on the model of English 'may, might' is well established. The present is periphrastic as described above, and the imperfect (durative and iterative) is formed in the same way. The perfect (and pluperfect) is also periphrastic, the prep. *er* (OIr **iar**) with the verbnoun parallel to the *ag* of the present, and the past conditional similarly. As early as EM the inflected tenses are paralleled by alternatives formed with auxiliary 'do', a feature found also in earlier Irish,[13] but which never became systematic as it is in Manx.

Thus the inflected tenses exhibit the following endings in EM: Future – 1sg. *-ym,*. lpl. *–meid;*[14] 2nd and 3rd pers. absolute *-i* + pronoun,[15] conjunct -Ø + pronoun,[16] affirmative relative (3rd person) *-ys,* Conditional -1sg. -*in;* other persons *-agh* + pronoun;[17] Preterite -all persons - Ø + pronoun;[18] Imperative -2sg. - Ø; 2pl. *-i, -igi, -ji.*[19]

The impersonal/passive is represented in EM by only one verb *breh* 'give birth to'; the present *rwggyr* 'is born' (also translating 'was born') OIr **ructhar**, preterite *rwgg* 'was born' (also once as active 'gave birth to') OIr **rucad**.

As an illustration of the 'irregular' verbs we may take *chiit* 'come' OIr **tíchtu**: imperative sg. *tar*, OIr **tair**, pl. *targi;* future 1sg. *higgym*, OIr **ticim**, 3sg. *hig*, OIr **tic**, conj. *gha jigg*; 1pl. (later) *higmayd*; conditional 1sg. (later) *harrin*, 3sg. *horragh*, OIr **tergad**, conj. *gy dorragh;* preterite, *haink*; OIr **tánic**, conj. *gha daink*.[20]

The external influences on the language are most clearly seen in the foreign elements in the vocabulary. For this there are four principal sources, in chronological order, Latin (also as a channel for Greek), Norse, (Norman-) French, Middle (and later) English. It is not always possible to be sure of the immediate source, as words from the first three sources may in some cases have been introduced to Man as English, having been already domesticated in England; in other cases there are features of the Manx form which point more definitely to their having been taken directly from the languages to which they originally belonged. The Latin and Norse lists are fairly complete; the Romance and English lists are a selection only. Almost all the words of Latin origin are recorded in 1610, the exceptions are marked ā; 1610 spellings are marked ā; in the Romance and English lists words recorded by 1610 are marked ā:

Latin: *aer* 'air, firmament' (a_r), *agglish* 'church' (ecclesia), *ainle* 'angel' (angelus), **ally* 'oil, ointment' (oleum), *altar*, **altyr* 'altar' (altare), *annym* 'soul' (anima), *arg* 'ark' (arca), °*armyn* pl. 'arms' (arma), *asbyrt* 'vespers, evening prayer' (vesper; cognate in *fastyr* 'evening'), *aspick* 'bishop' (episcopus), *assyl* 'ass' (asellus), °*baghyl* 'crozier' (baculum), *bannaght* 'blessing' (benedictio), °*caashey* 'cheese' (caseus), °*cabbal* 'chapel' (capella), *cabdil* 'chapter' (capitulum), *cainle* 'candle' (candela), *casherick* 'holy' (participle of Gaelic borrowing of consecrare), *Caisht* 'Easter' (Pascha; the earliest Irish had no *p*, and substituted *q*, which became *c*), *Cargys* 'Lent' (quadragesima), *chiamble* 'temple' (templum), *cleragh* 'clerk, man in orders' (clericus), °*coagerey* 'cook' (*coquarius), °*cloaie* 'down, feathers' (pluma; cf. *Caisht*), *corp* 'body' (corpus), *crea* 'creed' (credo), *credjal* 'believe' (credo, with Gaelic verbnoun suffix), *Creest* 'Christ' (Christus), °*criy* 'gallows' (crux; acc/dat. of *crogh), *croghey* 'hang' (crucio), *currym* 'duty, responsibility' (cura), *doonaght* 'Sunday, church' (dominicus 'belonging to the Lord' with dies 'day' or domus 'house'), *erin*, **ayryn* 'morning service, mass' (offerenda), *feailley* 'holiday, feast-day' (vigilia), *teeyn* 'wine' (vinum), *fockle* 'word' (vocalis), *gloyr* 'glory' (gloria), *Jylhune, Jymayrt, Jysarn* 'Monday, Tuesday, Saturday' (dies Lunae, Martis, Saturni), *jouyl* 'devil' (diabolus), °*juist* 'dish' (discus), °*kail* 'cabbage' (caulis), *keeill* 'church' (cella; acc/dat. *cill*, nom. * *kiall*), *keesh* 'tax' (census), °*kelk* 'chalk' (calx), °*kiarkyl* 'circle' circulus, °*Kingeesh* 'Pentecost' (Quinquagesima), *kishtey* 'chest' (cista), (*Laa-)Innyd* 'Shrove Tuesday' (initium; the beginning of Lent), *lhaih* 'read' (lego), *lioar* 'book' (liber), *maarderagh* 'adulterer' (meretrix, -icius), *mainshtyr* 'master' (magister; or perhaps Middle English), °*managh* 'monk' (monachus), °*mannishter* 'monastery' (monasterium), °*meoir* 'moar, bailiff' (maior), *mirril* 'miracle' (mirabile), *mollaght* 'curse' (maledictio), *mwyllin* 'mill' (molina), *(n)iurin* 'hell' (infernum), *Nallick* 'Christmas' (Natalicia), °*oalan* 'communion wafer' (oblatio), *obbyr* 'work' (opera), *oik* 'office, function' (officium), *oor* 'hour' (hora), _*Orynan, *Iurynan_ 'R. Jordan' (Iordanen), _ostyl, *awstyl_ 'apostle' (apostolus), *oural* 'sacrifice, offering' (offero; with vbn suffix -al, cf. *credjal*), *Raue* 'Rome' (Roma), *reill* 'rule' (regula), *saggyrt* 'priest' (sacerdos), *scoillar* 'pupil' (scholaris), *screeu* 'write' (scribo), *seihll* 'world, lifetime' (saeculum), °*sheayney* 'bless, charm' (signo), °*shoggyl* 'rye' (secale), *side* 'arrow' (sagitta), °*skeab* 'broom' (scopa), *spyrryd* 'spirit' (spiritus), *soalt* 'barn' (stabulum), *straid* 'street' (strata [via]), °*surn* 'fireplace' (furnus; in this and the next Latin f- is treated as the lenition of s- in those cases when s- arises from *sw-; cf. *feailley*), °*soost* 'flail' (fustis), *trinaid* 'trinity' (trinitas), *Yeesey* 'Jesus' (Iesus), *Yuaase* 'Judas' (Iudas).

Norse: °*aker* 'anchor' (akkeri), °*baatey* 'boat' (bátr), °*baie* 'bay' (vágr), °*bekk* 'bench' (bekkr), _*brod_ 'goad' (broddr), °*clett* 'rock' (klettr), *eearley* 'earl' (jarl), _garey, *garr_ 'garden' (gar _r), °*giau* 'narrow inlet' (gjá), *greie* 'instrument, tool' (cf, grei _a), °*grinney* 'gate' (grind), *leigh* 'law' (*lagu), °*laut* 'upstairs room' (lopt; or English), *margey* 'market' (marka _r), *naboo* 'neighbour' (nábúi), °*oalsum* 'hobble, from head to leg' (halsband), *ronsaghey* 'search' (rannsaka), *sheshey* 'companion' (sessi), *sker* 'sea-rock' (sker), °*sprettal* 'start, shy' (spretta), *treishteil* 'trust' (treysta), °*uinnag* 'window' (vindauga), °*wappin* 'weapon' (vápn; or English).

Romance elements are difficult to distinguish with certainty from those that came through English, and vice versa. Source-forms are cited only where the meaning is inadequate to explain the origin. Words occurring in 1610 are marked * when quoted in the original spelling, otherwise by >:

Anglo-Norman and Romance: >*ammys* 'respect' (homage), >_ashoon, *atiwn_ 'nation', *bardoon* 'dirge' (bourdon), >*barrant* 'trust' (warrant), >*biallagh* 'obedient' ([o]bey + verbnoun and adj. suffixes), >*boteil* 'bottle', *caabyl* 'cable', *caboon* 'capon', >*captan* 'captain', >*cashtal* 'castle', >*cloagey* 'cloak', >*coardail* 'agree' ([ac]cord), >*conaant* 'covenant, condition', *combaasal* 'encompass', *cooat* 'coat', >*coontey* 'account, count', >_coorse, *kws_ 'course', >*cooyrt* 'court', >*corneil* 'corner', *costrayl* 'jar' (costrel), >*couyral* 'recover, get better', *coyrd* 'cord', >*cubbyl* 'couple',

>*cumrail* 'impede' ([en]cumber), *curlead* 'coverlet', *danjeyr* 'danger', >*daunsin* 'dance', >*dooble* 'double', >*dooyt* 'doubt', >*eirey* 'heir', *entreil* 'enter', >*failleil* 'fail', *flooyr* 'flour', >*foalsey* 'false', >*foayr* 'favour', *goon* 'gown', *greeishyn* 'stairs' ([de]grees), *jatter* 'debtor', >*jinnair* 'dinner', *koir* 'box' (coffer), *lindeyr* 'lintel', >*livrey* 'deliver', >*lowal* 'permit' ([al]low), >*manjoor, *bainshwyr* 'manger', *marchan* 'merchant', *naunt* 'aunt', *oast* 'host', >*ooill* 'oil', >*recortys* 'record', >*resoon (*reswnagh)* 'reason', *resowir* 'receiver', *rowlal* 'roll', >*sambyl* 'example', >*sauail* 'save', *scapail* 'escape', *scrial* 'espy' ([de]scry), >*shamyr, *shiambyr* 'chamber', >*sharvaant* 'servant', *shecktar* 'executor', >*shiartanse* 'some' (certains), >*shibber* 'supper', >*shirveish* 'service', >*soar* 'smell' (savour), *sorch* 'sort, kind', *spooilley* 'despoil', *staabyl* 'stable' (or English), >*stayd* 'state, condition', *stoyr* 'store, treasure', >*streeu* 'strive, contend', >*stroie* 'destroy', *studeyr* 'student', >*surranse* 'suffer', *tendeil* 'attend', *thurneyr* 'attorney', >*tooilleil* 'toil, labour', >*troailt* 'travel, travail', *use* 'usury, interest', >*vondeish* 'advantage', **wardwni* '[church]wardens'.

English: *ansoor* 'answer', *arpin* '[n]apron', >*boayrd* 'table', *bwooishal* 'wish', >*coau* 'chaff', >*cramp, *knapp* 'plague' (knap), *crankal* 'knock', >*crout* 'craft', *crowal* 'crave', >*dellal* 'deal', *dree* 'dull, miserable', >*farling* 'farthing', *fordrail* '[af]ford', >*frourtagh* 'froward' (with adj. suffix), *gamman* 'game, play', >*giat* 'gate', >*gioot* 'gift', *gyrnal* 'snarl, pull faces', *hollyn* 'holly', *jeebin* 'kind of fishing net' (deeping), *jerlyn* 'darnel', *keeak* 'cake', *kiarail* 'care', >*laadey* 'load', *laccal* 'lack, want', >*leeideil* 'lead' , >*lhiettal* 'hinder, prevent' (let), *maail* 'rent, tribute' ([black]mail), *meeiteil* 'meet', >*moidyn* 'maiden', *naim* 'uncle' ([n]+eme), *oaseir* 'overseer', **okyr* 'usury, interest' (ocker), >*reejerey* 'knight' (rider), *roddan* 'rat', *rouail* 'rove', *rubbey* 'rub, dry', *saaue* 'saw', *shelliu* 'salve', >*shickyr* 'sure' (sicker), **shout* 'beam' (shaft), *skelloo* 'shelf', *sneg* 'sneck', >*soorid* 'leaven, yeast' (sour, with nom. suffix), *spaarail* 'spare, use sparingly', *sparroo* 'sparrow', >*stampey* 'tread' (stamp), *sthappal* 'stop', *sthock* '[live]stock', *sthook* 'stook' (derivative **stwckan* 'piece'), >*stiurt* 'steward', *stowal* '[be]stow', >*stoyl* 'stool, chair', >*voalley* (wall).

Notes

1 C.R. Cheney (ed.), in *Cambridge Medieval Celtic Studies*, 7 (1984), 63–89 (text), and 8 (1984), 51–63 (translation); see 7, pp. 85, 86.

2 K.H. Jackson, 'Notes on the Ogam inscriptions of Southern Britain', in *The Early Cultures of North- West Europe*, ed. Fox and Dickins, 199–213, at pp 209–10.

3 David N. Dumville, *The Churches of North Britain in the First Viking-Age*, Whithorn Lectures 5 (1997), 23–24.

4 Ludwig Bieler (ed.) *The Patrician Texts in the Book of Armagh* (Dublin, 1979)

102–7.

5 Bede, *Historia Ecclesiastica Gentis Anglorum*, ed. C. Plummer, 1896, 11.5, 9, III. 3, pp. 89, 97, 132–3.

6 Maud Joynt (ed.) *Tromdámh Guaire* (Dublin, 1941), lines 1169ff. For these and other Gaelic literary notices of Man, see McQuarrie's discussion in chapter 13 below.

7 William J. Watson, *The History of the Celtic Place-Names of Scotland* (Edinburgh, 1926) 172–4.

8 Margaret Gelling, 'The place-names of the Isle of Man', *JMM*, 7 (1970), 130–9, (1971), 168–75; see pp.173–4.

9 K.H. Jackson, 'Common Gaelic: the evolution of the Goedelic languages', *Proceedings of the British Academy*, 37 (1951) 71–97, at p.78.

10 A fuller account of the external history will be found in the papers of the conference *Centred on Mann* held in July 1998.

11 Kenneth Jackson, *The Gaelic Notes in the Book of Deer* (Dublin, 1972), 149–52.

12 Jackson, 'Common Gaelic'; AFM, *s.a.* 1258 (*tria san nGaoidhilcc nAlbanaigh*), following T.F. O'Rahilly, *Irish Dialects Past and Present* (Dublin, 1932), 162, n.3.

13 The 1pl. ending is OIr **-mai**; the *-d* is the survival of a 3rd pers. suffixed object pronoun. Cf. R. Thurneysen, *A Grammar of Old Irish* (Dublin, 1946), §431.

14 The 2nd sg. frequently ends in *-yt,* the OIr pron. 2sg **tú**, normally lenited to *w* in Manx, losing its lenition after the ending **-idh** > *-i,* and the *t-* being transferred to the verb.

15 The ending is **-adh**, which fell together with **-agh** in the thirteenth century, and is unvoiced to **-ach** before pronouns beginning with a voiceless sound (e.g., *t, s*), and then generally.

16 In derivative verbs with the suffix *-agh-* the endings **-igh** and **-ighidh** both > *-i* so that there is no distinction here between absolute and conjunct.

17 The initial consonant is lenited in the pret.; before initial vowels *d/j* is prefixed, a relic of the perfective particle **do** < **ro** (see above). The final consonant of the stem may be palatalised, regularly so with the *-agh-* verbs.

18 The final consonant may be palatalised in the 2sg., regularly so in the *-agh*-verbs. The pl. is historically **-idh** > *-i;* the *-agh-* verbs had **-ighidh** with **-gh-** later stopped as **-igidh, -idigh** > *-igi, -iji.*

19 T.F. O'Rahilly, *Celtica*, 1, part 2 (1950), 318.

20 This verb is a blend of forms from OIr **do-ic** (future and preterite) and **do-téit** (imperative and conditional). The lenition in the future absolute is common to Manx and Scottish Gaelic in these verbs which were originally deuterotonic, e.g., *thig, theid, bheir, gheibh = hig, heidg, verr, iew* (but *their, tha = jirr, ta).*

12 *The Manx Place-name Evidence*

GILLIAN FELLOWS-JENSEN

Place-names are one of the best sources of evidence for the settlement history of a country. If treated circumspectly, they can reveal a great deal about the various waves of settlers and the resulting linguistic contact. There are, however, many problems to be confronted. The greatest of these is probably the fact that the modern nomenclature is a palimpsest and many of the present names must have replaced older names that have apparently been lost without trace. In order to be able to present an authoritative discussion of the place-names of the Isle of Man in the period 1000–1405, it would be necessary to have access to reasonably full lists of names from the years 1000 and 1405 respectively. The differences between these two lists could then be assumed to reflect the developments that had taken place in the intervening years. This is a counsel of perfection, however, and the situation in the Isle of Man renders it impossible to adopt. The only Manx name to be recorded in a source earlier than the year 1000 is that of the island itself, which occurs in varying forms in sources from the Roman-British period, all of which can perhaps be explained as going back to a form **Manavia*, a derivative of **man-*, meaning 'mountain island'.[1] On the other hand, the Irish form *Manu*, which clearly lies behind the Norse *Mön*, seems to have the same declensional pattern in Irish as other old island-names in the region, e.g., *Aru*, gen. *Arann* for Arran, *Ériu*, gen. *Érenn* for Ireland. These names may all be of pre-Celtic origin.[2]

There is not even a comprehensive source of Manx names from the early fifteenth century. Fortunately, various monastic sources have yielded records of scattered place-names from before this date and these are of inestimable value as a yardstick against which to assess the evidence in later sources.[3] The first reasonably comprehensive sources of Manx place-names that we have are the rent rolls, the so-called *Libri Assedationis* or setting books, in which the names of tenants paying rent to the lord of Man are entered on a parochial basis, grouped under their respective treens.[4] These have survived from 1506 to 1911 for the administrative north side of the island (the sheadings of Glenfaba, Michael and Ayre) and from 1515 to 1911 for the south side (the sheadings of Garff, Middle and Rushen). It was not, however, until after the revision of the Lord's Composition Book in the middle of the seventeenth century at the instigation of the then lord of Man, James, seventh earl of Derby, that an attempt was made to find

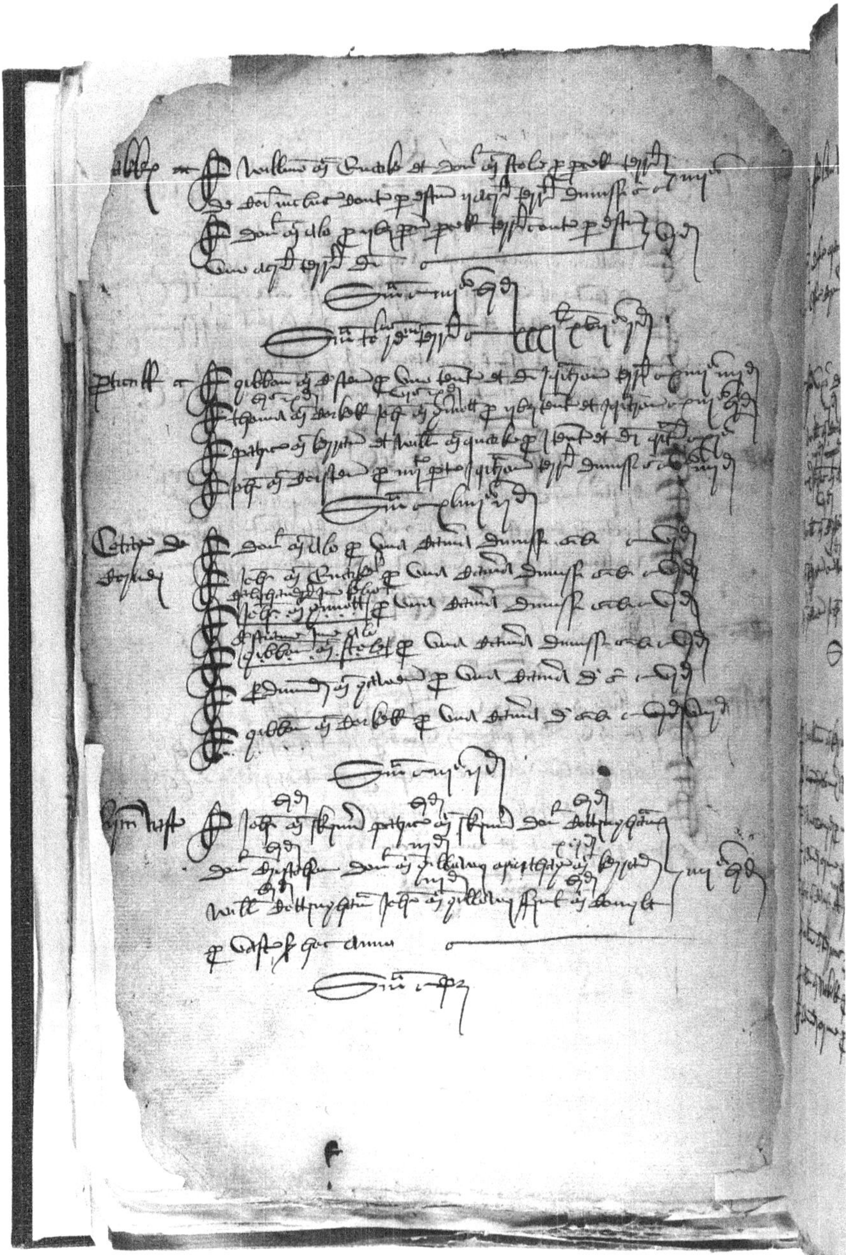

Fig. 12.1 *A page of the* Liber Assedationis *or setting book of 1511.*

out exactly who held land from the lord and for what rent. This process involved the recording of a number of quarterland- and intack-names. The Composition Book from 1704 was greatly expanded and can therefore be looked upon as the main source for early attestations of the majority of minor settlement names.

Man has been fortunate in that much attention has been paid to its place-names throughout the twentieth century. The pioneering work of collection and presentation was done by a Manxman, J.J. Kneen.[5] A Norwegian scholar, C.J.S. Marstrander, subsequently studied the place-names in the light of his knowledge of Old Norse and Manx phonology and the already well-advanced research into Norwegian place-names, and he was able to correct a number of Kneen's interpretations.[6] More recently there has been a good deal of discussion of the evidence provided by the place-names for the extent of survival of Gaelic speech on Man in the period of Norse hegemony.[7] Now George Broderick has published a new edition in seven volumes of the place-names of Man.[8] There are also useful treatments of the names in Maughold and Ramsey and Kirk Bride.[9]

Any place-name has something to reveal about the history of the region in which it appears. As a general rule it will reveal the language that was spoken by the namers. There are naturally exceptions. Ohio in Lezayre is first recorded in 1831.[10] This name does not, of course, show that native Americans settled here and gave the place as a name this vague Iroquoian term of commendation 'fine, good'; it simply reflects the fact that Ohio was the main destination for Manx emigration in the nineteenth century and that its name was employed by returning exiles or their relations to name localities in the homeland. Another possible example of a transferred name is that of a quarterland called Belfast in Andreas, first recorded in this form in 1794.[11] It could be explained as a Gaelic name **béal feirste* 'sandy-spit mouth', identical with that of the Irish city, but it is more likely to be a name transferred from Ireland in relatively modern times than one coined from scratch by Gaelic-speakers, in the light of the fact that all the recorded forms show the anglicised spelling and pronunciation of the name.

A full survey like Broderick's of the place-names of Man is naturally committed to recording all possible name-corpora, that is, all the names that can be culled from written sources or elicited from local informants. Such a composite corpus will include many names that are without relevance for a study of place-names in the period 1000–1405. In addition to really exotic names like Ohio, it has also been thought reasonable to omit from the present survey all the names which are obviously of English coinage, for example many of the names in the urbanised settlements, such as Big Cellar, Castle Street and Parr's Brewery in Peel. It is doubtful whether many English names would have been coined in the first turbulent century of English rule. We shall then be left with a corpus of place-names of which the majority are of Manx Gaelic origin, while a substantial minority are certainly, probably or possibly of Scandinavian origin.

The most striking fact about the Gaelic names in Man is the comparatively low status of the settlements bearing the names. Only about one third of the treen-names recorded in the early sixteenth century are Gaelic by comparison with no less than 90 per cent of the quarterland-names recorded in the early eighteenth century.[12] These figures have been used as an argument for a relatively slight survival of Gaelic names (and the Gaelic language) in the period of Viking rule and a subsequent reintroduction of the Gaelic language to Man.[13] The situation is, however, more complicated than might appear on the surface. Admittedly, hardly any of the Gaelic names can be proved to be of pre-Norse origin. The sheading- and parish-name Rushen and the treen-name Douglas are both recorded in the Manx chronicle and for that reason alone may perhaps be thought to be of pre-Gaelic Celtic origin. Rushen, a derivative *roisean* of *ros*, a word with several meanings, is described by Broderick as being of a type extremely rare in Man.[14] The British loanword in Manx, *ros*, may simply have been used by Manx speakers to create the name **Roisean*. There are similar formations **rosan* in Cornwall and **rhosan* in Wales, and probably in Lancashire, Cheshire and Yorkshire.[15] Douglas, too, has parallels in mainland Britain. The Manx form Doolish < **Dubhghlais*, implied, apart from the final palatal *s*, in the Manx chronicle's *Dufglas*, has parallels in Dowlish in Somerset, and Dulas in Herefordshire and Wales.[16] The modern English form of the name, Douglas, must reflect the post-Stanley influence of either the Lancashire river-name or the Scottish place-name or surname.

It is reasonable to assume that Celtic names used by the Norse-speaking rulers of Man in the middle of the thirteenth century, at the time when the Manx chronicle was compiled, had been taken over from the Celtic-speaking population. In common with the Gaelic names of Ireland and Scotland, however, the Manx Gaelic names are notoriously difficult to date on linguistic grounds and the lateness of the sources intensifies this problem. Many of the surviving Manx names are undoubtedly post-Norse formations, but the comparative modernity of the structure of the names and the transparency of their meaning cannot be taken as proof of the lateness of their coining. The preferred structure of Manx Gaelic names, with post-modification of nouns and retention of the definite article, that is as syntactic groups rather than compounds, tends to protect the elements in the names from being reduced and obscured and to encourage their development to follow that of the rest of the language.[17]

A few names might seem from their semantic content likely to have arisen in the pre-Norse period. George Broderick has argued, for example, that place-names such as Appyn in Patrick and probably Nappin in Jurby and Nappin in Lezayre may point to pre-Norse settlement associated with the early Christian church in Man.[18] These names are reflexes of a Manx **apainn*, from Old Irish *apdaine*. This word has been thought to be derived from Latin *ab(ba)thania* 'abbey estate' but R.L. Thomson has suggested that the Latin word might rather be a derivative of Old Irish *ap* [ab], gen. *apad*, earlier *apath*, from Latin *abbas*, gen. *abbatis*, with Irish syncopation of the second syllable to [-bth], followed by unvoicing of [b] to [p] when [-th] becomes [h]. The sense 'abbacy' is the only one given for Irish; the extension to ecclesiastical or monastic property is only recorded in Scotland but must obviously have extended to Man. Broderick has also pointed to a few names whose structure would seem to be of some antiquity, although parallel formations survive in the Hebrides, some of which involve Norse loanwords, e.g. *Dubh Sgeir* 'black skerry'. In Man we find, for example, Dollagh in Ballaugh, Doolough in Jurby and *Dufloch* in Lezayre *c.*1280, in which the adjective *dubh* 'black' is prefixed to the generic, here *logh* 'miry area', in a close compound and bears initial stress, in contrast to a name such as Doo-halloo in Ballaugh, in which *doo* bears unexpected secondary stress.[19]

By far and away the most frequently occurring generic in the Gaelic treen-names in Man is *baile* 'settlement'. The names containing this element have been thought to be young because Liam Price had argued that there was no evidence for the use of this generic to form place-names in Ireland before the middle of the twelfth century.[20] Some of the Manx names in *Balla-* are definitely young, containing as they do surnames of English or Anglo-Norman origin, e.g., Ballafletcher and Ballaharrison in Patrick.[21] Some of the names in *Baile-* in Galloway, however, may date back to the pre-Norse period,[22] and there is good reason to believe that some *Bally-* names in Ireland date from the Viking period, for example Ballyfermot in co. Dublin and Ballygunner and Ballytruckle near Waterford, which contain the Norse personal names *Þormóðr*, *Gunnarr* and *Þorkell* respectively. An early Manx source, the Malew Abbeyland Bounds from *c.*1280, includes one Gaelic name in *Balla-*: Ballasalla. In Man the primary centres of Norse archaeological remains, both early pagan burials and later Christian cross-slabs, tend to be found along the west coast in treens which, with the exception of Jurby, have Gaelic names in *Balla-*.[23] Even Tynwald is in a *Balla-*treen. This tends to suggest that the Norse often took over earlier Gaelic settlements in Man without interfering with their names, in the same way as the Danes who settled in English-named settlements in the

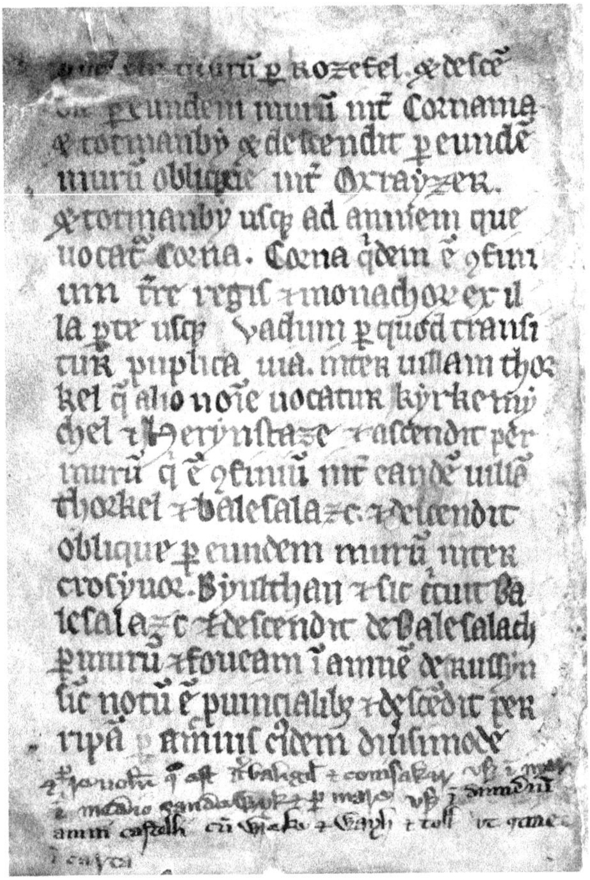

Fig. 12.2 *Abbeylands Bounds 1280:* Limites Terrarum Monachorum *folio 54v, entered in Cotton Julius A vii (fol. 53v). The following placenames can be read: Skynnescor, Laxa, Gretastaz, Tofthar, Asmund, Rynkurlyn, Orumsouz and*

ÞURLIBR : NHAKI : RISTI : KRUS : ÞĄNĄ : AFT : FIAK : SU[N] SIN : [B]RUTH UR : SUN : HABRS X

Fig. 12.3 *The inscription on the Braddan rune-stone, Thorleif's cross (Kermode no.108): a) sketch of the runes by P M C Kermode and b) transliteration. Translated it reads: 'Thorleif Hnakki put up this cross in memory of Fiacc his son, brother's son to Hafr'. The man who erected the cross has a Norse personal name and a Norse by-name meaning 'back of the head'. The dead man has a Gaelic name but his nephew has a Norse name meaning 'he-goat'.*

Danelaw continued to use the English names.

That the Scandinavians did not avoid contact with the native population is shown by the Norse runic inscriptions on some of the Christian gravestones that have survived from the tenth century and later (Fig. 12.3). These reveal that intermarriage between Gael and Scandinavian cannot have been uncommon.[24] The very existence of these stones and inscriptions is a reflection of a fruitful combination of two traditions, the Celtic one of raising crosses over the dead and the Norse one of raising runic memorials. Even the Norse kings would seem to have acquired some Manx. Several of them had Gaelic by-names, such as Crovan (**crobh bhán*, 'white hand'), Don (**donn*, 'dun-coloured') and Duf (**dubh*, 'black'), while none of them had a Scandinavian by-name.[25] In the course of time it would seem that the descendants of the Norse settlers became fully gaelicised and abandoned Norse speech. Patronymics began to be formed by the prefixing of Gaelic *Mac* to Scandinavian personal names, perhaps originally by Manx-speakers rather than the Norse themselves. There is an early example in the Abbeyland Bounds of *c.*1280, where the present Ballakeigan is recorded in latinised form as *villam Mac Akoen*, where the Latin *villa* might represent Gaelic *baile*. There are certainly numerous modern Manx place-names that go back to a formation with *Baile-* and a Manx patronymic in *Mac-* formed on a Scandinavian personal name, such as Ballacottier from Óttarr and Ballacorlett from Þorljótr,[26] but these are Manx formations and most probably post-date the Viking period. The treen-name Aryhorkell in Michael is of rather more significance, for it contains the personal name Þorkell as a personal name and not as a patronymic and is therefore most probably to be dated to the Norse period.[27]

Names such as Ballacottier are just one type of Manx name involving Scandinavian linguistic material whose formation is to be ascribed to Manx-speakers. The fact that the surnames in question are based on Scandinavian personal names does, of course, show that there were once Scandinavians resident on the island, but the place-names cannot be used as an indication of a Viking presence at the localities in question.

Rather different questions are raised by another type of compound, that in which the generic is a Manx word and the specific is a place-name of Scandinavian origin, for example Ballelby in Patrick, a lost *Ballacgniba* in German and Knoksewell in Jurby.[28] Ballelby is a quarterland-name, first recorded in 1704. It is difficult to explain satisfactorily but would seem to consist of Manx *Balla-* prefixed to a Scandinavian place-name in *-bȳ*. Marstrander has suggested that this latter name might have been **hala-bȳ* 'farm on a tail of land' and he associated it with the name Elby Point, borne by a deep-water cliff by Niarbyl reef, and the Manx name Niarbyl itself (**yn arbyl* 'the tail').[29] George Broderick considers that *Balla-* might have been prefixed to **Elby* to distinguish this settlement from the original farm, which has since disappeared. Other explanations of this *bȳ*-name are possible. It might, for example, contain Scandinavian *hellir* 'rocky cavern' or *hjallr* 'flat shelf'. Although the name Ballelby is a Manx formation, it is not without significance for the assessment of the Scandinavian influence on Manx place-names because it contains a Scandinavian name that would otherwise be unknown to us. Knoksewell is a similar case. It is a Manx treen-name that probably includes an older Norse name **sjá-ból* 'farm by the sea'. To this has been prefixed Manx *knock* 'hill', presumably to form a hill-name, and this hill-name displaced the settlement name before the compilation of the earliest list of treen-names. What makes this name particularly interesting is that it may contain a lost Scandinavian name in *-ból*, a generic not certainly evidenced in Man. The absence of other names in *-ból*, however, does throw some doubt on the explanation. The lost name *Ballacgniba* in German, which is found in an early sixteenth-century transcript of a charter from 1228 has occasioned a good deal of interest as being either a possible early example of a place-name in *Balla-* or a misreading of a latinised form **Villacgniba*. It seems rather unlikely that the Manx word *Balla-*, although still perhaps not of very frequent occurrence in place-names, should not have been recognised by the scribe or transcriber of the charter and replaced by Latin *villa*. In any case, there is good reason to think that the original generic was not *Balla* but Gaelic *Bealach* 'pass', as in the place-name Balloch in Dumbartonshire.[30] The name *Ballacgniba* is thus a compound of Gaelic *bealach* 'pass' with the Scandinavian hill-name Greeba (**gnípa*). Since the Scandinavian hill-name survives in use as a hill-name, however, the lost Manx name is of no relevance for an assessment of Scandinavian influence on the place-names.

Other problematical place-names are those consisting of, or including, a Scandinavian word that had been adopted into Manx as a loanword. The sheading of Ayre, for example, takes its name from the Ayre, now Ayres, a sandy, gravelly bank at the north-east of the island.[31] This is a very prominent topographical feature and it seems reasonable to assume that it was the Vikings who bestowed the name **eyrr* 'gravel bank' upon it. *Eyrr* was also adopted into Manx as a common noun, occurring in several place-names in which it is declined as a Manx word and accompanied by a Manx definite article, for example the quarterland-name Ballanayre in Sartedale.[32]

The situation is even less clear with the Scandinavian word *gata* 'hedged or fenced road in open country', which may occur as a loanword in the form *gat* in Manx place-names such as Gat Beary in German.[33] A Manx word *giat* meaning 'field', perhaps cognate with Gaelic *gead*, has been explained as an anglicised form of *gata*,[34] which was used in northern England with the meaning 'right of pasturage', but it is more likely that *giat* reflects Old English *geat* 'gate, gap'.[35] R.L. Thomson has suggested to me that the Manx spellings *gat(t)* and *gha(a)it*, rather than being direct reflexes of Scandinavian *gata*, probably represent a late importation of the word from northern English in the sense 'field'. The name containing *gat* which is most likely to be of Scandinavian formation is probably Raggatt in Patrick, which is first recorded in 1801 as *the Ragged* but has been explained convincingly enough as Norse **rák-gata* 'drove road' or **rak-gata* 'straight track'.[36] The main reason for assuming that Raggatt is likely to be a place-name coined by Norse speakers is that it is a close compound of two Scandinavian elements in Germanic word-order.

Quite a number of such names are recorded in the Manx chronicle and these can all be assumed to have been current in the Norse period, although several of them can no longer be precisely located on the map. Most of these names originally denoted topographical features. The name *Mirescog*, *Mirescohc* (**mȳra(r)-skógr* 'miry wood') refers to an area of originally wooded mire in what is now known as The Curragh.[37] It is described in the chronicle as a *boscum* or 'wood'. The names *Ramsa* and *Rognalswaht*, on the other hand, originally **hrams-á* 'wild-garlic river' and **Ragnalds-vað* 'Rögnvaldr's ford', are both said to be borne by a *portus* or 'harbour' and are thus secondary settlement names.[38] The present bearers of the names are the town and treen of Ramsey and Ronaldsway airport respectively. Another name in *-vath* 'ford' recorded in the chronicle is *Santwat* 'sand ford', the site of a decisive and bloody battle fought between Manxmen of the north and the south in 1098.[39] The name is only known from this one reference in the chronicle. The final Norse compound place-name to be recorded in this source is *Tyngualla*, the site of a battle between Oláfr, son of Guðröðr, and his brother Rögnvaldr in 1227.[40] It is described as a *locus* or 'place' and no mention is made here of its function as the site of the judicial assembly. Since the Manx assembly probably provided the immediate inspiration for the establishment of Thingwalls in Wirral and Lancashire, it must be assumed to have come into existence by the end of the ninth century at the latest.[41]

When the Abbeyland Bounds were redated to *c.*1280, the argument for a survival of the Gaelic language in the Norse period was greatly strengthened, for while Norse names predominate in the two sets of bounds from the administrative south of the island – around Castletown and Laxey, in the third set, from the area immediately to the north of the mountains, it is Gaelic names that predominate. It is nevertheless significant that so many

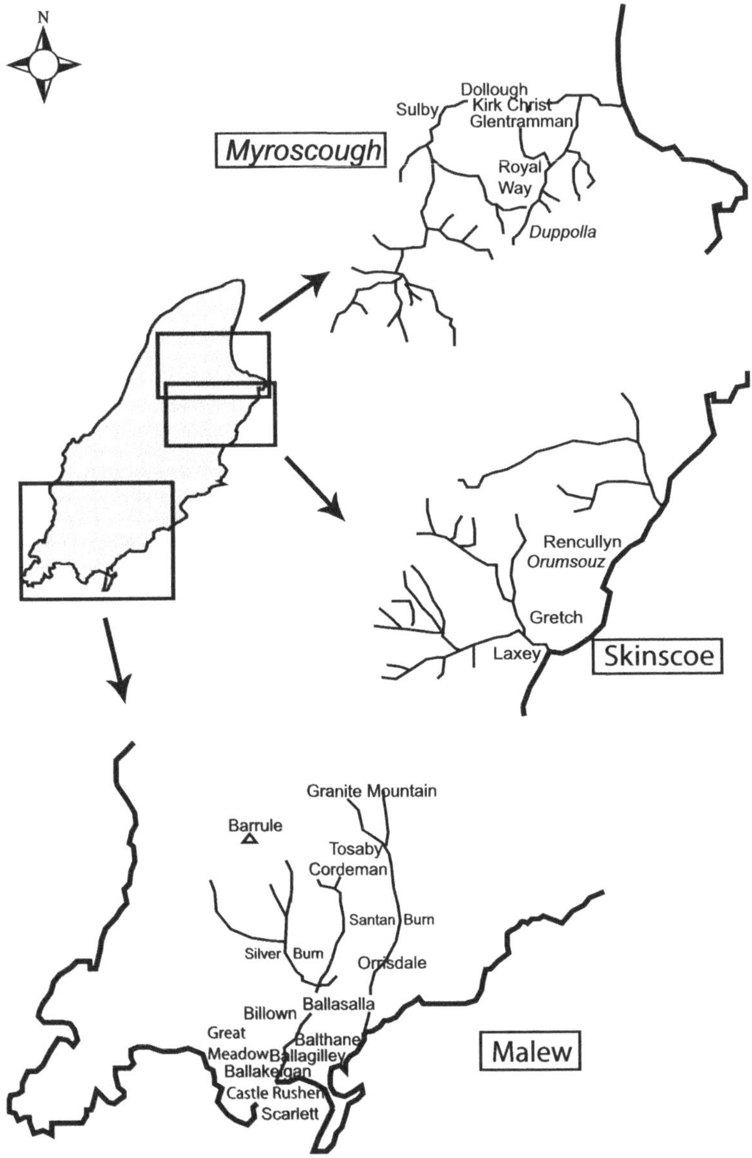

Fig. 12.4 *The locations described in the monastic bounds of c.1280 often referred to as* Limites Terrarum Monachorum *(Broderick, CKMI, ff. 53r–54v). With the exception of Orumsouz and Duppolla which do not have modern day equivalents, the places are shown with their modern names.*

natural features bear Norse names, including rivers and mountains, features whose earlier names might have been expected to survive anything other than a massive Norse immigration. We find the river-names *Corna*, now Santanburn,[42] and Cornaa in Maughold,[43] (**kvern-á* 'mill-river'), and *Laxa* (**laks-á* 'salmon river'), now Laxey,[44] and the mountain-names *Worzefel* (**varðar-fjall* 'look-out mountain' or less likely **vörðu-fjall* 'cairn mountain'), now Barrule,[45] and *Rozefel* (**rauth-fjall* 'red mountain', referring to the colour of the weathered granite), now Granite Mountain.[46] Other Norse topographical names are borne by features of less prominence. In the Castletown area there are the now-lost *Oxwath* (**oxa-vath* 'ox ford') and *Oxrayzer* (**oxa-hreysar* 'ox cairn'), a lost *Staynarhea*, whose specific is Norse *steinn* and whose generic might have been thought to be Manx *eary* 'shieling', if there were other evidence for the use of this element in Germanic compounds in Man. In the Laxey area there is *Skynnescor*, now Skinscoe, possibly from the occupational term *skinnari* 'skinner' and *skor* 'cleft', although the later form of the generic points to *skógr* 'wood',[47] and the lost *Orumsouz*, which would seem to be identical with a Scandinavian name in Wales, Ormes Head, which has been thought to have been given its name **Orms-höfuð* because of the startling resemblance of the promontory seen from the sea to the undulating body of a snake.[48] Finally, in the northern area there is one certain Norse topographical name, *Myrosco*, discussed above under the form *Mirescog* in the chronicle, and a possible one, *Duppolla*. Megaw considered that this latter name might be either Scandinavian or Gaelic,[49] but Thomson has argued that it is doubtful whether *Dup-* could represent Old Norse *djúp*, in the light of the development of that element to *Gib-* in Gibdale in Malew, which is assumed to be a reflex of **djúp-dalr*.[50] On the other hand, it should be noted that Old Norse *djúr* is represented as *Dur-* in a form of the name Jurby that is approximately contemporary with the Abbeyland Bounds, namely *Dureby* 1291,[51] and Deepdale in Lancashire is recorded as *Dupedale* in 1228.[52] Thomson and Broderick both assume that the generic of *Duppolla* is Gaelic *poll* and the specific Gaelic *dubh* with the *bh* assimilated to the *p* of the generic. I believe, however, that the name may be a purely Scandinavian compound **djúp-pollr* 'deep pool'.

The Abbeyland boundary marks also include a number of settlement names. Two of these belong to a very characteristic group of Manx names, those consisting of the word *Kirk* 'church' and the name of the saint to whom the church in question is dedicated. These are the now-lost *Kirkemychel* and the parish-name *Kyrk Christ* (Kirk Christ Lezayre). The reference to the lost settlement is particularly interesting, for it reveals that it was also known by the name *villam Thorkel*. This suggests that the Kirk

Michael type names are secondary names that have replaced older names. To judge from the citing of two names for the one place in 1280, the substitution must have been fairly recent at that time. The Kirk Michael name-type seems likely to have been introduced to Man from south-west Scotland and north-west England, where it would seem to have arisen as a compromise between the Scandinavian name Kirkby (**kirkju-bȳ* 'church village'), which had spread north-westwards from the Danelaw, and Gaelic names such as Kilbride, which had spread eastwards from Ireland to south-western Scotland in the pre-Norse period. The names would seem to be associated with a reorganisation of the parochial system. It is only indirectly that they reflect Scandinavian influence.

Others of the settlement names in the Abbeyland Bounds are, however, of purely Scandinavian origin. Apart from Laxa, which is used as a primary name of the river itself and secondarily of the harbour at its mouth, these settlement names are primary habitative formations. There are two names in *-staðir*, two in *-bȳ* and two in *-toft*. The two *staðir*-names, *Herynstaze*, now Orrisdale in Malew (**Hærings-staðir*),[53] and *Gretastaz*, now Gretch in Lonan (**Grettirs-staðir*),[54] both seem to have Norse personal names as their specifics and thus compare closely with the *staðir*-names in Norway and Iceland that would seem to have originated as names for some kind of dependent settlement.

The two names in *-bȳ* might also be thought to have been given to dependent settlements, as was often the case in the Danelaw. *Totmanby*, now Tosaby in Malew, and *Sulaby*, now Sulby in Lezayre, are both treens, however, and it seems likely that these names were given to pre-existing settlements that were taken over by Norse-speakers. Tosaby (**toftmanna-bȳ*, 'the settlement of the toft-holders') was perhaps some kind of collectively owned settlement in which the farmers each had his own individual plot of land or *toft*,[55] while the specific of Sulby is probably *súla* 'cleft, fork', perhaps referring to a fork in the river.[56]

The two names in *-toft* probably also referred to some form of minor settlement. The element *toft* denoted a building plot. Neither of the *toft*-names in the Bounds has survived to the present day. *Toftha(r) Asmund*, now Ballellin, apparently has the elements in Celtic word-order with the generic preceding the specific, but there are both older and later records of this name with the elements in the usual Germanic order, *Asmundertoftes* *c.*1154 and 1329.[57] The spelling *Tofthar* presumably reflects the Norse plural form *toftir*. In England many of the *toft*-names originated as simplex names, such as *Toft* or *Toftes*. As a need for distinction from other places with the same name arose, distinguishing elements were added, occasionally in post-position, as in Toft Monks in Norfolk. The sequence *Asmunder* *toftas-Tofthar Asmund-Asmundertoftes* is curious. The first and third forms reflect the original Scandinavian genitive singular in *-ar* of the personal name and a secondary English plural form of the generic, while the form in the Bounds reflects the Scandinavian nominative plural of the generic. The survival of the *Asmunder*-spelling in the third form probably merely reflects that it is a copy of the form in the original twelfth-century grant. Megaw assumed that the form in the Bounds is a gaelicised one that was coined at a time when the Scandinavian nominative plural of *toft* still survived in the spoken language. The personal name would either have been left uninflected or inflected in the most common Gaelic fashion by palatalising the final consonant(-group), a palatalisation that would not be reflected in the orthography, as in, for instance, *Villa Thorkel* and *Crosyvor*.[58] The second name in *-toft* is the lost *Trollatofthar* in Malew, whose specific is more likely to be the genitive plural of the appellative *troll* 'troll' than a personal name *Trolli*.[59] It has a parallel in Troldtoft in Denmark (*Trolletofftt c.*1450).[60]

The six Scandinavian habitative names in the Abbeyland Bounds are not representative of the names of this class in the island as a whole, at least not in the frequency of occurrence of the individual generics. There are altogether about a dozen names in *-staðir* in Man, all except two of which lie north of a line running from Peel to Douglas, one of the two exceptions being *Herynstaze* in Malew. Various interpretations have been proposed for the *staðir*-names in Man but since the specifics of most of the names are personal names and the localities bearing the names are still only farms, it seems likely that in Man, as in Iceland, the generic *staðir* was used for dependent settlements that were granted to the followers of the men who had settled in the primary settlements. The element *staðir* is typically west Scandinavian and the names were presumably coined by men coming directly from Norway or from the Norwegian colonies in the Scottish islands.

There are no other recorded names in *-toft* in Man. The two names in the Bounds could have been coined by Norwegians or Danes, but a third possibility is that the men who coined the names came from the Danelaw, where names in *-toft* are of fairly common occurrence and where the structure *Toft* + specific also occurs.

The element *bӯ*, *bœr* is of frequent occurrence in all the Scandinavian countries but, although the Norwegians did take it with them to their Atlantic colonies, it is of rare occurrence in the Northern and Western Isles, except for secondary names such as simplex **Bœr* and compound **Húsabœr* and names for parts of the homefield such as *Evrabi*. An explanation is therefore required both for the cluster of *bӯ*-names in Man and for the

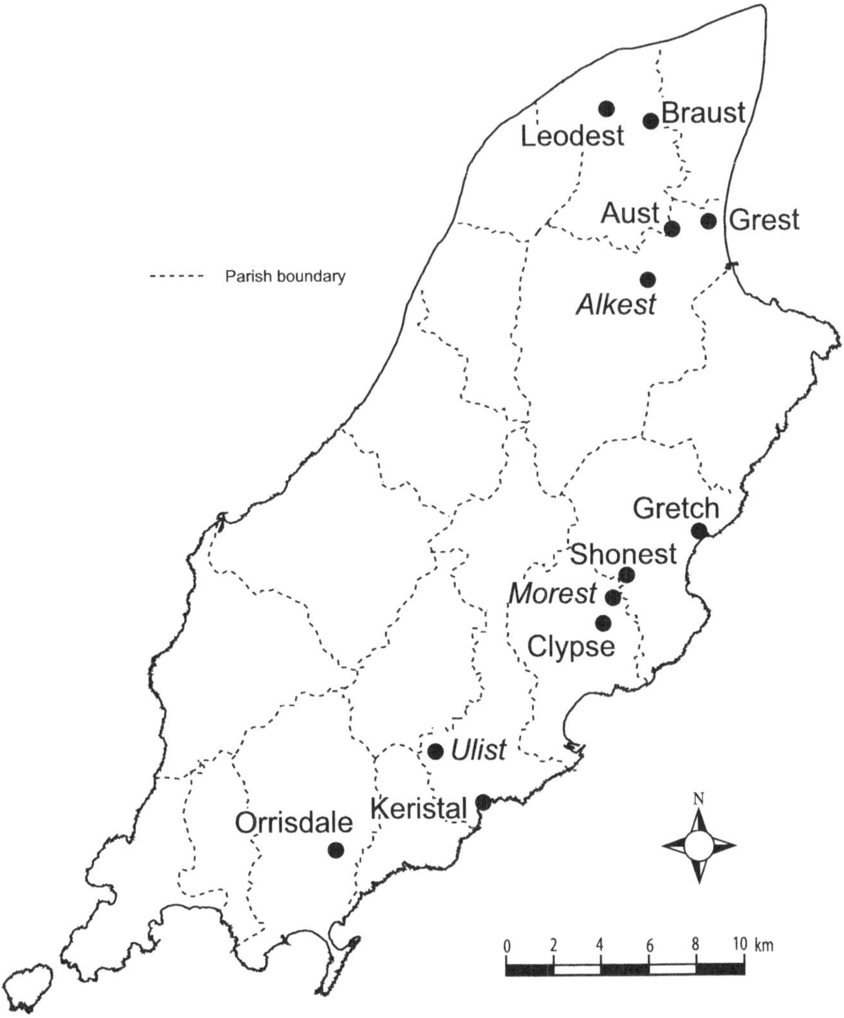

Fig. 12.5 *The distribution of place-names in* staðir.

comparatively high status of several of the Manx settlements bearing these names. To judge from the rents that were levied on them, they were among the more considerable on the island; six of them had been subdivided or expanded into two or three parts by 1500, and eight of them contained ten or more tenements.

No fewer than 15 of the 26 Manx names in *-bȳ* have exact parallels in either north-west England or North Yorkshire. The 15 names are two Colbys, two Crosbys, Dalby, Jurby, Kirby, two Rabys, Regaby, Scholaby, Surby and three Sulbys. There are several possible explanations for the presence of these names in Man. The distribution of names in *-bȳ* over the British Isles is in general outline a reliable indication of the spread of Danish or Danelaw influence.[61] It was in the last quarter of the ninth century that an organized settlement of Danes took place in eastern England. To begin with the Danes took over existing English settlements, sometimes without interfering with their names, sometimes replacing the English names with secondary names such as Kirkby 'church village' or Derby 'village with a deer-park'. At the end of the ninth century and the beginning of the tenth the large English estates began to be split up into small, independent, agricultural units, many of which received names consisting of the tenant's personal name and the element *-bȳ*, such as Grimsby (*Grím*). Other Danes, however, moved out across the Pennines, particularly along the Eden valley. Having reached Carlisle, some of the Danes moved northwards into eastern Dumfriesshire and others southwards into the coastal plain of Cumberland. From there it seems likely that some made their way across the Irish Sea to Man. This anti-clockwise movement can be traced in a trail of settlement names in *-bȳ*. Eventually there would seem to have been a movement back across the sea from Man to Wirral and south-west Lancashire. It is impossible to date this penetration of Danish settlement across the Pennines at all closely, but the presence of pagan Viking burials along the routes followed by settlers entering Cumbria from the Danelaw and in the coastal plain of Cumberland has been interpreted as an indication that the settlement in the north-west must have begun comparatively early.[62] The reoccupation of northern Cumbria by the Strathclyde Britons at some date before 927 and the fact that English rule had been restored over Cheshire and southern Lancashire by 934 imply that most of the Scandinavian place-names in these areas must have been coined before these dates at least and the same must apply to the names in Man, if the *bȳ*-names in south-west Lancashire and Wirral were in fact coined by settlers from Man.

Contact between England and Man did not come to an end early in the tenth century, however, although Michael Dolley has noted that to judge from the lack of coin hoards Man would seem to have held itself aloof from the Viking world in the first half of that century.[63] From the second half of the tenth century and the middle 50 years of the eleventh century, however, altogether about 15 hoards containing Viking-Age coins have been found in Man.[64] The hoard found at Kirk Michael in 1972 contained six tenth-century English coins, all of which came from mints in north-eastern

England, and there were no contemporary coins from the north-west, a fact which suggests that the coins had been introduced into Man quite recently before their concealment, for other Manx hoards show a preponderance of coins from the Chester mint.[65] The eleventh-century coins in the hoard are also predominantly from the north-eastern mints. Michael Dolley has therefore suggested that the coins might have been brought together in Orkney. A squadron of Orcadian ships had sailed south in 1066 to support Tosti's rebellion against his brother, King Harold Godwinesson, but after the Norwegian defeat at Stamford Bridge, the Orcadians had been forced to come to terms with the English and retreat northwards. Among these ships was one under the command of Godred Crovan, who would then seem to have decided to try his luck in Man, and Dolley has suggested that it may have been on this occasion that the coins in the Kirk Michael hoard were brought to the island. The question is, however, whether Godred Crovan might not have recruited men in the Danelaw or north-west England before his victory at the battle of Sky Hill in 1079. Marstrander tentatively linked the names in *-bȳ* in Man with Crovan's subsequent partition of the island, in which those of his own followers who wanted to stay on the island were granted lands in the southern and most fertile portion, while the native Manxmen were allowed to retain the northern part, then largely swamp.[66] If Crovan's men had been recruited in northern England, there would then be a natural explanation for the Manx *bȳ*-names with parallels in England.

The next immigration to Man from England for which there is evidence is that of the English administrators who were brought in after the island had been ceded to the English crown. Over 500 surnames of an essentially non-Gaelic nature are recorded in Manx sources and most of these are in fact English place-names functioning as surnames.[67] Almost all the original bearers of these surnames would have come to Man after 1405 and they are strictly speaking outside the scope of the present paper, but in the light of the fact that their influence on the written records was marked, they cannot be ignored in an assessment of the place-name evidence. To judge from the surnames, about two-thirds of the immigrants in the period down to 1540 came from Lancashire. This is natural enough, since this is where most of the Stanley estates were situated and the Stanleys would presumably have looked first to their tenantry when making appointments to the insular administration.

I should like to illustrate some of the problems involved in the assessment of the recorded evidence by reference to the forms noted for Manx place-names in *-bȳ*. Jurby is identical in origin with the English name Derby. While the original form **djúra-bȳ* developed in Man via *Dureby*

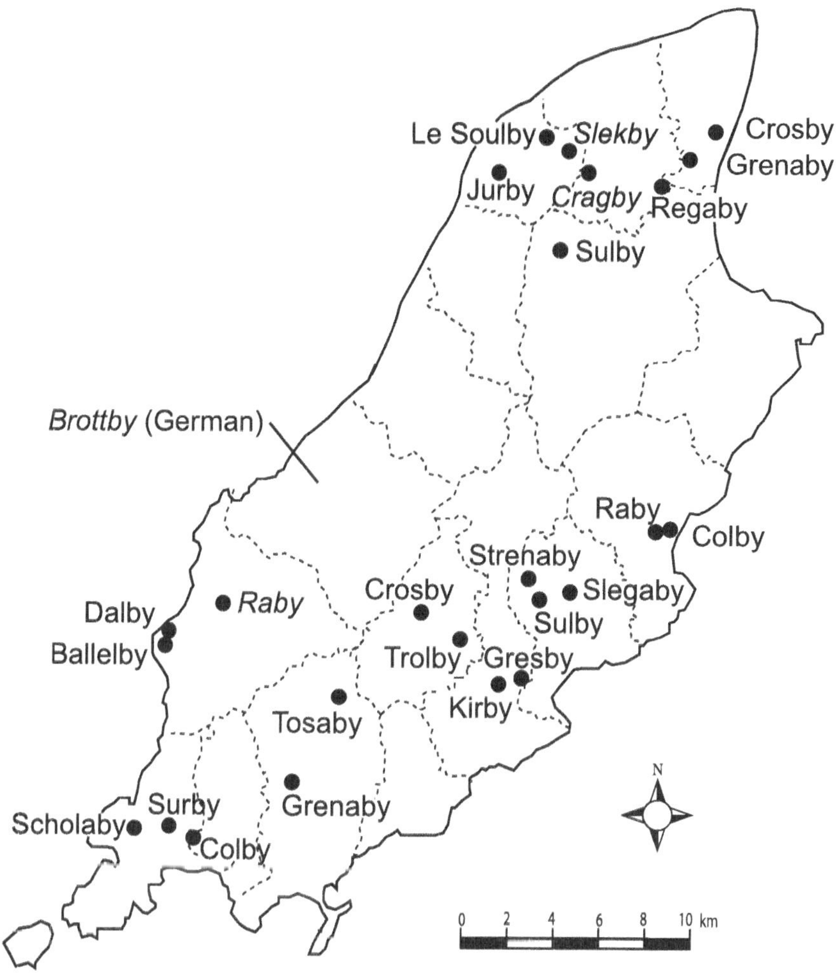

Fig. 12.6 *The distribution of place-names in* by.

to Jurby, in England it developed via *Deoraby* to Derby. The Stanley administrators do not seem to have recognised the ultimate identity of Jurby and Derby, for they registered the treen- and parish-name as *Jourby*.[68] The failure of the Stanley administrators to recognise the name would presumably have been because the palatal *d* of the Scandinavian form had already been assibilated in Manx. Their reaction to some of the other *bȳ*-names, however, was different. Sulby in Lezayre[69] is identical in origin with two Soulbys in Cumberland and Westmorland respectively,[70] and shares the same development as Sulby in Onchan whose earliest record is as Sulaby in 1280 and which has later forms such as Sulby 1713.[71] The modification of the pronunciation in the Manx names may reflect the shortening in Manx surnames. Regaby in Andreas, an original **hrygg-bȳ* 'ridge village', is recorded as *Rygby* in 1515, probably under the influence of the form taken by the name Ribby in Lancashire (*Rigbi* 1086),[72] but it is the three-syllabled Manx form that survives.[73] The insertion of the medial vowel in Regaby is a Manx feature to avoid the consonant cluster. The treen-name Dalby in Patrick is identical with two Dalbys in the North Riding of Yorkshire,[74] and spellings such as *Dawby* 1708 and the modern pronunciation reflect English influence.[75] The treen-name Slegaby in Onchan has a spelling *Slekby* 1511, perhaps because the English administrators recognised that its first element was *slakki* 'slope',[76] and that it is in fact identical with the now-lost treen-name Slekby in Jurby, all of whose recorded forms retain the spelling with *-k*.[77] The development to Slegaby is what would be expected in a Manx environment, with voicing of *k* to *g* and insertion of a medial consonant. The treen-name Surby in Rushen is recorded in 1511 as *Saureby*, a spelling showing its identity with several Sowerbys in north-west England,[78] but it is the Manx development to Surby that survives.[79] The shortening of the vowel may be a result of the shortening in surnames. In the treen-name Scholaby in Rushen, the 1511 spelling *Scaleby* seems to show that the name is identical with Scaleby in Cumberland,[80] while the later spellings, *Scaldeby* 1643 and *Scoalaby* 1840,[81] make this explanation perhaps seem less likely, although it is possible that the Scholaby-type spellings reflect the normal English development of long *a* to long *o* in southern Lancashire, where place-names containing Scandinavian *skáli* have forms in *Schole-*.

If it were not that the mountain of Barrule is named in the Manx chronicle, it might not have been realised that its name probably originated as Scandinavian **varðar-fjall* 'look-out hill', for the initial bilabial has been radicalised to *b*, the intervocalic *-th-* has been lost and *fjall* has developed to *-ūl*, as a result of Manx voicing of [f] to [v] and subsequent vocalising of [v] so that the Scandinavian loanword ends up by falling together with the Manx adjectival ending *-amhail* '-like'.[82] Another *fjall*-name whose origin was not recognised in the sixteenth century is Camall/Cammall, the name of a treen and quarterland in Michael.[83] It occurs in a sixteenth-century historical poem in the form *Keamool*, rhyming with *Barrool*.[84] Kneen and Marstrander, however, both identified the name correctly as a Scandinavian **kamba-fjall* 'ridge mountain'. In the case of the treen- and quarterland-name Lambefell/Lambfell in German, the identity with Scandinavian **lamba-fjall* 'lamb mountain' was also recognised by the sixteenth-century scribes, who recorded the form *Lambefell* in 1515, even though spellings reflecting the Manx developments, such as *Lammell*, continued to occur.[85] For some other *fjall*-names the situation is even more complex. The mountain known as Sartfell (**svart-fjall* 'black mountain') is recorded in young documents in forms both with and without *-f-*,[86] but an intack which took its name from the mountain is recorded in 1728 as both *Sartall* and *Sartfield*, suggesting that the *-f-* must have survived and led to substitution of English *feld* 'field'. The treen of Sertfell in Jurby is recorded with this spelling in 1515 and has some spellings in *-field* in the eighteenth century, while the quarterlands Sartfield Mooar and Veg show spellings in *-field*, with the exception of *Sartal Veg* in 1771. Forms such as *Sartal* probably reflect an alternative development of *-fjall* as the second element of a compound, in which the stress remains initial and the long vowel of the Manx form of the second element is shortened. An interpretation as 'black mountain' is not topographically appropriate here so the generic has been taken to be *hóll* 'hill', which would have fallen together with *fjall* in Manx.[87] The most complex problem is connected with the name of the island's highest mountain, Snaefell, whose present form causes the thoughts to fly across the Atlantic to Iceland. This form, however, is a comparatively modern antiquarianising one, with its first record dating from 1733.[88] The Manx form of the name, *Sniaul*, represents the normal development of Scandinavian **snæ-fjall* 'snow mountain', while the earliest recorded forms such as *Snawble* 1586 and *Snafeld* 1595 suggest that English scribes associated the name with the English words *snāw* 'snow' and *feld*.[89] The substitution of *-feld* for *-fell* in some forms of Sartfell and Snaefell is probably a result of hypercorrection, reflecting the fact that the loss of *-d* in this word is a dialect feature.

The Scandinavian element *nes* 'promontory' occurs in a small number of Manx treen-names and would seem to have been recognized by the English scribes. Agneash in Lonan is recorded as *Hegnes* in 1511,[90] Cregneash in Rushen as *Crokenesse* in 1511,[91] and Rheneash in Bride as *Rennesse* in 1515.[92] Marstrander explained the spellings in *-nesse* as reflecting a genitive of Manx **neash* from *nes*, but it is perhaps more likely to reflect English orthography. The Lancashire name Amounderness, for example, has spellings in *-nesse* from 1086 to 1540.[93] The subsequent development to *-sh*, however, is clearly a Gaelic feature. Langness is not a treen-name but the name of the long, flat promontory that juts out from Derby Haven into Castletown Bay. The name looks like a Scandinavian formation but early records such as *Longnese* 1428, *Langnase* 1511, *Lang Nouse* 1595 point rather to an English name in **nesu*, **nosu* 'nose' or perhaps they merely reflect the fact that the original Scandinavian name was associated by the

Fig. 12.7 *Modern sign posts.*

scribes with English names containing the word for 'nose'.[94]

It is at all events clear that many of the place-name forms recorded in early sixteenth-century sources in Man reflect English influence. The English administrators must often have recognised the identity of the Scandinavian names or elements with names or elements with which they were familiar in their homeland. Such names would have presented much less difficulty to them than the Manx names and would have had a better chance of surviving. Detailed studies of place-names in Ireland have shown that quite a number of these were translated into English, sometimes incorrectly.[95] It is of particular significance for the present paper to note that where settlement names in Ireland had both an Irish name and a Scandinavian one, generally unrelated coinages, it was always the Scandinavian name that was taken over by the incoming English and that has persisted in use by English-speakers ever since. This is presumably because the Norse names were less lexically opaque to the English settlers than the Irish ones.

It is not my impression that the English in Man deliberately renamed places in the fifteenth century or later but it seems clear that they exercised a strong influence on the form in which some of the Scandinavian names survived. There would also seem to have been some deliberate scandinavianisation in later years of names which had been gaelicised or anglicised. With these qualifications in mind, it is not unreasonable to look upon the Scandinavian and Manx names recorded in the early sixteenth-century setting books and the early eighteenth-century Lord's Composition Books as representative of the names in use in the island in the period of Norse rule and in the first century after its cessation.[96]

Notes

1 A.L.F. Rivet and Colin Smith, *The Place-Names of Roman Britain* (London, 1979), 411.

2 Pointed out to me by R.L. Thomson. Cf. Joan N. Radner, *Fragmentary Annals of Ireland* (Dublin, 1978), 236. There is some doubt as to whether the battle known as *Cath Manann* was fought on Man or at the place at the head of the Forth in Stirlingshire whose name survives in the place-names Slamannan (*Slefmannyn* 1275) and Clackmannan (*Clackmanan* 1147). Cf. Watson, *Celtic Place-Names of Scotland*, 103.

3 Cf. Gelling, 'The place-names of the Isle of Man'; Megaw, 'Norseman and native', in the Kingdom of the Isles; a reassessment of the Manx evidence', *Scottish Studies*, 20, 1–44 (1976), revised version in Davey (ed.), *Man and Environment*, 265–314 (citations are from the latter version).

4 For a discussion of Manx land divisions, see chapter 19 below.

5 J.J. Kneen, *The Place-Names of the Isle of Man with their Origin and History*, 6 vols (Douglas, 1925–8; repr. 1970, in one vol.).

6 C.J.S. Marstrander, 'Det Norske Landnåm På Man', *Norsk Tidsskrift for Sprogvidenskap*, 6 (1932), 40–386, and 'Remarks on the place-names of the Isle Of Man', *Norsk Tidsskrift for Sprogvidenskap*, 7 (1934), 287–334.

7 Gelling, 'Place-names'; Megaw, 'Norseman and native'; R.L. Thomson, 'The interpretation of some Manx place-names', in Davey (ed.), *Man and the Environment*, 319–25; Gillian Fellows-Jensen, 'Scandinavian settlement in the Isle of Man and Northwest England: the place-name evidence', in *The Viking Age*

in the Isle of Man. Select papers from the Ninth Viking Congress, Isle of Man, 4–14 July 1981, ed. Christine Fell *et al.* (London, 1983), 37–52; Margaret Gelling, 'The place-names of the Isle of Man', in Sture Ureland and George Broderick (eds), *Language Contact in the British Isles. Proceedings of the Eighth International Symposium on Language Contact in Europe, Douglas, Isle of Man, 1988* (Tübingen, 1991), 141–55.

8 George Broderick, *Placenames of the Isle of Man*, 1 Sheading of Glenfaba (Tübingen, 1994), 2 Sheading of Michael (1995), 3 Sheading of Ayre (1997), 4 Sheading of Garff (1999), 5 Sheading of Middle (2000), 6 Sheading of Rushen (2002), 7 Douglas and Appendices (2005) (hereafter cited as *PNIM*).

9 William and Constance Radcliffe, *Maughold and Ramsey Place-Names* (Ramsey, 1978), and *Kirk Bride – a Miscellany* (Ramsey, 1983).

10 Broderick, *PNIM* 3, 448.

11 Broderick, *PNIM* 3, 73.

12 Marstrander, 'Det Norske Landnåm På Man', 307, 315, 330–1.

13 Gelling, 'Place-names'.

14 Broderick, *PNIM* 1, xxvi.

15 O.J. Padel, *Cornish Place-Name Elements*, English Place-Name Society, volume 56/7 (1985), 203.

16 K.H. Jackson, *Language and History in Early Britain* (Edinburgh, 1953), 674–6.

17 Alan Crozier, 'On the transparency of place-names in Ireland, England, and Sweden', *Ainm*, 3 (1988), 42–58.

18 Broderick, *PNIM* 1, 19; 2, 257; 3, 441; 7, 340.

19 Broderick, *PNIM* 2, xxix–xxx, 171, 239; 3, 378.

20 Liam Price, 'A note on the use of the word *Baile* in place-names', *Celtica*, 6 (1963), 119–26.

21 Broderick, *PNIM* 1, 33, 35.

22 W.F.H. Nicolaisen, *Scottish Place-Names* (London, 1976), 133.

23 Megaw and Megaw, 'The Norse heritage in the Isle of Man', in Fox and Dickins (eds), *The Early Cultures of North-West Europe*, 141–70, fig.13.

24 D.M. Wilson, 'Manx memorial stones of the Viking period', *Saga-Book of the Viking Society*, 18 (1970–3), 1–18; R.I. Page, 'The Manx rune-stones', in Fell *et al.* (eds), *The Viking Age in the Isle of Man*, 133–46.

25 Megaw, 'Norseman and native', 276–8.

26 Broderick, *PNIM* 1, 31; 2, 25.

27 Broderick, *PNIM* 2, 18.

28 Broderick, *PNIM* 1, 48, 179; 2, 251.

29 Marstrander, 'Det Norske Landnåm På Man', 207–8.

30 It was R.L. Thomson who first suggested that the *c* in *Ballacgniba* was not merely a superfluous velar consonant but belonged to the generic; in Thomson, 'Some Manx place-names', 320.

31 Broderick, *PNIM* 3, 268, 423.

32 Broderick, *PNIM* 1, 192–3.

33 Broderick, *PNIM* 1, 250.

34 Marstrander, 'Det Norske Landnåm På Man', 230.

35 Broderick, *PNIM* 2, 177.

36 Broderick, *PNIM* 1, 155.

37 Broderick, *PNIM* 3, 440–1.

38 Broderick *PNIM* 4, 167; 6, 161–2.

39 Broderick, *PNIM* 1, 158.

40 Broderick, *PNIM* 1, 295.

41 Gillian Fellows-Jensen, 'Tingwall, Dingwall and Thingwall', *NOWELE [North-Western European Language Evolution]*, 21/2 (1993), 53–67. A revised and expanded version printed under the title 'Tingwall: the significance of the name', in Doreen J. Waugh (ed.), *Shetland's Northern Links: Language and History* (Edinburgh, 1996), 16–29.
42 Broderick, *PNIM* 6, 93, 168.
43 Broderick, *PNIM* 4, 83.
44 Broderick, *PNIM* 4, 326.
45 Broderick, *PNIM* 1, 53.
46 Broderick, *PNIM* 6, 165.
47 Broderick, *PNIM* 6, 350.
48 Gillian Fellows-Jensen, 'Scandinavian place-names of the Irish Sea province', in James Graham-Campbell (ed.), *Viking Treasure from the North West. The Cuerdale Hoard in its Context* (Liverpool, 1992), 31–42.
49 Megaw 'Norseman and native', 309.
50 Thomson, 'Some Manx place-names', 323; Broderick, *PNIM* 3, 378–9.
51 Broderick, *PNIM* 2, 245.
52 Gillian Fellows-Jensen, *Scandinavian Settlement Names in the North-West*, Navnestudier, 25 (Copenhagen, 1985), 119.
53 Broderick, *PNIM* 6, 153.
54 Broderick, *PNIM* 4, 311.
55 Broderick, *PNIM* 6, 182–3.
56 Broderick, *PNIM* 3, 468.
57 Megaw 'Norseman and native', 273, 299, 308; Broderick, *PNIM* 4, 25, 162.
58 I owe this comment to R.L. Thomson.
59 Broderick, *PNIM* 6, 184–5.
60 Gordon Albøge, Stednavne: Ringkøbing Amt, *Danmarks Stednavne*, 17 (1976–84), 408.
61 Gillian Fellows-Jensen, 'Anthroponymical specifics in place-names in *-bȳ* in the British Isles', *Studia Anthroponymica Scandinavica*, 1 (1983), 44–60, and *Scandinavian Settlement Names in the North-West*, 411–12.
62 D.M. Wilson (ed.), *The Archaeology of Anglo-Saxon England* (Cambridge, 1976), 396–99.
63 Michael Dolley, 'New light on the 1894 Douglas hoard', *JMM*, 7, no.85, 121–4.
64 See chapter 18 below, and A.M. Cubbon, 'The 1972 Kirk Michael Viking treasure trove. The hoard: its discovery, composition and general historical implications', *JMM*, 8, no.89, 5–11.
65 Michael Dolley, 'The numismatic element of the hoard, and a possible historical context', *JMM*, 8, no.89, 11–20.
66 Marstrander, 'Det Norske Landnåm På Man', 327.
67 Michael Dolley, 'Toponymic surnames and the pattern of pre-1830 English immigration into the Isle of Man', *Nomina*, 7 (1983), 47–64; Gillian Fellows-Jensen, 'How old are the Scandinavian place-names in Man?', *Proceedings*, 9:3 (2004), 423–36.
68 Broderick, *PNIM* 2, 205, 245.
69 Broderick, *PNIM* 3, 468.
70 Fellows-Jensen, *Scandinavian Settlement Names in the North-West*, 40.
71 Broderick, *PNIM*, 4, 418.
72 Fellows-Jensen, *Scandinavian Settlement Names in the North-West*, 38.
73 Broderick, *PNIM* 3, 160, 165.
74 Gillian Fellows-Jensen, *Scandinavian Settlement Names in Yorkshire*,

Navnestudier 11 (Copenhagen, 1972), 25.
75 Broderick, *PNIM* 1, 95.
76 Broderick, *PNIM* 4, 416.
77 Broderick, *PNIM* 2, 268–9.
78 Fellows-Jensen, *Scandinavian Settlement Names in the North-West*, 40.
79 Broderick, *PNIM* 6, 484, 498.
80 Fellows-Jensen, *Scandinavian Settlement Names in the North-West*, 39.
81 Broderick, *PNIM* 6, 484, 486
82 Broderick, *PNIM* 1, 53.
83 Broderick, *PNIM* 2, 53.
84 Information supplied by R.L. Thomson.
85 Broderick, *PNIM* 1, 267.
86 Broderick, *PNIM* 2, 95.
87 Marstrander, 'Det Norske Landnåm På Man', 236; Broderick, *PNIM* 2, 267–8.
88 Broderick, *PNIM* 3, 464.
89 Cf. perhaps the name Goatfell in Arran, an anglicised form of Scandinavian **geita-fjall*, which was gaelicised as *Gaotabeinn*; cf. G. Henderson, *The Norse Influence on Celtic Scotland* (Glasgow, 1910), 131, 204.
90 Broderick, *PNIM* 4, 217–18.
91 Broderick, *PNIM* 6, 392–3.
92 Broderick, *PNIM* 3, 260–1.
93 E. Ekwall, *The Place-Names of Lancashire* (Manchester, 1922), 139.
94 Broderick, *PNIM* 6, 137–8.
95 Éamonn de hÓir, 'The anglicisation of Irish place-names', *Onoma*, 17 (1972–3), 192–204.
96 I am very grateful to R.L. Thomson and Richard A.V. Cox for kindly reading a draft of the present paper and giving me much good advice on Manx and Gaelic names. My thanks are also due to Margaret Gelling and Eva and David Wilson, who made it possible for me to visit the sites of almost all the places whose names I have ventured to discuss.

13 *The Isle of Man in Medieval Gaelic Literature*

CHARLES W. MACQUARRIE

Despite its close proximity to the east coast of Ireland and the west of Scotland, the Isle of Man usually appears as a markedly exotic location in medieval Gaelic literature. Although it is mentioned in the annals as an important prize in the colonial ambitions of various Irish and Scottish dynasties from the sixth century, in most of the tales it is a place associated with magic and isolation rather than with conquest and secular power politics.[1] In other tales, which probably extrapolate the Lordship of the Isles back into the mythic past of the region, Man is a centre of power from which a highking comes to make a circuit and to put in order the affairs and households of a disorderly Ireland. Another notable feature of its appearance in most of the tales is a lack of detail in the descriptions of the island. While medieval Gaelic literature is rich in onomastics there is seldom a mention of any particular location on the Isle of Man, and our impressions of the island, based on the tales, are of a dark and misty place, the sea pounding its tall craggy cliffs, and populated by very few and rather strange creatures.

There are consistencies then, as well as contradictions, in the portrayal of the Isle of Man in medieval Gaelic literature. It is sometimes presented as marginal and sometimes as central to the mythical geography of the culture. One of its most important and consistent associations in the tales is with the character Manannán mac Lir, the sometime god of the Irish Sea. The Isle of Man, according to the authority of early medieval texts such as *Sanas Cormaic* ('Cormac's Glossary') and *Tochmarc Luaine* ('The Wooing of Luan'), and to the meaning of his very name 'the little one of Man', is the home of Manannán. But the relationship between the character and the island is more complex than that between a man and his homeland. The character and the island sometimes bear a synecdochic relationship to one another in the literature – in some cases Manannán even seems to be a personification of the island – and the association with Manannán is central to Man's place in medieval Gaelic literature.[2]

Nevertheless, Man is not Manannán's only home and Manannán is not the only important character to be associated with the Isle of Man. A.W. Moore, in his study of the folklore of the Isle of Man, first published over

100 years ago, briefly discussed the connections between the magically powerful Midir, Cú Roí, the smith Culann, and the Isle of Man. Culann, as Moore notes, is located on the Isle of Man in versions of the 'Boyhood Deeds of Cúchulainn' and it is to Man that Conchobar mac Nessa goes in order to have Culann forge his battle armour. When, with the help of the magically powerful armour, Conchobar takes the kingship of Ulster, he brings Culann from Man to live in honour in Ireland.[3] Moore also discusses a tale he calls the story of the Isle of Falga, which, as he relates, is sometimes taken to be either the Isle of Man or the Western Isles of Scotland. In this story, which is better known as *Aided Con Roí* ('The Death of Cú Roí'),[4] Midir is the king of the Isle and Cú Roí is the king's enemy who conspires, along with the Ulstermen, to raid the king's palace and steal his jewels. The Isle of Man in both these tales is associated with supernatural power that is imported into Ireland, but it is only briefly mentioned, and its association with Cú Roí and Culann is exceptional. The supernatural power that flows from the island, however, is characteristic of its presentation in other tales as well. The Isle of Man appears to be far enough away from Ireland to be exotic and magical, but, at the same time, close enough to be a repository of Gaelic culture – the rich and strange people and things that are located there are clearly Gaelic rather than foreign in nature.

This combination of exotic and mysterious marginality and cultural centrality is also characteristic of the Isle of Man in the story of the journey of the possibly mythical early poet, Senchán Torpéist. There are a number of versions of an episode in which Senchán travels to the Isle of Man in search of a poetess who had gone on a circuit of Ireland, Scotland, and Man. Kuno Meyer included three versions of this story in his edition of *Sanas Cormaic*, a glossary of obsolete and difficult Irish words, compiled in the early tenth century by the famous king-bishop of Cashel, Cormac mac Cuilennáin.[5] While there are a number of variant readings among the three versions the episodes are very similar. But one significant difference is the fact that the poetess is described in two versions as having gone on a circuit of Ireland, Scotland, and Man, while in the other her circuit is said to have included only Ireland and Scotland.[6]

One of the most significant questions about the episode is why Senchán and his troop go to Man at all. It seems, at first, that they go there only to visit the island on a 'journey of pleasure'.[7] This makes it sound like a sort of vacation, which it may have been, at least in part, but the other word used to describe the trip here is *cúairt* 'circuit', which word suggests either that Senchán is making an official or semi-official tour of households of the island in his role as chief poet, or that he is searching the island for someone or something. While it is also possible to take the word *cúairt* to mean that Senchán and his troop went to the island on a journey of exploration, the word more usually denotes a tour during which travellers receive hospitality from the local luminary. Senchán is used to being looked after in grand style by his hosts, and can anticipate that he will get a welcome on Man. Unfortunately for our purposes, however, Senchán never actually lands on the island in the three versions included in Meyer's edition, and we are not given a picture of the thriving social life on Man that Senchán may have been expecting.

In fact, the impressions that we do get of the island are of a barren and all but depopulated place. All that Senchán and his men see as their ship approaches the shore is a large nobly proportioned but unkempt and shabbily (and it seems scantily) dressed woman.[8] The woman is the only person whom the poets encounter. She is positioned on the *carraic* 'cliffs' and is said to be collecting seaweed and other sea-produce. The implication of her appearance and her industry is that she is a lonely exile on the island. One explanation of her reason for going to Man is that she was seeking isolation.[9] She is apparently in mourning for her household who have all died (*ba marb a muintir uile*),[10] and her 'circuit' of Man seems to be more like the wanderings of a *gealt* (a roaming lunatic) than those of a famous poetess seeking the largesse of the Manx aristocracy. Did she go to Man to be alone, to commune with nature and live off seaweed much as the most famous *gealt* of medieval Gaelic literature, Suibne, escaped to the wilds of Ireland and lived on watercress? Certainly, considering her state of discomposure, she was not living in luxury on Man. If Man is seen as a place where the poetess went in order to get away from people and be in touch with nature, then it is analogous to the natural Ireland to which Suibne flees – a place not apart from the Irish way of life but rather a source of it.

Still another important association that the episode makes is between the Isle of Man and magic. After the troop spot the poetess from the ship, and before she allows them to land, she challenges them to a poetic contest, which they are only able to win with the help of a grotesque and apparently supernatural churl who has stowed away on the ship against Senchán's will. The cryptic verse or riddle she recites is *Níbsa éolaig imnig odbaigh/Ciasa femmain [m]bolgaigh bung*, which translates 'I do not comprehend a difficult problem/What is blistered seaweed?'. The churl, after a long pause in which Senchán and his poetic troop try desperately and unsuccessfully to come up with a response, jumps up before Senchán, and with the poetess's permission, recites the proper *lethrand* (couplet): *de muin cairge máre Manann/do rónad mór saland sund* ('From the top of the tall cliffs of Man/was made a great deal of salt there'). As with many other verse-capping episodes in medieval Irish literature, the correct interpretation of the verses is not immediately obvious. Perhaps the riddle asks why seaweed has such strange shapes and the answer, in two parts, is that it is because the sea is salty and that the salt in the sea comes from the cliffs of Man. The Isle of Man is connected with sea-salt here, but the exact nature of that connection, whether as a part of a mythic explanation for the origin of salt (and the appearance of seaweed) or as a place where salt was produced, is by no means clear. The other association that comes out of the verse-capping episode is that between the island and the mysterious and hideous churl who answers the riddle, and who is revealed at the end of the episode to be the spirit of poetry in disguise. It is this character, with his preternatural appearance, poetic skill, and arcane knowledge about Man, who finds the right verses for Senchán.

A version of Senchán's journey to Man that is different in significant ways from those versions edited by Meyer in *Sanas Cormaic* appears at the end of the early modern Irish tale *Tromdámh Guaire* ('Guaire's Troublesome Guest-Company').[11] This tale is notable both for its length, one of the longest of medieval Irish literary texts, and for its lively parody of the presumption of Irish poets. The Isle of Man is mentioned only briefly in *Tromdámh Guaire*, but here again it is clearly associated with magic and mystery. In this version Senchán goes to the Isle of Man not for a pleasant vacation, not for an outdoor adventure, and not to search for a woman poet; rather he goes there in search of the most celebrated of all medieval Irish sagas *Táin Bó Cúailnge* – actually, Senchán and his troop of poets stop on Man on their way to search for the *Táin* in Scotland. It is notable that Man is presented as a natural midpoint between the north of Ireland and Scotland in this story. In fact, Senchán and his troop would have to go out of their way to stop at the Isle on their way from Ulster to Scotland. The trip is not long enough for them to stop for supplies, and reprovisioning is not given as a reason.

The island functions in part as a barrier in this story.[12] The *carraic*, or cliffs, suggest an actual barrier and the required verse contest a virtual one. Is there some ritual reason that the poets must stop at Man before they can go on to Scotland to search for the *Táin*? When the troop reaches Man they are challenged to a poetic contest not by the poetess, but rather by a lone man stationed high up on the cliffs. They win the contest and are allowed to land on the island only because of the intervention of a supernatural character disguised as a *lobur* 'leper' – later in this version of the tale revealed to be the holy swineherd Marbán.[13] Once they navigate this barrier, by passing this test, they are able to resume their quest.

In *Tromdámh Guaire* the Isle of Man appears as a place where fine hospitality is to be had. While only two residents are mentioned, the man who plays the role of gate-keeper to the island from his cliff-top lookout, and a woman doctor (*banliaigh*) who entertains and rewards them, Man here is a less isolated and a richer location than it was in the *Sanas Cormaic*. Senchán and his troop, on the leper's instructions, go in search of the woman doctor 'who makes salt every other year' and has a chest containing 60 marks (i.e. 40 pounds) hidden in her stone house. They are very well received by the woman who, having put them up for the night, gives them 30 marks the next morning before they set out for Scotland to continue their search for the *Táin Bó Cúailnge*. The woman poet's home, where they are entertained, may be conceived either as a thriving estate or as an isolated, perhaps supernaturally appointed, retreat. In any case, when they move on to Scotland, the poetic troop is entertained, in not markedly superior style, by the king of Scotland. And Scotland is described in even less detail than Man. The fact that the king of Scotland is mentioned suggests, however, that it is conceived as a more socially sophisticated place than the Isle of Man (which does not seem to merit a king).

Although none of the versions of Senchán's journey to Man mention him by name, the most important association of the Isle of Man in medieval Gaelic literature is with Manannán mac Lir. (In fact, the role of the supernatural 'spirit of poetry', who is disguised as a churl, is very similar to roles Manannán plays in a number of tales.) Manannán's very name, which translates as 'the little one from Man son of the sea', signals the connection, and every time this rather popular character appears in a tale the place-name is also evoked. While Manannán is clearly a supernatural character in origin, and manifests his powers to some degree in most of his appearances in Irish literature, he is also euhemerised in a number of stories. There is an entry for Manannán in *Sanas Cormaic*, which both connects him with the Isle of Man and insists on his mortal nature. A nearly identical passage also appears in a text called *Cóir Anmann* ('The Fitness of Names'). *Cóir Anmann* is similar to *Sanas Cormaic*, in that it provides brief stories to explain the origin of the names of traditional personages, as well as poems and triads referring to them, and genealogies,[14] and is of generally similar date and provenance. The entries referring to Manannán are:[15]

Sanas Cormaic

Manandán mac Lir, cendaighe amra robúi a nInis Manann. Is hé luamaire is dech robúi a n-iarthur domuin. Rofindad trie nemgnacht .i. tria déicsin gné in nime, .i. ind aeoir, ind airet nobíth ind thsoinind ocus in donend ocus intan conclaochbadh cechtar de a rré. Inde Scoti [et]

Britones eum deum uocauerunt maris, et inde filium maris esse dixerunt (is aire sin dogairdis Scoitice [*sic*] ocus Brethnaig dee in mara de ocus adeirdis corba mac don muir hé) .i. mac lir. Dé nomine Manannán Manand insula dicta est (ocus is uaide aderar Inis Manand).

Manannán mac Lir, a wonderful trader who was from the Isle of Man. He was the best pilot who was in the West of the world. He would know through his sky-gazing, that is through looking at the state of the heavens, that is the air, the length of time the fine weather would last, and the bad weather, and when it would change from one to the other. The Gaels [and] the British called him the god of the sea, and they said that he was the son of the sea. (Hence the Irish speakers and the British speakers called him the god of the sea and they said that he was the son of the sea) that is *mac lir*. The Isle is called Man from the name Manannán (and it is from him that the Isle of Man is called).

Cóir Anmann

Manannán mac lir .i. Oirbsin a ainm .i. cendaighi amhra robi a n-Inis Manann .i. isse luamhaire is dech robhi for muir a n-iarthar domain. Rofinnadh triana engnacht .i. tria dheicsin ghne ind neime .i. ind aeoir, ind airet nobhith in tsoininn no in doininn, ocus intan conclaechlobadh araile, ocus is aire sin rothoimnetar Bretnaigh ocus fir Erenn essiumh gurbha dee in mhara e ocus Mac lir aderthi fris .i. mac in mhara. Manannán dano do radh ris a Manainn.

Manannán mac Lir, Orbsen his name, that is a wonderful trader who was from the Isle of Man. He was the best pilot who was upon the sea in the West of the world. He would know through his expertise that is through his looking at the state of the heavens (that is the air), how long the weather would be fair or foul, and when it would change again, and it is for this reason that the British and the men of Ireland were of the opinion that he was the god of the sea, and he used to be termed Mac Lir, that is son of the sea. Manannán was, then, named after Man.

Whatever the precise textual differences, the stories in *Sanas Cormaic* and in *Cóir Anmann* have a similar purpose, which is to emphasise the contention that Manannán mac Lir was a skilled sailor rather than a deity, and the obvious impulse of the entry is to correct what the author sees as a heretical belief in a native god. Whether a god, or a famous sea trader who plied his goods across the Irish Sea, the glossator says that he was known by both the medieval Irish and the Welsh; that is, Manannán Mac Lir and Manawydan fab Llyr (of the *Mabinogi* group of Welsh tales) are homologous, the latter simply being a Welsh version of the former. Manannán therefore seems to have been connected to the Irish Sea cultural province from an early stage, and this role is clearly consonant with, and may even to some degree explain, the fact that his name is so intimately linked with that of an island that is a pivotal point between Ireland, Scotland, and Wales. The Isle of Man, the above entries suggest, was a place of central commercial and cultural importance to the medieval insular Celtic world.

There is some disagreement between *Sanas Cormaic* and *Cóir Anmann* about the nature of Manannán's first name. *Sanas Cormaic* claims that the character was named after the island, while *Cóir Anmann* makes the opposite claim. If Manannán was merely a famous sailor, it would seem unlikely that the Isle of Man would have been named after him. The author of *Sanas Cormaic* does not give us any hint about what the island would have been called before Manannán, though it would have been easy enough for him to have done so, if he had chosen. No doubt he did not realise that his naming sequence created a potential problem. The *Cóir Anmann* account of the character having been named after the island, rather than vice versa, is a better argument if he is to sustain his claim that Manannán was merely a skilled sailor based on Man. However, the nature of the name *Manann* + *án*, a genitive singular with a diminutive suffix, suggests that the character's name was based on that of the nominative singular name for the island, and hence that the island acquired its name first.[16]

Probably the earliest appearance of Manannán in Irish literature is in *Immram Brain* ('The Voyage of Bran').[17] In this appearance the Isle of Man is not mentioned by name at all, although it may be alluded to in the place name *Mag Mon*, which is usually translated as 'Plain of Feats'.[18] Stanzas three and four of the poem in question read:

A n-as muir glan don nói bro(i)nig i tá Bran, is mag meld co n-immut scoth damsa i carput dá roth.	What is a clear sea to the prowed ship in which Bran is, is Mag Mell with plenty of flowers to me in a two wheeled chariot.
At-chí Bran lín tonn tibri tar muir glan At-chíu ca-déin i Maig Mon scotha cennderca cen on.	Bran sees many smiling waves upon the clear sea. I myself see in the Plain of Feats red topped flowers without fault.

In the story Manannán appears in the middle of the Irish Sea and recites a poem to Bran. His role and position are analogous to that of the man who appears on the cliffs of Man and requires Senchán and his troop to pass the verse test before they can land on the island. His role also, however, incorporates that of the disguised spirit of poetry mentioned in *Sanas Cormaic* whose help allows Senchán to succeed in his quest. Manannán in *Immram Brain* functions as a synecdoche for, even a personification of, the Isle of Man, as well as a tester and initiator.[19]

There are a number of tales, like *Immram Brain*, in which Manannán appears, but in which the Isle of Man is not mentioned by name. Rather than discuss them individually it is perhaps enough for our purposes here to point out that the most common function of Manannán in these stories is that of a supernatural tester/benefactor associated with wisdom and learning. This description fits his roles in *Immram Brain*, as well as in *Cuach Cormaic* ('Cormac's Cup'), and other tales such as *Altrom Tige Dá Medar* ('The Fostering of the House of the Two Vessels').[20] Another important role that is characteristic of Manannán is that of king of the Otherworld. This role, which is implicit in some of his appearances and manifest in others, has substantial implications for our understanding of the importance of the Isle of Man in the literature. The chain of reasoning, one suspects, was as follows: since Manannán's realm is the Isle of Man, and since Manannán is king of the Otherworld, the Otherworld must be on the Isle of Man. The notion that the Isle of Man was the oversea Otherworld might predate and/or be independent of the Manannán connection, but because the Isle of Man is usually associated with the Otherworld only by association with Manannán, one suspects it is not.[21]

In *Echtra Airt* ('The Adventures of Art), a tale, like *Cuach Cormaic*, which is part of a cycle of tales dealing with the adventures of Conn, the king of Tara, and his family, the association between Man and the Irish Otherworld is again mediated through Manannán.[22] Manannán is connected with Cormac's father Art in the story, which concerns the effect of a sinful Otherworld maiden on Art's life. The tale is named in one of the medieval lists of Irish tales (the B list), but the only extant version is in the much later Book of Fermoy (fifteenth century).[23] It is a curious tale in its own right, not least in that it begins by recounting an act of sin in an Otherworld that is usually described as being sinless. A woman, Bécuma, is banished for her illicit sexual union with Manannán's son Gaidiar, and she goes to Ireland in search of Art with whom she had fallen in love from afar.[24] When Bécuma marries Conn, whose wife Eithne had recently passed away, the story echoes details of *Fingal Rónáin*, with the stepmother lusting after her stepson Art.[25]

Manannán gives only a cameo performance in the story, but his appearance does provide us with some evidence concerning the literary reputation of the Isle of Man in the Middle Ages. In fact, the third paragraph contains all of the references to Manannán that occur in the tale. The context of the passage is that Conn's wife Eithne has died, bringing dejection upon Conn, who proceeds to the Hill of Howth (Benn Edair):

> One day, however, he was all alone; and he [Conn] went from Tara straight out until he came to Ben Edair meic Etgaith. There he bewailed and lamented his wife and helpmate. It was on that very day the Túatha Dé Danann happened to be gathered in their council and assembly in the Land of Promise, because of a woman who had committed a transgression, and whose name was Bécuma Cnesgel, daughter of Éogan Inbir, that is wife of Labraid *Luathlam-ar-Claideb* ('Quick-hand-on-Sword'), and Gaidiar, Manannán's son, it was that had committed the transgression. And this was the sentence passed on her as regards herself: to be driven forth from the Land of Promise, or to be burned according to the counsel of Manannán, and Fergus Findlíath, and Éogan Inbir, and Lodan son of Lir, and Ilbrec son of Manannán. And their counsel was to drive her out of the Land of Promise. And Manannán said not to burn her lest her guilt should cleave to the land or to themselves.

The date of *Echtra Airt* has not been established with any certainty, but it seems to be from around the thirteenth century. Bécuma's banishment from the Otherworld (Man?) to Ireland reverses the usual path taken by fugitive outcasts in Irish history and literature. Man is mentioned repeatedly in historical sources as a resort for 'those forced to flee from neighbouring lands until their fortunes mended',[26] and people were banished to Man: the English, like the Irish and the Scots, both banished people to and imprisoned people on Man, but Bécuma is one of the few characters who was seemingly banished *from* Man. For instance, in the prehistoric section of the annals of Tigernach, the Ulaid are said to have been expelled from Ireland to Man by Cormac grandson of Conn (the text explains that this is the reason Cormac was called Ulfada 'since he put the Ulaid afar (*i fot*))'.[27] In literary sources such as the *Lebor Gabála Érenn* ('The Book of Invasions of Ireland'), escapes and banishments to Man occur repeatedly, as when the mythological inhabitants of Ireland known as the Fir Bolg escape to Man after they are defeated by invaders known as the Túatha Dé Danann ('the people of the goddess Danu'); the latter in turn were banished by the ancestors of the Gael, known as the sons of Míl.[28] Bécuma may have been sent by the Túatha Dé Danann, the former rulers of Ireland, as a punishment not only to Bécuma herself, but also as a curse on the sons of Míl for vanquishing the Túatha Dé Danann and banishing them from Ireland.[29]

Is Man the location of the Otherworld (*Tír Tairngire*) in this story? The fact that *Tír Tairngire* is over the sea is revealed by the fact that Bécuma is 'banished beyond the expanse of the sea and the great deep', but the link between the ideas of the underground and the oversea Otherworld(s) is shown in that Manannán and the council sent messengers out to ensure that Bécuma was not allowed into any magical *síd* (fairy mound) in Ireland (the messengers are ineffective and Bécuma is welcomed into a *síd* by her sister). The most logical location to associate with *Tír Tairngire*, the pristine overseas Otherworld that Manannán governs, is the Isle of Man.[30]

Tír Tairngire, however, is not the only name associated with Man in medieval Gaelic literature. Another popular Otherworld name associated with Man is *Emain Ablach*, 'Emain of the Apples'. In the epic tales of ancient Ireland the capital of Ulster is Emain Macha (Navan Fort, near Armagh), and it perhaps no coincidence that a variant on the name is attached to Man in the literature. *Emain Ablach* is the name used for Man in the tale *Altromh Tige Dá Medar* ('The Fostering of the House of Two Vessels').[31] While the most complete version is found in the fifteenth-century Book of Fermoy, the story itself is potentially significantly older then either the manuscript or the language in which it was recorded. Certain aspects of the tale at least seem archaic. The story concerns the conversion of the Otherworld maiden Eithne to Christianity; Manannán appears as an Otherworld king who helps Eithne come to understand the change that has come over her. According to M.E. Dobbs, *Emain Ablach* is 'on the West coast of the Isle of Man near the city of Peel, which is the district associated with Manannán'.[32] Since Dobbs does not give evidence for her contention, and because the Isle of Man is not specifically mentioned in the tale, it is difficult to evaluate her identification, but it seems likely enough that medieval readers too must have connected *Emain Ablach*, Manannán's kingdom, and the Isle of Man. The location of Manannán's Otherworld realm is not always specified in the tales in which he appears. Sometimes, as in *Cuach Cormaic*, he is not associated either with the sea or with an oversea Otherworld. But his connection with the sea and with Man must always have remained obvious to audiences – his very name specifies such connections and he is associated with the Isle of Man and the sea in many other contexts.

The Isle of Man's special qualities in the story include the notion of it as the place of perfect order. Manannán, in fact, comes on a circuit of Ireland from his kingdom in order to show the Túatha Dé Danann how to set their house in order, as it is done in *Emain Ablach* and *Tír Tairngire*. When Elcmar heard that Manannán was making a tour of the courts he sent his foster-son Óengus to invite him to feast as well at *Brug na Bóinne* (the complex of megalithic tombs at Newgrange and its sister sites near the mouth of the river Boyne). Manannán accepted the invitation and came to the 'green watered Boyne'. In what some scholars think reflects a particular Manx ritual connected with Manannán, rushes were strewn before him.[33] He later identifies Eithne's ailment (her demon has abandoned her because of an insult she received and an angel has taken its place) and is able to feed her by serving milk from a holy cow in a magical vessel. Though it is not mentioned by name, it seems that the Isle of Man, or some part of it, functions as the capital of Manannán's kingdom in the story, with a sister capital in Ireland ruled by Óengus at *Brug na Bóinne*.

A more detailed and less fantastic portrayal of Manannán and the Isle of Man in medieval Gaelic literature occurs in the tale *Tochmarc Luaine ocus Aided Athairne* ('The Wooing of Luaine and the Death of Athirne').[34] This tale, which clearly draws on texts such as *Sanas Cormaic* and *Lebor Gabála*, describes four Manannáns. One is Manannán mac Athgno (*ri Manand ocus Insi Gall*, 'King of Man and the isles of the foreigners'), who appears in the tale to avenge the deaths of Derdriu and the sons of Nóise on King Conchobar mac Nessa. The story itself, as suggested by the title, concerns the wooing of the maiden Luan and the death of the warrior Athirne. The primary setting is Conchobar's Ulster, and the plot involves the finding of a new wife for him after Derdriu has killed herself rather than marry him. Conchobar who was dejected after the suicide of Derdriu sends two messengers to search Ireland and to find him a new young wife. The messengers find in an outlying area of Ulster a suitable young girl named Luan. When they return and describe the girl to Conchobar, he cannot resist going out to take a look for himself. At first sight he falls deeply in love with her and asks her to marry him. Luan assents to marry Conchobar, the latter agrees to pay her bride price to her father, and so they are betrothed. Conchobar then returns to his palace at Emain Macha and his kingship, apparently hoping to be married to Luan in a short time.

It is at this point in the tale that Manannán mac Athgno appears in the tale and seeks to avenge the deaths of Derdriu and the sons of Nóise on Conchobar. What Manannán's appearance does for the plot is delay the marriage of Conchobar and Luan and thereby facilitates the tragedy that follows this delay. For while Conchobar is busy trying to fend off Manannán, Athirne and his two sons approach Luan and attempt to seduce her. The technique that they use is to threaten her with a satire. When Luan refuses to betray Conchobar, they recite three satires against her, which cause three blotches on her cheeks, i.e., Shame and Blemish and Disgrace, black and red and white. Luan dies subsequently on account of the humiliation. The remainder of the tale recounts the planning and execution of

Conchobar's revenge on Athirne and his sons, who are eventually walled into their own house and burned alive:[35]

6. At that time then Manannán mac Athgno, the king of Man and the Isles of the foreigners (*rí Manand ocus Insi Gall*), came with a vast fleet of large boats to raid and ravage Ulster [and] to avenge the sons of Uisnech; since that Manannán was a friend to them and he fostered the children of Nóise and Derdriu, namely Gaíar their son and Aíb Gréni their daughter.
7. There were four Manannáns there and they were not contemporary. Manannán son of Allót was a druid of the Túatha Dé Danann and he lived in the age of the Túatha Dé Danann. Oirbsen then was his proper name. That Manannán lived on Aran/Arran and from him Emain Ablach is named and he was killed in the battle of Cuilleann by Uillean of the Red Eyebrows, son of Cathaír, son of Nuada Silverhand, while in contention for the kingship of Connacht. And when his grave was dug, Loch Oirbsen broke out from the ground so that Loch Orbsen is named from him, that is the first Manannán.
8. Manannán son of Cirp [was] king of the Isles and Man (*rí na nIndsi ocus Manann*) and that Manannán lived in the time of Conaire son of Etersceól, and he is the one who wooed Tuad the daughter of Conall Collamrach, the foster son of Conaire, and Tuag Inbir is named after her.
9. Manannán mac Lir, that is the famous merchant throughout Ireland, Scotland, and Man (*cendaigi amra ro baí eter Érinn ocus Albain ocus Manaind*), and he also [like Manannán son of Allót] was a druid and he was the best pilot who used to frequent Ireland and he used to know through studying the heavens, through examining the air, the time when there would be good or bad weather, and on account of it one Manannán was named. Thereafter, the Scoti and the Britones called him the god of the sea because they said he was the son of the sea (*mac Lir*), that is to say a god, and therefore he was worshipped by the people as a god who transformed himself into many shapes during the time of the pagans (*per gentilitatem*).
10. Manannán mac Athgnai is the fourth Manannán. It is he who came in the large fleet to avenge the sons of Uisnech and it is he who supported the sons of Uisnech while they were in Scotland. The sons of Uisnech were in Scotland for sixteen years and they conquered from Man northwards to Scotland (*ro gabsad ó Manaind fo thuaid don Alpain*) and they expelled the three sons of Gnáthal son of Morgan, namely Iatach and Triatach and Mani Rough-hand from that territory, since it is their father who had been ruling that land, and the sons of Uisnech killed him [Gnáthal]. So that the three [sons of Gnáthal] came in exile to Conchobar, and it is they who

killed the sons of Uisnech while under orders of Éogan son of Durrthacht.
11. Then Manannán began to plunder extensively in Ulster. The Ulstermen gathered together to give battle to Manannán. The Ulstermen said that the battle of Conchobar against the sons of Nóise was unjust. An act of peace was made between them and Manannán, and during the peace he, that is Bobarán the poet, the fosterer of Gaíar son of Nóise, was sent along with a message. Then Bobarán said:

Gaíar son of renowned Noíse,
foster-son of great-pure Manannán,
[it is] for this he came here,
to raid this country.

I am white Bobarán
the great-good druid of Manannán,
It is I who raised, no secret,
Gaíar son of modest Nóise.

The evil which you did there was ample
O Conchobar of the noble race
the slaying of the sons of Uisnech together
on account of the swift elopement with Derdriu.

Let the blood-price (*éric*) of his father be given
to noble nimble Gaíar
your honour is sufficient for healing [appeasing?]
rough Aindle and Ardán.

There shall be a friendship from it
between you and yellow-haired Manannán,
there will be peace without division
between Man and Ireland (*eter Manaind is Érinn*)

[There will be] two secure sounds from the
proud keen-weaponed Manannán
he will give to him every good thing before day
It will be a joint pact which will be made.

He will give nobly the Isle of Man to him (*Do-bir Manaind dó co bán*),
to the foster-son of good Manannán,
He will give land to him, no secret,
He will do every good thing for Gaíar.

12. And peace was made with Manannán and friendship with Conchobar after that and the blood-price of his father was paid to Gaíar according to

the wishes of the nobles of Ulster and those other two, that is Aindle and Ardán, were left against the honour of Conchobar. And a *trícha cét* (lit. 'thirty hundreds') of the land of Liathmain was given to Gaíar, that is the land of Dubthach Chafer-tongue, since he was along with Fergus at war against the Ulstermen. So they parted in peace and there was friendship between them afterward.

The tale obviously relies heavily on the Derdriu story, the oldest version of which, *Longes mac nUislenn*, was originally composed in the late eighth or early ninth century.[36] The most recent editor the late medieval version of the Derdriu story, Oidheadh Chloinne hUisneach ('The Violent Death of the Children of Uisneach'), Caoimhín Mac Giolla Léith, points out that it 'refers on two occasions to Derdriu and Nóise receiving gifts from a Manannán', and conjectures that it 'seems more than likely that this was originally the Manannán mac Athgno of *Tochmarc Luaine*. That some eighteenth-century manuscripts... would later convert him into his infinitely better known namesake Manannán mac Lir is hardly surprising'.[37] In fact, the reason that Manannán mac Lir is 'infinitely better known' is that the other Manannáns exist only as particular articulations of his character. There is really only one Manannán in Irish literature, and the other Manannáns named here are merely convenient multiforms.

The author of *Tochmarc Luaine*, drawing on the pseudo-historical texts of *Cóir Anmann*, *Sanas Cormaic*, *Lebor Gabála Érenn*, and the *Dindsenchas*, as well as the sagas, surely created multiple Manannáns in order to add verisimilitude to his tale and to explain the contradictory genealogies for Manannán in the tradition. Manannán *mac Athgno*, for example, may be a pun on *aithgeinn*, 'rebirth, regeneration', having the legal sense of 'restitution, compensation', and hence the name probably refers to Manannán's role in *Tochmarc Luaine*, meaning something like 'Manannán the avenger', the enforcer of the *éric* ('blood-price'). As with mac Allót, mac Lir, and possibly mac Cirp, the name Mac Athgno does not designate a true patronymic as much as a sobriquet. And none of these three plays an important part in the early literature due to the fact that they are not real characters at all, but rather secondary constructions used to describe Manannán.

While the four-part division is artificial, Manannán's portrayal in *Tochmarc Luaine* is a conflation of tradition and innovation. It is possible that Manannán seemed an appropriate overseas avenger from the fact that in other tales, such as *Altromh Tige Dá Medar* and *Immram Brain*, he appears both as a powerful transmarine or submarine ruler who was invested in the 'proper' order of Irish culture. He appears in *Tochmarc*

Luaine, as he does most often, to teach the hero a lesson. The 'hero' in this case is the anti-heroic Conchobar, and the lesson is that Conchobar cannot behave dishonourably without suffering serious consequences. The direct consequences are a conditional surrender to Manannán, as a part of which Conchobar must pay the proper compensation to Nóise's son Gaíar for murdering his father. As with Manannán's intervention in *Altrom Tige Dá Medar* where Elcmar leaves *Brug na Bóinne* to Óengus, here a part of the settlement involves the transfer of land from Conchobar to Gaíar. As Stokes notes, the land which is given to Gaíar is 'Liathmain i n-Ultaib', which according to one of the topographical poems in the *Dindsenchas* becomes the bed of Lough Neagh,[38] from which, of course, tradition has it that the Isle of Man was scooped.

Manannán, here again, is interested in justice and proper order, or at least that is how it seems from his function in the plot of the tale. Certain aspects of Manannán's role in the story, however, lend themselves to multiple interpretations. For example, he does not seem to be in any way complicit in the attempted rape and eventual shaming to death of Luan. Luan's shaming, at least, is reminiscent of the shaming of Eithne in *Altromh Tige Dá Medar*. After Eithne is insulted, she loses her Otherworld spirit, is then possessed by a Christian spirit, and finds that she is unable to eat anything but the milk of one of two special cows. She is saved by Manannán's diagnosis that she has become Christian, but she loses her ability to live in the unchristian Otherworld on account of the insult, and eventually dies when she moves to Christian Ireland and is baptised. Manannán seems to be a benefactor to Eithne, but his 'help' results in her death. In *Tochmarc Luaine* Manannán's proper role involves not only avenging the murder of the sons of Uisnech, but also, secondarily, preventing the corruption of the pure Luan by the depraved Conchobar (that is, he does not allow Conchobar to rejuvenate himself and his kingship by means of marrying a young virgin). Despite the nominally pseudo-historical description of Manannán in the text, underlying the whole complex of this and other tales surrounding the Derdriu story is myth, as Gantz points out, 'the familiar regeneration pattern of old king-goddess-young king: Conchubur-Derdriu-Noísiu'.[39]

In *Tochmarc Luaine*, Conchobar is again defeated in his attempt to reinvigorate his kingship by taking a young beautiful girl to wife, a fresh sovereignty goddess, by the interruption of Manannán. The transfer of power from old king to young king nevertheless seems finally to be completed in *Tochmarc Luaine* as a large portion of Conchobar's power is ceded to Gaíar, the young son of Nóise. This interpretation is reinforced by a related text on the descendants of Ír son of Míl, progenitor of the

Gael.[40] Here, Gaíar, by Manannán's advice, took the kingship of Ulster from Conchobar, and exiled the former king for a year to the islands of *Orcc* ('pig') and *Catt* ('cat'). Gaíar only retains the kingship of Ulster for a year. As with Bécuma in *Echtra Airt*, who is banished rather than burned on the advice of Manannán, Conchobar is granted mercy. After he has been in exile for a year, Gaíar, again acting on the advice of Manannán, restores the kingship to Conchobar and returns himself to Manannán's kingdom – the Isle of Man. The reconciliation between Conchobar and Manannán, after the paying of Nóise's *éric* ('blood-price) to his son Gaíar, would seem premature if Manannán were concerned to seek justice for either Derdriu or Luan. Once Manannán's duty as a friend to Nóise and as foster-father to Nóise's son Gaíar has been fulfilled, he is willing to make peace with Conchobar. He serves on one level as an enforcer of the *éric*, which is owed for the murder of a man of high status to the man's son, and on another to assure that the kingship is not improperly monopolised. It is possible that Manannán's function here is related to the 'suretyship of the gods', which is mentioned in medieval Irish and Welsh texts.[41] Manannán, while presented as a mortal, does therefore function as a sort of vengeful god in the story of the sons of Uisnech.

Neither Manannán, nor Nóise and Derdriu's son Gaíar, is mentioned in *Longes mac nUislenn*. Derdriu and Nóise, when they flee from Ireland, spend time both in Scotland and on 'an island in the sea'.[42] If Manannán is meant to be the king of Scotland in *Tochmarc Luaine*, then his role has shifted radically from that of the king in the original story. For in *Longes mac nUislenn* the king of Scotland sends a messenger to Derdriu who seeks to convince her to leave Nóise and to take up with the king. When Derdriu refuses the Scots king first tries to kill Nóise off (*á la* Uriah) by sending him out to fight in dangerous battles, and when Nóise and his brothers survive all these treacherous missions, the king sends his troops to chase them out of Scotland. The brothers take Derdriu to 'an island in the sea'. No information is given about this island or about the length (or any other details) of their stay there. It is from this island, however, that they are summoned home by Conchobar. Presumably then, since Manannán is portrayed as an ally of Nóise in *Tochmarc Luaine* (and *Oidheadh Chloinne nUisneach*), he, rather than the king of Scotland, must be the unnamed ruler of this mysterious island. Nevertheless, according to *Tochmarc Luaine*, Manannán mac Athgno supported Derdriu and Nóise during the 16 years that they were in Scotland. He is not, however, called the 'king of Scotland' but rather 'the king of Man and the isles'. In *Oidheadh Chloinne nUisneach*, Manannán is referred to by Derdriu in a poem she recites to Nóise as having given 'the cup' and 'the very swift hound' to them, and

Nóise offers the magic sword which Manannán gave him, as the means by which all three of the brothers might be decapitated in one blow, and thus die simultaneously.[43]

The portrayal of Manannán (with various second names) as the king of the Isle of Man, and the Isle of Man as a centre of political power in the time of Conchobar, is the product of historical and fictional cutting and pasting. It is probable that either the Lordship of the Isles, or perhaps a slightly earlier manifestation of political and martial power on Man, such as that of Godred Crovan, was the model upon which the *Tochmarc Luaine* portrayal was based. The character and the island remain powerful in this portrayal, but the power is mundane and military rather than supernatural. The Isle of Man is again, however, presented as an integral, in some sense even central, part of the medieval Gaelic cosmos.

One notable reference to Manannán and the Isle of Man in the Fenian lays, which hints at their importance in Gaelic tradition, occurs in the last part of 'The Fray at Loch Luig'. In this poem the narrator speaks nostalgically of '[from] the house of Muireadhach, son of Flann, and of Manannán from Man (*Mhanainne ó Mhaonuinn*) I used to seek crags and havens and chilly heights)'.[44] The house of Manannán from the Isle of Man seems here to intend an ideal residence which was open to the Fíanna in the good old days. It is possible that it is a reflex of the idea expressed elsewhere, that Manannán's Otherworld dwelling was an example of ideal living – one imagines a Platonic Otherworld of forms, and Manannán's house as the ideal house, perhaps like the house with which Manannán is associated in *Cuach Cormaic*. The 'crags and havens and chilly heights' may intend the cliffs of Man, where the narrator presumably sought solitude and communion with nature. But the reference is rather too brief to support a more sustained analysis, and the character Muireadhach mac Flainn is unknown to me. Nevertheless, the reference clearly indicates the association between Manannán and the Isle of Man, an association which remains in play even when it is not explicitly articulated.

In contrast to the brevity of the above reference, one of the most extensive poetic uses of the Isle of Man in all of medieval Gaelic literature occurs in a poem in praise of Ragnall (ON Rögnvaldr), king of Man and the Isles (1187–1229). Ragnall was the great-grandson of Godred Crovan or Gofraid Mérach as he is named in this poem. In 1187 Ragnall took over a kingdom that had been founded by his great-grandfather on the Isle of Man but that also, at times, incorporated Dublin and some of the Hebrides. Ragnall had strong Norse connections and is noted for his military prowess in *Orkneyinga saga*. An edition of this poem was prepared by Brian Ó Cuív in 1957 and a new translation by Thomas Clancy has since appeared in a

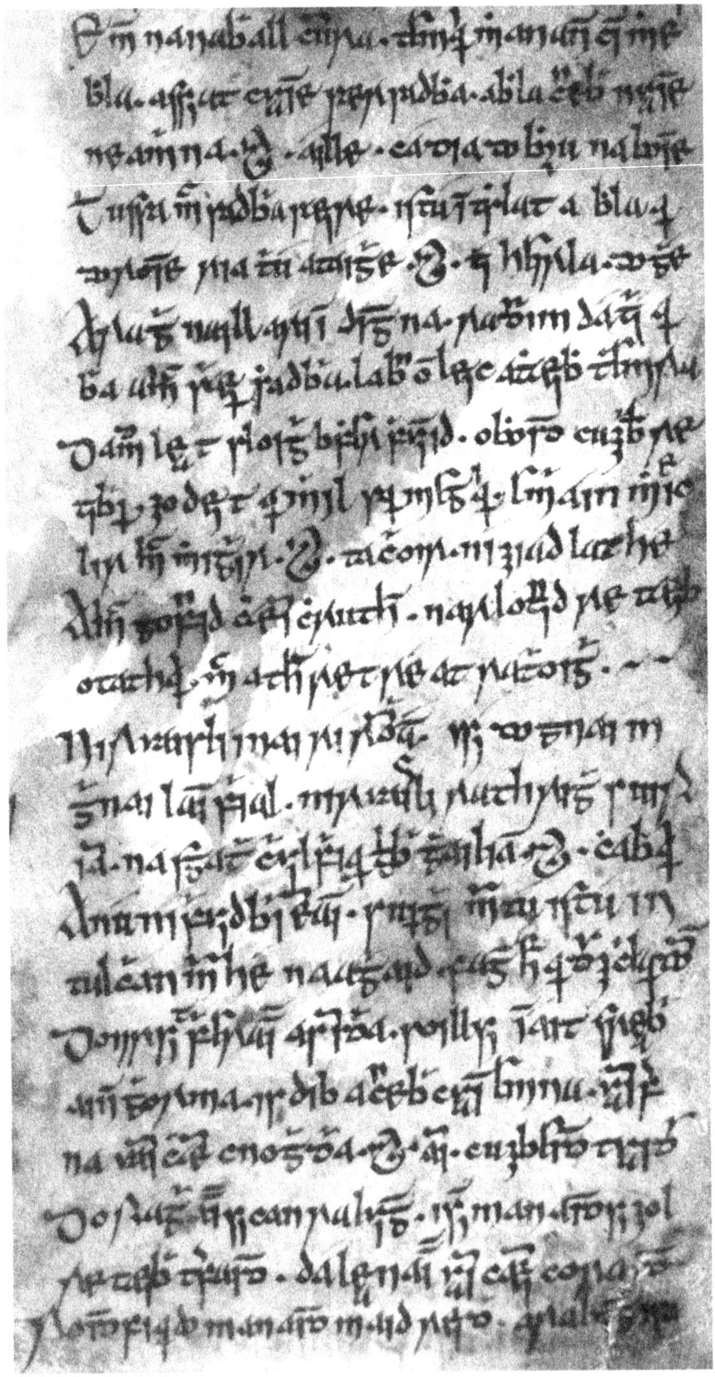

collection of medieval 'Scottish' poetry.[45] In his brief analysis of the poem Clancy points to the 'otherworld quality' attributed to the Isle of Man and to the importance of a certain mound or *síd* on Man which seems to be parallel with a sister *síd* at Tara. *Emain Ablach*, the name used for Man here, as in other texts we have discussed, is one name for the Gaelic Otherworld. The Isle of Man is equated with the Otherworld paradise and Ragnall with the ideal Otherworld king. Furthermore, Ragnall is positioned as a successor to a historical king and kingdom. Manannán and his kingdom on Man are not merely useful here as mythic ideals, but also function, to some extent, as past glories that have been reincarnated in Ragnall and recovered in his rule. That is to say, Manannán and Man serve both as mythic and historical precedents for the ideal kingdom and king.

In the poem *Emain*/Man is described as a fruitful, shapely land abounding in apple trees. It is 'rich in steeds' and apparently has a substantial population, 'many men'. Much of the description, while clearly hyperbolic, is concerned with the beauty and lushness of the island, but the supernatural connections of the island are also emphasized:

7. Emain Ablach na n-ibor	Emhain Abhlach of the yews,
sleamain barrdath a bile*d*h,	glossy its trees' crests' colour,
baili nua fan dub droighen	fresh place of the dark blackthorn,
'nar hoiled Lugh ua in fhile*d*h.	where Lugh was raised, poet's offspring.
8. Emain na n-aball cumra	Emhain of the fragrant apples
Teamair Mhanann cin mhebhla,	is without lie Man's Tara;
as siat cuaine saer Sadbha	the noble brood of Sadhbh, they
abhla craebh n-uaine nEamhna.	are Emhain's green-branched apples.
9. Tussa, mac Sadbha saeire,	You, the son of noble Sadhbh,
tusa in tslat abhla as áille,	are the fairest apple sceptre.
cá dia do bhrú na Bóin[n]e	What god from beside the Boyne
do-róine ria thú a táighe?	conceived you with her in secret?
11. Dá mad leat slóigh Fher bhFuinid	Were yours the hosts of Ireland's men,
ó Bhóind cu mben re Tibhir,	from Boyne as far as Tiber,

Fig. 13.1 *A poem in praise of Ragnall, King of Man 'Eamhain of the fragrant apple trees'. Verses 7–17 are shown.*

mó deit ar mhil's ar megair	better to you for honey and mirth
Emhain mheic Lir m[e]ic Mhighir.	were mac Lír mac Midhir's Emhain.
16. Do-raghainn-si can raluing	I would arrive, with no great ship,
isin Manaind-si molaim,	in this Man which I extol,
cu mbeind tuaidh re taeibh t'fheraindso	I'd be north beside your land,
dá leanainn uaim caeim Coraind.	should I follow Corann's fair cave.
17. Roindfí ár do Manaind maidréidh,	You will deal death from smooth-plained Man,
a raluing is ár iondshlóigh;	slaughter by a great ship's host;
sléibti ar fhut do ghort nglanréid	amidst your smooth fresh fields, hills
tuc dagmhéin ort a FindBhóind.	have lured you from the fair Boyne.

The mac Lír mic Midhir named in the poem must be a reference to Manannán, though why Manannán is not mentioned more directly is somewhat of a mystery. Ragnall is deified in the above stanzas, though the reference to his father, the 'god from beside the Boyne', probably intends Óengus or the Dagda rather than Manannán. The implication of the final stanza above seems to be that it is better, more fun and more profitable, to rule the Isle of Man than the entire western world.

Other Gaelic poems, including some written in praise of the Irish king of Bréifne Feargal O'Reilly (d.1291) found in *Book of the Dean of Lismore*, contain references to Manannán, and by implication to the Isle of Man.[46] Most of these poems read as long excuses for the poet to show off his knowledge of tradition. Manannán appears in two poems in the *Book of the Dean,* which is remarkable for its Scottish origin and its unique orthography, as well as for its literary content. The most interesting of these poems, for our purposes, was written by Baron Ewen M'Omie. In the poem the 'Baron' complains about how long it is taking his doctor to come and attend him. He mentions the herds and flocks of Manannán, presumably from the Isle of Man, as among the invaluable items that he would give, if he had them, for a cure for his sickness.[47]

> I'd give besides the heavy bull,
> If for my cure I had the price.
> The herds and flocks of Manannán,
> The sword and horn of Mac Cumhaill,
> The trumpet of Manallan I'd give,
> And the quiver of Cú Chulainn.

Plainly, Manannán is used here to indicate the preciousness of the animals associated with him. Its author may have had in mind texts in which Manannán is associated with magic animals, such as *Altromh Tige Dá Medar* and *Cuach Cormaic*. The name, Manallan, is almost surely an altered form of Manannán, although a 'trumpet' does not appear to be associated with Manannán in any other context. These references from the *Book of the Dean*, however, are typical of other poetic references to Man and Manannán in medieval Gaelic literature; a brief mention, usually in the form of a flattering equative construction, which juxtaposes a mundane Irish king or kingdom with Manannán the ideal ruler and Man the ideal land.

The ambiguous roles of the Isle of Man as exotic Otherworld location, remote and forbidding place of exile, and thriving centre of Gaelic culture, are not easily reconciled either with each other or with the historical record. How could a place so nearby, a place that was important to the power politics of the medieval Gaelic world, a place that was for long periods a centre of commerce under Norse domination, remain an idealised and largely uncharted location in the literature? The Isle of Man in medieval Gaelic literature is far enough out on the margins of the map to be described both fantastically and inconsistently. This stands in marked contrast to Anglo-Saxon texts such as 'The Marvels of the East' where the supernatural tends to be placed relatively far away from England, at the margins of the world as it was then known. Medieval Gaelic literature imagines a multi-dimensional universe, and the Isle of Man, while nearby on one plane, was potentially worlds away on another. It might be conceived of as a paradise, or a wasteland, or both, not because the medieval Gael did not know what the actual place was like; they no doubt did know much about Man, from either direct experience or word of mouth. But while some medieval literatures seem to prefer to position the incredible in the long ago or far away (or both), medieval Gaelic literature, in the case of the Isle of Man at least, placed the fantastic and the forbidding in a proximate and perennial near and now.

Notes

1 Dáibhí Ó Cróinín, *Early Medieval Ireland 400–1200* (London, 1995), 50.

2 It seems unlikely that Manannán is thought to shift into the shape of the island. Manannán, and all the other Celtic shape-shifters, seem to take on animate forms exclusively. The association of Manannán with Man is parallel to the associations of Ériu, Banba and Fódla with Ireland, and Bóand with the River Boyne. See G.A. Wait, *Ritual and Religion in Iron Age Britain* (Oxford, 1985), 217–20.

3 A.W. Moore, *Folklore of the Isle of Man* (London, 1891), 8.

4 Versions of the story are to be found in R.I. Best's edition of *Aided Con Roi* in *Ériu*, 2 (1905), 20–31; *Keating's History of Ireland*, II, ed. P.S. Dinneen, Irish

Texts Society Vol. VII (1908), chapter XXXVI; the prose *dindshenchas* version of the tale 'Findglais', edited and translated by Whitley Stokes, 'The Rennes Dindshenchas', *Revue Celtique*, 15 (1894), 448–50; and in Standish Hayes O'Grady's *Silva Gadelica* I (London, 1892), 482ff. Thanks to Tina Hellmuth, who is working on a new edition of the Cu Roí material, for these references.

5 Kuno Meyer, *Sanas Cormaic* (London, 1913).

6 Nevertheless, Senchán and his troop do find her on the Isle of Man later on in all three versions of the episode.

7 *fecht a aínessa/fecht nainiusa/fecht n-áinius*[*a*]: The first spelling is from Harleian 5280, the second from 23 N 10, and the third from the Yellow Book of Lecan (see Meyer, *Sanas Cormaic*, viii, xiii, and 91). I include the variant spellings to give the reader some sense for the sorts of variations to be found among the redactions.

8 She is described variously as *acht nat mbúi étach maith n-impe* ('without good clothes on') and as *nad mbui etag impe* ('without clothes on'). See Meyer, *Sanas Cormaic*, x and 92.

9 According to a story summarised by Ó hÓgain, St Patrick orders a tyrant named Mac Cuill to set himself adrift as penance for murder: 'he did so and reached the Isle of Man, where he became a hermit'. Daithi Ó hÓgain, *Myth, Legend and Romance: An Encyclopædia of the Irish Folk Tradition* (New York, 1991), 357.

10 See Meyer, *Sanas Cormaic*, 92.

11 Maud Joynt (ed.), *Tromdámh Guaire* (Dublin, 1931). In yet another version of Senchán's search for *Táin Bó Cúailnge*, the Isle of Man is not mentioned at all. See A. O'Kelleher and G. Schoepperl (eds and trans.), *Betha Colaim Chille. Life of Colum Cille (compiled by Manus O'Donnell in 1532)* (Urbana, Illinois, 1918). *Tromdámh Guaire* is mentioned at 160–5, but there is no specific mention of the Isle of Man.

12 The *Dindshenchas* (toponymical) story of *Umall*, in which Manannán is said to have used druidry to raise a protective cliff of bronze, may refer to a phenomenon on Man. See Edward Gwynn (ed.), *Poems from the Dindshenchas* (Dublin, 1913), 274.

13 The verse capping contest this time between the man on the cliffs and the leper runs as follows: 'Giarsat eolach a mbi h'adbhuidh / giarsat taman bolgaig bunn / Dixit in lobar /Ar bru chairrgi mhara Manann/dorínes mor salann sunn… Ar mu loscadh, ar mu mescadh,/ar mu mescadh ar an tuine/Dixit in lobur;/A bainnliaigh doni in cerd choimsi,/is mor do thoirrsi ar an tuinn.' (Joynt, *Tromdámh Guaire*, 37).

14 Alwyn Rees and Brinley Rees, *Celtic Heritage* (London, 1961), 27.

15 Taken respectively from Meyer *Sanais Cormaic*, 78 and from Whitley Stokes 'Cóir Anmann', *Irische Texte*, 3.2 (Leipzig, 1895), 356.

16 A.W. Moore speculated that there was first of all a character Man whose name was given to the Isle of Man, and that at a later period the diminutive was added to the character's name (*Folklore*, 845). Mercier believed that Manannán gives his name to the Isle of Man. See Vivian Mercier, *The Irish Comic Tradition* (Oxford, 1962), 23.

17 Seamus Mac Mathúna, *Immram Brain* (Dublin, 1985). Kuno Meyer (ed. and trans.) *The Voyage of Bran* (London, 1895).

18 Heinrich Wagner suggested that *Mon* here might be a reference to Anglesey. See 'Origins of pagan Irish religion', *Zeitschrift für Celtische Philologie*, 38 (1981), 1–28 (at p. 22).

19 In some later texts, such as 'The Kern in the Narrow Stripes', the Isle of Man is

also closely connected with Manannán. Man is mentioned in all but one of the type-scenes as one of the places the kern has been: 'i ndún monaidh i mbaile ríg Alban do chodlas aréir ar in cetharnach. I nOilech na ríg do rugad mé. bím lá in Ile, lá i gcionn tíre, lá i Mann, lá i Rachlainn': Standish Hayes O'Grady, *Silva Gadelica*, 277.

20 Whitley Stokes (ed. and trans.) 'Cuach Cormaic', *Irische Texte*, 2 (1891), 193–9.

21 An exception to this rule occurs in the thirteenth-century poem to Ragnall, discussed below. For *Altrom Tige Dá Medar* see note 31 below.

22 See R.I. Best (ed. and trans.), 'The Adventures of Art Son of Conn, and the Courtship of Delbchaem', *Ériu* (1907), 149–73.

23 See Proinsias MacCana, *The Learned Tales of Medieval Ireland* (Dublin, 1980).

24 According to some late versions of 'The Fate of the Children of Uisliu' Gaidiar is actually the son of Nóise and Derdriu who was left by the couple with Manannán before they returned to Ireland and were murdered. See Eugene O'Curry, 'The Tri Thruaighe na Scéalaigheacht' (i.e., the 'Three Most Sorrowful Tales') part 2, *Atlantis* 4 (1863), 113–240.

25 Tomás Ó Cathasaigh has suggested that 'this tale can be read as a development of the theme of king and goddess which is pervasive in the Irish literature of kingship'. See Ó Cathasaigh, *The Heroic Biography of Cormac mac Airt* (Dublin, 1977), 28.

26 See Megaw and Megaw, 'The Norse Heritage in the Isle of Man', in Fox and Dickins (eds), *The Early Cultures of North-West Europe*, 148.

27 'Indarba Uladh a hErind a Manaind la Cormac hua Cuind. as de ba Cormac Ulfada dia rochuir Ultu a fad (Expulsion of the Ulaid from Ireland into Mann by Cormac, grandson of Conn. Hence he was called Cormac Ul-fota, since he put Ulaid afar)'. See Whitley Stokes, *The Annals of Tigernach* (Lampeter 1993; repr. from *Revue Celtique* (1895–6)).

28 See See R.A.S. Macalister, *Lebor Gabála Érenn* parts 1–4 (Dublin, 1938–41), vol. 4, 110–11 and 172–3.

29 Kim McCone suggests that Bécuma's banishment to Ireland, and the trouble that she causes there, is 'a microcosm of the behaviour and fate of the fallen angels'. But, while Bécuma does threaten order by her transgression of sexual mores in both worlds, she is closer, as McCone also observes, to a corrupt and corrupting Eve, than to a dark angel. See Kim McCone, *Pagan Past and Christian Present* (Maynooth, 1990), 152–3.

30 The connection between Manannán and the Isle of Man and between the Isle of Man and the Irish Otherworld is also suggested by stories in which Otherworld visitors, sometimes Manannán himself, bear magical apple branches on their visits to Ireland. See discussion of Ragnall poem below.

31 See M.E. Dobbs, 'Altrom Tige Dá Medar', *Zeitschrift für Celtische Philologie* 18 (1930), 189–230 and Lilian Duncan, 'Altrom Tige Dá Medar', *Ériu* 11 (1932), 184–225.

32 Dobbs, 'Altrom Tige Dá Medar', 230.

33 This rush-strewing may have ritual overtones. James Frazer points to a Manx rush-strewing ritual involving St Brigit. See James Frazer, *The Golden Bough* (London 1922), 134–5. The folklorist David Spaan, elaborating on observations of the Manx historian James Gell, specifically connects rush-strewing rituals, which he suggests survive in the custom of strewing green rushes along the road from St John's Chapel to the Tynwald Hill when Tynwald courts are being held, with a 'cult of Manannán'. See David Spaan, 'The place of Manannán mac Lir in Irish mythology,' *Folklore*, 76, (1965), 177. But rush-strewing does not always

have such mythical overtones in the Celtic context: 'It was common practice to strew the floor of the house with rushes or with fresh straw', (Donncha Ó Corráin, *Ireland before the Normans* (Dublin, 1972), 62–3).

34 See Liam Breatnach, 'Tochmarc Luaine ocus Aided Athairne', *Celtica*, 13 (1980), 1–31. *Tochmarc Luaine* appears in three manuscripts: YBL (Trinity College, Dublin, H.2.16), col. 880.1–885.26 (late 14th century); Book of Ballymote (Royal Irish Academy, 23 P 12) 257a46–259b13 (14th–15th century), and TCD MS. H 2.17, 464b1–468a18 (15th-16th century)'. See Whitley Stokes, 'Tochmarc Luaine ocus Aided Athairne'. *Revue Celtique* (1903), for a facing-page translation of the prose portions of the tale, and Eugene O'Curry 'The Tri Thruaighe na Scéalaigheacht' (i.e., the 'Three Most Sorrowful Tales') part 2, *Atlantis* 4 (1863), 113–240, for a facing-page translation of part of the tale.

35 The following text is from Breatnach, *Tochmarc Luaine*, 1–31.

36 Caoimhin Mac Giolla Léith, *Oidheadh Chloinne hUisneach* (London, 1993), 9.

37 See Mac Giolla Léith, *Oidheadh Chloinne hUisneach*, 19.

38 Stokes, *Rennes*, see note 4 above, 153 and 413.

39 Jeffrey Gantz, *Early Irish Myths and Sagas* (New York, 1981), 256.

40 MS. MS H. 3. 17, col 865, 10–20; Breatnach, 'Tochmarc Luaine', 3–4.

41 See Robin Stacey, *Road To Judgment: From Custom to Court in Medieval Ireland and Wales* (Pennsylvania, 1993), 200.

42 Gantz, *Early Irish Myths and Sagas*, 262.

43 See Mac Giolla Léith, *Oidheadh Chloinne hUisneach*, 19, 110–11 and 128–9. In an obscure verse from the tale, which Mac Giolla Léith attempts to untangle in a footnote, Derdriu is described as being *ar ghallán mara Manann* ('on the pillar [hero?] of the sea of Man' (106–7 and 158).

44 See Eoin Mac Néill, *Duanaire Finn*, vol. 1 (Dublin, 1904), 19 and 116.

45 See Ó Cuív, 'A poem in praise of Raghnall'; and T.O. Clancy, J.P. Clancy, G. Márkus, P. Bibire and J. Jesch, *Scotland's Earliest Poetry, 550–1350* (Edinburgh, 1998), 236–41.

46 For the description of Feargal as 'a Manannán for protection', see James Carney, *Poems on the O'Reillys* (Dublin, 1950), 106.

47 Thomas M'lauchlan (ed. and trans.) and William F. Skene (intro. and notes) *The Dean of Lismore's Book* (Edinburgh, 1862), 102.

14 *The Chronicles of the Kings of Man and the Isles*

BERNADETTE WILLIAMS

The Manx chronicle, a mid-thirteenth century parchment manuscript, has been transcribed and translated many times, most recently by George Broderick in 1979.[1] The study that follows investigates the character of the Manx chronicle and its chronicler, rather than the historical evidence of the events recounted therein. Unless an account is contemporary with the event described – and then left completely untouched by future chroniclers who consult the account as their source – it has limited value as historical evidence of contemporary events. However, a later chronicler's adaptation, selection and manipulation of his earlier source can reveal the purpose of his work and his bias. This investigation will concentrate on analysing both the manuscript and the text in order to reveal, as far as practicable, the identity, if not the name, of the scribe behind the events recorded and his purpose in writing. Once that is established, the political events, as recounted, can be more fully explored and due weight can be given to statements made by the scribe when his bias is taken into account.

This manuscript is of immense value to the history of the island as it is the only Manx narrative source for a period covering the years from 1000 (*recte* 1016) to 1316. The main literary sources for the history of the island in the earlier period are the Icelandic sagas and the Irish annals and these external references are comparatively scanty and obscure.[2] The geographical position of the Isle of Man made the island very attractive to anyone who required passage through the Irish Sea. It was inevitable that Man, with its low-lying rich agricultural land, and its rocky indented coastline, dotted with good natural harbours which offer shelter for ships, should arouse the interest of the Vikings and indeed Norse incursions into Man began shortly before AD 800; the first record of Viking raids in this part of the Irish Sea can be found in the Annals of Ulster in 795.[3]

Theoretically, all districts conquered by the Norse were claimed by the king of Norway, but, in practice, powerful Viking chieftains fought each other for supremacy. Thus, at one time, Man might be ruled by a king who lived in Dublin, by a king who lived on the island itself, by the Scandinavian king of Limerick or Waterford, or the earl of Orkney. Only from 1079 was the Isle of Man ruled by a king with known previous Manx associations,[4] and it is the history of these kings of Man that is recounted in the chronicle of Man.[5]

The manuscript known as *Cronica Regum Mannie & Insularum* is bound together with two other related documents. The Manx chronicle itself is contained on folio 31 recto to folio 50 recto; the second document (fol. 50v. to fol. 52r.), is an account of the bishops of the church of Sodor (the diocese of Man and the Isles), and the final document (fol. 53r. to fol. 54v.), is an account of the boundaries of the monastery of the Cistercian abbey of Rushen. The principal scribe was responsible for the chronicle from the year 1000 (*recte* 1016) to 1257. A second hand wrote the entries for the years 1263, 1265, 1266 and 1274, a third hand wrote the entry for 1275, a fourth hand was responsible for 1313 and a fifth hand wrote the last entry ascribed to 1316.[6] These same scribes were also writing, contemporaneously, the history of the bishops of Sodor.[7] Once the principal scribe had ceased writing in 1257, the subsequent scribes used the chronicle merely to add items of exceptional interest. It is the character of the principal scribe that is under consideration in this study.

The scribe does not identify himself to the reader; but neither do most medieval scribes. Only from a close examination of both the parchment itself and the content of the entries can a picture of the scribe begin to emerge. It is evident from the chronicle that the scribe was an ecclesiastic; the overall tone is that of a man of God and three miracles are recounted in the chronicle at significant moments. There are only two drawings in the manuscript and those are marginal drawings of churches, the first beside the year 1098,[8] where the scribe notes the foundation of Cîteaux, and the second beside the year 1126,[9] where he states that Furness, the mother house of Rushen, was founded. This evidence would support the theory that the scribe was Cistercian.[10] Furthermore, the presence of the document detailing the boundaries of the Cistercian abbey at Rushen substantiates this Cistercian provenance.

Two suggestions have been forwarded in the past concerning the identity of the scribe. One is that he was a monk at Furness, the other that he was a monk at Rushen.[11] Certainly the presence of a drawing beside Furness points to the importance of Furness to the scribe, but Furness was, as noted, the mother-house of Rushen,[12] and, as such, together with Cîteaux, would deserve special recognition. But it is impossible to believe that a monk of Furness, or from Furness, would give an incorrect date for the foundation of his house as this scribe has done.[13] Furthermore, Furness was a royal foundation (founded originally in 1123 by Stephen, count of Boulogne and Mortain, later king of England),[14] and it is difficult to imagine a monk from

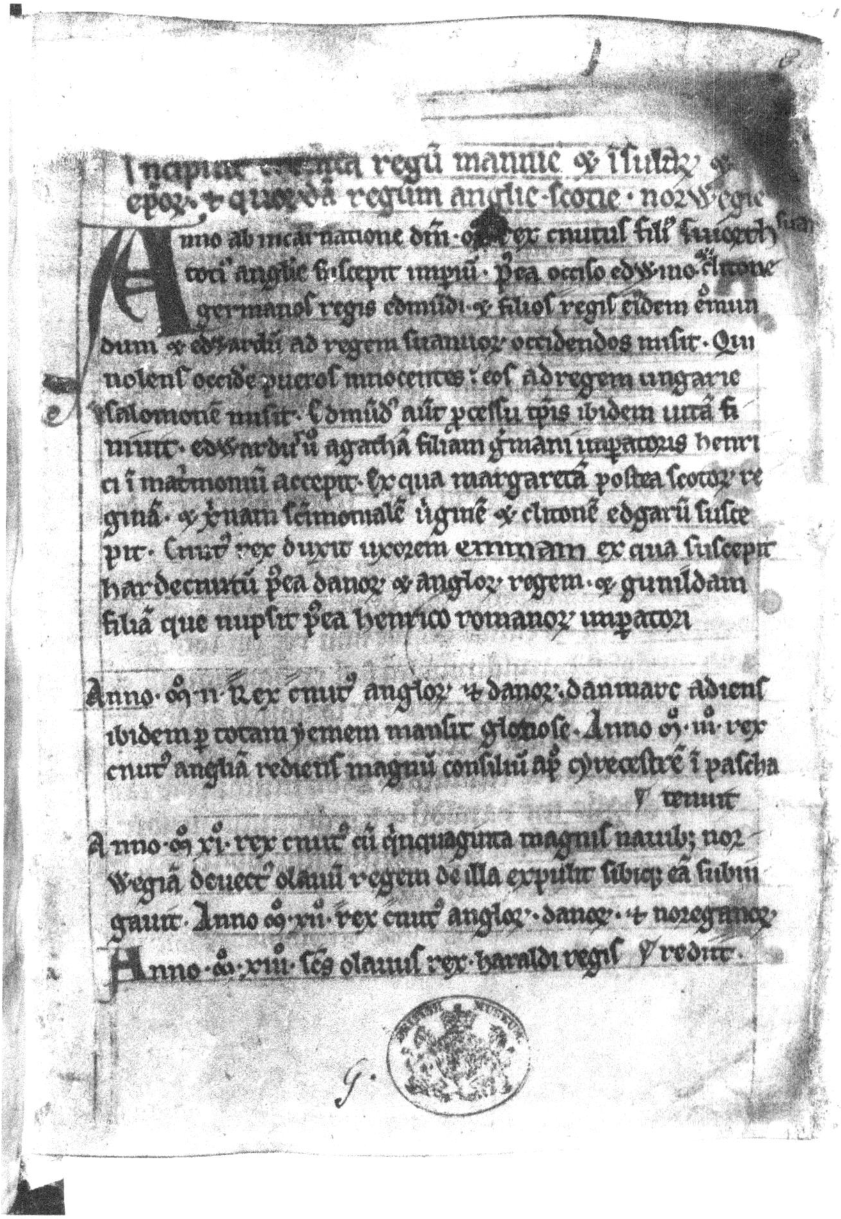

Fig 14.1 *The first page of the* Chronicles, *folio 31,* recto, *begins with the two lines translated from the Latin as 'Here begin the Chronicles of the Kings of Man and the Isles, and of the bishops, and some of the Kings of England, Scotland (and) Norway'. Copyright: British Library.*

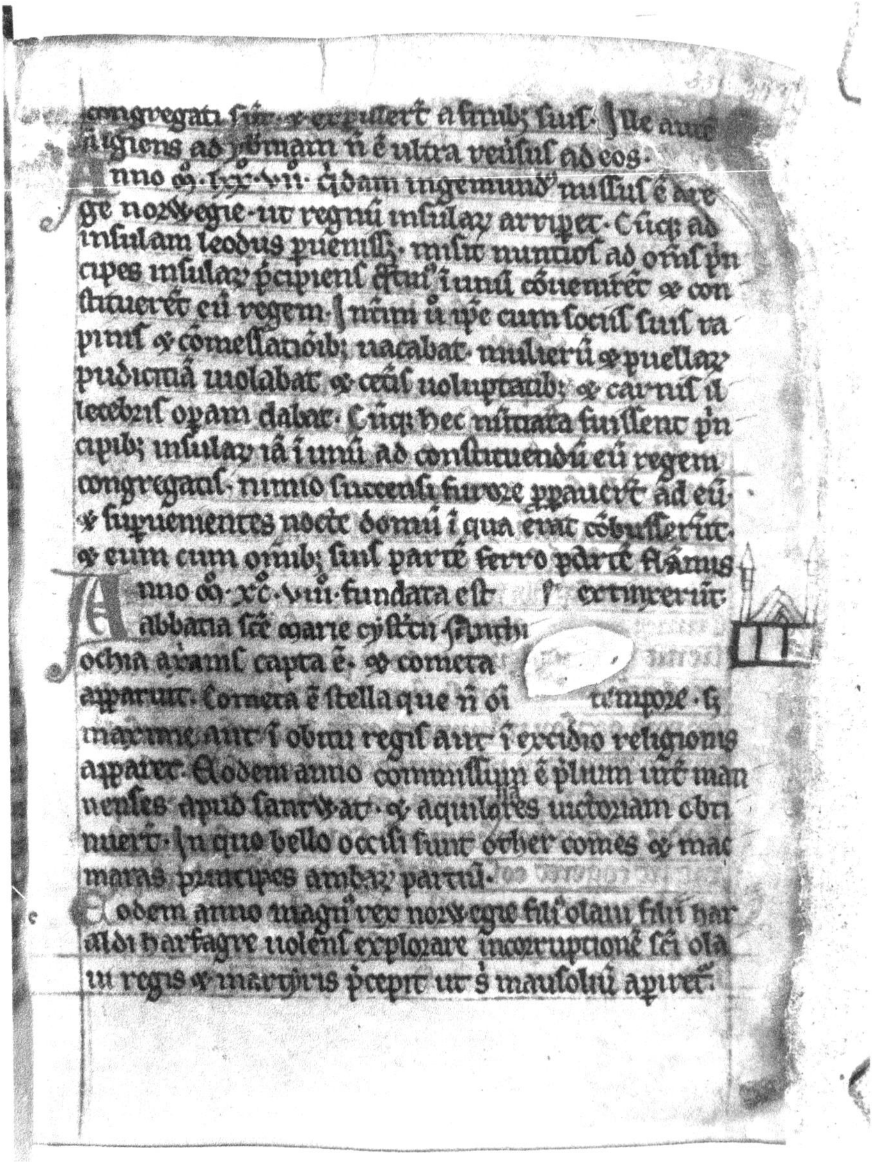

Fig 14.2 (a) **and** (b) *Marginal sketches of abbeys. Drawn alongside the texts that translate from the Latin: a) 'In the year 1098 the Abbey of St Mary of Cîteaux was founded' and b) 'The same year [1133] the Abbey of St Mary of Furness was founded' (folio 34r and folio 35v). Copyright: British Library.*

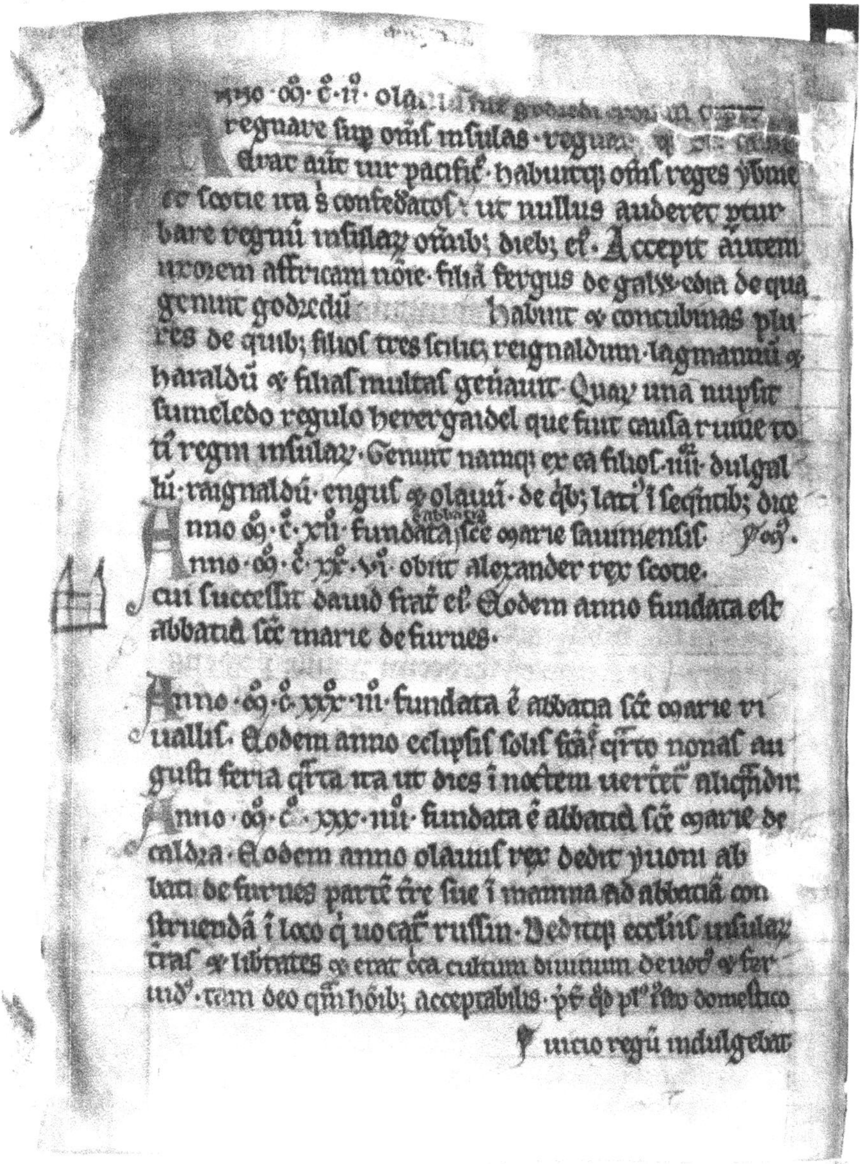

a royal foundation claiming that William the Bastard, the ancestor of their founder, had 'subjected the English to perpetual slavery'.[15] In fact it appears that the scribe had an anti-Norman bias. When, in 1047 (*recte* 1066), reporting the death of Edward, the scribe informed the reader: 'Of him it is said that he was the honour and glory of the English while he lived and their ruin when he died.'[16] It is also difficult to imagine that a monk at Furness would refer to the king of Man as coming home to Man.[17]

There is some evidence to support the conjecture that the scribe was a Manxman. He furnishes detail about the island and its landscape, and describes Man as beautiful.[18] The scribe is very single-minded; after 1079, he has no interest in the affairs of other countries unless they actually impinge on the affairs of Man. He is, in fact, very insular, reflecting the comparative isolation of the island and presents the impression of a man very familiar with and empathising with the sea, such as one might expect of an islander. The scribe's awareness of the all-pervasive presence of the sea, the coastline and the dangers to shipping posed by the environment paints a view of Man in the thirteenth century that is very immediate and evocative. When reporting a shipwreck he states: 'The entire ship was so full of water to its upper decks, that the sea seemed to be in the ship and not the ship in the sea'.[19]

Accepting that the Cistercian scribe was a monk at Rushen, the question arises as to the purpose of the chronicle. It has been conjectured that the inspiration for the writing of the chronicle was the dedication of the church of Rushen in 1257.[20] Rushen abbey is certainly mentioned on occasions in the chronicle, but only very briefly, the longest entry indeed being the dedication of the church of Rushen when the scribe states:

> In the year 1257 St Mary's church at Rushen was dedicated by the venerable father and lord Richard bishop of Sodor in the fifth year of his pontificate and in the presence of lord Magnus king of Man and the Isles in the fifth year of his reign, lord Simon was then abbot'.[21]

Apart from that concise entry the scribe rarely mentions Rushen. Even the foundation date of Rushen, in 1134, is treated casually.[22] In 1192 the scribe merely notes in passing that 'St Mary's abbey, Rushen, was transferred to Douglas, and there they lived for four years, then returned to Rushen'.[23] The scribe offers no explanation of this event; a true monastic chronicle would at least relate the reason. So, although it can be accepted that this is a chronicle written by a Cistercian monk at Rushen, the theory that the inspiration for the writing of the chronicle was the dedication of the church of Rushen in 1257 is questionable. There is no drawing beside the foundation of Rushen or the dedication of the church, although there is a cross in the margin beside the report of the transfer of Rushen to Douglas in 1192.

Clearly the chronicle of Man is not a monastic chronicle within the normal meaning of the term. A typical monastic abbey would produce a chronicle that would be read aloud to the monks and would relate how their predecessors at the abbey sustained tribulations and oppressions, want and labour for the hope of eternal glory.[24] Also, a typical monastic chronicle would give the names of benefactors and abbots and similar information. In this chronicle the abbot of Rushen is mentioned only once and that is when his presence at the dedication of the church at Rushen is noted; and the notice referring to the abbot has the appearance of being a later addition. So, although the scribe is almost certainly a Cistercian monk at Rushen, he is most definitely not writing a monastic chronicle.

Once again an examination of the manuscript itself suggests the scribe's purpose. Apart from the depictions of two Cistercian abbeys, the only other marginal notations are crosses drawn beside the report of the deaths of Guðröðr, king of Man, in 1187, Rögnvaldr, king of Man, in 1228, and Óláfr Dubh, king of Man, in 1237. Therefore we can state that the scribe was a Cistercian monk exhibiting a particular interest in the kings of Man. In point of fact the chronicler is quite explicit. He states his purpose very clearly in the opening words of the chronicle: 'Here begin the chronicles of the kings of Man and the Isles, and of the bishops, and of some of the kings of England, Scotland and Norway'.[25] (X-ref to Fig. 14.1) Again, an examination of the manuscript itself is important as the manner in which the scribe has entered his information on the manuscript can give vital clues that can be missed by just relying on a transcript however excellent. In this case, although the script is uniform, the use of rubrics is one method by which the scribe signifies what he considers to be important areas of his material.

Traditionally, rubrics are used to highlight the beginning of the document and the letter A of *Anno* and indeed the scribe follows tradition in this manuscript. Sometimes however, apart from the A of *Anno*, a scribe will rubricate some word or letter that is of particular importance to him. In this manuscript the most noteworthy rubrication is to be found on folio 32v. where, after a significant gap of 4 lines, the scribe then inserts the one and only very large A for *Anno* at the beginning of an entry.[26] This is the entry that records that Godred Crovan came to Man in 1056 (*recte* 1079) and, by his victory at Skyhill, firmly established the kingdom of Man and the Isles which was then ruled by Godred's descendants from that date to 1265 when Magnús son of Óláfr Dubh, king of Man and the Isles, and direct descendent of Godred Crovan, died and was buried in Rushen abbey.

The chronicle was intended for some degree of public perusal; this is evident from the statement: 'For the benefit of the readers'.[27] From the historian's point of view it is reassuring to know that the scribe regarded accuracy as important. When beginning the history of the bishops of Sodor he states:

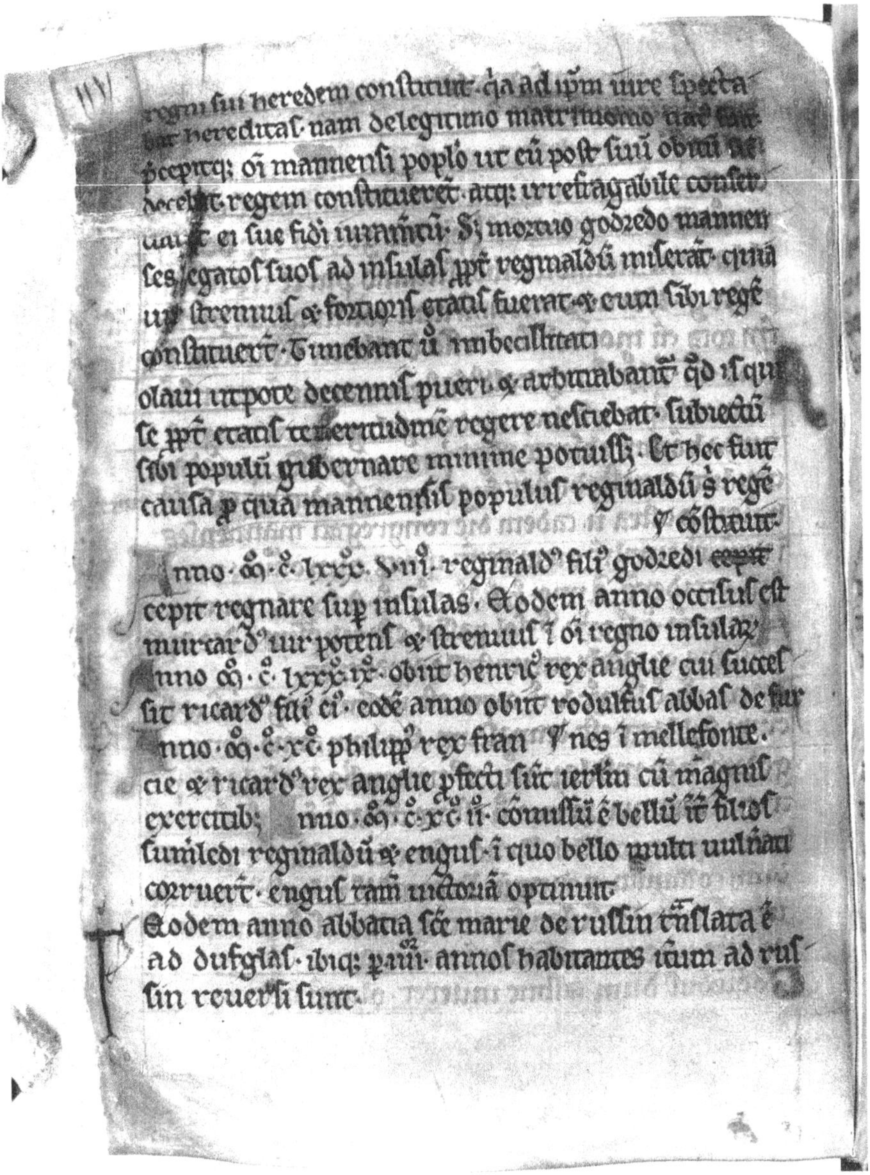

Fig. 14.3 (a) and (b) *Crosses drawn in the margin beside mentions of St Mary's Abbey, Rushen, translated as: a) 'In the same year [1192] … St Mary's Abbey, Rushen, transferred to Douglas, and there they lived for four years, then returned to Rushen.' and b) 'In the year 1237 … Olaf … King of Man and the Isles died on St Patrick's Isle and was buried in St Mary's Abbey, Rushen' (folio 40v and folio 44v). Copyright: British Library.*

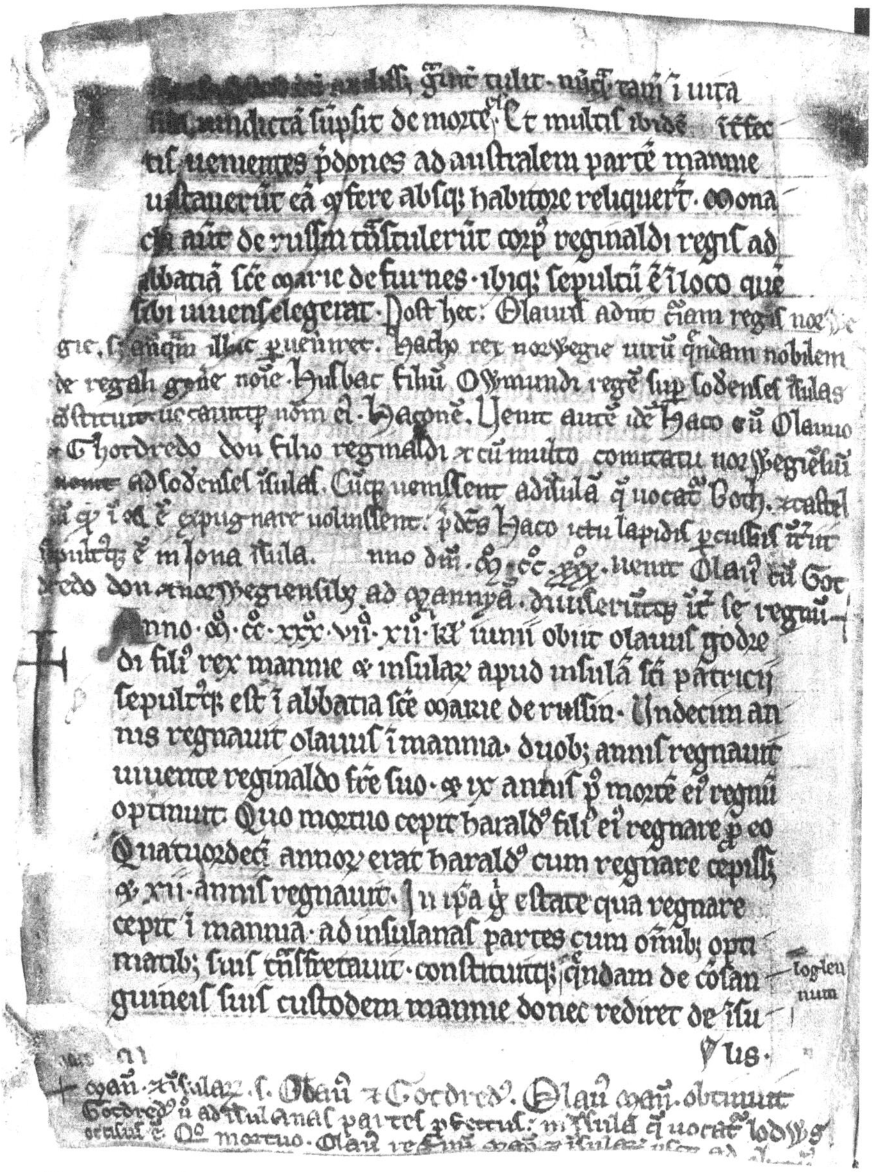

There were bishops who assumed the episcopal seat in Man from the time of Godred Crovan and some time before… but it is sufficient to begin the account of the bishops from Roolwer. We say it is sufficient because we are very ignorant of who or what sort of bishops there were before him and because we have found no record, nor can we learn for sure from what our elders tell us.[28]

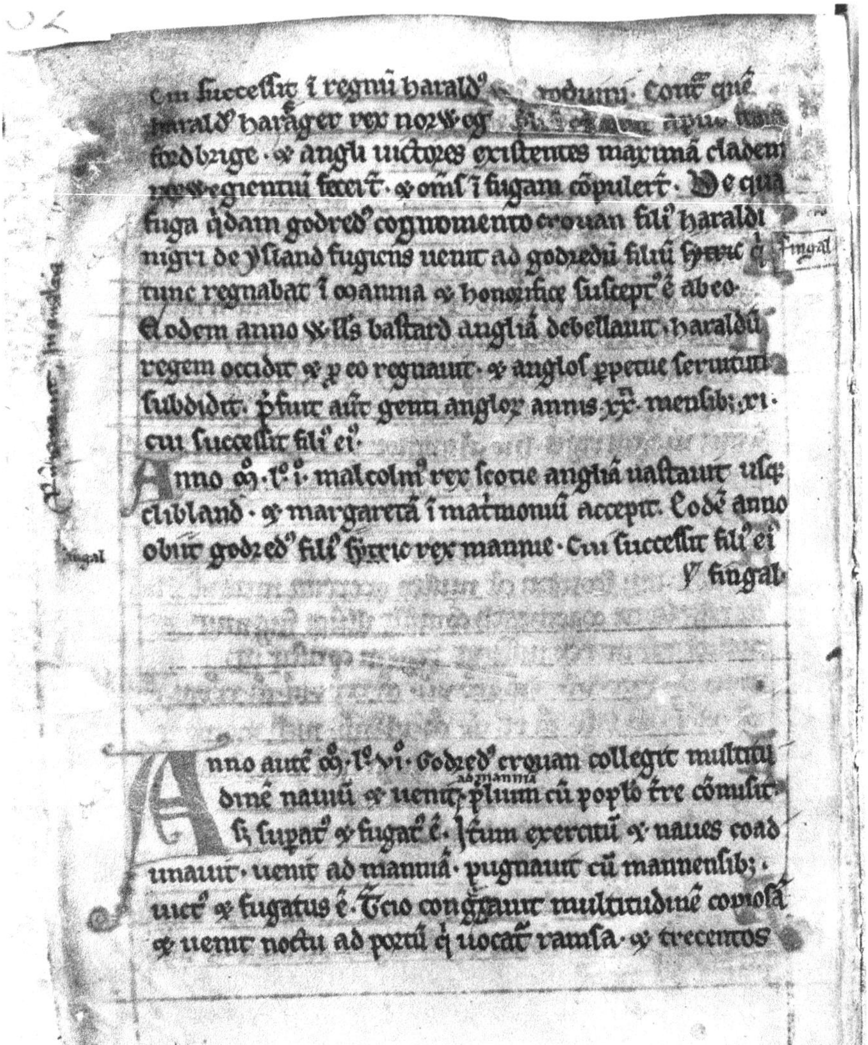

Fig. 14.4 *A gap of four lines and rubrication of the 'A' of Anno mark start of the section about Godred Crovan mustering a great number of ships and coming to Man.* 'Anno autem m.l.vi. Godredus crouan collegit multitudinem nauium & uenit ad manniam prelium cum poulo terre commisit', *folio 32v of the* Chronicles of the Kings of Man and the Isles. *Copyright: British Library.*

Incidentally, the phrase, 'from what our elders tell us', may be merely a statement of respect but might also indicate that the scribe was a comparatively young man. Occasionally he tells us his source. His entry in 1249 states: 'This we have written just as we learned it from the man himself'.[29] An attempt at accurate reportage is implicit in that statement. Some information the scribe has obtained from oral tradition; concerning Guðröðr, king of Man (d. 1187), he tells us: 'There are many anecdotes about him worthy of narration, but for brevity's sake we have omitted them.'[30]

The chronicle covers the period 1000 (*recte* 1016) to 1316 and is clearly a combination of compilation and original material and therefore it is not remarkable to find a problem with the dates given by the scribe for the period 1000 to 1144. The year 1000 should be corrected to 1016 and, following that, the sequence of error is approximately 17 years behind.[31] The years attributed to reigns and bishoprics also contain inaccuracies for this period. It is always possible that the scribe did not consider strict accuracy of dating important for the purpose of his chronicle and used his own memory and deduction to fill in the dates at least in the correct order of the events.[32] Alternatively, the scribe may have been using a source that contained those inaccuracies. The fact that the scribe states 'In the year 1036, 1037, 1038, 1039, 1040, 1041, 1042, 1043, 1044, nothing to record',[33] suggests that the scribe had some written source before him which had either no entries for those years or, alternatively and more probably, no entries of interest to a Manx chronicler. The chronicle was written as one continuous exercise. This is evident from a statement, under the year 1102, where, when the scribe is referring to Somerled's sons by the daughter of the king of Man, he states: 'about whom we shall later go into in greater detail in subsequent chapters.'[34] The uniformity of appearance of the manuscript itself also bears out this assumption.

The question that next arises is: what was the source used by the scribe for the early period of the chronicle? The obvious approach in such a situation is to look to the mother-house for source material, but a problem of chronology arises here. The monks in Furness did have a chronicle. The Cistercians of Stanley abbey in Wiltshire loaned their chronicle (which was a continuation of the chronicle of William of Newburgh to 1270) to the monks in Furness who copied, expanded and continued it to 1298.[35] The Manx chronicle was written in 1257, too early to have made use of a Furness chronicle. Another suggested source for our scribe was the chronicle of Melrose, Scotland's principal monastic chronicle covering the years 781–1257. This would certainly be a viable proposition; we know, for instance, that the abbot of Dundrennan in Galloway borrowed the chronicle of Melrose in the thirteenth century.[36] The chronicle of Melrose was also used as a source for the chronicle of Lanercost, the chronicle of Holyrood and the chronicle of Roger of Howden.[37] However, although it is true that there is some material present in the Manx chronicle similar to entries in Melrose, that alone is not sufficient to claim Melrose as a source. Furthermore, the foundation date for the abbey of Melrose is incorrectly entered in our chronicle, under the year 1139 instead of 1136, a virtual impossibility if the scribe had the chronicle of Melrose as his source.

To seek a Cistercian source might appear logical for a Cistercian monk but it appears very unlikely that this scribe had access to any Cistercian source. The Cistercian order is mentioned ten times, very briefly, between 1098, the foundation of Cîteaux, and 1143 when the scribe records the death of St Bernard of Clairvaux at Clairvaux. Of those ten dates seven are incorrect. The foundation dates of Cîteaux, in 1098, Savigny in 1112 and Rushen in 1134,[38] are the only correct ones. To enter incorrectly the foundation dates of Rievaulx, Calder, Holm Cultram and Melrose is one thing but to record the death of St Bernard as 1143 instead of 1153 must be the final proof that our scribe did not have a Cistercian chronicle as his source. Interestingly, there is no mention of any further Cistercian foundations after 1141. This lack of accuracy, or indeed interest, in Cistercian affairs would probably account for the dismissive comment concerning the chronicle made by the Savignac, Dom Avory, who in his *History of the Savignian Order* (written *c.*1700) declared, 'I think that one ought not to place too much faith in this chronicle in which many mistakes are to be found'.[39]

There is no clear solution to the question of the source used by the chronicler.[40] Whatever source the scribe used, he did not deviate from his purpose of telling the history of the legitimate line of the kings of Man. He was not alone in producing a history of kings; in Scotland, one version of the *Chronicle of the Kings of Scotland* ends in 1251 and must have been written within a few years of that date.[41] At the time of his writing, *c.*1254, there was an evident interest in royal circles in the idea of legitimate kingship. The influence of the Capetians and the Salian emperors had spread to many areas of Europe, and Scotland was receiving and absorbing the same ideas concerning monarchy as was her immediate neighbour, England.[42] This is not surprising as from the eleventh century onwards there was much foreign influence at the Scottish court; the kings were partly of English blood, the queens were English or French, some nobles originated from northern France, and French manners were cultivated.[43]

Perhaps of even greater interest is that in Norway, shortly before the time when our scribe was writing, there was a strong promotion of the concept of the divine right of kingship. Sverrir, king of Norway 1184–1202, in his own saga which he commissioned, and in a remarkable document known as the *anecdoton Sverreri*, was concerned with defining the power of monarchy: 'For kingly rule is created by god's command... and no man obtains kingly rule except by divine dispensation'.[44] Following this interest, a document was written in Norway in the 1240s, during Hákon IV's reign called the *King's Mirror*, in which is stated:

> [The king] is so highly honoured and exalted upon earth that all must bend and bow before him as before God. So great is his power that he may dispose as he likes of the lives of all who live in his kingdom; he lets him live whom he wills and causes him to be slain he whom he wills.'[45]

This Norwegian interest in kingship is very significant to an understanding of the purpose of the Manx chronicle. In 1252 Magnús son of Óláfr Dubh successfully claimed his rightful place as king of Man and the following year he was in Norway at the court of King Hákon IV, the man who commissioned the *King's Mirror*, where, we are told, he remained for a year. Other chronicles of kings written in this area of Europe at this time include the *Knýtlinga saga*, or *History of the Kings of Denmark*, written *c.*1240–50.[46] With all this literary interest in kingship in north-west Europe it would not be remarkable if Magnús, king of Man, commissioned a similar history from a monk at Rushen: the scribe records in his chronicle, therefore, the history of the legal claim of Magnús son of Óláfr Dubh to the divine right to be king of Man.

The concept of kingship rested on both lay tradition and biblical authority. By ancient custom a king must protect and defend his people, be a member of an ancient warrior family and be chosen by the free consent of the people. Added to this list was the church's qualification, when promoting the ideal of kingship, that he should be a man of spirituality, compassion and liberality, giving his full support to the church. Once duly chosen as king there should be no rebellion against the one chosen by God. Our scribe clearly held these views. He portrays the legitimate dynasty of the kings of Man protecting and defending the people of Man, stresses the legitimacy of the ancient family of proven leaders and, whenever possible, includes the information that the people chose the king – even when he does not agree with the king so chosen, as in the case of Rögnvaldr in 1187. The rightful kings are referred to at all times as supporters of the church. We find them going on pilgrimages, giving land to the church and receiving papal legates whose instructions they obey. Rebellion against God's chosen king is reprehensible. The scribe states that King Óláfr of Norway, the future saint, was unjustly put to death, that Harold, rightful king of England, was killed by the Normans and as a result the English were subjected to perpetual slavery. Plots against a king are described as villainous,[47] tyranny is wrong even when a legitimate king is the culprit, and disaster inevitably follows tyranny.[48] Usurpation is wrong and will be corrected by God's intervention in the form of a miracle when human attempts fail. Most importantly the scribe promotes the legal and moral entitlement of the legitimate heir to inherit the kingdom. These beliefs can be clearly demonstrated in our chronicle, which details the rightful descent of Magnús son of Óláfr Dubh, king of Man.

Although the story of the kings of Man begins with the battle of Skyhill in 1056 (*recte* 1079), the scribe begins his chronicle with the year 1000 (*recte* 1016), the start of a new millennium. The early section from 1000 (= 1016) to 1056 (= 1079) is concerned with affairs in England, brief entries concerning Scottish kings and events of importance in Norway and Denmark. The first mention of Man occurs in 1047 (= 1066) where we are informed that, 'Godred nicknamed Crovan', who was part of the Norwegian contingent under King Haraldr *harðráði* of Norway at the battle of Stamford Bridge, had fled to the Isle of Man and had taken refuge with Guðröðr, son of Sigtryggr, the then king of Man. After Guðröðr's death and the succession of his son Fingal, Godred Crovan conquered Man.

The scribe's interest in the dynasty of Magnús son of Óláfr Dubh, king of Man, begins on the second folio,[49] when, after the only large gap in the manuscript, the scribe uses an extra large rubrication to begin the account of the battle of Skyhill, and it is now that detailed entries appear in the chronicle and the history of the kings of Man truly commences. When describing the battle, the scribe displays local knowledge and detail. He relates how Godred came by night to Ramsey harbour with a massive force and hid 300 men in a wood that was, the scribe tells us 'on the sloping brow of the mountain which is called Sky Hill'. Battle commenced at dawn and when the 300 men emerged from their place of hiding the battle was over. It is at this point that the first intimation of the favoured status of this dynasty comes. We are told: 'those who were left begged Godred with pitiful cries to spare them their lives. Moved with compassion and taking pity on their plight... he called off his army and forbade them to pursue them further'.[50] Godred, and his dynasty, are portrayed as good Christian men worthy of the title king. It is in this entry that the most significant remark appears. The scribe states:

> Godred... granted the southern part of the island to the few [Western] Islanders who had stayed with him, and the northern part to the remainder of the Manxmen, on such terms that none of them should at any time dare to usurp any part of the land for himself by right of inher-

itance. Whence it has come to pass that up until the present day the entire island is the property of the king alone, and that all its dues belong to him.[51]

With the death of Godred a problem arose that is repeated many times in the chronicle until eventually the rule of primogeniture becomes established. Godred had left three sons, Lögmaðr (Lagman), Haraldr and Óláfr. Lögmaðr, the eldest, seized the throne for seven years and then his brother Haraldr rebelled. Lögmaðr captured Haraldr whom he blinded and castrated. The scribe now relates that Lögmaðr regretted his treatment of his brother and abdicated the kingdom of his own accord and went on a pilgrimage to Jerusalem but died en route.

The third brother, Óláfr, was still too young to rule and it was at this time that the noblemen of the isles sent an embassy to Ireland to Muirchertach Ua Briain for a regent to govern until Óláfr should reach maturity. Domnall, son of Tadc, was sent from Ireland to govern the island and the scribe significantly states that Domnall was to do so 'with all due kindness and modesty as it was not his'.[52] It was evidently God's wish to ensure that Óláfr should rule because the first substitute, Domnall, was guilty of tyranny and after three years of cruelty the chieftains rebelled and drove him away. The second substitute, Ingimundr, sent by the king of Norway to seize the island, also proved unsuitable. We are told that he and his companions 'indulged in rapine and orgies, violating the chastity of maidens and matrons, and gave themselves up to every other variety of entertainment and pleasure of the flesh',[53] clearly not suitable behaviour for a Christian king. We are told that when this was reported to the chieftains of the Isles they killed him and all his men.[54]

The next intruder into the kingship was Magnus Barelegs, king of Norway. The scribe opens this report with the account of a miracle showing Magnus in an unfavourable light. According to the scribe, Magnus wanted to find out if the body of St Óláfr had decayed and wished to open the tomb. The bishops and clergy opposed him, but he went ahead boldly and had the tomb opened by royal mandate. The body was indeed intact and we are told that a great fear rushed upon him and he departed in great haste. The following night St Óláfr appeared before him in a dream and told him to choose between two things: either to stay in Norway and die within 30 days or to leave at once permanently. Naturally, Magnus left. He eventually came to Man and chose to live there, because 'the beauty of the island was pleasing to his eye'.[55] It is difficult to see the purpose of the insertion of the story of the opening of St Óláfr's tomb – against the advice of the bishops – if not to demonstrate the unsuitability of Magnus as king of Man. After he had ruled for six years he died while attempting to conquer Ireland and now the chieftains sent for Óláfr, son of Godred Crovan, who had been living with the king of England. Óláfr was the legitimate heir and now had also been chosen by the acclaim of the people.

The true line was now restored in the person of Óláfr who ruled for 40 years. The scribe immediately launches into a panegyric: 'He was a peaceable man and had all the kings of Ireland and Scotland as confederates in such a way that no one dare disturb the kingdom of the Isles during his lifetime.'[56] It is not surprising to find such an accolade at this point as it was King Óláfr who granted to Ivo, abbot of Furness, part of his land in Man in order to establish the abbey of St Mary at Rushen. Furthermore, we are told, he also granted lands and privileges to the churches of the Isles; he was in effect a good Christian king. However he had one failing, which the scribe, as a cleric, cannot ignore. Óláfr had a wife, Affreca, daughter of Fergus of Galloway, by whom he had a son called Guðröðr but he had also many concubines by whom he had three more sons and many daughters. The scribe, writing in 1257, after the period of church intervention in marriage laws, cannot condone this conduct, even though Óláfr was such a praiseworthy king. We are told: 'he [Óláfr] was devout and enthusiastic in matters of religion and was welcome both to God and man, for all that he over-indulged in the domestic vice of kings'.[57]

While Guðröðr, the legitimate son, was in Norway, Óláfr was murdered by his nephews, the sons of the blinded and castrated Haraldr. The author describes this event as 'so grave a crime' and 'a villainous plot' to assassinate the king. The legitimate heir, Guðröðr, eventually returned from Norway and we are told: 'All the chieftains of the Isles were overjoyed and when they heard he had come at an assembly unanimously elected him their king';[58] again the legitimate heir was chosen by the people. The rebels had to be dealt with and King Guðröðr 'punished them with the death they deserved'; the scribe agrees with this punishment for the sin of regicide. In fact, he tells the reader: 'It is even said that he blinded two of them and killed one'.[59] The legitimate line now continues to rule Man in the person of Óláfr's son Guðröðr who, as both the legitimate son of the king and unanimously elected by the assembly, ruled for 33 years. He was apparently such a paragon that, according to the chronicle, the people of Dublin sent for him to rule over them and he was 'received graciously by its citizens with much dancing'.[60] The scribe tells us that: 'There are many anecdotes about him worthy of narration, but for brevity's sake we have omitted them'.[61]

A different aspect of Guðröðr's character emerges as we are told that when he was firmly established on the throne he began to exercise tyranny against his chieftains, with the result that in 1156 one of the chieftains went to Somerled of Argyll, and invited him to give his son Dubgall to be made king. The inevitable confrontation between King Guðröðr and Somerled resulted in Guðröðr's flight to Norway. Despite many vicissitudes, the dynasty of Guðröðr was destined to survive and at this point the scribe inserts a miracle concerning the local St Machutus.[62] The incident involved the plunder of St Machutus's church by one of Somerled's men and resulted in Somerled and his men fleeing in terror. Somerled had tried to usurp the kingdom but we are told that eventually, 'by divine vengeance', he was overcome by a handful of men.[63] One presumes that Guðröðr had been sufficiently punished for his tyranny and now God was once again on the side of the legitimate line of kings. Guðröðr was worthy of God's intervention because he was a man who respected church authority. When the papal legate, Cardinal Vivian, came to Man in 1176 he must have been received with great accord by the king because Vivian is described as 'fulfilling his duty as legate [when he] caused Godred to be lawfully betrothed with his wife called Phingola', the mother of his three-year-old son Óláfr Dubh. This is one of the instances where the scribe stresses the importance of following canon law in respect of marriage. The importance of the occasion is underlined by the presence of Silvanus, abbot of Riveaux, who performed the actual ceremony.[64] Óláfr must have been legitimised by the church at this time because later we are told that 'he had been born in lawful wedlock'.[65]

With Óláfr Dubh now recognised by the church as the legitimate heir, Guðröðr attempted to safeguard the dynasty:

> While Godred was still alive, he established Olaf his son as heir to his kingdom, as this inheritance was his by right, for he had been born in lawful wedlock, and he gave instructions to all the Manx people that after his death they should make him king, as was fitting, and to keep their oath of allegiance to him inviolable'.[66]

The best-laid plans go awry and the Manxmen, who had not yet endorsed the principle of primogeniture and the idea of hereditary kingship, did not find the ten-year-old Óláfr Dubh wholly acceptable. We are told that they worried about Óláfr's inexperience and believed that, 'because he did not know how to look after himself on account of the slenderness of his age, he would be quite unable to govern a people subject to him'.[67] This, we are told, was why the Manx people in 1188 sent for Rögnvaldr, one of Óláfr Dubh's illegitimate half-brothers, 'a sturdy man of maturer years', and made him king.[68]

King Rögnvaldr presents the scribe with a problem. He is, in effect, in a quandary. His purpose in writing the chronicle is to uphold the legitimate line of kings and, as such, he must support Óláfr Dubh's claim as the legitimate son of a king who had been born of a union recognised by the church. But King Rögnvaldr had some legitimate claim to the kingship; he also was the son of Guðröðr and he was duly elected by the Manxmen and went on to rule as king of Man for 38 years. Furthermore, King Rögnvaldr was a benefactor of Furness abbey where he was eventually buried (Óláfr was buried at Rushen). The scribe's bias is evident with regard to Rögnvaldr, in that he is economical with the truth. This is most particularly evident in the omission of the fact that King Rögnvaldr ceded the Isle of Man to the pope as a papal fief.[69] That a monk should ignore this important action clearly demonstrates his bias against Rögnvaldr. Not all medieval writers shared his bias; a poem in praise of King Rögnvaldr was written by a Gaelic poet in the earlier part of his career.[70]

Óláfr Dubh spent years trying to regain his throne. The scribe depicts Óláfr Dubh in an Old Testament light – willing to accept all the misfortune with which God chose to test him. Óláfr comes across as positively angelic, with a hint of the sanctimonious. When he was not satisfied with the island of Lewis given to him by his brother, King Rögnvaldr, he went to him, and we are told that 'he came in all faith', saying: 'My brother, lord and king, you know that the kingdom of Isles belongs to me by right of inheritance, but because the Lord chose you to govern it I do not envy you, nor am I angry that you have been raised to royal heights'.[71] According to our scribe, the self-effacing Óláfr Dubh, now merely asked his brother for some other portion of land, as Lewis was unable to sustain him. King Rögnvaldr's response was to arrest him and send him in chains to William, king of Scotland, to be kept as a prisoner. After seven years had passed, King William died, but before he died he ordered an amnesty for all prisoners and Óláfr was freed. God's purpose was again evident.

Óláfr Dubh returned to Man, but we hear nothing from the scribe of what happened between the two brothers. Peace of some sort evidently existed and Óláfr set off on a pilgrimage to the shrine of St James at Compostela. Upon his return, Óláfr Dubh was prevailed upon to marry King Rögnvaldr's sister-in-law, Lauon, and once more retire to live in Lewis. This Óláfr did, presumably under some duress, because he soon appears to use the church to escape from the unwelcome marriage. This action however is presented by the scribe as Óláfr Dubh acting as an obedient son of the church. When Reginald, bishop of the Isles and Óláfr Dubh's nephew, came to the island of Lewis to visit him we are told that Óláfr joyfully hastened to meet him and ordered a banquet to be prepared, but Bishop Reginald said:

> 'I will not partake with you, brother, until the catholic church has released you by canon law from your illicit marriage bond... Are you not aware that you were previously wedded to the first cousin of the woman whom you now have as wife?' Óláfr did not deny that it was true and admitted that he had kept her cousin as a concubine for a good while.[72]

Although the scribe does not say so, there was a second reason why the marriage was canonically unlawful; it was not permitted to marry those linked to you by affinity – in this case Óláfr Dubh had married his brother's sister-in-law. A synod was now assembled and Bishop Reginald, upholding canon law, annulled the marriage between Óláfr and Lauon. While it is true that the marriage was canonically unsound on two counts, nevertheless this was obviously an occasion when the church laws were used to political advantage as, after this, Óláfr married Christina, daughter of the earl of Ross.[73] This episode, which occurred *c.*1217, is the last mention of concubines in the chronicle.

This annulment infuriated King Rögnvaldr's wife (Lauon's sister) and we are told that, 'stimulated by bitterness and resentment', she 'sowed the seeds of all disharmony between Reginald [Rögnvaldr] and Olaf'. [74] The result was that King Rögnvaldr's son, Guðröðr, at the instigation of his mother, sought to kill his uncle, Óláfr Dubh. This move gave Óláfr the justification he needed to attack and in 1223 Óláfr's men cut down all whom they found, but we are told that they did so 'outside the confines of the church'.[75] Óláfr Dubh's men seized Guðröðr in 1223 and blinded and castrated him. The scribe is quick to assert: 'Olaf did not agree with this action nor was he able to stop it.'[76] The kingdom was then divided between Rögnvaldr and Óláfr Dubh. In 1228 King Rögnvaldr tried to regain his lost kingdom, in the course of which he plundered churches, but the scribe relates that Óláfr put him to flight, and 'the Manxmen... began to come together and to live in safety.'[77]

King Rögnvaldr was finally deposed by the Manxmen, for fraud. According to the chronicle, Rögnvaldr, under the pretext of going to the king of England, received 100 marks from the men of Man, but instead used the money to proceed to Alan of Galloway to marry his daughter to Alan. The Manxmen were extremely angry and, we are told, sending for Óláfr Dubh, they made him their king. The legitimate heir had now been chosen by the people. With the words 'Olaf recovered his inheritance... which his brother Reginald had governed for 38 years',[78] the scribe suggests that King Rögnvaldr had done so illegally. Rögnvaldr was finally killed by 'a band of wicked men', a deed that the scribe cannot condone and he is quick to inform us that Óláfr was not involved in the crime and indeed protested about the death. Interestingly though, the scribe adds that Óláfr Dubh did not in his lifetime exact vengeance for King Rögnvaldr's death.[79] The implication appears to be that such a deed would have to be punished at some time either in this life or the next. The fact that it was the monks of Rushen who conveyed the body of King Rögnvaldr for burial to St Mary's abbey at Furness illustrates the difficulty encountered by the scribe in his treatment of Rögnvaldr in a chronicle intended to recount the history of the 'true' dynasty of King Magnús son of Óláfr Dubh.

When Óláfr Dubh himself died in 1237, he was buried at St Mary's abbey at Rushen, another explanation for the bias shown towards him. Haraldr, Óláfr's 14-year-old son, succeeded and after encountering some problems with the king of Norway eventually settled into a productive reign. The people of Man, we are told, received him with great joy and he began ruling quietly and peacefully in Man and held a very stable peace with the king of England and the king of Scotland and was an ally of theirs in friendship until drowned in a shipwreck off Shetland in 1249.[80] His brother Rögnvaldr son of Óláfr Dubh succeeded him, but was killed within a month. Trouble arose again as another Haraldr, grandson of the late King Rögnvaldr, 'usurped the title and dignity of king in Man for himself and banished practically all the chieftains'.[81] At this crucial juncture the scribe introduces his third miracle – this time about St Mary and Rushen abbey.[82] The only purpose of the story is to indicate that heaven was not on the side of Haraldr, and eventually, in 1252, 'Magnus son of Olaf [Dubh] came a second time to Man and all the Manxmen received him gladly and made him their king.'[83] In 1254, we are told that Hákon IV, king of Norway, 'established Magnus son of Olaf king over all the isles which his predecessors possessed by right of inheritance and he confirmed them to him and to his heirs and successors'.[84] After this, we are told that Magnús son of Óláfr Dubh 'came' home – the phrase implying that the scribe was writing on the island. The final entry by this scribe is the dedication of the church of Rushen in the presence of Magnús. It is logical to suggest that it was on this occasion that the scribe was asked to write a history of the dynasty.

Following a space of two lines, brief entries of special interest are recorded by later scribes, which include the death of Magnús, who was buried at St Mary's abbey, Rushen. In 1275, a new scribe wrote the entry recounting the battle between the men of Man and the army of the king of Scotland where, we are told, the Scots were victorious, killing 537 Manxmen in that engagement. There then occurs a 38-year gap before the entry of 1313, which describes the siege of Castle Rushen by Robert Bruce, king of Scotland. The date of the final entry, entered in the chronicle under the year 1316, has been challenged by W.R. Serjeant and others.[85] This entry, written by the fifth hand, refers to the arrival on the Isle of Man of Richard de Mandeville and a group of Irish mercenaries who proceeded to plunder the island for a month.[86] Serjeant claims that the date, in fact, should be 1329. He bases his argument on the contention that because there is a record of activity by Richard de Mandeville in 1329, then the date should in fact be 1329. This is the only basis for his claim. While it is always possible that there is an error it seems at least as likely, in view of the following points, that the date is correct.

The first point to be noted is that the date on the manuscript is quite clear. There is no way that the roman numerals m.ccc.xvi could be an error for m.ccc.xxix; that is to say, xvi bears no relationship to xxix. This is a single entry by a new hand. Why would the scribe give an incorrect date for such an account? Furthermore it is an account of considerable detail. He tells us that the raid began at sunrise on Ascension Day when Richard de Mandeville and his brothers with other magnates and evildoers from Ireland landed at the port of Ronaldsway with a large fleet. He tells us that troops, standards and large siege equipment were put ashore. He recounts the interesting fact that when the Irish became angry they sounded a battle cry.[87] He knows the detail that the enemy formed themselves into two squadrons and went to an open field under the mountain-side of Barrule and that the Manxmen turned tail and about 40 fell in the conflict. He describes the pursuit as 'both on foot and on horse'. He gives details of the demand by the enemy: they 'asked for land, or that aid should be given to them in terms of victuals, animals and money because they had been plundered and weakened by starvation by enemies continually waging war on them'. He reports that when the enemy was subsequently plundering the land, it came upon 'much silver which had been hidden for a long time in many places throughout the country'. Taking all this into account, it is difficult to conceive of a scribe, knowledgeable enough to recount such detail, making such a fundamental error as to enter the year as 1316 instead of 1329. The most telling argument in favour of the scribe's date of 1316 is contained in the next sentence: 'After this they came to Rushen abbey and plundered it so extensively of its furniture, cattle and sheep, that they left nothing at all'. A monk at Rushen abbey could hardly make an error in the date his abbey was attacked and plundered for the first time. The most logical conclusion, therefore, is that the scribe did not make an error when entering the last item: however convenient it might be to embrace the alternative date it is untenable to accept an error of such magnitude.

It is clear that the chronicle as a whole must be viewed in two parts; the chronicler to 1257 and the later additions. After the year 1257 the manuscript was used only as a convenient place in which to note significant incidents that occurred on the Isle of Man and which an inmate of the Cistercian monastery at that time considered to be of sufficient importance to be added to the existing chronicle. The first part of the chronicle was clearly written by a Cistercian monk of Rushen abbey to substantiate the right of Magnús son of Óláfr Dubh to be the king of Man; this he does with great skill. It was the very purpose of the chronicle to recount and justify the legitimate line of Magnús, king of Man. While the scribe does not actually state that it was God's wish that those men should be kings, the belief is implicit in his writing. The scribe believes that God sanctioned this dynasty and his retelling of events is adapted to this purpose. The insertion of three miracles in the chronicle occurs when it is necessary to discredit possible usurpers of the kingdom. Furthermore it is possible that the scribe might even have been commissioned to write this history in 1257 when Magnús, in the fifth year of his reign as king of Man, was present at the dedication of the church at Rushen.[88] The great historical importance of the chronicle is enhanced by identifying the purpose behind its composition. That done, a great deal more can be revealed by reading the lines, and between the lines, penned by the main scribe of this manuscript.

Notes

1 Broderick, *CKMI*.

2 Duffy, 'Irishmen and Islesmen', 98.

3 AU, vol. i, 274.

4 Concerning Godred Croven and the battle of Skyhill, the scribe of the chronicle writes: 'Moved with compassion and taking pity on their plight, since he had been reared among them for some time', (Broderick, *CKMI*, fol. 33r.).

5 The chronicle begins with the year 1000 (1016) but, apart from a very brief statement in 1066, the history of Man begins in 1079 with the first long entry.

6 See Fig. 14.3 (b).

7 Broderick, *CKMI*, iv-v.

8 Broderick, *CKMI*, fol. 34r.

9 Broderick, *CKMI*, fol. 35v.

10 Broderick, *CKMI* , i.

11 *Ibid.*

12 A.G. Taylor, 'The monastic orders of Rushen abbey (Savignac and Cistercian)', *Proceedings*, 3 (1930), 250–7; William Cubbon, 'History of Rushen abbey, Ballasalla, Isle of Man, to 1134', *Proceedings*, 4 (1936), 98–115.

13 Additionally, such a monk would have had information available to him which was not available to our scribe.

14 *History of Furness Abbey* (London, 1965), 3–4.

15 Broderick, *CKMI*, fol. 32v.

16 Broderick, *CKMI*, fol. 32r.

17 'Magnus... came home': Broderick, *CKMI*, fol.49r.

18 Broderick, *CKMI*, fol. 32v-33r; fol. 38r; fol. 48v; fol. 34v.

19 Broderick, *CKMI*, fol. 45v.

20 Broderick, *CKMI*, i–ii.
21 Broderick, *CKMI*, fol. 49v.
22 Cubbon, 'History of Rushen Abbey', 98.
23 Broderick, *CKMI*, fol. 40v.
24 Antonia Gransden, *Historical Writing in England c.550 to c.1307* (London, 1974), 290.
25 Broderick, *CKMI*, fol. 31r. For a genealogical table of the Manx kings, see p. 12 above.
26 Broderick, *CKMI*, fol. 32v.
27 Broderick, *CKMI*, fol. 41v.
28 Broderick, *CKMI*, fol. 50v.
29 Broderick, *CKMI*, fol. 48r. The scribe rarely names a day, but when he does so it suggests that it can be relied upon. In 1228 he gives a date as 'the fourteenth day of the month of February, that is on the feast of St Valentine the martyr': Broderick, *CKMI*, fol. 44r. Another date occurs in 1237: 'the twenty fifth day of the month of October', when an assembly was held at the Tynwald. The remarkably immediate account on this occasion suggests that either the scribe himself was present or else he was recording the information from an eye witness. Apart from naming the day the scribe adds that it was the third day since the arrival of Niall's sons in Man and that at the assembly there was much abuse and vilification. Broderick, *CKMI*, fol. 45r.
30 Broderick, *CKMI*, fol. 36v.–37r .
31 The error ranges from plus 20 to minus 2 years.
32 Once the initial mistake had been made then all the subsequent dates in that section would follow suit.
33 Broderick, *CKMI*, fol. 32r.
34 Broderick, *CKMI*, fol. 35v.
35 Gransden, *Historical Writing*, 421.
36 Anderson, *Early Sources*, i, xliv.
37 *Ibid.*
38 For information about the date of the foundation of Rushen, see Taylor, 'The monastic orders of Rushen abbey', 257.
39 Quoted by Taylor, 'The monastic orders of Rushen abbey', 257, and by Cubbon, 'History of Rushen abbey', 104.
40 An examination of the early section of the chronicle reveals that there are strong similarities to the Anglo-Saxon chronicle and to the chronicle of Florence of Worcester.
41 Anderson, *Early Sources*.
42 G.W.S. Barrow, *Scotland and its Neighbours in the Middle Ages* (London, 1992), 32.
43 See, for example, Dauvit Broun, 'Anglo-French acculturation and the Irish element in Scottish identity', in *Britain and Ireland 900–1300. Insular Responses to Medieval European Change*, ed. Brendan Smith (Cambridge, 1999), 135–53.
44 Quoted by Cowan, in 'Norwegian Sunset – Scottish Dawn', 124.
45 *Ibid.*, 123–4.
46 In *Danakonunga sogur*, ed. Bjarni Guðnason, Íslenzk fornrit xxxv (Reykjavik, 1982).
47 Broderick, *CKMI*, fol. 36r.
48 Broderick, *CKMI*, fol. 37v.
49 Broderick, *CKMI*, fol. 32v.
50 Broderick, *CKMI*, fol. 33r.

51 Broderick, *CKMI*, fol. 33r.
52 Broderick, *CKMI*, fol. 33v.
53 Broderick, *CKMI*, fol. 34r.
54 Broderick, *CKMI*, fol. 34r.
55 Broderick, *CKMI*, fol. 34v.
56 Broderick, *CKMI*, fol. 35v.
57 Broderick, *CKMI*, fol. 35v.
58 Broderick, *CKMI*, fol. 36v. This scribe does not numerate the kings; this Guðröðr is never called Godred II nor is the second King Óláfr so designated.
59 Broderick, *CKMI*, fol. 36v.
60 Broderick, *CKMI*, fol. 37r.
61 Broderick, *CKMI*, fols 36v.-37r.
62 Broderick, *CKMI*, fols 38r.-39r.
63 Broderick, *CKMI*, fol. 39r.
64 After the ceremony, Guðröðr gave land at Myroscough to Silvanus who built a monastery there but we are told that, 'in the course of time the whole estate, monks and all, was ceeded to St Mary's abbey, Rushen' (Broderick, *CKMI*, fol. 40r.).
65 Broderick, *CKMI*, fol. 40v. The legitimising by the church of the liaison of Finnguala and King Guðröðr, and their son Óláfr Dubh, indicates an approval and encouragement of church-recognised marriages and the support of the church for the offspring of such marriages. This inevitably demotes the sons of the other liaisons and makes them no longer eligible to inherit the kingdom.
66 Broderick, *CKMI*, fol. 40r.
67 Broderick, *CKMI*, fol. 40v.
68 Broderick, *CKMI*, fol. 40v.
69 Johnsen, 'Payments from the Hebrides', 25. In the document in question Rögnvaldr declared that the Isle of Man belonged to him by hereditary right.
70 Ó Cuív, 'A poem in praise of Raghnall'.
71 Broderick, *CKMI*, fol. 41v.
72 Broderick, *CKMI*, fols 42r.–42v.
73 Broderick, *CKMI*, fol. 42v.
74 Broderick, *CKMI*, fol. 42v.
75 Broderick, *CKMI*, fol. 43r.
76 Broderick, *CKMI*, fol. 43r.
77 Broderick, *CKMI*, fol. 44r.
78 Broderick, *CKMI*, fol. 43v.
79 Broderick, *CKMI*, fols 44r.–44v.
80 Broderick, *CKMI*, fol. 46r.
81 Broderick, *CKMI*, fol. 47v.
82 Broderick, *CKMI*, fols 47v.–48r.
83 Broderick, *CKMI*, fol. 49r.
84 Broderick, *CKMI*, fol. 49r.
85 W.R. Serjeant, 'The Isle of Man and the Anglo-Scottish War, 1296–1328', *JMM*, 77 (1960–1), 126–8. See also C. McNamee, *The Wars of the Bruces: Scotland, England and Ireland 1306–1328*, (East Linton, 1997).
86 Broderick, *CKMI*, fol. 50r.
87 It is of more than passing interest to note here that the persons that we would term Anglo-Irish are merely 'Irish' to the Manx scribe: he sees no distinction between the Anglo-Irish and the native Irish.
88 Broderick, *CKMI*, fol. 49v.

15 *The Early History of the Diocese of Sodor*

ALEX WOOLF

From the death of Bishop John Duncan, who held the see from 1374 until 1387, the ancient bishopric of the Isles was divided between bishops located on Man who were drawn increasingly into the English church and bishops based in the Hebrides who at first claimed to be dependent only upon the Holy See and who later found themselves integrated into the Scottish hierarchy. Unfortunately the beginnings of the bishopric of Sodor (from Norse *Suðreyjar*, 'the southern islands') are more obscure.

A number of bishops allegedly active in the fifth century were remembered in later times. The Life of St Patrick written by Muirchú in the last quarter of the seventh century, and preserved in its oldest surviving manuscript in the Book of Armagh (c.807),[1] records the story of a curious character from the territory of the Ulaid (the ancient occupants of County Down in Ireland) named Macc Cuill moccu Greccae. Macc Cuill is presented as a bandit chief who sets out to ambush Patrick as he passes by. One of his men feigns sickness in order to lure the charitable saint into their clutches but God intervenes by causing the man who is feigning actually to die. Macc Cuill, overcome with the fear of God, confesses his crimes to Patrick and converts. Patrick, clearly not in a good mood on this occasion, orders Macc Cuill to fetter his legs together and throw away the key and to have himself put out to sea in an oarless and rudderless craft. The penitent is eventually washed up on the shores of Man and rescued and cared for by two bishops, Conindrus and Rumilus, who, we are told, have just converted the island. He becomes their disciple and eventually succeeds them in the episcopate.[2]

Whether this story was originally part of Muirchú's work or something added between his time and the compilation of the Book of Armagh, it probably reflects an attempt by the Patrician *familia* to claim some sort of superiority over the church on Man, a claim that is probably also connected to the naming of St Patrick's Isle. If so, it seems likely that this Patrician line was plugging into a pre-existing and strong tradition that the apostles of the island were Conindrus and Rumilus. The fact that no attempt is made to claim that they were themselves acolytes of Patrick may indicate that a strong tradition of their origins survived which could not be readily distorted to fit the Armagh agenda. Unfortunately for us, no independent trace of this tradition survives. We might wonder, however, whether the presence of a pair of evangelists might indicate a division of the island into two dioceses even at this early period. We should also be wary, of course, of assuming that Rumilus and Conindrus were originally thought of as contemporaries of St Patrick. They might conceivably belong to any period between the fourth and sixth centuries. That Macc Cuill had some existence outwith the fantasies of an Armagh propagandist would seem to be supported by the dedication to him at Maughold, for which ancient church he also appears to be the eponym. Indeed at Maughold one of the inscribed stones, dated by Kermode to the later seventh or eighth century, appears to commemorate a bishop with the rather curious, and perhaps misread, name Neitspli![3]

In the late twelfth century the professional hagiographer Jocelin of Furness was employed to rework the Patrician material to suit the ecclesiastical standards of the day. He introduced a visit to Man by St Patrick himself, which included the establishment of St German as bishop.[4] This story was probably developed to explain the importance of St German in Jocelin's day, although according to the Manx chronicle the church of St German on St Patrick's Isle was only begun in the days of Bishop Simon (1226–48).[5] There seem to be two possible explanations for a cult of St German springing into being in the course of the twelfth century. One possibility is that it results from Jocelin's own Armagh work. The Book of Armagh contains an account of Patrick visiting the famous Germanus, bishop of Auxerre, in which this Gallic saint is described as *episcopum Alsiodori*.[6] Auxerre is otherwise reproduced as *Autessiodurum* and it may be that Jocelin misread, or construed, this contracted form, or a similar one elsewhere in the Irish materials he was working with, as a form of *Sodorensis*, and thus translated Germanus from Gaul to Man.

The other possibility for a twelfth-century introduction of the cult of St Germanus is that it is linked to the foundation of Rushen abbey. Rushen was founded *c.*1134 when King Óláfr, son of Godred Crovan, granted the Savignac community of Furness (Jocelin's own house, it should be remem-

Fig. 15.1 *Drawing of a cross slab from the monastery at Maughold with the name of a bishop of the island in the inscription. Trench-Jellicoe suggests that the encircled inscription cryptically records the name of the bishop as ARNEIT and that he was not only a priest and bishop but also an abbot. (Trench-Jellicoe, R. 'Manx Sculptured Monuments', 1–34 in Davey P.J. and Finlayson D.,* Mannin Revisited *2002).*

bered) the *monasterium Sancti Leoc* together with other lands in order to found a daughter-house.[7] St Leoc, the original dedicatee, appears to have been the same person as the better-known Mo-Luóc, and was also known in Man as St Lua. The house of Rushen, however, identified this Lua with the Gaulish St Lupus of Troyes. Since this St Lupus is best known for having accompanied Germanus of Auxerre on his visit to Britain in 429,[8] it is possible that the presence of a supposed Lupus dedication on Man led to the inference that Germanus must also have visited the island. In either case, the cult of Germanus was probably a development of the twelfth century and tells us little of the early history of the church on Man.

Our knowledge of the state of the church on Man from the days of Conindrus and Rumilus is indeed very limited. The corpus of early medieval crosses and other sculpture bears witness to a thriving Christian community amongst the Britons and subsequently amongst the Norse, but we have no records of bishops or even of diocesan organisation in this period. The account of the episcopal succession is taken up by the Chronicle of Man both in its main text and in an addendum account of the bishops. The chronicle, which is a product of the thirteenth and fourteenth centuries, begins its narrative of the island's history with the career of Godred Crovan who reigned from 1079 to 1095. Although Godred's reign is unlikely to have marked a major break in the cultural or political trajectory of the kingdom he was the apical figure, the common ancestor of all subsequent successful claimants to the kingship and was thus fetishised by his descendants in order to legitimise their exclusion of other kinsmen from the

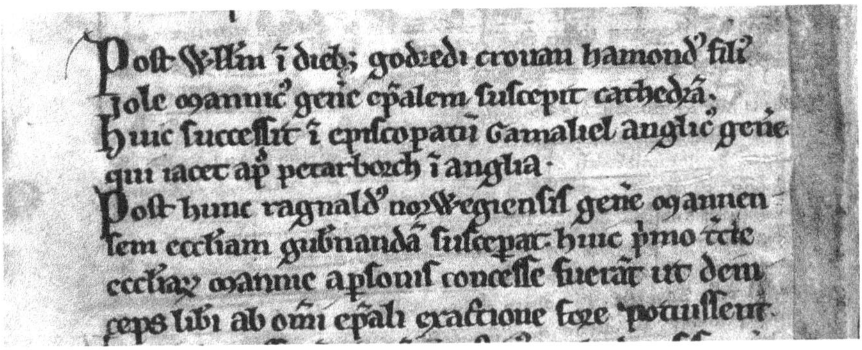

Fig. 15.2 *Part of a page from the* Chronicles, *folio 50v, showing the names of several bishops. It reads: 'After William in the days of Godred Croven Hamond, son of Iole, a Manxman by birth, assumed the Episcopal seat' and continues by mentioning Gamaliel and Reginald who 'was the first to receive the thirds of the churches of Man from their incumbents, so that from that time they could be free from all Episcopal demands.*

succession. Consequently the chronicle's account of the bishops also starts in the latter part of the eleventh century, but this should not be taken to mean that there was necessarily a reorganisation of the church at this period.[9]

The first bishop to appear in the chronicle account is one Roolwer. This rather odd-looking name probably stands for the Scandinavian name Hrólfr or something similar. We are told that he was the first bishop before Godred Crovan began to rule and this has been taken to mean that he had died before Godred's accession.[10] This may be the case, but it might simply mean that he was incumbent at the beginning of Godred's reign. We are told nothing more about Roolwer save that he was succeeded by one William. It seems likely from his name that this William was Anglo-French and his appearance may indicate something about the relations established between Godred and his neighbours, the new Norman dynasty in England. Those who believe that Roolwer was the first bishop after a Viking-Age break in the succession (and it should be emphasised that this is not implied at all by the chronicle) link his episcopate with the near contemporary episcopate of Dúnan, generally termed bishop of Dublin (d. 1074).[11] Dúnan is the first recorded 'bishop of Dublin' (excluding a dubious tradition of very early bishops in Continental sources), and it is usually assumed that he was the first bishop there. Since in the early to mid eleventh century Man and Dublin were ruled by the same dynasty it may be, the argument runs, that the sees were established at the same time. In fact this is not at all certain.

Dublin, so far as is known, had never previously been an episcopal centre, so this was a new see. Man had, however, had bishops since antiquity and there is no reason to suppose that pagan Norse political occupation would necessarily put an end to the see. This does seem to have been what happened at York or in Orkney. Indeed, given the fact that the bishops of Sodor seem to have possessed a diocese coextensive with the kingdom of the Isles it seems most likely that Dublin owed its elevation to its separation from the kingdom of the Isles. Dúnan himself is called simply *ardespoc Gall* – 'high-bishop of the Foreigners' – in his obituary and the first allusion to Dublin specifically comes with his successor Patrick or Gilla Pátraic who was sent to Lanfranc of Canterbury for consecration by Toirrdelbach Ua Briain of Munster, at that point the most powerful ruler in Ireland, and his Dublin sub-king Guðröðr, a member of the Mac Ragnaill family of Waterford.[12] It may well be that the death of Dúnan in 1074 opened the way for Toirrdelbach to create a new see in Dublin, which he had conquered in 1072, thus separating the Ostmen of the city from those of the Isles. If this interpretation were correct then Dúnan, as 'high-bishop of the foreigners', may well have been Roolwer's predecessor in the Isles.

The establishment of the see of Dublin, in this scenario, would thus mark the recognition that the town was now firmly part of the Irish political scene and no longer an integral part of the Dublin Hiberno-Norse empire.

Roolwer, then, may have commenced his episcopacy *c.*1074 and died sometime between 1079 and 1095. William, whose episcopacy ran its course entirely within the reign of Godred Crovan, must have also died in or before 1095, when he was succeeded by Hámundr 'son of Iole', whom the chronicle tells us was a Manxman.[13] As we enter the twelfth century, however, our records become very confusing. The episcopal list attached to the chronicle claims that Hámundr was succeeded directly by an Englishman named Gamaliel. Records from York make it clear that a Bishop Gamelin, presumably the same man, was consecrated by Archbishop Roger (1154–81).[14] It is very unlikely that Hámundr, if he was consecrated in Godred Crovan's time, held the bishopric for 50 years, so the Manx record is apparently inaccurate.

A letter survives from King Óláfr son of Godred Crovan to an Archbishop 'G' of York, asking him to consecrate Óláfr's bishop.[15] 'G' has been identified as Archbishop Gerard who reigned from 1100 to 1108,[16] but current thinking would place the beginning of Óláfr's reign at about 1113.[17] There is no York record of a consecration at this period so the simplest way out of this conundrum is to suggest that the initial 'G' is the result of miscopying and originally represented an epistle to one or other of the bishops who were in office during Óláfr's reign; Thomas II (1109–14), Thurstan (1114–40), William (1141–7), Henry (1147–53) and Roger (1154–81). A 'T' for Thomas or Thurstan would seem the most likely.

Our period of uncertainty enters a new phase with the remarkable career of Bishop Wimund. Our best account of Wimund comes from the northern English chronicler William of Newburgh (1136–98), who was acquainted with Wimund in the latter's old age.[18] According to William, Wimund was a monk of Furness abbey who went to Man with some of his *fratres*. Furness was founded in 1127 by the Savignac order (which later merged with the Cistercians). In 1134 King Óláfr, as we have seen, granted the church at Rushen to the monks of Furness and this is likely to have been the occasion of Wimund's arrival in Man. The grant of Rushen was connected with a further grant to Furness of the right to elect a bishop for the kingdom since, Óláfr complained, episcopal authority was divided amongst foreigners.[19] Óláfr's grant to Rushen was confirmed by his son Guðröðr in 1154, by his grandson Rögnvaldr between 1188 and 1190, and by the pope in 1195.[20] Shortly after Óláfr first made this grant he confirmed the choice by the monks of Furness of one of their own number, presumably Wimund.[21] Assuming that we have not lost some vital link in the chain it seems likely that Bishop Hámundr had died at some point, perhaps not too long before 1134, and that episcopal duties in the kingdom had fallen to various neighbouring bishops. A vacancy of a few years in a see was no unusual thing in the twelfth century, particularly in the neighbourhood of northern Britain and Ireland where the metropolitan provinces were still not firmly established and the rights to consecrate new bishops were in dispute. Wimund, it should be noted, is almost certainly the same bishop as the Wimund whose profession of obedience to Archbishop Thomas (1109–14) is recorded by a late twelfth-century York source.[22] Wimund's consecration by Thomas is not recorded in Hugh the Chantor's account written in 1127,[23] and it seems likely that once again we have a false assumption of the full form represented by an initial, in this case 'T' being taken for Thomas rather than Thurstan by our source. The fact that Wimund describes his see, in his profession, as the *sancta ecclesia de Schith* – the holy church of Skye – simply serves to emphasise that in the early twelfth century the seat of the diocese was not yet fixed in Man.

William of Newburgh's account of Wimund goes on to say that the bishop behaved in a very unepiscopal fashion and invaded the territories of the king of Scots claiming to be the son of an unnamed earl of Moray. After unsuccessfully attacking a Scottish bishop, Wimund eventually gained from King David (1124–53) a province to rule that included Furness. Most commentators have presumed that Wimund's putative father was that Áengus earl of Moray who was killed at Stracathro in 1130.[24] However, the fact that Wimund was born in England, that he professed at Furness, and that he received a province adjacent to Furness from King David, suggests an alternative identification. The most likely province in the region of Furness for a man to receive who had links to the Isles would seem to be Copeland (also Coupland), now the west coast of Cumbria. For much of David I's reign the lord of Copeland was David's nephew, William fitz Duncan, who held the lordship in the right of his wife Alicia, the daughter of William de Meschin.

Now, although this William invariably appears in Scottish royal acts as 'the king's nephew' or 'my nephew' there is one thirteenth-century Cumbrian genealogy, dealing with the descent of the lords of Copeland and Allerdale, which refers to him as earl of Moray.[25] While this genealogy remains unsupported, there seems no reason for the claim to be invented, and William's status as a member of the royal house has certainly masked any titles or lordships that he may have held in Scotland, despite his clear position as a man of the first rank in the kingdom. If Wimund was in fact claiming to be the son of William fitz Duncan, his invasion of Scots territory must surely be dated to after the death of his 'father'. William fitz Duncan's death is not noted by any chroniclers but he disappears from the witness lists of charters between 1147 and 1151. He was certainly dead by the time his widow founded Bolton Priory in Wharfedale in 1151.[26] Nevertheless there is a curious reference in John of Hexham's chronicle under the year 1152 that associates the visit of the papal legate in that year with an expedition by King David to 'confirm his nephew William fitz Duncan in the honor of Skipton and Craven'.[27] Now, although William fitz Duncan was actually dead by this time his recognised heir in his northern English lands was his son by Alicia, also named William, and it would require little emendation to see John's account as the confirmation of this William's rights and as the final suppression of Wimund. Wimund's story, as told by William of Newburgh, ended when he was betrayed by his own followers and handed over to King David. He ended his days blinded and mutilated in the abbey of New Byland in Yorkshire.

We can thus tentatively summarise the episcopal succession in the early twelfth century by suggesting that Hámundr son of Iole occupied the see from *c.*1090 to some time in the twelfth century, perhaps *c.*1125 (the re-establishment of Whithorn in 1128 may be a response to a vacancy in the Isles, as discussed below). At some point in or shortly after 1134 Wimund was elected by the monks of Furness and subsequently consecrated by Thurstan. At some point between 1147 and 1151 Wimund attempted to seize territory under the control of David I of Scotland and, after temporary success, was captured and mutilated in 1152.[28]

It must be assumed that Wimund's bid for secular power led to his abandonment of his see. King Óláfr seems to have tried to persuade the dean and chapter of York to accept his candidate for consecration, one Nicholas. The fact that Óláfr addressed the dean would suggest that this occurred during the interregnum between the deposition of Archbishop William fitz Herbert (1147) and the return from his consecration in Rome of the new archbishop, Henry Murdac (1148).[29] King Óláfr seems to have failed in his attempt to get Nicholas consecrated, possibly because the Wimund situation was still unresolved. Henry Murdac waited until 1152 before consecrating a new bishop, described by the chronicler Robert of Torigni as the 'second bishop' (presumably the second consecrated by an archbishop of York), John, a Benedictine monk from Normandy.[30] John, however, does not appear in the Manx list and was therefore probably unacceptable to the Islesmen and may never have entered his see.[31]

On 30 November 1154 the papacy approved the establishment of Nidaros (now Trondheim) as a metropolitan see and the transfer of the diocese of Sodor into the province of the new metropolitan. However, the

Fig. 15.3 *Nineteenth-century view of Trondheim (Nidaros) Cathedral, from the south-east, showing the south transept (restored in 1666) with decorations of Anglo-Norman style presumed to be constructed by Augustine c.1160. Other features survive from the thirteenth-century. This etching is plate 5 in a book presented to the Manx Museum in 1951 on the occasion of the Festival of Britain, by the Bishop of Trondheim:* The Cathedral of Trondheim *published by order of the Norwegian Government in 1859, text by Professor P.A. Munch and drawings by Architect H.E. Schirmer.*

next bishop of whom we hear, the Englishman Gameliel, was consecrated in York by Archbishop Roger who himself only took office in October 1154.[32] One might imagine that news of the papal confirmation may not have reached York or Man until the New Year and so Gamaliel's consecration probably took place between October 1154 and the first few months of 1155. Since Gamaliel is recognised both in English sources, where he is called Gamelin, and in the Manx list, it is safe to infer that he took up his office, and the switch of metropolitans need not have interfered with his own ministry. His place of burial is recorded as Peterborough,[33] which does suggest that he may have retired from his see at some point, although he may have died while on a journey (we know from Robert of Torigni that a bishop of the isles visited Mont St Michel in the company of William I of Scotland in 1166).[34]

Gamaliel's successor Reginald is described as a Norwegian by the chronicle, and was probably nominated by the archbishop of Nidaros. He may be the same man as the Reinar (for Ragnarr?) mentioned in the Icelandic annals *s.a.* 1210 as having died about 40 years previously.[35] If this identification is correct then Reginald must have died *c.*1170. His episcopacy must have seen the break up of the kingdom into two parts, one owing allegiance to the descendants of Somerled and another recognising the claims of King Guðröðr and his heirs. This dispute has been dealt with in detail in other chapters but we must here consider its implications for the church.

At first the struggle between Somerled and Guðröðr must have seemed to be a succession dispute like so many before. The Hiberno-Norse kings of Man and the Isles had rarely achieved their goal without some conflict. As the twelfth century drew to a close, however, it must have become clearer and clearer that the kingdom itself was divided, and this had implications for the diocese. In the Gaelic and Scandinavian worlds it was still very much the case that ecclesiastical provinces mirrored political ones, and the idea of a bishop administering to a flock engaged in long-term conflict amongst themselves was hardly acceptable.[36] At some point in the late twelfth century Clann Somurli (the descendants of Somerled) seem to have received a bishop for their territories. Somerled's rapid rise to power in the 1150s had been at the expense of the Scottish kingdom as well as of the kingdom of the Isles. Most of his mainland acquisitions were parts of the diocese of Dunkeld, and the new bishopric of Lismore (or, as it was to be called eventually, Argyll) seems to have included these portions of the mainland. The appropriation of Dunkeld territory was probably facilitated by the long vacancy following the death of Bishop Richard (1178) and the disputed election of his successor John Scot who, although recognised by the pope in 1183, did not gain full royal recognition until 1188. The see was certainly in existence by 1193.[37] It was not mentioned in the papal bull *Cum Universi* of March 1192, which named all nine Scottish sees.[38] This, if not a simple error, may suggest either that Haraldr (Aralt in Gaelic), allegedly the first bishop of Lismore, if already bishop at this point, was claiming to be bishop of the Isles, or that Lismore was not at this point recognised as being within the kingdom of the Scots.

The effect on the bishops of Sodor of the foundation of the see of Lismore, with its chief seat on the island of Lismore in the Firth of Lorn, was that the former became increasingly identified with the Isle of Man. This process may already have begun in Bishop Reginald's time, for the episcopal list attached to the chronicle claims that he was the first bishop to receive the 'thirds' (a third part of the tithes) of the churches of Man from their incumbents, so 'that from that time on they could be free from all episcopal demands'.[39] This looks very much as if a peripatetic episcopacy was finally settling down and establishing centres of consumption and administration. We might imagine earlier bishops sailing constantly from island to island, with a chief church in every district from which they administered their episcopal duties. It is interesting to note that both Lismore and Rushen, the premier churches of the two sees, shared the same dedication, to Mo-Luóc, as did several churches in the north end of Skye, another region closely associated with the bishopric.

The Icelandic annals claim that after the death of Ragnarr/Reginald the see of the Isles lay vacant for 40 years, until the consecration of John in 1210.[40] The Manx records, however, name two intermediate bishops between Reginald and John. The first of these is Cristinus who is said to be an Argyll man and who was buried at Bangor in County Down. It is perhaps worth noting that the bishop of Whithorn from 1154 until his death in 1186 was also called Cristinus.[41] Given not only the cultural and linguistic links between Galloway and Man, but also the close kinship between Roland of Galloway and King Guðröðr son of Óláfr, his cousin, it is quite possible that the bishop of Whithorn administered part of the diocese during this confused period.

Michael, whom the chronicle names as Cristinus's successor, was said to have died in 1203 and to have been buried at Fountains abbey in Yorkshire.[42] His place of burial suggests that he was a Cistercian, and therefore probably a monk of Rushen (the Savignac order had merged with the Cistercians in 1140), and Watt suggests that he is the unnamed Cistercian monk expelled from the order in 1194 for accepting consecration while his successor still lived.[43] If the suggestion is accepted that Cristinus was in fact the bishop of Whithorn and not formally bishop of the Isles, then he cannot be the predecessor referred to in the Cistercian judgement. Possibly the contender was Bishop Haraldr of Lismore; although not reliably attested before 1228, he is generally thought to have acceded before 1189.[44] His name suggests Norwegian extraction, and the beginning of his episcopacy, if it is indeed 1186/9, may have coincided with a period when Ragnall son of Somerled appeared to be the dominant king in the Isles. If so, Haraldr may have been sent from Nidaros but thrown his lot in with Clann Somurli rather than the Manx branch of the dynasty.

To summarise a complex period once again, it might be suggested that after Bishop Reginald's death the see lay vacant and was administered by Cristinus of Whithorn. On his death in 1186 Haraldr, or an unknown predecessor, was elected by clergy loyal to Ragnall mac Somurli, but after Ragnall's fall from power in 1192 King Rögnvaldr son of Guðröðr of Man secured the election of Michael. The Cistercian order expelled Michael for assuming the episcopacy whilst Haraldr was still in office, but the papacy regularised the situation by recognising the see of Argyll/Lismore.[45]

The vexed problem of metropolitan jurisdiction is complicated in this period due to the fact that successive archbishops of Nidaros fell out with the Norwegian kings. Archbishop Eysteinn was in exile in England between 1180 and 1183 and his successor Eiríkr was in exile in Denmark from 1190 to 1202. Even when they were in Norway, both Eysteinn and Eiríkr were frequently in conflict with the crown and sometimes in open warfare against it.[46] In a situation like this it is hard to tell whether the intervention of the province of York in the person of archbishops, and perhaps the bishop of Whithorn, reflects conflict with the claims of Nidaros or simply a response to the vacuum at metropolitan level created by these conflicts. It may well be that necessity made a virtue out of vice and the church of York was able to pursue its own agenda whilst appearing to act charitably.

After Bishop Michael's death in 1203 we next hear of the consecration of Bishop Nicholas, called Kolli, in the Icelandic annals under the year 1210.[47] What the situation was between these two points is unknown. The most likely alternatives would seem to be the following: first, that the see lay vacant from 1203 to 1210, second, that the see was administered from Lismore during the ascendancy of Áengus son of Somerled (d. 1210),[48] or third, that Nicholas was elected shortly after Michael's death but did not receive consecration in Nidaros until 1210. There seems to be no good reason for preferring any one of these alternatives over the others. Nicholas died in 1217 and was buried at Bangor in Ulster. Bearing in mind the close relations between Ulster and the Isles in both political and religious terms there is no reason to believe that Nicholas's death there indicates that he was in exile.

The next bishop was a grandson of King Guðröðr (d. 1187) called Reginald II. He appears not to have been elected by the monks of Furness since they elected a rival, Nicholas II, whom they sent to Dublin for consecration. King Rögnvaldr refused to accept this candidate, obviously preferring his own nephew, and the pope had to issue a mandate (9 November 1219) ordering him to do so. The king, however, does not seem to have been alone in his support for Bishop Reginald, for as late as May 1224 the pope had to issue a second mandate, this time to the archbishop of York, ordering the recognition of Nicholas.[49] Despite papal backing, Nicholas is not recognised in the list of bishops attached to the chronicle and so was probably never accepted in his see.

Bishop Reginald II is the first bishop after Wimund about whose activities in the diocese we can say anything. The chronicle tells us how on a visit to Lewis he called a synod to annul the marriage of King Rögnvaldr's half-brother, Óláfr Dubh. The grounds for this annulment were that Óláfr had previously kept a first cousin of his wife as a concubine and was therefore, technically, committing incest. This seems an extremely neat distinction for medieval Gaeldom, and the sequel to this story probably explains the real motive. On being released from his first marriage to Lauon, a daughter of a nobleman in Kintyre, Óláfr married Christina, the daughter of Ferchar earl of Ross.[50] Lauon's father is nowhere named in our sources but it is likely that he was Ruaidrí son of Ragnall mac Somurli who ruled Kintyre in the early thirteenth century. Ruaidrí appears to have lost his lands, and perhaps his life, in the course of King Alexander II's expedition(s) to the west in 1221 and/or 1222.[51] Following its account of Óláfr's marriage to Christina, the chronicle tells us that Lauon's sister, queen to King Rögnvaldr, provoked the latter's son Guðröðr into attacking his uncle Óláfr. Despite initial discomfiture, Óláfr, with the help of Earl Ferchar, overcame his nephew. This incident is dated to the year 1223.[52] The dating would suggest that it was the collapse of Ruaidrí's position in Kintyre that led Óláfr, now based in the north, to seek a more appropriate ally in Ferchar of Ross. If this interpretation of events is correct, then we should see Bishop Reginald as the tool of Óláfr's policy rather than as an officious reformer. It would be interesting to know whether the Ruaídrí's descendants, the Clann Ruaidrí of Garmoran and the Long Island, owed their later position of strength there to Óláfr's patronage.

Bishop Reginald, as we have seen, appears to have been still active *c.*1222 and his successor but one, Simon, was consecrated in Bergen by the bishop of Nidaros in the autumn of 1226. The intervening incumbent, John son of Hefare (ON *Hávarr*?) is known only from the list in the chronicle in which he is said to have been buried at Jervaulx after being burned to death in an accident, presumably in Yorkshire.[53] It would be tempting to surmise that John never visited his see, but his inclusion in the Manx list suggests otherwise. Perhaps he was a monk of Rushen, elected by Furness and accepted in Man, who was on his way to York for consecration at the time of his death. Simon was a far more successful incumbent who not only held his see for 18 years but also, following Haraldr's demise, administered the see of Argyll between *c.*1230 and *c.*1238.[54] This period of joint administration, coinciding with a low point in the fortunes of Clann Somurli, is perhaps further evidence that Argyll and the Isles were in origin a single diocese. In 1238 William, chancellor of the diocese of Moray, was elected bishop of Argyll and he held the see until his death in 1241, after which time at least part of the see was administered by Clement of Dunblane.[55] Simon was an Argyll man by origin and is credited by the chronicle with

Fig. 15.4 *St German's Cathedral on St Patrick's Isle, Peel. Viewed from the south-west. Photo: Peter Davey.*

the building of St German's cathedral.[56] This may mark the final settling of the episcopal seat at Peel.

After Simon's death in 1248 the chronicle records that the see was vacant for 'about six years'. Simon's archdeacon, Laurence, was elected bishop by the chapter of Man and went to Norway for consecration. King Haraldr son of Óláfr Dubh, king of the Isles, had been in Norway at the court of King Hákon since the previous autumn. He refused to allow the archbishop of Nidaros to consecrate Laurence because of a letter he had received denouncing him. It was agreed that Laurence should return to the Isles with the king to be elected publicly. Leaving Norway towards the end of September the king and bishop-elect with all their retinue were drowned in a shipwreck off Shetland.[57]

It was not until early 1253 that a new bishop was finally consecrated. It is possible that once again the irregular position in the Isles can be explained with reference to the see of Argyll. As we have seen, Simon of the Isles held episcopal authority in Argyll until *c.*1238. He relinquished this authority to William of Moray who was consecrated in 1240 but was dead by the end of 1241. After Bishop William's death the see of Argyll remained vacant for the duration of Simon's life, but sometime between

1248 and 1250 one Alan was elected as bishop there. This election may have been connected to Alexander II of Scotland's ill-fated expedition to Argyll in 1249.[58] Alan continued in office until his death in 1262.[59] In this light it is interesting that when the election of a new bishop of the Isles occurred, in 1253, it happened when the archbishop of Nidaros was actually in Rome, and the new bishop was a canon of St Andrews in Scotland who had been working in the Curia for some time.[60] It may be that the archbishop of Nidaros had complained at the interference in his province by the Scottish church and that the pope had achieved a compromise by providing a candidate for the cathedral at Peel who was acceptable to Scottish royal interests, if not necessarily to Clann Somurli, and who was known personally to the pope. Once more we seem to see relations between the sees of Argyll and the Isles mirroring the relationships between Clann Somurli and the descendants of Godred Crovan.

Bishop Richard was an Augustinian canon. He ruled the diocese for 23 years and dedicated the new church of St Mary at Rushen in 1257.[61] He died in Copeland returning from a church council in 1275 and was buried at Furness.[62] Richard's episcopacy saw the treaty of Perth (1266) and the Scottish conquest of Man, and although there is no record of his involvement in these great affairs of state it is hard to imagine that he did not have some part to play in them. On Richard's death, however, the tensions of the new political situation revealed themselves. The clergy and people of Man elected Gilbert abbot of Rushen to succeed as bishop, but Alexander III, king of Scots, vetoed the election and instead sent his own nominee, Mark of Galloway, to Nidaros for consecration.[63] The Manx refused to accept him for three years and an interdict was placed on the island.[64] Mark ruled the diocese until 1303 and died, blind and aged but well loved. He was buried at St German's.[65] In 1305 Antony Bek, the bishop of Durham, who held the lordship of Man under the English crown, imposed on the cathedral chapter another Gallovidian, Alan. The latter, like earlier Gallovidian bishops, was a Gaelic-speaking native of the province of York. He died in 1321 and was buried at Rothesay on Bute. His successor Gilbert MacLellan (1325–8) was also a Gallovidian and was also buried on Bute.[66] This association with Bute may mark the growing influence of another secular force, the House of Stewart, in the outer Clyde.

This Stewart connection can perhaps also be detected in the election, late in 1327 or early in 1328, of Bernard, abbot of Arbroath and chancellor to Robert I of Scotland. Bernard had first risen to prominence as abbot of Kilwinning in Ayrshire, within the Stewart sphere of influence, and returned there to be buried in 1331. This Scots intervention seems to have been resented by some at least of the clergy in the Isles and at some point after Gilbert's death the canons and clergy of Snizort in Skye elected one Cormac as bishop and, on Bernard's death, sent to Nidaros for confirmation of his election.[67] They do not seem to have been successful in their bid and Cormac does not appear in the chronicle. The next Scottish candidate was Thomas, notable for introducing a tithe on the herring fishery; he also introduced a 20-shilling 'procuration' fee which he levied from the churches of Man.[68] It is not clear if this was a one-off payment or a regular levy. Thomas ruled the diocese from June 1331 until his death in September 1348. The fact that he was buried at Scone may suggest that he was an Augustinian canon. Thomas was the last of the Scottish bishops and was succeeded by William Russell, allegedly a Manxman, who had been abbot of Rushen since about 1330. He was elected by the Manx clergy and sent to Avignon for consecration by Clement VI in April 1349. He died in 1374 and was buried at Furness abbey.[69]

William's successor, John Donkan, was the last bishop of the united see of Sodor. He was a Manxman by origin, but was an archdeacon in the diocese of Down in Ireland at the time of his election. He was sent, like his predecessor, to Avignon for papal confirmation. This he received, but was delayed in his return to his see when imprisoned in Boulogne. Upon being ransomed he returned to Man and was installed in his cathedral in 1377.[70] Ten years later the see was split when John sided with the English church and crown in the Great Schism, recognising Urban VI as pope while the Scottish crown, together with the Lord of the Isles, recognised Clement VII. Clement ordered John's deposition and in the Scottish territories he was replaced by Michael of Cashel.[71] From that time forth the bishops in Man became increasingly bound into the English ecclesiastical hierarchy.

The diocese of Sodor was always a problematic entity. As we have seen, it seems to have originated as the pastoral aspect of the *imperium* of a dynasty of Hiberno-Norse background, and as this *imperium* crumbled so the diocese itself fragmented. The establishment of sees at Dublin (1074), and Lismore (*c*.1189), as well as the ultimate separation of the Isles from Man in the fourteenth century, reflect the increasing political fragmentation. It may even be the case that the re-establishment of the see of Whithorn in 1128 likewise signals the removal of Galloway, or the western portion of it at least, from Hiberno-Norse control.[72]

We have little evidence of how the diocese was organised, but what hints survive suggest that different regions with their own distinct cultural traditions probably had their own head churches, which formed the basis for episcopal visitations. Rushen on Man, Kingarth on Bute, Snizort on Skye, and perhaps Lismore, seem to have been among these regional centres, and there may perhaps have been others. We should probably imagine ordina-

Fig. 15.5 *Site of the Episcopal centre of St Columba's Snizort, Skeabost, Skye on an island in the abraided River Snizort: a) viewed towards the west and b) plan of visible features.*

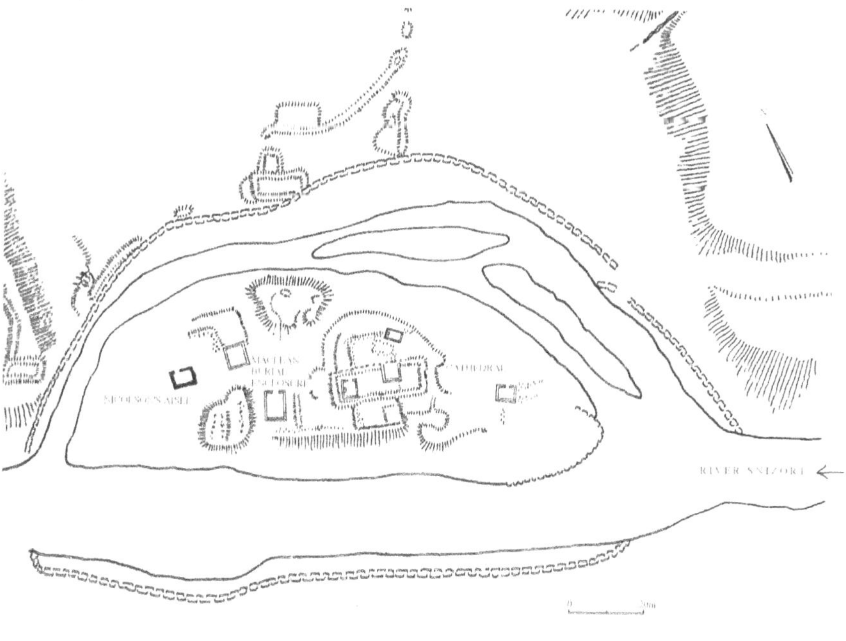

tions and confirmations for each region taking place at these centres. Just as the kings of the Isles began to lose control over the outlying parts of their realm as they became more closely identified with Man, so the diocese probably became more difficult to control as the episcopal centre became more permanently fixed at St German's. Wimund, as we have seen, was a monk of Rushen but was still able to operate from Skye as an episcopal centre. As time went by, however, the clergy in places like Snizort and Bute probably began to feel that their interests were not served by a cathedral chapter based at Peel. If the hypothesis put forward here about the origins of the see of Argyll is correct, it seems that the clergy of Lismore, with appropriate secular backing, eventually decided to elect their own bishop. The church at Snizort attempted the same thing in the fourteenth century, first with the abortive episcopacy of Cormac and subsequently, with more success, during the Great Schism.

In the eleventh and twelfth centuries it seems likely that the bishops would have circulated between these major churches, possibly appearing at a different place for each of the major festivals of the year. We might expect the bishop to travel in company with an extensive retinue, including warriors as well as clerics, living off the tithes that would be collected at the episcopal centres. From the reign of Óláfr son of Godred Crovan onwards, the creation of extensive estates in Man and eventually the development of money lenders reduced the need of the bishops to engage in a peripatetic lifestyle in order to support their household. The long-term trend, through the course of our period, was for the increasing territorialisation of the diocese and the establishment of an episcopal centre on Man, first at Rushen and then at St German's, which made the bishops of Sodor look and behave much more like the rank and file of bishops of western Christendom. As in the secular sphere, the economic development of the Isle of Man led to a withering away of influence in the outlying parts of the episcopal *regnum*.

Notes

1 Ludwig Bieler (ed.), *The Patrician Texts in the Book of Armagh* (Dublin, 1979), 61–121.
2 Bieler, 102–7.
3 P.M.C. Kermode, *Manx Crosses* (reprinted with introduction by D.M. Wilson, Balgavies, 1994), 111–12.
4 *Acta Sanctorum*, 17 March, ii (1866), 556 and 567–8.
5 Broderick, *CKMI*, fol. 46v.
6 Bieler, 70.
7 *The Coucher Book of Furness Abbey* (Manchester, 1886–7, 1915–19), ii, 708–9.
8 W. Levison (ed.), 'Constantius's *Vita Sancti Germani*', in *Scriptores Rerum Merovingicarum, Monumenta Germaniae Historica*, 7 (Berlin, 1920).

9 Broderick, *CKMI*, fol. 50v. ff.
10 E.g., D.E.R. Watt, 'Bishops in the Isles before 1203: bibliography and biographical lists', *Innes Review*, 45 (1994), 99–119, at 109–10.
11 AU, *s.a.* 1074.
12 J.F. Kenney, *The Sources for the Early History of Ireland: Ecclesiastical, an introduction and guide* (New York, 1929; repr. Dublin, 1997) ,758–9. See also Duffy, 'Irishmen and Islesmen', 102 and n.45, and chapter 1 above, p. 16.
13 Broderick, *CKMI*, fol. 50v.
14 J. Raine (ed.), *Historians of the Church of York*, Rolls Series (London, 1879–94), ii, 462.
15 Oliver, *Monumenta*, ii, 7.
16 For example, Watt, 'Bishops in the Isles', 110.
17 Duffy, 'Irishmen and Islesmen', 102.
18 P.G. Walsh and M.J. Kennedy (eds), *The history of English affairs [by] William of Newburgh*, Book 1 (Warminster, 1988).
19 Oliver, *Monumenta*, ii, 1–3.
20 Watt, 'Bishops in the Isles', 111–15.
21 Oliver, *Monumenta*, ii, 4–6.
22 Raine, *Church of York*, ii, 372.
23 C. Johnson (ed.), *Hugh the Chantor: The History of the Church of York 1066–1127* (London, 1961).
24 E. van Houts (ed.), *The Gesta Normannorum Ducum of William of Jumièges, Orderic Vitalis, and Robert of Torigni* (Oxford, 1992), OV, 8. xxx.
25 Wilson (ed.), *Register of St Bees*, 532, discussed in G.W.S. Barrow, *Regesta Regum Scottorum* II (Edinburgh, 1971), 12–13.
26 A.C. Lawrie, *Early Scottish Charters prior to A.D. 1153* (Glasgow, 1905), 271–3.
27 T. Arnold (ed.), *Symeonis Monachi Opera Omnia* (London, 1885), ii, 326.
28 This reading of Wimund's career has benefited from discussion with Alasdair Ross and Richard Oram.
29 Oliver, *Monumenta*, ii, 49–52. Discussed by Watt, 'Bishops in the Isles', 116 and n. 5.
30 Richard Howlett (ed.), *Chronicles of the Reigns of Stephen, Henry II and Richard I* (London, 1884–9), iv, 167.
31 Watt, 'Bishops in the Isles', 117.
32 Raine, *Church of York*, ii, 462.
33 Broderick, *CKMI*, fol. 50v.
34 Howlett, *Chronicles*, iv, 228–9.
35 Gustav Storm, *Islandske Annaler indtil 1578* (Christiania [Oslo], 1888).
36 Colmán Etchingham, *Church Organisation in Ireland, AD 650–1000* (Maynooth, 1999), 105–47.
37 P. Fabre and L. Duchesne (eds), *Le Liber Censuum de L'Eglise Romaine* (Rome, 1889), i, 230–2.
38 McDonald, *Kingdom of the Isles*, 211–12.
39 Broderick, *CKMI*, fol. 50v.
40 Storm, *Islandske*.
41 James Stevenson (ed.), *Chronica de Mailros* (Edinburgh, 1835), *s.a.* 1154 and 1186. Cristinus, bishop of Candida Casa [Whithorn], also witnessed an act of Roland of Galloway *c.*1176–85, for which see K. Stringer, 'Acts of lordship: the records of the lords of Galloway to 1234', in T. Brotherstone and D. Ditchburn, *Freedom and Authority, Scotland c.1050–c.1650: Historical and Historiographical Essays presented to Grant G. Simpson*, (East Linton, 2000),

203–34, at 217–18.

42 Broderick, *CKMI*, fol. 50v.

43 Watt, 'Bishops in the Isles', 119, citing J.-M. Canivez, *Statuta Capitulorum Generalium Ordinis Cisterciensis* (Louvain, 1933), i, 179.

44 Watt, *Fasti Ecclesiæ Scoticanæ*, 26.

45 For the complex politics of the period, see chapter 4 above.

46 B. Sawyer and P. Sawyer, *Medieval Scandinavia: from Conversion to Reformation, c.800–1500*, (Minneapolis, 1993), 117 and 226.

47 Storm, *Islandske*.

48 Broderick, *CKMI*, fol. 41r.

49 Watt, *Fasti Ecclesiæ Scoticanæ*, 200.

50 Broderick, *CKMI*, fols 42r.–42v.

51 Duncan and Brown, 'Argyll and the Isles', 200; Sellar, 'Hebridean sea kings', 201.

52 Broderick, *CKMI*, fols 42v.-43r.

53 Broderick, *CKMI*, fol. 51r.

54 Watt, *Fasti Ecclesiæ Scoticanæ*, 26.

55 Watt, *Fasti Ecclesiæ Scoticanæ*, 26.

56 Broderick, *CKMI*, fol. 51r.

57 Broderick, *CKMI*, fol. 46v.

58 I owe this suggestion to Stephen Boardman.

59 Watt, *Fasti Ecclesiæ Scoticanæ*, 26.

60 Watt, *Fasti Ecclesiæ Scoticanæ*, 201.

61 Broderick, *CKMI*, fol. 49v.

62 Broderick, *CKMI*, fol. 51r.

63 Watt, *Fasti Ecclesiæ Scoticanæ*, 201.

64 Broderick, *CKMI*, fol. 51r.

65 Broderick, *CKMI*, fol. 51r.

66 Broderick, *CKMI*, fol. 51v.

67 Watt, *Fasti Ecclesiæ Scoticanæ*, 201–2.

68 Broderick, *CKMI*, fol. 51v.

69 Broderick, *CKMI*, fol. 51v.

70 Broderick, *CKMI*, fol. 51v.

71 Watt, *Fasti Ecclesiæ Scoticanæ*, 202.

72 Watt, *Fasti Ecclesiæ Scoticanæ*, 128, and Daphne Brooke, *Wild Men and Holy places: St Ninian, Whithorn and the Medieval Realm of Galloway* (Edinburgh, 1994), 78.

16 *Medieval Monasticism and the Isle of Man c. 1130–1540*

P.J. DAVEY

The background

By the middle of the thirteenth century, with the consecration of St German's cathedral in Peel,[1] the Norse kings of Man had brought the island into the mainstream of contemporary western Christianity. The bishop of Sodor and Man ceased to be peripatetic in the old style,[2] and had a permanent seat on St Patrick's Isle. The present parish structure had been substantially created, together with resident priests and an elaborate tithe system, all based on coherent episcopal policy and authority.[3] The Cistercians at Rushen abbey, their sister nunnery in Douglas, together with a complex of alien monastic interests were all deeply interwoven into the ecclesiastical and economic life of the island.[4] It is not clear how much of the organisation and structure of the early Christian church survived the Viking raids and subsequent settlement of Man. Did the monastic communities at Maughold and Peel continue to thrive under Norse rule or did the developments of the twelfth century take place in a religious vacuum created by the new political order? Despite a mid-twelfth-century reference to a monastery of St Leoc in Rushen,[5] the traditions linking St Brigit with Douglas,[6] and finds of lintel graves at a number of medieval sites with later monastic associations,[7] the nature and scale of any continuity between Early Christian monasticism on the island and the new order which developed in the twelfth century is uncertain. However indeterminate is the nature of monastic activity and interest in the tenth and eleventh centuries, during the 100 or so years from 1130 until 1250 the 'sea kings' of the Isle of Man and the Isles[8] succeeded in bringing the island within the orbit of high-medieval European monasticism.

High medieval monasticism and the Isle of Man: an historical summary

The first new development was initiated by Godred Crovan's son, Óláfr I, who had been brought up in the English court and presumably was fully aware of the religious, political and economic significance of the reformed orders which had spread so rapidly from France to England during his youth.[9] In 1134 he appears to have donated land 'in Russin' for the foun-

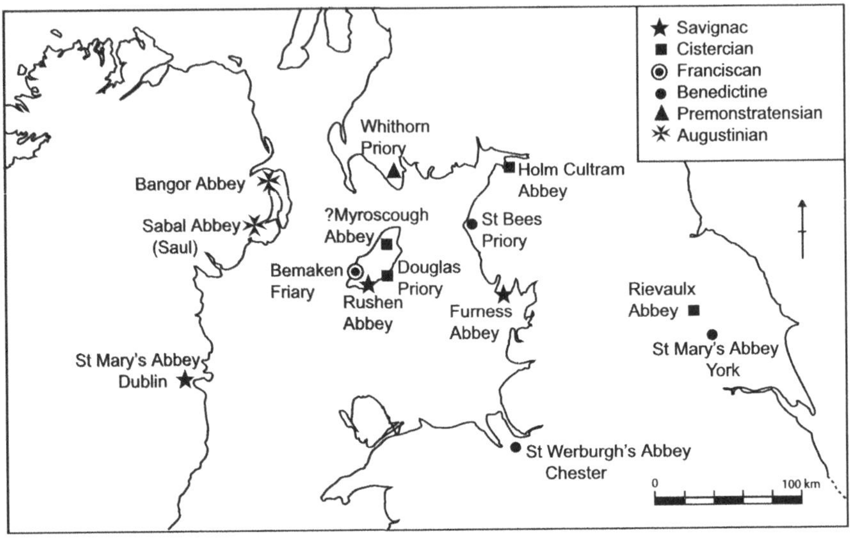

Fig. 16.1 *Monastic sites around the Irish Sea mentioned in the text.*

dation of a daughter-house by the Yorkshire Cistercian abbey of Rievaulx.[10] His offer was not taken up, probably because building at Rievaulx which had itself only been founded in 1131, had only begun in March 1132,[11] and the Yorkshire abbey had already sent out a number of missionary groups to found new abbeys.[12] Apparently in the same year Óláfr repeated his offer, this time to Abbot Ivo of the Savignac abbey of Furness from where a founding colony was despatched to Rushen, thus beginning the history of the most important monastic house on Man.[13] According to the Manx chronicle, Óláfr's son Guðröðr (Godred II) having been married to 'Finguala, a daughter to Mac Lochlann, son of Muirchertach, king of Ireland' by Silvanus, abbot of Rievaulx, granted the Yorkshire abbey land in the north of the island at Myroscough where 'he presently built a monastery'. Well before the main text of the chronicle had been completed 'the whole estate, monks and all' had been taken over by Rushen abbey.[14] At some point during his reign Guðröðr's son Rögnvaldr (Ragnall or Reginald, 1187–1228) founded a Cistercian nunnery at Douglas.[15]

The interest of these sea-kings in the expansion of monastic influence was not restricted to the endowment of monasteries located on the island. Grants of Manx lands and vicarages were made to a number of houses, of different orders, which were located at sites around the northern Irish Sea.

St Bees (Benedictine, Cumbria), Whithorn (Premonstratensian, Galloway), Bangor (Augustinian, County Down), Saul (Augustinian, County Down) and Furness itself were all endowed to a greater or lesser extent.[16] St Bees was also given favourable trading rights.[17] Thus, by the mid-thirteenth century the monastic orders owned a significant proportion of Manx farmland, and tithe income from at least half of the parishes. Other neighbouring abbeys such as Holm Cultram (Cistercian, Cumbria),[18] and the important Benedictine abbey of St Werburgh's, Chester,[19] were given economic advantages on the island and in its waters.[20] The other major landholder on the island during the medieval period, apart from the king himself, was the Bishop of the Isles who, because the power of election had been given to the monks of Furness, was often a Cistercian himself or a man with strong monastic affiliations.[21] The history of medieval monasticism on Man is completed by the foundation of the friary of Bemaken (Ballabeg) for the Dublin-based order of Friars Minor by William Montacute in 1367.[22] The dissolution took place in 1540.[23]

Myroscough Abbey

In 1176, as noted above, Abbot Silvanus of Rievaulx officiated at the marriage of King Guðröðr II (1153–87) to the granddaughter of the Irish highking Muircheartach Mac Lochlainn. He was rewarded by a grant of land in the north of the island: 'The same day King Godred gave as an offering to the venerable Abbot Silvanus a portion of land at Myroscough where he presently built a monastery. But in the course of time the whole estate, monks and all, was ceded to St Mary's abbey, Russin.'[24] There is no other contemporary reference to this abbey. By the time of the writing down of the *Limites terrarum monachorum* ('Boundaries of the monks' lands'), around 1280, the landholding had already been incorporated into Rushen abbey property.[25] The nine quarterland farms of East Kella, Carrick, Ballamanagh, Narradale, Grange, Knockshamerk, Kerrowmoor, Nappin and Glenduff continued to be classified as 'abbeyland' until the twentieth century.[26] It seems probable that before the transfer to Rushen an abbey was built, or at least begun, and that, given the distance to Ballasalla, the estate would have been administered as a grange located on the core of the remaining conventual buildings. The most likely candidate is the Grange Farm, pronounced locally 'grangee',[27] which lies at the focus of the landholding and where, in the nineteenth century, early building remains were discovered beneath the present farm.[28] Taking into account the evidence from the rent books and the *Limites*, it is possible to reconstruct the enclosed medieval holding with some degree of accuracy.[29]

Rushen Abbey

As alluded to above, in 1134 Óláfr I (1113–53), having failed to attract a colony from the Yorkshire Cistercian abbey of Rievaulx, offered, in 1134, the same foundation to the Savignac abbey at Furness which was accepted.[30] The actual date at which settlement began is difficult to determine. The Furness *Coucher Book* gives 1138 as the date of foundation,[31] which seems reasonable and is accepted by Coppack.[32] In the 1153 bull of Pope Eugenius III, confirming its landholdings to Furness, now an enforced Cistercian house, its lands in the Isle of Man are named.[33] The grant is again confirmed by King Rögnvaldr *c.*1190.[34] The history of the abbey in the later twelfth century is complicated by the reference in the Manx chronicle that in 1192 'St Mary's abbey, Rushen, was transferred to Douglas, and there they lived for four years, then returned to Rushen'.[35] No reason

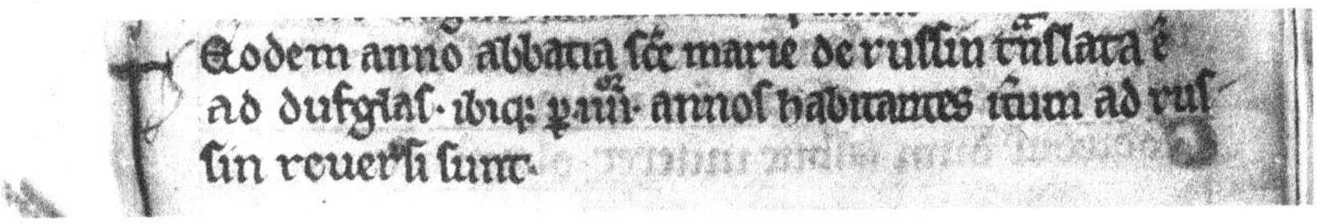
Eodem anno abbatia sce marie de russin translata e
ad dufglas· ibiq: ·iiii· annos habitantes iterum ad rus
sin reuersi sunt·

Fig. 16.2 *Three lines from the* Chronicles, *folio 40v, describing the transfer to Douglas for four years. It begins* Eodem anno *'The same year'.*

for this move is given. There is no indication that the site at Ballasalla had become impossible through flood, famine, pestilence or fire. Neither is it clear where in Douglas the monks resided. The implication is that it was the whole convent which moved and not a party sent out to found a new abbey in Douglas, which, in any case, by Cistercian rules, was too close to Ballasalla. Was the intention to cause a confrontation with the new house at Myroscough, which would also have been closer than the 12-mile limit?

Basil Megaw has suggested that, based on the uncertainty of the location of Rushen in the original grant of land to the abbey, the first site had been further to the south, close to the site of Castle Rushen. He suggests that the king persuaded the monks to move in order that the castle could be built and that the monks lodged temporarily in Douglas while a new site was developed in what is now Ballasalla.[36] Although the transfer of monasteries to new sites was quite common in the Middle Ages,[37] and the sequence which Megaw suggests is perfectly possible, the dating methods available are insufficiently accurate to establish that the present site was or was not the original one. For example, the style of the one surviving arch in the north transept at Ballasalla has been dated to between 1190 and

1230,[38] a range which would allow Megaw's interpretation but does not prove it. Recent excavations have retrieved a number of small architectural fragments from the sixteenth-century demolition, which are probably of twelfth-century date. Again, they cannot be dated with sufficient precision to support Megaw's thesis or to deny it.[39] The name Rushen, however, is not so puzzling as it appeared to Megaw. Roscow has recently discovered from a study of the 1540 *Computus*, contrary to Kneen and others, that the abbey farms were grouped in treens and that the block of land between Castletown and Ballasalla constituted the Treen of Rushen.[40]

Whatever the reason for the move, by the early thirteenth century Rushen abbey's dominant position as both a major religious and secular power in Man was established. The Myroscough lands were added in the middle of the thirteenth century,[41] and a block of land at Eskdale was inveigled from St Bees in 1312,[42] thus increasing its income and sphere of influence. In religious matters the abbey was also powerful. It enjoyed the advowson of the vicarages of Lonan, Santon, Arbory, Rushen and Malew and a proportion of their tithes.[43] The parish church, vicarage and glebe of Rushen actually lay within the abbey demesne. For a time at least the abbey also had a voice, through its mother-house at Furness, in the election of the bishops of Sodor and the Isles, who were frequently Cistercian themselves.[44] In the absence of a fixed seat until the mid-thirteenth century, the abbey also probably provided a local power-base for the bishop.

The medieval landholdings of the abbey can be determined with some degree of accuracy partly through study of contemporary documents including the important *Limites terrarum monachorum*, but mainly through the post-dissolution records, in which the abbey lands, their incomes, and the baron courts continued to be treated as distinct entities up to the early twentieth century.[45] There is no surviving charter for the main blocks of land in Malew, Skinscoe, Myroscough or Knocksharry. The papal bull of 1153 appears to describe the Malew lands,[46] but much of the detail is difficult to relate to actual areas of terrain. The *Limites* describe in some detail the Malew, Myroscough and Skinscoe properties in a manner which allows them to be defined on the ground with some degree of confidence.[47] There is no medieval documentation for the sizeable holding between Peel and Knocksharry which had become abbeyland by the early sixteenth century.[48] Such a large, coherent unit, was almost certainly obtained by the abbey by royal charter, rather than by purchase.

The site of Rushen abbey itself lies on a broad river terrace on the north-eastern boundary of its demesne farm. Recent excavations have revealed much of the plan of the core of the site as it was at the time of the dissolution.[49] A number of aspects of the choice of site and its design are worthy

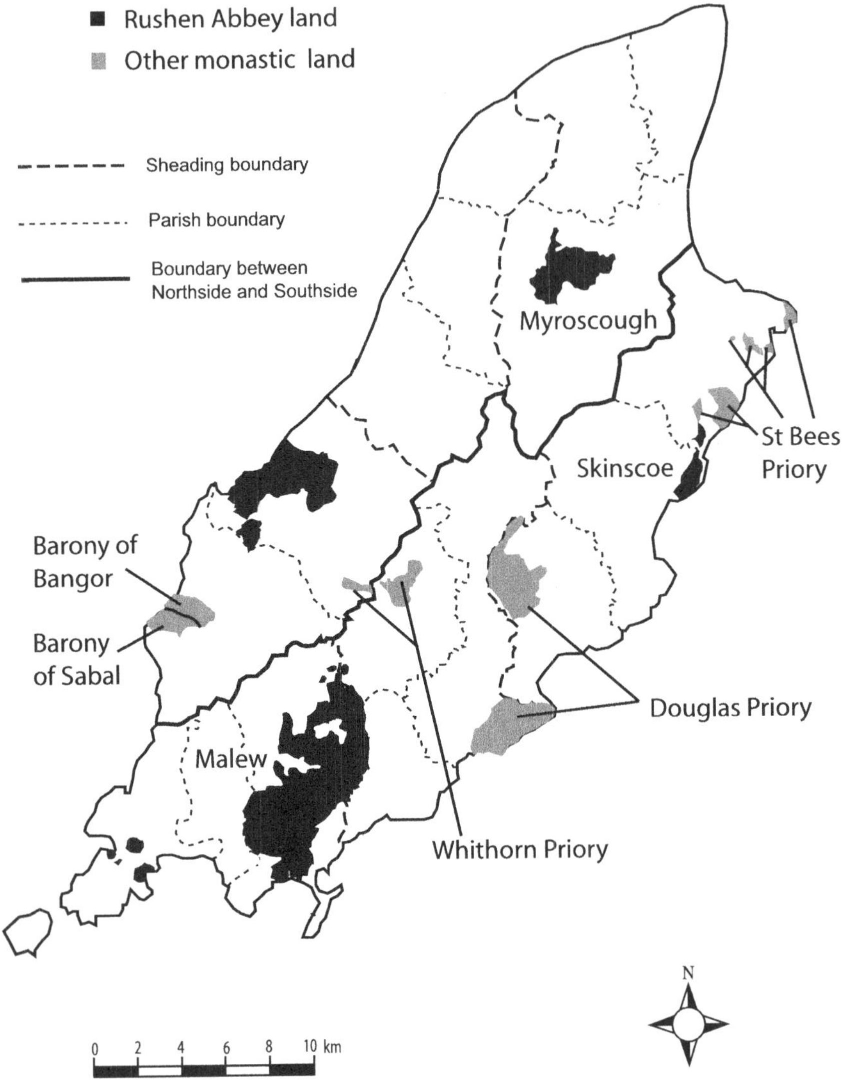

of notice. The abbey is very small. It is one of the few Cistercian houses in the British Isles in which the church has no aisles. The area of the cloisters, at around 10m square, is much smaller than any comparable site.[50] Contrary to normal Cistercian practice the abbey is situated very close to a major seat of power, Castle Rushen, in other words, it cannot really be regarded as remote. Its lands, especially the demesne – a farm of over 1,000 acres – are the most fertile in the island and have been such since the Neolithic.[51] It seems to have functioned as a royal mortuary chapel, rather

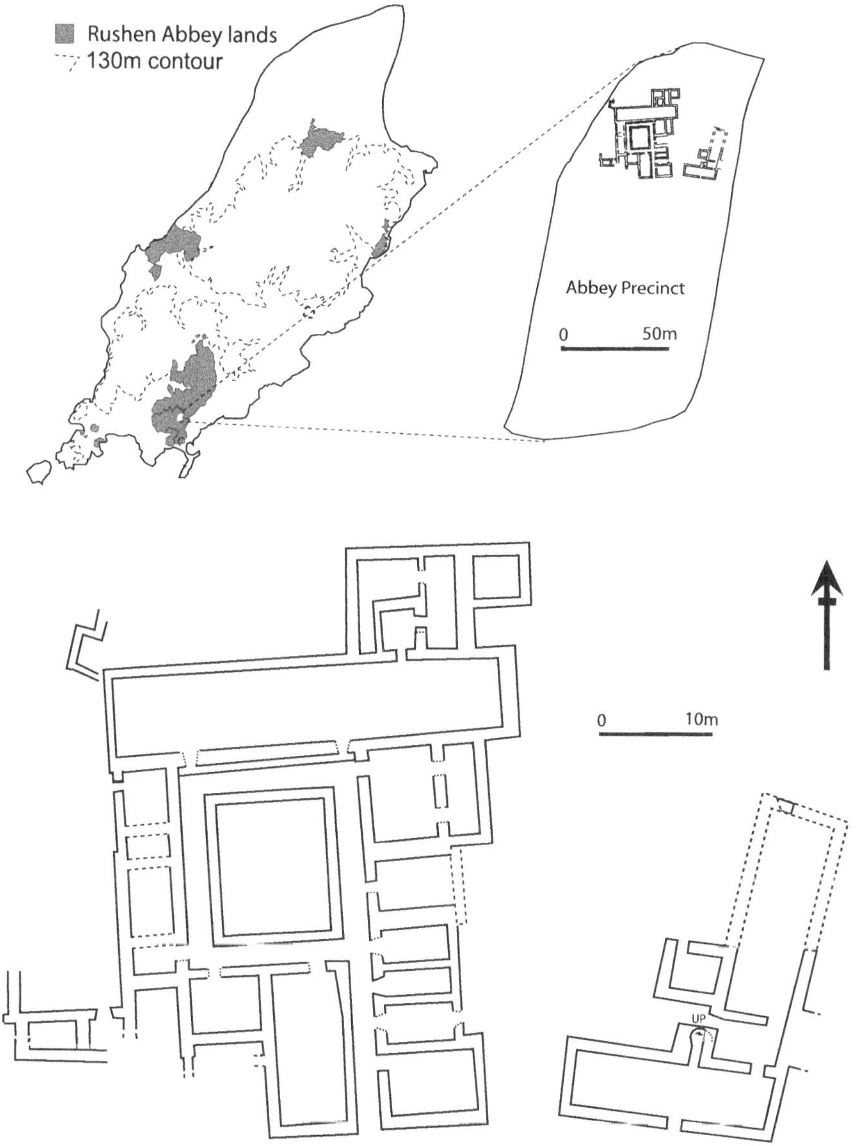

Fig. 16.3 *(opposite) Monastic land-holdings in the Isle of Man shown on an outline of parish and sheading boundaries (see also Fig. 19.2).*

Fig. 16.4 *(above) Location of Rushen Abbey (inset map); and plan of abbey buildings as excavated 1999–2004. Dashed lines indicate walls and doorways deduced from limited evidence.*

in the manner of Westminster abbey in England, though there is no direct indication that the Manx kings were crowned there.[52]

Part of the explanation for these unusual features may lie in its Savignac origins, part in Rushen's special relationship with the kings of Man and the Isles. Although the Savignac order was taken over by the Cistercians in 1147, it is clear that the process of assimilation was not a smooth one. First, the Savignacs successfully held out for the retention of their rights and privileges at the time of the takeover.[53] These included forms of endowment such as the acceptance of the patronage of churches, tithe income and gifts from the faithful, all of which had been violently rejected for the Cistercians by Stephen Harding, the abbot of Cîteaux from 1109 to 1135.[54] Neither did the Savignacs seem to enforce strict observance in such matters as poverty, manual labour and simplicity. Their ethos was so different from that of St Bernard of Clairvaux, the dynamic force behind the expansion of the Cistercians,[55] that some writers have seen the takeover as the principal cause of the decline in Cistercian impetus towards the end of the twelfth century.[56] In England there was considerable resistance to the move, led especially from Furness, the most important Savignac house in the British Isles.[57] Even after the merger, for some time English abbots were regularly getting into trouble with the General Chapter in Cîteaux for failing to attend the annual meetings.[58] Despite subsequent Cistercian propaganda and the imposition of 'right thinking' abbots from outside, it seems clear that, in many respects, the Savignac houses remained an order within an order throughout the Middle Ages.

At the dissolution Rushen abbey received annual rent from lands and cottages and tithe incomes amounting to around £200. Only the demesne farm remained under the direct control of the monks.[59] Whilst this may merely reflect changes in the economic activities of all Cistercian abbeys in the century or so before the dissolution, it is tempting to suggest that the size and location of the original donations of land to Rushen abbey by the Manx kings and its Savignac ethos was intended, from the first, to provide a significant rent income. For an abbey that was physically small (excavations suggest that the dormitory may barely have slept 20 monks at a maximum),[60] the management of a demesne farm of over 1,000 acres would have stretched human resources to the limit.

The atypical elements of siting, endowment and ground plan of Rushen abbey should also be considered in a twelfth-century political context. During the decade of instability which followed the death of Magnus Barelegs in 1103, Óláfr, the youngest son of Godred Crovan, had been living in the court of Henry I of England and must have been aware of the significance of the monastic reformation which was taking place and of its economic significance. He had also probably observed the role which was played by Westminster abbey, as the focus of both coronations and funerals of the royal family. Once Óláfr returned to Man to claim his kingdom in around 1113, the creation of such a focus of religious power, and driving force for economic development, was a logical move. In the absence of an existing Benedictine abbey he chose one of the new reforming orders, probably because of their reputation as innovating agriculturalists, and established them with a generous endowment on the best land on the island. In the context of his successful attempt to reassert authority over the whole Hebridean empire, Rushen abbey provided both a focus for kingly power, a royal mausoleum, and a direct indication that the king was in tune with the times. It should be noted that Rushen abbey was founded before the first Savignac house in Ireland (St Mary's, Dublin),[61] and earlier than any of the Cistercian houses in Ireland, Wales or Scotland.[62] Coincident with the foundation of Rushen abbey, this consolidation of royal power was further emphasised with the grant to Furness of the right to elect a bishop for the kingdom and with the election of the Cistercian monk Wimund, who may have been of Manx descent, as bishop.[63] He was followed by John, a Savignac monk, and Nicholas, formally abbot of Furness.[64] The creation of the see of Nidaros by Pope Anastasius IV, in 1154,[65] confirmed the Norwegian basis of the kingship of the Isles and the later construction of Castle Rushen provided a physical seat of power which lay at the boundary of the abbey demesne.[66] The abbey thus formed an integral part of the corporate royal identity. This identification with the Norse kings is very much reflected in the tone and bias of the Manx chronicle, which was almost certainly written by monks at the abbey.[67] This royal function of the abbey, along with its Savignac origins may together explain its location, relative wealth and internal organisation. Given these factors it is even more difficult to explain why the church and claustral buildings are so small.

Lacking medieval documentation it is hard to determine the way in which the abbey managed its lands, the kinds of crops it grew or the livestock it held. A key issue is the number and role of lay brothers, especially during the first two centuries after foundation. The excavated plan of the claustral buildings reveals a short, narrow west range, which would indicate that by the mid-sixteenth century the lay brothers did not represent a significant element in the economy of the abbey. The receiver's accounts at the dissolution in 1540 show that the monks had almost £50 tied up in grain, £43 in cattle, £4 in horses and less than £3 in sheep – not a typical Cistercian profile – all presumably deriving from the abbey demesne and not the tenanted farms.[68] The sharp rise in cottage rents in Ballasalla between the abbey rent roll of 1539/40 and the lord's roll in the following year, which is not paralleled in the equivalent properties in Peel, may well imply that the tenants close to Rushen were still providing 'boon' labour to the abbey and that, once that had ceased, the rents were increased to a more realistic 'market' level.[69] The movement from the abbey precinct of its main labour force to nearby tenancies may have occurred at quite an early date. It is clear from a 1368 dispute over his income between the vicar of Malew and the abbey that, already by that date, cash income, whether from tithes or rents, was a major feature of the monastic economy.[70] On the other hand, once the Myroscough monks and their lands had been assimilated it seems likely that some kind of presence was retained at the site of the abbey buildings which then operated as a grange farm. The presence of a farm named Ballagrangey in the northern part of the Malew abbeylands suggests that, at least for part of its existence, the abbey was using the standard Cistercian grange/lay brother system over much of its estate.[71]

A more distant holding of the abbey, in Copeland in Cumbria, was granted to it between 1160 and 1180 by Benedict Pennington.[72] A confirmation of the charter, dated 1278–83, shows that the abbot of Rushen was receiving rent of one mark for the land.[73] It consisted of an area called Skeldou Moor in Birkby, Westmorland and was still in Rushen's hands in 1292 at the time of the papal *Taxatio* of England and Wales. The '*Abbas be Mannia*' was assessed at 6s. 8d. (1 mark) and a footnote states '*in Decanatu Coupland*'.[74] The reasons behind this particular grant are nowhere stated. Unless it was retained solely for its rent income from the beginning, it is tempting to suggest that a benfactor of Furness gave land to Rushen for a particular purpose. Given that the island is virtually self-sufficient in minerals (Furness itself possessing prospecting rights and a smelt at Ronaldsway), that fuel supplies were not a problem, and that the holding in question is moorland, free-stone or timber for building seems most likely. Access to its Cumbrian lands would be by sea from Derbyhaven to the estuary at Ravenglass. After the main buildings at Rushen had been completed the lands were then rented out. The lease of the lord's land at Totnanby, recorded in the 1506 Rent Roll,[75] may have secured the abbey mineral supplies such as lead which would have been needed not only during its construction phase, but for glazing, roof maintenance and water-pipe construction throughout the life of the site.

Rushen abbey in the later Middle Ages

The treaty of Perth in 1266 saw the demise of Norse hegemony over Man.[76]

Although nominally Scottish from that date, the island experienced over a century of political uncertainty, until, eventually, passing into the hands of the English crown and then to the Stanleys in 1406.[77] During this period the abbot of Rushen, as the largest independent landowner, provided a resident, consistent and powerful secular authority as well as a pervasive religious influence on the island. In a series of charters the Scottish kings generally confirmed the rights and properties of Rushen and the other monasteries with lands on Man.[78] The Scots did, however, attempt to become involved in the election of the bishops. Alexander III succeeded, against considerable Manx opposition, in vetoing in 1275 the election of Abbot Gilbert of Rushen and installed instead as bishop Mark of Galloway.[79] During the short period in which Antony Bek ruled the island he also imposed a Gallovidian, Alan, as bishop,[80] and attempted to wrest the vicarages of Kirk Michael and Maughold from Furness.[81] A series of Scottish bishops followed, ending with Thomas (1333–48).[82] These clerics did not have authority over the abbey, which resided with the Cistercian order itself, and, although barons of the island, were not major landowners. In any case, because of the size of the see, they would have spent a good deal of time away.

Once English power was established, there were a number of developments which can, in part, be interpreted as an attempt to reduce the power of Rushen abbey. Perhaps the most important was the introduction of the order of Friars Minor from Dublin by William Montacute in 1367.[83] Although the Franciscans depended entirely on alms and were committed to absolute poverty, possessing no estates of their own, they would have provided a foil to the Cistercians in matters of faith and practice rather that in terms of secular power. The choice of site in Ballabeg, only a few hundred metres from the boundary of the Abbey farm, might itself be considered provocative. On the other hand William Russell, the bishop at the time, who was a Cistercian, having previously been abbot of Rushen himself, appears to have given the friars every assistance.[84] Once the island was in the hands of the Stanleys there was a much more overt move by the secular authority to exercise power over both resident and alien barons when Sir John Stanley II summoned them to a Tynwald in 1422 to do fealty under threat of confiscation of their lands.[85] This attempt to put the abbey, nunnery and bishop in their place in the feudal order of things was successful. As the alien barons do not appear to have turned up within the required 40 days, and neither were their lands confiscated, the inference is that the exercise was largely one directed towards insular discipline and mainly aimed at Rushen abbey.[86] Although there are recorded clashes of authority between the lord and the abbot later on in the early sixteenth century, there is no longer any threat to the latter's position and, on occasions, the abbot was brought in to support the secular power and even to preside over a civil inquest.[87]

St Mary's chapel

According to Cubbon the chapel of St Mary in Castletown was constructed at some time in the late twelfth or early thirteenth century,[88] the details of construction and materials of its three supposed Romanesque nave arches being extremely similar to the surviving arch in the east wall of the north transept at Rushen. Although excavations at Castle Rushen have suggested a phase of fortification prior to the present standing tower,[89] there is no evidence for any sort of urban development until the late fifteenth century at the earliest. It is difficult to see why such a chapel would have been constructed in the twelfth century, at a point when the principal focus of power was at Peel. The presence of at least one aisle is also remarkable in that at the abbey itself the church has a simple nave, making St Mary's the earliest aisled church on the island after the cathedral of St German at Peel. One explanation, made by Canon Quine, is that the arches at St Mary's were brought from Rushen abbey at the dissolution.[90] This seems unlikely given the archaeological evidence,[91] and the fact that the chapel was clearly

Fig. 16.5 *The Renaissance arcade at St Mary's, Castletown (the old Grammar School). Photo: courtesy Manx National Heritage.*

in existence well before 1540.[92] In the *Computus* 4s. 4d. is charged against Rushen abbey income for the 'the salary of the chaplain celebrating below the Castle of Castletown of ancient foundation (*ex antiqua Fundacione*)',[93] showing that the chapel was a Cistercian responsibility.

Another possibility following Megaw's reintepretation of the original site of Rushen Abbey itself, is that, despite the rather unlikely physical nature of the site, so constricted and near the sea, might not St Mary's contain the core of the first stone-built Rushen abbey? Although the width of the chapel's nave is barely five metres and that at Rushen abbey is nearly seven, both are compatible with the size of the earliest structures at other sites.[94] If the abbey was moved because it was in the way of the development of Castle Rushen as a new royal seat of power – the sort of move imposed by Edward I on Aberconwy when he needed to build a castle and town at Conwy[95] – Megaw's interpretation of the 1192 move to Douglas and return to Ballasalla described in the chronicle might appear justified. A further point in its favour lies in the geography of the original grant of land to Furness for the construction of the abbey. The abbey demesne farm extends right to the river at Castletown; and abbey lands impinge directly on the town.[96] It would be very surprising if King Óláfr gave land to the abbey which so clearly impinged on an existing secular site of any importance. It looks much more likely that the castle and later town were imposed on the abbey's holdings and not the reverse. If this is the case, the presence of a small, innovative, aisled church in Castletown, as the survivor of the original stone building of Rushen abbey, might provide a further component in support of Megaw's argument.

These arguments founder, however, in light of a close examination of the structure and context of the arches in the chapel First, the blocks out of which they are constructed are very large and deep and are of a size that twelfth-century masons could not have managed with the blocks and tackle available at the time. Secondly, the surfaces of the stones are punch-dressed, a technique of stone preparation that did not appear until the late Middle Ages. Thirdly, examination of the coursing of the walling above the arches shows that they have been inserted into an existing structure. The arches are, therefore, of Renaissance design, probably dating to around AD 1500 and probably represent the extension of an existing small chapel in response to an expanding urban population.[97]

The Nunnery

In common with the majority of women's houses in the British Isles, the Douglas nunnery is very poorly documented.[98] It was presumably the 'monastery' in which Robert the Bruce, according to the Manx chronicle, stayed the night on his punitive expedition to Man in 1313.[99] Inserted in a space on a page of early sixteenth-century accounts contained in the Castle Rushen Papers is a note about the nunnery which gives three separate pieces of information which are not independently stated elsewhere.[100] First, the house was founded in the reign of King Rögnvaldr, that is, between 1187 and 1228. Secondly, it was of the Cistercian order, and thirdly that Antony Bek as lord of Man (1298–1310) had granted the monastery the advowson of the parish church of St Conchan. This information had, apparently, been obtained by Bishop Richard in 1414, probably in order to confirm the tithe income. The first reference to nuns as such comes in 1408 when a 'Cristina, prioress of Douglas', signed, along with others, a declaration against a claim for lordship of the island by Sir Stephen Scrope.[101] We have seen that, according to the Manx chronicle, in 1192 Rushen abbey was transferred to Douglas for four years.[102] It is usually assumed that the monks resided at the nunnery for this period, in which case its foundation would have to have been in the earlier part of Rögnvaldr's reign. As the nunnery is not specifically mentioned it is possible that the monks went somewhere else or that the nunnery was founded on the site which they had occupied after they had returned to Ballasalla. Unfortunately, therefore, this reference in the chronicle cannot be used as evidence for the existence of the Nunnery at this time.

The reference to the nuns belonging to the Cistercian order is interesting in view of the reluctance of the order to receive female houses.[103] From its foundation in the late eleventh century, it took until 1213 before any women were accepted into the order.[104] Of the 27 'Cistercian' nunneries in England and Wales only two were ever officially accepted.[105] The remainder were organised on Cistercian lines and occasionally claimed Cistercian privileges, such as exemption from tithes, although not always successfully.[106] The bishop's confirmation of the nature of the Douglas nunnery's affiliation was probably important to them for the same reason. The advowson of the church of St Conchan would have involved the nuns receiving a proportion (one third in 1540) of the tithes of the parish.[107] The vicar, whose stipend would be paid from the revenues, would also act as their priest and thus be their own appointee. As the nunnery was not officially accepted into the Cistercian order its visitor would have been the bishop. The prior(ess) of Douglas was one of the barons of the island who made fealty to John Stanley in 1422,[108] and at the dissolution in 1540 the 'Abbess', Eleanor Calcotte was given a pension of £3 6s. 8d. and her two remaining nuns Margaret Egliston and Agnes Inlowe pensions of £1 6s. 8d. each. The portable property of the nunnery at the time was valued at

Fig. 16.6 'The Prospect of the Nunry in y^{e} Isle of Man on the East side', *from The Vale Royall of England published in 1656 by Daniel King. Courtesy, Manx National Heritage.*

£28 2s. 10d., including £4 5s. 4d. for *jocalia* (items, such as chalices, in precious metal). The nunnery's share of the tithe income from St Conchan amounted to £6 13s. 4d. and would have almost covered the cost of the pensions, £7 0s. 0d., on its own. The landholdings which were worth an additional £6 19s. 2d. in customary rents, were in two parts, one in Braddan parish, along the coast south of Douglas, and the second, the modern 'abbeylands' in Onchan.[109]

That some substantial building fragments survived the dissolution is clear from the descriptions of William Blundell (c.1618–56) and George Waldron (c.1726). Blundell notes only 'a piece of ye cloyster yet standing, wherein ye religious were used to goe in processions'.[110] Daniel King's *Prospect*, originally published in 1656 seems to show two substantial pieces of ruined masonry in the foreground with the 'modern' buildings behind.[111] Waldron refers to 'some of the cloisters remaining including ceilings and pillars supporting arches'. He also describes the chapel and what appears to be an undercroft with benches, possibly the chapter house.[112] These descriptions imply that a full set of claustral buildings did once exist.

St Trinian's barony

According to a copy made of the Registry of Whithorn in 1504 which is now preserved amongst the Ellesmere Papers in the Huntington Library, California, a charter of Óláfr Dubh, of around 1215, grants to the

Premonstratensian canons of *Candida Casa*, Whithorn, two blocks of land at 'Ballacgniba' and 'Dalhamer', the church of St Ninian and the hospital of Ballacgniba and the church of 'Saint Runan' (Marown).[113] The specific mention of the hospital, in particular, suggests that the charter is, in fact, a confirmation of an earlier donation, possibly by King Óláfr I. A number of later thirteenth-century confirmations repeat the same information.[114] In 1285 King Alexander of Scotland added the advowson of Holy Trinity, Ramsey (Lezayre) to the Whithorn interest in Man. This gift was confirmed by both bishop and pope soon afterwards.[115] Using the post-dissolution rentals, Basil Megaw has successfully unpicked the topographical and place-name evidence for the landholdings and has shown that the main holding, 'Ballacgniba', consisted of the four quarterlands below Greeba on which both hospital and chapel stood. The smaller holding, 'Dalhamer', he equates with the present quarterland of Ballachurry.[116]

Whilst very similar Romanesque mouldings and capitals have been recorded from both St Trinian's chapel and Old Kirk Marown,[117] the site of the hospital is not known.[118] It seems likely to have stood in the same field as the chapel where, even today, subdued earthworks can be observed under low sunshine. The discovery of lintel graves under the floor of the

Fig. 16.7 *St Trinian's Chapel from the south.*

chapel, during the restoration of the building in 1910,[119] may suggest that the building was erected on an early Christian site, although it seems more likely that the involvement of Whithorn with the Isle of Man during the twelfth century and later was the result of the political or dynastic interests of the Manx kings. The description in the Manx chronicle of the murder of Óláfr I, himself married to a daughter of the lord of Galloway, implicitly states that there was a significant presence of Galloway men in the north of the island at that time and that this settlement had been the cause of considerable unrest.[120] Once the Scottish interest in Man had waned, the strength of the Whithorn influence seems to have declined. The case of Michael Magbrayer, in 1472,[121] shows a lack of authority over Lezayre which is soon being gifted to the Manx bishops.[122]

The barony of St Bees

The Benedictine priory of St Bees, a cell of St Mary's York, was given land in Man by King Guðröðr (1153–87). The charter, witnessed by Bishop Gamaliel who died in 1181, refers to two areas of land one called 'Eschedale' (modern Kerrowdhoon), the other 'Asmunder toftas' (Ballelin).[123] Confirmation of the grant by King Rögnvaldr (1187–1228) adds half of 'Ormeshar' (the Howe/the Barony) to the holding.[124] The three plots of land lie on the east coast of the island south of Cornaa, facing Cumbria.[125] Kerrowdhoon was lost to Rushen abbey in 1312 following a lawsuit.[126] At some time before the dissolution the priory acquired some 70 acres of Staff Lands on Maughold Head. The Prior of St Bees was one of the barons who failed to do fealty to Sir John Stanley in 1422.[127] His refusal to appear does not seem to have resulted in the land being confiscated, as had been threatened. Soon after the dissolution the lands were in the hands of the Christian family of Milntown who were not regarded as tenants of the crown. Thus, the Act of Settlement did not apply to these estates.

The baronies of Bangor and Saul

The first unequivocal reference to these baronies is in the *Lex Scripta* for 1422 in which the abbots of Bangor and Saul in County Down were among the barons summoned to do 'faith and fealty' to Sir John Stanley, the lord of Man.[128] Post-dissolution papers show that the baronies consisted of six quarterland farms on the coast of Patrick parish south of Glenmaye (see Fig. 19.2).[129] Although the later rents were kept in a single book (*Liber Bangor et Sabal*) and the lands were granted as a whole by Charles II to the Sherburnes of Stonyhurst in Lancashire, references in Irish records suggest that Bangor had the three quarterlands adjacent and south of Glenmaye, that is Ballachrink, Cronkmoor and Balnalargy, and Saul the three farms of Ballaquayne, Ballelby and Ballahutchin further to the south.[130] In the Quayle Bridge House Book the ancient rent for the combined barony was set at £6 7s. 0d. In addition tenants had to pay 'customs' of 21 hens at 6d., 63 boon days (of labour) at 4d. and 118 loads of turf at 1d., which came to an additional £2 1s. 4d., making a grand total of £8 8s. 4d. As it was presumably impractical for tenants of alien monasteries to provide their boon labour, or hens and peat at the mother-house, their customs appear to have been commuted into cash amounts which were then added to the rent.[131] This practice, which probably also occurred at St Bees and Whithorn, appears to have become general by the time of the dissolution.[132] This sum is very close to the £8 7s. 6½d. which was actually charged in 1916 when the rents and customs were redeemed under the Lord's Rents Purchase Act of 1913.[133]

It is not at all clear when this monastic interest from Ulster began. Both Bangor and Saul were, originally, early Christian foundations, the latter intimately connected with the life of St Patrick. It is possible that these landholdings were of long standing, dating from a Patrician mission to Man.[134]

The influence of Furness abbey

Although Furness, as the mother-house of Rushen, was clearly the most influential alien abbey with the power for a time to elect the bishop of Sodor and Man, it held the smallest amount of land on its own account of all the medieval barons. In a charter of King Haraldr son of Óláfr Dubh (1237–48) the abbey is given mineral rights on the island and 'a messuage containing three acres of land at a fitting place at Bakenaldwath to build a house as well for the reception of their men as for a repository for their minerals and other property'. Basil Megaw has convincingly argued that the place in question is on land at Ronaldsway described in the Furness abbey rental of 1539 as 'a parcel of land called Ronateswath lying between the monastery of Russhen and Castletowne' for which unpaid income of two

Fig. 16.8 *The Ronaldsway smelt under excavation in 1935, photo E H Stenning, with a sketch plan showing various features identified. This lead smelt is thought to have been in use between the fourteenth and fifteenth centuries. The bins contained masses of burnt domesticated animal bones, numerous samples of galena and two types of medieval pottery. Megaw, B. (1960–61) and 'Bakenaldwath' and the Medieval Lead Mines,* JMM *7 (77), 105–7.*

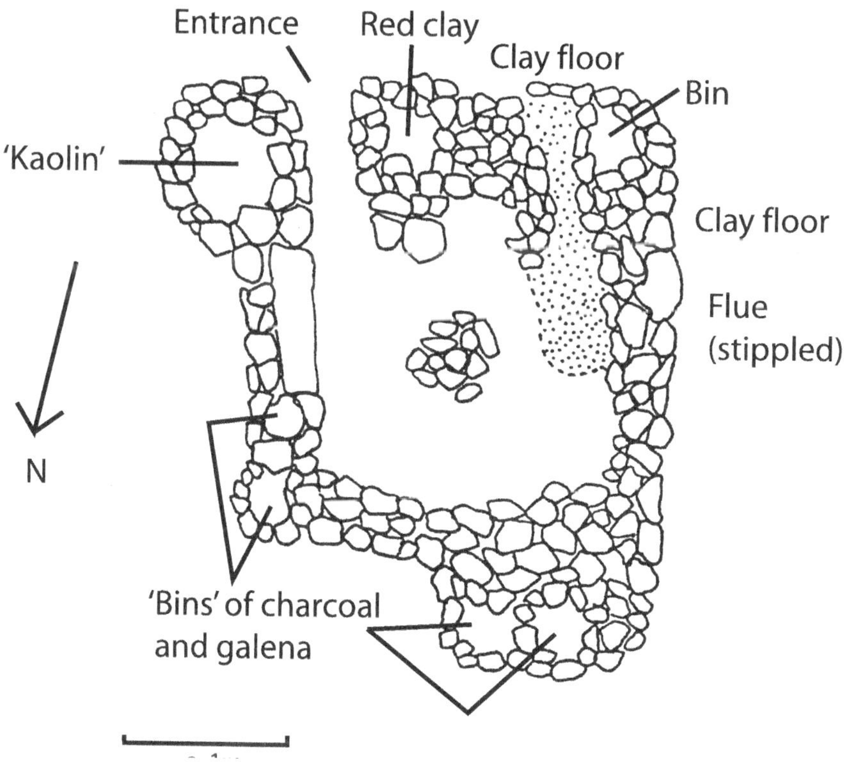
Entrance
Red clay
Clay floor
Bin
'Kaolin'
Clay floor
Flue
(stippled)
N
'Bins' of charcoal
and galena

shillings was due.[135] Excavation by Canon Stenning in 1935 of a medieval smelt, probably for lead, which appears to have been located on this land strongly suggests that Furness used the site as a metal processing area, convenient for the incoming transport of ore and export of the refined metal. By the time of the abbey rental, and in a survey of the post-dissolution lordship of the Manor of Furness, dated 1649, the land is being rented out to Manx farmers.[136] In 1300 Furness had also been granted the vicarages of Michael and Maughold,[137] which provided in 1540 an income of £13 6s. 8d. a year.[138]

The precise relationship between Furness and its daughter at Rushen is difficult to determine. It is likely to have been close. Furness would have provided the Visitor for Rushen. A number of bishops of Sodor had been either abbots of Furness,[139] or Rushen.[140] From the evidence of the *Coucher Book*, Rushen was clearly involved in the election of bishops when that prerogative was held by Furness. When Furness was trying to get its candidate Nicholas consecrated as bishop in around 1217, it enlisted the support of Rushen, the entire convent signing the appeal.[141] Although disputes did occur,[142] the weight of evidence is for a close collaboration and co-operation over many issues.[143]

Bymaken Friary

The introduction of monastic orders to the Isle of Man is completed by the arrival of the order of Friars Minor from Dublin in the late fourteenth century. William Montacute and the Irish provincial prior of the Franciscans both petitioned the pope in 1367 for permission to construct

> a church or oratory, together with a bell-tower; bell, cemetery, houses and other necessary offices, provided that twelve brethren of the said order can be fittingly and properly maintained at the place; without however infringing on the rights of the parochial church.

Montacute, as lord of Man, would provide the site in Kirk Arbory. The pope agreed.[144] Building was apparently complete in 1373 when the pope issued a mandate for the consecration of the buildings.[145] There is no further direct reference to the friary extant in medieval documents. There is no reference to the friars in the 1422 Tynwald, presumably because they were insignificant landowners.[146] The dissolution documentation of 1540–3 is more informative. Robert Calcott, the earl of Derby's receiver, reported that 'of Bemakin there is no return as there was nothing left there to be sold, the house being left for the farmer'. The first payment of rent by the farmer describes the property as a 'quarter of land comprising 40 acres enclosed by a ditch' with a *parva capella* and a *domus fratrum minorum* on the site, the latter implying that the living quarters of the friars were still in use, presumably by the farmer.[147]

Substantial parts of the eastern half of the chapel survive today to roof height, the building having been used as a barn (see Fig 7.1). It seems likely that elements of the *domus fratrum* survive within and beneath the present farmhouse. The landholding probably equates with the almost 120 acre estate within which the Friary Farm now lies.[148] This would have provided about 40 acres of kitchen gardens, orchards, farm buildings, etc., together with outfields which could provide subsistence for the friars, who, theoretically at least, paid 20 s. rent to the lord throughout their occupancy of the site. The friary was included in the 21–year lease between Henry VIII and Thomas Hungate, which included both the abbey and nunnery.[149] In 1610 it was granted back to the earl of Derby by the crown.[150]

An interesting sidelight on the inter-relationships between the friars and the other monastic orders on Man is given in a Papal letter of 1471:

> To the bishop of Sodor, the abbot of St. Mary's, Rwythin, in the diocese of Sodor, and Gilbert Vrytht, archdeacon of Sodor.
> Mandate to collate and assign to Alan Hobuntar, a Friar Preacher, the perpetual vicarage of Holy Trinity by Ramsey, in the diocese of Sodor (dependant on the Premonstratensian priory of St. Ninian in the diocese of Whiteherne *(candide case)*, and wont to be governed by canons thereof, and value 6*l.* sterling), so long void that its collation has lapsed to the apostolic see; summoning and removing Michael Magbrayer, a Premonstratensian canon, who without any title, and without having obtained any dispensation on account of illegitimacy, as the son of a Cistercian monk and an unmarried woman, has detained possession for between nine and ten years. As soon as the said Alan has obtained possession, they are to transfer him from the order of Friars Preachers to the said priory of St. Ninian, and cause him to be received as a canon thereof, etc. *Religionis etc.*
> *11 Kal Jan 1472* St Peter's Rome[151]

Not only is there evident lack of control of the appointments to Lezayre vicarage from Whithorn, but the solution is to put a friar into the parish and, in order to do so, to make him a Premonstratensian canon.

The Dissolution

Edward, earl of Derby, having been chosen by Henry VIII as one of the commissioners to oversee the dissolution of Furness abbey in April 1537 does not seem to have been backward in dealing with the Manx situation. Initially, it seems, the earl thought that, as 'king' of Man, he would benefit from the monastic estates himself. He was overruled by Henry who insisted that the Manx lands and revenues should be dealt with by the Court of Augmentations in London. The dissolution of Rushen abbey and the nunnery took place on 24 June 1540, and the abbot, prioress, and the remaining monks and nuns were pensioned off. The court paid for the pensions and the other costs of running the estates from the rent and other income derived from them.[152] The first leasing of the dissolved abbey lands, including the friary, was to a Sir Thomas Hungate for 21 years and is dated 18 March 1543. Only in 1609 did the lands revert to the lord of Man. Although Whithorn was not dissolved until 1587, its Manx lands and interests appear to have been appropriated by the lord of Man before that date.[153] A survey of 1649 shows that the Manor of Furness, the successor of the abbey, retained its Manx land at Ronaldsway and the rectories of Kirk Michael and Maghauld at their earlier rents.[154] The barony of Bangor and Saul passed into private possession, as did the St Bees lands. In the case of the latter the owners were not regarded as crown tenants, so that, as late as 1986,[155] the Manx government had to enact new legislation in order to be able to let the rights for offshore oil and gas prospecting.

The administration of the abbey lands, with their own sergeants, stewards and baronial courts, continued until 1916 when the Lord's Rents Purchase Act of 1913 allowed tenants to buy out their customary rents which, in most cases, had been unchanged since the sixteenth century.[154] The monastic legacy survives today in buildings such as Rushen abbey and St Trinian's, in place-names such as the abbeylands and the Grange, and in the network of monastic holdings still felt by many of their occupants to be 'abbey farms'.

Notes

1 Broderick, *CKMI*, fol. 51r.

2 Etchingham, *Church Organisation in Ireland AD 650 to 1000*, esp. 455–60.

3 See the ordinances of Bishop Simon, 1229, in Oliver, *Monumenta*, iii, 176–82.

4 For details and references see below.

5 Oliver, *Monumenta*, ii, 10–11.

6 This seems very doubtful as is demonstrated in detail in an unpublished paper by Talbot (MM Ref 9587, Box 3) entitled 'The Priory and Nunnery of Douglas: its alleged ruins and relics: founder and first occupants'.

7 Such as Rushen abbey (J.R. Bruce, *The Manx Archaeological Survey, Sixth Report 1966: keeils and burial grounds in the sheading of Rushen*, Manx Museum and National Trust (Douglas, 1968), 16; St Trinians (P.M.C. Kermode, 'S. Trinian's', *Proceedings*, new ser. 1 (1910), 332; and the Friary (J.K. Barratt, 'The Franciscan friary at Bymacan', *JMM*, No 80 (1965), 209.

8 The phrase 'sea kings' is borrowed from W.D.H. Sellar, 'Hebridean sea kings: the

successors of Somerled, 1164–1316', in E.J. Cowan and R.A. McDonald (eds), *Alba: Celtic Scotland in the Middle Ages* (East Linton, 2000), 188.

9 For Óláfr's youth in the English court, see Broderick, *CKMI*, fol. 35r.

10 'Certa terra in *Mannia* data fuit Abbathiae de *Rievalle* as construendam Abbatiam de *Russia*. Postea tamen data fuit Abbatiae de *Furnesio* as construendam eam de Ordine Cisterciensi ubi modo situata est, et sic non de *Rievalle* sed de *Furnesio* exivit' (T.A. Beck, *Annales Furnesiensis: history and antiquities of Furness Abbey* (London, 1844), 122; *Coucher Book of Furness*, ii, 11–12.

11 G. Coppack, *The White Monks: the Cistercians in Britain 1128–1540* (Stroud, 1998), 20–1.

12 Colin Platt, *The Abbeys and Priories of Medieval England*, 2nd edn (London, 1995), 40–2.

13 Broderick, *CKMI*, fol. 35v.

14 Broderick, *CKMI*, fol. 40r.

15 Anon., 'Document No 6', *JMM*, ii, No.27, 21.

16 The details are given below in the paragraphs dealing with each monastery in turn.

17 Óláfr Dubh granted them licence to purchase from the island in any one year '60 oxen or so many sheep and pigs as may be bought in my land or of my heirs for the price of 60 oxen'. (Wilson (ed.), *Register of St Bees*, no. 45.

18 F. Granger and W.G. Collingwood (eds), *The Register of Holm Cultram*, Cumberland and Westmorland Antiquarian and Archaeological Society, Record Series Volume 7 (1929), 94. Óláfr Dubh granted Holm Cultram 'free entrance and exit to his land with one ship and its boat for monks, lay brothers and their men, goods and chattels, and leave to buy and sell for their own use whatever they need, without tolls'.

19 The monks of Chester were granted 'free entrance and exit from his land, of licence to buy and sell, of exemption from tolls, etc. in all his ports, and of fishing rights off his coast', (J. Tait (ed.), *The Chartulary or Register of the Abbey of St Werburgh, Chester*, Chetham Society, new ser., 79 (1920), 211.

20 K.J. Stringer, *The reformed church in medieval Galloway and Cumbria: contrasts, connections and continuities. The Eleventh Whithorn lecture 14 September 2002* (Friends of Whithorn Trust, Whithorn, 2003), 54.

21 Oliver, *Monumenta*, ii, 1–6; W. Harrison, *An account of the Diocese of Sodor and Man and St German's cathedral also a record of the bishops of Sodor and Man and a tabular statement of the rectors, vicars and chaplains in the seventeen parishes in said diocese with the date of their appointment and cause of vacancy*, Manx Society, Vol.29 (Douglas, 1879), 55–7; see also, Alex Woolf in chapter 15, this volume.

22 Barratt, 'The Franciscan friary at Bymacan', 209.

23 P.J. Davey and J. Roscow, *Rushen Abbey and the Dissolution of the Monasteries on the Isle of Man*, Isle of Man Natural History and Antiquarian Society Monograph, forthcoming.

24 Broderick, *CKMI*, fol. 40r.

25 Broderick, *CKMI*, fol. 54r.

26 See, for example, J. Woods, *A new atlas & gazetteer of the Isle of Man, consisting of seventeen highly-finished maps, compiled from original and authentic sources, describing the civil and ecclesiastical boundaries of each parish, and the boundaries of the several baronies, freeholds, and quarterlands, as well as the boundaries of the several farms as they are now held in possession* (London, 1867), 24.

27 Broderick, *PNIM*, *s.n.* Grange Farm.
28 *Manx Advertiser*, 46, 1818.
29 See Davey and Roscow, *Rushen Abbey and the Dissolution of the Monasteries on the Isle of Man*, forthcoming.
30 Oliver, *Monumenta*, ii, 1–3.
31 *Coucher Book of Furness*, 11.
32 Coppack, *The White Monks*, 48.
33 Oliver, *Monumenta*, ii, 10–11.
34 Oliver, *Monumenta*, ii, 17–18.
35 Broderick, *CKMI*, fol. 40v.
36 B.R.S. Megaw, 'The original site of Rushen abbey and its significance', in P.J. Davey (ed.) *Recent Archaeological Research in the Isle of Man*, British Archaeological Reports, British Series 278 (Oxford, 1999), 261–5.
37 For Wales, see for example, D.H. Williams, *The Welsh Cistercians* (Pontypool, 1969), 28–34.
38 A.M. Cubbon, 'The medieval chapel of St Mary's, Castletown later the Castletown Grammar School', *Proceedings*, VII, No 3 (1971), 307–42.
39 P.J. Davey (ed.), *Rushen Abbey, Ballasalla, Isle of Man: second archaeological report*, Centre for Manx Studies Research Report 7 (Douglas, 1999).
40 In Davey and Roscow, *Rushen Abbey and the Dissolution of the Monasteries on the Isle of Man*, forthcoming.
41 These lands had certainly been taken over by the time of the *Limites terrarum monachorum c.* 1280.
42 Wilson (ed.), *Register of St Bees*, no. 46.
43 In Davey and Roscow, *Rushen Abbey and the Dissolution of the Monasteries on the Isle of Man*, forthcoming.
44 W. Harrison (ed.), *A History of the Isle of Man written by William Blundell, Esq of Crosby, County Lancaster 1648–1656*, printed from a manuscript in the possession of the Manx Society, Volume 11 (Douglas, 1877), 56–8.
45 In Davey and Roscow, *Rushen Abbey and the Dissolution of the Monasteries on the Isle of Man*, forthcoming.
46 Oliver, *Monumenta*, ii, 8–12.
47 In Davey and Roscow, *Rushen Abbey and the Dissolution of the Monasteries on the Isle of Man*, forthcoming.
48 In Davey and Roscow, *Rushen Abbey and the Dissolution of the Monasteries on the Isle of Man*, forthcoming.
49 Davey (ed.), *Rushen Abbey*.
50 See Roger Stalley, *The Cistercian monasteries of Ireland* (London and New Haven, 1987), 53–4, for the size of Irish Cistercian cloisters; only Bective II, a fifteenth century rebuild, approaches the smallness of Rushen.
51 See especially the series of interim reports of the Billown excavations, Darvill 1995–9.
52 See J. de Pange, *Comment se fait un roi* (Paris, 1937) for a discussion of the unusual role of Westminster abbey in relation to English kingship.
53 B.D. Hill, *English Cistercian monasteries and their patrons in the twelfth century* (Chicago, 1968), 92–3.
54 Coppack, *The White Monks*, 17.
55 Coppack, *The White Monks*, 18–19.
56 Hill, *English Cistercian monasteries*, especially chapter 3 on 'the congregation of Savigny and its impact on the Cistercian order' (pp.80–115).
57 Hill, *English Cistercian monasteries*, 105–6.

58 Hill, *English Cistercian monasteries*, 108–10.
59 In Davey and Roscow, *Rushen Abbey and the Dissolution of the Monasteries on the Isle of Man*, forthcoming.
60 Davey (ed.), *Rushen Abbey*.
61 See Stalley, *Cistercian monasteries of Ireland*, 198, 244
62 Melrose in the Borders comes nearest, being founded in 1136 and dedicated in 1146.
63 See chapter 15 above, pp. 334–6.
64 Harrison (ed.), *History of the Isle of Man written by William Blundell*, 55; see also Surtees Society, vol. 113, 'The records of the Northern Convocation', 374–5.
65 See Munch (ed.), *Chronica Regum Manniae*, ii, 274–84.
66 Broderick, *CKMI*, fol. 49v.; the first actual mention of the castle is under the year 1265.
67 See the discussion by Bernadette Williams, in chapter 14 above.
68 In Davey and Roscow, *Rushen Abbey and the Dissolution of the Monasteries on the Isle of Man*, forthcoming.
69 In Davey and Roscow, *Rushen Abbey and the Dissolution of the Monasteries on the Isle of Man*, forthcoming.
70 Munch (ed.), *Chronica Regum Manniae*, ii, 387–8.
71 See R.A. Donkin, *The Cistercians: studies in the geography of medieval England and Wales*, Pontifical Institute of Medieval Studies (Toronto, 1978), 110–11.
72 *Coucher Book of Furness*, ii, 95, and iii, 510–13.
73 *Coucher Book of Furness*, ii, 792–3.
74 *Taxatio Ecclesiastica Angliae et Walliae Auctoritate P Nicholai IV, circa A.D. 1291* (London, 1802), 309.
75 The rent was £1 6s. 8d. and in the early eighteenth the land was recorded as 'the Four Nobles', that is four time. 6s. 8d. or £1 6s. 8d. See also, Davey and Roscow, *Rushen Abbey and the Dissolution of the Monasteries on the Isle of Man*, forthcoming.
76 Broderick, *CKMI*, fol. 49v.; Munch (ed.), *Chronica Regum Manniae*, ii, 323–33; R.I. Lustig, 'The Treaty of Perth: a re-examination' *SHR*, viii (1979), 35–57.
77 Oliver, *Monumenta*, ii, 235–46 for a transcription and translation of the charter from Henry IV to Sir John Stanley.
78 For example, the confirmation of grants to Whithorn by Prince Alexander of Scotland *c.*1280 and of the St Bees lands by Thomas Randolph, earl of Moray, in 1329.
79 Harrison (ed.), *History of the Isle of Man written by William Blundell*, 58.
80 Broderick, *CKMI*, fol. 51r.; see the discussion by Alex Woolf in this volume, chapter 15.
81 Oliver, *Monumenta*, ii, 133–34.
82 W. Harrison (ed.), *A description of the Isle of Man: with some useful and entertaining reflections on the laws, customs, and manners of the inhabitants, by George Waldron, Gent., late of Queen's College, Oxon. Printed for the widow and orphans, MDCCXXXI*, Manx Society, Vol.11 (Douglas, 1865), 59–60.
83 Munch (ed.), *Chronica Regum Manniae*, ii, 382–4.
84 Barratt, 'The Franciscan friary at Bymacan', 209–10.
85 J.F. Gill (ed.), *The Statutes of the Isle of Man, Volume 1, from A.D.1414 to A.D. 1824* (London, 1883), 8–20.
86 Gill (ed.), *Statutes of the Isle of Man*, 20–2; Gillespie 1994, 43–4.
87 Gill (ed.), *The Statutes of the Isle of Man*.
88 For a detailed account of this building and its history see Cubbon, 'The medieval

chapel of St Mary's, Castletown'.

89 P.J. Davey, D.J. Freke, and D.A. Higgins, *Excavations in Castletown, Isle of Man 1989–1992* (Liverpool, 1996), 8–9.

90 J. Quine, 'Rushen abbey', *Yn Lioar Manninagh*, III (1899–1902), 405.

91 Cubbon, 'The medieval chapel of St Mary's, Castletown', 26–7, found no evidence for inserted masonry.

92 In 1506 one Thomas Clerke rented '1 chamber near the Chapel' for 4d (J. Roscow, 'Appendix 1 – Castletown cottages', in Davey *et al.*, *Excavations in Castletown*, 157–60, 158).

93 Cubbon, 'The medieval chapel of St Mary's, Castletown', 326.

94 For example, at Fountains abbey the early timber church had an internal width of 4.8m and the first stone building about 6m (Coppack, *The White Monks*, 27–33).

95 Williams, *The Welsh Cistercians*, 29–30.

96 In Davey and Roscow, *Rushen Abbey and the Dissolution of the Monasteries on the Isle of Man*, forthcoming.

97 Roscow in Davey *et al.*, Excavations in Castletown, 157–60.

98 S. Thompson, 'Why English nunneries had no history: a study of the problem of English nunneries founded after the conquest', in J.A. Nichols and L.T. Shank (eds), *Medieval religious women 1, Distant echoes*, Cistercian Publications (Kalamazoo, 1984), 131–49.

99 Broderick, *CKMI*, fol. 50r.

100 Anon 1931, 21.

101 Oliver, *Monumenta*, ii, 247–50.

102 Broderick, *CKMI*, fol. 40v.

103 See S. Thompson, *Women Religious: the founding of English nunneries after the Norman Conquest* (Oxford, 1991), 94–6; Coppack, *The White Monks*, 57–60.

104 Coppack, *The White Monks*, 94.

105 Coppack, *The White Monks*, 96–8.

106 Thompson, 'Why English nunneries had no history', 136.

107 In Davey and Roscow, *Rushen Abbey and the Dissolution of the Monasteries on the Isle of Man*, forthcoming.

108 G. Jefferson, 1819, *Lex Scripta*, Douglas and London, 5.

109 In Davey and Roscow, *Rushen Abbey and the Dissolution of the Monasteries on the Isle of Man*, forthcoming.

110 Harrison (ed.), *History of the Isle of Man written by William Blundell*, 163.

111 J.G. Cumming (ed.), *A short treatise of the Isle of Man, digested into six chapters, by James Chaloner, one of the commissioners under Lord Fairfax, for settling the affairs of the Isle of Man in 1652; and afterwards Governor of the island, from 1658 to 1660. Originally published in 1656, as an appendix to 'King's Vale Royal of England; or, the County Palatine of Chester, illustrated*, Manx Society, Vol.10 (Douglas, 1864), plate opposite p.16.

112 Harrison (ed.), *A description of the Isle of Man*, 44–6.

113 T. Talbot, *The Priory of Whithern (Candida Casa), and its lands and churches in Mann*, privately published (*c.*1990) (MML F22/17), Charter 1.

114 Talbot, *The Priory of Whithern*, Charters 2 to 8.

115 Talbot, *The Priory of Whithern*, Charters 9 to 11.

116 B.R.S. Megaw, 'The Barony of St Trinian's in the Isle of Man', *Transactions of the Dumfriesshire and Galloway natural History and Antiquarian Society*, xxvii (1950), 173–82.

117 Megaw, 'The Barony of St Trinian's', 180–1.

118 E. Megaw, 'The cult of St Leonard and Manx medieval hospitals', *JMM*, vii, No.88 (1976), 225–31, 229.
119 Kermode, in *Proceedings*, new ser., 1, 328–32.
120 Broderick, *CKMI*, fol. 36v.
121 See p. 370 below.
122 For example, in the 1505 charter from Thomas, earl of Derby, in Oliver, *Monumenta*, iii, 29–30.
123 Wilson (ed.), *Register of St Bees*, no.43.
124 Wilson (ed.), *Register of St Bees*, no.44.
125 In Davey and Roscow, *Rushen Abbey and the Dissolution of the Monasteries on the Isle of Man*, forthcoming.
126 Megaw suggests that this dispute was the occasion for the writing of the *Limites terrarum monachorum* as a ligitimisation of Rushen's claim (Megaw, 'Norsemen and native', 271).
127 G Jefferson, 1819, *Lex Scripta*, Douglas and London, 5.
128 *Lex Scripta*, 5.
129 B.R.S. Megaw, 'The barony of Bangor and Sabal in Kirk Patrick: remarkable survival of the Middle Ages', *JMM*, 4, no. 60 (1939), 135–8, 135.
130 George Broderick, 'The baronial possessions of Bangor and Saul in Man', *Bulletin of the Ulster Place-name Society*, Ser 2, 4 (1981–2), 25; he is confused about directions – the farms centred on Dalby are south (and not north) of those centred on Glenmaye.
131 B.R.S. Megaw, 'The barony of Bangor and Sabal in Kirk Patrick: an account of its origin', *JMM*, iv, no. 61 (1939), 159–60, 160.
132 See Roscow on the increase of cottagers' rents in Ballasalla at the dissolution, in Davey and Roscow, *Rushen Abbey and the Dissolution of the Monasteries on the Isle of Man*, forthcoming.
133 Megaw, 'The barony of Bangor and Sabal in Kirk Patrick: remarkable survival of the Middle Ages', 137.
134 Megaw, 'The barony of Bangor and Sabal in Kirk Patrick: an account of its origin', 159.
135 *Coucher Book of Furness*, 658; cf. also Oliver, *Monumenta*, iii, 36.
136 Oliver, *Monumenta*, iii, 145.
137 *Coucher Book of Furness*, 713.
138 *Coucher Book of Furness*, 658.
139 Such as Eudo and Nicholas de Meaux, (Harrison (ed.)), *History of the Isle of Man written by William Blundell*, 55–6.
140 Such as William Russell who was abbot for 18 years and bishop for 26 in the mid-fourteenth century (Harrison (ed.)), *History of the Isle of Man written by William Blundell*, 60.
141 *Coucher Book of Furness*, 711–12.
142 For example, one recorded in the Castle Rushen Papers in the Manx Museum in 1511 that also involved Whithorn.
143 Furness even collected the one mark rent for Bretby (*Coucher Book of Furness*, iii (1887), 511–13).
144 Munch (ed.), *Chronica Regum Manniae*, ii, 382–4.
145 *Calendar of Papal Letters*, Vol.IV, 1902, 186.
146 Gill (ed.), *The Statutes of the Isle of Man*, 20–2.
147 Barratt, 'The Franciscan friary at Bymacan', 211–13.
148 See Woods, *A new atlas & gazettteer of the Isle of Man*, 45.
149 In Davey and Roscow, *Rushen Abbey and the Dissolution of the Monasteries on*

the Isle of Man, forthcoming.

150 Oliver, *Monumenta*, iii, 101–2.

151 J.A. Twemlow (ed.), *Calendar of entries in the Papal Registers relating to Great Britain and Ireland*, Vol.XIII, Papal Letters 1471–84, HMSO (London, 1955), 324.

152 In Davey and Roscow, *Rushen Abbey and the Dissolution of the Monasteries on the Isle of Man*, forthcoming.

153 Megaw, 'The Barony of St Trinian's', 182.

154 Oliver, *Monumenta*, iii, 145.

155 Section 1 (1) of the Minerals Act 1986 vests all mines and minerals in the Isle of Man in the Department of Industry. Schedule 1(1) excepts mines or minerals 'in any land which was not subject to the provision of section 16 of the Act of Settlement 1704 until the expiry of 27 years from the commencement of section 1.' *Acts of Tynwald 1986*, 1199–1200; 1230–1.

156 For example, Bangor and Sabal (Megaw, 'The barony of Bangor and Sabal in Kirk Patrick: remarkable survival of the Middle Ages', 138).

17 *Economy and Trade in Medieval Man*

DAVID DITCHBURN and BENJAMIN T. HUDSON

The Isle of Man possessed the finest land in the Isles. That, at least, was the verdict of the thirteenth-century Icelandic writer Snorri Sturluson.[1] Snorri was not alone in holding this view. The relative lushness of Man when compared with surrounding regions seems also to be reflected in a late twelfth-century Irish poem, written in praise of the Manx King Rögnvaldr (r.1187–1228), which employs the symbolism of apple trees to depict the island's fruitfulness.[2] (see Fig. 13.1) While caution must be applied in reading too much into such flattering comment – and the Northumbrian writer Bede was adamant that Anglesey was more fertile than Man – the economy of the Isle of Man in the Middle Ages was undoubtedly a product of its environment.[3] With its upland grazings, heathland, streams, patches of blanket peat and more fertile coastal land, it was an environment similar to that of Ireland: two-thirds of the total flora and fauna found in Ireland are also evident in Man, which has only two-fifths of the total found in Britain.[4]

Yet the medieval centuries witnessed significant alterations in the Manx landscape. At the root of these changes were climatic and demographic factors. Climatological studies suggest that from about 1000 until the later thirteenth century northern Europe generally witnessed a period of comparatively mild weather, which facilitated agricultural production. Climatic warming was accompanied by population growth, which continued in most parts of Europe until the later thirteenth century. Old forests, especially stands of oak, disappeared throughout Christendom as land was newly ploughed to feed the growing population – to the extent that when Suger, abbot of St Denis, near Paris, was supervising the construction of his great church, his discovery of oak trees tall enough to complete the building was considered a miracle and a sign of divine favour.[5] From the fourteenth century, however, cooler and wetter meteorological trends prevailed and the frequency of poor harvests increased. Population levels began to stagnate and in many areas fall, even before the massive haemorrhage in numbers in the mid-fourteenth century caused by the Black Death. This, and subsequent outbreaks of plague, were to scourge Christendom repeatedly for the remainder of the Middle Ages.

It seems unlikely that Man was isolated from the climatological and demographic trends that affected its neighbours. Specifically Manx evidence of these developments is, nonetheless, scarce. Still, if farmsteads were, indeed, established at higher, less fertile altitudes between 1050 and 1250 – for instance on the hills above Sulby River – this was presumably because lower, more productive land was already occupied.[6] Meanwhile, the disappearance of the great oak forests that had once covered the island is also suggestive of population growth between *c.*1000 and *c.*1300: presumably trees were felled in order to cultivate land, as well as for fuel and to build houses and ships. On the Isle of Man deforestation was ultimately severe. By the Early Modern era 'all timber for construction work and other purposes had to be imported'.[7] The change was, of course, gradual. Gaelic and Norse place names indicate the presence of ash, elder, holly, oak and yew. In 1079 King Godred Crovan was still able to hide his 300-strong army in a wood and there appears to have been at least a 'thicket' at Myerscough at late as 1249.[8] Still, the increasing scarcity of Manx timber is reflected early. In 1098 Magnus Barelegs ordered the shipment of timber from Galloway to Man. While this arguably reveals more about Gallovidian submission to the Norwegian king than it does of Manx deforestation, the gesture would have been pointless had Man been awash with woodland. Even more tellingly, perhaps, the Viking house at Braaid boasted wooden gable ends but its walls were made of turf.[9] With timber apparently scarce even by the eleventh century, the collection of peat and turf for fuel and construction seems to have become an essential, its cutting and drying carried out while livestock was herded on the summer pastures.

If timber shortage is, indeed, indicative of population growth in the high Middle Ages, it seems unlikely that demographic expansion continued into the fourteenth century, despite the surely inaccurate claims of the vicar of Malew in 1368 that his parish was then more populous than it had once been.[10] Admittedly, he did not define 'once'. Admittedly too, evidence of the Black Death's impact on Man is elusive. It seems unwise, however, to interpret the silence of Manx sources as indicative of insular isolation from this deadly virus.[11] An Icelandic report of 1349 suggests that the Western and Northern Isles did not escape the ravages of plague; and adjacent parts of both Ireland and England certainly suffered.[12] In surrounding countries, as plague became endemic, population continued to decline, reaching a nadir in the later fourteenth and early fifteenth centuries. By then some landlords could no longer find any tenants to farm their lands: the ensuing labour shortage had enabled peasants to bargain for better tenurial terms and conditions from their increasingly impecunious landlords. That in 1422 Manx peasants had to be reminded of ancient agricultural duties, suggests a high turnover in peasant manpower; that, by then, draconian laws had also been introduced to forbid emigration without the lord of

Man's specific licence smacks of an attempt to conserve the island's manpower.[13] Yet, if these are indications of later medieval depopulation, the demographic crisis was probably not as profound as that encountered in some other countries. The abandonment of up to half the farms in some areas of Norway stimulated reforestation.[14] No such trend is evident on the Isle of Man.

Environmental changes were not, however, merely the result of demographic expansion and contraction. The Manx landscape was also moulded by the dietary and financial expectations (of landlords in particular) and by tenurial traditions and the limitations of agricultural technology. Remarkably little is known about the island's landowners and tenants before the sixteenth century. Still, it is clear that the demise of the native kingship in 1265 presaged a fundamental change in the character of the island's chief landholder. Normally resident and originally of Hiberno-Norse stock, and presumably with tastes and demands fashioned by such a background, the ruling dynasty was replaced in 1265 by a series of usually absentee lords of originally Anglo-French descent. In their wake came other, lesser men too, such as the Yorkshire knight Brian Stapleton, whose signet ring was recently excavated at Peel, and who was granted land at Appyn in Glenfaban in 1377.[15] The culinary fads of these newcomers were born of northern French agricultural circumstances and by choice this was a wheat-eating and wine-drinking aristocracy. This is not to argue that previous Manx rulers had not enjoyed their imported wheat and wine; at least some clearly had. Nevertheless, their consumption of these products is likely to have been tempered by a sensitive appraisal of the agricultural potential of their insular homeland. Vine cultivation was, of course, an environmental impossibility in the Isle of Man. Wheat was different. Some was certainly grown on Man, but, as we shall see presently, it was not the cereal crop best suited to the Manx climate. It is significant that wheat and wine were deemed honourable gifts to Manx kings in the thirteenth century; and that local bishops found it necessary to stipulate that the Host should be made of wheat and that communion wine should not be diluted with vinegar.[16] Wheat and wine were scarce commodities. They were also status symbols and natives recognised luxuries when they devoured them. On the other hand, for the new lords of the later medieval period these were not luxuries. They were culturally determined necessities. Their acquisition required either shipments from abroad or instruction to tenants to skew arable production in order to deliver a higher proportion of wheat – something that seems to have been attempted by Scottish landlords in the fifteenth century.[17] But there was also a third option. With significant landed possessions elsewhere, Man's new lords could choose to live abroad; and most did. Indeed, although absenteeism is perhaps best explained in political terms, the island's inability to provide adequate and fitting fare for its lords may have been a contributory factor in their decision to reside elsewhere.

Absenteeism and, in origin, French culinary tastes were not an attribute unique to the island's secular overlords. These were characteristics shared by many ecclesiastical landlords too. From the twelfth century extensive Manx estates were owned by the local bishop and by monastic houses, many of which were based in adjacent countries. The acquisition of these properties is perhaps best explained in terms of conventional piety. This was expressed in terms of landed donations granted to the church by both Manx kings and private individuals such as Benedict of Penigtona and his brother Maldred, who bequeathed Skeldou to the abbey of Rushen.[18] Pieced together, these donations made for sizeable territorial agglomerations. The extent of Rushen's acquisitions is evident from the partial survey of the abbey's holdings appended to the Manx chronicle.[19] Rushen's monks were not, however, the only beneficiary of such pious generosity. The Manx king Guðröðr (r.1153–87) donated lands at Eschedal (now Groudle Glen) and Asmundertofts (now Ballellin) to the Cumbrian priory of St Bees, which by then already possessed Evastad (unidentified). More followed. Guðröðr's son, Rögnvaldr (r. 1187–1228), was soon to grant the same monks Ormesham (possibly now Onchan) while Cornaa was among further lands bestowed upon the priory by Thomas Randolph, earl of Moray, the island's Scottish overlord, in the early fourteenth century.[20] St Bees was exceptional only in that its acquisitions have been preserved in the priory's register. Although we are less well informed about other recipients, the Lancastrian abbey of Furness certainly acquired property on the island, along with patronage of the churches of Kirk Michael and Maughold;[21] the Irish houses of Bangor and Saul obtained a barony in the parish of Kirk Patrick;[22] and, despite the vicissitudes of Anglo-Scottish warfare in the fourteenth century, the Scottish cathedral abbey of Whithorn managed to obtain, and then retain, possession of the inland barony of St Trinian's, together with patronage of the churches of St Bride (near Point of Ayre), St Runan (at Old Kirk Marown) and Holy Trinity (at Lezayre).[23]

These ecclesiastical landlords and their secular counterparts expected rents from their lands and these might be delivered in either cash or kind. Several ecclesiastical institutions further benefited from the collection of tithes owed to those churches whose patronage they had appropriated. Payable by all parishioners, tithes were based upon Old Testament enactment and intended for the upkeep of the entire church and its clerics. In ecclesiastical theory it mattered not if a significant proportion of one parish's income (let us say, that of St Bride's) was diverted into the coffers of another ecclesiastical body (say, that of Whithorn cathedral). Supposedly levied at the rate of a tenth on the proceeds of all agricultural and manufactured produce, tithes were a potentially lucrative asset. The specific obligations of Manx tithe payers are outlined in the synodal statutes of the Manx church, which date from the thirteenth century. Nevertheless, probably because they are one of the few extant sources to reveal much about the island's medieval economy, these statutes have generated much uninformed discussion of allegedly hapless Manx peasants being exploited by a greedy Catholic church.[24] In the early thirteenth century there was, indeed, some resentment against the attempt to extend tithe collection to butter and cheese production in the diocese of the Isles, though it seems not to have provoked the wrath which led unusually disgruntled parishioners in Caithness to murder the local bishop, a particularly innovative and zealous collector of tithes, in 1222.[25] This discontent was a perhaps predictable development as local anomalies and exemptions in collection were gradually eradicated across Christendom. Indeed, local peculiarities were never fully snuffed out and in Man too it remains uncertain whether the theoretical range of titheable assets, described in the synodal statutes, correlated with what was actually collected from lay society. Of course, all tithes were burdensome to the poorest among the peasantry. But since tithes of some description were a universal exaction, common to all of Christendom, it is quite misleading to argue that the Manx population was unduly burdened by them. To suggest as much smacks more of later Protestant hubris than of historical accuracy.

Rents and tithes were not the only exactions imposed on the island's population. Taxes too were levied, at least occasionally: the Manx chronicle notes that between 1223 and 1226 King Rögnvaldr levied 100 marks from the islanders ostensibly to pay for his expenses for travelling to England; and that Bishop Mark (1275–1303) levied a tax of one penny, on households boasting a fireplace, to pay for the lifting of an interdict.[26] Further exactions, though of a different genre, were also imposed on some of the island's chief landholders. The papacy collected tribute from Manx kings of the thirteenth century in recognition of their feudal subservience.[27] The Cistercian order of monks also raised funds from its houses throughout Christendom in order to pay papal taxation and to defray the costs of its annual assembly of abbots, held at Cîteaux in France. It seems unlikely that Rushen abbey was exempted from these mandatory levies, which were imposed from 1250. Rushen, admittedly, is not readily identifiable in the order's earliest tax book, which dates from the later thirteenth or early fourteenth century. If, however, it can be equated with the otherwise unidentifiable house of 'Appennea', its assessment amounted to 15 *livre tournois*. This was a comparatively modest sum. Although roughly on a par with that of poorer Scottish abbeys such as Deer and Newbattle, it was considerably less than the exaction imposed upon Rushen's mother-house of Furness.[28] Rushen, we may suppose, may have been a wealthy landowner in Manx terms, but it was small fry in the wider Cistercian family.

Individual clergymen too were subjected to papal levies. By the thirteenth century, for example, the newly established papal penitentiary was charging supplicants a fee for processing dispensations from canon law. The early penitentiary records have not survived, but by the fifteenth century some Manxmen – such as Christian Prior, the illegitimate son of a Rushen monk – were paying dues for such favours.[29] During the fourteenth century the papacy also began to impose a one-off tax on a number of appointments to ecclesiastical office. Bishops, for instance, who were appointed directly by the pope, became liable for payment of 'common services'. These normally amounted to a third of the estimated gross annual income of their office, and after William Russell was elevated to episcopal office in the diocese of Sodor in 1349, his common services were assessed at 600 gold florins. Though markedly higher than the assessments for both the nearby sees of Argyll and Galloway in Scotland and for those of Bangor and St Asaph in Wales, when set in a wider context the Manx assessment amounted to a comparatively small valuation – smaller than that for every English diocese and less than that for a majority of those in Scotland too.[30] Nevertheless, Russell appears to have been unable to raise his dues immediately. To meet these and other expenses of office he was granted papal permission to raise a loan of 1,200 gold florins.[31]

Russell's financial problems and his recourse to moneylenders were far from unique. Many of his episcopal colleagues elsewhere in Christendom responded to similar demands with similar measures. Of far greater significance for present purposes is the indication that Man's ecclesiastical landlords were part of an international system of taxation. This meant not just that money had to be raised to pay international obligations, but also that mechanisms had to be devised for the transfer of capital abroad. Absentee landowners, of course, were faced with the similar predicament: how, exactly, were the profits from their Manx landholdings and tithes to be transferred to their own distant coffers? We may suppose that rents, tithes and taxes paid in kind could be sold on the open market. This, at any rate, was a practice well established among absentee Irish landlords by the thirteenth century.[32] Alternatively, levies paid in both cash or kind could be shipped abroad for more distant enjoyment by their recipients – in the case of Whithorn, in the company of monastic agents who perhaps travelled with the Manx pilgrims who were apparently visiting St Ninian's shrine on a regular basis by at least the 1420s.[33] More certainly, on at least one occasion Bishop Russell entrusted part of his papal dues to 'the hands of brother Thomas of Cakan and Alexander of Carlisle, his domestic' for direct delivery to the papal treasury in Avignon. Given the dangers posed by pirates and brigands on such a lengthy journey, this was a risky undertaking and perhaps explains why, in the early thirteenth century, King Rögnvaldr had arranged to dispatch his annual papal tribute no further than Furness abbey, where it was presumably collected by agents or bankers acting on the pope's behalf. Indeed, on a subsequent occasion, Bishop Russell preferred the even safer option of engaging the services of the Alberti, a Florentine banking house, to deliver a further instalment of his common services.[34] However geographically and commercially remote from the great cities of Christendom, where the still largely Italian cohort of medieval bankers plied their business, Manx kings and clerics still found access to banking services. Sadly how they did so, and whether others on the Isle of Man did likewise, remains unknown.

We may doubt, however, whether the great majority of the Manx population had need of banking services. If prayer (on behalf of all) was the primary social function of clerics, and combat (in defence of all) the accepted social function of nobles, it was the duty of the third and largest section of medieval society to work, and through its toil to support the clerics and nobles as well as itself. For the vast majority of the medieval Manx population, work meant agricultural endeavour. Throughout the period the basic farming unit on the Isle of Man remained the quarterland, the estate of a single family. Approximately four quarterlands were originally encompassed in a *treen*, a term possibly derived from *tír uinge*, literally 'an ounce of land' – an ounceland being the amount of land which originally paid tax (or rent?) to the value of one ounce of silver. The origin of these units, which can be found in western and northern Scotland too, remains a matter of debate. Many have argued that they were of earlier Celtic, rather than of later Scandinavian, origin and they may have been an arable equivalent of the seventh-century cow lands (*tír-mbó*) to be found in Ireland. A more recent argument favours a Welsh or English derivation. There is also the possibility that land divisions and administration were influenced by Carolingian practices in continental Europe. On Man, local authority was represented by the *moar*, equivalent to Welsh and Irish *maer*, the name derived from the *major domus* of late antiquity who among the Franks had become the so-called 'mayor of the palace'. It is not impossible that the clergy from Britain and Ireland who frequented the Carolingian courts used the land divisions found among the Franks for the organisation of church lands; from there it could have passed to the general populace.[35] Yet, whatever the origin of quarterlands, it is significant that they survived, for this suggests little innovation in the use to which land was actually put during the medieval period. Treens, however, were apparently less enduring. What lies behind their hitherto unexplained absence from church lands remains conjectural. Their disappearance, if such it was, may reflect nothing more than the desuetude of the ancient tax system to which they owed their name or the mere chance of onomastic survivals elsewhere. Alternatively, the lack of treens on ecclesiastical lands may reflect tenurial tampering by ecclesiastical landlords, among whom the Cistercians, in particular, were internationally famed for their pioneering methods of agricultural cultivation.[36]

It is difficult, however, to detect significant differences between the uses to which secular and ecclesiastical land was put. Arable farming was already well established by the medieval period. The Viking settlers appear, at least to some extent, to have been dependent on cereals. A Norse burial at Cronk Moar has plough lines running under it and it has been postulated that Hiberno-Norse immigrants of the eleventh century were responsible for land reclamation along the morainic northern shores of the island.[37] More specifically, wheat, barley, and oats were all grown, as apparently were some vegetables. All are mentioned as commodities upon which the church might expect to claim tithes.[38] Nevertheless, Gerald of Wales noted for Ireland, and it was probably true of the Isle of Man too, that the Irish varieties of grain – he specifically includes wheat, rye and oats – produced small kernels which were difficult to separate from the chaff during threshing.[39] The relative importance of these crops, and their yields, remains uncertain. It may be presumed that the aristocracy and monastic communities preferred their bread wheaten, as they did elsewhere, and that either market forces or aristocratic diktat encouraged peasant farmers to sow their fields accordingly. Nevertheless, it was barley and flour made from unspecified corn that was delivered to the Scottish crown from the island in 1329.[40] Oats, together with the hardy variety of barley known as bere, certainly predominated over climatologically more sensitive wheat in the more northerly isles, Galloway and Gaelic Ireland. Medieval returns on all crops were, however, miserly when compared to the norms of twenty-first-century agriculture. Cultivators of wheat expected a return of as low as 2:1 in parts of northern Europe, and many French, Irish and Scottish wheat producers expected no more than a yield of 4:1.[41] In part such poor returns were a reflection of soil exhaustion and inadequate fertilisation. It seems likely that Man too suffered from such afflictions, for in 1422 tenants had to be reminded of the importance of manuring their lands.[42] Yet, though grain was undoubtedly grown on Man, and delivered in rent to landlords, it is perhaps significant that the Manx chronicle includes not one reference to grain.[43]

If the cultivation of cereals, albeit in limited quantities, was of ancient tradition, other crops were newly introduced into the island during the medieval period, especially through the conduit of the new monastic orders. The local distribution and densities of herbs nowadays is a sign of cultivation in the past, as plants from cottage gardens seeded their immediate environs. In Man this could explain the concentrations of claimint in the north and elecompane in the south, to take two examples. It has also been suggested that the introduction of watercress in the south of the island, and rabbits, might have been pioneered by the monastic community at Rushen.[44] Mention of rabbits leads on to consideration of livestock farming which is better documented than arable cultivation. Stock-raising had an ancient importance on the Isle of Man and physical reminders of it are to be found throughout the island. Evidence for peasant co-operation in stock-tending is provided by the dikes and hedgerow lanes. These barriers would not only have enclosed livestock; they were also useful for directing the movement of livestock. Indeed, the remains of hedgerows have been used to identify early drove roads. A rough estimation of the antiquity of these roads can be gauged by the number of bramble varieties to be found in adjacent hedgerows; a hedge with ten species may date to the later ninth or early tenth centuries (the early Norse period), while nine varieties suggest an eleventh-century date, contemporary with King Godred Crovan.[45] The maintenance of some early medieval roadways illustrates the continued importance of grazing and herding in the later medieval Manx economy. Charter evidence dating from the later twelfth century further illustrates the value placed on cattle, sheep and swine herds. A charter granted by Óláfr son of Godred Crovan (r. *c.*1113–53) to the priory of St Bees gave the community licence to graze 60 head of cattle, although, if they desired, the monks could substitute an equivalent number of sheep or swine; and when Rushen abbey was pillaged by Irish forces, apparently in 1316, it was 'so extensively stripped of its furniture, cattle and sheep, that there was nothing left at all'.[46] The lack of any reference to grain in this report is striking; and the evident importance of livestock, rather than arable farming, to the Manx economy is further demonstrated in the detailed quantities of beef, mutton, pork, lamb and goose with which the first Stanley lord could expect to victual his household in 1422.[47]

It is not only the scarcity of grain that is striking among these examples. So too is the prominence accorded to cattle as opposed to sheep, pigs and horses, a balance also reflected in archaeological excavations.[48] Of course, some sheep and pigs were certainly nurtured on the Isle of Man, as were horses, even if the developments in warfare associated with the arrival of Anglo-French settlers in the British Isles placed a greater worth on heavier horses than the native Manx species. Still, the lighter Manx horses probably retained a local significance and they were perhaps to be numbered among the unspecified colts, which (along with pigs, bullocks and calves) were destined for tithe delivery at Easter.[49] Yet, for all the mixed animal husbandry which characterised agriculture in the British Isles generally, it was wool that in many areas proved the most profitable agricultural product – to such an extent that the early thirteenth-century Scottish landscape had allegedly been transformed by the 'multitude of sheep'.[50] This seems not to have been the case on the Isle of Man. Manx wool is scarcely mentioned outwith the island. Although some might have been mixed with that sold in the Netherlands by Furness abbey, which was not only a landholder on the island but also the mother-house of Rushen, it seems unlikely that the Manx landscape resembled the sheep-ridden pastures familiar to many parts of the British Isles.[51] Instead, the similarity is likely to have been with Gaelic Ireland where sheep and pigs were of secondary importance in animal farming. In Gaelic Ireland and Man cattle were supreme.[52]

Cattle-raising made for a pastoral society characterised by seasonal transhumace. This is illustrated by the place name element *eary* (Old Irish *áirige*, 'dairy'), found in names such as Aresteyne and Eary Glas, which was similar to the *shieling* (cognate with Old Norse *sel*, 'shed on a mountain pasture'), found in many areas of Scandinavian settlement.[53] An *áirige* was the milking place used when the cattle had been moved to the hill pastures for summer grazing; *sel* originally had the same general meaning as *áirige*, but later also came to be used for the hill-grazing of sheep and goats. The Manx *eary* was located at an average altitude of 600 feet, showing the importance of the upland fields in the local economy. Traces of the importance of herding in the medieval Manx economy are further suggested by festivals. It was probably at the beginning of May when cattle were moved from winter to summer pastures; and Old May Day (11 May), which continued to be observed on the Isle of Man into the modern era, might have coincided with the driving of cattle from their winter to summer grazings, as it did in Wales and Ireland. In Old Norse vocabulary the term used to indicate the date for herding livestock to the mountain pastures is *selmána_r*, 'the month for the removal to the *sel*'.

The significance of livestock, and above all cattle, to the Manx economy ensured that meat, and especially beef, figured prominently in the diet of the locals, especially perhaps in the male population.[54] That, at least, is the implication of dental remains from the medieval period: those that belonged to men had accumulated smaller amounts of calculus than those belonging to women – perhaps a consequence of the greater mastication associated with meat consumption. But, in addition to meat, both cattle and sheep yielded milk and at the end of the thirteenth century each house was expected to supply the church with its tithe of 18 cheeses in summer and a further 18 in the autumn, clean and slated. Any house that processed other dairy products was expected also to provide a tithe of them and the penalties for not doing so were, in theory, severe.[55]

The medieval Manx diet was probably further supplemented by large quantities of fish. Fish constituted an important part of medieval menus because of the religious proscription of meat and dairy consumption on Wednesdays, Fridays and Saturdays, during Lent and at other special times. These conventions were introduced in token recognition of human sinfulness and God's retort to Adam: 'cursed is the ground for thy sake'. Since they lived in water fish evaded this curse and, in theory at least, roughly half the days of the year were 'fish days'. Hierarchical notions of society were extended to the water and its inhabitants. At the top of the piscine scale of perfection were porpoise, sturgeon and whale; they were destined for the table of the lord of Man.[56] Humbler folk satisfied themselves with more common species of both sea and fresh-water fish. The right to fish rivers was, however, often guarded by the king: when Rögnvaldr granted Ormesham to the priory of St Bees, he included fishing rights.[57] By the early sixteenth century salmon and white fish occasionally filled the holds of Manx vessels visiting England; and remnants of cod, eel, hake, ling, mackerel, piper, plaice, ray, sea bream and turbot have been excavated at Peel.[58] Herring, however, was the most commonly excavated fish species. It was also the staple of those cargoes sent to England in the sixteenth century and it is reasonable to assume that this was the most abundant species in earlier centuries too, as well as that which was consumed most frequently on the island itself.[59] The archaeological evidence suggests a major expansion of the fishing industry in the eleventh or twelfth centuries and there is some circumstantial documentary support for this hypothesis. During the period of Norse sovereignty over Man and the Isles the legal code *Frostaþing*, compiled in the reign of Hákon IV Hákonarson (1204–63), claimed that Pope Alexander III (1159–81) had recognised the importance of herring and permitted its daily catch except on the most holy of days in the Christian calendar such as Christmas and Easter. The indulgence recognised the need to fish when the opportunity presented itself and demonstrates an unexpected leniency to the otherwise severe penalties for working on Sundays and holy days.[60]

Although Manx medieval society was of an essentially rural

complexion, cereal and animal products were important in the establishment of small-scale industrial activity, which involved women as well as men.[61] Grain, for instance, was used for the brewing of ale, which was probably the staple drink of most of the population.[62] Meanwhile, sheep produced wool and this constituted the essential raw material for a small textile industry. In Man, as well as in the Hebrides and Ireland, woollen cloaks known as *röggvarfeldr* (*fallaing* in Gaelic) were manufactured, their protruding tufts giving them the appearance of shaggy fur. These mantles were widely worn in the island and were even known of in Iceland.[63] In addition, it seems likely that some linen cloth was manufactured. Biologists have noted the presence of flax plants in coastal regions of the island and flax and hemp, the key raw materials for linen manufacture, were among the produce upon which the church expected to levy tithes in the thirteenth century.[64] Initially a tithe of 2d. per year was levied on the sale of three pieces of cloth, although that was the total sum demanded by the church, regardless of the eventual amount of production.[65] Limited ecclesiastical expectation suggests a cloth industry that was small-scale. Its manufactures were probably intended for primarily Manx, rather than overseas, consumers, even though weaving appears to have been a full-time profession for some, since the tithe regulations envisaged contributions from those 'who pay not on other things'.[66] Meanwhile, as elsewhere in the Latin West, animal carcasses probably provided other material for craft activity. Animals provided leather, the essential raw material for the production of jackets, leggings, belts and footwear.

Other industrial activity included the production of pottery, probably for domestic rather than commercial purposes.[67] There was clearly also a metalworking industry of some importance. Even in the tenth century the famous cross at Kirk Michael was made for Melbridge (Máel Brigte), 'the son of Athakan the Smith'.[68] By the late thirteenth century mineral deposits

Fig. 17.1 *The smith's tongs, shown on the left hands side of the photograph, were found with other metal work finds such as the sword, bone-handled knives, harness pieces, stone sharpening hone in the well-furnished burial of a typical farmer-warrior by P.M.C. Kermode in his excavations at Knock y Doonee along with large number of iron bolts that had been used for the construction of the boat in which the man and his horse were buried. Phot courtesy Manx National Heritage.*

Fig. 17.2 *Landscape of the Calf of Man where lead was mined. Edward, First Lord of Man in 1292 issued a warrant to his ally John Comyn which, from the Calendar of the Patent Rolls, read "For Comyn, Earl of Bogham ... he may dig ore of lead in our mines of Calf in the Island aforesaid for covering eight turrets in the Castle of the same John of Cringleton and Gallaweye".*

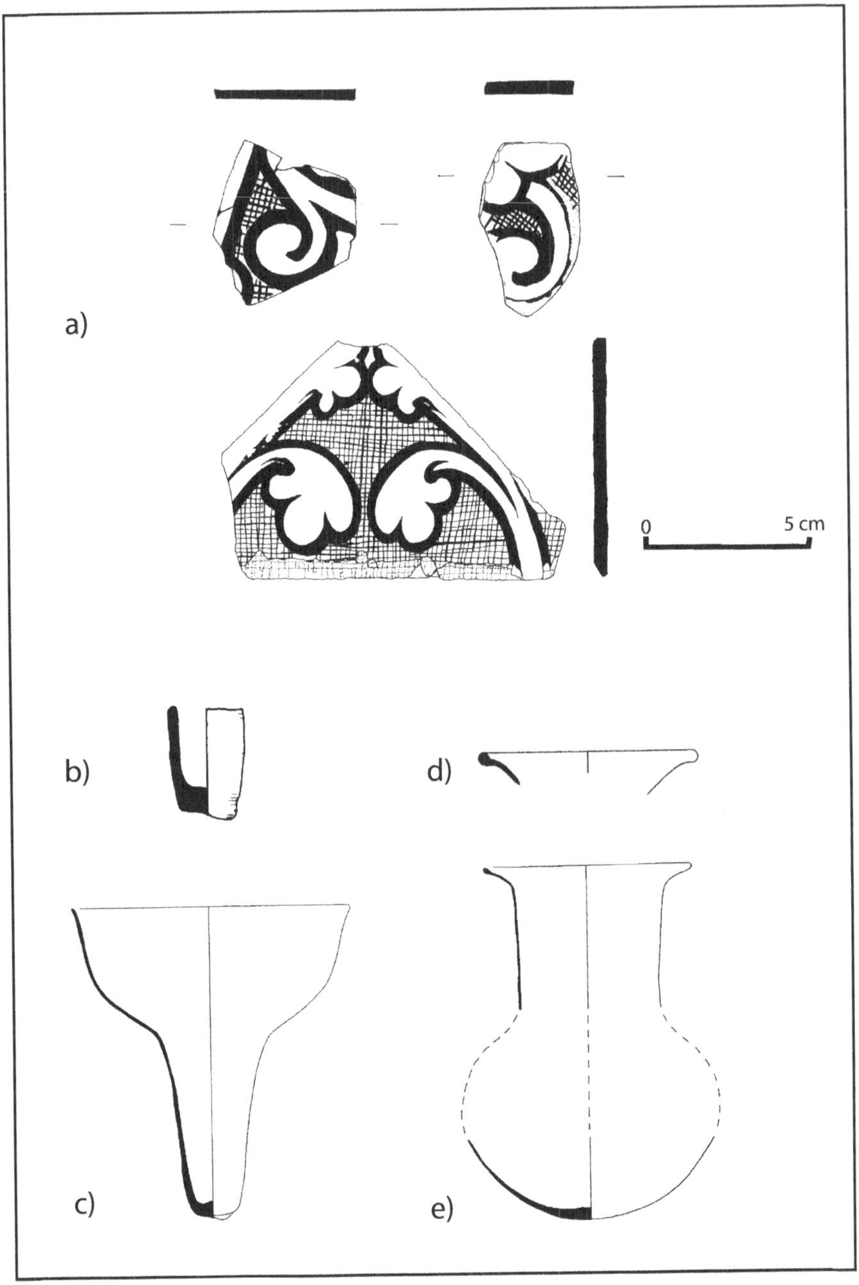
a)
0
5 cm
b)
d)
c)
e)

extracted on the Calf of Man were being sold for use in the construction of Edward I's Welsh castles. Likewise, in 1292, the earl of Buchan received permission to acquire lead in the Calf to cover eight turrets of his castle at Cruggleton in Galloway.[69] There were also reserves of zinc, copper and iron, and archaeology attests to the exploitation of at least the iron deposits, in now otherwise obscure metal workings excavated at Ballavarry, Ballataere and Braddan.[70] Mines and metalworks required metalworkers and the thirteenth-century synodal statutes provide allusions to goldsmiths and makers of scythes or sickles as well as to more mundane smiths.[71] Scythes and sickles, of course, were the essential implements of agricultural activity.

It seems reasonable to assume that medieval Man was not only an overwhelmingly rural society, but one in which industrial production was, by and large, closely related to agricultural activity and undertaken, in the main, as an adjunct to such activity. This, too, is the implication of place names such as Balynessar and Balystere ('farm of the craftsman'), which suggest a lack of industrial exclusivity in the working lives of craftsmen.[72] Yet, it remains difficult to discern the extent to which economic activities focused on individual households were supplemented by commercial interaction and transaction between the island's inhabitants as a whole. Elsewhere in Christendom the classic signs of such activity are to be found in the existence of markets, fairs and towns. Markets (normally weekly events) were chiefly intended for the sale of local produce required for routine daily use. By contrast, fairs (normally annual events) tended to attract merchants from further afield with a correspondingly more exotic range of commodities. Both, however, usually emerged in the vicinity of castles, monasteries, ports or at the intersection of land routes – locations where significant numbers of people congregated, either routinely or for specific occasions, and where merchants and craftsmen expected to find an identifiable group of consumers to purchase their wares and services.

There were several locations on the Isle of Man where one might expect proto-urban nuclei of this variety to have developed. The chronicle of Man indicates that Ramsey, Ronaldsway and St Patrick's Isle (now Peel) all possessed havens. We may assume that these ports were used regularly, not

Fig. 17.3 *Medieval glass from excavations at St Patrick's Isle and Rushen Abbey. a) three sherds of potash window glass from Peel showing traces of reddish drisaille painting on one surface, dating from fourteenth or fifteenth-century; b) base fragment of a hanging lamp probably of the form with a cup-top and narrowing tapering as shown (c); d) rim sherd from a urinal similar to the form shown in (c), not to scale; (e) a spherical bottle with a cylindrical neck and wide, horizontal rim.*

just for the military purposes outlined in the chronicle, but also by the fishing vessels that operated off the Manx coast. This being so, one might expect groups of craftsmen and merchants to have gathered in these places, in order to service the needs of both the maritime community and each other. Moreover, at Peel, where the diocesan cathedral was located by the mid-thirteenth century, a steady flow of visitors transacting spiritual and other business with the bishop of Sodor and his officials is likely to have swelled the resident population of clerics. These people too constituted a potential market, as did the garrison that manned Peel's newly constructed fortifications of the fourteenth century. Similarly, the garrison of Castle Rushen (parts of which appear to date from the later twelfth century) made for a demographic concentration, overlooking the small natural harbour at the mouth of the Silver Burn. Nevertheless, evidence of proto-urban settlement on the island remains scant. So far, at Peel alone have archaeologists found the remnants of domestic habitation dating from the medieval period. On the other hand, excavation of Castletown has revealed disappointingly little about medieval settlement while other potential urban nuclei remain archaeologically unexplored.[73] Meanwhile, documentary evidence of urban activity is even more jejune. Weekly markets were held in Castletown, Peel and Ramsey (and for that matter in Douglas too) by the Early Modern period, but their origins remain obscure. By then at least one annual fair was also held in each of the island's parishes. Several (including those at Douglas and Peel) were held on the feast days of Celtic saints to whom local churches were originally dedicated. This suggests a pre-Reformation origin, although there is no positive evidence to substantiate this.[74] Yet, even if Castletown, Douglas, Ramsey and Peel did function as market centres before the Early Modern period, it remains altogether less certain that they possessed the other common characteristics of medieval urban life: communal commercial privileges and a resident population, a significant proportion of which lived off trade, industry, administration and other non-agricultural occupations.[75]

The lack of recognisably urban insular foci did not preclude overseas trading activity. The western Highlands and Islands of Scotland also had no recognisable towns in the medieval period, but this did not prevent their inhabitants from trading as far away as Bristol and Dublin in the thirteenth century. Indeed, their rulers found it profitable to tax such activity. At some point before 1202, when the future Manx king Óláfr Dubh (r.1228–37) was ruling the outer Hebrides, Hrafn Sveinbjarnarson's ship was blown off course to the Isles. There a bailiff demanded landing dues or tolls (*laudaurar*) from Hrafn at the rate of 120 lengths of *vaðmál* (rough woollen cloth) for each Icelander on board – the equivalent of about five ounces of silver *per capita*.[76] Similar tolls, which appear to have originated during the reign of St Óláfr (r.1015–30), were levied in Norway and the Northern Isles and perhaps also Man, for in the thirteenth century the monks of St Werburgh's abbey in Chester were granted exemption from the payment of unspecified tolls on fish landed on the island.[77]

Tolls were clearly a source of royal income, although specific Manx customs data, with information regarding who traded and what they traded, does not survive before the later sixteenth century. It might be assumed, however, that in the early part of the period sea-faring Norsemen were among the most frequent visitors to Manx ports. The Isle of Man was, after all, part of the Scandinavian political world. Scandinavian merchants were certainly active in both the Irish Sea zone and the more northerly Isles and their activities may explain the circulation of Hiberno-Manx coins as far away as the Baltic.[78] Aside from Scandinavians, there are literary references from the tenth, eleventh and twelfth centuries which indicate the involvement of Hebrideans too in commerce. The *Orkneyinga saga*, for instance, notes that the Tiree chieftan Holdboði owned a fleet of ships and that some of his men participated in trading activities.[79] More unusually, given her gender, an Isleswoman named Þorgunna is mentioned in *Eyrbyggja saga*; she sailed to Iceland with clothes and fabrics which excited the envy of Icelandic women.[80] Þorgunna's voyage is especially interesting because the ship on which she sailed was owned jointly by Islesmen and Dubliners, a partnership found elsewhere in literature too, and joint ventures by the Islesmen and Dubliners probably reflect the occasions on which the two areas were politically united, for example, 1036–8, 1046–52, 1061–72, 1091–4 and 1156.

Of perhaps greater antiquity was the southern extension of these commercial routes, from the Irish Sea to Biscay and the North Sea: Adomnán noted that one of St Columba's prophecies was confirmed by sailors from Gaul, probably transporting a cargo of wine;[81] a bishop from Gaul named Arculf was said to have been Adomnán's guest and his informant on the Holy Lands;[82] and in the eleventh century the chronicler Adémar of Chabannes recorded the arrival of fleets from the Irish Sea which had sailed through St George's Channel to raid around the Bay of Biscay.[83] Not all traffic went south, however: some veered east into the English Channel. A charter of the mid-twelfth century issued by Henry of Anjou, the future King Henry II of England, provides a synopsis of the landmarks followed by ships coming from Ireland and the Irish Sea region as they approached the mouth of the Seine on their way to Rouen.[84] The longevity of commercial traffic along this route is suggested by the similarities between the sculputural reliefs extant in Normandy, at Evrecy, and

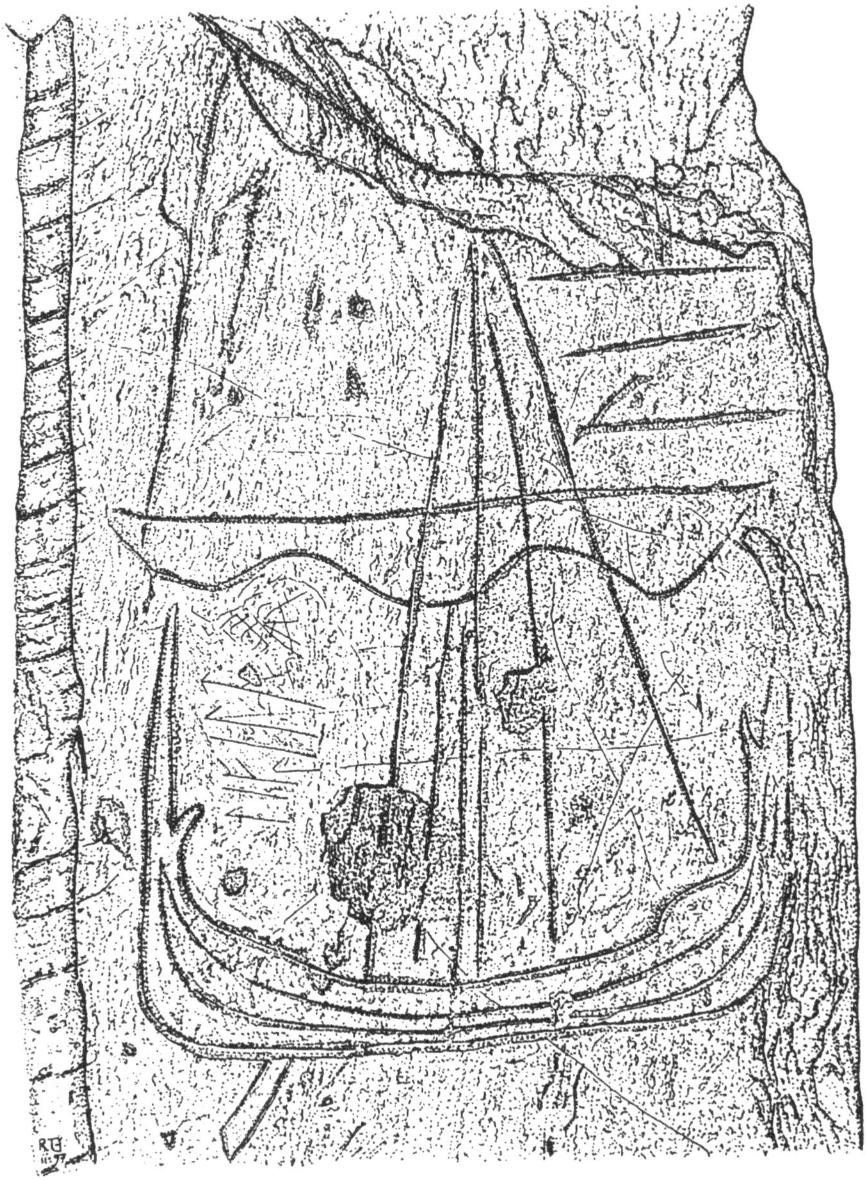

Fig. 17.4 *Ship representation on Maughold cross no.142, possibly eleventh-century (see also runes). Drawing R. Trench-Jellicoe.*

tenth- and eleventh-century designs found on Man, as well as by the Manx deposits of pottery manufactured in Normandy, dating from the eleventh and twelfth centuries.[85]

Nevertheless, trade was not the only reason for travel and none of the preceding examples provide irrefutable evidence of specifically Manx-focused commercial activity. Indeed, it would be unsafe to assume, simply on the basis of geographical determinism, that the Manx population 'must have' regularly participated in a far-flung trading nexus which incorporated the rest of the Irish Sea and Hebridean worlds. Indeed, documentary evidence of specifically Manx commercial contact, not only with the more distant north and south, but even with surrounding lands is remarkably scant before the thirteenth century. This may, of course, simply reflect the paucity of documentary sources; alternatively, it perhaps suggests that such trade was, at most, rare. Save for two brief periods, numismatic evidence tends to suggest that trade was, indeed, infrequent. The exceptions were in the 960s and 970s and again between *c.*1025 and *c.*1080. Hoards buried during both periods contain a substantial amount of silver 'ring-money'. These arm rings or bracelets of Scotto-Viking type circulated widely in the Western and Northern Isles as a substitute for coin. Their presence clearly points to contact, probably of a commercial nature, with the Western Isles at least, during the eleventh century.[86] Moreover, that cordial relations between the Manx king Magnús Haraldsson and the English king Eadgar coincided with the development of Anglo-Manx trade is implied by coin hoards buried at Ballaqueeney, Ballakilpheric, Ballaquayle and Kirk Andreas in the 960s and 970s. An examination of the coins found in these hoards has shown that the majority date to the reign of Eadgar. While these hoards could represent the proceeds of looting, no raiding activity is known of in the Irish Sea during Eadgar's reign (959–75).[87] There is also some marginally more positive evidence for construing the Manx hoards as the product of economic rather than military interaction. A hoard buried in *c.*988 at the Castle Esplanade in Chester included fragments of a brooch and an armband, which resemble similar items found at Ballaquayle and it has been suggested they may have been manufactured on the Isle of Man.[88]

The numismatic evidence from the second period (*c.*1025–*c.*1080) is even more impressive and derives from hoards buried in the north of the island which included not only 'ring-money', Anglo-Saxon coins and Norman *denier*, but also a significant number of both Hiberno-Norse and Hiberno-Manx coinage. Indeed, more Hiberno-Norse coins have been found on the Isle of Man than anywhere else in Britain.[89] Although this is striking enough, even more remarkable is the incontrovertible evidence that a mint was operative on Man itself, producing coins similar to those struck by the Dublin moneyers of the 1020s.[90] The Manx mint was operative during the reign of Echmarcach Mac Ragnaill (*c.*1030–64), who for much of the period (1036–8 and 1046–52) was simultaneously king of Dublin. This, at the very least, points to close interaction with Dublin, which, while under the control of Echmarcach and his predecessor Sigtryggr, had rapidly emerged into a great commercial centre. Given its limited circulation – no Hiberno-Manx coins have been found in Ireland – it remains uncertain whether the coinage was issued for commercial purposes; but Professor Dolley is persuasive in further arguing that the mid-eleventh century witnessed nothing less than a sustained attempt to bring the Isle of Man, and especially the north of the island, into a close dependency on Dublin. Moreover, he surmised, the attempt was invigorated by the settlement of emigrants from Dublin's hinterland on the northern shores of the island.[91]

Yet, if such was the plan, both it and the independent Manx mint soon floundered. In 1052 Man and Dublin parted political company, once Echmarcach was ousted from Dublin by the Leinster king, Diarmit mac Maíl na mBó. Although on three, brief subsequent occasions Man and Dublin were politically reunited, the experiment of the Manx mint was not to be repeated in the medieval period. Indeed, it was not only the mint that disappeared; only one Manx coin hoard (buried in *c.*1180) can be identified positively to the period between *c.*1080 and the end of the thirteenth century.[92] While infrequent taxes levied on the island continued to be computed in monetary sums we cannot be sure that they were paid in coin rather than kind. Man, it would seem, had returned to the numismatic isolation that characterised the island in the first half of the tenth century and again during the 50 years or so which straddle the tenth and eleventh centuries. 'Numismatic isolation' suggests commercial isolation – an isolation that was the norm rather than the exception before the thirteenth century. It also suggests economic self-sufficiency.

Moreover, evidence from the later medieval period, or the lack of it, strongly suggests that even if Manx trade with distant foreign lands had been frequent before the thirteenth century, it soon withered. In 1349 it was reported that Bishop Russell did not 'dare to face the dangers of the long voyage' to Norway, where he ought to have journeyed to profess his obedience to the archbishop of Trondheim.[93] The bishop's comments were personal and they perhaps reflect nothing more than his own queasy anticipation of seasickness. Nonetheless, his views are also symbolic of a society that seems to have lost its taste for distant maritime adventure. To the north, Icelandic trade became increasingly focused on Bergen from the thirteenth century and it was only from the fifteenth century that English and

Hanseatic vessels began independently to voyage to Iceland.[94] There is no evidence that Manx ships did likewise at this juncture. Meanwhile, although the Isle of Man was included in an early thirteenth-century geography compiled at the Hanseatic town of Hamburg, Hanseatic vessels rarely ventured into the Irish Sea and no evidence suggests that they visited Man on even the rare occasions when they did so.[95] Likewise, there is little evidence of direct contact between Man and either France or the Low Countries in the later medieval period. Although some Saintonge pottery, dating from the thirteenth or fourteenth century, has been discovered on the island, there is no reason for supposing that it arrived directly from south-western France.[96] Indeed, the Bordeaux customs accounts of the fourteenth and fifteenth centuries make no reference to Man; Man does not appear on the itinerary of vessels recorded in fifteenth- and sixteenth-century Bordeaux notarial agreements; and, perhaps most significantly of all, it is difficult to detect Manx references in Netherlandish records, even though the Low Countries were the principal focus of commercial activity north of the Alps in the Middle Ages.[97] Manx trade, if it ever did extend further afield, had been ringed in to the Irish Sea zone by the later Middle Ages.

Within this more confined orbit there are more sustained indications of commercial interaction than exist for the earlier period. For a start, coin was clearly once again in circulation. Buried coins minted during the reigns of Alexander III (r.1249–86) and Robert I (r.1306–29) indicate the circulation of Scottish currency, as well as of English and Irish issues, on the island. Indeed, Scottish coins were apparently still commonly circulating before 1375 when it was stipulated that, whereas previously they had been of equal parity with English pennies, now they were to be exchanged for only three-quarters of their previous value.[98] Nevertheless, there may have been some reluctance to accept the face value of Scottish coins even before 1375, for as early as 1367 their silver content had been reduced by almost 15 per cent. Debasement could lead to inflation and this may explain the complaints of the vicar of Malew in the following year that his predecessors had been able to live better with an income of six marks than he could with 40 marks.[99] There are, of course, other possible explanations for the inflation about which the vicar moaned. Shortages resulting from a poor harvest might well have inflated prices and there is, indeed, evidence that the 1360s was a decade of poor harvests in parts of England, though there is little indication that similar conditions prevailed concurrently in either Ireland or Scotland.[100]

More concrete evidence of trade with Scotland is afforded by a report from August 1342 that two Manx ships, laden with wheat, horses, cows

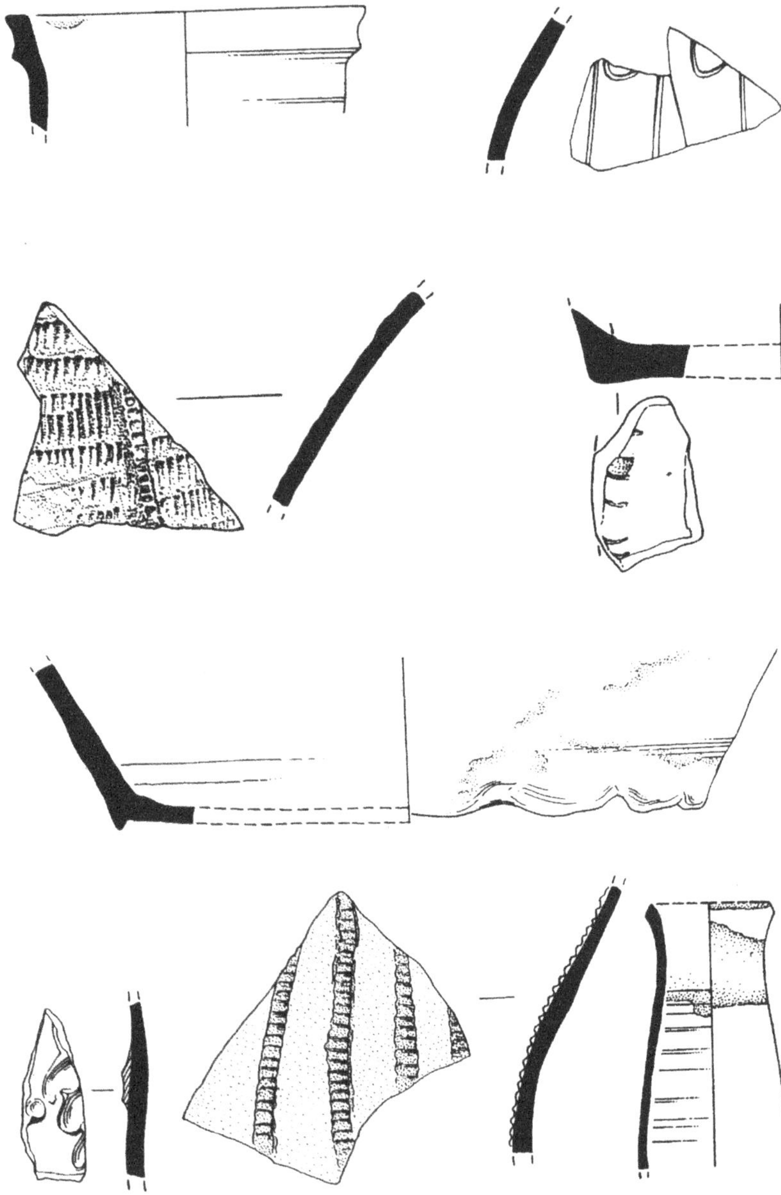

Fig. 17.5 *Fragments of British imported pottery, mainly of jugs, from excavations at Peel Castle and Castle Rushen indicate the range of imports of this period from places such as Ham Green, Bristol, Somerset, Cheshire and Cheam in Surrey, scale is one half. From Davey, P.J., 'Medieval and later pottery from the Island of Man',* Proceedings Isle of Man Natural History Antiquarian Society XI, *Figure 2, pp.94–5.*

and other unspecified goods to the value of 40 marks, had been bound for Scotland in the company of the abbot of Rushen and other Manxmen when the vessels were arrested by Irishmen from Drogheda and Ulster claiming to police the sea on the crown's behalf.[101] The inclusion of cows and horses in the cargo is as might be expected given the emphasis of pastoral farming on the island. The reference to wheat is more surprising, though its derivation cannot be ascribed with any certainty to Man: it may have been a re-export of a product originally grown elsewhere. A month later Edward III permitted the Manxmen to make a truce with the Scots and to trade with them in all goods except armour and victuals.[102] Yet such evidence does not necessarily bespeak of vibrant and regular commercial contact with Scotland; and if Manxmen were to adhere to Edward III's conditions, it is difficult to imagine what, other than metals (the *sine qua non* of armour) and victuals, they might have dispatched to Scotland. Nevertheless, in 1422 it was enacted that Scots 'voyde the Land with the next vessell that goeth into Scotland upon paine of forfeiture of theire goods, and their bodies to prison'. It may be presumed that such legislation was necessary because by-passing Man was exactly what Scottish-bound vessels were by then, unaccustomedly, doing.[103]

This statute invites speculation. Obviously, that Scottish ships were, by the early fifteenth century, avoiding Man was considered detrimental to Man's prosperity. It is perhaps significant, however, that the complaint refers to ships going to, rather than coming from, Scotland. Now, it is probably safe to assume that Manxmen were not worried about the loss of Scottish markets *per se*. The economy of western Scotland (and for that matter northern Ireland too) was not dissimilar to that of Man and the opportunities for selling Manx produce in Scotland (and Ulster), despite the attempts to do so in 1342, were probably limited; western Scotland and Ulster, like Man, were predominantly pastoral economies, and while there was a demand for wheat in such areas, it seems unlikely that it was one which Man could routinely furnish. Indeed, that Man's own arable cultivation was often insufficient to meet aristocratic preferences for wheat seems far more likely. In 1212 part of the *quid pro quo* for Rögnvaldr's submission to King John of England was a pension of 100 'seams' of wheat to be collected annually at Easter.[104] Similar sustenance (amounting to 100 crannochs of wheat, also payable at Easter) was granted to Rögnvaldr's brother and successor, Óláfr Dubh, in 1235 in return for naval service to the English king.[105] The timing for the collection of these pensions – Easter – is significant, for spring was often accompanied by the exhaustion of winter provisions and summer crops would not yet have ripened. Later lords probably faced similar problems. Both wheat and barley were imported to victual Castle Rushen in 1395, and licences to deliver further consignments of wheat to the castle were granted in 1402, 1406 and 1407, on the two latter occasions together with malt.[106] Local supplies, it may be presumed, were insufficient to meet these demands on a routine basis; and since western Scotland too frequently imported wheat it seems unlikely that grain could readily be procured there.

Instead, then, the Manx interest in north-bound vessels is likely to derive from the cargoes which these vessels were carrying to Scotland and, indeed, Ulster. Scottish sources would suggest that these included wine, iron and probably salt, of French and Spanish origin; wheat from Ireland; and perhaps also cloth from England;[107] and presumably in 1422 it was believed that vessels laden with goods such as these had traditionally called at Man while sailing north, offloading part of their cargoes in the process. That, certainly, is the trading routine suggested by the itinerary of the *Jesus*, a Bristol ship, laden among other things with Gascon wine, salt, woollen cloth, silk, saffron, wheat flour and salmon, which in 1553 called at Man before intending to sail north for Lough Foyle.[108] If this voyage was at all typical it would seem that Man was a stopping-off point, rather than a final destination, for northward bound vessels. Indeed, arguably the island's principal attraction to foreign mariners was as a convenient landfall (where supplies of drinking water might be replenished, ship repairs undertaken in quiet waters and legs stretched on dry land) rather than as a marketplace for the sale of goods, important though the latter may have been to the Manx men and women themselves. There is much to commend this hypothesis for the conduct of trade in earlier centuries too, and not just for vessels sailing along the south-north axis. In 1312 Edward II informed his lieges on Man of a safe conduct which he had granted to men whom the Cumbrian abbey of Holm Cultram might dispatch to Ireland in order to acquire supplies of corn and other goods: it was apparently envisaged that these men and their ships would call at Man while traversing the Irish Sea, but not that they would undertake their chief commercial purpose there.[109]

More concrete evidence of Man's commercial links with south-eastern Ireland, western England and Wales is limited. If Man was indeed generally a port of call for vessels in transit, rather than a final destination, this would explain why English and Welsh customs officials rarely recorded the island in their accounts (the best source for the medieval trade of the Irish Sea zone); at most customers usually noted only one destination (or origin) for ships which passed through their ports. At any rate, the fragmentary customs accounts of Wales provide no firm evidence of Manx connections in that direction.[110] This is hardly surprising given the similarity of the Manx and Welsh economies and, as with western Scotland, it is difficult to see the potential for sustained commercial exchange between the two areas. Even the Manx lead, dispatched to Wales in the 1290s, was probably exceptional since north Wales was normally furnished with local supplies from Flintshire.[111] With England, however, the possibilities of exchange were greater. The fisheries around the island certainly attracted English interest: in the thirteenth century the monks of St Werburgh's abbey in Chester were permitted to fish off the Manx coast and exempted from payment of toll when their catch was landed, and by the early sixteenth century fish dominated the Manx cargoes which arrived in Chester.[112] At least occasionally, the island's mineral deposits were also alluring: it was merchants from Chester and the Welsh marches who were granted a safe-conduct to deliver lead to Wales in 1290.[113] By way of return, merchants from the same area and from Cahors in France (at least one of whom, William Servant, was prominent in the English wool trade) were granted safe conducts to deliver unspecified merchandise to Man in 1290;[114] and in 1395 the supplies sought for Castle Rushen were to be shipped from Liverpool or Chester.[115] Chester may also have been the origin of the Saintonge pottery excavated in Castletown, for it was found commonly in Chester too, and it seems reasonably safe to assume that the pottery manufactured in Cheshire itself found its way to the island directly from the Dee.[116] Indeed, Chester, the most important port in north-western England, is likely to have been the town with which the island had the closest commercial contacts in the medieval period, even though there is no indication of Manx shipping in the town's earliest extant customs account of 1397.[117] A few Manx ships were recorded there in subsequent decades and it is possible that some of the numerous Irish ships visiting Chester both before and after called at Man while en route.[118] There is also evidence of contact further south. Pottery manufactured in the south-west of England has been excavated at Castletown and Peel, and Manx trade is noted in some fifteenth-century Bristol customs accounts, for instance in 1437.[119] Nevertheless, direct sailings between Man and Bristol were apparently of an irregular rather than annual nature: there is, for instance, no evidence of Man among the destinations recorded for ships departing Bristol in 1461–2.[120]

Information regarding the Isle of Man's trade with Ireland is marginally fuller. It seems likely that the commercial attraction of Man to the Irish, like the English, was fish. Evidence for this is sparse, but in 1217 herring fishermen from Waterford, Wexford, Derry, and probably the ports in between, are recorded in the island, where they committed violence and were slain.[121] By the fourteenth century foreign (perhaps including Irish) involvement in the sea fisheries was substantial enough for Bishop Thomas

(1331–48) to claim a tenth of the taxes paid to the clergy by foreign workers in the herring industry.[122] If fish was what attracted Irishmen to Man, they probably soon discovered that here was a market in which they could offload wheat. In the thirteenth century Ireland was an exporter of wheat to both Scotland and England, and Man too was furnished with grain from the same source. King Rögnvaldr arranged to collect his pensions of wheat, wine and cash in Drogheda, suggesting trading links with that port; and a few Manxmen were to be found in thirteenth-century Dublin too. Richard Taylor of Man and Yole of Man both became members of the town's guild merchant before 1223, and Elias de Ramseye (possibly of Manx origin) and Siward son of Paul of Man (more certainly from Man) were admitted to the same body in 1232–3 and in 1246–7 respectively.[123] In addition Reginald the Black of Man was enrolled as a free citizen of Dublin before 1234 and Mathie de Trig from Man owned property in the town during the same century.[124] What they were doing there remains uncertain, but it is credible to suppose that they tapped into Dublin's extensive trading nexus, which by now extended from its own rural hinterland to the Iberian and Gascon ports, in order to procure supplies of wheat and wine. Whether these Irish contacts continued in the fourteenth century remains difficult to ascertain because of the scarcity of Irish urban records and the lack of detailed Irish customs accounts for the period. Still, it was from unspecified locations in Ireland that the supplies of grain, malt, wine, salt and fresh-water fish were sought to provision Manx fortifications in 1402, 1406 and 1407.[125]

The absence of more detailed information regarding the Isle of Man's domestic production and overseas trade makes it difficult to reach judgements about the wealth of the island's inhabitants in the Middle Ages. Still, in attempting to reach such a judgement, it is important to consider other sources of income too. By the fifteenth century (and perhaps ever since the labour shortage caused by the Black Death) some Manxmen and women were working in England. One Manxwoman by the name of Isabella is, for example, recorded in the East Riding of Yorkshire in 1440.[126] Described as a 'vagabond', she was probably a transient labourer, lured abroad by the prospect of higher wages. Like others of her standing, she perhaps returned home eventually with the fruits of her labour. In earlier centuries labour of a different sort was also sold to foreigners. There seems, for instance, to have been an economic importance to the fleet of the native Manx lords that was not recognised by contemporary writers more interested in military activities. The Manx fleet was hired by Gwynedd prince Gruffudd ap Cynan in 1094 and it again found Welsh employment in 1193. Five years later the earl of Orkney sought the fleet's services for battle in

Caithness, the Orcadian adventurer Sveinn Ásleifarson having procured its services against a Welsh pirate earlier in the century.[127] The Irish, however, are the most frequently recorded customers. The fleet was hired by the men of Dublin in 1094, by the northern Irish in 1154, and by the Irish highking in 1171.[128] Anglo-French lords also sought its assistance. While in 1205 John de Courcy, lord of Ulster, may have acquired its assistance by virtue of his kinship ties to the Manx king, the English king Henry III paid the expenses of a fleet of 50 galleys under the command of King Óláfr Dubh to protect the northern Irish sea – a markedly more sizeable fleet than the six ships of 26 oars each which Robert I of Scotland later expected in return for his grant of the lordship of Man to Thomas Randolph, earl of Moray.[129]

More double-edged were the effects of warfare and piracy. The Manx chronicle, brief though it is, is littered with accounts of battle and slaughter dated to 1056, 1075, 1098, 1158, 1182(?), 1192, 1210, 1224, 1228, 1229(?), 1237, 1250, 1275, 1313 and 1316.[130] Even though pastoralism perhaps mitigated the worst effects of such conflict, since cattle could be more readily removed than crops from areas of conflict, these events can only have had a disruptive effect on the Manx economy. To what extent this was so remains uncertain, but conflict on land was exacerbated by maritime insecurity. In 1214 King John of England ordered Irish sailors not to enter the kingdom of Man and the Isles, perhaps because of depredations which they had been committing before the king took the island under his protection. More certainly, the seas around Man were periodically infested with pirates and privateers during the Anglo-Scottish 'Hundred Years War' of 1296–1403. This was especially the case between 1313 and 1317, as Robert I attempted to wrest the island from English control, though it did not escape during later episodes of the same conflict. In 1388, for instance, it was reported that Sir William Douglas of Nithsdale and his accomplices 'plundered the Isle of Man' on return from a raiding expedition on Carlingford, a thirteenth-century fief of the Manx king.[131] Of course, on occasions the Manx population itself was able to profit from similar activities. Sveinn Ásleifarson, in a leisurely moment while resident on Man, captured an English ship bound for Dublin along with its cargo of cloth, and this was perhaps not an isolated incident. When, in 1218, King Rögnvaldr was given safe passage to the English court in order to render homage, some of his subjects accompanied him to make amends for their 'excesses' (perhaps a euphemism for piracy) in England and Ireland.[132] Yet, given that Man was surrounded by sea, examples of illicit Manx maritime activity are remarkably rare. Perhaps, once again, this is nothing more than a reflection of incomplete sources; alternatively it may be an indication that the fruits of the sea were less significant to ordinary Manx livelihoods than those of the land.

It was, however, the sea that gave the Isle of Man its international significance in the Middle Ages. The Manx fleet was a useful weapon to those who sought mastery of the Irish Sea zone, while the fish that inhabited Manx waters were of great commercial interest to a society which, in theory at least, was prohibited from the consumption of animal-based foodstuffs for roughly half the year. The sea too brought a measure of prosperity and dietary variation to the Manx population itself. But fishing and military endeavours were seasonal occupations and for much of the wherewithal for daily life the Manx population relied upon the land, not the sea. That land was not infertile. Indeed, the extensive building works carried out at Peel and at Rushen Abbey from the later fourteenth century suggest a degree of affluence among those who owned it.[133] Even for those who worked it, it seems likely that basic diet was comparatively healthy when compared with supposedly more developed and prosperous regions such as south-eastern England. Although the paucity of references to vegetables and above all fruit probably made for a deficiency of vitamin C, the dietary emphasis on fish, beef and dairy produce provided protein and calories. Meanwhile, grain products (especially oats) provided carbohydrates, especially, to judge by the dental evidence, for women. For both genders, dairy produce was an additional source of not just calcium but, together with herring, also of vitamins A and D, the former supplemented further by the consumption of offal.[134] Yet, there was little unique about an economy that produced such a balance of foodstuffs. It was similar to that of Gaelic Ireland and Scotland. Besides, it seems unlikely that the island produced vast agricultural surpluses or sufficient wealth to stall peasant migration after the Black Death. It is this that surely explains the island's comparative commercial isolation during the medieval centuries. The Manx population might have desired the luxury produce of foreign countries, but there was little on the Manx landscape to interest foreign traders. Medieval maps reflect this. The Isle of Man is clearly discernible in the British Library's Anglo-Saxon world map of the tenth or eleventh century, on the famous Hereford *mappa mundi* of the later thirteenth century, and on Matthew Paris's thirteenth-century maps of the British Isles. It is there too on Pietro Vesconte's late thirteenth-century Venetian portolan chart and on his world map of *c.*1320, and on Angelino Dulcert's mid fourteenth-century portolan chart.[135] But while for Snorri Sturluson the Isle of Man possessed the finest land in the Isles, for the cartographers and merchants of medieval Europe it was nothing more than a featureless, and often nameless, clump of rock.

Notes

1 Snorri Sturlson, *Heimskringla*, ed. Bjarni Aðalbjarnarson (Reykjavík, 1941–51), iii, 221.
2 Ó Cuív, 'A poem in praise of Raghnall', 288–89.
3 Bede, *A History of the English Church and People*, ed. Leo Sherley-Price and R.E. Latham (rev. ed., Harmondsworth, 1968), 114.
4 D.E. Allan, 'The present-day fauna and flora of Man as indicators of the date of the Flandrian Severance' in Davey (ed.), *Man and the Environment*, 9.
5 Jean Gimpel, *The Medieval Machine* (London, 1976), 76–7.
6 L.S. Garrad, 'Some thoughts on Manx woodland', *Proceedings*, 7 (1964–72), 668.
7 J.R. Dickinson, *The Lordship of Man under the Stanleys: Government and Economy in the Isle of Man, 1590–1704* (Manchester, 1996), 275.
8 Kay Muhr, 'Manx Place-Names: an Ulster View', in Peter Davey and David Finlayson (eds), *Mannin Revisited: Twelve Essays on Manx Culture and Environment* (Edinburgh, 2002), 47; Broderick, *CKMI*, fols 33r., 47v.
9 Broderick, *CKMI*, fol. 34v.; P.S. Gelling, 'The Braaid site: a re-excavation of one of the structures', *JMM*, 6 (1964), 201–5.
10 Augustinus Theiner (ed.), *Vetera Monumenta Hibernorum et Scotorum Historiam Illustrantia* (Rome, 1864), no. 677.
11 Moore, *Isle of Man*, i, 284–5.
12 Gustav Storm (ed.), *Islandske Annaler indtil 1578* (Christiania [Oslo], 1888), quoted by Rosemary Power, 'Scotland in the Norse Sagas' in G.G. Simpson (ed.), *Scotland and Scandinavia 800–1800* (Edinburgh, 1990), 21; P.H.W. Booth, *The Financial Administration of the Lordship and County of Chester*, Chetham Society (1981), 3, 89–90; M.C. Lyons, 'Weather, famine, pestilence and plague in Ireland, 900–1500' in E.M. Crawford (ed.), *Famine – The Irish Experience* (Edinburgh, 1989), 44–6; M. Kelly, *A History of the Black Death in Ireland* (Stroud, 2001).
13 William Mackenzie (ed.), *Legislation by Three of the Thirteen Stanleys, Kings of Man*, Manx Society (1860), 90–1.
14 M.L. Parry, *Climatic Change, Agriculture and Settlement* (Folkestone, 1978), 128–33.
15 R.H. White (ed.), *Peel Castle Excavation. Final Report I: The Half Moon Battery* (Oxford, 1986), 13; Charter to Brian de Stapleton, 19 February 1377 (MML, Derby Papers, MD401/1400/3). We are greatly indebted to Ms Wendy Thirkettle of The Manx Museum for sending us a copy of the 1377 charter. 'Appyn' (on which see Broderick, *PNIM* (Tübingen, 1994–), I, 19) remains unidentified. Stapleton's absenteeism is suggested by his active political and military career in England and France, on which see Carole Rawcliffe, 'Stapleton, Sir Brian (*c*.1322–1394)', *Oxford Dictionary of National Biography* (Oxford, 2004): http:www//.oxforddnb.com/view/article/26299.
16 C.R. Cheney, 'Manx Synodal Statutes, A.D. 1230(?)-1351. Part I: Introduction and Latin Texts', *Cambridge Medieval Celtic Studies*, 7 (1983), 87 (no. 2); C.R. Cheney, 'Manx Synodal Statutes, A.D. 1230(?)-1351. Part II: Translation of Latin Texts', *Cambridge Medieval Celtic Studies*, 8 (1984), 61 (no. 2).
17 *APS*, ii, 51 (no. 28).
18 *Coucher Book of Furness*, i, 510–12.
19 Broderick, *CKMI*, fols 53r.-54v.
20 Wilson (ed.), *Register of St Bees*, nos. 43–4, 46–8.
21 *Coucher Book of Furness*, iii, 658, 695, 713.

22 George Broderick, 'The baronial possessions of Bangor and Saul in Man', *Bulletin of the Ulster Place Name Society*, 2nd ser., 4 (1981–2), 24–6; B.R.S. Megaw, 'The Barony of Bangor and Sabal in Kirk Patrick', *JMM*, 4 (1938–40), 135–8, 159–60.

23 [B.R.S. Megaw], 'The Barony of Saint Trinian in Kirk Marown: a memorial to St Ninian of Galloway', *JMM*, 4 (1938–40), 175–7; B.R.S. Megaw, 'The Barony of St Trinian's in the Isle of Man', *Transactions of the Dumfriesshire and Galloway Natural History and Antiquarian Society*, 3rd ser., 27 (1950), 173–82.

24 See, for example, Kinvig, *Isle of Man*, 88–90; and most recently D. Freke, 'History' in Vaughan Robinson and Danny McCarroll (eds), *The Isle of Man: a Sense of Place* (Liverpool, 1990), 115.

25 *Diplomatarium Norvegicum* (Christiania [Oslo], 1848–1919), VII, no. 10; Anderson, *Early Sources*, ii, 449–52.

26 Broderick, *CKMI*, fols 43v., 51r.

27 Theiner (ed.), *Vetera Monumenta*, nos 26, 51.

28 A.O. Johnsen and Peter King (eds), *The Tax Book of the Cistercian Order* (Oslo, 1979), 56–7, 72–3.

29 Rome, Archivio Segreto Vaticano, Penitenziera Apostolica, Reg. Mat. et Div., vol. 20, fol. 253v. We are very grateful to Jennifer McDonald for this reference, dated 1472. For fees levied by the penitentiary, see Emil Göller, *Die päpstliche Pönitentiare von ihrem Ursprung bis zu ihrer Umgestaltung unter Pius V* (Rome, 1907–11).

30 A.D.M. Barrell, *The Papacy, Scotland and Northern England, 1342–1378* (Cambridge, 1995), 29–30; W.E. Lunt, *Financial Relations of the Papacy with England 1327–1534* (Cambridge, Mass., 1962), 725–800.

31 W.H. Bliss and C. Johnson (eds), *Calendar of Entries in the Papal Registers relating to Great Britain and Ireland: Papal Letters III: 1342–1362* (London, 1897), 305.

32 Kevin Down, 'Colonial society and economy in the high Middle Ages' in Cosgrove (ed.), *A New History of Ireland*, 459–61, 467, 472, 479.

33 J.M. Thomson *et al.* (eds), *Registrum Magni Sigilli Regum Scotorum* (Edinburgh and London, 1882–1914), ii, no. 107.

34 P. Munch (ed.), *Chronicle of Man and the Sundreys* (Manx Society, 1874), nos. 35–6.

35 This aspect of the Manx economy has attracted considerable scholarly attention. Useful studies include: Megaw and Megaw, 'The Norse heritage in the Isle of Man' in Fox and Dickens (eds), *Early Cultures of North-west Europe*, 141–70; Megaw, 'Norsemen and native'; Elwyn Davies, 'Treens and quarterlands', *Transactions of the Institute of British Geographers*, 22 (1956), 97–116; R.A. Moore, 'The Manx multiple estate: evidence for undertones in the Manx landsystem?' in P.J. Davey (ed.), *Recent Archaeological Research on the Isle of Man* (Oxford, 1999), 171–82; and, for comparative purposes, L.J. Macgregor and B.E. Crawford (eds), *Ouncelands and Pennylands* (St Andrews, 1987). See chapter 19 below.

36 Glyn Coppack, *The White Monks: The Cistercian Order in Britain 1128–1540* (Stroud, 1998), chapter 5.

37 P.G. Foote and D.M. Wilson, *The Viking Achievement* (London, 1970), 176; Michael Dolley, *Some Irish Dimensions to Manx History* (Belfast, 1976), 21.

38 Cheney, 'Synodal Statutes I', 77–8 (no. 13), 80 (no. 15); C.R. Cheney, 'Synodal Statutes II', 53 (no. 13), 55 (no. 15).

39 Gerald of Wales, *History and Topography of Ireland*, ed. J.J. O'Meara (London, 1985), 34.

40 *ERS*, i, 53, 189.
41 W.C. Jordan, *The Great Famine: Northern Europe in the Early Fourteenth Century* (Princeton, 1996), 25–6; Guy Bois, *The Crisis of Feudalism: Economy and Society in Eastern Normandy c.1300–1550* (Cambridge, 1984), 204–7; Down, 'Colonial society', 471; Elizabeth Gemill and N.J. Mayhew, *Changing Values in Medieval Scotland: a study of prices, money, and weights and measures* (Cambridge, 1995), 145. English returns were better than most: Joan Thirsk (ed.), *The Agrarian History of England and Wales* (Cambridge, 1967), II, 289–93, 381–2, 394, 407–8, 449–50.
42 Mackenzie, *Legislation*, 90.
43 Broderick, *CKMI*, *passim*.
44 Allen, 'Plant distribution', 51–2; L.S. Garrad, 'Evidence for the history of the vertebrate fauna of the Isle of Man' in Davey (ed.), *Man and the Environment*, 71.
45 Allan, 'Plant Distribution', 56.
46 *Register St Bees*, no. 45; Broderick, *CKMI*, fol.50r.
47 Mackenzie, *Legislation*, 86.
48 David Freke (ed.), *Excavations on St. Patrick's Isle, Peel, Isle of Man, 1982–88: Prehistoric, Viking, Medieval and Later* (Liverpool, 2002), 249.
49 Cheney, 'Synodal Statutes I', 76 (no. 5); Cheney, 'Synodal Statutes II', 52 (no. 5).
50 *APS*, i, 382.
51 Francesco Balducci Pegolotti, *La Practica della mercatura*, ed. A. Evans (Cambridge, Mass., 1936), 260; J.H. Monro, 'Wool price schedules and the qualities of English wools in the later Middle Ages, *c*.1270–1499', *Textile History*, 9 (1978), 121, 160.
52 Kenneth Nicholls, 'Gaelic society and economy in the high Middle Ages' in Cosgrove (ed.), *A New History of Ireland*, 415; P.J. Davey, D.J. Freke and D.A. Higgins (eds), *Excavations in Castletown, Isle of Man, 1989–1992* (Liverpool, 1996), 127–43.
53 For a discussion of *eary*, see Eleanor Megaw, '"Eary" and its significance' in Davey (ed.), *Man and the Environment*, 327–45.
54 Davey *et al.* (eds), *Excavations in Castletown*, 132; White (ed.), *Peel Castle*, 9. The evidence from Peel relates mainly to the sixteenth century.
55 Cheney, 'Synodal Statutes I', 77 (no. 7), 80 (no. 15); Cheney, 'Synodal Statutes II', 52 (no. 7), 55 (no. 15).
56 Mackenzie, *Legislation*, 83.
57 *Register of St Bees*, no. 44.
58 Chester customs accounts, 1538–9; 1540–1; 1542–3 (CCRO, Sheriffs' Book [hereafter cited as SB]/7, fols 122r., 137r.; SB/8, fol. 39d.); White (ed.), *Peel Castle*, 11; Freke (ed.), *Excavations on St. Patrick's Isle*, 258–61.
59 Chester customs accounts, 1510–11; 1524–5; 1533–4; 1534–5; 1536–7; 1538–9; 1539–40; 1540–1; 1541–2; 1542–3; 1543–4 (CCRO, SB/5/1, fols 101, 104, 162; SB/7, fols 22r., 38d., 74r., 90d., 98r., 137r.; SB/8, fols 7d., 39d., 65r., 70d., 71r.).
60 L.M. Larson (trans.), *The Earliest Norwegian Laws* (New York, 1935), 236.
61 Cheney, 'Synodal Statutes I', 77 (nos. 11–12), 82 (no. 19); Cheney, 'Synodal Statutes II', 53 (nos. 11–12); 56–7 (no. 19).
62 Cheney, 'Synodal Statutes I', 77 (no. 11); Cheney, 'Synodal Statutes II', 53 (no. 11).
63 Cheney, 'Synodal Statutes I', 78 (no. 2); Cheney, 'Synodal Statutes II', 53 (no. 2); Foote and Wilson, *Viking Achievement*, 172, 202.
64 Allan, 'Plant Distribution', 52–3; Cheney, 'Manx Synodal Statutes I', 81 (no. 15);

Cheney, 'Manx Synodal Statutes II', 56 (no. 15).

65 Cheney, 'Manx Synodal Statutes I', 77 (no. 12); Cheney, 'Manx Synodal Statutes II', 53 (no. 12).

66 Cheney, 'Manx Synodal Statutes I', 82 (no. 19); Cheney, 'Manx Synodal Statutes II', 56–7 (no. 19).

67 L.S. Garrard, 'Medieval pottery in the Isle of Man' in Davey (ed.), *Man and Environment*, 357–9; *Medieval Archeaology*, 28 (1984), 251; Davey *et al.* (eds), *Excavations in Castletown*, 18–19; R. Barton, 'Manx Granite Tempered Ware' in Davey (ed.), *Recent Archaeological Research*, 221–40.

68 David Wilson, 'Manx memorial stones of the Viking period', *Saga-book of the Viking Society for Northern Research*, 18 (1970–3), 2–7.

69 *CPR, 1281–1292*, 358, 497.

70 Roger Dackombe, 'Solid geology', in Robinson and McCarroll (eds), *Isle of Man*, 39; *Medieval Archaeology*, 28 (1984), 251; 29 (1985), 209; 32 (1988), 293.

71 Cheney, 'Manx Synodal Statutes I', 82 (no. 22); Cheney, 'Manx Synodal Statutes II', 57 (no. 22).

72 P.S. Andersen, 'To what extent did the *balley/balla (baile)* names in the Isle of Man supplant place-names of Norse origin?' in C. Fell *et al.* (eds), *The Viking Age in the Isle of Man*, 162, though it should be noted that the meaning of Balystere offered here differs from that advanced in Broderick, *PNIM*, ii, 40–1.

73 Davey *et al.* (eds), *Excavations in Castletown*, 156 (for Peel) and *passim* (for Castletown).

74 J.J. Kneen, 'Manx fairs and festivals', *Proceedings*, 3 (1927–32), 38–82; Dickinson, *Lordship of Man*, 193–8.

75 The definition of a town is based loosely on that offered by Susan Reynolds, *An Introduction to the History of English Medieval Towns* (Oxford, 1977), pp. ix–x.

76 Guðrún P. Helgadóttir (ed.), *Hrafns saga Sveinbjarnarsonar* (Oxford, 1987), 22.

77 James Tait (ed.), *The Cartulary or Register of St Werburgh's Chester*, Chetham Society (1920–3), i, no. 314.

78 Anderson, *Early Sources*, ii, 477; G.J. Marcus, 'Norse trade with Iceland', *Economic History Review*, 2nd ser., 9 (1956–7), 408; K. Bornholdt, 'Myth or mint? The evidence for a Viking-Age coinage from the Isle of Man' in Davey (ed.), *Recent Archaeological Research*, 209–10.

79 Finnbogi Guðmundsson (ed.), *Orkneyinga Saga* (Reykjavik, 1965), 180–1.

80 E.Ó. Sveinsson and Matthías Þórðarson (eds), *Eyrbyggja Saga* (Reykjavik, 1935), 137–39.

81 Adomnán, *Life of Columba*, ed. A.O. Anderson and M.O. Anderson (Oxford, 1991), 54.

82 Adomnán, *De Locis Sanctis*, ed. B. Meehan (Dublin, repr. 1983), 36.

83 Adémar of Chabannes, *Chronique*, ed. Jules Chavanon (Paris, 1897), 176.

84 Benjamin Hudson, 'William the Conqueror and Ireland', *Irish Historical Studies*, 29 (1994), 157.

85 Maylis Baylé, 'Reminiscences Anglo-Scandinaves dans la sculpture romaine de Normandie', *Anglo-Norman Studies*, 13 (1990), 36; P.J. Davey, 'Medieval and post medieval continental ceramics from the Isle of Man' in Davey (ed.), *Recent Archaeological Research*, 241.

86 James Graham-Campbell, 'The Viking-Age Silver Hoards of the Isle of Man' in Fell *et al.* (eds), *The Viking Age in the Isle of Man*, 62–3; see the discussion by Bornholdt in chapter 18, pp. 419–20.

87 Michael Dolley, 'Some preliminary observations on three Manx coin-hoards appearing to end with pennies of Edgar', *Spink and Son's Numismatic Circular*,

83 (1975), 146.

88 G. Webster, R.H.M. Dolley and G.C. Dunning, 'A Saxon treasure hoard found at Chester', *Antiquaries Journal*, 33 (1953), 26–9.

89 Dolley, *Irish Dimensions*, 17–19; R.H.M. Dolley, 'The palimpsest of Viking settlement on Man' in H. Bekker-Nielsen, P. Foote and O. Olsen (eds), *Proceedings of the Eighth Viking Congress* (Odense, 1981), 173–81.

90 See chapter 18; Bornholdt, 'Myth or mint?' in Davey (ed.), *Recent Archaeological Research*, 199–218; and the earlier more tentative discussions by R.H.M. Dolley, 'Hiberno-Manx coinage of the eleventh century', *Numismatic Chronicle* (1976), 75–84; *idem*, 'Some insular(?) imitations from the 1030s of contemporary English pence of Cnut', *Spink and Son's Numismatic Circular*, 88 (1980), 86.

91 Dolley, *Irish Dimensions*, 21.

92 The find contained several Scottish coins from the reigns of David I, Malcolm IV and William the Lion: Ian Stewart, 'An eighteenth-century Manx find of early Scottish sterlings', *The British Numismatic Journal*, 33 (1964), 48–56; Bornholt, below, p. 453.

93 W.H. Bliss (ed.), *Calendar of Entries in the Papal Registers relating to Great Britain and Ireland: Petitions, 1342–1419* (London, 1896), 168.

94 E.M. Carus Wilson, 'The Iceland trade' in Eileen Power and M.M. Postan (eds), *Studies in English Trade in the Fifteenth Century* (London, 1933), 155–82; Sigurður Skúlason, 'Hafnarfjörður: Ein Beitrag zur Geschichte des Islandhandels', *Hansische Geschichtsblätter*, 63 (1938), 170–226; Else Ebel, 'Kaufmann und Handel auf Island zur Sagazeit', *Hansische Geschichtsblätter*, 95 (1977), 1–26.

95 *Insulae Britannicae* in Adam of Bremen, *Gesta Hammaburgensis Ecclesiae Pontificum*, ed. B. Schmeidler (Hanover, 1917), 286.

96 Davey *et al.* (eds), *Excavations in Castletown*, 18; Freke (ed.), *Excavataion on St. Patrick's Isle*, 376; Davey, 'Medieval and post medieval continental ceramics' in Davey (ed.), *Recent Archaeological Research*, 241–60.

97 TNA, E101/158–95, *passim*; Jacques Bernard (ed.), *Navires et gens de mer à Bordeaux vers 1400–vers 1550* (Paris, 1968); L. Gillidots van Severen (ed.), *Inventaire des archives de la ville de Bruges* (Bruges, 1871–82); *idem* (ed.), *Cartulaire de l'ancienne Estaple de Bruges* (Bruges, 1904–8); H.J. Smit (ed.), *Bronnen tot de Geschiedenis van den Handel met Engeland, Schotland en Ierland, 1150–1485* (s'Gravenhage, 1928).

98 J.D.A. Thompson, *Inventory of British Coin Hoards A.D.600–1500* (Royal Numismatic Society, 1956), nos 23, 25; *CCR, 1374–1377*, 203.

99 Theiner (ed.), *Vetera Monumenta*, no. 677.

100 Christopher Dyer, *Standards of Living in the Later Middle Ages: social change in England c.1200–1520* (Cambridge, 1989), 262

101 *CCR, 1341–1343*, 654.

102 *CDS*, iii, no. 1396.

103 Mackenzie, *Legislation*, 98.

104 *CDI*, i, no. 428; see also *ibid.*, nos 898 (wherein the grant was amended to 120 crannocks, a crannock equating to eight bushels), 944, 977, 1040, 1240.

105 *CDI*, i, nos 2269, 2271, 2327.

106 *CPR, 1391–96*, 562; *CPR, 1401–1405*, 61, 189; *CPR, 1405–1408*, 145, 329.

107 Alexander Stevenson, 'Trade with the south, 1070–1513' in Michael Lynch, Michael Spearman and Geoffrey Stell (eds), *The Scottish Medieval Town* (Edinburgh, 1988), 183, 186.

108 Jean Vanes (ed.), *Documents illustrating the Overseas Trade of Bristol in the*

Sixteenth Century (Bristol Record Society, 1979), no. 45.

109 *CPR, 1307–1313*, 509.

110 E.A. Lewis (ed.), 'A contribution to the commercial history of medieval Wales', *Y Cymmrodor*, 24 (1913), 86–188.

111 E.A. Lewis, 'The development of industry and commerce in Wales during the Middle Ages', *Transactions of the Royal Historical Society*, new series, 17 (1903), 146, n.1.

112 *Register St Werburgh's*, I, no. 314. See also, notes 56 and 57, above.

113 *CPR, 1281–1292*, 358.

114 *CPR, 1281–1292*, 341; on Servant, see also T.H. Lloyd, *The English Wool Trade in the Middle Ages* (Cambridge, 1977), 47, 296–8.

115 *CPR, 1391–1396*, 562.

116 Davey *et al.* (eds), *Excavations in Castletown*, 18–19; White (ed.), *Peel Castle*, 3, 12.

117 Chester customs accounts, 1397 (CCRO, Mayor's Book [hereafter cited as MB]/1, fols 50–1).

118 The 1404 Chester customs account includes the names of several merchants from 'Rush', which may be either the Manx Rushen or the port of Rush in Co. Dublin (CCRO, MB/2, fols 38–40, 42). There apart the first Manx vessel in these accounts, John Stanley's *Marie de Man*, appears in 1416 (CCRO, MB/3, fol. 33d).

119 Davey *et al.* (eds), *Excavations in Castletown*, 18; Freke (ed.), *Excavations on St. Patrick's Isle*, 384–96; H. Bush, *Bristol Town Duties* (Bristol, 1828), 17–25, cited in W. Childs, 'Ireland's trade with England in the later Middle Ages', *Irish Economic and Social History*, 9 (1982), 15.

120 TNA, E122/19/1.

121 *ALC*, i, 257.

122 Broderick, *CKMI*, fol. 51v.

123 Philomena Connolly and Geoffrey Martin (eds), *The Dublin Guild Merchant Roll, c.1190–1265* (Dublin, 1992), 31, 40, 64, 84.

124 Connolly and Martin, *Dublin Guild*, 113; J.T. Gilbert (ed.), *Historic and Municipal Documents of Ireland, AD 1172–1320*, Roll Series (London, 1870), 113, 475.

125 *CPR, 1401–1405*, 61, 145, 329.

126 TNA, E122/270/31, m. 18, 42. See too S.L. Thrupp, 'A survey of the alien population of England in 1440', *Speculum*, 32 (1957), 270–2.

127 *Orkneyinga Saga*, 179.

128 *AFM*, ii, s.aa.

129 Broderick, *CKMI*, fol. 41r.; *CDI*, i, no. 2269; J.M. Thomson *et al.* (eds), *Registrum Magni Sigilli Regum Scotorum* (Edinburgh and London, 1882–1914), I, appendix 1, no. 32.

130 Broderick, *CKMI*, *passim*.

131 *Scotichronicon*, vii, 415; *CDI*, i, no. 428;

132 Herman Pálsson and Paul Edwards (eds), *Orkneyinga Saga: The History of the Earls of Orkney* (Harmondsworth, 1981), 215; *CDI*, i, no. 828.

133 Freke (ed.), *Excavations on St. Patrick's* Isles, 11–14; Glynn Coppack, 'The planning of Cistercian monasteries in the later middle ages: the evidence from Fountains, Rievaulx, Sawley and Rushen' in J.G. Clark (ed.), *The Religious Orders in Pre-Reformation England* (Woodbridge, 2002), 208–9. We are grateful to James Clark for bringing this article to our attention.

134 R.A. McCance and E.M. Widdowson, *The Composition of Foods* (London, 1960), 128–69, 190–206; White (ed.), *Peel Castle*, 9.

18 *Coinage*

KRISTIN BORNHOLDT COLLINS

Man has produced more than 30 tenth- to fourteenth-century coin hoards,[1] including the large and important mixed hoard from Glenfaba (*c.*1030), discovered in March 2003.[2] This is an impressive total when the island's size (221 square miles) is taken into consideration. No other region bordering the Irish Sea can boast such an overall concentration of monetary wealth from this period. The premeditated accumulation and deposition of hoards and their ultimate non-recovery is, however, governed by complex social and political factors, and the presence of hoards alone is not adequate evidence of a thriving or regulated local economy. The Manx hoards must therefore be seen in conjunction with contemporary single finds, stray or casual losses, to ascertain the extent of everyday coin use and monetisation. This type of evidence is fundamentally different from hoards because each find represents an unconscious or unplanned loss, resulting in a more reliable reflection of circulation. Single finds thus act as a useful control group with which to compare the hoards, but with less than 40 medieval single-coin finds on record for Man, a distinctive and perplexing situation is observed.[3] The chronology and concentration-peaks of the two types of evidence essentially mirror each other, indicating that there are no major external variables dictating and distorting the deposition patterns except in terms of the scale and density. The disparity between hoards and single finds is therefore a central theme in this examination of coin use in medieval Man.

The currencies of England, Scotland and Ireland mixed, and were the mainstay of Man's monetary 'system', to whatever degree that existed. At different times each region enjoyed a distinct and predominant role in the Manx economy, and this is taken to reflect Man's political and/or economic orientation at that time. Silver and gold bullion, cut up and weighed for each transaction, as was the habit of Vikings in Scandinavia, Scotland and Ireland, was also a mode of currency in Man during the earlier part of this period, and this is witnessed in three coinless hoards as well as mixed coin and bullion deposits. For a time, this metal-weight system functioned together with a coin-based economy, giving rise to a situation where two very different concepts of measuring wealth coincided in a 'dual economy'.[4] The one notable exception to these main types of foreign currency occurred in the eleventh century when a local Manx coinage was introduced and

Fig. 18.1 *Hiberno-Manx coin.*
Manx Museum 76-84/1, Manx National Heritage, Kirk Michael 1972/5 hoard (1.04 g/16.1 gr.)

minted *c.*1025–*c.*1065 (Fig. 18.1). It did not supersede other currencies, but circulated with foreign money and bullion in Man. It appears not to have left the island in any great number, but must have been produced for a specific purpose. We are left asking not only what inspired this mint but also, once instituted, why did coin production later cease? The function of money throughout the period appears always to have been in some way limited, even at the time a mint functioned on the island.

The numismatic evidence is particularly important for Man, not just because there is a relative abundance of it, but because it is one of the few ways we can access and elucidate this period of history in Man. The island is rich with archaeological material of the early and later Middle Ages, and the hoards and stray coins make up one of the most accessible and comparatively straightforward bodies of archaeological data. Michael Dolley studied the important Manx collection of coins in the 1970s, and published assiduously on the subject,[5] followed soon after by James Graham-Campbell who contributed a survey of the hoards and associated ornaments in 1983.[6] The material in the Manx Museum is currently being catalogued for the British Academy's *Sylloge of Coins of the British Isles* series and is the subject of a general reappraisal.[7]

OVERVIEW OF THE NUMISMATIC EVIDENCE

Hoards

There are 33 tenth- to fourteenth-century coin hoards recorded from Man. Details of the specific discoveries, contents and principal references are summarised in Appendix I,[8] to which the running numbers in the text refer. The hoards fall into two main chronological groupings, the distribution of which is illustrated in figure 18.2.[9] Hoards that are positively dated and for which the details are relatively certain appear in the chart in solid black, while hoards that are definite but cannot be dated with the same accuracy are hatched and 'floating'. Both concentrations are significantly, if enigmatically, narrow and specific. The first occurs in the later Viking Age,

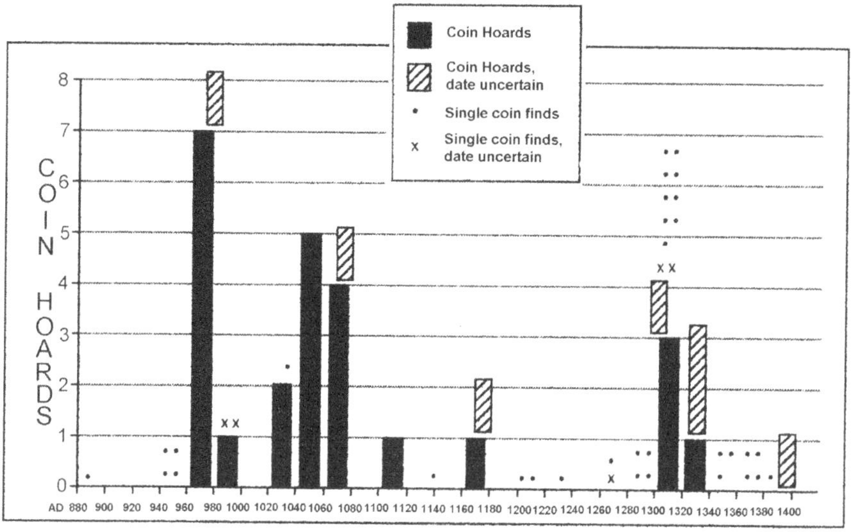

Fig. 18.2 *Name of histogram*
Extended caption text, up to 2 lines. Extended caption text, up to 2 lines. Extended caption text, up to 2 lines. Extended caption text, up to 2 lines.

*c.*955–60 until *c.*1075, while the later hoards aggregate in the early fourteenth century, and only a handful of finds fall between the two. Many of the hoards were discovered in the eighteenth or nineteenth centuries and are no longer extant, or are only partially preserved, and have been carefully reconstructed based on clues from contemporary written accounts and based on the patination and condition of coins which are associated. Only a few hoards have been recovered or investigated using modern methods, and their discovery may be attributed to both professional archaeologists (15, 16, 24, 26) and metal detectorists (9, 25, 27).

Since so few hoards have been properly excavated this century, little is known about the precise context of most finds. Nevertheless, enough clues are provided in the sources to indicate that several hoard depositions (where a general provenance is known) appear to be in some way associated with a keeill or keeill cemetery. This applies to the Viking-Age hoards in particular, but at least two of the medieval hoards (24 and 26) also derive from keeills. As many as 200 of these early Christian chapels dot the island, dating from about the sixth century, and they were probably rebuilt and/or used continuously through the Viking Age, falling out of use *c.*1200. Indeed, the structures would have been ruins by the time the later hoards were deposited. The exact relationship between Manx hoards and their apparent sacred contexts is not yet clear, and the subject will remain contentious until the sample of modern discoveries is larger and allows a more precise analysis of contexts. The Viking-Age pattern might have social significance as the result of a tradition in which deposits were made as a kind of offering, without the intention of retrieval (e.g., 1). This is at odds with what is usually quite reasonably assumed about hoarding (normally regarded as a kind of banking system), but coins and hoards in graves are known in this period from Scandinavia,[10] and the suggestion of a similar situation in Man is not without basis. If such a ritual were fashionable for a time, perhaps due to a thriving economy (ritual and economic use of coins need not be mutually exclusive), it might at least help to explain the remarkable concentration of hoards remaining on one island. Alternatively, such sites may have been chosen because they were deemed protected and 'safe', or because they were convenient and easily relocated. In other words, the pattern may simply reflect practical developments in an island where one was never too far away from a keeill site. This is at least assumed to be the rationale behind the later hoards, but the interpretation is less straightforward for depositions made when the sites held religious significance. Unfortunately there is no clear interpretation, and discussions of context remain theoretical. The existence of a potentially significant pattern must at least be noted in the hope that new discoveries will clarify and enhance our understanding of the situation.

Single Finds – There are 39 single-coin finds, casual losses rather than conscious depositions, recorded for the period up to AD 1400 in the Isle of Man. Other single finds may exist in private hands or in collections off Man but, since its foundation in 1886 (and opening of the museum in 1922), the Manx Museum and National Trust has generally been the first port of call for those wishing to report and identify finds. A listing of the known single finds and their principal references is found in Appendix II.[11] These are represented in Fig. 18.2 as small, black dots (•) where the coin is known for certain to come from a Manx context and where the date of the coin is positive. An 'x' is used instead of a dot where there is some question about the discovery, provenance and/or date of the coin. The finds fall into three general types of discovery: first, those that came to light in a completely random fashion, for example, during gardening and building, and were then recorded by antiquarians or reported to the Manx Museum (17 coins); second, those found during formal archaeological excavations (13 coins); and third, representing a phenomenon of the last three decades, those found in the course of metal detecting (9 coins).

The extensive excavations on St Patrick's Isle, Peel, in the 1980s produced several rare tenth-century Anglo-Saxon single-coin finds, as well as one

Fig. 18.3 *A selection of Phase III Scandinavian pennies from the Peel Castle 1982 hoard.*
Manx Museum 82-150, Manx National Heritage (left to right, 0.84 g/12.9 gr.; 0.57 g/18.8 gr., 0.77 g/1 1.9 gr., 0.85 g/13.1 gr.)

coin each of the eleventh, thirteenth and fourteenth centuries; an eleventh-century hoard of Dublin-minted pennies was also unearthed (Fig. 18.3).[12] Excavations in recent years have also taken place in Castletown (1989, 1991–2)[13] and have been ongoing at Rushen Abbey since 1998, both sites adding a small number of coin finds to the total. Metal detecting has proved itself a fairly popular hobby in Man, and its own club of amateur archaeologists was founded in 1979. Members have an exemplary history of working in co-operation with Museum archaeologists, and they are responsible for retrieving much material, medieval as well as later.[14] One might have expected this category of find to outnumber dramatically the former two, as in England, where the hobby has brought on an explosion of new material and has revolutionised our perceptions of coin use amongst peasants in the Middle Ages.[15] Dyer's work on the subject demonstrated that the comparatively low number of coins from settlements is not a genuine reflection of who used money on a regular basis, especially since high-status sites were only moderately more productive than poorer sites. Detectorists in England have observed that the majority of single finds derive from fields, not from within settlements, but in agricultural land quite a distance from them (in part because this land is available for metal-detecting). It seems that money was a widespread phenomenon in the English countryside, and stray losses in fields might indicate the presence of occasional marketplaces or fairgrounds, or coins may have been lost by peasants during agricultural work, or swept up and transported with household debris, which was periodically spread on fields as a kind of fertiliser.[16] No matter how they got to the fields, their presence today is proof that coin use was not restricted to an élite, but a habit that transcended social boundaries.

So far, however, concentrations of single finds have not been found in the fields of Man. A total of nine detector finds on record from within the given date parameters is a paltry sum indeed.[17] Time and more systematic efforts could alter the emerging pattern, and the unfortunate reality must be factored in that some finds are likely to have been made but not added to the official archaeological record. Nevertheless, preliminary impressions based on the known material are telling, and it will be shown that in contrast to England, and despite the concentration of hoards, the evidence for widespread coin use in the Middle Ages does not exist in Man.

Viking-Age Finds

Hoards

There are 20 documented, closely dated, and (in all but one case) at least partially extant hoards of the Viking period. The blank interval from AD 995 until about 1030 creates two distinct phases of hoarding during this period. This roughly fits the wider trend in the Irish Sea region, where for some as yet unexplained reason a lull in hoarding occurred just after AD 1000 until the 1020s.[18] With one exception, the tenth-century hoards aggregate in the geographical south of Man, while the eleventh-century hoards are concentrated in the north of Man, with the focus on the west coast and north of Peel. Hoards dating to the tenth century (Appendix I: 1–8) are composed almost entirely of Anglo-Saxon pennies, as one would expect, with just a few issues from Viking rulers of the kingdom of York (1, 6 and 7) and a single mid-tenth-century Continental coin from Melle (1). At least three irregular types or imitations of tenth-century Anglo-Saxon pennies are also known (6 and 7). There is a possibility that early Hiberno-Scandinavian coins based on the *Crux* type of Æthelred II were present in the Bradda Head 1848 hoard (8), but this is unconfirmed and most of the coins were lost to a watchmaker's pot. Based on the composition of these hoards, and in particular the scarcity of hack-silver, it appears that Man's closest economic and political ties were probably with Anglo-Saxon England rather than Ireland in the second half of the tenth century. The impact and extent of this connection and the form it took is impossible to gauge based on the coinage alone, but a written clue indicates a formal alliance with England during the reign of Edgar, and lends weight to the suggestion that Man's interests lay in this direction at least in the early 970s.[19]

The eleventh- and early twelfth-century hoards (9–20) are sometimes

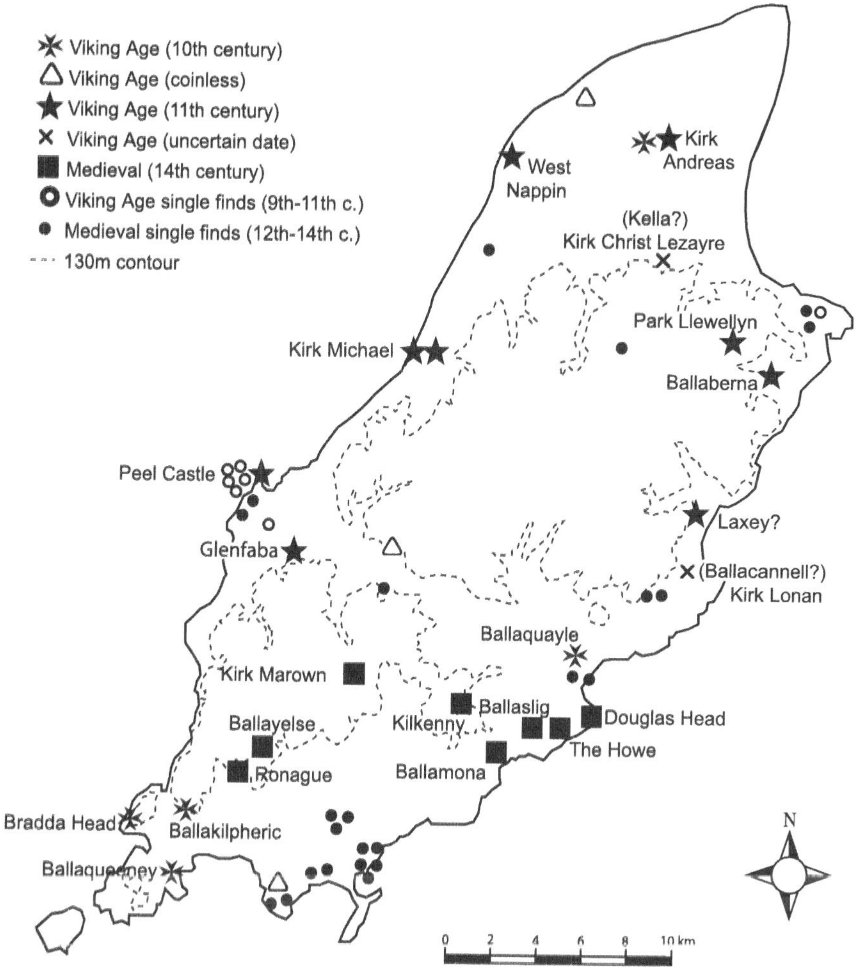

Fig. 18.4 *Hoards and single coin finds from the Isle of Man to c.1405.*

of a single series only, such as several which appear to have been entirely from Dublin (11, 15, 18, 19 and 20) and one which may have contained primarily coins of Edward the Confessor (17), but it is equally common to have a mixture, with two, three or more currencies (Anglo-Saxon, Hiberno-Scandinavian, and Hiberno-Manx and other types) combined in a single deposit (9, 10, 13, 14, 16). In one case Normandy deniers were included in the diverse array (16), and in another there were also four anomalous 'Knútr' imitation pennies (13). At least six of the above coin hoards, including two tenth-century hoards, also contained a bullion element in the form of arm-rings, hack-silver, ingots or other ornaments (5, 7, 9, 13, 14, 16). This tendency for an eclectic mixture of currencies illustrates the cosmopolitan nature of trade, and is most spectacularly illustrated by the new hoard from Glenfaba found in 2003 (9) *c.*1030, as well as the Kirk Michael 1972/5 'savings hoard' (16), buried *c.*1065, both of which contained locally produced coinage in addition to foreign coins and bullion.

These carefully selected accumulations provide insights into what was regarded as valuable at the time of deposition. They are also windows onto the workings of an economy that was apparently flexible enough to sustain a need for such an assortment of currencies, some of which would have been regarded as anachronistic and unacceptable in the more tightly regulated markets of England. In short, the Glenfaba and Kirk Michael 1972/5 finds epitomise Man's role as a well-situated island along a busy trade route. Perhaps it was practical to maintain a diverse purse adaptable to various payment needs, ready for trade and negotiation with any merchant, whether a bullion- or coin-user. Above all, they introduce questions about the implications and practicality of such a heterogeneous economy, and tell of a situation in which a degree of economic chaos was acceptable and prevailed. This situation may on the one hand be the impetus for an attempt to move towards a standardised monetary economy with a single local currency. At the same time, these mixed hoards illustrate that such a move was contrary to an existing mindset that favoured monetary options over loyalty to a single currency, or was perhaps even indifferent on the subject of coinage.

Some details are known about two additional eighteenth-century hoards (21 and 22), but the information is incomplete and they cannot be precisely dated, except that they are almost certainly 'Viking-Age'. The former contained Anglo-Saxon pennies of unknown type, while the other hoard was from the eleventh century (described by an eighteenth-century observer as 'Danish', thus probably Hiberno-Scandinavian). They are hatched and floating in Figure 2, to avoid giving a misleadingly precise date, but that each existed in some form is certain. Also difficult to date with precision are three coinless hoards belonging to this general period (I, II and III). Although this is not the place for a detailed examination of this class of find, they are included in this study because the ornaments would have functioned as money to a Viking trader. The plain arm-rings, probably used as currency by Vikings in Scotland in particular, occur with coins in other finds from Man (5, 7, 13, 14, 16), and circulated in the Irish Sea region from *c.*925–*c.*1075.[20] The Ballacamaish 1868 deposit (II) of two neck-rings (both broken) and a twisted silver arm-ring has been dated by

Graham-Campbell to *c.*950–*c.*1025, 'possibly during the troubled 970s'.[21] The exceedingly rare find of gold from Greeba (III) may be confidently dated to the eleventh century and will form the subject of a future publication by Sir David Wilson and James Graham-Campbell.

The first group of hoards begins *c.*960 (or a little earlier), which is curiously later than the start and main phases of hoarding in Scotland and Ireland, where hoards are prevalent from the start of the tenth century onwards. This is not the case in Man despite other archaeological evidence attesting to a permanent Viking presence from the early tenth century, a revised date that is later than once assumed but strongly suggested by the material evidence.[22] The settlement of Man therefore did not follow on the heels of the earliest Viking activity in Ireland, although one might have expected Man, with its seemingly advantageous situation in the Irish Sea, to be contemporary and to have had early and close ties in this direction. Even if there was no parallel settlement during Dublin's ninth-century *longphort* phase, Man would at least seem a logical and convenient haven for the Vikings expelled from Dublin in 902, or perhaps a natural stopping place in their return in 917. Several prominent pagan burial mounds,[23] generally thought to be of the first generation of settlers, may date to about this time and the burials contain some artefacts of Insular manufacture and inspiration. This may at least hint at the beginning of a connection with the Vikings in Ireland, though perhaps only in a minor way when the lack of numismatic evidence is taken into account. For most of the tenth century the Vikings in Ireland did not mint their own coinage, but conducted business using a mixture of foreign coins (predominantly Anglo-Saxon pennies, as well as Continental, Arabic, and Viking issues from East Anglia and Northumbria) as well as ingots, arm-rings and cut pieces of silver. Tenth-century Hiberno-Viking silver hoards are therefore characteristically diverse, and can be entirely coinless, mixed coin and bullion, or else made up only of coin.[24] These hoards are also distinctive in their extended age-structures[25] and in their mint-structures (north-eastern mints predominate),[26] which are quite distinct from the composition of mints found, for example, in Irish hoards. It is difficult to say for certain by which route silver reached Man in the middle decades of the tenth century but, as mentioned above, one would expect comparable mint-structures as well as more bullion had it arrived via Ireland. The numismatic evidence therefore suggests closer economic and political ties in the mid tenth century with England – specifically York and the north-east – than to somewhere with a dominant or transitional metal-weight economy, like Ireland.

It is perhaps most remarkable of all that a whole class of material produced by Vikings in Ireland is absent from the Manx archaeological record: stamped, broad-band arm-rings, prevalent in the period AD 850–950 (*c*.880–*c*.930–40).[27] They are found both whole and cut up into hack-silver, and are present in 23 hoards from Ireland and in at least a dozen more from England, Scotland, Wales, and Norway.[28] For example, broad-band arm-rings were found in the north-west of England in the Cuerdale hoard *c*.905, and in Scotland, in the hoards from Storr Rock, Skye *c*.935 and Skaill, Orkney *c*.950–970. Examples are also known from Wales, where a piece of one was most recently unearthed at the early tenth-century Norse settlement at Llanbedrgoch, Anglesey.[29] Similar arm-rings were also found in Wales at Red Wharf Bay,[30] and a fragment of one is known from the Bangor hoard, buried in or after 921.[31] With sound evidence for the dispersal of this class of material across the Irish Sea and beyond, it seems significant indeed that Man was bypassed at this early stage. There is, then, no indication of an overbearing Dublin influence in the tenth century and the implication so far seems to be that Man was detached from Hiberno-Viking affairs until after the turn of the millennium, perhaps even several decades after Vikings began minting coins in Dublin (*c*.995).

It is interesting to note that the tenth-century hoards are more infrequent than the eleventh-century hoards, and these appear to be characterised by generally larger assemblages of wealth, although the sample is small. Overshadowing all is the great Ballaquayle hoard of 1894 (7), which contained several hundred coins, if not 1,000, and the Kirk Andreas 1866/7 (6) and the Bradda Head 1848 (8) hoards each contained over 100 pennies, the latter being the greater of the two. The Ballaqueeney 1874 (1) hoard, however, is significantly smaller than previously thought,[32] while the sizes of (2) and (3) are uncertain as they may have been relatively small finds, or else parcels of larger deposits. In the eleventh century there is evidence for more intensive hoarding activity over a longer period, and the hoards appear to be small and medium-sized (practical sums), rather than vast stores of wealth removed from circulation (e.g., 7). The logical conclusion would then be that there was a great deal of silver reaching the island in the tenth century, but it landed in fewer hands, where it accumulated and did not continue in general circulation. As noted by Wilson,[33] the profusion of monumental stone sculpture during the tenth century is interesting in this connection, supporting the inference that the earlier hoards occur at the height of Manx prosperity, but it seems that this wealth was not very evenly distributed. The eleventh-century trend indicates a more general proliferation and acceptance of coinage at a local level, possibly even for common transactions and market use, although the single-find evidence is too sparse to take this suggestion further. A short-term or experimental shift towards a more general usage of coinage in Man in the eleventh century is, however, indicated by the introduction of a local coin type at this time.

Finally, falling outside the main concentration of hoards and thus apparently representing an anomaly rather than reflecting a wider pattern, is one small, late eleventh- or early twelfth-century (Phase VI) Hiberno-Scandinavian deposit (20). This hoard was integrated into the National Museum of Scotland's collection in the late eighteenth century, but it can be positively traced back to a Manx donor, Mrs Wood, wife of Governor John Wood (1761–77). The hoard was lost sometime during the reign of Magnus Barelegs (1098–1103), who used Man as a base for raiding in Wales and Ireland, or during the scramble for power after his death, when Godred Crovan's line was reinstated with the return of his son, Óláfr, from the court of Henry I of England.[34] It is interesting to note that connections between the ruling families of Man and England are seen to be in place at this time, although the political orientation based on the lingering numismatic evidence seems to be still with Ireland at the turn of the twelfth century.

The cessation of intensive hoarding from *c.*1075 is interesting and somewhat surprising if conventional interpretations of hoarding are applied. If an increase in hoarding signifies a time of unrest or acute danger, when more people than usual are victims of the calamitous cocktail that involved hiding money in the ground for safe-keeping and dying due to that danger, preventing them from recovering the secreted treasures, then it would seem particularly appropriate at this juncture, a time of warfare and political upheaval with the rise of Godred Crovan in 1079, to witness a sudden increase in hoarding. In fact, it is written in the Manx chronicle that, after defeating the Manxmen in his third attempt:

> ... Godred gave his army the option of either dividing Man among themselves and living in it, if they so preferred, or of plundering the land entirely and returning home. It pleased them more to lay waste the whole island and to enrich themselves with its valuables, and thus to return to their homes.[35]

According to the chronicle Godred subsequently stayed to rule Man, and divided the island in two, allowing the native Manx to inhabit the northern half. The chronicle for this time paints a picture of upheaval and bloodshed on a grand scale, but the evidence from the hoards falls silent. Even if he proved to be an acceptable ruler after the disturbance, and if Man then entered a period with some semblance of 'self-sufficiency',[36] convention would still expect some reflection in the hoarding pattern of this major turning point in Manx history. In the same way, the traditional interpretation falls short of explaining the gap in hoarding between *c.*995–*c.*1030, which divides the Viking-Age hoards into two distinct phases (discussed above). Ironically, the only Viking raid on the island recorded in the Anglo-Saxon Chronicle (in 1000) occurred during this hiatus.[37] Similarly, there is no peak in hoarding (not even one hoard) at the time of the battle of Ronaldsway in 1275 when the Scots defeated and killed 537 Manxmen,[38] and the list could go on.

There is no simple explanation as to why people hoard at some times and not others, or why there are no traces left of hoarding activity at certain times. The traditional explanation does apply in some cases, but diverse social practices and evolving local traditions, due perhaps to an influx of new people, might also be a potential factor in hoard-deposition and non-retrieval. Hoards could even be the result of another lethal combination: surplus and a vibrant economy coupled with the outbreak of disease. The absence of hoards is not necessarily a sign of peaceful times, but may be because depositing coins in the ground was not fashionable or was thought unsafe, or because fewer coins were available to be hoarded. In this case, the negative evidence may even be an indicator of economic decline, but again there are many variables and external corroboration is necessary. If politics are to blame it should be remembered that many, many events that could have affected people's economic behaviour are wholly unknown to us today, and it is unwise to assume hoards are always tied in with the major recorded incidents. The gaps in hoarding cited above serve to remind us that political strife alone does not dictate the hoarding pattern, and we must be conscious of the other factors that create a complex pattern such as that in Man, even if we cannot fully or satisfactorily explain it.

Single Finds

The Viking-Age single finds begin with one extremely unusual ninth-century find from Kirk Maughold churchyard, a Frisian(?) imitation of a Louis the Pious gold solidus (possibly made from an official obverse die paired with a blundered reverse),[39] the only definite ninth-century coin from the island. A gap follows until the middle decades of the tenth century, when four Anglo-Saxon pennies of Edmund, Eadred and Eadwig appear, all from the Peel Castle excavation. It is interesting to note that these date to the decades just before the start of hoarding in Man; thus while the types occur in hoards, the deposition dates are later than the earliest date possible for each single coin. The single coins may have been old when lost, as they were in the hoards, or alternatively this may indicate a presence of coinage in Man at a time when there was no political or social impetus for hoarding.

Two were associated with graves, one an offering in a child's grave, and the other possibly included accidentally with the grave fill, although equally it may have been intentionally thrown in during the burial ritual, a custom known from Scandinavian contexts. There are three alleged single finds of Æthelred II, type unknown, and noted from passing references only (one has been excluded as a probable stray from hoard no. 8, as recently suggested by James Graham-Campbell[40]). Their presence seems unlikely based on the wider single find pattern from this century, but it is not impossible. Finally, one mid-eleventh-century find (Hiberno-Scandinavian Phase III) was also found at Peel Castle. No other random or excavated single finds are known from the late Viking era, and the next recorded find dates from a whole century later. The meagreness of single finds from this period is not surprising, but is much as would be expected elsewhere around the Irish Sea and in western England and Wales, where coins from this time are much more likely to be part of hoards than found singly.[41] This is evident especially in contrast to the later group which, as is typical based on finds elsewhere, sees a steep increase in the number of single finds, particularly during the Edwardian period.

The Manx Mint

One of the most important monetary developments for the Isle of Man was the opening of a local mint in the eleventh century. The mint was short-lived, functioning from *c.*1025 to *c.*1065 or slightly later, and may have produced coins only sporadically between these years. It is enigmatic that the Manx coins appear not to have left the island in any great number, and must have been minted with an intention other than to facilitate overseas trade. They also did not replace other currencies on the island, but circu lated with foreign money and silver bullion, as demonstrated by the hoard evidence. The coins are present in at least six hoards (10, 12, 13, 14, 16, 19) as well as (9), where there is a large group of coins from the transitional Dublin/Manx obverse die,, and with the excellent dating evidence provided by this range of deposits it has been possible to suggest date brackets for the duration of the series, and also to establish a relative internal chronology for the coinage, with discernible Early, Middle and Late Styles (Fig. 18.5). This is based also on changes in overall appearance and epigraphy, a steady decrease in weight, as well as variations in the silver alloy over time. Though the mint did not become a permanent fixture in Man, its appearance was momentous and the act was profound in initiating the idea of a local currency where previously there had been none. The series was first identified by Michael Dolley, who published his theory in 1976,[42] just a short time after the discovery of the Kirk Michael 1972/5

Early Style (1.05g)

Middle Style (0.95g)

Late Style (0.58g)

Fig. 18.5 *Three Hiberno-Manx Coins: Early, Middle and Late Styles.*
i. Manx Museum 83-326, Manx National Heritage, Park Lewellyn 1835 hoard (1.05 g/ 16.2 gr.)
ii. Manx Museum 76-84/13, Manx National Heritage, Kirk Michael 1972/5 hoard (0.95 g/14.7 gr.)
iii. Manx Museum 76-84/2, Manx National Heritage, Kirk Michael 1972/5 hoard (0.58 g/8.9 gr.)
Scale of photographs is 2:1

hoard which contained 21 examples of the type he termed 'Hiberno-Manx'. Specimens had been known previously and attributed to the Hiberno-Scandinavian series from Dublin,[43] but it was only with the discovery of such a substantial number that their distinctiveness – in both style and distribution – became apparent. Previously there was simply not enough evidence to postulate a mint on Man. Our understanding of the origin of the Manx series was sharpened by the discovery, by W.A. Seaby, of a die-link with the Dublin coinage.[44] Recently a corpus of Hiberno-Manx coins has been compiled, and a reassessment of the evidence with the benefit of metallurgical analyses conducted by Peter Northover has supported and refined Dolley's identification of a Manx coinage.[45]

It is apparent that the Hiberno-Manx series was established with the transfer of a die or pair of dies from the Dublin mint to an unknown location in Man. An obverse die, the 'Transfer Die' (Fig. 18.6/i, ii and iii), was removed from Dublin and used in Man with locally made reverse dies, until it became worn out or broken, and had to be discarded. Signs of die wear are indeed apparent in the later coins produced from this die. A replacement obverse die was prepared by closely copying this transitional die, although the result was in a different, rougher style (Fig. 18.6/iv). Coins produced from the second obverse die, and subsequent obverses, bear the same cardinal features: a pellet cross behind the head and at two points in the obverse legend, and a prominent slash before the face. One reverse die provides a critical link (Fig. 18.6/iii and iv), for it is found with both the prototype obverse and the copy of it. Subsequent dies were cut locally, copying the original die but in a fashion which reinterpreted the intended design. The portrait becomes increasingly more stylised, and the eye in particular is simpler, represented by a solitary pellet. This is never the case with contemporary coins of the Hiberno-Scandinavian series, where the facial expression appears different because an oval always encircles the eye-pellet. A second mint had to be involved to account for the stylistic changes, and there are tell-tale signs of a less experienced die-cutter being involved. This is true not just in terms of artistic ability and execution of the design, but witnessed in a much higher proportion of retrograde and nonsensical legends than is seen in the Hiberno-Scandinavian series. This is not to imply that the coins were inferior in terms of market value, and it should be emphasised that literacy and outward appearance are not indicators of a viable coinage, but only that the die-cutter was more careless or less familiar with the art of die-cutting. In fact, EPMA analysis of the Hiberno-Manx silver alloy has demonstrated that the coins were produced to a consistently high standard of fineness,[46] ranging between 91–97 per cent 'silver' (Ag+Au+Pb),[47] and suffered a significant decrease in fineness only

i: Hiberno-Scandinavian Prototype

ii: Hiberno-Scandinavian/Hiberno-Manx?

iii: Hiberno-Scandinavian/Hiberno-Manx

iv: Hiberno-Manx

Fig. 18.6
Sequence of the Hiberno-Scandinavian/ Hiberno-Manx Transitional Die
i . Fitzwilliam Museum, Henderson bequest 1933, no. 2339 (1.44 g/ 22.2 gr.)
ii. Manx Museum 74-130/2, Manx National Heritage (1.04 g/16.1 gr.)
iii. Royal Irish Academy, National Museum of Ireland, no. 3092 (1.06 g/ 16.4 gr.)
iv. Royal Irish Academy, National Museum of Ireland, no. 3140 (1.21 g/1 8.7 gr.)
Scale of photographs is 2:1

<u>HIBERNO-NORSE</u> (PHASE II)	<u>HIBERNO-NORSE</u> (PHASE III)	<u>HIBERNO-MANX</u>
+SIHTRCRE + DYFLNI	+IINITRCREIDIFNI	:: IIIIIIIIIIII :: DIIC
+SIHTRCRE + DYFL	+NNTRCR + DNICII	:: IIIIIIIIII :: DIIIIC
+NHTRCRE + DNN	+RNEINRNEL	:: IIIIIIIIIIII :: D.IIIC
+HNTRCRE + INDI	+RINRIDI + INNO	:: IIIIIIIIIII :: D.I.I.I.C.
+NHTRCRE + DYFLI	+IINDHNONDNHN	:: IIIIIIIIIIIIII: :: DIII.C

Fig. 18.7 *Hiberno-Scandinavian and Hiberno-Manx Obverse Legends 2*

during the Late Style. This generally mirrors the contemporary Hiberno-Scandinavian standard and indicates a well-regulated and relatively sophisticated mint on a par with that in Dublin, whose product had no intrinsic reason to be rejected in foreign markets.

The reverse legends at first closely imitate those of Dublin, one factor allowing us to date and identify earlier and later stages in the Hiberno-Manx series, and a wedge cross appears (when an initial cross is employed) rather than the distinctive pellet-quadrants on the obverse. Errors, however, were rapidly incorporated, suggesting that the legends were being copied rather than understood. The die-cutter even seems unfamiliar with the shape of individual letters, often replacing them with symbols or slashes. This is also witnessed in the obverses, and it is interesting to see the divergence when samples of Hiberno-Manx and Hiberno-Scandinavian obverse legends are compared. Figure 18.7 looks specifically at Hiberno-Scandinavian Phase II (*c.*1020–35), which would have had the most influence on the initial stages of the Manx coinage, and Phase III (*c.*1035–55), when the Hiberno-Scandinavian coins become smaller and less literate, but with obvious continuity from Phase II. The contrast provides an immediate and dramatic impression of the individuality of the Manx series. The almost stubborn rigidity of the Manx obverse legend is maintained throughout the series, reflecting not only a certain insecurity about introducing new ideas to the design, but also a sense of isolation in the business of die-production. The Hiberno-Manx coins are also larger in diameter than contemporary coins from Dublin, and whether this was an intentional move to distinguish the coins from other issues, or a mere coincidence based on available resources, it is evidence again that they emanate from a different source. The coins are also thinner, resulting occasionally in a production flaw known as 'ghosting', where the image on one side of the coin shows through and distorts the other side.

In a sample of 60 Hiberno-Manx coins of which the photographs were available, a total of 18 different obverse dies were identified and these are paired with 43 different reverses. Based on the degree of die-linking in the sample, it was possible to estimate the number of dies used to strike the Hiberno-Manx coinage (approximately 26 obverses and 132 reverses).[48] This provides a sense of the extent of the series without suggesting a total output figure, which would be misleading since we cannot know whether a die was used to its full capacity, or what that capacity might have been for a Manx die. The numbers support the suggestion of the hoard evidence, which indicates that the series was not minor and insubstantial, nor could it represent a one-off minting incident, and that it developed gradually over time to incorporate changes in weight standard, style and alloy. The mint must have functioned for about 35 to 45 years, within the range of *c.*1025–*c.*1065, and it may even extend later, but the hoarding pattern is such that there are no finds after 1075. Indeed, our knowledge of the Late Style dies is more incomplete than for the earlier styles, and the demise of the mint is therefore less understood than the initial stages of the series. It is also significant that it took five times more reverse dies than obverses to produce the Manx coinage. While reverses were naturally more susceptible to breakage as the top die received the direct impact of the hammer, a typical ratio at Anglo-Saxon mints was less than two to one,[49] and during the *Helmet* and *Quatrefoil* types of the early Hiberno-Scandinavian coinage the ratio was one to one.[50] The astounding Manx statistic suggests that in Man there may have been fundamental difficulties in manufacturing strong dies, a highly specialised craft, and this points once more towards a novice establishment. Thus, the series became distinctive in many respects, and though it owed its conception to Dublin, it evolved along an entirely separate path. The Manx mint provides yet another example, along with ones from English, Hiberno-Scandinavian and Scandinavian contexts, of valuable, skilfully cut and manufactured dies being moved - whether bought, commissioned, stolen or presented as gifts - for use in a distant mint.

There are 64 Hiberno-Manx pennies currently known, as well as 43(+) examples of different states of the 'Transfer Die' (up from 13 after the discovery of the Glenfaba hoard), some of which must have been struck in Man, but earlier examples may derive from the Dublin mint before the die was removed. The contentious transitional group is therefore treated separately and awaits further examination before additions can be confidently added to the Hiberno-Manx total. Two examples are positively provenanced to Manx hoards (6 and 9) and one from the 1902 Garde hoard from Gotland (*c.*1050),[51] while the rest are unprovenanced and scattered in a variety of collections. Excluding the transitional group coins, there are 31 Hiberno-Manx pennies that derive from secure Manx provenances and seven from Scandinavian or East Baltic hoards. That there are some finds from Scandinavia is not at all surprising, but rather to be expected based on the overall pattern of coin finds of the first half of the eleventh century when through trade, and through tribute payments, vast amounts of foreign coinage reached Scandinavia. In addition to the provenanced coins, there are 25 that have lost all record of original find location, so could have been found in Man, or not. The absence of pecking in this group, a common practice in Scandinavian marketplaces that involved testing the silver with a sharp instrument, and in effect mutilating the coin, at least rules out Scandinavian provenances. It is also notable that not a single example can be positively tied with any other Irish Sea location. Even if some were to be found in Ireland or elsewhere today, it would not undermine the suggestion of a Manx mint.

There is a high degree of die-linking among the Hiberno-Manx examples on the island, and between those in Manx hoards and the coins without provenance, forming a positive bond between those without provenance and the tight-knit group on the island. Along with the estimate of the total obverse and reverse dies used to produce the series, it was determined that a fairly complete picture exists of the population of obverse dies in particular, especially for the Early and Middle Styles, with 85 per cent of the obverses represented in the corpus.[52] The fact that a good majority (68 per cent) occurs amongst the Manx-provenanced group again supports the premise of a Manx source.[53] The distinctive physical attributes and the die evidence, and above all the dispersal of the series over several variously dated hoards on one island, not just a single chance deposit from a trader or pirate in transit, makes the theory of a Manx-based mint virtually incontrovertible.

There are no historical sources specific to the island until the mid-thirteenth-century chronicle, and only a smattering of early references to Man exist in Irish sources. Indeed very little is known of the administration in Man before Godred Crovan's take-over in 1079, but Seán Duffy's careful scrutinising of the Irish annals has turned up evidence of a mid-eleventh-century involvement in Manx affairs by Dublin rulers. This is seen specifically in the personages of Echmarcach mac Ragnaill (d. 1065), who may have sought haven in Man and ruled the island in or before *c.*1052 until 1061, and Murchad son of King Diarmait mac Maíl na mBó, who subsequently reunited it with Dublin and presumably reigned in both until his death in 1070.[54] Though the sources are not explicit, Duffy also deduces an earlier involvement and growing interest (*c.*1000) in Manx affairs based on aggressive moves by the Hiberno-Scandinavians of Dublin towards the east Ulster kingdom of Ulaid, the Irish region closest to Man. The numismatic evidence certainly bears out Duffy's suggestion of a Dublin involvement in Man by the third decade of the eleventh century, if not earlier. This is seen both in the frequency of Hiberno-Scandinavian pennies in eleventh-century hoards and in their predominantly northern, almost 'Ireland-facing' distribution, and most eloquently of all in the Manx coinage which traces back to the essential Dublin obverse. The political connection with Dublin at this time is therefore not just hinted at by the sources, but has important tangible manifestations. Dolley suggested that the Battle of Clontarf in 1014, in which Manxmen allegedly participated and fell, contributed to the circumstances that gave rise to the Manx mint a decade later.[55] It is difficult to see how it could have had a direct impact, and provides at best the long-term backdrop of general unrest and political upheaval after the deaths of many key players in the region. Of more immediate and plausible relevance may be the sea battle between the Dubliners and the Ulaid that took place in 1022, around the time the Manx mint emerges. Duffy suggests this was fought due to tension over Man, or to secure safe access in the seas near the Ulaid for unencumbered trade and to reach the Isles.[56] The crises in this region point towards a political and strategic interest in Man and the territory around it, even if the sources do not expound further. The sea battle itself therefore marks one possible turning point in this conflict, and, perhaps, an opportunity for a mint to be established upon the arrival of a new ruler from Dublin who sought creative ways to assert his authority and legitimacy, and to raise funds and facilitate trade.

The decades around the turn of the millennium saw the spread of minting in many Viking spheres, including Dublin (from *c.*995) and Man (*c.*1025), and there may have been other mints in the Irish Sea region, such as in the Wirral where Knútr *Quatrefoil* imitations appear to have been produced in the early 1020s.[57] Though there had been earlier, sporadic minting activity in Scandinavia (such as at Ribe and Hedeby) in the eighth to tenth centuries, it was at the tail end of the tenth century that royal mints emerged in Sweden, Denmark and Norway. It has been suggested that the institution held profound symbolic weight as the right and privilege of a king, an extension of royal power, and was manipulated for propaganda purposes.[58] The metal-weight economies had functioned long and well, relying on a variety of foreign coins and bullion, and monetisation was 'a development that had not so much to do with trade as with the expression of growing royal authority and strength'.[59] The brief but significant interlude in which the

Manx mint functioned therefore raises larger questions about the impetus behind a new mint and the factors that contribute to the formation of an organised economic structure, or at least at an apparent attempt to establish one. It seems that in this case political factors could have been as important, if not more important, than economic considerations. At the same time, care was taken to assure its commercial viability and the intention behind it was not just egocentric – the coinage had to be 'good' to engender respect. Coinage was a convenient medium for royal revenue, an 'economic weapon',[60] and may have been intended to raise funds as well as to unite people in the ritual of paying dues, and respect, to a central figure. Essentially, it was an act of control and a method of channelling the formal recognition of a leader. A new mint in Man may therefore have been one part of a strategic legitimisation process to broadcast a new king's authority, and ultimately to emulate the success of King Sigtryggr of Dublin.

The fact that the Manx coinage did not block out foreign currencies despite being of a conscientiously high quality seems to indicate that the king did not have sufficient political or economic power to exclude alien coins. Or, he may never have intended it to function in this way if its inspiration was first as a propaganda mechanism, and it never realised its full potential as an effective coinage. Trade was nonetheless one aspect of the coinage's natural function, and the hoard evidence indicates that the coins were indeed circulating on the island, and even in the Baltic in small numbers, but trade may not have been its primary or initial role. The Manx coinage apparently ceased within a few decades of its inception and most likely with the demise of the political power that created it, but was it a failure? Though it was not a resounding or lasting economic success, it served a political function and its presence must have provided a tangible sign of autonomy and authority for the ruler who instigated it. That Godred Crovan and subsequent rulers appear not to have continued the tradition of local coinage is not a sign of its failure as much as a symptom of its immediate and limited function. It may also be a reflection of a decline in the supply of silver, and perhaps the resources to make a practical and viable coinage were not reaching the island by the last quarter of the eleventh century.

Medieval Period Finds

Hoards

From the medieval period there are five securely dated hoards, appearing in solid black in Fig. 18.2. Only one hoard derives from the later twelfth century (23), while the others date to the first decades of the fourteenth century (24, 25, 26, 27).[61] The provenanced hoards have an exclusively southern distribution (Fig. 4). The earliest hoard in this group is an eighteenth-century find known from an illustration (23), while three others are new discoveries since 1977 (24, 25, 26). The fifth, from Ballaslig, has been recovered in stages over a very long period, the first coins discovered in 1839 presumably belonging to the very large, ploughed-out hoard recovered in several batches from a single field by skilled metal detectorists in 1978 and 1979–80 (27). There are five additional medieval hoards of uncertain date for which only vague or incomplete details are known (28, 29, 30, 31, 32). These are included to demonstrate the volume of material from this period in Man, even if they cannot contribute to a specific analysis of the numismatic material. As with the less certain Viking-Age examples, these are listed in a separate category in Appendix I, and they, too, appear hatched and floating in Fig. 18.2. The absence of hoards from the first half of the twelfth century, after the late Viking-Age deposit *c.*1100 (20), is not too surprising, since finds of coins of the early twelfth century are also relatively scarce in England. This is especially so during the reign of Henry I and, with the exception of a group of hoards coinciding with the Civil War, the situation persists until about 1160, due to a depleted bullion stock in England.[62]

The two subsequent hoards, one dated with good accuracy to after *c.*1174 (23) and the other appearing in the 'uncertain' category, but evidently dating to sometime after 1165 (28), were made up predominantly of Scottish pence. Scottish coins of this time are rare, and their occurrence at this stage is positive evidence of an orientation towards Scotland about the time of the third quarter of the twelfth century. Similarly, the total absence of hoards of English coins supports the idea that Man's political and economic axis lay in a direction other than England in the later twelfth century. It seems significant that lordship over the Hebrides, a unified kingdom in the first half of the twelfth century extending from Lewis to Man, was divided between two competing dynasties in the mid-1150s.[63] Man at this time lost control of Islay and Mull, and sporadic feuding continued between Guðröðr of Man (1153–87) and his successors, and the descendants of Somerled of Argyll (d. 1164). Their interests were mainly Hebrides-based and dynastic, or focused in the direction of their Norwegian overlords, and in this context the absence of English coinage in Man in the later twelfth century, and perhaps the presence of neighbouring Scottish issues, begins to make sense.

The absence of English coins at this stage becomes even more significant with the knowledge that a drastic increase in the volume of available currency in England occurred under the early Plantagenet kings, particularly after 1180. Mint output numbers for London and Canterbury, available in detail from 1220 onwards, serve to illustrate the vast amount of silver being released into circulation.[64] The numbers rocket between 1180–1280, and the substantial increase in the quantities of coinage leaving the mint is reflected in the wider archaeological record with the burgeoning of coin finds of the Short Cross and Long Cross types in England.[65] It is also significant that Henry II and John were pursuing English interests in Ireland from 1171 onwards, and one might have expected to see more signs of English contact considering their intensified activities in the region. In 1210 King John extended his power further in Ireland, and the Manx chronicle tells us he also sent an army led by an Earl Fuco to Man, where hostages were taken and 'in a fortnight they laid waste almost the whole island'.[66] Despite this, not a single deposit of the period has been discovered in Man, and only two halfpennies of the reign of John have occurred as stray finds. Based on the positive and negative numismatic evidence together, one must conclude that the coinage we might have expected to see was not reaching the island in significant quantity. The incident described in the chronicle was noted precisely because it was extraordinary, and there was no significant or lasting connection with England at this time.

In the 1240s, under the leadership of King Haraldr son of Óláfr Dubh, it is noted in the chronicle that a 'very stable peace' was achieved with the kings of England and Scotland,[67] and in 1247 Haraldr was knighted by Henry III of England, just as his father had been.[68] One would expect such circumstances to coincide with evidence of flourishing trade and enhanced economic exchange, but there are only three, possibly four, single coin finds of Henry III from Man and no hoards. Once again, the situation is baffling in view of the vast amount of coinage produced during his reign and its prevalence in finds elsewhere. Crovan's descendants ruled Man and the Isles under Norwegian suzerainty until 1266, when Mágnus Hákonarson (1263–80) renounced Norway's rights to the Isle of Man and the Hebrides in the treaty of Perth, and authority in the Isles was transferred to Alexander III, king of the Scots. Scottish lordship in Man, however, was not uncontested, and disputes over its ownership between England and Scotland continued into the fourteenth century. Man's final attempt to reinstate its own leader, the son of the last Norse king of Man, was crushed by the Scots in 1275, when Alexander III invaded and defeated the islanders at the battle of Ronaldsway. Scotland's interests in Man were suspended when Alexander III died in 1286 with no obvious heir, and a period of dynastic crisis ensued. This gave Edward I the opportunity to take possession, and Man was being ruled under his aegis by the 1290s. Yet, only a handful of single finds and possibly one or two hoards (29 and 30) coin-

Fig. 18.8 *Composition of the Ronague 1996 Hoard (c.1310)*

cide with the turbulent events of the later thirteenth century.

A concentration of hoards together with the majority of single finds finally occurs in the first decades of the fourteenth century. New and intensified contacts with England are indicated by the composition of these hoards, the largest of which (25, 26, 27) each contain over 90 per cent pennies from England plus small proportions of Scottish, Irish and, in the case of Ballaslig (27), Continental types. The composition of the Edwardian hoards is typical of English finds, and nothing stands out as significant or distinctive regarding their general make up. Man was much antagonised at about this time. Robert the Bruce reasserted Scotland's claim and laid siege on Castle Rushen in 1313, after which the island fell to Thomas Randolph, earl of Moray. The weakened island was apparently attacked again in 1316, in a raid launched from Ireland led by Richard de Mandeville. He and his men demanded land, or aid 'in terms of food, animals and money',[69] but the Manx people refused and were subsequently defeated in a battle fought near Barrule. It is written that de Mandeville's men 'plundered the land of all its more valuable goods and came upon much silver which had been long hidden in many places throughout the country',[70] and a particular focus of the month-long raid was Rushen abbey, where allegedly they 'left nothing at all'.

It is tempting to make a direct connection between the concentration of depositions and these precise events, but this is tenuous upon closer examination, since the nature of the evidence allows us to date each hoard with a high degree of precision. A re-examination of the material has enabled the dating of the Edwardian hoards to be refined and brought into line with recent scholarship.[71] The Ballayelse (24) and Kilkenny (25) hoards were deposited in or after *c.*1305, Ronague (26) *c.*1309, and the Ballaslig hoard (27) *c.*1325. The dates provided are *termini post quem* (or *t.p.q.*), the earliest date of the latest coin in each deposit, and this provides an accurate guide to the date at which the hoard was abandoned. In theory the coins could have remained in circulation longer than the latest coin without the introduction of another type, but this is unlikely at this stage of monetary history, and certainly could not persist for a protracted time without newer types creeping in. There are then clues in the overall composition and proportions of types represented, as well as in the excellent condition of the coins, which shows that they did not circulate for an extended period. The abrupt cut-off points of the Edwardian hoards provide good evidence that the deposition dates provided above are accurate within a few years. Each hoard is therefore either too early or too late to be convincingly associated with the events recorded in the Manx chronicle. The attacks were relatively isolated incidents, even if disastrous at the time, and it is unrealistic to propose that related circumstances and unrest led to the deposit of these hoards, except perhaps in the case of the Ronague hoard (26). Other factors, now lost to us, must have inspired their deposition and non-retrieval. The southern distribution of the Edwardian hoards is interesting in light of the plundering of Rushen abbey in 1316, but this is more likely to reflect the shift in political focus which had taken place, with Castle Rushen the centre of power on the island.[72]

The hoards and the significant peak in English single finds in the first decades of the fourteenth century reflect a dramatic shift in Man's political orientation and economic connections. The coin finds are therefore direct evidence of the strengthened English presence in Man established by Edward I at the end of the thirteenth century. While the number of single finds is still low by English standards and cannot reflect a fully monetised economy, the contrast is noteworthy and this sudden increase may also be a sign of a step having been taken towards the wider acceptance of coin use.

Single Finds

The medieval single-coin finds from Man are significantly more abundant than those of the Viking Age, if still meagre in contrast with the hoard evidence and the situation of single coins in England. Following on in chronological sequence from the Viking-Age material is a coin of Stephen, dating to 1135–45, excavated at Block Eary shieling. This is the only twelfth-century single find, but this is not too surprising considering the general scarcity of twelfth-century single-finds from the British Isles. More significant is the dearth of finds of the later twelfth and thirteenth century (discussed above), which only consist of two cut halfpennies of John (1199–1216), and one (possibly two)[73] whole coins, a cut halfpenny and one cut quarter of Henry III (1216–72). Such coins of the Short and Long Cross types are prolific as finds from England, so their rarity among Manx single finds lends powerful support to the conclusion drawn from the hoard evidence, namely that little coinage reached Man from England during the twelfth and thirteenth centuries.

The cut fractions are characteristic of English single finds of the Short and Long Cross types, while cut coins are much rarer after the introduction of round halfpennies and farthings in 1279–80.[74] Coins were cut to convert them into more practical amounts for small transactions, so the practice is an indicator of a society moving towards a higher degree of monetisation by adapting the available currency to suit monetary needs. It would be interesting to know whether the halfpennies of John and and halfpenny and farthing of Henry III were cut on or off Man, as this would reveal something about the monetary needs of the islanders, but it is impossible to tell. The fact that there are so few examples of thirteenth-century coins, and no hoards, argues against a significant advance towards monetisation at this time, and in turn supports the idea that the coins arrived already cut. That is, they were probably not cut especially for local use, but functioned 'as is' upon arrival.

In England the proportion of fractions to whole coins found in excavations drops from one in less than three to one in almost five in the Edwardian period, and one in 11 between 1351–1412.[75] There are no cut coins amongst the Manx Edwardian single finds, but two out of 22 are round halfpennies. This is less than one might expect of the smaller 'everyday' denominations and again appears to reflect a situation in which coinage was not needed for small transactions. It may be that the Manx numbers are distorted by the nature of the discoveries, since coins have been more often found by chance rather than in careful excavation or as detector finds, which are more likely to turn up the small denominations. The statistic may change, but the evidence so far indicates that small denominations are a distinct minority amongst the coin finds. It is only from the 1280s that the first significant aggregate of single finds appears, four coins of Edward I, one a halfpenny (Fig. 18.9/i). The concentration becomes more pronounced after 1300, with a string of six pennies of Edward I and Edward I or II and three pennies of Edward II, while two

Fig. 18.9 *Edwardian Single Finds from the Isle of Man*
i: Edward I halfpenny (0.36 g/ 5.56 gr.) Manx Museum 1970-115. Appendix II, Part 2 no. 17.
ii: Edward I penny (1.34 g/20.68 gr.) Manx Museum 1978-1. Appendix II, Part 2 no. 20.
iii: Edward III groat (4.28 g/66.05 gr.) Manx Museum 1956-93. Appendix II, Part 2 no. 31.
iv: Edward III half noble (3.11 g/48 gr.) Manx Museum 1954-1285. Appendix II, Part 2 no. 34.

more are unidentifiable, but 'Edwardian' (Fig. 18.9/ii). Seven coins are known from the reign of Edward III, an array of his denominations including a halfpenny, three groats, and, unusually, three gold coins, a noble, a half noble and a quarter noble (Figs 18.9/iii (groat) and 18.9/iv (gold half noble)). It is perhaps useful to appreciate the chronological distribution of single finds analysed by century (Fig. 18.10), where distinct peaks are seen in the tenth and thirteenth centuries, and in the fourteenth century in particular. The burst of Edwardian stray coins is quite in keeping with the overall trend noted by Rigold,[76] and Dyer,[77] but it too underlines the dearth of Short Cross and Long Cross issues of the period 1180–1279.

The total number of single finds from Man is suspiciously low for a population apparently familiar with coinage, but Man's excavated site totals are not out of keeping in a British Isles context. Where something is known of the function of a site which has produced coins, for example settlements like Cronk ny Merrieu or Block Eary, or a religious site like Rushen abbey, the single find numbers are generally comparable to similar sites in England.[78] Surprise at the infrequency of finds at these sites has also been expressed in England, and the situation is demonstrably the norm even where coinage is known to have passed through a household at a rapid pace.[79] The discrepancy is due on the one hand to practical variables like recovery methods and excavation conditions, but it is also due to the concerted efforts made at the time of loss to rescue coins, for 'at no time in medieval England were there denominations so small that their loss might be ignored and not worth the trouble of searching'.[80] The same principles must have applied in Man, if not doubly so, since coins may have seemed even rarer and more precious than to an English coin-user. Thus, it is not the low number of single coins from settlements that indicates limited coin use in Man, but rather the complete lack of concentrations in the countryside. In Man the detectorists have been instrumental in retrieving hoards in fields, but a single 'productive site' for single finds has

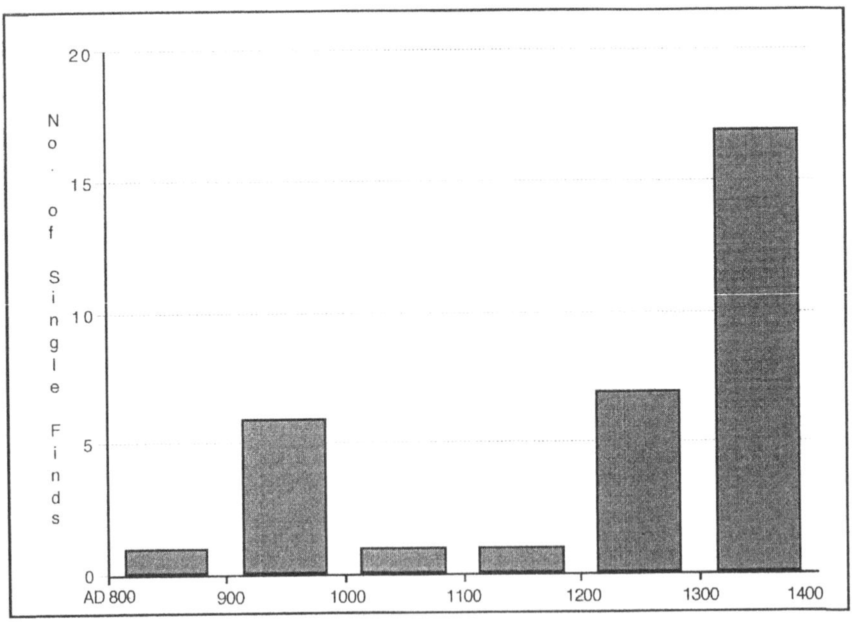

Fig. 18.10 *Single-Coin Finds from the Isle of Man.*

not yet been isolated. While a first glance at Appendix II seems to suggest the Freeport site, near Ronaldsway airport, as one possibility, it must be noted that this particular field had been spread with night soil, general rubbish and waste collected from around Castletown and used as fertiliser, much as in the medieval period.

In the light of the data currently available, one must conclude that currency was not used regularly by the majority of folk in Man during the Middle Ages. Nevertheless, the presence of money was still felt in Man, and it must have had some role in this island community. This role appears to have been special, perhaps mainly limited to larger payments and taxes, and it is interesting that it is with this specific purpose that money makes its appearances in the Manx chronicle, as will be seen below.

Possible hoards and single finds

In addition to the material summarised above, there are no less than ten 'possible hoards' of this period, unconfirmed finds for which only vague or insufficient details were found, primarily drawn from late eighteenth- and nineteenth-century sources.[81] Most of these hoards cannot be dated at all, and could be Viking or medieval (as the majority of Manx hoards demonstrably are), but could also be of any period, from Roman to relatively modern. These possible hoards, as well as at least six or seven single coins for which the details are unknown, have been excluded from the present study because of their ambiguous status. They warrant a note in passing if only to emphasise the fact that not every discovery has been reported or sufficiently recorded. There is an element of chance not just in the discovery of such finds, but in notice being taken of a find, and proper documentation being made. Furthermore, the very nature of the material, highly desirable to coin collectors of the last three centuries, has made this kind of find prone to clandestine dealings, and no doubt over time such antiquities have been smuggled off the island eluding the record completely.[82]

Money in motion: coinage in the Manx Chronicle

Of special interest are three instances in the Manx chronicle that provide glimpses of money changing hands and operating in Man. Oddly, the three putative citations of coin use in this source coincide with the most striking gap in Man's record of finds. The first occurs in around 1225, during a feud between two brothers competing for power, Rögnvaldr and Óláfr Dubh. Rögnvaldr raised funds to make a trip to the English court (then under Henry III), taking a hundred marks from the islanders.[83] Instead he used the money to visit and collude with Alan, lord of Galloway, deceiving and enraging the people of Man. The second mention is in 1228, when the island was briefly but savagely taken over and plundered by the same Rögnvaldr and Alan, together with Alan's brother Thomas, earl of Atholl. Alan is said to have 'left his bailiffs in Man to pay over to him the country's taxes'.[84] They were not successful in doing so before Óláfr Dubh regained his kingdom, but the implication remains that taxes were to be taken by one ruler rather than another and a system of taxation, for which money may have been required, was already in place on the island. Taxation is noted a third time in 1238, when Gospatrick and Gilchrist were sent by the king of Norway to expel Haraldr son of Óláfr Dubh, who at this stage had offended the Norwegian king by refusing to visit his court. The duo seized power and 'collected the king's dues for the use of the king of Norway', although coin is not specifically alluded to.[85] However, the list of bishops of Sodor and Man included at the end of the chronicle records a tax commencing in the 1270s of one penny per house to be paid to bishops.[86] And, under Bishop Thomas in the first half of the fourteenth century, 'administration charges' were exacted for the first time from Manx churches, perhaps payable in coin, while tithes were placed on fish.[87] There is, it seems, written evidence for the existence and need for coinage in Man in the thirteenth century specifically, and thereafter, at least to pay taxes if not for use in the marketplace.

Conclusion

The story of coin use, production and circulation in the Isle of Man in the medieval period is told through the substantial number of silver hoards and, in contrast, its few single-coin finds. This divergence, an abundance of hoards alongside a marked dearth of single coins, is key evidence in itself. The significant presence of coin as seen through the hoards indicates something other than a monetised economy where coin circulated on a day-to-day basis. In other words, coin presence does not necessarily indicate regular coin use. Coinage must have had a different status and limited purpose on the island, making it behave differently in the archaeological record when compared to a place like England where coin use was not an event, but an everyday act. If not for convenience at the marketplace, why were coins saved and safeguarded in such large numbers? Some people, such as traders and political leaders for whom it was most beneficial, adopted a 'coin mentality' at various points in the period, and the important appearance of the Manx mint in the eleventh century is evidence of an attempt to spark (or even enforce) the 'coin habit' in others. Full monetisation, however, met resistance and was not achieved at this stage of Man's history. Nevertheless, there were certainly coin users as well as reasons to need coin, even if coinage was not fully accepted or integral to the routine functioning of society. Money was instead reserved for special occasions, used for larger payments and for taxation. This accounts for its presence in hoards, and its dearth in small denominations and stray losses.

From the coin evidence we also learn something about the politics and economic orientations of Man, even if it is difficult to say what form such alliances took, and this is seen to shift over time. The pattern is distinct and interesting, even when summarised in the most general terms. In the tenth century Man appears to be aligned (if only in a trading nexus) with England, while the eleventh-century orientation is most definitely towards Ireland. The twelfth and thirteenth centuries are noteworthy for their dearth of numismatic evidence, but the two hoards dating to the second half of the twelfth century indicate stronger connections with Scotland than at any time before or after. Finally, the fourteenth-century evidence reflects another dramatic shift, and England is suddenly seen to be in Man's sphere of influence after an extended period when there must have been limited economic interaction with England. While the persistent and staunch resistance to a standardised economy remains a central mystery in Manx monetary history, an examination of the numismatic evidence brings us one step closer to understanding the unique and limited role of coinage in Man during the medieval period.

Appendix I:
COIN HOARDS FOUND IN THE ISLE OF MAN TO *c.*AD 1405[88]

Part 1: Viking Age

Securely dated hoards

(1) Ballaqueeney (Port St Mary), 1874, Kirk Christ Rushen: a small hoard deposited *c.*960 (or slightly earlier) associated with human remains in a lintel grave in the burial ground of a keeill, disturbed in the course of removing gravel for railway construction. The majority are characteristically cut and/or in fragmentary condition. Extant in the Manx Museum are: one coin of Edmund, three of Eadred, three of Eadwig, one of Óláfr son of Guðröðr and one Continental 'Type Immobilisé' penny of Melle, There is no evidence to support Dolley's suggestion that coins of Edgar were present (1975a), and an earlier deposition date is now suggested. **Refs:** *1876 Archaeological Commission Report*, see 'Parish Rushen' for account of discovery, condition and specific

provenance, and 'Miscellaneous antiquities: coins' (MNHL, M.M. MSS. 258 C); Constable Monro to the Lieutenant Governor, 17 April 1874 (MNHL, GO 29/73); Constable Monro to the Lieutenant Governor, 21 May 1874 (MNHL, GO 29/80); William Kneale, a handwritten list headed 'Anglo-Saxon coins recently found in a tumulus at Port St Mary' (post-1870) (MNHL MS.); Henry Kelly, 'Ballaqueeny Cronk, the Clagh-Ard or Crosh Ballaqueeny, and Cronk How Mooar', *Yn Lioar Manninagh*, II (Douglas, 1901 [written c.1892/3]), 47–51; P.W.P. Carlyon-Britton, 'On Some Coins of the Tenth Century, Found in the Isle of Man, With Special Reference to a Coin of Anlaf Struck at Derby', *BNJ* 5 (1908), 85–96; P.M.C. Kermode *List of Manx Antiquities* (Douglas 1930) [A revised and 'entirely re-written' edition of the original 1901 (compiled in 1894) List in *YLM* II.], 85 no. 8 and 87; J.R. Bruce, *The Manx Archaeological Survey, Sixth Report 1966* (Douglas, 1968), 55–60, at p. 57; Michael Dolley, 'The pattern of Viking-Age coin-hoards from the Isle of Man', *Seaby's Coin and Medal Bulletin* (1975a), 296–302, 337–40, at pp. 298–9, no. 3; Michael Dolley, 'Some preliminary observations on three Manx coin-hoards appearing to end with pennies of Eadgar', *Spink's Numismatic Circular*, LXXXIII (1975b), 146–7, 190–2. R.H.M. Dolley, and K.F. Morrison 'A note on four 'Type Immobilise' coins of Melle from British finds', *Numismatic Chronicle* (1962), 157–60; James Graham-Campbell, 'The Viking-Age silver hoards of the Isle of Man', in Fell *et al.* (eds) *The Viking Age in the Isle of Man* (1983), 53–80, at pp. 55 and 56–7, plus Appendix A no. 2 for further references; Mark Blackburn and Hugh Pagan, 'A revised check-list of coin hoards from the British Isles, *c.*500–1100', in M.A.S. Blackburn (ed.), *Anglo-Saxon Monetary History* (Leicester, 1986), no. 143.

(2) Unprovenanced, pre-1908: an otherwise unrecorded Manx hoard (or parcel of a larger hoard) deposited *c.*955–60, which was unearthed sometime in the later nineteenth century and amalgamated into the collection at the Government Office (where artefacts were stored in anticipation of the museum opened in 1922) without record of provenance or donor. The hoard has been reconstructed based on the material comprising the early collection as catalogued by Carlyon-Britton in 1908 after the coins relating to the two lists compiled by William Kneale have been accounted for. The pre-Edgar composition and uniformly fragmented condition of the remaining group forms a distinct and plausible unit that does not fit neatly with any other Manx hoard, but which is hardly anomalous in the Irish Sea context. The 11 coins associated with this find comprise one of Edward the Elder, three of Athelstan, three of Edmund and four of Eadred. **Ref.:** Carlyon-Britton 1908.

(3) Unprovenanced, *c.*1880s?: this find deposited *c.*965 was catalogued by

William Kneale sometime after 1870 (The watermark date in the paper) under the heading: 'Anglo-Saxon Coins found in the Isle of Man' (MNHL M.M.MS.). The text was reproduced by Kermode (1902) as part of a catalogue of the collection of artefacts being kept in storage at the Government Office in anticipation of the Manx Museum, and the coins appear to have been amalgamated into the pre-Museum collection without record. Dolley assumed that the coins represented a further parcel of the Ballaqueeney hoard, not having traced the contemporary evidence indicating the true size and character of that small find. The discovery most likely dates to the period after the dissolution of the Archaeological Commission in 1879, since the hoard is not mentioned in the Commission's survey of archaeological sites and finds,[89] suggesting a probable date of discovery in the 1880s. The fact that the 18 coins listed by Kneale were catalogued together on one occasion suggests that they are related, while the age-structure and uniform condition of the surviving coins strongly recommend its classification as a single deposit. Furthermore, the overall condition of the find and the fact that it extends into the reign of Edgar (yet is not dominated by coins of this reign) distinguishes the assemblage from all other recorded Manx hoards. The coins include three of Edmund, six of Eadred (one of Baldwin was not traced), six of Eadwig and three of Edgar. It is possible that this group may correspond with the lost Ballakilpheric find (4), the discovery of which dates to this time and which is said to have included at least one coin of Edgar; there is, however, no concrete reason to link Kneale's list with this find, and until further evidence can demonstrate otherwise the two must be treated as separate discoveries. **Refs:** Kermode 'Museum Catalogue (Collection at Government Office)', *YLM* III (1902 [compiled in 1897]), 276–80 at p. 279; Carlyon-Britton 1908; Dolley 1975b, 190–1.

<u>(4) Ballakilpheric, pre-1885, Kirk Christ Rushen</u>: a presumed-lost hoard of the *c.*960s–70s (including at least one coin of Edgar) unearthed in the cemetery associated with Keeill Pherick. There is reason to suspect that the 18 coins listed by Kneale in an untitled post-1870 manuscript (see 3), most of which can be identified in the Manx Museum collection, may correspond with this hoard, but there is as yet no positive evidence to demonstrate such a connection. **Refs:** E.B. Savage, *Some Notes on Manks Antiquities* (*c.*1880) (MNHL, M.M.MS. 78A, xvi.A.6); Bruce (1968), 48; Michael Dolley, 'A supplementary note on the 1874 Ballaqueeney find from the Isle of Man', *Spink's Numismatic Circular,* LXXXVII (1979), 123–4, at p. 124; Graham-Campbell (1983), 57 and Appendix A, no. 4; Blackburn and Pagan (1986), no. 159.

<u>(5) Unprovenanced, pre-1994</u>: no details are known of the circumstances of discovery of this find (or parcel of a larger hoard) deposited *c.*970s?, formerly

part of the collection of the late Sir Sidney Nolan, which appeared on the market in 1994. The assemblage consists of seven pieces of silver bullion (both fragmentary and whole) and one fragment of a cut halfpenny of Edgar. An Irish provenance was postulated by Graham-Campbell and Blackburn (1995), but the distribution of pre-Reform tenth-century Anglo-Saxon half-pennies, the dearth of plain silver arm-rings in Ireland and parallels with other Manx finds more convincingly suggest a Manx origin for this find. **Refs:** Christie's, 6 July 1994, lot 466; James Graham-Campbell and Mark Blackburn, 'An Unprovenanced Viking-Age Silver Hoard of Tenth-Century Date', *Numismatic Chronicle* 155 (1995), 279–82.

(6) Kirk Andreas, 1866 or 1867: a hoard of approximately 100 coins deposited *c.*970 and rapidly dispersed after workmen discovered it while digging foundation trenches for the new tower at the Kirk Andreas parish church. At least 18 coins can be identified in the Manx Museum (one of Eadred two of Eadwig, eleven of Edgar, three Viking and one irregular Anglo-Saxon type; a cut halfpenny of Edgar remains untraced) while nine are known to be in two separate private collections (including two of Eadred, one of Eadwig, five of Edgar and one irregular type). **Refs:** Charles Clay, *Currency of the Isle of Man*, Manx Society XVII (Douglas, 1869), 43–4; J. Harris Gibson, 'A penny of Eadgar recently found in the Isle of Man', *Journal of the Liverpool Numismatic Society*, part II, vol. ii (1877–8), 69–70; Dolley (1975a), 299 no. 4; Dolley (1975b), 146–7; Michael Dolley, 'Promised further light on the 1866 Kirk Andreas find', *Spink's Numismatic Circular*, LXXXVII (1979), 548–9; Graham-Campbell (1983), 57 and Appendix A, no. 3; Blackburn and Pagan (1986), no. 155.

(7) Ballaquayle, 1894: also known as the 'Woodbourne' or 'Douglas' hoard, from Upper Douglas, is the largest Viking-Age deposit known from Man, discovered in a stone-lined pit. The find, deposited *c.*970, consisted of several hundred coins, possibly even 1,000 (many reputedly destroyed upon discovery and/or widely dispersed), and 21 ornaments, including one gold arm-ring, an array of silver rings, a small silver ingot and a variety of hack-silver, including the ornate heads of two ball-type brooches. The remaining coins and objects were divided up between the British Museum (eight ornaments and 19 coins), the Royal Mint (five coins), and the Manx Museum (71 coins and 13 objects). Several strays and additional parcels were acquired by the Manx Museum over the years, while a significant number of dispersed Ballaquayle coins have also been traced to other private and public collections. The coins are predominantly of Edgar, but also include types of Æthelstan, Eadmund, Eadred, Eadwig, and Óláfr son of Sigtryggr. **Refs:** Rev. John Quine, 'The Douglas

treasure trove', *Yn Lioar Manninagh*, II (Douglas, 1901), 242–5; H.A. Grueber, 'The Douglas find of Anglo-Saxon coins and ornaments', *Numismatic Chronicle*, XIII (1913), 322–48; P.M.C. Kermode, 'The Woodbourne treasure-trove, 1894', *Proceedings*, new ser., vol. 1 (1915), 437–40; B.R.S. Megaw, 'The Douglas treasure trove', *JMM*, IV no. 57 (1938), 77–80; H. Shetelig (ed.), *Viking Antiquities in Great Britain and Ireland*, IV (Oslo, 1940), 51–3, figs 17–22; C.E. Blunt, 'A new parcel from the Douglas, I.O.M., 1894 hoard (?)', *British Numismatic Journal*, XXXV (1966), 7–11; Michael Dolley, 'New light on the 1894 Douglas hoard', *JMM*, VII, no. 85 (1969), 121–4; Dolley (1975a), 299, no. 5; H.E. Pagan, 'The 1894 Ballaquayle hoard: five further parcels of coins, Æthelstan-Eadgar', *British Numismatic Journal*, L (1980), 12–19; Graham-Campbell (1983), 57, 68–71 and Appendix A, no. 5 and Appendix B, no. 5; Blackburn and Pagan (1986), no. 165; Kenneth Jonsson, *The New Era: The Reformation of the Late Anglo-Saxon Coinage*, Commentationes De Nummis Saeculorum IX-XI in Suecia Repertis. Nova Series 1, The Royal Coin Cabinet (Stockholm and London, 1987), 43 and 64.

<u>(8) Bradda Head, 1848, Kirk Christ Rushen</u>: this large hoard was deposited *c.*995, and consisted of several hundred pennies of Æthelred II's *Crux* type (some, now lost, may have been of the Hiberno-Scandinavian *Crux* type). The hoard was found in a roll near the surface on a hillside near Bradda Head. Three coins, characteristically broken, are preserved in the Manx Museum; four are known in private hands. In addition, several coins in other public collections (e.g., Belfast and Chester) are believed to derive from this find, while the majority were dispersed or melted down by a Castletown watchmaker. **Refs:** W.B. Dickenson, 'Find of Anglo-Saxon coins in the Isle of Man', *Numismatic Chronicle*, XVI (1853–4), 99–104; W.B. Dickenson, 'Saxon coins found in the Isle of Man', *Numismatic Chronicle*, XVII (1854–5), 130; Clay (Douglas, 1869), 41–3; *1876 Archaeological Commission Report*, 'Miscellaneous antiquities: coins' (MNHL, M.M.MSS. 258C); Dolley (1975a), 299, no. 6; Michael Dolley, 'The neglected Norwegian dimension to the 1848 coin-hoard from Bradda Mountain (Isle of Man)', *NNF-NYTT: Meddeleelser fra Norsk Numismatisk Forening*, 2 (1980), 15–24; Graham-Campbell (1983), 57–8, and Appendix A, no. 6; Blackburn and Pagan (1986), no. 186.

<u>(9) Glenfaba, 2003</u>: this large mixed hoard deposited *c.*1030 contains a diverse selection of coins, 464 in all: 326 coins are from Dublin (Phases I and II); 79 coins are from Anglo-Saxon England (ending in Knútr's *Quatrefoil* type), deriving from 25 different mints; 30 are from the Hiberno-Scandinavian/Manx transitional die group, and were probably struck in Man; 12 appear to be related to this group, but their origin and place in the Hiberno-

Scandinavian/Manx series is uncertain; 11 are from a mint somewhere in the 'Irish Sea', perhaps the Wirral, as recently recognised by Mark Blackburn (*Quatrefoil* type); one is apparently a Scandinavian imitation; and five are at present unidentified or uncertain types. In addition, the hoard contains 24 ingots (cut and whole), a rounded, hammered piece of silver and most of a heavy plaited silver arm-ring. Finally, there are fragments of the lead container in which the coins and objects were deposited, and which acted as a shield to corrosive elements so that the coins and metalwork are in an extraordinary state of preservation. **Ref.**: Allison Fox and Kristin Bornholdt Collins, 'The 2003 "TT": A Viking-Age Silver Hoard from Glenfaba, Isle of Man', *Viking Heritage Magazine* 1/2004, 3–5.

(10) Park Lewellyn, 1835, Kirk Maughold: a hoard of *c.*1030, or slightly earlier, found contained in a ram's horn, confused with the Ballaberna hoard in early literature. The site was somewhere on the southern slopes of the mountain range running north-eastwards from Snaefell, North Barrule. At least six coins in the Manx Museum are from Park Lewellyn (one Æthelred *Long Cross*, one Hiberno-Scandinavian Phase II, four Early Style Hiberno-Manx), while an additional five are likely candidates (three Hiberno-Scandinavian Phase II and one from the Hiberno-Manx transitional group). **Refs**: Clay (Douglas, 1869), 39, muddling Ballaberna and Park Llewellyn; *1876 Archaeological Commission Report*, 'Miscellaneous antiquities: coins' (MNHL, M.M.MSS. 258C), provides the Park Llewellyn date with Ballaberna details; Dr John Bradbury, journal entry 183 (*c.*1860–90s), (M.M.MSS. 2202A); Dolley (1975a), 300 no. 7; Michael Dolley 'A Hiberno-Manx coinage of the eleventh century', *Numismatic Chronicle,* CXXXVI (1976a), 75–84; Michael Dolley, 'The two near-contemporary findings of Hiberno-Norse coins from Maughold', *JMM,* VII, no. 88 (1976c), 236–40; Graham-Campbell (1983), 58 and Appendix A; Blackburn and Pagan (1986), no. 219; K. Bornholdt, 'Myth or mint? The evidence for a Viking-Age coinage from the Isle of Man', in P.J. Davey (ed.), *Recent Archaeological Research on the Isle of Man,* BAR British Series 278 (1999), 199–218, at p. 208 and Appendix.

(11) Ballaberna, 1833, Kirk Maughold: this hoard of the 1040s, confused with the Park Lewellyn hoard in early literature, was contained in a small urn and was discovered by workmen in September 1833 in (or near) a stone quarry where iron ore was once mined.[90] At least two Ballaberna coins are in the Manx Museum, both Hiberno-Scandinavian Phase III (1035–55), one with a note attached which is contemporary with the discovery. In addition there are at least five other probable Ballaberna candidates (three additional Phase III pennies, as well as one Hiberno-Scandinavian fragment and an imitation type)

in the museum, while a third definite Ballaberna coin, corresponding in type and condition and with another note indicating the provenance attached, exists in a private collection on the island. **Refs:** Joseph Train, *An Historical and Statistical Account of the Isle of Man*, II (two volumes, Douglas, 1845), 71; Clay (Douglas, 1869), 39, muddling Ballaberna and Park Llewellyn; *1876 Archaeological Commission Report*, 'Miscellaneous antiquities: coins' (MNHL, M.M.MSS. 258C); Bradbury, journal entries 181 and 183 (*c*.1860–90s), (MNHL, M.M.MSS. 2202A); Dolley (1975a), 301, no. 11; Graham-Campbell (1983), 58 and Appendix A; Blackburn and Pagan (1986), no. 228.

(12) Unprovenanced, pre-1783 (Hunterian Museum): the provenance of this closely die-linked group of seven Early Style Hiberno-Manx coins dating to the *c*.1030s–40s is unknown, but it is more than likely to have been Man based on the peculiar distribution pattern of this type of coin. The coins, acquired by Dr William Hunter between 1770 and 1783, are not peck-marked, ruling out a Scandinavian provenance. One coin is pierced with part of a loop attachment remaining. It was suggested by W.A. Seaby that a group of four closely-linked Phase III coins also in the Hunter cabinet may be associated. **Refs:** Dolley (1976a), 77, 78; W.A. Seaby, 'Die-links of an Eleventh-Century Dublin Penny in the Isle of Man', *Irish Numismatics* 74, 13 (2) (1980), 61–4.Graham-Campbell (1983), 60, Appendix A; Bornholdt (1999), 209.

(13) Kirk Andreas, 1874: this chronologically wide-ranging, mixed bullion and coin hoard deposited *c*.1045 was unearthed in the Kirk Andreas churchyard while digging a grave and was at first concealed by workers, but the bulk of the find (excluding an unknown number of silver rings) was eventually submitted to the Manx Museum. At least 42 coins believed to be from this find are identifiable in the collection, five of which are uniformly pierced (all Phase II Hiberno-Scandinavian). These include three coins of Knútr, two of Edward the Confessor, 15 Phase II Hiberno-Scandinavian, 15 Phase III Hiberno-Scandinavian, four 'Knútr' *Short Cross* imitations and one Hiberno-Manx (transitional or 'Transfer Die' type). One additional Knútr and one Early Style Hiberno-Manx penny may also be associated with this hoard. **Refs:** Head Constable D. Monro to the Lieutenant Governor, 24 June 1874 (MNHL, GO 29/86); *1876 Archaeological Commission Report*, 'Miscellaneous antiquities: coins'; *Yn Lioar Manninagh*, III, 1897 (pub. 1902), 279–80 and Kermode (1930), 34, reveals confusion between the two Andreas hoards; Dolley (1975a), 300–1, no. 9; Michael Dolley, 'Some Insular (?) imitations from the 1030s of contemporary English pence of Cnut', *Spink's Numismatic Circular*, LXXXVIII (1980), 86–8; Graham-Campbell (1983), 60, Appendix A and

Appendix B, no. 10; Blackburn and Pagan (1986), no. 230; Bornholdt (1999), 208 and Appendix.

(14) West Nappin, *c.*1880s, Jurby: a small mixed hoard deposited *c.*1045 discovered in a mound, now eroded away, near Jurby Head. The find included one plain silver arm-ring and at least two identical Hiberno-Scandinavian coins which are mentioned in 1935 Museum correspondence with the finder's daughter. Eight coins (one of Knútr, one Phase II Hiberno-Scandinavian, four Phase III Hiberno-Scandinavian and two Early Style Hiberno-Manx), with corresponding breakage patterns and distinctive patination, including the Phase III Hiberno-Scandinavian die-duplicates, are preserved in the Manx Museum and presumably make up the whole find. **Refs:** A.W. Moore (ed.), 'Meetings of Societies', *The Manx Note Book*, II (Douglas, 1886), 139; Museum correspondence, not accessioned: William Cubbon to Mr Smith, British Museum, 27 August 1935 and William Cubbon to Miss Clarke, 31 August 1935; Annie C. Clarke to Mr Megaw, 17 October 1939 (MNHL, MS. 5293c); Shetelig (Oslo, 1940), IV, 53; Dolley (1975a), 301, no. 10; Dolley (1976a), 76; Michael Dolley, 'The 'forgotten' Viking-Age silver hoard from the West Nappin, Jurby', *Proceedings,* VIII, no. 1 (1977), 54–64; Graham-Campbell (1983), 58, Appendix A and Appendix B, no. 9; Blackburn and Pagan (1986), 298 no. 231; Bornholdt (1999), 208 and Appendix.

(15) Peel Castle, 1982, St Patrick's Isle: this *c.*1050 hoard was found in a roll-like configuration in the keeill area during the course of archaeological excavation. It was composed of 42 Hiberno-Scandinavian pennies, comprising two Phase II and 39 closely die-linked Phase III, plus one that remains undetermined due to its poor condition. An inquest declared it treasure trove on 16 December 1981. **Refs:** Graham-Campbell (1983), Addenda; Blackburn and Pagan (1986), 298, no. 239; W. Seaby in David Freke (ed.), *Excavations on St Patrick's Isle, Isle of Man* (Liverpool, 2002), 320–5 ; A.M. Cubbon, 'A remarkable decade of Manx coin hoards, 1972–1982', *Proceedings,* XI, no. 1 (2000).

(16) Kirk Michael 2, 1972/5: this mixed, chronologically wide-ranging, savings hoard deposited *c.*1065 was contained in a linen-type fabric pouch, and was unearthed while digging a grave in the 1911 extension of the Kirk Michael graveyard. The grave was re-excavated in 1975 to recover any overlooked pieces and to confirm the find-spot. Two inquests took place at which the finds were declared treasure trove, 2 March 1976 and 13 January 1981. Two silver arm-rings, one nearly complete arm-ring and two small, cut arm-ring fragments accompanied the 81 coins. The coins included one of Edmund, five of Edgar, eight of Knútr, one of Harðaknútr, five of Edward the Confessor, 21

Hiberno-Scandinavian (7 Phase II, 11 Phase III, 1 Phase V, plus 2 undetermined/Phase V?, very weakly struck); 21 Hiberno-Manx (encompassing Early, Middle and Late Styles); and 17 Normandy deniers. **Refs:** Dolley (1976a), 75–6; Françoise Dumas, 'Les monnaies Normandes (X-XII siècles) avec un répertoire des trouvailles', *Revue Numismatique*, XXI (1979), 84–140; Cubbon and Dolley, 'The 1972 Kirk Michael Viking treasure trove', *JMM*, VIII, 89 (1980), 5–20; Graham-Campbell (1983), 60–1, Appendix A and Appendix B, no. 14; Blackburn and Pagan 1986: 299, no. 248; Bornholdt (1999), 208 and Appendix; A.M. Cubbon (2000).

(17) Unprovenanced, pre-1785a: a hoard of Edward the Confessor pennies and Hiberno-Scandinavian Phase V, deposited *c.*1065. The find appears not to have been recorded in the early literature, but became apparent with the 1992 Gelling bequest; a second parcel of four coins at the National Museum of Scotland (believed to be from Man, ex Wood 1785) appears to be associated with the Gelling parcel and indicates a pre-1785 date for the find. The possibility exists that this (or 20, below) may correspond with the 1772 find of 37(+) 'sundry pieces of ancient coin' from Ballaugh (MNHL B.H. 4389c), but there is no positive evidence to demonstrate a connection with either, and it remains pure speculation that the Ballaugh find dates to the Viking-Age or medieval period. The larger parcel of 14 whole coins (plus a number of fragments) was acquired either by James Gelling, vicar at Peel in the early nineteenth century, or by his son, Frederick Gelling of Castletown, in the mid-nineteenth century. The whole collection was taken to Canada near the turn of the twentieth century. This hoard is apparently distinct from that of the 'Norman Edward' recorded by Train (1845, 71), found while ploughing a field on the Howe ('hill'), south of Douglas, with London, York and Canterbury mints equally represented, see (33) below. Clay (1869, 41, following Train) adds: 'Edward the Confessor is perhaps meant', and J. Harris Gibson (1877–8, 69) simply assumes it to be the latter. However, aside from the composition sounding 'Edwardian', in volume one of R. Ruding, *Annals of the Coinage*, 3 vols (3rd edn, London, 1840, 204), a likely source for Train, the same otherwise obscure term is used to denote Edward I/II/III. Train's word is therefore to be trusted, particularly in the light of his almost contemporary perspective (an 1845 report of the 1842 find). It seems that the confusion arose not just from the obscure phrase employed, but because a hoard of the earlier Edward had also been discovered within memory, if several decades earlier, and suppressed; the details of the two finds were subsequently muddled. The known coins of this unprovenanced hoard are primarily of Edward the Confessor (1 Pointed Helmet, 12 Hammer Cross, 3 Pyramids, plus fragments) of various mints, including Chester, Huntingdon, Lincoln, London, Norwich,

Stafford and York; there are also two Phase V coins from Dublin that appear to be associated with the find. **Refs:** Dolley (1975a), 301–2, no. 12 (regarding the coins in Edinburgh); Blackburn and Pagan (1986), 299 no. 249 ('Ballaugh').

(18) Laxey? pre-1950, Kirk Lonan: this unprovenanced but tightly linked group of seven Hiberno-Scandinavian Phase V, small flan pennies, *c.*1070 or later, was acquired by P.J. Seaby from a collector at Laxey and presented to the Manx Museum about 20 years later, 1974. **Refs:** Dolley (1975a), 302, no. 13; Graham-Campbell (1983), 61, Appendix A; Blackburn and Pagan (1986), 299, no. 278.

(19) Kirk Michael 1, 1834: this hoard of predominantly late Hiberno-Scandinavian pennies (57 Phase V plus two Late Style Hiberno-Manx pennies) *c.*1075 was discovered under the foundation of the old parish church during demolition work, and was subsequently dispersed by workmen. The British Museum acquired 46, donated by William Ward, bishop of Sodor and Man (d. 1838), and a parcel of 12 came to the Manx Museum with the 1992 Gelling bequest; at least 4 additional coins are known to exist in a private collection on Man, while a parcel of seven Phase V coins sold at Glendining and Co. in 1980 appear to derive from the same find. The four parcels are in similar condition and are closely die-linked, demonstrating that a representative portion of this hoard is known. **Refs:** Anon., 'Coins found in the Isle of Man', *Numismatic Chronicle* (1849), 180 plus two plates; Clay (Douglas, 1869), 38; J. Harris Gibson (Liverpool, 1877–8), 69; R.H.M. Dolley, 'A "Pseudo-Orans" on a Hiberno-Norse penny of the Dublin mint', *Spink's Numismatic Circular,* LXIX, 2 (February 1961), 32–3; Michael Dolley, 'A Hiberno-Norse penny misattributed to the 1834 hoard from Kirk Michael', *Spink's Numismatic Circular,* LXXXI (January 1973), 2; Dolley (1975a), 302 no. 14; Dolley (1976a), 76, 83; Michael Dolley, 'Additional light on the 1834 coinhoard from Kirk Michael (Isle of Man)', *Irish Numismatics*, 74, 13: 2, (March-April 1980), 82–4; Glendining & Co. auction catalogue, 1 October 1980, lots 185–91; Graham-Campbell (1983), 61 and Appendix A; Blackburn and Pagan (1986), 299, no. 283.

(20) Unprovenanced, pre-1785b: an obviously associated group of four early twelfth-century pennies, Phase VI Hiberno-Scandinavian. The coins were given to the National Museum of Scotland in 1785 by Mrs Wood, wife of John Wood (d. 1777), Isle of Man governor from 1761 until his death. The provenance remains uncertain, but is presumed to be Manx based on the donor's background. Mrs Wood donated a wide variety of coins that were probably, but

not necessarily, found or acquired in Man. A connection with the 1772 Ballaugh find of 37 ancient coins (type unknown), discovered during Wood's office, is possible, although this (as for 17) cannot be substantiated. **Refs:** Mr Ludwidge to John Quayle 9 September 1772 (MNHL, B.H. 4389c); *Archaeologica Scotica*, III (Edinburgh, 1831), 36; Graham-Campbell (1983), 61 and Appendix A.

Hoards of uncertain date

(21) Unprovenanced (the Kella,?), Kirk Christ Lezayre, 1750: a hoard of 39 or 40 coins (one larger than the rest) found near, although not directly associated with, a Viking-Age lintel grave with sword and battleaxe. The coins are now lost and the hoard is of uncertain date, deposited sometime in the ninth-eleventh centuries. **Refs:** William Christian to Atholl, 2 December 1750 (MNHL, AP/X19/30a); John Quayle to Atholl, February 1751 (MNHL, AP/54–27); Clay (Douglas, 1869), 36; D.M. Wilson, *The Viking Age in the Isle of Man: The Archaeological Evidence*, C.C. Rafn Lecture III (Odense, 1974), 18, 36, 44 and 46; Dolley (1975a), 298, no. 2; Graham-Campbell (1983), 56 and Appendix A.

(22) Unprovenanced (Ballacannell?), Kirk Lonan, 1786: this large hoard contained at least 237 'Danish' coins, including one 'square coin', probably eleventh-century Hiberno-Scandinavian and/or Hiberno-Manx pennies, and is known today only from contemporary administrative correspondence relating to this find. The coins were dispersed amongst three men upon discovery, and some were lost to a watchmaker's pot before the remainder were seized as treasure trove; an inquest took place on 7 September 1786. According to Heyward's first letter to the duke of Atholl, the coins were found 'not far from Laxey', while Train (1845, 69) adds that it was found by a person digging near the church at Lonan, 'and several others had been previously found at the same place'. **Refs:** Peter John Heywood to Atholl, 13 May 1786 (MNHL, AP 122 (4th)-2); Thomas Moore (Deemster) to the Coroner, 17 May 1786 (MNHL, AP X66–1); Heywood to Atholl, 17 June 1786, (MNHL, AP 122 (4th)-3; Heywood to Atholl, 7 August 1786 (MNHL, AP 122 (4th)-5; Exchequer Court, Treasure Trove, the King *v.* Heywood (MNHL, Castle Rushen Papers, Box 1, file 8); Heywood to Atholl, 8 September 1786 (MNHL, AP 122 (4th)-8; Heywood to Atholl, 1 October 1786 (MNHL, AP 122 (4th)-11; Heywood to Atholl, 9 July 1788 (MNHL, AP 122 (4th)-24); Atholl to Heywood, 9 July 1788 (MNHL, AP 122 (4th)-25; Report of the Commissioners of Enquiry (1792), Appendix A, no. 41 (MNHL, AP 133(2nd)-2; George Woods, *An Account of the Past and Present State of the Isle of Man* (London, 1811), 174; Robert Airey (ed.), *Feltham's Tour through the Isle of Man, in 1797 and 1798*,

The Manx Society, VI (Douglas, 1861), 215; Train (Douglas, 1845), 69–70; Clay (Douglas, 1869), 37; Dolley (1975a), 300, no. 8; Graham-Campbell (1983), 58 and Appendix A; Blackburn and Pagan (1986), 298, no. 223.

Coinless hoards

(I) Unprovenanced (Balladoole?) pre-1842: a hoard of four plain silver arm-rings (mid-tenth to mid-eleventh century) known from a labelled drawing in the sketchbook of Sir William Betham (*c.*1824–42), 25 in the National Library of Ireland (Tx 1959), brought to light by Graham-Campbell (1983), 62, 64, Fig. 6, and Appendix B, no. 18. The arm-rings may now be identified in the collections of the National Museum of Ireland (formerly believed to be Irish finds) thanks to recent work by John Sheehan and James Graham-Campbell, 'A Viking-Age Silver Hoard of 'Ring-Money' from the Isle of Man Rediscovered', *PIOMNHAS* (forthcoming). The provenance is unknown, although one possibility may be near Keeill Vael, Balladoole, Arbory, indicated by Oswald in his *Vestigia*, Manx Society, V (Douglas, 1860), 77 (quoted by Bradbury *c.*1860–*c.*1890, journal entry 136) where it is written that, at Keeill Vael, 'ancient rings have been found in the immediate vicinity within the memory of man'. While the objects in Betham's drawing may be strays from other known or unrecorded hoards of this time (such as Park Lewellyn 1835, Ballaberna 1833 or Kirk Michael 1834), it seems even more likely that they represent an independent find. In the light of the dating of the two, it is reasonable to connect, but impossible to confirm, the Oswald reference with the Betham drawing.

(II) Ballacamaish, 1868, Kirk Andreas: this deposit *c.*970s? (*c.*950–*c.*1025) consisted of two plaited silver neck-rings (both broken, one nearly whole with a hook, the other a shorter segment) and one arm-ring (whole, made of twisted silver rods) and was recovered from a marl pit by workmen. The objects are held in the British Museum. **Refs:** Manx Note Book (1885), 40, 71; Shetelig (Oslo, 1940), IV, 53, figs 22–3; Graham-Campbell (1983), 63, 65, Fig. 7, 68 and Appendix B, II, no. 19, and Appendix C.

(III) Greeba, German, 1981 and 2002: these detector finds of gold, comprising one whole plaited-rod finger-ring and two fragments, including a piece with eleventh-century ornamentation, were recovered from the same field and derive from a single coinless deposit that has been scattered by the plough. The objects, with a total weight of 24.45g, represent at least part of a high-value store of wealth, for gold was valued at about ten times that of silver. Finger-rings similar to the whole plaited ring are generally from late Viking-Age contexts and are known from Ireland and Scotland, while the only coin-dated example in Britain is from Hampshire, England (deposited *c.*1068). **Refs:** Graham-Campbell 1983, 80; Cubbon 2000, 39–40; D.M. Wilson, 'A Ring from Greeba', Proceedings of the Isle of Man Natural History and Antiquarian Society XI no. 3 (April 2001 – March 2003), 437–9.

Part 2: Medieval Period

Securely dated hoards

(23) Unprovenanced eighteenth century (I): this hoard of *c.*1174 or later was probably discovered shortly before its first publication in 1769. It comprised at least one coin of Stephen of England, two of David I of Scotland, one of his successor Malcom IV, and one of the latter's brother, William the Lion. **Refs:** Thomas Snelling, *Miscellaneous Views: A View of the Coins Struck in the Isle of Man* (London, 1769), 40–1; John Pinkerton, *An Essay on Medals*, II (London, 1789), 363 and vol. II, plate 1; Ian Stewart, 'An eighteenth-century Manx find of early Scottish sterlings', *British Numismatic Journal,* XXXIII (1964), 48–56.

(24) Ballayelse 1977, Arbory: a small hoard of five English coins deposited in or after *c.*1305 in the wall of a keeill, discovered by two schoolboys and subsequently excavated by the Manx Museum and investigated with a metal detector. An inquest held 2 June 1977 declared the find treasure trove. The types include four Edward I (1272–1307): Class 2b, London (1279–80), Class 3c, Bristol (1280), Class 4a, Canterbury (1281–2), Class 9b, Durham (1300), and one Edward I/II: Class 10cf, Canterbury (*c.*1305–*c.*1310). **Refs:** *British Numismatic Journal*, XXXXVII (1977), 164; *Coin Hoards*, 4 (1978), no. 359; A.M. Cubbon, 'Some chance finds of archaeological importance in the Isle of Man, 1962–1977', in Davey (ed.), *Man and the Environment*, 413–28, at pp. 424–8; Cubbon (2000).

(25) Kilkenny 1982, Kirk Braddan: a very large hoard deposited in or after *c.*1305, scattered in a field by ploughing, and recovered in eight separate parcels by metal detectorists in the course of a systematic investigation of the field. A concentration of 80 or so coins indicated the original deposition location. The find was declared treasure trove at an inquest held 6 September 1983. A total of 565 coins plus 22 fragments were found, including two halfpennies. These comprised 529 English: Edward I (1272–1307), Classes 1c-10ab minted between 1279 and *c.*1305 (317 London plus three fragments?, 103 Canterbury plus three fragments?, 28 Durham plus three fragments?, 22 Bristol, 15 York, 14 Lincoln, 10 Bury St Edmunds, 8 Berwick plus one fragment?, 7 Newcastle upon Tyne, 4 Kingston upon Hull, one Exeter); 26 Scottish: 24 Alexander III

(1249–86), 2 John Balliol (1292–6), and 10 Irish: Edward I, second coinage (1279–1302), (8 Dublin, 2 Waterford). **Refs:** *British Numismatic Journal*, 54 (1984), 304; Cubbon (2000).

(26) Ronague 1996, Arbory: a hoard of 65 coins deposited in or after *c.*1309–*c.*1310, found under some large stones at a keeill site during fencing work, and subsequently excavated by the Manx Museum. The hoard included 60 English pennies: Edward I (1272–1307) and Edward II (1307–27) Classes 1c-10cf5 minted between 1279 and *c.*1310 (44 London, 7 Canterbury, 2 Bristol, 2 York, 2 Bury St Edmunds, 1 Durham, 1 Lincoln, 1 Newcastle), as well as one Irish: Type 1a Edward I, *c.*1279–84, (Dublin), and four Scottish pennies: Alexander III (1249–86), second coinage *c.*1280–6.

(27) Ballaslig *c.*1839, 1978 and 1979–80, Kirk Braddan: the first documented parcel of this large fourteenth-century hoard was said to include coins minted at London, Canterbury and Durham, and was possibly found with the remains of a container, which was scattered by the plough. It was discovered in a field where Edwardian coins had 'so frequently been found that it is called silver field' (Clay, Douglas, 1869, 40). The remainder of the same disturbed hoard was rediscovered by metal detectorists, from which it was possible to determine the probable date of the deposit, *c.*1325. A systematic metal detecting investigation produced a number of parcels (249 coins) that were consistent in character, clearly deriving from a single hoard. Two inquests declared the finds treasure trove, 12 December 1978 and 15 July 1981. The hoard was composed of 241 English pennies: Edward I (1272–1307) and Edward II (1307–27): Classes 1–15c minted between 1279–*c.*1327 (126 London, 60 Canterbury, 22 Durham, 7 York, 7 Bury St Edmunds, 5 Bristol, 4 Lincoln, 3 Berwick, 3 Newcastle, 2 Exeter, one Chester). In addition, 2 Irish pennies: Edward I, second coinage 1279–1302, (Dublin), 3 Scottish: Alexander III (1249–86), second coinage *c.*1280–6?, one Flemish: Robert de Bethune (1305–22), Alost, and 2 continental forgeries of English pennies. **Refs:** *Coin Hoards*, V, (1979) no. 284; Cubbon (2000).

Hoards of uncertain date

(28) Unprovenanced eighteenth century (II): a lost hoard unearthed in 1780, which included 'a number of silver coins' of William the Lion of Scotland. No details are known about the coins, and therefore the dating remains imprecise, 'after 1165'. This find appears to be distinct from (23) which, though also of Scottish sterlings, was illustrated for the first time in 1769, before this find was discovered. **Refs:** Train (Douglas, 1845), 69; Clay (Douglas, 1869), 37, following Train.

(29) Kirk Marown 1828: a lost, small late thirteenth- or early fourteenth-century hoard which included Irish pennies of Edward I, second coinage (1279–1302), found in the debris while taking down a wall. **Refs:** Train (Douglas, 1845), 70; Clay (Douglas, 1869), 38, following Train.

(30) The Howe 1842: a lost, late thirteenth- or fourteenth-century hoard of about 200 coins that was discovered in a field on a hill near Douglas during ploughing. See (17) above regarding confusion in the literature between this hoard and an unrecorded hoard of Edward the Confessor pennies that was found around the same time. London, York and Canterbury mints were said to be equally represented in this hoard. **Refs:** Train (Douglas, 1845), 71; Clay (Douglas, 1869) 41; Gibson (Liverpool, 1877–8), 69, probably following Clay.

(31) Ballamona 1840 or 1841, Kirk Santan: a lost hoard of around 250? ('about a troy pound in weight') fourteenth-century pennies (deposited in or after 1318), contained in an earthen jar which was lost or destroyed. The coins are further described by Clay (Douglas, 1869, 40–1) as 'nearly all of Edward I', and included York, Canterbury, Bury St Edmunds, Bristol, Newcastle, and Durham mints, as well as an Irish coin of Edward I, and Scottish coins of Alexander III and Robert I, although he admits that some of his facts about this hoard were confused with the separate, but apparently comparable, find at Ballaslig. This, however, does not justify Dolley's conclusion that the hoards, reported from separate parishes, are one and the same. **Refs:** R.H.M. Dolley, 'The Irish mints of Edward I in the light of the coin-hoards from Ireland and Great Britain', *Proceedings of the Royal Irish Academy*, 66 (1967–8), 235–97, no. 5 and 257.

(32) Strandhall 1921, west of Castletown, Arbory/Rushen: a lost late fourteenth-century deposit comprising at least two silver coins, one a groat of David II (1329–71) struck at Edinburgh, the other a half-groat from 'Dalkeith' (recte Perth) of Robert II (1371–90). As Dolley suggested, the find may have been deposited in the 1370s or 1380s, although this is speculative based on the evidence of only two coins. Nevertheless, the deposition is unlikely to date later than a few years after the introduction of Robert III's light coinage in 1403. **Refs:** *The Manx Quarterly* VI, no. 25, April 1921, 85; Michael Dolley, 'A Neglected Minor Find of Later Fourteenth-Century Scottish Silver Coins from the Isle of Man', *Seaby's Coin and Medal Bulletin* 690, Feb. 1976, 43–5; Pers. comm. Martin Allen, Department of Coins and Medals, Fitzwilliam Museum, Cambridge.

(33) Douglas Head 1859, Kirk Braddan: a lost and otherwise unrecorded late

fourteenth-century hoard, only known from the *1876 Archaeological Commission Report,* 'Miscellaneous antiquities: coins' (MNHL, M.M.MSS. 258C), where it is written: 'In 1859 a small silver coin... of Robert III of Scotland (1390–1406) was found on Douglas Head, with others enclosed in a small box.' The same passage indicates that the coin was minted at Perth, and according to its description it is probably a halfpenny or penny.

Appendix II:
SINGLE COINS FOUND IN THE ISLE OF MAN TO *c.*1405

Part 1: Viking Age

(1) Frisian(?) imitation of Louis the Pious, gold solidus (mid? ninth century). Manx Museum 1609. Kirk Maughold churchyard, 1884. **Refs:** A.W. Moore (ed.), *The Manx Note Book* (Douglas, 1885), I, no. 1, 30 and I, no. 2, 65–8; John Evans, 'A gold solidus of Louis le Débonnaire', *Numismatic Chronicle*, IV (1884), 259; Philip Grierson 1951 'The Gold Solidus of Louis the Pious and its Imitations', *Jaarboek voor Munt- en Penningkunde 38*, 1–41 at 17, C [reprinted in Grierson, *Dark Age Numismatics*, London 1979, XXII]; Mark Blackburn, 'Gold in England During the Late Anglo-Saxon Period', in J. Graham-Campbell and G. Williams (eds), *Silver Economy in the Viking Age*, Institute of Archaeology Occasional Papers Series, (London, 2005), appendix A15.

(2) Edmund (939–46) penny, North-west Mercia, moneyer Eadmund. HR1. Manx Museum 82–150. Peel Castle excavation 1984 (ref. 84.16/L/420 NM), found in an adult lintel grave by the left femur (in the fill?) **Ref.:** Marion Archibald in Freke (ed.), *Excavations at St Patrick's Isle,* 326.

(3) Eadred (946–55) halfpenny, Northern or Western?, moneyer Hildulf. Flower type (very rare). Manx Museum 82–150. Peel Castle excavation 1985 (ref. 85.60/L/683 JN), found near the jaw in a child's grave. **Ref.:** Marion Archibald in Freke (ed.), *Excavations at St Patrick's Isle,* 326.

(4) Edmund (939–46) or Eadred (946–55) cut quarter-penny, North-west Mercia. HR1. Manx Museum 82–150. Peel Castle excavation 1986 (86.53/I/262 DG), found near the north-east wall/oven area(?). **Ref.:** Marion Archibald in Freke (ed.), *Excavations at St Patrick's Isle*, 327.

(5) Eadwig (955–9) penny, Derby?, moneyer Elf(r)e(d). HR1. Manx Museum 82–150. Peel Castle excavation 1986 (ref. 86.53/I/357 CT), found in the fill

of a lined drain. **Ref.:** Marion Archibald in Freke (ed.), *Excavations at St Patrick's Isle*, 327.

(6) Æthelred II (978–1016). Lost, details unknown, allegedly of 'gold' although this is highly unlikely (it may have had a gold-like appearance upon recovery). Found around 1830 in a mound that was being levelled in the north, at the farm of Gordon, Patrick. **Refs:** Train (Douglas, 1845), 69; Clay (Douglas, 1869), 35; Gibson (Liverpool, 1877–8), 69.

(7) Æthelred II (978–1016). Lost, details unknown, allegedly of 'gold' (see previous). Found pre-1860 'in the north of the island', and is apparently a distinct find from no. 6. **Ref.:** H.R. Oswald, *Vestigia Insulae Manniae Antiquiora*, Manx Society V (Douglas 1860) 60, note 6.[91]

(8) Æthelred II (978–1016). Lost, details unknown. Found pre-1869 in the garden of Rushen Abbey. This coin is likely to have been a stray from the Bradda Hoard as recently suggested by James Graham-Campbell, and should now be excluded from the total of true single coin finds of this period. **Refs:** Clay (Douglas, 1869), 35; J. Harris Gibson (Liverpool, 1877–8); James Graham-Campbell, 'The Lost Coin of Æthelred II from Rushen Abbey, Isle of Man' (*BNJ* 75 (2005), 161–3).

(9) Hiberno-Scandinavian penny, Phase III (1035–55), Dublin. Manx Museum 82–150. Peel Castle excavation 1985 (ref. 85.60/F/482 FP), found in the hall area, in the fill of a cut of a gulley. **Ref.:** Marion Archibald in Freke (ed.), *Excavations at St Patrick's Isle*, 327.

Part 2: Medieval Period

(10) Stephen (1135–54) penny. BMC type i, 1135–*c.*1145, mint and moneyer illegible. Block Eary shieling excavation, 1958, from the top of the solid turf in the lower part of Mound B. Manx Museum 1959–154. **Ref.:** P.S. Gelling, 'Shielings in the Isle of Man', *JMM* VI, no. 77 (1960–1), 124; P.S. Gelling 'Medieval shielings in the Isle of Man', *Medieval Archaeology*, 6–7 (1962–3), 158.

(11) John (1199–1216) cut halfpenny, Short Cross. London (off coin), Willelm L, Class 5b2, 1205–7. Castle Rushen excavation, 1989. **Ref.:** M.M. Archibald in P.J. Davey *et al.* (eds), *Excavations in Castletown, Isle of Man 1989–1992* (Liverpool, 1996), 35.

(12) John (1199–1216) cut halfpenny, Short Cross. London, Ilger or Rener, Class 5c, 1207–*c.*1209. Rushen Abbey excavation, 1998. Manx Museum 1998–508.72. **Ref.:** Kristin Bornholdt in P.J. Davey, *Rushen Abbey, Ballasalla, Isle of Man: First Archaeological Report*, Centre for Manx Studies, University of Liverpool, Research Report 7 (Douglas 1999), 64.

(13) Henry III (1216–72) penny, Short Cross. London, Adam, Class 7b2, 1230–early 1230s. Metal detector find from the Freeport site, Malew, 1984. Manx Museum 1995–263.

(14) Henry III (1216-72) cut halfpenny (0.45 g), Long Cross, Bristol, Iacob, Class 3b, c. 1250. Peel Castle excavation 1984 (84.16/E/202 IV). **Ref.:** Marion Archibald in Freke (ed.) *Excavations at St Patrick's Isle*, 327.

(15) Henry III (1216–72) penny, Long Cross. London, Ricard, Class 5g, 1258–*c.*1270. Purchased in 1943 from W.C. Wells, allegedly from Man. Manx Museum 1974–131.

(16) Henry III (1216–72) cut farthing, Long Cross. Canterbury, Durham or London, moneyer Willem, Class 5g, *c.*1258–*c.*1270 (or mid-1260s). Rushen Abbey excavation find 2004.

(17) Edward I (1272–1307) penny. London, Class 1c, 1279. Found while digging a grave at Malew parish churchyard, 1998. Loan accession no. 1262.

(18) Edward I (1272–1307) halfpenny. London, Class 3c-e, 1280. Cronk ny Merriu, 1970, found immediately under the sod near the north-east corner of the defended promontory. Manx Museum 1970–115.

(19) Edward I (1272–1307), penny. Uncertain mint, Class 3g1, 1281–2. Metal detector find from Rhenab, Maughold, 1984.

(20) Edward I (1272–1307) penny. Canterbury, Class 4a-4c, *c.*1281–*c.*1287. Metal detector find from the Freeport site, Malew, 1984. Manx Museum 1995–262.

(21) Edward I (1272–1307) penny. London, Class 10ab3/9b1 mule, *c.*1302–*c.*1303. Unprovenanced, from a Manx donor. Manx Museum 1978–1.

(22) Edward I (1272–1307) penny. London, Class 10cfl, *c.*1305–*c.*1306. Metal detector find from the Freeport site, Malew, 1984. Manx Museum 1995–265.

(23) Edward I or II penny. Canterbury, Class 10cf, *c.*1305–*c.*1310. Douglas shore, pre-1951. Manx Museum 1979–185.

(24) Edward I or II penny. Canterbury, Class 10cf2, *c.*1306–*c.*1307. Maughold parish church, 1899. Manx Museum 1954–1290.

(25) Edward I or II penny. Canterbury, Class 10cf2, *c.*1306–*c.*1307. Brunswick Road, Douglas, *c.*1954. Manx Museum 1954–2361.

(26) Edward I or II penny. Durham, Class 10cf3b, *c.*1307–*c.*1309. Metal detector find from the Freeport site, Malew, 1984. Manx Museum 1995–264.

(27) Edward II (1307–27) penny. Canterbury, Class 10cf4, *c.*1309. Found in the garden of the manse at Peel, *c.*1939. Manx Museum 1974–74.

(28) Edward II (1307–27) penny. Canterbury, Class 11c (or 11c reverse with obverse of 11b3, 12 or 13), 1311–*c.*1314. Metal detector find from Scarlett, 1982. Manx Museum 1995–266.

(29) Edward II (1307–27) penny. Canterbury, Class 12(b?), 1311–*c.*1314. Gift of P.M.C. Kermode, probably from Maughold, 1922. Manx Museum 1954–1288.

(30) Edward III (1327–77) halfpenny (fragments). London, Second Coinage, 1335–44. Castle Rushen Stores excavation, 1992 (92.104/23). **Ref.:** Davey *et al.* (eds), *Excavations in Castletown*, 118.

(31) Edward III (1327–77) groat (broken). Pre-Treaty series E, 1354–5. Metal detector find from Greeba, German, 1981.

(32) Edward III (1327–77) groat. London, Pre-Treaty series F, *c.*1356. Found in a garden at Onchan, 1956. Manx Museum 1956–93.

(33) Edward III (1327–77) groat. London, Pre-Treaty series Gb, *c.*1356–1361. Metal detector find from Ballaugh, 1984. Manx Museum Loan 21883.

(34) Edward III (1327–77) noble (gold). Lost, but Train's description is adequate to identify the coin as Treaty B, 1361–9. Found around 1845 at Slegaby, Kirk Onchan. **Refs:** Train (Douglas, 1845), 71–2; Waldron (Douglas, 1865), 119; Clay (Douglas, 1869), 35.

(35) Edward III (1327–77) half noble (gold). London, Treaty B, 1361–9. Gift of Rev. W. Kermode, Peel Harbour, 1840. Manx Museum 1954–1285. **Ref.:** P.M.C. Kermode, *List of Manx Antiquities* (Douglas, 1930), 18.

(36) Edward III (1327–77) quarter noble (gold). London, Treaty B, 1361–9. Recent metal detector find from Rushen Abbey.

(37) Richard II (1377–99) penny. York, Type Ia1, 1377–80s. Unprovenanced, possibly Douglas, 1937. Manx Museum 1954–3880.

(38) Edwardian penny, London, 1279–1335. Uncertain class. Metal detector find from Scarlett, 1982. Manx Museum 1995–267.

(39) Edwardian penny, 1300–51. Lost, details uncertain. Clay describes it as 'a small silver coin of the reign of Edward II', but coins of Edward II were not distinguishable from other Edwardian coins at the time he was writing. Clay's identification is based on the form of the legend and indicates a Class 10 or later Edwardian penny. Found pre-1869 at Ronaldsway, Malew. **Refs:** Clay (Douglas, 1869), 35; *1876 Archaeological Commission Report*, 'Miscellaneous antiquities: coins' (MNHL, M.M.MSS. 258C).

(40) Philip IV of France (1285-1314) Denier Tournois (0.67 g). Peel Castle excavation 1986 (86.53/G/870 KL). Archibald identified the coin as belonging to the issue of 1307, but notes that its very poor condition suggests that it may have been old by the time of deposition, perhaps sometime around the mid fourteenth century, or later. **Ref.:** Marion Archibald in Freke (ed.) *Excavations at St Patrick's* Isle, 327.

Notes

1 This paper incorporates material that is earlier than the date parameters of the volume, since the numismatic data does not conform naturally to the cut-off dates.

2 Allison Fox and Kristin Bornholdt Collins, 'The 2003 "TT": A Viking-Age Silver Hoard from Glenfaba, Isle of Man', *Viking Heritage Magazine* 1/2004, 3–5.

3 40 coins are listed in the appendix, but no. 8 has been excluded since it is appears more likely to be a stray from a known hoard, while the true provenance of (15) is less than certain.

4 See for example Mark Blackburn in 'Expansion and Control: Aspects of Anglo-Scandinavian Minting South of the Humber', ch. 7 in Graham-Campbell *et al.* (eds), *Vikings and the Danelaw*, (Oxford, 2001) 125–42. Here, Blackburn identified a comparable development in the Danelaw in the late ninth and early tenth centuries, where 'for the first forty or fifty years of Scandinavian presence… there were two co-existing types of economy' (p. 135). This situation arose despite the fact that the Scandinavian settlers began minting their own coins in East Anglia and the East Midlands from the mid-880s.

5 Some of Michael Dolley's main contributions to the study of the Manx collection include: 'The pattern of Viking-Age coin hoards from the Isle of Man', *Seaby's Coin and Medal Bulletin* (1975), 296–302, 337–40; 'A Hiberno-Manx coinage of the eleventh century', *Numismatic Chronicle*, 136 (1976), 75–84; 'Some Irish dimensions to Manx history', Inaugural Lecture delivered before the Queen's University of Belfast (1976); 'The palimpsest of Viking settlement on Man', in Bekker-Nielsen *et al.* (eds), *Eighth Viking Congress*, 173–81.

6 James Graham-Campbell, 'Viking-Age silver hoards in Man', in Fell *et al.* (eds), *The Viking Age in the Isle of Man*, 53–80.

7 Kristin Bornholdt Collins, *Manx Museum, Douglas: Anglo-Saxon, Hiberno-Scandinavian, Hiberno-Manx and other Coins to 1280*, Sylloge of Coins of the British Isles (Oxford, forthcoming); Kristin Bornholdt Collins, 'Viking-Age Coin Finds from the Isle of Man: A Study of Coin Circulation, Production and Concepts of Wealth During the Viking Age' (Cambridge University, unpublished PhD, 2003). Some results of my PhD research have been drawn on here, and I wish to thank my supervisors, Catherine Hills and Mark Blackburn, for their insights, support and guidance. I am most grateful for the practical advice, inspiring discussions, expertise on local matters and generous hospitality provided on numerous occasions by Peter Davey and colleagues at the Centre for Manx Studies; Marshall Cubbon; Frank Cowin; and, in particular, Sir David and Lady Wilson. I am also indebted to Hazel Simons, Sue Palmer and Allison Fox, past and present Assistant Keepers: Archaeology, The Manx Museum and National Trust, who fielded my questions and helped collect the data for this paper; to Professor James Graham-Campbell, especially for sharing with me his latest epiphanies on Manx matters; and to Martin Allen, Assistant Keeper, Department of Coins and Medals, Fitzwilliam Museum, for his assistance in identifying the medieval-period coins and for advising on the discussion and interpretation of this material. Finally, I am profoundly grateful to Manx National Heritage for its generous financial support, and to Stephen Harrison, Director, The Manx Museum and National Trust, who was instrumental in making possible my study of the Manx coin collection.

8 The appendix is divided into two parts to distinguish the distinctively Viking-Age cluster from the later hoards, which are labelled 'medieval period' in the loosest sense only, since both groups technically fall under this term. Sub-sections indicate the degree of confidence in the dating of the depositions.

9 Fig. 18.2 is designed to give an immediate visual impression of the quantity of material over time, with the chronological spread of all the relevant hoards and single finds together. It does not provide a sense of the size of each hoard nor an idea of composition and type, but this information is found in the relevant appendices.

10 For example, single coins and hoards dating to the eleventh century have been found in the burial ground at Grødbygård, Bornholm: Hanne Wagnkilde and Torben Pind, 'Tæt på 1000-tallets indbyggere I Aaker sogn: Gravpladser fra tidbig kristen tid ved Ndr. Grødbygård', *Bornholmske Samlinger*, 3rd ser., 10 (Rønne, 1996), 167–86.

11 The appendix is based on those coins held permanently in the Manx Museum collection or which are known to the Museum and waiting to be accessioned, as well as some examples known from references only, but believed to be true single finds. Coins for which there was sufficient reason to doubt a Manx provenance, or which may not be true single finds, have been rejected (for example, the coin-group Manx Museum 1954–7057B). The coins are listed in running

chronological order, and those with less certain identifications are indicated, but are not separated into a distinct category as with the hoards.

12 Contributions by Marion Archibald and W. Seaby in Freke (ed.), *Excavations on St Patrick's Isle, 1982–88* (Liverpool, 2002), 326–7 and 320–5.

13 Davey *et al.* (eds), *Excavations in Castletown, 1989–1992* (Liverpool, 1996); see contributions by M.M. Archibald on the coins, 35 and 117–18.

14 I am most grateful to Robert Farrer for information about the practice of metal-detecting in Man.

15 Christopher Dyer, 'Peasants and coins: the uses of money in the Middle Ages', *British Numismatic Journal*, 67 (1997), 30–47.

16 Dyer, 'Peasants and coins', 36; D.M. Metcalf, *An Atlas of Anglo-Saxon and Norman Coin Finds, c.973–1086* (Royal Numismatic Society and Ashmolean Museum, London, 1998), 14.

17 Robert Farrer, former Chairman of the Manx Detector Club, personal communication.

18 Mark Blackburn and Hugh Pagan, 'A revised check-list of coin hoards from the British Isles, c.500–1100', M.A.S. Blackburn (ed.), *Anglo-Saxon Monetary History* (Leicester, 1986), 291–313, see 297. An updated version is now available on the Web at www.medievalcoins.org

19 The Anglo-Saxon Chronicle (northern recension) and John of Worcester, who names a Manx king, 'Maccus, king of many islands' (amongst others), describe a gathering of Celtic leaders which took place in Chester to honour and submit to Edgar in 973. The six (or eight) sub-kings are said to have rowed the newly-crowned Edgar along the river Dee in a demonstration of their loyalty, and gave him pledges of their allegiance 'on sea and on land'. The event is corroborated by Ælfric, abbot of Cerne Abbas, Dorset, who refers to the same event in his *Life of Saint Swithun*, written in the early eleventh century. Dorothy Whitelock (ed.), *English Historical Documents c.500–1042* (2nd edn, London, 1979), 228 and 927.

20 Graham-Campbell, 'Viking-Age silver hoards in Man', 63. Referring to the results of 'preliminary studies', he notes that ring-money occurs mainly in Scotland, dating between 950–1050.

21 Graham-Campbell, 'Viking-Age silver hoards in Man', 68.

22 David Dumville, *The Churches of North Britain in the First Viking-Age*, Fifth Whithorn Lecture (Friends of the Whithorn Trust, 1997), 24–6; James Graham-Campbell, 'The Irish Sea Vikings: Raiders and Settlers', T. Scott and P. Starkey (eds), *The Middle Ages in the North-West*, Leopard's Head Press and Liverpool Centre for Medieval Studies (Oxford, 1995), 59–83, at pp. 75–8; also, Graham-Campbell, 'The early Viking Age in the Irish Sea area', Howard B. Clarke, Máire Ní Mhaonaigh and Raghnall Ó Floinn (eds), *Ireland and Scandinavia in the Early Viking Age* (Dublin, 1998), 104–30, at pp. 116–20.

23 Gerhard Bersu and David M. Wilson, *Three Viking Graves in the Isle of Man*, The Society for Medieval Archaeology Monograph Series: No. I (London, 1966); Graham-Campbell in Clarke *et al.* (eds), *Ireland and Scandinavia*, 117–18.

24 On Irish hoards see: James Graham-Campbell, 'The Viking-Age silver hoards of Ireland', in B. Almquist and D. Greene (eds), *Proceedings of the Seventh Viking Congress, Dublin 15–21 August 1973* (Dublin, 1976), 39–74; Michael Kenny, 'The geographical distribution of Irish Viking-Age hoards', *Proceedings of the Royal Irish Academy*, 87 C (1987), 507–25; John Sheehan, 'Early Viking Age silver hoards from Ireland and their Scandinavian Elements', in Clarke *et al.* (eds), *Ireland and Scandinavia*, 166–202.

25 D.M. Metcalf, 'The monetary economy of the Irish Sea province', in James Graham-Campbell (ed), *Viking Treasure from the North West: The Cuerdale Hoard in its Context*, National Museums and Galleries on Merseyside Occasional Papers Liverpool Museum No. 5, (Liverpool, 1992), 89–106.

26 A detailed analysis is provided in the author's PhD thesis, chapter 5.5 and table 5.9. p. 268. It was previously assumed that north-west Mercian mints (Chester in particular) dominated the finds, but the evidence instead demonstrates much closer ties with north-east England.

27 James Graham-Campbell, *The Viking-Age Gold and Silver of Scotland (AD 850–1100)*, (Edinburgh, 1995), 26–7; John Sheehan, in Clarke *et al.* (eds), *Ireland and Scandinavia*, 177–80.

28 John Sheehan, in Clarke *et al.* (eds), *Ireland and Scandinavia*, 178.

29 Mark Redknap, interim report in *Archaeology in Wales*, 35 (1995), 58–9.

30 G. Boon, *Welsh Hoards 1979–81* (Cardiff, 1986), 98–102.

31 G. Boon, *Welsh Hoards*, 92 and Fig. 38 (no. 14).

32 This hoard was discovered in the burial ground at Ballaqueeney according to the near-contemporary report of the *1876 Archaeological Commission*, MNHL MSS. 258 C, which also indicates that it was a small find. A post-1870 hand-written list of the coins by William Kneale is headed, 'Anglo-Saxon coins recently found in a tumulus at Port St Mary', MNHL MS. The coins identified in this list are characteristically cut in half or in fragmentary condition and end before the reign of Edgar, forming a unified group. A second longer and untitled list exists, also by Kneale, but compiled on a different occasion. These coins together were assumed to be part of the same hoard, but coins of Edgar are present in the second list and full inscriptions indicate that the coins were whole, unlike the first group. It is evident that Kneale examined two separate and distinct hoards, and that the one from Ballaqueeney most likely contained only the eight coins from his first list.

33 D.M. Wilson, *The Viking Age in the Isle of Man: The Archaeological Evidence*, C.C. Rafn Lecture 3 (Odense, 1974), 39.

34 Broderick, *CKMI*, fol. 35r.

35 Broderick, *CKMI*, fol. 33v.

36 Michael Dolley's explanation of the cessation of hoarding, in 'Some Irish dimensions to Manx history', 21.

37 Whitelock (ed.), *English Historical Documents*, 237.

38 Broderick, *CKMI*, fol. 50r.

39 M. Blackburn, 'Gold in England during the "Age of Silver" (Eighth–Eleventh Centuries)' in James Graham-Campbell and Gareth Williams (eds), *Silver Economy during the Viking Age* (London 2005), Appendix A15.

40 J. Graham-Campbell, 'The Lost coin of Aethelred II from Rushen Abbey, Isle of Man', *BNJ* 75 (2005), 161–3.

41 Metcalf, 'The monetary economy of the Irish Sea province', 15, Map 1: All finds.

42 Dolley, 'A Hiberno-Manx coinage of the eleventh century'.

43 J. Lindsay, *A View of the Coinage of Ireland* (Cork, 1839), plate 2, 48 and plate 3, 50; B. Roth, 'The coins of the Danish kings of Ireland; Hiberno-Danish Series', *British Numismatic Journal* 6 (1909), 55–146, plate 2, 34.

44 Dolley, 'A Hiberno-Manx coinage of the eleventh century', 79.

45 K.A. Bornholdt, 'Myth or mint? The Evidence for a Viking-Age coinage from the Isle of Man', in P.J. Davey (ed.), *Recent Archaeological Research on the Isle of Man*, BAR British Series 278 (Oxford, 1999), 199–220.

46 Bornholdt, 'Myth or mint?', 206–7 and Appendix.

47 Metcalf and Northover define 'silver' as silver plus its associated trace elements and lead, since the other elements could not be separated from the silver at this time and would have been incorporated as part of the weight: D.M. Metcalf and P.J. Northover, 'Interpreting the alloy of the later Anglo-Saxon coinage', *British Numismatic Journal*, 56 (1986), 35–63, at p. 36.

48 Bornholdt, 'Myth or mint?', 207–8, using the formula discussed by W. Esty, 'Estimation of the size of a coinage: a survey and comparison of methods', *Numismatic Chronicle*, 146 (1986), 185–215.

49 H.R. Mossop, *The Lincoln Mint c.890–1279* (Newcastle upon Tyne, 1970), 17 and table 4.

50 Mark Blackburn, 'Hiberno-Norse and Irish Sea imitations of Cnut's Quatrefoil Type', *British Numismatic Journal*, 156 (1996), 1–20, see 2–3.

51 Stockholm Collection Inv. 11619/2; G. Hatz, *Handel und Verkehr zwischen dem Deutschen Reich und Schweden in der späten Wikingerzeit*, (Lund, 1974), 226, no. 272.

52 The confidence interval is much wider for the reverses, with about 45 per cent coverage in the sample: Bornholdt, 'Myth or mint?', 207.

53 Bornholdt, 'Myth or mint?', 209 and Fig. 9.

54 Duffy, 'Irishmen and Islesmen', 98–101.

55 Dolley, 'A Hiberno-Manx coinage of the eleventh century', 82; Dolley, 'Some Irish dimensions to Manx history', 19–21.

56 Duffy, 'Irishmen and Islesmen', 98.

57 Blackburn, 'Imitations of Cnut's Quatrefoil Type'.

58 This has been observed in Scandinavian contexts by Lotte Hedeager, 'Warrior economy and trading economy in Viking-Age Scandinavia', *The Journal of European Archaeology*, 2:1 (1994), 130–47.

59 Hedeager, 'Warrior economy and trading economy', 141.

60 Hedeager, 'Warrior economy and trading economy', 141.

61 Several of the relevant finds are discussed in Marshall Cubbon, 'A remarkable decade of Manx coin hoards, 1972–1982', *Proceedings*, XI, no. 1 (2000).

62 D.M. Metcalf, 'A survey of numismatic research into the pennies of the first three Edwards', N.J. Mayhew (ed.), *Edwardian Monetary Affairs (1279–1344)*, British Archaeological Reports 36 (Oxford, 1977), 1–31, at p. 6.

63 See chapter three above.

64 C.E. Challis (ed.), *A New History of the Royal Mint* (Cambridge, 1992), Appendix I; M. Allen, 'The Volume of the English Currency, 1158–1470', *Economic History Review* LIV, 4 (2001), 595–611.

65 Metcalf's estimates ('Pennies of the first three Edwards', 7) are now considered to be too high, but the discussion still provides a sense of the scale of increase underway at this time.

66 Broderick, *CKMI*, fol. 41v.

67 Broderick, *CKMI*, fol. 46r.

68 King Magnus of Man and the Isles was also knighted by Henry III later, in 1256, Broderick, *CKMI*, fol. 49r.

69 Broderick, *CKMI*, fol. 50r. On the date of this raid, see Colm McNamee above, p. 140, and, for a contrary view, Bernadette Williams, p. 325.

70 Broderick, *CKMI*, fol. 50r.

71 I am grateful to Martin Allen, Fitzwilliam Museum, for providing expertise in this respect.

72 David Freke, 'History', in Vaughn Robinson and Danny McCarroll (eds), *The Isle of Man: Celebrating a Sense of Place*, (Liverpool, 1990), 118.

73 The later Henry III penny was purchased from W.C. Wells, who is known to have confused or perhaps even fabricated provenances on other occasions, and the coin is therefore only 'allegedly' from Man.

74 Metcalf, 'Pennies of the first three Edwards', 10.

75 S.E. Rigold, 'Small change in the light of medieval site-finds', in Mayhew (ed.), *Edwardian Monetary Affairs*, 59–80, at p. 69.

76 Rigold, 'Small change', 61.

77 Dyer, 'Peasants and coins', 37, Fig. 2.

78 Rigold, 'Small change', see site totals 70–8; Dyer, 'Peasants and coins', in his study of 33 medieval rural settlements in England and Wales, each of which met the criterion of having at least one fully excavated house, found that most sites produced only 'one, two or three finds' (p. 32). Manor houses and urban sites produce more coin finds on average, but the difference is not overwhelming, and 'peasant sites do not seem exceptionally deficient' (pp. 34–5).

79 Dyer, 'Peasants and coins', 33–4, calculates a minimum figure, based on the money that would have been circulating from rent payments alone in the thirteenth and fourteenth centuries, concluding that excavations produce 'about one coin of every 33,000 which came into the hands of the original inhabitants'.

80 Rigold, 'Small change', 59.

81 These finds will be discussed elsewhere by the author. A brief list of unconfirmed hoards is provided here in the hope that readers may be able to provide additional details: Castletown pre-1789; Ballaugh 1772; Peel? 1868; Cronk Beck, nineteenth century?; Knockaloe pre-1820; Tower of Refuge, Kirk Michael 1836; King Orry's Castle 1857; Beary Chapel 1800s; 'The Craves' 1800s; Corrody, Kirk Christ Lezayre, early twentieth century?

82 For example, an incident is recorded in the journal of Dr John Bradbury *c.*1860s-*c.*1890s, (MNHL MS. 2202A) entry no. 187: 'About 1857, two men discovered in a sod fence near King Orry's Castle, a black earthenware pitcher full of coins. They employed a sharp man in the neighbourhood to go with them to Liverpool, where they disposed of their treasure for a considerable sum of money.'

83 Broderick, *CKMI*, fol. 43v.

84 Broderick, *CKMI*, fol. 44r.

85 Broderick, *CKMI*, fol. 45v.

86 Broderick, *CKMI*, fol. 51r.

87 Broderick, *CKMI*, fol. 51v. See also the evidence adduced by Ditchburn and Hudson in chapter 17, pp. 380–3.

88 For full details of coin types, moneyers and mints and detailed discussions relating to the discovery, reconstruction and significance of each find see Kristin Bornholdt Collins, unpublished PhD thesis (University of Cambridge, July 2003), Appendix viii vol. 2, 'Corpus of Viking-Age Coin Hoards from the Isle of Man with a Summary of Later Medieval Hoards and Single Coin Finds'. As information regarding additional finds can be made available to the public, these details will be made available through the iMuseum web site of Manx National Heritage.

89 Kneale's involvement in both should have ensured its inclusion in the Commission's report had the hoard been known before 1879.

90 This hoard was previously thought to have been unearthed in 1834, but a reference to it in *Mona's Herald* on Saturday, 28 September 1833 (under the heading 'Local intelligence') verifies the revised date (personal communicaion, James Graham-Campbell).

91 I am most grateful to James Graham-Campbell for bringing this reference to my attention.

19 *The System of Land Division and Assessment*

GARETH WILLIAMS

Like many aspects of the social and political structure of medieval Man, the study of land assessment is complicated. There are three main reasons for this. Firstly, although a number of units of land assessment are known from Man, these are only documented clearly from the end of the Middle Ages, although most appear to be much earlier in origin. Secondly, it appears from the wider context of land-divisions in the Norse settlements in Scotland and Man that elements of the system of assessment may well have been imposed in the late tenth or early eleventh centuries, a period in which political authority over the Isle of Man is difficult to trace with any certainty. Thirdly, it appears that while some at least of these units of assessment were introduced during the period of Norse rule, they may have been imposed on pre-Norse land-divisions. This raises the general problem of the extent to which the pre-Norse population, and particularly pre-Norse social structure, survived after the Norse settlement. Subsidiary to this is the question of the extent to which the *treen*, one of the main assessment units on the island, may be associated with a group of small chapels, known as *keeills*, which have been seen as a pre-Norse precursor of the parochial system. There is also a question, when considering survival of pre-Norse institutions, of precisely where such institutions might have originated. Man's position in the Irish Sea exposed the island to influences from a number of directions. A final point of caution is that while the land assessment units of Man as they survive in the sources show a clear hierarchical structure (the island is divided into two 'deemster' divisions, each of which contains three *sheadings*, further subdivided into parishes, treens and quarterlands), it is by no means certain that all the layers of this structure were introduced simultaneously as part of a single unified structure.

Three major studies of land assessment on Man have been published.[1] The first of these was by the Norwegian philologist Carl Marstrander, who was interested in the Norse settlement of Man, and the extent to which pre-Norse elements survived in language and place-names as well as in systems of administration and social structure. A monograph on Norse settlement on Man included discussion of the treen and quarterland, which

Marstrander believed to be Norse assessment units imposed on a pre-existing pattern of Celtic land divisions.[2] This point was picked up by the Orcadian historian Hugh Marwick, although he differed with Marstrander on the precise origins of the treen/quarterland assessment. Inspired by the work of the Norwegian historian Asgaut Steinnes on the Norwegian *leiþangr* (a national system of military obligations and taxation),[3] Marwick suggested that the same system could be traced in land assessment units throughout the Norse settlements in Scotland, including both the earldom of Orkney and Caithness, and the kingdom of Man and the Isles. He suggested that a single assessment unit, the ounceland, divided into quarters, could be traced throughout the area of Norse settlement, although he saw this as superimposed on pre-Norse land divisions. In Orkney the ounceland was known in Old Norse as *eyrisland*, 'land of an ounce', and in the west of Scotland as Gaelic *tír unga*, with the same meaning. Marwick took treen to be a Manx version of Gaelic *tír unga*, and therefore to be part of the same system of assessment.[4] This idea was enthusiastically endorsed by Marstrander in preference to his own earlier etymology, and he produced a second monograph on the subject. This was particularly concerned with the relationship between treens and keeills. Based on the Manx traditionary ballad of *Mannanán Beg Mac Y Lir* (a text of debatable antiquity; for which see below), he suggested that originally there had been a keeill in every treen, and that the treen thus represented a pre-Norse proto-parochial unit, on which the Norse ounceland assessment was superimposed.[5]

A second major study, this time from a geographical perspective, was published by Elwyn Davies in 1956.[6] This was less concerned with the political and historical background to the introduction of the various units of land assessment than with the relationship between those units and the physical landscape. Davies pointed out that the island is physically dominated by an upland mass, which divides coastal plateau ledges to the north-west and south-east. This physical relief naturally creates the division of the island into 'Northside' and 'Southside', while the smaller treen and quarterland units are largely confined to the coastal plateau ledges and the lower slopes of the central mass, mostly below a height of around 600 feet above sea level. Davies also noted that most of the parishes formed physically distinct units, although he suggested that the parishes of Santon and Marown may originally have formed a single parish, giving a total of 16 parishes rather than the 17 which exist today. While this argument is based on the facts that the southernmost treen in Marown and the neighbouring treen in Santon share the same name, and that Marown is the only parish on the island lacking access to the sea, it finds support from the number of 16 representatives originally sent to the Tynwald (ON *Þing-völlr*, or 'assembly place'), the meeting place of the Norse law assembly which later became the Manx parliament (see below).

The third major study combined history and archaeology with computer-aided statistical analysis.[7] Paul Reilly's work contains two main features. He pointed out the similarity between the hierarchical system of land assessment in the Isle of Man and other systems of land assessment in the British Isles, following a model of a 'multiple estate' system, in which small estates are grouped together to form multiple estates which in turn are grouped into even larger units for the purpose of taxation and royal administration. At the same time he listed a number of references to Man in sources of the pre-Norse period, which indicated that Man had at various times been linked politically with a number of neighbouring kingdoms around the Irish Sea, although Reilly was inclined to link the land assessment system with the kingdom of Gwynedd and especially the island of Anglesey. Reilly's conclusions supported Marstrander's earlier suggestion that the assessment units of the Norse period and later were superimposed on pre-Norse land divisions. However, Reilly's second main argument was to challenge Marstrander's link between the treen unit and the keeill chapels. Marstrander based his calculations on sites identified as keeills in Kermode's Manx archaeological survey. According to these calculations, out of a total of 162 identifiable 'original treens':

84 treens showed evidence of a single keeill;
21 treens showed evidence of two keeills;
3 treens showed evidence of three keeills;
53 treens showed no evidence of any keeills at all.

Thus, while treens with a single keeill form the single largest group, this group represents only 51.9 per cent of the total number of treens listed. Reilly's computer analysis plotted the number of keeills against the total amount of settled land, and the number of treens into which this land was divided, and found that the distribution noted by Marstrander was consistent with a completely random distribution of keeills.[8] This challenge to Marstrander's theory meets with further support from the work of Christopher Lowe, who has suggested that not all sites identified by Kermode (and thus by Marstrander) as keeills can safely be accepted as such. He points particularly to burial grounds of lintel graves with no physical remains of a keeill structure. Because lintel graves are often associated with keeills, Kermode had accepted such burial grounds as keeill sites, but there is no firm evidence to support this assumption.[9] The traditional association between treens and keeills is thus highly questionable.

None of the three studies summarised above fully explains the development of land assessment in the Isle of Man, although all three make significant contributions. While Davies's article provides a useful background survey of the various land divisions, Reilly raises important points about the origins of the land divisions, and the combined work of Marwick and Marstrander focuses on the assessment system based on those divisions. The distinction between the land divisions and the assessment system is an important one, and the remainder of this chapter will address each of these in turn.

Land divisions in the written sources

As mentioned earlier, the physical geography of Man creates a division into 'Northside' and 'Southside', each of which contains three sheadings, which in turn each contain either two or three parishes (Manx *skeerey*). Within each parish there are varying numbers of treens, which are further divided

Fig. 19.1 *The Isle of Man showing parishes, sheadings and the Northside/Southside boundaries.*

into quarterlands (Manx *kerroo*). Although these units have a variety of functions, it is notable that nowhere does a land-unit of one type overlap the boundaries of another, i.e., each smaller unit is completely contained within all larger units of which it forms a part.[10] This gives an impression of a unified hierarchical system, but given the late date of most of our evidence, one cannot safely say that this was originally the case.

There is no early evidence for the existence of the Northside/ Southside divison. Each possessed in post-medieval times a court known as the Deemster Court, presided over by the deemster, who also functioned as a speaker in the House of Keys (the Manx parliament). The word 'deemster' is probably of northern English extraction, and is thought to have been introduced to Man by the Stanleys in the fifteenth century.[11] However, the office of Deemster seems to correspond closely in function with the Norse lögmaðr, or 'lawspeaker', and may thus represent a renaming of an earlier title. It should also be noted that 'the North part' and 'the South part' of the island are portrayed as separate entities in the late eleventh century in the chronicle of Man; Godred Crovan is reported as having granted the southern part to his supporters, and the northern part to the conquered Manx *sub anno* 1056 (= 1079), while *s.a.* 1098 a battle between the Manxmen is recorded in which the 'men of the north' had the victory. Furthermore, use of the name 'Lögmaðr' (Lagmann) in the royal house during this period, together with a reference in Irish Annals to the *lagmenn* of the Isles,[12] suggests the existence of the role of lögmaðr, as one might in any case expect within a Norse kingdom. This does not prove that the deemster division dates back to the eleventh century, since the role of lögmaðr does not presuppose an administrative division, and since the chronicle references may simply reflect the physical division of the island. Nevertheless, the possibility of an early administrative division cannot be ruled out.

The sheading division is certainly of medieval origin, although no precise date can be given for the introduction of the unit. The first reference to the sheading as such comes in the Manx Statutes of 1422, after the beginning of the Stanleyan period (1405–1627). The *Oxford English Dictionary* derives the word from ME *scheding*, which could suggest that the unit was introduced by the Stanleys.[13] However, both Gaelic and Norse origins have also been suggested for the word;[14] it is notable that there are six sheadings and that both the Gaelic etymology, and the more satisfactory of two Norse etymologies,[15] refer to 'sixths'.

The names of three sheadings appear in sources of the Norse period, although it is not certain that the sheading unit is referred to in these cases. The Manx chronicle refers to a *loco qui vocatur Russin* (identified with the sheading name Rushen) *s.a* 1134, which has been taken to refer to the sheading,[16] but Marstrander argues that the word *loco* would never have been used for so large a district, and that this is a reference to the actual place from which the sheading took its name, rather than to the sheading as a whole.[17] A reference to the sheading names of Glenfaba and Lezayre in a papal bull of 1231, however, is accepted by Marstrander, because of the phrase *Ecclesia Sanctae Trinitatis in Leayre*, since the church is some six miles from the Point of Ayre from which the sheading takes its name.[18] Again, however, this does not constitute firm evidence for the division to predate the fifteenth century.

There are currently 17 parishes on the island, thus:

Sheading	*Parishes*
Ayre	Andreas, Bride, Lezayre;
Michael	Jurby, Ballaugh Michael;
Glenfaba	German, Patrick, Marown;
Rushen	Rushen, Arbory, Malew;
Middle	Santon, Braddan, Onchan;
Garff	Lonan, Maughold.

Before 1796, however, Marown was in the sheading of Middle, and Onchan was in Garff.[19] The parishes seem to have been laid out with an eye to the equitable distribution of the land resources necessary to a mixed farming economy; arable land, pasture, and rough grazing.[20] With the exception of Marown, each parish touches on the sea (valuable for fishing, transportation, and the fruits of the sea, e.g., seaweed, beached whales, etc.), and as mentioned above, it is possible that Marown and Santon originally formed one parish. The case for an original pattern of 16 parishes is strengthened by a reference in a declaration of the Deemsters and the House of Keys to Sir John Stanley in 1412, which states that

> Also we give for Law, that there was never xxiiij in Certainty, since they were first that were called taxiaxi, those were xxiiij free Houlders viz. viij in the Out Isles, and xvj in your Land of Mann, and this was in King Orry's Days.[21]

It seems likely that the 16 'taxiaxi' from the Isle of Man itself represented a parish each.[22] However, this view has been questioned by Reilly, on the grounds that if the habitable areas of Marown and Santon were added together, this would create a much larger habitable area than any other parish possesses, while with the two separate, all the parishes have roughly the same area of habitable land.[23]

Although no precise date is known for the introduction of the parochial system, it may well be attributable to the reign of Óláfr I (*c.*1133–54), who reformed the church on Man along more modern lines, as a result of his upbringing in Norman England.[24] References to parishes exist from the thirteenth century,[25] and Marstrander points to a Norse origin for the Manx term for parish, *skeerey*. While this could plausibly derive from ME *scír*, Marstrander points out that by the fifteenth century this would already have been pronounced shire in English, and would thus have given *sheerey*, not *skeerey*. ON *skíri*, or Scottish Gaelic *sgire* thus seem more likely. *Sgire* in Gaelic has the meaning of parish, whilst *skíri* was used by the Norse as a general term for a district, as in *Dyflinnarskíri* for the area around Dublin.[26]

Treens are first mentioned explicitly in manorial rolls of the early sixteenth century. The roll of 1510 covers Southside, that of 1513 covers Northside, and thus a complete picture can be gained of the island from these two documents combined.[27] Holdings are listed under the names of the treens in which they were located, and listed as quarters, or fractions of quarters,[28] although the term 'quarterland' is not used as such. The word 'quarterland' first appears in the Manx Statutes of 1593,[29] but it is clear that the unit already existed by the time that the manorial rolls were written, and individual estates mentioned there are also referred to in a sheading court roll of 1417–18.[30] A possible reference to the treen of Rowany exists in a declaration of 1408,[31] and the list of monastic boundaries contained in the same manuscript as the chronicle, *c.* 1280, contains the names of estates which can be identified with treens and quarterlands known from later evidence.[32]

An even earlier date (fifth–sixth century) is suggested by a reference in the Manx traditionary ballad of *Mannanán Beg Mac Y Lir* to St Germanus building a keeill (chapel) 'in every treen balley'.[33] However, this ballad only survives in a nineteenth-century record, the language of which suggests an earlier sixteenth-century form. Megaw has argued that this may derive from a twelfth-century original,[34] but even so, it can hardly be regarded as a reliable source for the fifth–sixth century. Although quarterlands cover most of the island below approx. 600 feet above sea level, not all of this land is divided into treens. Treens are not recorded in the abbeylands and baronies (church estates),[35] although the presence of quarterlands on these

Fig. 19.2 *An example of treen and quarterland divisions in southern Patrick; showing five treens, each with between three and six quarterlands. Note the position of the keeills and two of the Barony lands referred to in chapter 16. From P.J. Davey and J. Roscow, 'The Dissolution of the Monasteries on the Isle of Man',* Isle of Man Natural History and Antiquarian Society *monograph.*

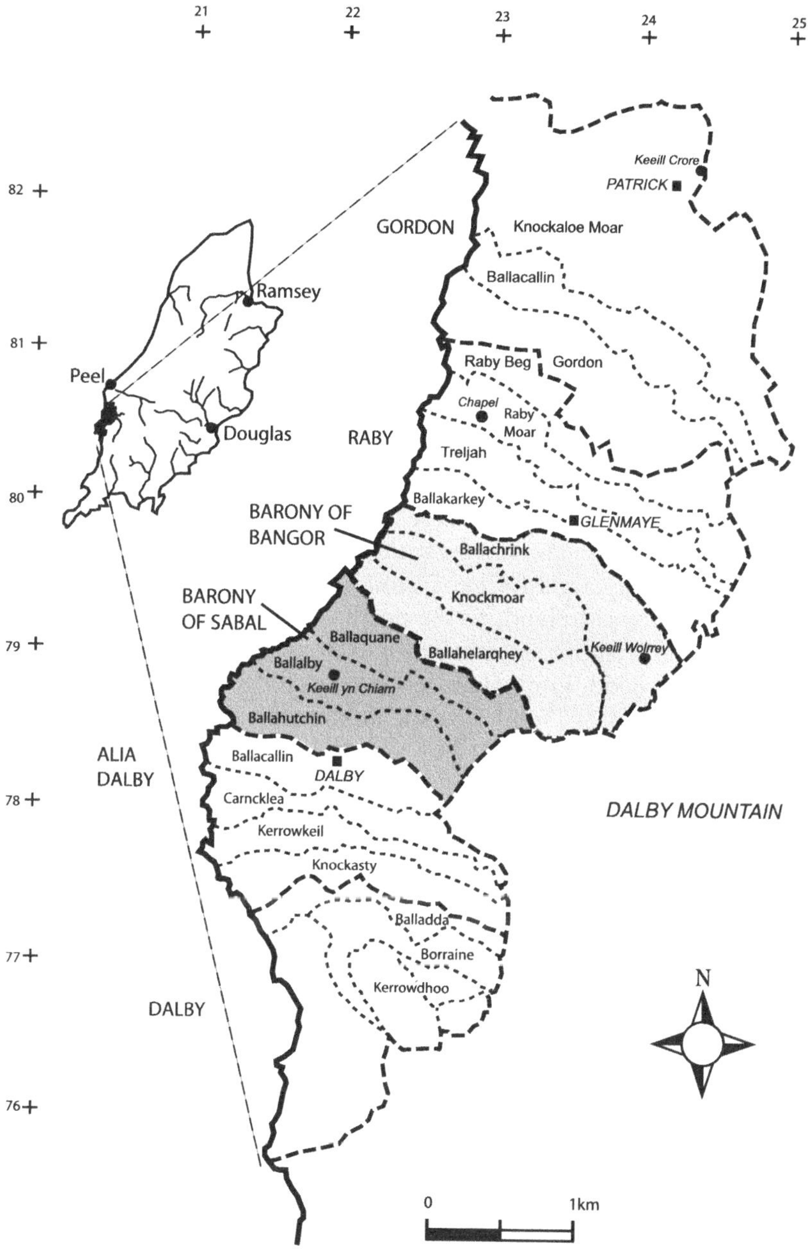
21
22
23
24
25
82
81
80
79
78
77
76
Keeill Crore
PATRICK
GORDON
Knockaloe Moar
Ballacallin
Ramsey
Raby Beg
Gordon
Peel
Chapel
Raby Moar
Douglas
RABY
Treljah
Ballakarkey
BARONY OF BANGOR
GLENMAYE
Ballachrink
Knockmoar
BARONY OF SABAL
Ballaquane
Ballahelarqhey
Keeill Wolrrey
Ballalby
Keeill yn Chiam
Ballahutchin
ALIA DALBY
Ballacallin
DALBY
Carncklea
DALBY MOUNTAIN
Kerrowkeil
Knockasty
Balladda
Borraine
Kerrowdhoo
DALBY
N
0
1km

estates suggests that formerly there may have been treens there as well. This suggests that the treen assessment predates the establishment of Rushen abbey, but that the church became exempted from the dues associated with the treen assessment. The absence of treens from church estates probably partly accounts for the apparent discrepancy between the numbers of known treens and quarterlands; 171 treens to 752 quarterlands.[36]

Pre-Norse influences

It appears that while none of the assessment units can be clearly identified in documentary sources before the later Middle Ages, all of them could potentially date back to the period of Norse rule *c.* 900–1266, or even further. Before moving to the origins and nature of the assessment system itself, it is necessary briefly to consider the possible pattern of land-units on which the assessment was imposed. The population of the Isle of Man before the Norse settlements reflects the island's central location in the Irish Sea; its position made it valuable for strategic reasons, as well as for trade, and it was a tempting target for expansion for powerful neighbours on all sides. To the west was Ireland, to the north the Scottish kingdom of Dál Riada, to the east Brythonic Strathclyde and Anglian Northumbria, and to the south lay Gwynedd. Limited evidence exists for the connections of all with early medieval Man, solid dynastic links in the case of Gwynedd.[37]

Matters are further complicated by the fundamental similarity between assessment systems in the different kingdoms around the Irish Sea. The *Senchus fer nAlban* provides a record of land assessment in Dál Riada, based on the *tech* ('household'), which has parallels in England, Wales, and Francia, as well as Ireland. The Anglo-Saxon 'hide' (OE *híd* or *híwisc*) derives from the root *híw-*, meaning 'household' or 'family', and was the holding of the normal freeman from at least as far back as the late seventh century (the Laws of Ine of Wessex refer to tribute from ten hides).[38] The hide is almost certainly identical to the Latin *terra unius familiae* of Bede s 'History', and the *terra primo familiarum quinquaginta* of the anonymous history of the abbots of Wearmouth and Jarrow. This family-based unit was the holding of a normal freeman, and was the basis for both taxation and military service.[39] Parallels are also found with the Welsh *tyddyn* and *tref*, both of which originally meant 'homestead', and later came to be used as units of land measurement.[40] The family unit also functions in the earliest surviving Norwegian laws; assessments tend to be based on individuals, whether free or unfree, but it is the responsibility of the householder to declare the numbers of all the individuals in his household, of whatever status, at the assessment meeting.[41]

This similarity of the likely systems that any of these races might impose, would make it very easy for later settlers of one race to take over the land systems of another, as long as there was sufficient continuity either in population, or in physical boundaries, for the earlier system to remain known. Thus it is perfectly plausible that Norse settlers, finding a Celtic (whether Welsh or Irish) system of land divisions in place, should continue to use that system, even if the names of those divisions, and the dues required of them, were to be changed. However, the same similarity means that where no concrete evidence exists for the origins of a particular unit, one cannot simply identify that unit with one particular pattern, since it might fit equally well with another. The Manx quarterland has been identified as a comparable 'household' unit,[42] but this does not help to indicate the particular origins of that unit. Arguments based on similarity of terminology can also be overly narrow. Marstrander points out that the fact that the treen and the Irish *baile biataigh* (as also the ounceland and the Scottish *dabhach*) are divided into quarters does not necessarily mean that they are fundamentally the same unit; a quarter is a simple division to make, and one can also find quarterlands in west Norway (where they signify a quarter of a large unit known as a *fylki*) and Iceland (where they signify a quarter of the whole island).[43]

Cross-racial similarities extend beyond the use of a 'household' unit. In Wales the *maenol* is equivalent to the treen, which is equivalent to the Orkney *eyrisland* and the Scottish *dabhach* and arguably to the Irish *baile biataigh*. These in turn can be grouped into larger units (Welsh *commote*, Manx *sheading*, Scottish shire, etc.), each with its focus on a particular estate owned by the overlord (king, earl, etc.) to whom any renders were due. Glanmor Jones's multiple estate system for England and Wales shows close similarities to Geoffrey Barrow's ideas on Scottish shires, and Asgaut Steinnes's views on the Orkney *huseby*.[44] It is against this broad background of common systems that any attempt to consider parallels for the Manx divisions must be made.

When considering treens and quarterlands, the obvious conclusion is either that the two units must be contemporary, or that the quarterland is the later of the two, since its name implies the existence of the larger unit. This need only apply, however, to the names of the assessment units, rather than to the actual land divisions themselves. Given the late evidence for the existence of either unit, there is no proof which of the two divisions is the earlier. Since the relationship between treens and quarterlands is far from regular, it is not impossible that the treen assessment was imposed on an existing system of 'household' units, with only a partial attempt at mathematical regularity, and that these 'household' units were subsequently renamed quarterlands in recognition of the fact that the most common relationship of 'household' unit to treen was 4:1.

For approximately 200 years before the Norse settlement, there were dynastic links between the dynasty of Man and the dynasty ruling Gwynedd. Anglesey was an important part of the kingdom of Gwynedd, and Bede and other early sources view Anglesey and Man as a pair. Thus, if one seeks for pre-Norse origins for the land-divisions of Man, Anglesey is an obvious starting point. The Welsh parallel of the *tref* for the 'household' unit, and the *maenol* for the grouping of four such units into a larger 'multiple estate', have already been mentioned. It is particularly striking that Anglesey, like Man, is divided into six larger territorial units (*commotes*), although when it comes to larger units still, Anglesey has three *cantrefs* as opposed to the two deemster divisons of Man.[45] The term *cantref* means 'a hundred *trefs*', and is thus parallel to the English 'hundred', and even is even closer to the *cet treb* of Islay in the *Senchus fer nAlban.*[46] Under Jones's multiple estate model, four *trefs* would constitute a *maenol*, or multiple estate. Twelve multiple estates plus two royally owned *trefs* (i.e., 50 *trefs*) would constitute a *commote*, and two *commotes* would constitute a *cantref.*[47]

The case for identifying the sheading with the *commote* is strengthened by similarities between Manx and Welsh administrative systems. The idea of a moderately large administrative unit containing a central estate, which acted as a focus for the collection of renders, has already been mentioned. In Wales, this estate was known as the *maerdref*, or 'steward's *tref*'. In each of the Manx sheadings there is one treen that has the same name as the sheading, and it is argued that the sheading takes its name from the treen rather than the other way round. Megaw suggests that these might be administrative centres equivalent to the *maerdref.*[48] Furthermore, each sheading was administered by a royal officer called a *moar*,[49] clearly related to the Welsh *maer*, or 'royal steward', and responsible for land tenure and crown revenues. This post is also known from a Scottish context, with the *mormaer*, or 'great steward' (possibly of Pictish origin) as the equivalent of an earl in early Scotland.[50] A similar system, based on the *huseby*,[51] may have existed in Norway and in Orkney, which would again have facilitated the continuity of such a system under bilingual Norse rulers. Furthermore, dues known from twelfth-century Man, *pecunia* and *(a)conveth*, show similarities not only to the Irish/Scottish dues of *caín* (tribute) and *coinmheadh* (hospitality), but also their Norse equivalents *skattr* and *veizla.*[52]

The physical divisions of quarterland, treen and sheading may well be pre-Norse, therefore, and very possibly a product of contacts with

Gwynedd. This does not, however, explain the origins of their surviving nomenclature. Sheading seems easy enough; if one accepts that the units already existed when the Norse arrived, an obvious name for the Norse to give to units which each constituted a sixth part of the island is *settungr*, 'a sixth', an etymology both Marstrander and Marwick accepted.[53] Similarly the term quarterland simply reflects that there were often four of these to a treen, although this was not invariably the case. More interesting is the term treen. If Marwick's etymology of *tír unga*, or 'ounceland', is accepted, this obviously implies a render of an ounce. The economy of the Norse settlements in Scotland and around the Irish Sea was firmly based on silver, initially in bullion and later in coin. Thus, if one seeks an origin for the Manx ounceland, a likely context would be that of tribute imposed on the island, in silver, by a figure who wielded authority over Man as well as the other areas where ouncelands are found, i.e., the Northern and Western Isles. Fortunately, we have an account of just such an occurrence, if not from a source of unquestionable reliability.

Although *Orkneyinga saga* does not explicitly connect Earl Sigurðr the Stout with Man,[54] both *Njáls saga* and *Eyrbyggja saga* record raids on Man and the Hebrides, and the imposition of tribute. *Eyrbyggja saga* tells us specifically that Sigurðr

> harried in the Hebrides and all the west as far as Man. He imposed tribute on the inhabited land of the Isle of Man. And when they had come to terms, the earl left behind men to wait for the tax, and that was mostly paid in refined silver (*herjat til Suðreyja ok allt vestr í Mön. Hann lagði gjald á Manarbyggðina. Ok er þeir höfðu sæzk, setti jarl eptir menn at bíða skattsins, en hann var mest goldinn í brenndu silfri*).[55]

Although one cannot take the evidence of a document such as *Eyrbyggja saga* as established fact, the account is quite detailed, and states specifically that the tribute was in silver. It also implies that some administrative structure was already in place, since Sigurðr left men 'to wait' for the tax, rather than actually to gather it, suggesting the use or adaptation of an existing system. This raid is likely to have taken place *c.* 980, and Sigurðr remained a powerful figure until his death at Clontarf in 1014.[56] It is certainly possible that he continued to levy tribute from Man and the Hebrides throughout this period, and his sons Einarr and Þorfinnr both showed interest in the West, while Þorfinnr in particular is remembered as having been a particularly powerful ruler until his death *c.* 1060–5.[57] There was thus a fairly lengthy period during which this tribute could have become regularly established, and with it the idea of the ounceland administrative unit.

One should note, however, a distinction between land assessment in Man and in the other areas in which the ounceland assessment is found. In both the Northern and Western Isles, ouncelands were subdivided into smaller units known as pennylands, with a relationship of 18 pennylands to the ounceland within the earldom of Orkney and Caithness, and 20 pennylands to the ounceland (probably as a result of the assimilation of early Dalriadic assessment units) in the Western Isles and along the western seaboard of the Scottish mainland. However, no trace of the pennyland assessment exists on Man.[58] This is particularly significant because while accounts in both Scandinavian and Irish sources of Sigurðr's dominions (including Man) agree closely with the ounceland distribution, accounts of Þorfinnr's dominions (not including Man) closely agree with the pennyland distribution.[59] This is consistent both with political and economic developments at this time. Seán Duffy has shown that after the battle of Clontarf in 1014, Man was closely linked with the kingdom of Dublin and with the political aspirations both of the Hiberno-Norse rulers of Dublin and of native Irish dynasties.[60] At the same time, Man seems to have drawn away economically from Norse Scotland, and closer to Dublin, with the establishment in the eleventh century of a 'Hiberno-Manx' coinage based on the Hiberno-Norse coinage of Dublin.[61] While no similar coinage was developed in Norse Scotland, it is likely that this area shared in the gradual monetisation of Scandinavia in this period, and that the pennyland assessment was introduced across the lands ruled by Earl Þorfinnr in the mid-eleventh century, with a penny assessment linked to the coinage of Cologne, probably the most dominant coinage at the time in northern Europe, and especially Scandinavia.[62]

This would be consistent with the introduction of the treen, or 'ounceland' assessment in Man under Sigurðr in the late tenth century. At this point, Man still seems to have been part of the same economic sphere as the Northern and Western Isles. From the evidence of hoards across these areas of Norse settlement, assessment in pennies would have been unlikely at this time, but assessments based on silver bullion measured in ounces would have been quite possible.[63] An ounce unit, or units, can be identified from Viking-Age weights from a number of sources, and the same units can be observed in ingots, jewellery and hack-silver. A particular type of arm-ring has been identified as corresponding roughly with this weight-standard, and has been identified as a form of 'ring-money' within a bullion-based silver economy across the Norse settlements in Scotland and Man.[64] While the precise nature of this economy is not yet fully understood, it seems likely that silver bullion fulfilled a quasi-monetary role, in as much as it probably served as a store of value in and of itself, but at the same time as a means of exchange for other goods. On this basis, an assessment based on ounces of silver might be paid directly in silver bullion, as in the episode in *Eyrbyggja saga*, or in other goods that could be recognised as equivalent in value. No record has survived of pricing in the area at this time, or of taxation in kind, but by analogy with tribute and taxation in other medieval societies, payment in livestock, grain, beer, fish, cheese and cloth are all likely. Thus, while it cannot be proven, a plausible origin for the treen land-unit may be found in the pre-Norse period, while a plausible occasion for the introduction of the treen assessment unit can be seen in the late tenth-early eleventh centuries. The treen assessment probably reflects the imposition of a set quantity of silver for the whole of the Isle of Man which was gradually subdivided across increasingly smaller units of land until it reached a unit from which an ounce was demanded. Once the treen assessment was introduced, the quarterland assessment would simply reflect further sub-division.

While a possible background for sheading, treen and quarterland has been established, the origins of the deemster divisions and the parishes are left unexplained. As mentioned above, the evidence for the deemster divisions is late, and while there may be oblique reference to their existence in the Manx chronicle, this cannot be taken as established fact. There is no obvious parallel elsewhere in Norse Scotland, and the Northside/Southside division may simply be a reflection of the geography of the island, with the inhabited land of Northside and Southside being divided by the central mountain ranges.

The parishes, however, are more interesting. As discussed, there is reason to suppose that there may originally have been 16 parishes rather than 17. In the later middle ages each parish had a double function as an ecclesiastical unit and as a unit of civil administration. Each parish was served by a *moar*, who fulfilled the same functions as the sheading *moar*, though at a more junior level.[65] It also seems likely that each parish had a representative in the House of Keys, the main court and legislative body of the island.[66] The parochial system itself may well be attributable to the reign of Óláfr I (*c.*1113–53), and certainly seems to have been established by the thirteenth century. It is less clear whether the parish divisions were newly established for the purpose of ecclesiastical administration, or whether the parochial boundaries simply took over those of an existing civil administrative unit. Following Marstrander's etymology of ON *skíri*, for Manx *skeerey*, an administrative origin cannot be ruled out. The *taxiaxi* of the 1422 Declaration may be identified with Gaelic *toiseach*, or 'chieftain'.[67] This could imply that each *skíri* was originally a chieftaincy. In Orkney, the parishes are related by J.S. Clouston with the powerful families of the area, each parish church being established on the site of the estate chapel of the main family in each parish.[68] It is certainly conceivable that the *taxiaxi* of Man are the equivalent of the *göðingar*, or chieftains of Orkney. These *göðingar* have been interpreted as a quasi-feudal chieftain class, holding earldom lands in addition to their family estates in return for military and administrative service to the earls.[69] The existence of similar chieftaincies on Man in the Norse period cannot be certain, but it is notable that the relationship between kings and chieftains portrayed in the Manx chronicle is very similar to that between the earls of Orkney and the *göðingar* portrayed in *Orkneyinga saga*.[70]

If the parishes do reflect earlier chieftancies, the origins of these may also be pre-Norse. The whole of the model of land assessment proposed here presupposes a degree of continuity of the pre-Norse population into the Viking Age. This is supported by archaeological evidence and, arguably, by toponymic and other linguistic evidence.[71] While this issue cannot be discussed in detail here, it seems that there is likely to have been continuity and intermarriage in the upper levels of society, and therefore that existing chieftaincies should have been taken over *in toto* by the new Norse aristocracy. The use of Celtic terms such as *toiseach* and *moar* for the leading figures within each parish also points to this, although it is conceivable that this could be the result of an influx of Gaelic speakers towards the end of, or after, the Norse period. Even so, such chieftaincies are in any case likely to have become established early in the period of Norse settlement, long before firm royal authority could have been established over the individual chieftains. It is thus likely that the parochial system was, like the treen assessment, superimposed on pre-existing land units. These units may also have served some role in the division of the silver assessment across the island, but this can only be conjecture.

To conclude, the evidence for medieval land assessment in the Isle of Man is too limited to permit a definite statement of the origins of the various units of land assessment. The evidence is both late and fragmentary, while it seems that both the units themselves and the assessments placed on them may well be of much greater antiquity. Nevertheless, comparison with Man's neighbours suggests that the origins of most, if not all, of the land-units found in Man in the later Middle Ages are likely to date back to pre-Norse times. By contrast, the names of the units reflect impositions by various incomers, from the Vikings to the Stanleys. The sheading is impossible to date closely, as it only reflects the division of the island into six. However, the treen and the quarterland can be seen in the broader context of Norse silver taxation of the late tenth–eleventh centuries, the parochial structure was probably introduced in the early twelfth century, and the division of the island into two deemster divisions perhaps only in the fifteenth century.

Notes

1 A more recent, but unpublished study can be found in D.G.E. Williams, 'Land Assessment and Military Organisation in the Norse Settlements of Scotland, *c.* 900–1266 AD', PhD thesis (unpublished), University of St Andrews, 1996. This provides the basis for much of this chapter, and will be referred to in passing throughout, along with various publications which touch on the subject of land assessment but do not focus on it in detail.

2 C.J.S. Marstrander, 'Det Norske Landnåm på Man', *Norsk Tidsskrift for Sprogvidenskap* [*NTSV*] 6 (1932), 40–386.

3 A. Steinnes, 'Leidang og Landskyld', *Videnskabs-Akademien i Oslo, Skrifter* (1927), II, no. 9.

4 Hugh Marwick, 'Leidang in the West', *Proceedings of the Orkney Antiquarian Society*, 13 (1934–5), 15–29.

5 C.J.S. Marstrander, 'Treen og Keeill', *NTSV*, 8 (1937), 287–442.

6 Elwyn Davies, 'Treens and quarterlands: a study of the land system of the Isle of Man', *The Proceedings of the Institute of British Geographers*, 22 (1956), 97–116.

7 Paul Reilly, *Computer analysis of an Archaeological Landscape: Medieval Land Divisions in the Isle of Man*, BAR, 190 (1988).

8 Reilly, *Medieval Land Divisions*, 155.

9 C.E. Lowe, 'Appendix 1: the problem of keeills and treens', in C.D. Morris, 'The survey and excavation at Keeill Vael, Druidale in their context', in Fell *et al.* (eds), *The Viking Age in the Isle of Man*, 124–5.

10 Davies, 'Treens and quarterlands', 102.

11 Kinvig, *Isle of Man*, 11, 73–4; Reilly, *Medieval Land Divisions*, 22.

12 AFM, *s.a.* 974.

13 Reilly, *Medieval Land Divisions*, 22.

14 Kinvig, *Isle of Man*, 12–13; Marstrander, 'Norske Landnåm', 289–95; Marstrander, 'Treen og Keeill', 410.

15 *Séttungr*, 'a sixth', was suggested by Marstrander, in the light of Marwick's article 'Leidang in the West', in preference to his own earlier derivation from *skeiðarþing*, 'warship-assembly'.

16 Reilly, *Medieval Land Divisions*, 22.

17 Marstrander, 'Norske Landnåm', 292.

18 Marstrander, 'Norske Landnåm', 291–2. However, the authenticity of this charter is not beyond question. B.R.S. Megaw suggests that the bull may be a forgery of the late fourteenth century, further modernised *c.* 1500, ('Norseman and native', 29–34).

19 Davies, 'Treens and quarterlands', 98, 100, 115 note 2.

20 Reilly, *Medieval Land Divisions*, 14.

21 Marstrander, 'Treen og Keeill', 400.

22 Davies, 'Treens and quarterlands', 101.

23 Reilly, *Medieval Land Divisions*, 37–8.

24 Megaw and Megaw, 'The Norse heritage in the Isle of Man', in Fox and Dickens (eds), *The Early Cultures of North-West Europe*, 143–71, at p. 163; Reilly, *Medieval Land Divisions*, 20–1.

25 Marstrander, 'Norske Landnåm', 289–90, 341.

26 Marstrander, 'Norske Landnåm', 289–90. The Dublin-Norse point may well be significant given the connections between Dublin and the Isle of Man in the eleventh and twelfth centuries.
27 Davies, 'Treens and quarterlands', 103. Fragments of an earlier manorial roll also survive, but this does not provide so comprehensive a record. M. Crellin, 'An early manorial roll', *JMM*, vii (1969), 98–9; Megaw, 'Norseman and native', 35.
28 Davies, 'Treens and quarterlands', 103.
29 Reilly, *Medieval Land Divisions*, 19.
30 Megaw, 'Norseman and native', 12–13.
31 Marstrander, 'Treen og Keeill', 302.
32 Although this document was at one stage attributed to the fourteenth century, more recent opinion concurs that it was written in the same hand as continuations to the Manx chronicle dated *c.* 1275, although perhaps a little later than those continuations. Megaw, 'Norseman and native', 6–7; M. Gelling, 'Norse and Gaelic in medieval Man: the place-name evidence', in Davey (ed.), *Man and the Environment*, 258.
33 Marstrander, 'Treen og Keeill', 301–2.
34 Reilly, *Medieval Land Divisions*, 20.
35 Davies, 'Treens and quarterlands', 103.
36 Davies, 'Treens and quarterlands', 102.
37 Reilly, *Medieval Land Divisions*, 3.
38 *Ine*, 70.I, cited in T.M. Charles-Edwards, 'Kinship, status, and the origins of the hide', *Past and Present*, 56 (1972), 3–33, at p. 4; J.W.M. Bannerman, *Studies in the History of Dalriada* (Edinburgh, 1974), 142–6; A.R. Easson, 'Systems of Land Assessment in Scotland before 1400', PhD thesis (unpublished), University of Edinburgh, 1986, 35–8.
39 Charles-Edwards, 'Kinship', 7; Bannerman, *Dalriada*, 145–6, 154.
40 Charles-Edwards, 'Kinship', 7; Bannerman, *Dalriada*, 142–3; Easson, 'Land Assessment', 37.
41 P.S. Andersen, 'When was regular, annual taxation introduced in the Norse islands of Britain? A comparative study of assessment systems in North-Western Europe', *Scandinavian Journal of History*, 16 (1991), 73–83, at p. 76.
42 Megaw, 'Norseman and native', 19–21; Reilly, *Medieval Land Divisions*, 11–12.
43 Marstrander, 'Norske Landnåm', 308–9.
44 G.R.J. Jones, 'Multiple estates and early settlement', in P.H. Sawyer (ed.), *Early Medieval Settlement*, 2nd edn (London, 1979), 15–40; G.W.S. Barrow, *The Kingdom of the Scots* (London, 1973), 7–68; A. Steinnes, 'The "Huseby" System in Orkney', *SHR*, 38 (1959), 36–46; Megaw, 'Norseman and native', 19–24; Reilly, *Medieval Land Divisions*, 38–43.
45 Megaw, 'Norseman and native', 23; Reilly, *Medieval Land Divisions*, 18–19. However, Reilly suggests that the sheadings, with around 100 quarterlands apiece in the earliest records, correspond more closely to *cantrefs*.
46 Bannerman, *Dalriada*, 142–3.
47 Jones, 'Multiple Estates', 15.
48 Megaw, 'Norseman and native', 23.
49 Megaw, 'Norseman and native', 23–4.
50 W.C. Dickinson, *Scotland from the earliest Times to 1603*, 3rd edn, revised and edited by A.A.M. Duncan (Oxford 1977), 54–5; Barrow, *Kingdom of the Scots*, 67–8.
51 Steinnes, 'Huseby System', *passim*; Crawford, *Scandinavian Scotland*, 83–4.
52 Williams, 'Land assessment', 235–7.

53 Marstrander, 'Treen og Keeill', 410–11; H. Marwick, 'Naval defence in Norse Scotland', *SHR*, 28 (1949), 1–11, at p. 10.

54 He is recorded as having authority over the *Suðreyjar* ('Southern Isles', a term used to describe the Hebrides, and often used in association with Man in the period of the kingdom of the Isles), and it is not impossible that Man was included in the author's mind in this more general statement.

55 *Eyrbyggja saga*, ed. E.Ó. Sveinsson and M. Þórðarson (Reykjavík, 1935), chapter 29, 76.

56 Crawford, *Scandinavian Scotland*, 65–8; Williams, 'Land assessment', 126–8.

57 Crawford, *Scandinavian Scotland*, 71–9; Williams, 'Land assessment', 128–32.

58 Crawford, *Scandinavian Scotland*, 86–91; Williams, 'Land assessment', 34–57.

59 Williams, 'Land assessment', 126–32.

60 Duffy, 'Irishmen and Islesmen'.

61 See the discussion by Kristin Bornholdt in chapter 18 above, pp. 423–31.

62 Williams, 'Land assessment', 131–2, 215–19. The relationship of 18 pennylands to the ounceland is consistent with the weight standard of the Cologne penny, but not with contemporary pennies in England or Scandinavia.

63 Williams, 'Land assessment', 196–211.

64 R. Warner, 'Scottish silver arm-rings: an analysis of weights', *PSAS*, 107 (1975–6), 136–43; Crawford, *Scandinavian Scotland*, 128–34; S.E. Kruse, 'Ingots and weight units in Viking Age silver hoards', *World Archaeology*, 20:2 (1988), 285–301; S.E. Kruse, 'Silver storage and circulation in Viking-Age Scotland', in C.E. Batey, J. Jesch and C.D. Morris (eds), *Caithness, Orkney and the North Atlantic* (Edinburgh, 1993), 187–203; Williams, 'Land assessment', 203–11.

65 Megaw, 'Norseman and native', 23–4.

66 Marstrander, 'Treen og Keeill', 401.

67 Megaw, 'Norse heritage', 167, note 2.

68 J.S. Clouston, *A History of Orkney* (Kirkwall, 1932), 154–6.

69 J.S. Clouston, 'Two features of the Orkney Earldom', *SHR*, xvi (1918–19), 15–28, at pp.21–7; J.S. Clouston, 'The Battle of Tankerness', in *Proceedings of the Orkney Antiquarian Society*, vi (1927–8), 21–5.

70 Williams, 'Land assessment', 256–61.

71 D.M. Wilson, *The Viking Age in the Isle of Man*, C.C. Rafn Lecture 3 (Odense and London, 1976); Megaw, 'Norseman and native', *passim*; Gelling, 'Norse and Gaelic', *passim*; R.H.M. Dolley, 'The palimpsest of Viking settlement on Man', in Bekker-Nielsen *et al.* (eds), *Eighth Viking Congress*, 173–81.

20 *Medieval Archaeology and Architecture*[1]

P.J. DAVEY[2] and A.C.C. JOHNSON[3]

Overview of the evidence

It is in the nature of archaeological evidence that only rarely at a given site will the events which constitute political or dynastic history be verifiable. The quality of the dating evidence available to archaeologists, often expressed in terms of plus or minus 50 years for pottery for example, means that even if a great fire deposit is located, or the foundations of a prominent building are investigated, the archaeologist will often be unable to support or deny the evidence of documentary sources which apply to the case. Indeed, it is much more common for excavators of medieval structures to rely entirely on documentary sources for dating, not only the sites, but also the association of artefacts which go with them. Thus, for Manx medieval history the story told by *The Chronicles of the Kings of Man and the Isles* – from the foundation of a local Norwegian dynasty by Godred Crovan in 1097 through to its demise at the treaty of Perth in 1266 – cannot be verified by archaeological evidence, despite the considerable amount of new research which has been carried out during the last 15 years. Even such a major monument as Castle Rushen, which figures prominently in thirteenth- and fourteenth-century accounts of the island, cannot be dated archaeologically even to the nearest 100 years. Events such as the attack by Robert the Bruce in 1313[4] and later Scottish efforts to control the island, for example in 1456,[5] are invisible to archaeology.

The aim of this chapter is to suggest ways in which the new evidence from excavations at Peel, Castletown and Rushen Abbey, in particular can, despite its chronological inadequacy, contribute to a better understanding of Man in the medieval period. The first part of the chapter will deal with the sites that still exist for examination discussed under the headings: seats of power, ecclesiastical sites, rural and industrial sites. The evidence from archaeological excavation will then be used as a basis for an evaluation of such issues as urbanisation, external trade and international relations and for the internal dynamics of island life in the Middle Ages.

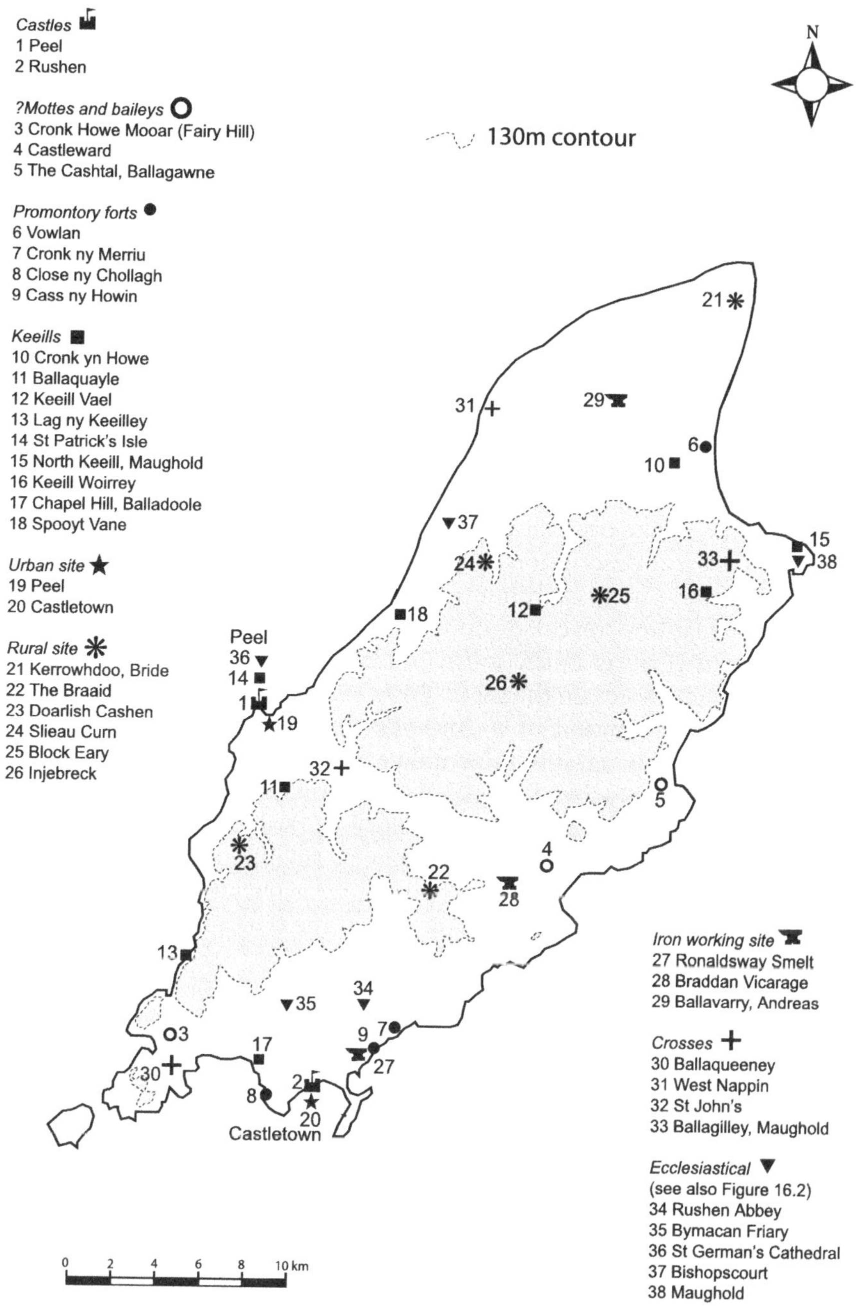

Fig. 20.1 *The location of medieval sites on the Isle of Man mentioned in the text, keyed by main class.*

Part 1: THE ARCHITECTURE AND ARCHAEOLOGY OF MEDIEVAL SITES ON THE ISLE OF MAN

Seats of power: Peel Castle and Castle Rushen

Peel Castle

Peel Castle is the most complicated and significant medieval structure on the Isle of Man, complicated in that there are so many different buildings, both above and below ground, and significant because it demonstrates the response to changing strategy, military tactics and fire-power to a degree which is found nowhere else on the island. Despite excavation and interpretation by archaeologists, historians and architects, there is no consensus on the precise development chronology of the castle up to the early fifteenth century.[6] The following therefore attempts a narrative while acknowledging that there are problems reconciling the differing published views.[7]

Until excavations at Peel Castle between 1982–8[8] enhanced detailed understanding of the occupation of St Patrick's Isle from the earliest times, the most coherent description of the castle was that proposed by Robert Curphey, and was necessarily limited to above-ground remains[9] (Fig. 20.2). Additional features revealed during the 1980s excavations suggest, however, that there is much still to understand from excavation about buried Viking defences on the islet.[10] Most significant of the newer discoveries was the recognition of a 5m wide twelfth-century stone rampart defending its low-lying and vulnerable eastern edge. This accorded well with the discovery nearby of a 'hall' of some structural sophistication, built of timber on stone sleeper walls. Only a small part of its floor area survived, but several episodes of reflooring, including a final floor of boards laid on joists, imply a relatively long-lived structure: a remanent magnetic date from the latest surviving hearth showed that the building was last used in the mid-twelfth century.[11]

It is instructive to note that the Chronicle tells us that Godred II died on St Patrick's Isle in 1187, and his son Olaf II in 1237; Olaf's fleet was destroyed there in 1228; the latter's son Harald landed at St Patrick's Isle when returning from exile in Norway in 1242. These entries only emphasise the royal and military importance of the islet and the harbour it guards. In 1257, however, Magnus gave St Patrick's Isle to the Church. The development of a soil on the stone rampart suggests that fortification ceased to be the dominating influence on life on St Patrick's Isle, as first the cathedral, and then associated ranges of domestic buildings to the north of it, were built. The latter comprised a stone hall, kitchen and living accommodation, and underlie the surviving apartments.[12] By 1313, St Patrick's Isle posed insufficient of a military menace to divert Robert Bruce's invasion.

Curphey[13] suggests that from 1333 onwards, when England wrested back control of the Isle of Man, some refurbishment of the Norse defences is likely,[14] perhaps justifying the application of the term 'pele', by which the neighbouring mainland harbour and settlement came to be known. By 1363, military use of his cathedral and precincts was such that the bishop was moved to complain to the Pope.

Despite such military occupation, and, one supposes, construction or at least maintenance of defensive structures, it was 1392 before William leScroop was licensed to build a castle, that is, a more permanent structure than a timber pele or palisade. LeScroop fortified the cathedral – which had been 'destroyed' – papal indulgences being granted to those who contributed to its restoration. This involved[15] removing the south aisle and walling-up the arcade,[16] raising the central tower and crenellating the

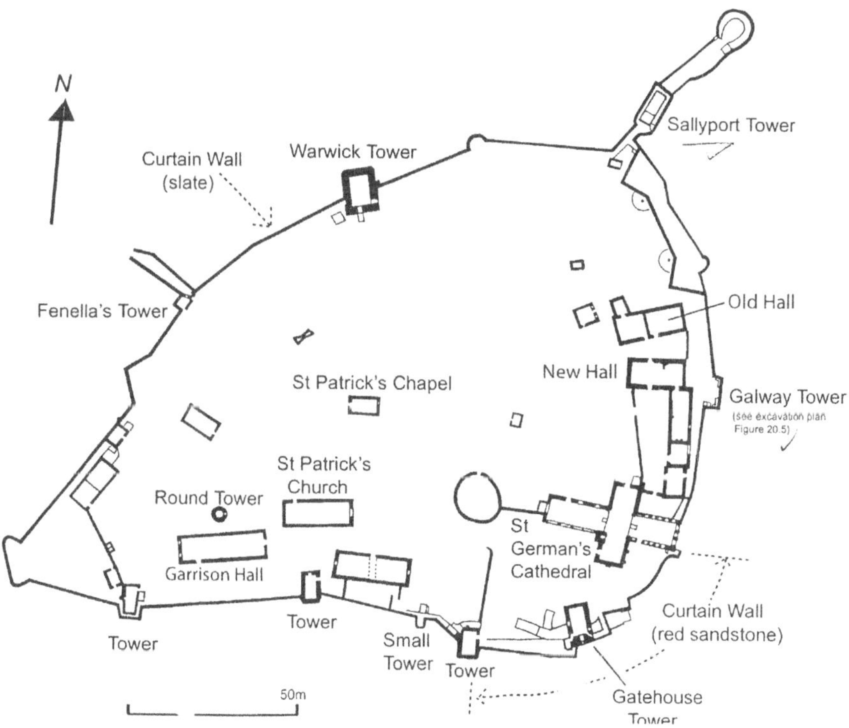

Fig. 20.2 *Plan of the above-ground structures at St Patrick's Isle showing the medieval tower houses and the curtain wall. The earliest military building is probably the late fourteenth-century Gatehouse Tower, followed by the Warwick Tower, the Sallyport Tower, the Galway Tower and possibly the tower to the left of the Gatehouse, all incorporated in an early defensive circuit.*

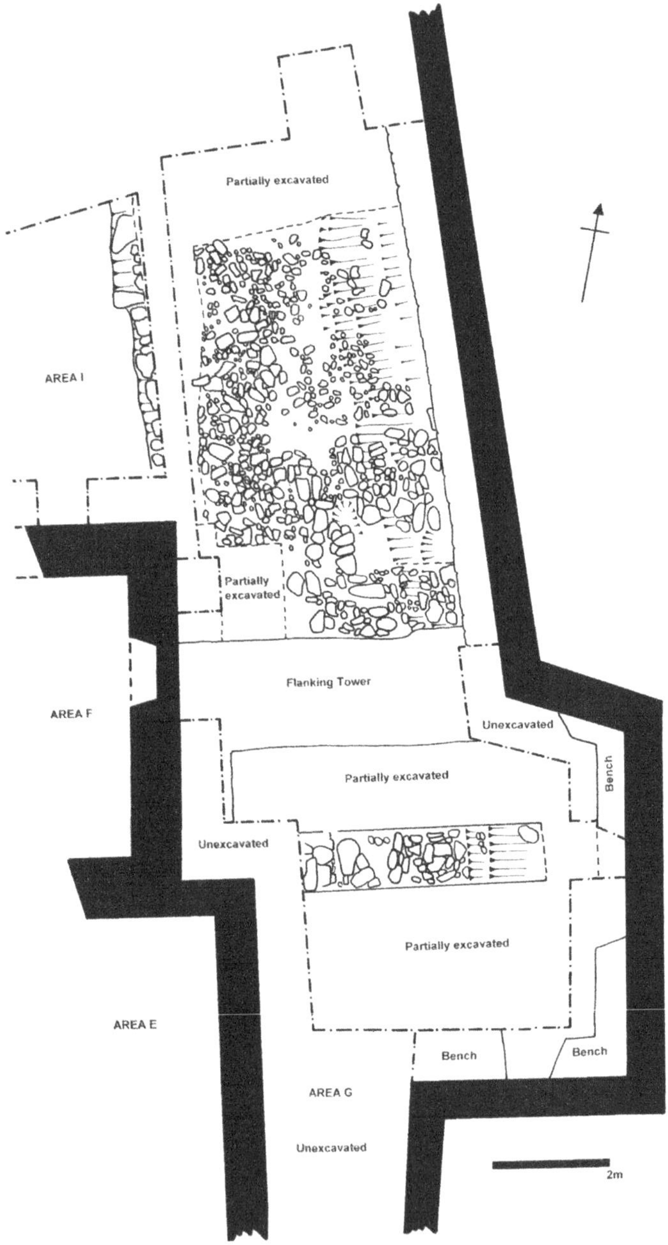

Fig. 20.3 *Excavation plan of the twelfth-century stone rampart at St Patrick's Isle. Area F is the New Hall (see Fig.20.2) and the Galway Flanking Tower is partially excavated, Fig.20.5 shows the detail. (from Freke 2002)*

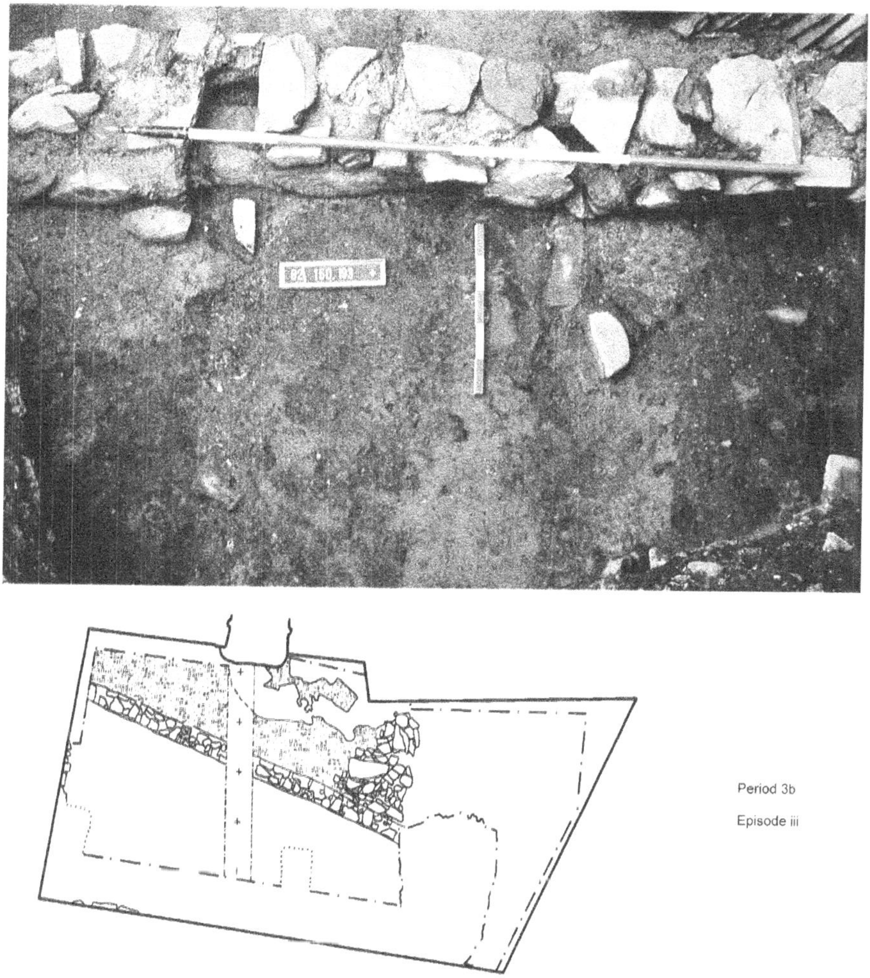

Fig. 20.4 *Excavations of the twelfth-century Norse domestic timber building at Peel Castle: a) photo of Area A in progress, scale 2m and b) plan of the final episode of reflooring the timber building.*

parapet, and similarly crenellating the transepts. A stair tower was added in the angle of the nave and south transept to provide access to these fighting tops, and a new, distinctly Gothic door was inserted in the south transept to re-establish liturgical and processional access lost with the removal of the south aisle (see fig. 7.3).

Close by the cathedral are the perimeter defences associated with the entrance to the castle, built from the distinctive and locally-won red sandstone (see fig. 1.4). Curphey suggests that there was already a wall here which was enhanced by leScroop, remarking on unspecified changes in the character of the masonry. With the benefit of a picture made fuller by excavation, Freke also has leScroop responsible for several stone towers built at intervals along the earth and timber ramparts – these are commonly referred to as the Gatehouse, Galloway, Sallyport, Warwick, and Causeway towers – and then, at a time unspecified, for a curtain wall. The

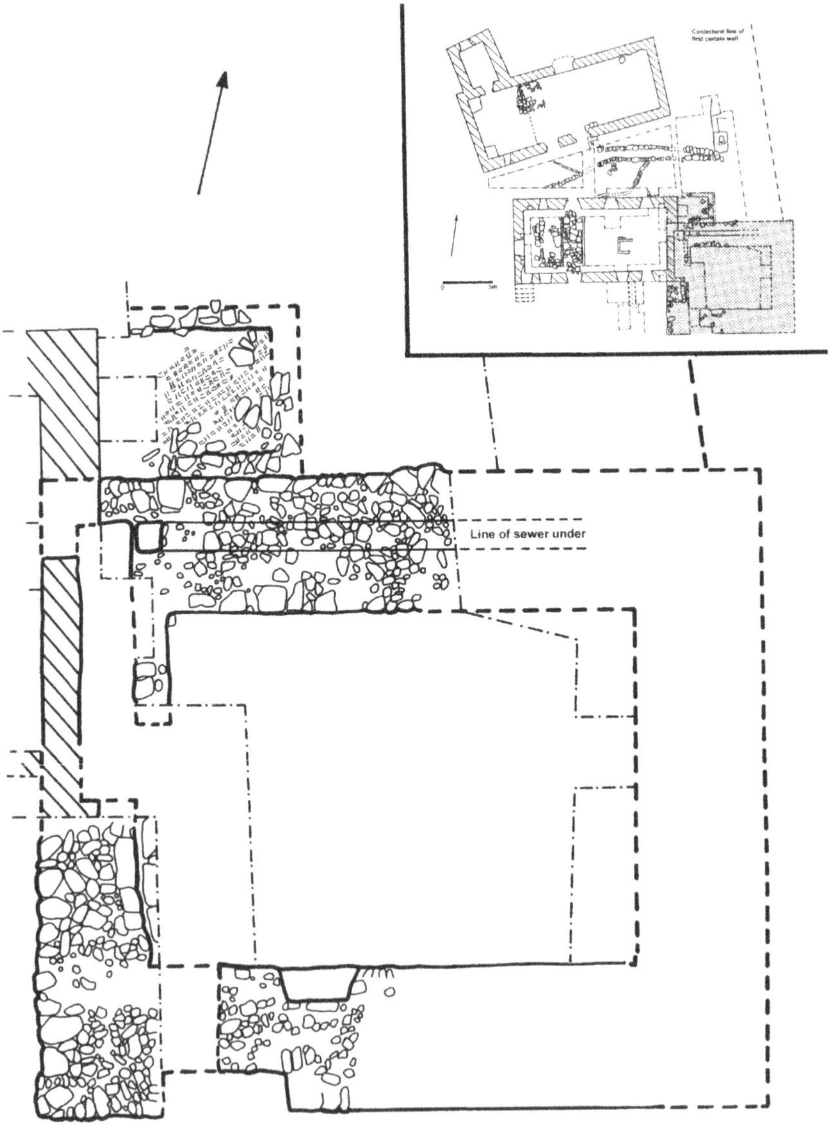

rationale for this – also followed by Gordon Slade[17] – is that a stone wall must have existed to retain the courtyard between the hall and the Galloway tower, which was at a height considerably greater than the present-day ground level outside the curtain.[18]

The towers referred to, with the possible exception of that which overlooks the causeway[19], are tower houses, providing secure and independent living accommodation and acting as strongpoints around the originally earth and timber perimeter of the castle (cross ref to Fig. 7.3). There can be no doubt that these towers, particularly the Warwick and Sally Port towers, sit uncomfortably and unconformably on the existing curtain wall, unlike, for example, the small towers along the southern side of the castle[20].

The curtain wall clockwise from the Causeway tower to the Galloway tower and slightly beyond is predominantly faced in irregular, vertically-hung slabs of slate with ladder pointing in between. The three tower houses affected by its construction were refaced in the same material – indeed the Galloway tower was substantially rebuilt, probably because it was unstable. This major building programme, however, falls outwith our period.[21] From the Galloway tower to the cathedral chancel the curtain is notably poorly built, and almost certainly reflects similar problems of stability to those which afflicted the tower. It is of similar, or later, date to the Green Curtain.

The completion of the perimeter wall did not mark the end of building activity at Peel Castle, as further refinements in the face of developments in artillery and musketry were constantly required until the early nineteenth century.[22]

Castle Rushen[23]

The Chronicles of the Kings of Man and the Isles inform us that Magnus, the last of Godred Crovan's dynasty to rule the Kingdom, died at Castle Rushen in 1265, and was buried at Rushen abbey. This is the earliest reference to the castle, but it seems possible that it was in existence for certainly 30 years prior to that, and possibly for as much as a century.[24] The earliest remains are represented by masonry which stands to a height of about 7m above existing ground level, and which is marked at just over half this height by a slight offset around the exterior façade of the core of the keep. This keep, as originally built, would have been a plain rectangular tower structure, probably with a fore-building protecting the first-floor entrance.[25]

Fig. 20.5 *Excavation at St Patrick's Isle, Period 5, Phase A, showing detail of the Flanking Tower, also known as the Galway or Galloway Tower.*

Fig. 20.6 *Castle Rushen. An aerial view of the castle from the east, illustrating its proximity to the rivermouth and harbour.*

Fig. 20.7 *Castle Rushen. The south-east corner of the keep: the horizontal step in the masonry clearly defines the early part of the keep from the later addition of further storeys and the towers.*

It is possible that at this time the keep was additionally protected by a ditch, identified during excavation in 1989:[26] it projected beyond the confines of the excavated area and would have had to be backfilled to allow the construction of the west tower described below. Alternatively, irregularities in its edge at the southern end of the excavation trench may signify its termination in front of the west tower. Certainly its upper fills contained small quantities of thirteenth- or early fourteenth-century pottery.

Subsequently, this simple tower was rendered far more defensible and sophisticated by the addition of mid-wall towers on the landward, and more vulnerable, west and south sides.[27] These new measures were insufficient, however, to prevent the fall of the castle to Robert Bruce in 1313; the extent to which he slighted the castle to prevent its re-use by the English is however not clear. Further building work and repair was probably not possible until after the Scottish loss at Hallidon Hill in 1333, and may even have been delayed further.[28] Such works comprised the construction of a third mid-wall tower on the east side, the complete remodelling of the north side to accommodate a gatehouse, and the raising of the entire edifice to contain two extra storeys.

Continuing Scottish predations required repairs and redevelopment at both Peel and Castle Rushen towards the end of the fourteenth century. At the latter, this refortification was substantially to improve the sophistication of the defences. The keep, now a rather large and over-engineered tower house, was vulnerable to advancing methods of warfare, and had to be protected by the addition of a large outer gatehouse with dog-leg barbican, and a full turreted curtain wall. The variation in design of the turrets has been offered as a justification for arguing their different age, but there seems no reason why this cannot be accommodated by their differing purposes and subsequent development. These very considerable additions to Castle Rushen also occasioned the raising still further of the wall walks and fighting tops on top of the keep, in order that the defenders might have an unencumbered field of fire over the new curtain wall.

By the beginning of the Stanley lordship, Castle Rushen had become a sophisticated medieval fortress; the Earls of Derby would soon have to see to its continuing impregnability by responding to the advent of artillery. This would require the construction of a glacis with corner redoubts beyond the curtain wall: whether this last great refortification masks an outer ditch[29] is unknown, although its existence is to be expected.

Fig. 20.8 *Fanc's plan of Castle Rushen dating from around 1736–65, viewed from the north-east. Courtesy: Manx National Heritage.*

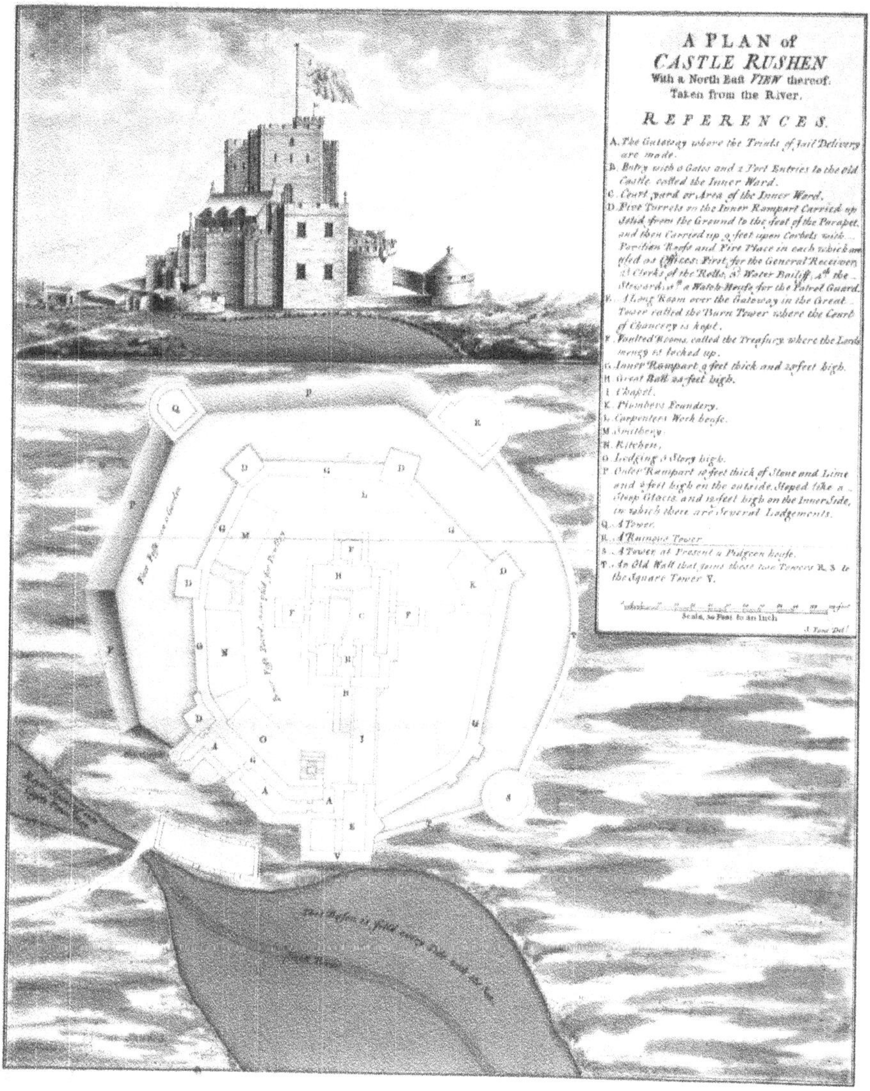

Mottes and baileys

Other defensive sites are rather less obvious, by virtue of their location and lack of above-ground structural remains: they are no less significant, however, and all the more intriguing because they are so little understood. Cronk Howe Mooar or the Fairy Hill is an earthwork mound, oval in plan, a maximum 70m in diameter at its base and 10m high. A possible bailey-like earthwork[30] extends from its east side, the further extent of which is

Fig. 20.9 *Cronk Howe Mooar, showing how the site appears today.*

still today perpetuated by modern boundary lines. The upper part of the mound and its regular profile are clearly artificial, though the base is likely to be natural, possibly glacial in origin. Excavation of the summit in 1912[31] revealed that the apparent hollow was in fact a carefully revetted rectangular space measuring 5.5 by 3m; the revetting took the form of orthostatic slabs with dry stone walling between. Outside of the wall was a substantial earthen bank, which may have been natural or created by the upcast of material dug out of the rectangular interior. The recent reconstruction shows how it may have appeared.[32]

Castleward is possibly more enigmatic than the last. On the valley floor of the River Glass stands a natural, rocky citadel enhanced by two approximately concentric earthwork ramparts on its weaker north and east slopes. A low bank surrounds its summit, enclosing a platform 16 by 14.5m; all three banks are broken by an apparently original entrance route from the east. The overall area enclosed measures approximately 70 by 40m. Several stone artefacts, such as spindle whorls and rubbing stones, have been recovered in the immediate vicinity, but the site has yet to be conclusively proved

Fig. 20.10 *Cronk Howe Mooar, as it may have appeared in the medieval period. Stone foundations on the summit of the hill point to the existence of a small defence structure whilst modern topography and field boundaries suggest the rudiments of an approach ramp and bailey.*

late Iron Age or Medieval through excavation.

Superficially, the Cashtal at Ballagawne, near Baldrine, is similar in location and natural defensive attributes to Castleward, but otherwise lacks the added artificial defences which give rise to the suspicion that the latter might be Iron Age. It is another natural rock feature, possibly enhanced, some 30m long and 15m wide. A strongly built stone structure stood on its summit, shown by excavation to be 14 by 6m.[33] Bersu's initial interpretation was that it was a fortified granary, and he believed Cronk Howe Mooar to be likewise; Marshall Cubbon thought otherwise, initially in 1967 considering it to be a dwelling, but later in 1983 suggesting instead that it might be cognate with the reoccupied promontory forts discussed below. One of the authors[34] has speculated along similar lines, and would now suggest that it is perhaps physically comparable to Cronk Mooar, but in a situation more reminiscent of Castleward.

The Promontory Forts

Four additional sites have been the subject of speculation as to their purpose, military or domestic. The first site to be investigated was that of Vowlan near Ramsey. In spite of the buildings surviving as little more than shadows in the sandy soil, the excavator[35] successfully revealed the remains of six rectangular buildings, several of them overlying each other, constructed on a promontory overlooking the estuary of the Sulby River. The largest building measured 10.5 by 4.6m internally, the smallest 7.4 by 3.4m. Bersu proposed that the walls had been of wattle, bedded in the ground in trenches that were sometimes packed with stones. A hearth lay along the long axis, and the interior was divided to form a central aisle (in which the hearth lay) with an aisle to either side along both long walls. Subsequent excavations at the three sites described below would suggest that these were wide 'benches' for sitting and sleeping on. It was inferred from the presence of a hearth in all six of the buildings that they were domestic structures. Small quantities of burnt clay and some splinters of calcined bone were found in the hearths, which were quite deep, containing up to 500mm of ash. No artefacts whatsoever were recovered. Bersu interpreted the site as temporary quarters, re-occupied on several occasions, belonging to guards left behind by Viking raiding parties whose longships were drawn up on the beach.

Until post-medieval times, when riverine erosion, longshore coastal drift, and the need to develop a modern harbour for the settlement of Ramsey combined to realign the old river-bed, the headland at Vowlan would have guarded the mouth of the Sulby River. In the light of this clear topographical relationship, and the subsequent excavation of other defended promontories, Bersu's interpretation of the purpose of the site is worthy of re-examination, and the site of comparison with the following three sites.

Between 1950 and 1957, Peter Gelling[36] excavated three promontory forts at Cronk ny Merriu, Close ny Chollagh and Cass ny Hawin. Of the three sites, Cronk ny Merriu provided the best preserved house structure. The house measured 11 by 4.3m internally, and had stone-faced walls. These were 1.2 to 1.5m thick, and were filled with an earth core. It appeared from the position and quantity of collapsed facing stone that the walls had been higher on the inside, and that the roof slope had continued across the thickness of the walls to within approximately 0.6m of ground-level on the outside. A reconstruction exercise based on the available collapsed debris, suggested that the interior wall facing may have stood as high as 1.4m above floor level. Earth benches were set along the long walls

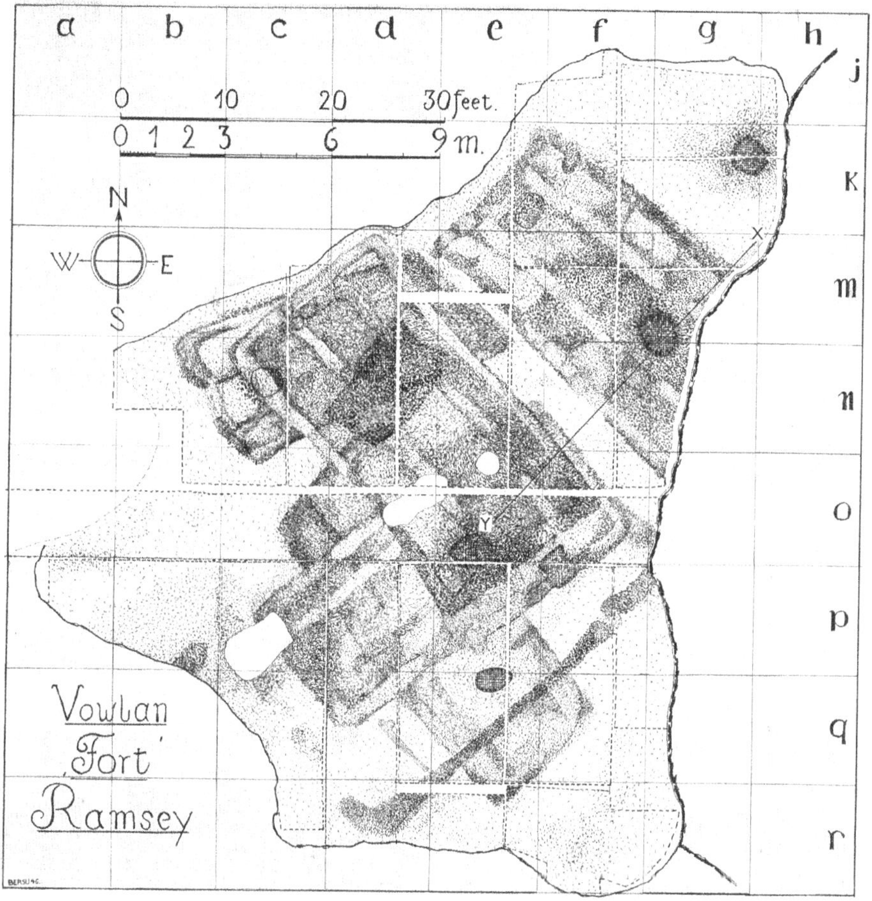

Fig. 20.11 *Vowlan. Gernard Bersu's remarkable naturalistic drawing of the six overlapping floor plans identified during his excavations.*

and possibly across one end wall, revetted with stones set on edge. Two original doors were positioned towards the end of the long walls opposite each other (a third door in one gable was believed to be later). There was slight and inconclusive evidence for a hearth, but the presence of a few fire-crazed stones in the floor implies that either cooking or heating must have occasionally occurred. Fired stones were also found towards the outer part of the promontory, together with a very few pieces of bone found within a post-hole in the same area. These remains scarcely constitute the amount of domestic rubbish to be expected at a domestic site.

No artefacts were found except for a few fragments of broken quernstone built into the walls, and a quartzite cobble that may have been used as a hammerstone. All of these may have related to an earlier Iron Age occupation of the site represented by the rampart and ditch on the landward side of the promontory

The lack of artefacts forced the excavator to suggest an occupation falling within a tenth- to twelfth-century time frame. A few years later, when embarking upon excavation at Close ny Chollagh, the house at Cronk ny Merriu was described as 'a permanent house of Viking type built on a small promontory whose defensive rampart was already ruinous in Viking times'.[37] Almost two decades subsequent to excavation, however, a silver penny of Edward I was found by chance close to the rampart. Although without secure context, its presence suggests activity at some, at least, of the promontory forts during the thirteenth century.

The lack of positive dating evidence led to the investigation of another promontory within which there were again surface indications of a longhouse: this was Close ny Chollagh. Here the substantial but collapsed defences, originally built to protect a group of roundhouses occupied into the first century AD, were made use of to shelter a rectangular house, which actually used the rampart for two of its walls. The house was the largest excavated on a promontory fort, measuring 12.5 by 5m, but was probably the least satisfactory in yielding up Scandinavian characteristics: there was only one door; the bench was narrow, a mere 400mm wide, and stretched the length of only one wall; there was no hearth, and no regular layout of posts supporting the roof: the excavator was moved to suggest that the roof was a single pitch, sloping back towards the rampart.

Three minor, poorly-built structures, interpreted as outbuildings and subsidiary structures, lay within the area enclosed by the rampart, and were adjudged broadly contemporary with the longhouse. These comprised a lean-to against the seaward rampart, a set of steps leading up to the rampart, and a circular structure built uncomfortably close to the longhouse but undoubtedly stratigraphically later than the roundhouses it resembled and overlay. Once again, no datable finds could be ascribed to the Medieval occupation. It was considered that only the form of the longhouse and its vestigial bench which was far narrower and less pronounced than either Vowlan or Cronk ny Merriu, gave any clue of Scandinavian antecedents. As a result, a twelfth-, and more probably a thirteenth-, century date was proposed for the occupation.[38]

Since excavation of Close ny Chollagh had not revealed a building of clearly Scandinavian style, a third promontory fort was investigated, this time at Cass ny Hawin. Excavation revealed a single rectangular house orientated west-east. The floor of the house was cut down into the bedrock, giving the effect of a central aisle and benches along either side and across each end; the benches were between 0.8m and 1.5m wide. The interior of the house measured 9.5 by 4.5m; its walls were only with difficulty identified in the trench sections, and appeared to have consisted entirely of turf. From the evidence of the trench sections, the walls of the house were approximately 2.4m thick; they survived to a height of no more than 0.25m, and must have been very much eroded.

Two entrances were identified, opening to the north and south close to the east end of the building. Only the southerly entrance was excavated completely, revealing a short passage through the thick turf side-wall which turned eastward through 90 degrees once outside. Two post holes marked the end of the passage, implying a doorway. Both doorway and passage are designed to avoid the prevailing wind.[39]

A substantial concentration of ash, spread across an area of 2.4 by 0.4m in the central aisle, under which the bedrock had been discoloured by heat, indicated the presence of a formal hearth, although no kerbstones were found. The post-holes were arranged in an orderly manner, two close to the west end, and four near the east end. It is possible that the posts in these positions supported and bolstered roof frames subjected to sideways pressures from a hipped roof, and that those towards the east end additionally had to support arrangements for a roof structure over the entrance.

More than 20 sherds, separated into three broad types were found, including the locally-produced granite-tempered ware.[40] Other finds included an incomplete pair of iron shears and an iron missile-head; six more pieces of iron, two pieces of copper alloy, and some fragments of lead slag. A thirteenth-century date is feasible for the finds, and hence for the house as well, but equally both pottery and the long-lasting design of the shears allow for a slightly more recent date.

Whilst the excavator of these three promontories originally favoured a domestic use for the sites, more recent reconsideration suggests that a military purpose may be more acceptable.[41] At Close ny Chollagh in particular, the poor quality of construction, lack of necessary domestic features, and lack of artefacts all mitigate against a true domestic use of the site, an interpretation reinforced by the careless discard of animal bones within the house and the relatively small numbers of shellfish found in the Medieval levels. In contrast, the suitability of the site as an observation post guarding one of the softest landing spots along the circumference of Bay ny Carrickey is clear.[42]

Ecclesiastical sites

The Isle of Man can boast the sites of almost 180 keeills – small chapels (or their attendant burial grounds) widely dispersed in the landscape – 17 parish churches, three or four resident monasteries, a number of larger medieval chapels, a cathedral and the residence of the Bishop of the Southern Isles. Although only two or three keeill sites and none of the larger chapels or parish churches have been excavated since the Second World War, important campaigns at Peel Castle by Bersu, Radford and Freke and at Rushen Abbey by Butler and the Centre for Manx Studies have provided a good deal of new evidence which throws some light upon the evolution of the church from its Early Christian origins and the nature of ecclesiastical organisation in the medieval period from the time of the Norse kingdom until the arrival of the Stanleys.

Fig. 20.12a *Ecclesiastical sites: a) keeills.*

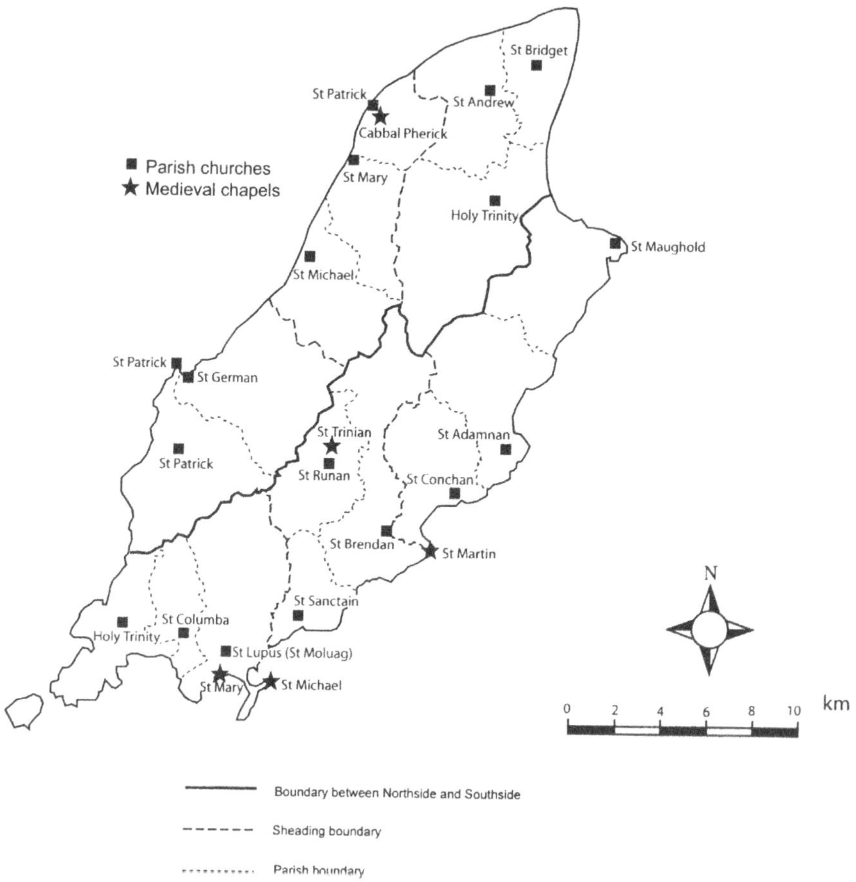

Fig. 20.12b *Ecclesiastical sites: b) parish churches and medieval chapels*

Keeills

Conventionally, the 174 known keeill sites are used as evidence for the nature of the Early Christian church in the island whose origins can be traced back to St Patrick or even earlier. In practice it is very hard to establish whether any of the buildings or earthworks, which survive at some 35 of the sites, date from that period. Although many of the keeills have produced cross slabs and altar frontals which typologically should date from the fifth to ninth centuries, the structures themselves have seemed reluctant to relinquish any dating evidence. Indeed in Marshall Cubbon's 1982 landmark paper 'The Early Church in the Isle of Man' he uses the evidence of the associated Norse crosses, runic inscriptions and architectural fragments to suggest that all of the upstanding remains date from the Norse period.[43] Whilst some are likely to have been constructed on earlier sites, others may well have been new.[44]

For example, at Cronk yn Howe, Lezayre, Bersu re-interpreted the results of Bruce and Cubbon's 1928 excavation and suggested that what they had found was a Viking ship-burial which had been replaced by a keeill, the original burial being reinterred once Christianity had been adopted. Although one of the cross slabs from the site (Cross 159) certainly dates from the Norse period, the others appear typologically to be earlier, so that it seems likely that the ship burial, as at Balladoole, had been placed in an existing Christian cemetery.

The excavation of a lintel grave cemetery at Ballaquayle between 1970 and 1977 by Sheila Cregeen[45] appeared to have located a timber building, probably an early keeill, but with no absolute dating evidence. The complete excavation of Keeill Vael in 1979, by Dr Chris Morris, in advance of the construction of the Sulby Reservoir, revealed a complex, multi-phased structure, but also with no dating evidence, not even any skeletons.[46] Johnson[47] has identified similar structural complexity in the remains of the equally isolated keeill at Lag ny Keeilley, which contained fourteenth-century pottery.

Fig. 20.13 *The excavated north-east angle of the Norse keeill on St Patrick's Isle viewed from the west (scale 2m).*

Only at Peel Castle has a keeill-type structure been examined within a good stratified sequence for which reasonable dating evidence is available. The foundations of a rectangular stone building some 9 by 5m in external dimensions, was located to the north of the cathedral. It lay beneath a wooden floored timber 'hall', dated by remnant magnetic determination to the mid-twelfth century, which had itself been destroyed by the construction of the cathedral transept in the mid-thirteenth century. It formed the focus and alignment for many of the pre-cathedral graves. A coin hoard of *c.*1040 had been deposited in its recently levelled remains. The keeill, which Freke dates to the early part of his Period 3 (1000–1200) may have formed part of a monastic community on St Patrick's Isle represented by an earlier phase of St Patrick's Church, identified by Radford in his 1962 excavations, and by St Patrick's Chapel some 25m to the north.[48] This community may perhaps have survived into the eleventh or even the twelfth century.

Runic inscriptions have also been recovered from keeill sites which

Fig. 20.14 *Conjectural drawing of medieval buildings on St Patrick's Isle in the thirteenth century. The church of St Patrick, the round tower and the small keeill, were from an earlier period, but the building of St German's Cathedral commenced around 1226 and, as discovered in the 1980s excavations, to the north of the cathedral, buildings that were probably the quarters of the Bishop, or the Kings of Man would also have been constructed about this time. Drawing by Caroline Jamfrey.*

otherwise give no hint of Norse period use. For example at the North Keeill, Maughold, a cross fragment with runes and an incised drawing of a ship were found by the Manx Archaeological Survey.[49] Similarly, at Keeill Woirrey, Maughold the presence of a runic inscription strongly suggests that the site was in use during the Norse period. Scandinavian crosses have been recovered at Ballaqueeny, Rushen,[50] West Nappin, Jurby,[51] St John's, German[52] and Ballagilley, Maughold.[53]

Parish churches and chapels

Although there has been very little excavation and architectural evidence is meagre, the parish churches and large medieval chapels, taken as a group, do give some indication of the way in which a system that depended on many dispersed chapels gave way to the parochial organisation which is in evidence from later medieval documents, and which survives substantially today.

Whilst many of the 17 parish churches and four larger medieval chapels exhibit no medieval structural signs, at a number of sites there are suffi-

Fig. 20.15 *(opposite) Runic inscriptions on the stone slab from Keeill Woirrey (Maughold).*

Fig. 20.16 *(above) Detail of the herringbone coursing on the north wall of St Patrick's Church, Figure 10.1 shows the whole wall with its range of masonry types.*

cient survivals of earlier work to indicate the likely form of the churches and their dating.

St Patrick's Church within Peel Castle, according to Radford,[54] had Irish-type *antae* in the eleventh century, prior to a major redesign in the twelfth that is characterised by herringbone stonework in English style in both north and south walls.[55] Alongside the church, probably at the same time as this extension, an Irish round tower was constructed – the only one in Man and one of only three outside Ireland.[56] Traces of Romanesque work can be seen in the toothed ornament over the west porch at Maughold[57] and in the jambs in the west door at Marown.[58] At Maughold two narrow, red sandstone, single-light windows, also likely to be of twelfth-century date, were revealed during nineteenth-century repairs.

On St Michael's Island the east gable of the chapel contains a window that, despite some restoration, appears to be of twelfth-century type.[59] The same may well apply to the west wall of Lonan Parish Church.[60] St Trinian's Chapel, Marown, now greatly restored, contains a number of Irish-type Romanesque sculptural features, as well as early window openings and doorjambs.[61] The existence of lintel graves on a different orientation, a pavement cross and a primitive cross-slab all suggest that the site is early.[62] At St Patrick's Chapel, Jurby, a typical keeill, only slightly larger than Balladoole and significantly smaller than Spooyt Vane, the Manx Archaeological Survey found a Romanesque pilaster capital with toothed ornament in the clearance. The site also boasts a Scandinavian cross slab that had been rebuilt into a later window lintel.[63] Old Kirk Braddan includes a number of worked stones around the windows on its south façade hinting at an earlier structure.

Although many of the parish churches were substantially restored or rebuilt in the late eighteenth and early nineteenth centuries, they nevertheless preserve more portable artefacts that argue for an earlier dating of the sites on which they stand. Braddan and Onchan, for example, both boast splendid gable crosses, possibly of twelfth-century date, which, with their collections of cross slabs, both Norse and pre-Norse, also suggest construction on an earlier site.[64] The same can be said of the crosses at Bride,[65] Ballaugh, Andreas[66] and Kirk Michael, Malew[67] and Marown[68]. A paten, a crucifix and thurible cover from Malew and a chalice from Jurby

Fig. 20.17 *Round Tower, Peel Castle. The Round Tower, viewed from the north, with the Garrison Hall and Peel Hill behind. The tower is built on the same east-west axis at St Patrick's Church, and is almost certainly of similar date, no doubt serving as a refuge like its Irish counterparts. The corbelled crenellations are a later addition.*

Fig. 20.18 *Romanesque stonework reconstructed in the north wall of St Trinian's, a) exterior view, b) (opposite) interior view showing original capital. Photographs: Harold Mytum.*

are similar survivals from earlier buildings on the sites.[69] The latter has also more recently produced a stone holy water stoup. A Latin inscription *AVITI MONOMENTI* was excavated from beneath the present Santon parish church during construction of the present building in 1782.[70] Another simple cross memorial was recovered from its reused position as a threshold slab in a southern doorway through an earlier wall overbuilt by an extension to Santon church. One of Maughold's most distinctive crosses was found in an outhouse in Ramsey and was thought by Kermode to derive from the keeill at Ballure.[71]

That many of the medieval churches and chapels were in continuous use during the Middle Ages can be seen in both the architectural and archaeological evidence. Fourteenth- or fifteenth-century windows are in evidence at St Trinian's and in both east and west gables at St Peter's Peel. Fragments of an east window survive at St Patrick's Chapel, Jurby together with a moulded piscina arch.[72] At Maughold a former east window, now built into the gable below the present one, together with a range of architectural fragments, a decorated holy water stoup, a gable cross and the fourteenth-century preaching cross were recorded by the Manx Archaeological Survey.[73] The quantity and range of material from this site underline its continued importance throughout the period.

No distinctively medieval features can be discerned in the chapel at Ballure, Ramsey, though lintel graves have been found disturbed by its

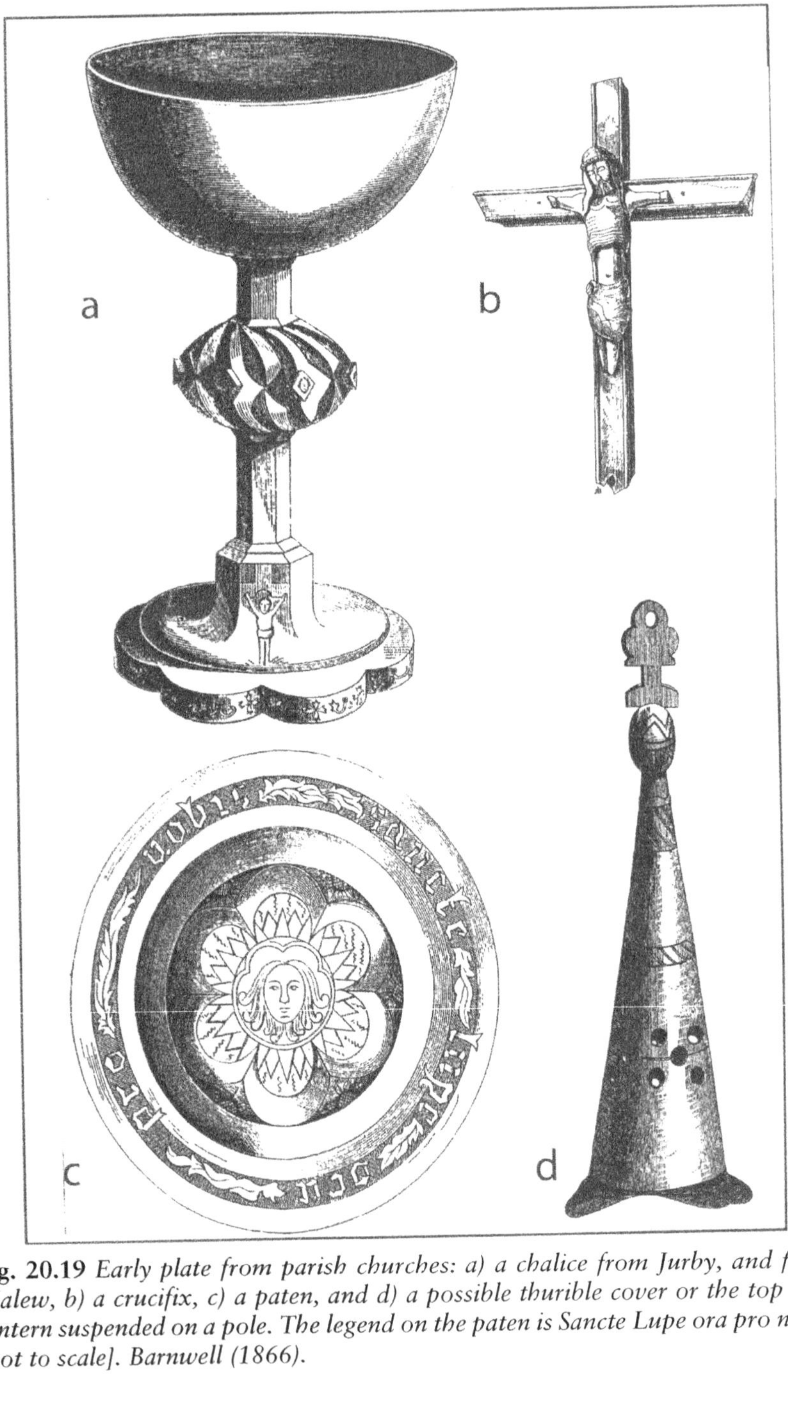

Fig. 20.19 *Early plate from parish churches: a) a chalice from Jurby, and from Malew, b) a crucifix, c) a paten, and d) a possible thurible cover or the top of a lantern suspended on a pole. The legend on the paten is Sancte Lupe ora pro nobis [not to scale]. Barnwell (1866).*

Fig. 20.20 *Preaching cross, Maughold. The high cross at Maugihold, the only one of its type on the island, bears a distinctive, early representation of the 'Three Legs' symbol. For safety, the cross now stands within the church.*

extension to the east,[74] or of the one that used to stand on Douglas Quay on the basis of the 1652 James Chaloner drawing.[75] The chapel at Castletown, more recently Castletown Grammar School, appears to have been significantly extended in the later fifteenth or sixteenth centuries when three relieving arches made of massive punch dressed sandstone were knocked through the existing fabric to produce a south aisle.[76] No earlier medieval architectural detail survives.

St German's Cathedral (X ref 15.2)
The Cathedral of St German is the largest single medieval building on St Patrick's Isle and by far the largest ecclesiastical structure on the Isle of Man. Although roofless and lacking its south aisle, the nave, chancel and both transepts survive to roof height. The crossing consists of early Gothic arches with dogtooth mouldings, the lancet window in the chancel walls and east end are early English in style. The remaining openings in the nave and transepts appear, stylistically, to be later.

Three features of the building are unusual. First, the floor level under the crossing and in the transepts is around one metre below that of the rest of the building. The position of the crossing pier plinths and those of the nave piers shows that this difference is an early, if not original feature.

Secondly, the upper levels of the tower and transepts have machicolations, usually dated to the refortification of the whole islet by the Lords of Man during the Anglo-Scottish wars in the early fourteenth century.

Fig. 20.21 *(opposite) St German's Cathedral, St Patrick's Isle. The Gothic arches at the crossing of the church, with their dogtooth mouldings, are amongst its most distinctive features, despite some previous restoration. The sunken crossing, fourteenth-century battlements and partially restored nave arcade also combine to make this a most eye-catching structure.*

Fig. 20.22 *(below) St German's Cathedral, St Patrick's Isle. A view eastwards across the crossing, showing the narrow early English windows that characterise the chancel. The east façade is heavily restored.*

Thirdly, the eastern gable of the cathedral forms an integral part of the castle defences.

Until Freke's 1982–8 programme of excavations the most coherent attempt to explain the existing structures was by Radford who carried out excavations in the nave in 1962.[77] Radford located the line of the south wall of the nave between the later and still surviving nave piers, the presence of which is still visible as a parch mark during dry weather. He also established that the north transept and nave foundations were bonded together and were of the same build. He went on to postulate that the nave and transepts were earlier than the present chancel and proposed a twelfth-century cruciform church with a short chancel, for which there is no surviving architectural evidence. Curphey in his detailed account of the building[78] accepted this dating and suggested that Bishop Reginald had constructed the first building soon after 1154, when the diocese had been created.

The most recent excavations at the castle have provided some new evidence for the dating of the building sequence.[79] Freke established that the north transept and north chancel walls were of the same character and bonded together at foundation level at least. He also identified a chamfered sandstone plinth course at ground level beneath the north wall of the present chancel that deviated from its present alignment and has been broken through at its eastern end to accommodate the entrance to the crypt. Although the existence of an earlier structure at this point rules out the possibility of Radford's shortened chancel, it does prove that an earlier building stood on the site.

The 1982–8 excavation also established something of the overall ecclesiastical sequence on the site. The keeill was replaced in the middle of the eleventh century by a timber-floored domestic building that remained in use for a century until itself destroyed by the construction of the north transept. Whilst some of the burials identified to the north of the cathedral are aligned on and conform to the structures of both the keeill and the cathedral, others appear to be related to the period between the use of the two structures. The cemetery appears to have been in continual use, arguing for a third ecclesiastical building on the site to provide the necessary focus. This building must have lain to the south of both the keeill (which has later burials cut into its foundations) and the domestic building; in other words it very likely lay beneath the present cathedral and is only represented today by the fragmentary plinth course beneath the north wall of the chancel.

Although the recent excavations have provided no explanation of the sunken floor level in the transepts, they have established that the fifteenth-century curtain wall collapsed during the latter part of the seventeenth century, and therefore, that, as built, the eastern end of the chancel lay within the castle defences.

Thus St German's Cathedral, a substantially thirteenth-century structure which was completed by Bishop Simon (*c.*1225–47), probably replaced a twelfth-century building which may have been constructed soon after the see was created in 1154. The relationship between the keeill to the north of the cathedral and St Patrick's Church – the only other sizeable ecclesiastical structure on the islet, remains unclear.

Bishopscourt

It seems likely that the bishop had a residence at Ballachurry, which became known as Bishopscourt, as early as the thirteenth century. Bishop Simon' death is 1247 is described by the *Cronica regum Mannie & Insularum* as taking place *apud ecclesiam Sancti Michaelis* which suggests a residence in Kirk Michael parish.[80] Although there is no trace today of a building of

Fig. 20.23 *Bishopscourt. The home of the bishop – though there were long periods when the Lord of Mann held the property and it is now a private residence – began as a fourteenth-century tower, which lies at the core of the tallest element visible here. Photograph: Harold Mytum.*

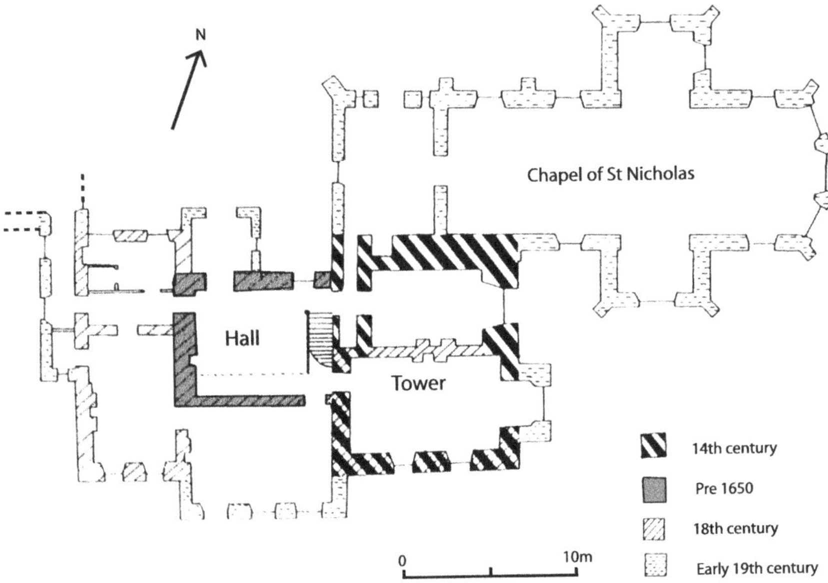

Fig. 20.24 *Ground floor plan of the fourteenth-to early nineteenth-century elements at Bishopscourt showing the tower, hall and chapel. The later domestic wing has been omitted. Based on W.T. Quayle's drawing in Curphy 1976.*

Fig. 20.25 *View of Bishopscourt from the south-east, published by Daniel King in 1656. Courtesy: Manx National Heritage.*

that date, at the core of the site a typical fourteenth-century peel tower can still be readily identified. Although the subject of many improvements and restorations over the years by succeeding bishops,[81] the main elements of an almost square tower with three floors, with a north-eastern entrance giving access to the upper floors by a staircase within the north wall, can be seen. Early views of the site, particularly those by Daniel King published in 1656 show some remaining medieval-style windows in the upper floors and a late medieval hall to the south and chapel to the north. Roof repairs in 1956 revealed the corbel to carry the original roof and fighting platform.[82] The site is important in Manx history not only because of its association with a succession of bishops from the thirteenth until the late twentieth century, but also as the only fortified medieval residence outside Peel Castle and Castle Rushen, which should be contrasted with the independent peel towers which stood on St Patrick's Isle before the curtain wall was built.

Monastic sites

From what has already been said about the churches and keeills at Maughold and St Patrick's Isle it seems highly probable that the monastic communities there survived the period of Viking raids and settlement and continued to exist in some form into the eleventh and twelfth centuries. Of the new orders that arrived in the twelfth century there is only a limited amount of surviving architecture. Apart from Rushen Abbey, founded in 1134, there are no upstanding remains of the Cistercian houses at Myroscough, founded in 1176 from Riveaulx, or at Douglas where the Nunnery was founded at the end of the century.[83]

Rushen Abbey

At Rushen Abbey extensive research and excavation by Cubbon and Bruce, by Lawrence Butler and, more recently by the Centre for Manx Studies has thrown some light about the history of this Savignac foundation out of Furness abbey. Above ground only a very simple chapter house with a pair of narrow, (?)lancet windows in its western gable is all that survives of the cloistral buildings.[84] No diagnostic architectural elements of the building remain *in situ*. Of the church only part of the north wall of the crossing and chancel together with a fragment of the north transept exist today. The dressed stones of the arch from the crossing into the transept have been removed and the opening partially blocked. It was clearly Romanesque in form, as is the surviving arch from the transept into the most southerly of its chapels.

The pair of linked buildings to the south-east of the church that stand,

Fig. 20.26 *Rushen Abbey. This Romanesque arch – here seen prior to conservation – lies within the church tower. The arch originally provided access from the north transept into a private chapel east of the transept and north of the presbytery. The tower was later inserted into the transept, and made use of existing masonry where this was possible. The arch was later filled in, probably post-dissolution.*

in part to full height, appear to have functioned, latterly at least, as the domestic quarters of the abbot. Excavation in 1998 of the foundations of the more northerly of the two structures showed that the present building had replaced two others of differing plans and orientation. Finds from the construction trenches together with the style of a window opening in the upper part of the east wall of this building suggests a date in the fourteenth or even fifteenth century for its construction. On the first floor a highly decorated sandstone supporter for one of the roof trusses suggests that this was the abbot's dining room. The more southern of the buildings retains medieval masonry, apparently involving three floors, to its full height. It seems likely that this building functioned, in part, as the public audience chamber for the abbot and survived the dissolution, as it continued to be used as the meeting place of the baronial court for a considerable period into the seventeenth century.

So far the excavations have found no clear evidence for any ecclesiastical presence which pre-dates the Savignacs, despite the presence of a cemetery to the south of the site which contains men, women and children buried over a considerable time, at least in part contemporary with the abbey, and despite the reference to a pre-existing monastery of St Leoc referred to in the papal confirmation of the Royal grant of land to the abbey.

Bymacan Friary

The Friary was founded in 1367 and apparently had been completed by 1373 when it was consecrated. The church building, *c*.12 x *c*.6m, a simple rectilinear structure, survives in part, but during its post-dissolution life within a farm complex has lost its west gable and seen a range of alterations. Although the east gable window has been blocked in two phases and perforated by a modern door, a pointed arch with chamfered sandstone mouldings survives. This feature is clearly original to the structure, is of fourteenth-century style and almost certainly dates to *c*.1370, as the church would have been constructed first on the site. On the inside of the gable there is a ledge above the window that probably carried a collar-beam for the medieval roof, no elements of which survive today. Part of

Fig. 20.27 *Bymacan Friary, Ballabeg. Window and door openings showing 'shouldered' lintel construction. The friary chapel serves as an outbuilding on the farm and is used for storage. Original features, including some of the distinctive shouldered doorways and windows are still apparent.*

both north and south elevations are clearly of medieval date and include a door and windows with 'shouldered lintel' construction, often referred to as the 'Caernarvon arch' technique[85].

Bruce, in his extensive unpublished description of the site,[86] shows clearly that the western gable had been taken down in post-medieval times and rebuilt some seven metres further west. He notes too that the lower courses of the north and south walls are constructed with 'unshamed and uncoursed' granite boulders, whereas the upper parts of the medieval structure are made with well-coursed, roughly squared limestone blocks. He makes the interesting suggestion that the friars having found that their own crude building techniques would not bear a wall of the size required for their church, called in help from the Lord of Man whose masons completed the job. Certainly the limestone coursing does bears some similarity to the fifteenth-century works at Peel Castle and may be contemporary.

The lesser baronies [Bangor, Sabal, Whithorn, St Bees]

Whilst Whithorn was responsible for the chapel at St Trinian's and its attendant hospital[87], there are no independent buildings clearly associated with the monastic houses of Bangor, Sabal and St Bees. In the case of the former, the baronies appear to have consisted of single treens containing three quarterlands each. Each treen includes a keeill site. It is tempting to think, given the Irish sites are themselves very early foundations from the time of St Patrick, that the keeills represent an Early Christian connection with the church in County Down and may have continued in use as temporary local bases well into the high medieval period.

In the case of the Benedictine cell of St Bees it is possible that its holding of the staff lands at Maughold Head which run right up to the parish churchyard boundary, may represent a similar continuity of interest from the Early Christian period. The smallholding belonging to Furness abbey at Ronaldsway is discussed below.

Part 2: THE ARCHAEOLOGICAL EVIDENCE FOR SOCIAL, POLITICAL AND ECONOMIC LIFE IN THE MIDDLE AGES

The questions which underlie the discussion include the degree to which the island was isolated from contemporary developments, the backwardness or otherwise of Manx social and economic life, the coherence of insular political and social institutions and the evolution of a distinctively Manx identity during the medieval period.

Urban development

Papal decrees, for example on the election of a new bishop of the Isles, often contained a phrase in greeting or direction to the people of the diocese such as: *In eundem modo populum civitatis et dioecesis Sodorensis.*[88] This formula, used in many such promulgations, presupposes that a diocese would have an urban centre at its core. Recent archaeological research has failed to find any settlement evidence on the island that could be construed as urban until the end of the fifteenth century, at the earliest.

In Peel itself extensive sampling excavations retrieved medieval evidence only from a very small area on the harbour edge, immediately opposite the castle.[89] Recent excavations just to the south of the promenade have located urban-type deposits of sixteenth-century date, with a few possible fifteenth-century residual artefacts.[90] These finds echo those recovered in 1985 from the silted up harbour.

In the historic core of Castletown much larger groups of sixteenth-century artefacts have been found, in association with what appeared to be an organised phase of town planning, only some 35m from the outworks of the castle.[91] In 1506 there were 86 'cottages' in Castletown.[92] There is no sign of typical urban structures or organisational features such as defensive walls, gates, markets, burgage plots, or town officials. The same is true at Peel. The papal instructions were directed at a rural population who happened to have the seat of a bishop located in their midst.

Rural sites and landscapes

In the countryside there existed a system of land division based upon the primary unit known as the treen, subdivided into quarterlands and progressively grouped upwards into parishes and sheadings: it is presumed that the treens and sheadings were the original units, later elaborated by increased pressure for land and by reorganisation for feudal and administrative purposes (X ref to 19.2 and 19.2). By the early 1500s, at the time of the earliest extant full manorial roll, a practice known as intacking – the enclosure under licence of common land – was already established, creating an additional class of (often poorer) holdings. Quarterland farmers could also augment their acreage by the licensed enclosure of nearby or adjacent common land, known as an intack of ease. Smaller cottage holdings also existed, almost exclusively in the lowland zone. The upland common was a rich source of grazing, fuel and other raw materials, and is now increasingly recognised as a remarkably rich archaeological landscape.[93]

No major farmstead has been fully excavated, although limited investigation at Kerrowdhoo, Bride, where thirteenth-century locally made granite-tempered ware was recovered in 1994,[94] tantalisingly demonstrates the potential of studying quarterland farms.

Whilst the re-use of the promontory forts has left behind houses which may not be domestic in the true meaning of the word, there still remain three other sites which might more truly be considered farmsteads and which have been subject to archaeological scrutiny: the Braaid, Doarlish Cashen, and Slieu Curn. The first two sites are vastly different. The Braaid lies at an altitude of 140m above sea level; the house encloses a space 20m long and up to 8m across at its widest point, and has slightly curved long walls. The interior has been disturbed by the later construction of small stone and turf shelters[95] reminiscent of shieling huts. Only very limited evidence has been found of benches, and no trace of a hearth survived in those areas investigated. There is still scope for further investigation in those areas not already affected by excavation. Downslope lies a second structure, 16.5m long and 6m wide, this time with straight long walls. The

Fig. 20.28 *The Braaid. An aerial view of the Viking Age homestead, showing a bow-sided dwelling, rectangular byre and round house. The latter is believed to represent a structure surviving from pre-Viking occupation of the site. The site was abandoned, probably due to waterlogging, and was later used as a shieling, with smaller huts built in the ruins of the dwelling house.*

tall stones that stand at intervals parallel to its north wall are taken to indicate that it served as a byre, with rudimentary stalls. The Braaid has the necessary attributes to be a substantial Viking period farmstead, provided with a house (so large it perhaps merits being called a hall) and a separate byre. The Braaid farmstead was abandoned, possibly because of flooding caused by its spring.

The modern status of the land on which the site stands is intack, which is very much at odds with the large scale of the buildings and the high status that this implies. It may be that climatic deterioration, population growth and soil impoverishment, which can be generally assumed from the post-Viking period onwards, had some hitherto undetected social, practical and economic effects on the land division system at the junction of farmland and commons which have yet to be understood.

In contrast, the farmstead at Doarlish Cashen is considered a more marginal site, located at 210m above sea level at the head of a valley draining northward from Dalby Mountain. Here Gelling found a group of structures associated with a field system. Survey revealed perhaps ten structures,[96] some of which were so ephemeral that they were only identified by changes in the vegetation. Investigation of three of the structures, grouped

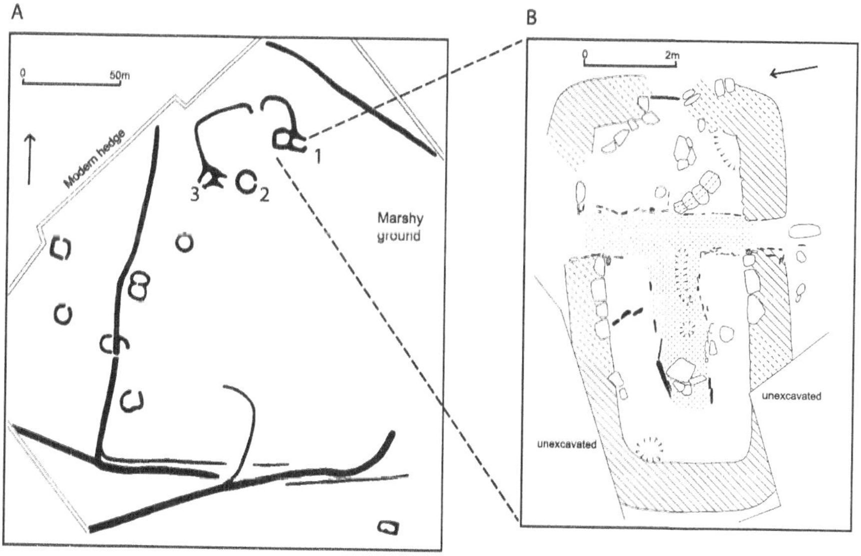

Fig. 20.29 *Doarlish Cashen shielings excavated by Peter Gelling. A: plan of field systems, including 1) dwelling house, 2) animal pen and 3) corn-drying kiln. B: detail of excavation of building 1. The diagonal lines indicate a thin layer of turf, the remains of the base of the wall. The stippling shows the spread of hearth material.*

around a farmyard-like enclosure, revealed a dwelling house, corn-drying kiln, and an animal pen.[97] The dwelling house was rectangular and built of stone, earth and turf; it had opposed doors, and benches lined the long walls and one gable: a hollow set into the bench at the other gable, perhaps served as cool storage, or as a basic dairy as the excavator suggested. The entire floor area between the doors and benches was covered in a spread of hearth material. Internally the house measured a mere 7 by 3m. On the strength of the internal arrangements, the excavator interpreted the house, and farmstead as a whole as Viking in date.

At a similar altitude, on the northern end of Slieu Curn overlooking Glen Dhoo, several complexes of banked enclosures and mounds representing collapsed structures have been surveyed.[98] These include three rectilinear features with low turf walls, ranging in size from 4.4 by 2.5m to 9 by 2m internally.

One of these features[99] has been investigated, revealing a rectangular building with turf walls. During its occupation three separate hearths were used; samples from stratigraphically the earliest and latest of the hearths produced calibrated radiocarbon dates from the early and late thirteenth century.[100] The latest hearth also produced fragments of burnt pottery, provisionally eleventh or twelfth century in date but, unless this is residual material, subject to revision in the light of the radiocarbon determination. This pottery is reminiscent of a single shard of very dark grey unglazed pottery recovered from the floor deposit within the house at Doarlish Cashen, and provides welcome confirmation of the age of the latter site. In contrast to Doarlish Cashen, however, there were no signs of benches, nor of the revetting for such structures, and the hearths were well defined rather than spread across the floor.

The structures at both Doarlish Cashen and Slieu Curn share the landscape with other features frequently classed as shielings. These remains were first investigated as a class on the island during the late 1950s and early 1960s.[101] Gelling initially identified around 50 sites, comprising groups of mounds – representing the collapsed remains of dwellings – and occasionally evidence for agriculture and animal control in the form of boundaries, enclosures and lazy beds. Excavation at two sites, Block Eary and Injebreck, demonstrated that the dwellings were simple, small, turf and stone-built huts, repeatedly repaired and rebuilt on the same site, and perhaps roofed with branches, turf, heather or bracken. Investigation at Block Eary also demonstrated that some of the huts were built on more substantial foundations of stone, and signified earlier, Iron or Bronze Age occupation.[102] Gelling was able to identify possible specialised uses for some of the structures, postulating cheese-making, corn drying,[103] and

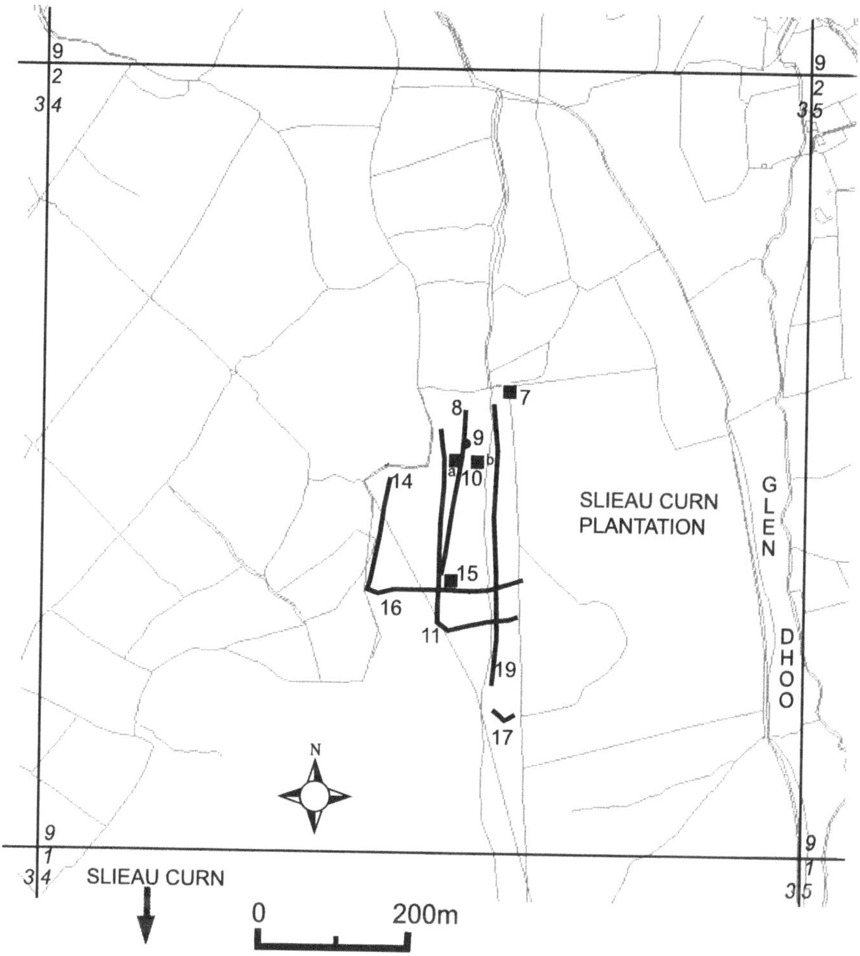

Fig. 20.30 *Map showing medieval structures and field system on the north-eastern slopes of Slieau Curn as surveyed in 1996. Linear features 8, 11, 14, 16, 19: rectilinear features 7, 10a, 10b, 15: and circular depression 9 and are numbered as in the published report. Note sites from other periods found during the survey are not shown. (Davey, P., Johnson, N.C. and Woodcock, J.J., 'Upper Glendhoo, Ballaugh, Isle of Man', Field Survey, September 1996, Fig. 4)*

accommodation for geese. Finds were sparse, but included a coin of King Stephen dating to 1135–41, and loom weights, which add spinning to the range of activities already mentioned. Boredom was assuaged with a stone merels board.

The growing number and range of features identified during field survey

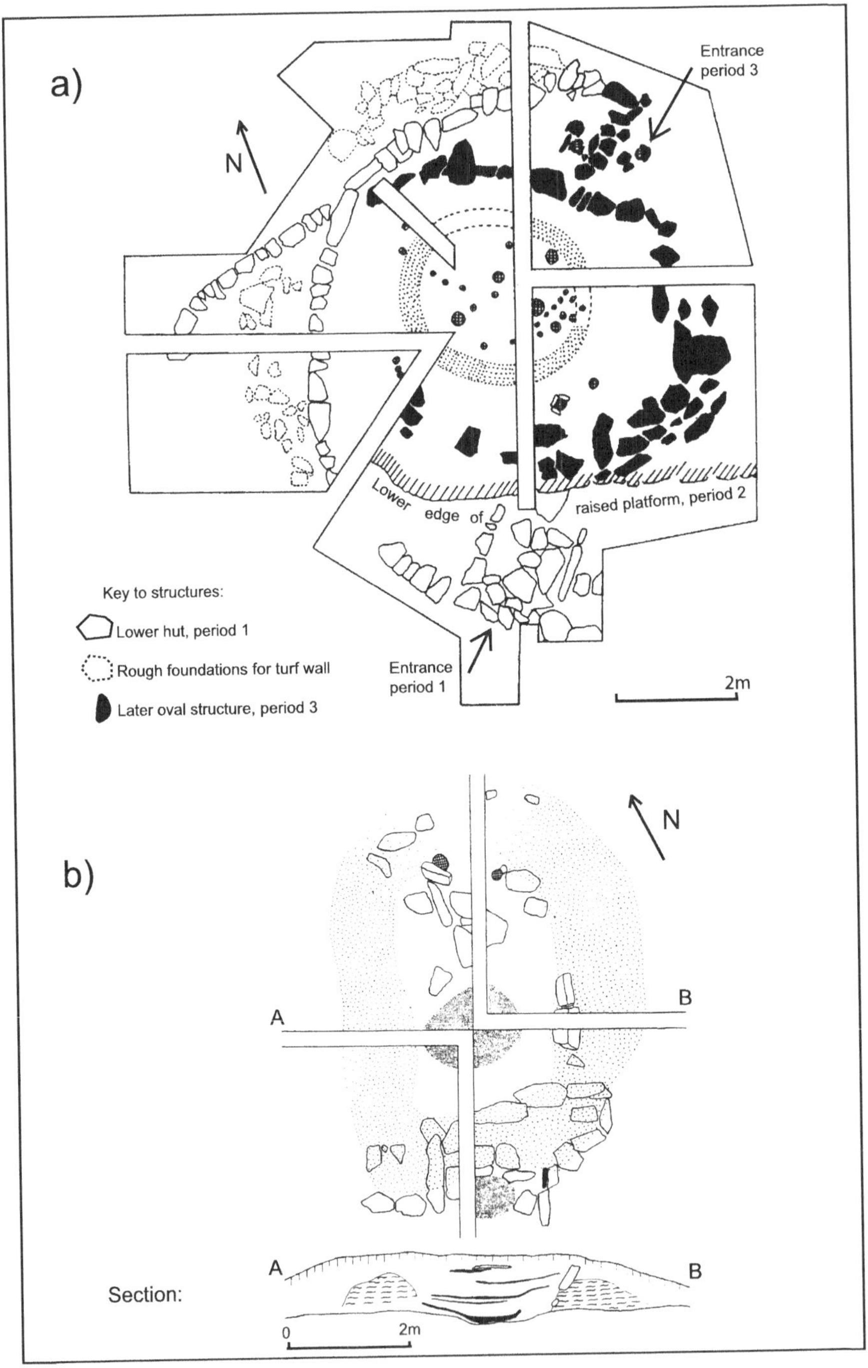
a)
N
Entrance
period 3
Lower edge of raised platform, period 2
Key to structures:
Lower hut, period 1
Rough foundations for turf wall
Later oval structure, period 3
Entrance
period 1
2m
b)
N
A
B
A
B
Section:
0
2m

in the uplands suggests much more intensive use of this landscape than might otherwise be appreciated. One last issue flows from discussion of shielings and seasonal activity, particularly the feasibility of raising crops. As previously considered in relation to the Braaid, the status of land as treen or intack is an important indicator of the pressures on land during this period and afterwards. Several upland farms are named using the generic element *eary*, meaning 'shieling'; such farms will have been named either after nearby shielings or after the seasonal settlements which they replaced.

Social and economic development

The archaeological evidence for economic activity on Man during the high medieval period is largely confined to three sites that can hardly be described as representative of the wider state of affairs in the island as a whole – Peel Castle,[104] Castle Rushen[105] and Rushen Abbey.[106] With the notable exception of the metalworking sites at Braddan Vicarage[107] and Ronaldsway smelt[108] (X ref to 16.12), there has been no serious attempt by archaeologists to investigate the nature of settlement or the quality of life beyond the centres of power. In particular, none of the 700 or so quarterland farms – the backbone of Manx social and economic life from the Norse period – has been the subject of serious excavation.

The level and quality of medieval economic activity on Man, as evidenced by the castles and abbey, can be partially assessed by looking at the evidence of artefacts such as pottery, metalwork, glass and coins which have been recovered from recent archaeological excavations. Questions of diet and food supply and, therefore, resource management can also be addressed.

The ceramic evidence has been discussed at length elsewhere.[109] In brief, with the exception of a handful of early medieval imports and the use of pottery crucibles in the later Iron Age and Early Christian periods, the island was aceramic from the middle of the Bronze Age (*c*.1000 BC) until the eleventh or twelfth century. With the establishment of Norse rule the production of a local hand-made cooking-ware, characterised by being grogged with freshly crushed Foxdale granite, was initiated. This 'granite-tempered ware' continued in production until late in the sixteenth century. For the first two or three centuries of local production a 'granite-free' ware was also in use for the production of jugs and other tablewares. Associated

Fig. 20.31 *Excavated structures of two turf and stone-built huts, shieling mounds: a) Block early plan and b) Injebreck plan and section, excavated by Peter Gelling in the 1960s.*

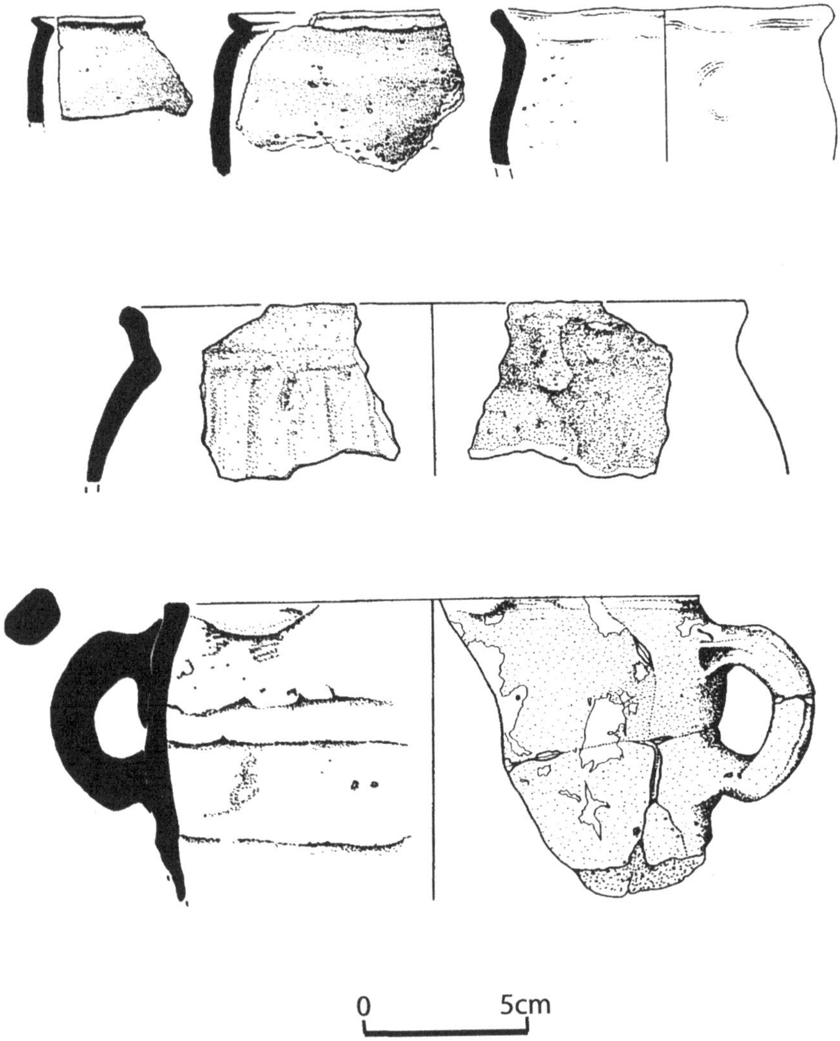

Fig. 20.32 *Medieval pottery. Examples of 'Manx granite tempered ware' from excavations at Peel Castle and Castle Rushen. Three unglazed cooking pots, above, date to the eleventh or twelfth century. An unglazed jar, middle, is fourteenth-century. The lower, large, handled jar is fourteenth- or fifteenth-century. See also Fig. 17.5. (Davey, P.J., 2000, 'Medieval and later pottery in the Isle of Man'* Proceedings, Isle of Man Natural History Antiquarian Society XI, *Fig. 1, p.92)*

with these insular wares, the island was in receipt of considerable quantities of imports from Britain and the continent (see fig. 17.5). The very limited evidence from other, lower status sites – such as the metalworking complex at Braddan or the small farm at Kerrowdhoo[110] suggests that, although imports were in general circulation on the island, they were present in only very small numbers outside the major centres.

Metalwork, whether of iron or copper alloy, does not survive well in Manx soils. Even at Peel Castle, outside the Norse grave groups, only small numbers of metal artefacts survived. The copper alloy finds consist for the most part of wire pins and needles, lace chapes and dress accessories such as strap ends and belt fittings.[111] Castle Rushen produced a similar though much smaller range of items that included metalworking evidence in the form of several cut fragments of sheeting and folded rivets for repairing bronze vessels.[112] At Rushen Abbey, whilst a majority of recent finds are from dissolution demolition deposits, small numbers of medieval copper alloy lace tags, studs, needles, dress fittings and repaired bronze vessel fragments have been found.[113]

Iron artefacts occur even less frequently. At Peel, apart from some 754 nails and rivets, and with the extensive use of X-ray photography, only seven items were recovered – a knife, a spur, a flesh hook, a fish hook, a projectile point and two chapes[114] – which must represent a very small proportion of the iron objects actually in use at any time in the medieval period. At Castle Rushen no medieval iron objects were recovered.[115]

These assemblages of metal artefacts, although extremely vestigial, do establish that at the main sites, metal was in widespread use for a range of purposes. The Manx finds exhibit no particularly insular features. They lie within the mainstream of the available technologies within the British Isles.

In addition, the presence of a smelt for lead and possibly silver, owned by Furness abbey and located on the coast at Ronaldsway together with a number of iron working sites such as the one excavated by Cubbon at Braddan Vicarage and that located by Larch Garrad at Ballavarry, Andreas,[116] show that the mineral resources of the island were certainly being widely exploited.

Medieval glass is even more rarely found. Four shards from a crumbling potash glass vessel were found at Peel,[117] together with some 220 shards of extremely weathered window glass, including ten with traces of grisaille decoration. Many fragments of window glass, fragments of a urinal and a lamp were recovered from Rushen abbey, the latter within a burial.[118] (X ref 17.6) There was no medieval glass from Castle Rushen.

To date five coin hoards, one of the late twelfth and the others of the early fourteenth century have been found on Man, together with 36 single

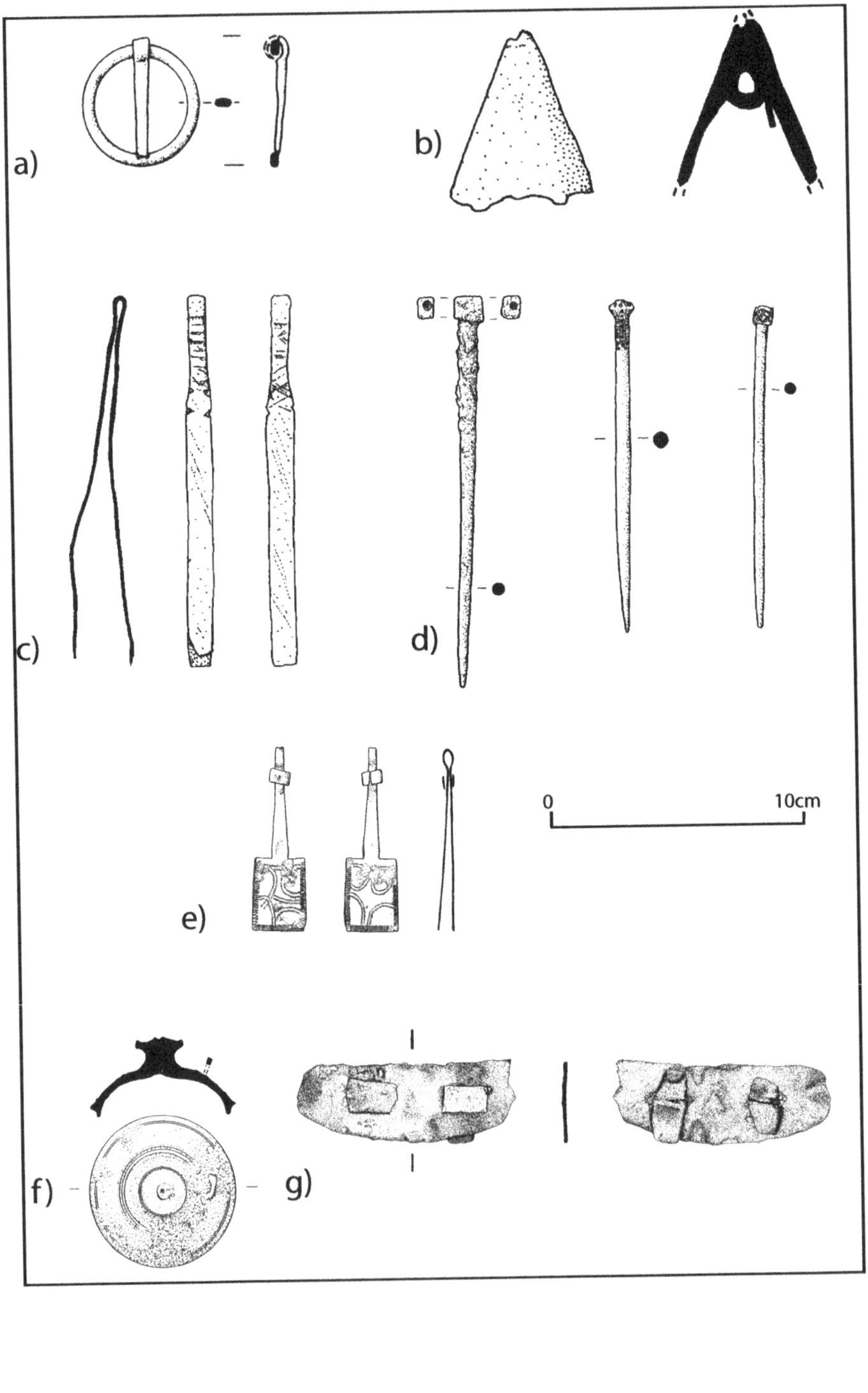
a)
b)
c)
d)
e)
0
10cm
f)
g)

coin finds. Bornholdt, in her recent study,[119] has commented: 'The total number of single finds from Man is suspiciously low for a population apparently familiar with coinage, but Man's excavated site totals are not out of keeping in a British Isles context.' The paucity of rural finds, compared with England, has led her to conclude '...that currency was not used regularly by the majority of folk in Man during the middle ages'. A number of factors suggest that this statement is rather too extreme. First, unlike England, medieval Man had no villages and, therefore, no deserted medieval villages. There has been no local tradition of fieldwalking *for medieval finds*; indeed the numbers of shards of pottery found outside formal excavations is also very small – a handful of shards from 11 sites.[120] In addition, the thirteenth- and fourteenth-century synodal statutes[121] show that tithes, payable by the majority of the 700 or so quarterland farms, were valued in monetary terms. Although payments in kind were also acceptable, it is clear from the records of episcopal payments of Papal taxa-

Fig. 20.33 *Medieval copper alloy artefacts from a) Rushen Abbey, b)–g) Peel Castle: a) brooch with tongue fond associated with burial in 1926 (from Butler, L.A.S. (1988), 'The Cistercian Abbey of St Mary of Rushen: excavations 1978–79',* Journal of British Archaeology Association, *60–104); b) hexagonal-shaped bell, possibly tenth-century; c) tweezers made from a folder strip of copper alloy sheet; d) three pins from eleventh–thirteenth century; e) tweezers with decorated, expanded terminals, likely to be medieval; f) lid with loop for a chain from post-medieval vessel; g) flat plate with wide 'paper clip' rivets, probably a strap mount, ?post-medieval (from Cubbon, A.M., Davey, P.J. and Gelling, M. (eds),* Excavations on St Patrick's Isle, Isle of Man, Prehistoric, Viking, Medieval and Later, 1982–88 by David Freke, *Liverpool University Press, Fig. 103).*

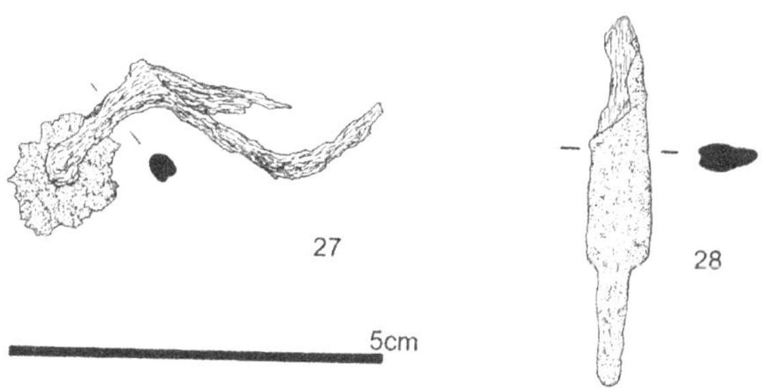

Fig. 20.34 *Medieval iron artifacts from Peel Castle: a) a rowel spur with a shank 90mm long, probably early fourteenth-century: b) projectile point 93mm long with a socketed tang and leaf-shaped blade, dated to the early medieval period up to the late thirteenth century.*

tion, via Nidaros, that commodities such as sheep, honey or grain must have been cash convertible, as Sodor and Man's valuation, at 660 florins for an incoming bishop, was a significant one in regional terms. The money was generally paid late, and in instalments, but it was paid.[122]

The few surviving medieval buildings on the island also give some indication of economic activity. With the exception of the residence of the bishop at Bishopscourt, no domestic buildings survive. Of the ecclesiastical buildings, the Cathedral of St German at Peel is pre-eminent. The construction of the crossing arch, vaults and chancel exhibits very good quality workmanship using varieties of Peel sandstone. Similarly, fine sculptured capitals are in evidence at St Trinians and decorated jambs at St Runius Church, Marown with local granite being exploited.[123] Although at Rushen Abbey most of the architectural fragments recovered from the excavations appear to be using imported sandstones, the principal walls of the cloistral buildings were constructed using large blocks of finely dressed local limestone.[124] In all of these cases it is possible that masons were brought in specially, from Furness or Whithorn (in the case of St Trinians). Even so, both Rushen Abbey and St German's Cathedral show a number of phases of workmanship and alterations in windows and doors which might imply resident skills in the Manx population. The wide time span over which major phases of work were carried out at Castle Rushen and at Peel tends to confirm this. All of these buildings have produced evidence for competent lead working, slating, carpentry and glazing of a quality equivalent to their architecture and status. Given the lack of fieldwork, how far these skills were available or appropriate to the wider population of the island remains unclear.

Recent archaeological excavations, especially those at Peel Castle have provided a wide range of information about the exploitation of natural resources, especially animals, birds and fish.[125] Over 50,000 fragments of large mammal bone were recovered from the excavations. In the medieval period cattle form by far the largest group, followed by sheep and pigs. A few horse, deer and dog bones were also recovered. Apart from rabbit that occurred in a number of genuinely medieval contexts, most of the small mammal bone was found in bulk sampling and represent elements of the contemporary fauna of St Patrick's Isle rather than human food. In contrast, of the 45 species of bird recovered, only five were of domesticated varieties (chicken, greylag goose, mallard, rock dove and peafowl), yet there was evidence of at least 38 of them forming part of human diet. Many of these latter were seabirds such as shag, shearwater, kittiwake, cormorant, goldeneye, long-tailed duck and tufted duck, some of which may also have been obtained for oil. Fish also formed an important element in the assemblage from Peel. Of the 28 species confidently identified in the 6,373 bones collected, some implied the organisation of deep-sea fleets, others inshore fishing, possibly with hand lines. If anything like Vikings in the north of Scotland, we should expect longline fishing from a variety of craft and for large individuals (of a size we would now only hope for from deep-sea) to have been caught inshore. There was very little evidence of fresh-water fish. Limpets, dog whelks and winkles were also consumed in quantity, as were oysters, which also formed part of a small medieval assemblage at Castle Rushen.[126]

These results from Peel show that Manx medieval society not only relied on domesticated animals and birds, but exploited local populations of wild birds, fish and shellfish to a much greater degree than previously thought.

Because of the lack of organic preservation within the sieved deposits, no medieval plant remains were recovered from either Peel or Castle Rushen. At Rushen Abbey two of the trial trenches produced charred grains of wheat, barley and oats.[127] Documentary sources suggest that cereal production, especially of wheat, was an important element in Manx medieval agriculture.[128] The limited surviving contemporary pollen evidence paints the same picture.[129] It remains for the right deposits to be examined to clarify the chronology and geography of cereal production in this period.[130]

Manx medieval landscape and society in an Irish Sea context

In what ways is the medieval architecture and archaeology of the Isle of Man distinctive in a regional context? The Island lacks evidence either for the open field systems of north-west England and lowland North Wales[131] or for the planned landscapes of Anglo-Norman Ireland.[132] There are no towns or villages as such; no sign of burgage plots or tofts and crofts. The beginnings of nucleation around the two medieval castles and at Ballasalla seem to date from the fifteenth century at earliest. The parish churches are diminutive affairs, simple, single-celled extensions of pre-existing keeills. Only the cathedral of St German at Peel Castle is aisled. A single probable motte and bailey at Cronk Howe Mooar and a possible one at Castleward are the only examples of a type of structure common in adjacent areas. There are no moated sites at all which are a major feature of medieval landscapes particularly in the south-east of Ireland,[133] north-west England[134] and North Wales.[135] There are no manor houses – Bishopscourt is the only quasi-domestic structure of the period. It is of a type common to urban structures in northern Ireland, such as Carrickfergus and widespread in south-west Scotland and northern England and Wales.[136]

All of these negatives appear to be a product of two factors. First, the island was in single ownership and was effectively treated as a single (or dual) manor by its kings and lords. Secondly, dispersed rural settlement persisted throughout the period and was not influenced by the Germanic patterns established in much of England or the Norman ones in Wales or Ireland. The lack of moated sites and manor houses is a clear indication that society was much less vertically structured than, for example, in neighbouring areas of England where in multiple-moated townships a chronological and social hierarchy can be discerned between the earliest, central site and a range of peripheral moats of lower status.[137] The two castles functioned as the manorial focus throughout the medieval period; the only other barons were monastic, the majority non-resident.

A distinctive feature of Manx medieval and later landscapes is the system of treen and quarterland divisions. Although there is evidence that in the eleventh to thirteenth centuries there was occupation at higher levels, now represented by earthwork field systems, farm and shieling sites above the present limit of enclosure, the boundaries that were retreated to in the later medieval period appear to be those represented in the early sixteenth-century Rent Rolls and can still be identified on the ground today. In the *limites terrarum monachorum* the boundaries mostly follow natural features, particularly streams. Where such features are lacking the boundary frequently follows 'a wall' *(per murum)*[138] or even 'an old wall' (*per ueterem murum*).[139] These are clearly built features used to separate estates such as *Villa Thorkel* and *Balesalazc* and are almost certainly to be equated with Manx 'hedges'. For example, the hedge that divides the King's land and the monastic estate of Skinscoe, on its western side, still runs for some 1,300m between the headwaters of two streams that flow into the Laxey River and Dhoon Glen respectively.

The overall pattern of treens and their subdivision into quarterlands is a fundamental element in Manx medieval and later economic and social structures. The whole land area was divided more or less equally into small estates called treens, a structure which appears to have been observed by the monastic landowners as well as the Lord. Beyond the King, his court and administrators, the abbot and bishop, lay the quarterland farmer who, latterly at least, paid rent for his land. There is no field evidence for any kind of intermediate social class. The lack of excavation, so far, of any of the structures associated with this land-holding system restricts greatly any understanding of it through archaeological evidence. But the potential is there. How old is the system? Are the quarterland divisions and their farms secondary elements or do they occupy later prehistoric sites?

The area of agricultural land enclosed in around 1500 was around 53,000 acres with significant areas of upland summer grazing.[140] In addition, the island was surrounded by rich sea fisheries and possessed important lowland wetlands[141] that provided fuel, fish and wildfowl. Quite apart from its strategic position, the density of these resources is in marked contrast to any of the Western Isles. The field evidence, both structural and artifactual suggests a successful economy, appropriate to a regional seat of power. The Island's maritime position provided easy contact not only with the lands around but with goods and material from the nearer continent. Whether the high proportion of French imports arrived directly or by coastal trade, the Manx King and Abbot could afford to buy wines and exotic ceramics on a scale not visible even in neighbouring trading centres such as Chester or Dublin. Serious excavation of a number of quarterland farm sites will be needed before it is possible to assess how far the life-style levels observed at Peel, Castle Rushen and Rushen Abbey permeated into the wider society.

Notes

1 The archaeological evidence for the Viking Age is to be presented in Volume 2.

2 Director, Centre for Manx Studies.

3 Field Archaeologist, Manx National Heritage.

4 G. Broderick, *Cronica regum mannie and insularum*, Manx Museum and National Trust (Douglas 1979), f.50r; cf. C. McNamee 1997, *The Wars of the Bruces: Scotland, England and Ireland, 1306–1328*, Tuckwell Press (East Linton, 1997) 58.

5 B.R.S. Megaw, 'The Scottish invasion of Man in 1456', *Journal of the Manx Museum* (1957), VI (74), 23–4.

6 The religious buildings are described elsewhere in this chapter except where they have undergone military adaptation.

7 The significant texts are R.A. Curphey, 'Peel Castle – Summer Excursion: June 1979', *Proceedings of the Isle of Man Natural History and Antiquarian Society* (1984), IX, 59–94; D.J. Freke, *The Peel Castle Dig* (The Friends of Peel Castle, 1995); D.J. Freke, *Excavations on St Patrick's Isle, Isle of Man, Prehistoric, Viking, Medieval and Later, 1982–88*, (Liverpool University Press, 2002) and H. Gordon Slade in D.J. Freke (2002).

8 D.J. Freke, *Excavations on St Patrick's Isle, Isle of Man, Prehistoric, Viking, Medieval and Later, 1982–88*, (Liverpool University Press, 2002).

9 R.A. Curphey, 'Peel Castle – Summer Excursion: June 1979', *Proceedings of the Isle of Man Natural History and Antiquarian Society* (1984), IX, 59–94.

10 This is particularly apparent when combined with the evidence so tantalisingly glimpsed in Bersu's 1947 excavations in the centre of the islet. This included a timber building, and perhaps also a palisade. See M.D. Wright, 'Excavation at Peel Castle, 1947', *Proceedings of the Isle of Man Natural History and Antiquarian Society* (1984), IX, 21–57.

11 It is tempting to recall that Magnus Barelegs is credited with fortifying the Isle of Man following his arrival in 1098, though there is no archaeological evidence to link him with these structures.

12 D.J. Freke, *The Peel Castle Dig*, (1995), 35–6.

13 R.A. Curphey, 'Peel Castle – Summer Excursion: June 1979', *Proceedings of the Isle of Man Natural History and Antiquarian Society* (1984), IX, 65ff.

14 D.J. Freke, *The Peel Castle Dig* (1995), 39, concurs, drawing attention to 'an earthen bank built on the stones of the earlier wall'.

15 R.A. Curphey, 'Peel Castle – Summer Excursion: June 1979', *Proceedings of the Isle of Man Natural History and Antiquarian Society* (1984), IX, 65–6.

16 One arch of the arcade survives in its walled-up state, the inserted window with a shallow-curved window head characteristic of this and other secondary windows found throughout the cathedral, far less architecturally impressive than the narrow Early English of the primary windows in the chancel and nave, and suggestive of utility rather than beauty of design.

17 D.J. Freke, *The Peel Castle Dig* (1995), 42; H. Gordon Slade, in D.J. Freke, *Excavations*, (2002).

18 None of the three authors referred to addresses in detail the sandstone masonry from which the Red Curtain and its turrets, the Gatehouse and its barbican are all built, which is considerably more complicated than implied. Recent observation by the writer (Johnson) suggested three or four major phases of construction. Gordon Slade also identifies masonry to either side of one tower that he proposes as remnants of earlier curtain wall. The present writer has not identified any such feature.

19 This tower is unlike any other at Peel, with sharp exterior corners and tapering sides. Of mixed slate and sandstone fabric, its form and construction reflects neither the Red Curtain, nor the later slate-faced curtain wall (sometimes called the Green Curtain).

20 Recent conservation work on the Warwick tower has demonstrated that it was much restored in the late 19th century, whilst the Sallyport tower has also been less recently repaired; neither has been investigated, and so their development, and that of the other tower houses, remains somewhat hypothetical. No two tower houses are the same size.

21 R.A. Curphey, 'Peel Castle – Summer Excursion: June 1979', *Proceedings of the Isle of Man Natural History and Antiquarian Society* (1984), IX, 71–2, and H. Gordon Slade in D.J. Freke, Excavations, (2002), give differing views on the date of the Green Curtain; either way, a fifteenth century origin is probable.

22 The entire curtain wall, together with the towers attached to, and built with it, would benefit from further detailed visual analysis as a means of more closely addressing the unresolved issues of their development.

23 The following description of the structural history of Castle Rushen relies upon the work of A. Rigby, *Castle Rushen, a historical and descriptive account* (1927); B.H.StJ. O'Neil, *Castle Rushen, Isle of Man, an archaeological report for the Manx Government*, typescript IoMNMR, Manx National Heritage, (1946); B.H.StJ. O'Neil, 'Castle Rushen, Isle of Man', offprint from *Archaeologia* (1951), XCIV; and R.A. Curphey, *Ancient Centres of Government on the Isle of Man* (1982), 17–34. The basic building archaeology is reasonably clear, but the latter two writers diverge in their interpretation and dating of it.

24 O'Neil originally proposed a date of around 1200 for the rectangular tower (O'Neil, *Castle Rushen, Isle of Man, an archaeological report for the Manx Government* (1946), 1), but later revised this date to the reign of Godred II, 1153–87 (O'Neil, 'Castle Rushen, Isle of Man', offprint from *Archaeologia* (1951), XCIV, 4). R.A. Curphey, *Ancient Centres of Government on the Isle of Man* (1982), 17, prefers to date this structure to the reign of Olaf II, and more specifically to a date after 1235. A. Rigby, *Castle Rushen, a historical and descrip-*

tive account (1927), 69, concludes, 'it is historically unlikely that there was a castle at Rushen at all events before 1220'.

25 As proposed by B.H.StJ. O'Neil, 'Castle Rushen, Isle of Man', *Archaeologia* (1951), XCIV, 3.

26 P.J. Davey, D.J. Freke and D.A. Higgins (1996), 8–9, 17–20.

27 Again there is a divergence of opinion on date: B.H.StJ. O'Neil, *Castle Rushen, Isle of Man, an archaeological report for the Manx Government*, (typescript IoMNMR, 1946), has the reign of Magnus, but later revises his view to *c.*1200 – see O'Neil, 'Castle Rushen, Isle of Man', offprint from *Archaeologia* (1951), XCIV, 4, Fig. 1, Plate X, whilst R.A. Curphey, *Ancient Centres of Government on the Isle of Man* (1982), also favours the reign of Magnus.

28 R.A. Curphey, *Ancient Centres of Government on the Isle of Man* (1982), 18–19, argues that rebuilding did not commence until the 1340s.

29 As proposed by A. Rigby, *Castle Rushen, a historical and descriptive account* (1927), Figs D and L; B.H.StJ. O'Neil, 'Castle Rushen, Isle of Man', offprint from *Archaeologia* (1951), XCIV, 13; and R.A. Curphey, *Ancient Centres of Government on the Isle of Man* (1982), 26.

30 B.H.StJ. O'Neil, 'Castle Rushen, Isle of Man', offprint from *Archaeologia* (1951), XCIV, 1–2.

31 P.M.C. Kermode and W.A. Herdman, (1914).

32 Terry Ball illustration commissioned by MNH.

33 G. Bersu, 'Excavation of the Cashtal, Ballagawne, Garwick, 1941', *Proceedings of the Isle of Man Natural History and Antiquarian Society* (1967), VII, 88–119, with notes by A.M. Cubbon.

34 A.C.C. Johnson, 'A View from the Hills: Some Thoughts on the Reoccupation of the Promontory Forts and the Possible Origins of the Manx Homestead', *Proceedings of the Isle of Man Natural History and Antiquarian Society* (2000), XI, 51–66.

35 G. Bersu, 'A promontory fort on the shore of Ramsey Bay, Isle of Man', *Antiquaries Journal* (1949), XXIX, 62–79.

36 P.S. Gelling, 'Excavation of a promontory fort at Port Grenaugh, Santon', *Proceedings of the Isle of Man Natural History and Antiquarian Society* (1952), V, 307–15; P.S. Gelling, 'Excavation of a promontory fort at Scarlett, Castletown, Isle of Man', *Proceedings of the Isle of Man Natural History and Antiquarian Society* (1957), V, 571–5; P.S. Gelling, 'Excavation of a promontory fort at Cass ny Hawin, Malew, Isle of Man', *Proceedings of the Isle of Man Natural History and Antiquarian Society* (1959), VI, 28–38.

37 P.S. Gelling, 'Excavation of a promontory fort at Scarlett, Castletown, Isle of Man', *Proceedings of the Isle of Man Natural History and Antiquarian Society* (1957), V, 571–5.

38 P.S. Gelling, 'Excavation of a promontory fort at Cass ny Hawin, Malew, Isle of Man', *Proceedings of the Isle of Man Natural History and Antiquarian Society* (1959), VI, 38, was later to consider the structural characteristics of the house so 'attenuated', as to suggest a fourteenth-century date more appropriate.

39 A.C.C. Johnson (2002) expresses doubts as to the existence of a northerly doorway.

40 R.S. Barton, 'Manx Granite Tempered Ware', in P.J. Davey (ed.), *Recent Archaeological Research on the Isle of Man*, (BAR British Series 278, 1999), 228.

41 A.C.C. Johnson, 'A View from the Hills: Some Thoughts on the Reoccupation of the Promontory Forts and the Possible Origins of the Manx Homestead', *Proceedings of the Isle of Man Natural History and Antiquarian Society* (2000),

XI, 51–66; A.C.C. Johnson (2002).

42 It is clear that Peter Gelling, 'Excavation of a promontory fort at Scarlett, Castletown, Isle of Man', *Proceedings of the Isle of Man Natural History and Antiquarian Society* (1957), V, 571–5, was predisposed to consider the site as a farmstead, comprising a house and outbuildings: 'The people who lived in this farmstead were probably descendants of Viking settlers. They bred sheep, pigs and possibly goats, but there was nothing to suggest that they raised any kind of crop. The flesh of their domestic animals provided part, at least, of their diet, and bones were found scattered all over the floor of the house, with particular accumulations at the foot of both short walls. It may be conjectured that they fished, and they certainly ate shellfish – periwinkle, limpet and dog-whelk – in considerable quantities. It is not clear where they did their cooking, as there was no trace of a hearth inside the house'.

43 A.M. Cubbon, 'The Early Church in the Isle of Man', in S.M. Pearce (ed.), The Early Church in Western Britain and Ireland, BAR British Series 102, (1982), 257–82.

44 A.M. Cubbon, 'The Early Church in the Isle of Man', in S.M. Pearce (ed.), The Early Church in Western Britain and Ireland, BAR British Series 102, (1982), 275–7.

45 A.M. Cubbon 1993–5.

46 C.D. Morris, 'Survey and excavation at Keeill Vael and Druidale in their contexts', in Fell, C. et al., *The Viking Age in the Isle of Man*, Proceedings of the Ninth Viking Congress, (1993).

47 A.C.C. Johnson, forthcoming, An Archaeological Investigation at Lag ny Keeilley [this is still forthcoming].

48 C.A. Ralegh Radford, 'St. Patrick's Isle, Peel. The medieval ecclesiastical remains and the excavations of 1962', *Proceedings of the Isle of Man Natural History and Antiquarian Society* XI, No. 3, (2004).

49 P.M.C. Kermode (1915), 23, Fig.34.

50 P.M.C. Kermode, *Manx Crosses*, 154–6, Plate XXXI, No. 76.

51 P.M.C. Kermode, *Manx Crosses*, (1907), 158–9, Plate XXXIII, No. 78.

52 P.M.C. Kermode, *Manx Crosses*, (1907), 159, Plate XXXIV, No. 81.

53 P.M.C. Kermode, *Manx Crosses*, (1907), 202, No. 106.

54 C.A. Ralegh Radford, 'St Patrick's Isle, Peel: The Medieval Ecclesiastical Remains and Excavations of 1962', *Proceedings of the Isle of Man Natural History and Antiquarian Society*, XI, (2004), 361–92.

55 P.M.C. Kermode, 24–6; R.A. Curphey 1984, 'Peel Castle – Summer Excursion: June 1979', *Proceedings of the Isle of Man Natural History and Antiquarian Society*, IX, (1910), 59–62.

56 The other two are in Scotland, at Brechin and Abernethy; like Peel, they are thought to date from the twelth century.

57 P.M.C. Kermode (1915), 17, Figs 17–18.

58 According to Quine (1906–12, 335), these jambs had been removed from St Trinian's in 1780. He provides no evidence for this statement.

59 J.R. Bruce (1968), 21–7.

60 P.M.C. Kermode (1915), 40.

61 P.M.C. Kermode (1906–12), 331–2.

62 P.M.C. Kermode (1909), 4.

63 P.M.C. Kermode (1911), 15–22, Figs 13 and 19.

64 P.M.C. Kermode (1918), 13, Fig. 34.

65 Excavated from the levelled earlier building in 1896, when the present structure

was erected; P.M.C. Kermode, *Manx Crosses*, 169, (1907), Plate xlii, 92.

66 e.g., The Sigurd Slab; P.M.C. Kermode, *Manx Crosses*, (1907), 177–8, Plate xlv.

67 P.M.C. Kermode, *Manx Crosses*, (1907), 176–7, No. 94.

68 A runic inscription from a keeill site at Rhyne Farm; P.M.C. Kermode, *Manx Crosses*, (1907), 208–9, No. 111.

69 E.L. Barnwell, 'Church furniture in Malew Church, Isle of Man', *Archaeologia Cambrensis*, XII, (1866), No. XLVIII, 472–6.

70 P.M.C. Kermode (1918), 21.

71 P.M.C. Kermode, *Manx Crosses*, (1907), 178–80, Plate XLVI, No. 96.

72 P.M.C. Kermode (1911), 15–19, Fig.14.

73 P.M.C. Kermode (1915), 10–19, Figs 9–16, 19–22, 25–30.

74 Personal commmunication A.C.C. Johnson.

75 P.M.C. Kermode (1918), Plate VI, Fig.8.

76 Marshall Cubbon, following Ralegh Radford, dates these arches to the early thirteenth century, cf. discussion in chapter 16 on medieval monasticism, this volume.

77 C.A. Ralegh Radford, 'St Patrick's Isle, Peel: The Medieval Ecclesiastical Remains and Excavations of 1962', *Proceedings of the Isle of Man Natural History and Antiquarian Society*, XI, (2004), 363–83.

78 R.A. Curphey, 'Peel Castle – Summer Excursion: June 1979', *Proceedings of the Isle of Man Natural History and Antiquarian Society*, (1984), IX, 64–7.

79 D. Freke *Excavations* (2002), Period 4, AD1200–1390.

80 G. Broderick 1995, *Cronica regum mannie and insularum*, Manx National Heritage, Douglas, f.46v.

81 cf. Curphey (1976).

82 Curphey (1976), Plate 58.

83 At Douglas some structures survived until the early eighteenth century Davey, in chapter 16 below, pp. 361–3.

84 But cf. Butler's interpretation of the same building in L.A.S. Butler, 'The Cistercian Abbey of St Mary of Rushen, Isle of Man: Excavations on the East Range, 1988–89', *Journal of the British Archaeological Association*, (2002), 155, 168–94, which is based on his reading of the *Site Guide*, without the benefit of the actual 1998 excavation evidence.

85 Barratt (1961), 210, Fig. 4.

86 J.R. Bruce, *The Friary Church of Bymacan: Notes on the Masonry and Construction*, unpublished MSS, (1964), MNHL MD 212, 6270.

87 The site is not known, but may well be in the same field as the chapel; a range of low earthworks are still visible in low sun. See E.M. Megaw, 'The cult of St Leonard and Manx medieval hospitals', *Journal of the Manx Museum*, (1976), VII, (88), 225–31.

88 In the same way to the people of the Sodor city and diocese.

89 R.A. Philpott and P.J. Davey, 'Peel Town sampling project 1985', in J.M. Lewis (ed.), *Peel Town: an archaeological and architectural assessment*, Isle of Man Government and University of Liverpool, (Douglas 1992), 55–74.

90 N.C. Johnson forthcoming, 'Rescue excavations at the IRIS site, Peel, 2000', in P.J. Davey (ed.), *Archaeological Research in the Isle of Man 1998–2000*, BAR, British Series.

91 D.A. Higgins, 'Excavations at Castle Rushen Stores, 1991–1992', in P.J. Davey, D.J. Freke and D.A. Higgins *Excavations in Castletown, Isle of Man, 1989–92*, Liverpool University Press, (1996), 49–125.

92 J. Roscow 'Castletown Cottages', in Davey *et al.*, *Excavations in Castletown*, 157–60.

93 e.g., A.C.C. Johnson, 'The Early Exploitation of the Upper Sulby Valley: a Field Survey', *Proceedings of the Isle of Man Natural History and Antiquarian Society*, (1998), X, 327–45; 'A Preliminary Gazetteer of Early Archaeological Remains in the Upper Sulby Valley'in P.J. Davey (ed.), *Recent Archaeological Research on the Isle of Man*, BAR British Series (1999), 278, 153–70; 'A View from the Hills: Some Thoughts on the Reoccupation of the Promontory Forts and the Possible Origins of the Manx Homestead', *Proceedings of the Isle of Man Natural History and Antiquarian Society*, (2000), XI, 51–66.

94 P.J. Davey, D.A. Higgins, N.C. Johnson, S.B. McCartan and J.J. Woodcock, *Kerrowdhoo, Bride, Isle of Man: fieldwork and excavations 1992–1994*, Centre for Manx Studies Research Report 4, Douglas.

95 P.S. Gelling (1964), 201, 202.

96 P.S. Gelling (1970), 75, Fig. 2.

97 A.C.C. Johnson, 'A View from the Hills: Some Thoughts on the Reoccupation of the Promontory Forts and the Possible Origins of the Manx Homestead', *Proceedings of the Isle of Man Natural History and Antiquarian Society*, (2000), XI, 51–66, reassesses the structures as well as reconsidering the relative status of Doarlish Cashen and the Braaid.

98 P.J. Davey *et al.*, (1997), 10–14.

99 *Ibid.*, 11, Site 15.

100 Laboratory reference Nos AA-28386 and AA-28387.

101 P.S. Gelling (1961); P.S. Gelling, 'Medieval Shielings in the Isle of Man', *Medieval Archaeology*, (1963a), VI–VII, 156–72, London; see also G. Quine, 'A Reconsideration of the Evidence of the Shieling in the Kingdom of Man and the Isles, with particular Reference to Man', unpublished PhD thesis, University of Durham, (1996); A.C.C. Johnson (1986); A.C.C. Johnson, 'Archaeological sites and fossil landscapes in the Isle of Man', *Proceedings of the Isle of Man Hill-Land Seminar*, (1997), 53–5. Manx Nature Conservation Trust; A.C.C. Johnson, 'The Early Exploitation of the Upper Sulby Valley: a Field Survey', *Proceedings of the Isle of Man Natural History and Antiquarian Society* (1998), X, 327–45; A.C.C. Johnson, 'A Preliminary Gazetteer of Early Archaeological Remains in the Upper Sulby Valley', in Davey, P.J., "Recent Archaeological Research on the Isle of Man", British Archaeological Reports (British Series) 278, (1999), 153–70; A.C.C. Johnson, 'A View from the Hills: Some Thoughts on the Reoccupation of the Promontory Forts and the Possible Origins of the Manx Homestead', *Proceedings of the Isle of Man Natural History and Antiquarian Society*, (2000), XI.

102 The preferred location of shieling huts and earlier roundhouses is usually, however, quite different: shielings tend to be much more closely associated with reliable water sources. The physical remains of typical shieling huts and roundhouses are also quite distinct.

103 The growth of corn during the short season at altitude is certainly possible, and presupposes the necessity to parch it before return to the lowland farms, but none of the three kilns excavated – at Block Eary, Injebreck and Doarlish Cashen – is entirely satisfactory. Later kilns exist at Forester's Lodge and Close Farm.

104 cf. D.J. Freke, *Excavations on St Patrick's Isle, Isle of Man, Prehistoric, Viking, Medieval and Later, 1982–88*, Liverpool University Press, (2002).

105 P.J. Davey, D.J. Freke and D.A. Higgins, *Excavations in Castletown, Isle of Man, 1989–92*, Liverpool University Press, (1996).

106 L.A.S. Butler, 'The Cistercian Abbey of St Mary of Rushen: Excavations 1978–79', *Journal of the British Archaeological Association*, (1988), 141,

60–104. L.A.S. Butler, 'Report on Excavations at Rushen Abbey: the East Range, 1988–89', *Journal of the British Archaeological Association*, (2002), 155, 168–94; P.J. Davey (ed.), Rushen *Abbey, Ballasalla, Isle of Man: First Archaeological Report*, Centre for Manx Studies Research Report, (1999), 7.

107 A.M. Cubbon,'Excavation of a medieval metalworking site, Braddan Vicarage 1966', *Proceedings of the Isle of Man Natural History and Antiquarian Society*, (1982–4), IX, 197–237.

108 E.H. Stenning, 'Ancient structures uncovered at Derbyhaven May 1935', *Proceedings of the Isle of Man Natural History and Antiquarian Society*, (1935–7), 4, 145–51.

109 P.J. Davey and N.C. Johnson, 'Pottery', in P.J. Davey D.J. Freke and D.A. Higgins 1996, *Excavations in Castletown, Isle of Man, 1989–92*, (1996), 16–22 and 65–88; P.J. Davey, 'Medieval and post-medieval continental ceramics from the Isle of Man', in P.J. Davey (ed.), *Recent archaeological research on the Isle of Man*, BAR British Series 278, (Oxford, 1999), 241–60; P.J. Davey 2000, 'Medieval and later pottery from the Isle of Man', *Proceedings of the Isle of Man Natural History and Antiquarian Society*, XI, 91–114; P.J. Davey, 'Identity and ethnicity: a ceramic case study from the Isle of Man', *Medieval Ceramics*, (2002), 24, 31–9; P.J. Davey 'The Pottery', in D.J. Freke, *Excavations at Peel Castle 1982–87*, Liverpool University Press, (2002).

110 P.J. Davey, 'The cultural affinities and dating of the ceramic finds', in P.J. Davey, D.A. Higgins, N.C. Johnson, S.B. McCartan and J.J. Woodcock, *Kerrowdhoo, Bride, Isle of Man: fieldwork and excavations 1992–1994*, Centre for Manx Studies Research Report 4, (Douglas, 1995), 61–2.

111 D.J. Freke and J. Graham-Campbell in Freke D.J. *Excavations at Peel Castle 1982–87* 'Metal artifacts' (2002).

112 G. Egan, 'Non-Ferrous Metal', in P.J. Davey *et al.*, *Excavations in Castletown*, (1996), 29–34.

113 P.J. Davey, 'The metalwork from the 1998 excavation', in Davey (ed.), *Rushen Abbey*, (1999), 62–3.

114 D.J. Freke, 'Iron', in D.J. Freke, *Excavations at Peel Castle 1982–87*, (2002), 317–19.

115 N.C. Johnson, 'Ironwork', in P.J. Davey, D.J. Freke and D. A. Higgins *Excavations in Castletown*, (1996), 29.

116 cf. her note in *Medieval Archaeology*, 28, 1984, 251.

117 R. Hurst-Vose, 'Vessel and Window Glass', in D.J. Freke *Excavations at Peel Castle 1982–87*, (2002).

118 Butler (1988), *op cit*, 99, Fig.17, No. 4.

119 K. Bornholdt, 'Coinage', this volume, chapter 18.

120 e.g., L.S. Garrad, 'Was pottery made in the Isle of Man in medieval times?, in P.J. Davey, *Medieval Pottery from Excavations in the north-west*, University of Liverpool, (1977), 109–12.

121 C.R. Cheney, 'Manx synodal statutes AD 1230(?) to 1351. Part 1: Introduction and latin text', *Cambridge Medieval Celtic Studies*, (1984), 7, 63–89.

122 G. Storm, *Exactions from the Norwegian Church Province to the Apostolic Chamber and College of Cardinals 1311–1523 from entries in the Papal Archives*, Special publication to His Majesty King Oscar II on the occasion of the Government Jubilee, (1897), Christiana. [Part translation from Norwegian (by J. Farrington) and latin (by W.R. Serjeant), 1956–7; Manx Museum Library F22/26].

123 P.M.C. Kermode *Proceedings of the Isle of Man Natural History and Antiquarian*

Society, New Series 1, 328–32.

124 G. Coppack and N.C. Johnson in preparation, 'The architectural fragments', in P.J. Davey (ed.), *Rushen Abbey, Ballasalla, Isle of Man: Second Archaeological Report*, Centre for Manx Studies.

125 Tomlinson P.R. 'Interim Report on the Larger Mammal Bones' 248–9, in D.J. Freke, *Excavations at Peel Castle 1982–87* (2002) *op cit.*; Crellin C. 'The Small Mammal Bones' 252–7, in *ibid*; Fisher C. 'The Bird Bones' 250–1, in *ibid*. A.R. Hutchinson and A.K.G. Jones, 'The Fish Remains' 258–61, in *ibid*; N. McMillan, 'The Molluscs' 262–3, in *ibid*.

126 P.J. Davey 1996, 'Molluscs', in P.J. Davey, D.J. Freke and D.A. Higgins, *Excavations in Castletown*, 151–4.

127 P.R. Tomlinson 1999, 'Biological Evidence from the 1998 excavations at Rushen Abbey', in P.J. Davey (ed.) *Rushen Abbey*, 72–6.

128 e.g., *De granis decimalibus* in Bishop Simon's Synodal Ordinances, *Manx Society*, xviii, 51. The implication of this is that each rector had his own store in which to receive the grain tithes, 'for the greater convenience of the bailiffs'.

129 e.g., Dhoo Valley core No. 44, Innes 1995, 11–13.

130 Grain production on the Island began early in the Neolithic; a recent C14 date for cereal pollen at Ballachrink, Jurby is one of the oldest in north-west Europe cf. P.J. Davey and J.B. Innes 2003, 'The Early Neoliothic and the Manx Environment', in I. Armit, E. Murphy, E. Nelis and D. Simpson (eds), *Neolithic Settlement in Ireland and Western Britain*, Oxbow Books, Oxford, 120–7. At Peel Castle a huge Iron Age grain store that had been destroyed by fire was uncovered cf. P.R. Tomlinson 'The charred cereal deposit', in P.R. Tomlinson, E.P. Allison, J.B. Innes and H.K. Kenward, 'Environmental evidence from the prehistoric period', in Freke, *Excavations* (2002).

131 e.g., D. Sylvester, *The historical atlas of Cheshire*, Cheshire Community Council, (Chester, 1958), 28–9 for Cheshire; G. Youd, 'The common fields of Lancashire', *Transactions of the Historical Society of Lancashire and Cheshire*, (1962), 113, 1–41 for Lancashire; J. Lewis, *Sefton rural fringes survey*, Archaeological Survey of Merseyside, (Liverpool, 1982), 70–87 for Sefton; G. Jones, 'Medieval settlement', in J. Manley, S. Grenter and F. Gale, *The archaeology of Clwyd*, Clwyd County Council, (1991), 186–202.

132 F. Mitchell, *Reading the Irish landscape*, Country House, (Dublin, 1986) 173–9.

133 F. Mitchell and M. Ryan, *Reading the Irish landscape*, Townhouse, (Dublin, 1997) 309–11, Fig.155d.

134 e.g., R. Newman, *The archaeology of Lancashire*, Lancaster University Archaeological Unit, (Lancaster, 1996), 109–17.

135 cf. J. Spurgeon, 'Mottes and moated sites', in J. Manley, S. Grenter and F. Gale (eds), *The archaeology of Clwyd*, Clwyd County Council, (1991), 157–72.

136 e.g., G. Stell, *Dumfries and Galloway*, The Stationery Office, (Edinburgh, 1996), 102–25, 'Castles and towers'.

137 e.g., in Merseyside cf. J. Lewis 'Medieval landscapes and estates', in P.R. Tomlinson and M. Warhurst (eds), *The archaeology of Merseyside*, *Journal of the Merseyside Archaeological Society*, (1991), 7.

138 cf. G. Broderick, *Chronica regum Mannie and insularum*, Manx National Heritage, (Douglas, 1995), f.53r.

139 G. Broderick, *Chronica regum Mannie and insularum*, Manx National Heritage, (Douglas, 1995), f.54v.

140 cf. R. Moore, 'The origins of the Manx land system debate', in P.J. Davey (ed.), *Recent archaeological research on the Isle of Man*, British Archaeological

Reports, British Series, (1999), 278, 175–6.

141 cf. P.J. Davey, J.J. Blackford, R.C. Chiverrell, J.B. Innes and P.R. Tomlinson, 'The curragh and other lowland wetlands of the Isle of Man', in M. Atherden (ed.), *Wetlands in the landscape: archaeology, conservation, heritage*, PLACE, (York, 2001), 12–40.

21 *Conclusion*
Man: The Medieval Legacy

TIM THORNTON

In some ways the medieval heritage of the Isle of Man seems relatively uncomplicated. The structure of these volumes, inevitably artificial, implies a significant break in Manx history at 1405/6. In doing so it implies that the Stanley lordship is in some way the major legacy of the preceding period, whether as fundamental continuity or discontinuity. Of course in many ways it was. By 1406, some form of English lordship had been in place for over half a century. One of the greatest factors for continuity in Manx history for pretty much the whole of the following 400 years was the Stanley lordship, its successors in the house of Athol and the repercussions of its end. There was direct dynastic continuity as far as 1594, and even then, despite the intervention of the crown and the competing claims of Alice, the dowager countess, and her daughters, Earl William's countess, and their son James, eventually managed to reassert a lordship which differed little from that of William's brother and father.[1] The Stanleys even achieved a succession before 1594 hindered by only one minority, that of the third earl, Edward, from 1521 to 1530.[2] The terms of their grant of lordship, which in turn followed closely those of the previous English lords examined in this volume, remained the framework for Manx government and politics, and, because of the extensive rights they exercised, for much of Manx social and economic life too.[3]

In addition, the Stanleys' close relationship with the English crown, which echoed the strong bonds between Henry Beaumont and Edward II, William Montacute I and Edward III, and William le Scrope and Richard II, remained a factor in the politics of these islands, through the fifteenth century and even more so in the sixteenth century, as closer kinship ties were developed with the Tudors.[4] As so much of the historiography of the last two centuries has emphasised, a major legacy of the medieval period was a powerful relationship between the island and the English crown, and between island society and economy and the society and economy of England, especially that of the north-west which remained the heartland of the Stanley connection.[5]

Yet to leave the story there would be very misleading. In many ways the end of this volume ushers in not some new phase in Manx history, one of greater continuities, but a continued instability which was itself a product of the medieval heritage. Stanley lordship was not uncontested – either in the context of English politics, or the relationship of the island with the Scots. The legacy of the changes of lordship described here in the fourteenth century, and in particular the more or less violent discontinuities of the passage from Salisbury to Scrope, from Scrope to Percy, and from Percy to Stanley, made for the continuing tensions of the fifteenth century between Scrope and Stanley.[6] They also provided more than a simple excuse for the way the island was treated by Elizabeth and James when the otherwise sure succession of Stanley son to Stanley father broke down in 1594.[7]

More generally, the unresolved nature of the Scottish interest in Man, and the English interest in Scotland, meant that far from settling under an uncomplicatedly English hierarchy of secular authority, the island remained awkwardly Scottish in so many of its political and constitutional associations, yet with an English noble as sovereign under the overlordship of an English king.[8] This meant that in moments of tension between England and Scotland – and even some moments of calm – the position of Man was debated in terms of this continuing Scottishness.[9] There was a distinct sense of purpose behind the resurrection of the Scottish claim to Man by James II in 1455 through his son Alexander, and the resulting raid and counter raid of 1456–7 had lasting impact on the consciousness both of the island and of south west Scotland.[10] It was therefore unsurprising that Anglo-Scottish hostilities in 1482–3, prominently involving Thomas, lord Stanley, should be perceived as, in part, involving a threat to the island, or that in 1513 potentially and in 1533 in fact Anglo-Scottish wars resulted in threats to Man.[11] Even the accession of James VI of Scotland to the English throne would not completely resolve the situation, given the tensions that emerged over the 'union' of the two kingdoms.[12]

This lasting instability originating from the Anglo-Scottish wars of the fourteenth century was particularly obvious in the ecclesiastical sphere. Before the schism, the church had continued to operate a relatively unified structure across territories with different lords.[13] The schism, in which English and Scottish rulers sided with different popes, played a role in reformulating the boundaries of ecclesiastical jurisdiction along lines more closely tied to *de facto* political divisions. The appearance in 1387, in the person of Bishop Michael, of a separate bishop for the Scottish portion of the diocese, was a major step in this direction.[14] Yet well into the sixteenth century the fact that Man, with the cathedral at Peel, was no longer under Scottish rule had not been accepted as final and therefore as grounds for the erection of a permanent new head of the diocese of the Isles. In 1498, more than a century after the effective division of the diocese, it was proposed that Iona should be the official seat of the Scottish bishop, but even then explicitly only as a temporary base, until 'his principal kirk in the Ile of Man be recoverit from Inglismen'.[15] Even this was not conclusive, with subsequent bishops simply holding the abbacy *in commendam* until the Scottish Reformation.[16] In 1472 metropolitan authority over the Scottish diocese was reallocated to St Andrews from Trondheim, which in some senses intensified the problem, although Norwegian authority had for some time been largely theoretical.[17] What might seem to us a rationalisation along 'national state' boundaries still left contemporaries describing complexity. Writing under the Tudors, Polydore Vergil noted the primacy over Scotland granted to the archbishop of St. Andrews in 1470, and the opposition to this voiced by Richard Neville from York; he included in the list of bishops over whom St. Andrews gained authority Sodor, but noted that the bishop's see was placed in Man, 'which ys thowght to be of the diocesse of York'.[18] Even well into the sixteenth century there was an occasional tendency to hark back to the medieval unity of the Irish Sea province, at least in its ecclesiastical aspect. In 1549, when Donald Monro, archdeacon of the Isles, toured his diocese, he still included Man as the first of the Western Isles.[19]

The events of the fourteenth century and the grants of 1405/6 had not therefore closed the island to the complex and multifarious influences which had characterised the medieval period. In the case of Scotland, more specifically, one important external influence remained that of Galloway. If the first period of Scottish rule, and especially the crushing of the rebellion of 1275, increased the influence of Galloway over the island, in the period after 1406 that influence remained important. The ecclesiastical connections fostered with Whithorn at the earlier period continued to have a real meaning through to the time of the Reformation;[20] even longer lasting were the economic and social ties between the two territories, with Galloway retaining for centuries a role as a key trading partner with the island.[21]

We can look more broadly too. The struggles of the fourteenth century left Man in the position of being a Scandinavian/Celtic/French/English borderland – a vulnerable and in some cases highly dangerous position, but also one which allowed for very fertile cultural interactions. To an extent, the solidification of ultimate English overlordship after 1400 reduced the potential for these interactions, but the stultifying nature of Stanley rule should not be overemphasised. The hugely widespread pattern of contacts which the island enjoyed before about 1080 was never fully renewed, but the relative isolation of the subsequent period was not replaced by a simple unilinear tie to England. The pattern of interaction even grew, with the increasing presence in the Irish Sea of, for example, Breton and Spanish interests.[22]

There are some more sturdy and concrete legacies to consider. In terms of language, the medieval period left the island as a stronghold of Gaelic. Norse had made little impact on the language of the mass of the islanders, and although English certainly made progress beyond the immediate ranks of officialdom and settlers under the Stanleys, and although there was little if any official support for the Manx language until the late eighteenth century, the need for island clergy to use Manx well into the seventeenth century demonstrates the hold of the language.[23] This also shows itself in the durability of the Manx place-names: it may be that some 'Scandinavianisation' took place, with the English administrators of the Stanleys (many of whom themselves came from areas of strong Danish and Norse influence) finding Scandinavian elements more easily understood, but there was little if any attempt to sweep away the Manx names which those administrators found.

Additionally, the medieval period left the island with its most impressive architectural expressions of civil and ecclesiastical power. Peel and Castle Rushen remained the most important civil buildings in the island until the nineteenth century, and even then Rushen in particular remained the centre of administration and justice for the island. Ruined as it was, St German's cathedral represented the bishopric in its most concrete form.

In memory and imagination, the medieval period provided a dynamic and unstable bequest to the island in the form of a reputation for association with mystery. The tales of Manx interests in magic and contacts with spirits, whether fairies or those of the dead, lived on. In a broader sense, the island retained and developed a liminal role, being seen as standing on the hazy boundary between the securely defined bounds of Britain and the far less substantial zones of the 'wild Irish' and beyond. That was the image possessed by many in England, even in the relative propinquity of the north-west and marches, as mentions of the island in the ballad literature suggest.[24] So it appeared, too, to visitors from and observers in continental Europe.[25] To the Spanish in the mid-late sixteenth century, amongst a British Isles heavy with prophetic expectations, the island seemed to possess particular supernatural significance.[26] One reason for this was the legacy of the chronicles. The texts most closely associated with the island were not continued to the end of the fourteenth century, and they had no significant successors of a similar kind for many decades.[27] In the absence of such a successor, much of the approach to the Manx past remained an approach to the period of the chronicles. Equally, the chronicle sources left by outsiders, and especially the *Polychronicon* of Ranulph Higden, had a powerful influence in sustaining an image of the Isle of Man which had its origins in the early fourteenth century and before.[28]

In some ways, however, it has been the malleability of the medieval legacy in Man which has made it so powerful. Without the density of documentary record and physical heritage to be found, for example, in England, which might have acted as a level of constraint on differing perceptions of the past, the centuries in Man covered by this volume have remained a highly fertile ground for the creative mind. This was true of the nineteenth century, when the efforts of the scholars such as A.W. Moore, associated with poets and novelists like Christopher Shimmin, T.E. Brown and Thomas H. Hall Caine achieved a gaelicisation of the island's culture. It was true too of artists like Archibald Knox. On the other hand, even as Irish nationalism meant Gaelic culture might become associated with violent dissent, it was possible for the culture of English tourism to season the hedonism of the dance hall and the TT track with some of the mystical and magical hues of a different and less threatening Manx medievalism.[29] So much of debate on the future of the island was (and still is) bound with a discussion of its medieval past, ultimately of whether the Manx were the sons of Orry or of Manannan.[30]

Notes

1 Moore, *Isle of Man*, i. 223–7; Kinvig, *Isle of Man*, 96–8; Barry Coward, *The Stanleys, Lords Stanley and Earls of Derby 1385–1672: The Origins, Wealth and Power of a Landowning Family*, Chetham Society, 3rd ser., 30 (1983), chapter 4; Joanna M. Williams 'The Stanley Family of Lathom and Knowsley, *c.* 1450–1504: A Political Study' (unpubl. MA dissertation, Manchester University, 1979), part 1; Katharine Walker, 'The widowhood of Alice Spencer, Countess Dowager of Derby, 1594–1636', *Transactions of the Historic Society of Lancashire and Cheshire*, 149 (2000, for 1999), 1–17.

2 Edward Stanley was a minor in wardship, but the regime did not use the opportunity to make any significant changes to the government of the island. Moore, *Isle of Man*, i. 218–19; PRO, SC6/HenryVIII/5676.

3 For the grants of 1405/6: *Foedera* (ed. T. Rymer) (3rd edn, 10 vols, London, 1739–45), iv/1. 90; *CCR, 1405–1409*, 2; *CCR, 1402–1405*, 525 (recognisance of 11 August 1405 to surrender the grant before Michaelmas next); *CPR, 1405–1408*, 201–2. Coward, *Stanleys*, 99–106; Moore, *Isle of Man*, i. 224–5.

4 G.E. C[okayne], *The Complete Peerage*, rev. Vicary Gibbs and others (13 vols in 14, London, St Catherine Press, 1910–59), iv. 205–14; xii/1. 248–51; Coward, *Stanleys*, chapter 1; Williams, 'Stanley family'; Michael K. Jones and Malcolm G. Underwood, *The King's Mother: Lady Margaret Beaufort, Countess of Richmond and Derby* (Cambridge, 1992), 58–60, 64–5, 144–54; Moore, *Isle of Man*, i. 211–23.

5 Most notably the work of Moore and Kinvig; cf. for economic and social connections, J.R. Dickinson, *The Lordship of Man under the Stanleys: Government and Economy in the Isle of Man, 1580–1704*, Chetham Society, 3rd ser., 41 (1996).

6 Contested by Stephen Scrope, B.L., Additional Charters 8482, 18, 267; cf. the order by Edward IV that John, lord Scrope should not use the arms of Man until after the 1475 French campaign, when a challenge to his doing so by Thomas, lord Stanley would be considered: B.L., Lansdowne MS 872, f.16 (*Foedera*, v/3. 60; *CPR, 1467–1477*, 529; Oliver, *Monumenta*, 24 (misdated to 1476)).

7 B.L., Lansdowne MS 82, f.26; *Calendar of State Papers, Domestic Series, of the Reigns of Edward VI, Mary, Elizabeth I and James I Preserved in the State Paper Department of Her Majesty's Public Record Office*, Robert Lemon and Mary Anne Everett Green (eds), (12 vols, London, 1856–72), *1595–1597*, 155; *1603–1610*, 359, 604; John Parr (1690), *An Abstract of the Laws, Customs, and Ordinances of the Isle of Man*, James Gell (ed.) (Manx Society, XII, 1867), 37–53; Coward, *Stanleys*, 45; Moore, *Isle of Man*, i. 224–5, 228–30.

8 Tim Thornton, 'Scotland and the Isle of Man, *c.*1400–1625: Noble power and royal presumption in the Northern Irish Sea province', *SHR*, 77 (1998), 1–30.

9 T. Thornton, 'The alleged French raid on the Isle of Man, 1377', *Northern History*, 35 (1999), 208–13.

10 Placed in 1507 by Moore, *Isle of Man*, i. 217–18; Kinvig, *Isle of Man*, 97, due to an error in transcription in their source, the Traditionary Ballad: R.L. Thomson, 'The Manx Traditionary Ballad', *Études Celtiques*, 10 (1962–3), 60–87, at 76–8. Nor was this, as Kinvig and Moore suggest, a response to an uprising among the Manx; the ballad refers to a 'troubling of the people', probably disturbance caused by the Scottish raid: 78. The raid is more accurately placed in the Stanley poem, *Palatine Anthology: A Collection of Poems and Ancient Ballads Relating to Lancashire and Cheshire*, J.O. Halliwell-Phillips (ed.), (London, 1850), 225. B.R.S. Megaw, 'The Scottish Invasion of Man in 1456', *JMM*, VI (1957), 23–4; Christine McGladdery, *James II* (Edinburgh, 1990), 100; Norman Macdougall, *James III: A Political Study* (Edinburgh, 1982), 42; Annie I. Dunlop, *The Life and Times of James Kennedy, Bishop of St. Andrews* (Edinburgh, 1950), 176–7, 202; *ERS* (23 vols, Edinburgh, 1878–87), vi. 204, 349.

11 1482–3: *Palatine Anthology*, 239; 1513: Matthew P. McDiarmid, 'Sir David Lindsay's report of the sack of Carrickfergus 1513', *Studies in Scottish Literature*, 9 (1971–2), 40–7; 1533: *Calendar of State Papers, Venice, 1527–1533*, item 956.

12 Sir Henry Savile, 'Historicall Collections', in *The Jacobean Union: Six Tracts of 1604*, Bruce R. Galloway and Brian P. Levack (eds), Scottish History Society, 4th ser., 21 (1985), 184–239, at pp.209–10; Robert Pont, 'Of the Union of Britayne', *Jacobean Union*, 1–38, at p.1; Sir Thomas Craig, 'De Unione Regnorum Britanniae Tractatus', C. Sanford Terry (ed.), (Scottish History Society, LX, 1909), 364–8.

13 E.g., the dispatch of letters confirming the election of William as bishop of Sodor in 1349 to the clergy and people of the diocese, the archbishop of Trondheim, William Montacute, Robert Stewart of Scotland, lord of the isle of Bute, and John Macdonald, lord of the Isles: *Papal Letters: 1342–1362*, W.H. Bliss and C. Johnson (eds) (Calendar of Entries in the Papal Registers relating to Great Britain and Ireland, III; London, 1897), 279.

14 Broderick *CKMI*, f.51v.; *Calendar of Papal Letters to Scotland of Clement VII of Avignon, 1378–1394*, Charles Burns (ed.), Scottish History Society, 4th ser., 12 (1976), 130 (provision, 15 July 1387); D.E.R. Watt, *Fasti Ecclesiae Scoticanae medii aevi ad annum 1638: Second Draft* (St Andrews, 1969), 197, 202–3.

15 *Registrum Secreti Sigilli Regum Scotorum: The Register of the Privy Seal of*

Scotland (8 vols in 9, Edinburgh, 1908–82), i (1488–1529), no. 184; I.B. Cowan, 'The Medieval Church in Argyll and the Isles', *Records of Scottish Church History Society*, XX (1978), 15–29, at p.17; Dunlop, *Life and Times of James Kennedy*, 191; John Dowden, *The Bishops of Scotland: Being Notes on the Lives of all the Bishops, under each of the Sees, Prior to the Reformation*, ed. J. Maitland Thomson (Glasgow, 1912), 290.

16 Watt, *Fasti Ecclesiae Scoticanae*, 207–8; *Highland Papers*, J.R.N. Macphail (ed.), 4 vols, Scottish History Society, 2nd ser., V, XII, XX; 3rd ser., XXII (1914–34), iv. 185–8.

17 *Vetera monumenta Hibernorum et Scotorum historiam illustrantia*, Augustin Theiner (ed.), (Rome, 1864), no. 852; Watt, *Fasti Ecclesiae Scoticanae*, p. 197; *Acts of the Lords of the Isles, 1336–1493*, Jean Munro and R.W. Munro (eds), Scottish History Society, 4th ser., 22 (1988), lv–lvi; R.G. Cant, 'Norse influence in the organisation of the medieval church in the Western Isles', *Northern Studies*, XXI (1984), 1–14.

18 Polydore Vergil, *Anglicae historiae libri xxvi* (Basel, 1534), 153 (*Three Books of Polydore Vergil's English History, Comprising the Reigns of Henry VI., Edward IV., and Richard III*, Henry Ellis (ed.), Camden Society, o.s. 29 (1844), 135–6).

19 *Monro's Western Isles of Scotland and Genealogies of the Clans, 1549*, R.W. Munro (ed.), (Edinburgh and London, 1961), 13–15, 46, 49, 62.

20 In 1472, the pope appointed Alan Hobuntar, a friar preacher, to the vicarage of Holy Trinity by Ramsey, allegedly occupied for the previous nine or ten years by Michael Magbrayar, a Premonstratensian canon; Alan was to be transferred to the priory of St Ninian immediately on getting possession: *Papal Letters: 1471–1484*, J.A. Twemlow (ed.), (Calendar of Entries in the Papal Registers relating to Great Britain and Ireland, XIII/i; London, 1955), 324. Whithorn enjoyed possessions, spiritual and temporal, in the Isle of Man well into the sixteenth century, although the Stanleys were in a position to dictate the choice of farmer and steward: *Correspondence of Edward, Third Earl of Derby*, T. Northcote Toller (ed.), Chetham Society, n.s., XIX (1890), 120.

21 Jeffrey Galloway, who settled in Castletown *c.* 1590, may be seen trading to Liverpool in the records of that port, but we can be fairly confident that it was in his eponymous homeland that he did much of his business; and John Martin, a Scot operating in Ramsey, definitely made frequent ventures to south-west Scotland, 1590–1620: J.R. Dickinson, 'Aspects of the Isle of Man in the Seventeenth Century' (unpublished PhD thesis, Liverpool University, 1991), 300–2. After the Restoration, vessels departing from Manx ports accounted for about 10 per cent of the heavy goods-carrying ships that traded into Dumfries and Kirkcudbright (figures from 1673–91, where port of departure known): Christopher Smout, 'The foreign trade of Dumfries and Kirkcudbright, 1672–1696', *Transactions of the Dumfriesshire and Galloway Natural History and Antiquarian Society*, 3rd ser., xxxvi (1960 for 1958–9), 36–47, at p.41. Galloway's influence evoked fear in the Irish Sea into the sixteenth century: Henry Bradshaw, *The Life of Saint Werburge of Chester*, Carl Horstmann (ed.), Early English Text Society, o.s., lxxxviii (1887), 157, 166.

22 Spain: *Chester Customs Accounts, 1301–1566*, K.P. Wilson (ed.), Record Society of Lancashire & Cheshire, 111 (1969). Although the island was just too far north, and just too far outside profitable opportunities for privateering, to be subject to Turkish piracy in the way that Lundy, for example, became in the seventeenth century. *Calendar of State Papers, Domestic Series, of the Reign of Charles I... Her Majesty's Public Record Office*, John Bruce, William Douglas Hamilton and

Sophia Crawford Lomas (eds), (23 vols., London, 1858–97), 1625–26, pp. 86, 89; 1633–34, pp. 157–58; A.F. Langham, *The Island of Lundy* (Stroud, 1994), 37.

23 George T.O. Bridgeman, *History of Wigan*, 4 vols, Chetham Society, n.s. 15–18 (1888–90), ii. 372–3; *A Description of the Isle of Man: with some useful and entertaining reflections on the laws, customs, and manners of the inhabitants* by George Waldron (1731), W. Harrison (ed.), (Manx Society, XI, 1865), 17–18; Victor Edward Durkacz, *The Decline of the Celtic Languages: A Study of Linguistic and Cultural Conflict in Scotland, Wales and Ireland from the Reformation to the Twentieth Century* (Edinburgh, 1983), 107, 214–29.

24 E.g. 'The Turke and Gowin', in *Bishop Percy's Folio Manuscript: Ballads and Romances*, John W. Hales and Frederick J. Furnivall (eds), (3 vols, London, 1867–8), I, 88–102, esp. pp.95, 102.

25 *Calendar of State Papers, Venice, 1534–1554*, 354 (*assai nominata e grande*; 1551).

26 Geoffrey Parker, 'The place of Tudor England in the messianic Vision of Philip II', *Transactions of the Royal Historical Society*, 6th ser., 12 (2002), 167–221; Albert J. Loomie, 'An Armada pilot's survey of the English Coastline, October 1597', *Mariner's Mirror*, 49 (1963), 288–300, at p.292.

27 E.g., Broderick, *CKMI*, f.50r.

28 John Taylor, *The 'Universal chronicle' of Ranulf Higden* (Oxford, 1966); *The Cronicles of Englond … Taken oute of Higden's Policronicon* ([Westminster]: [William Caxton], [1480]), and subsequent editions; Raphael Holinshed, *Chronicles of England, Scotland and Ireland* (6 vols, London, 1807–8), 66.

29 John Belchem, 'The Little Manx Nation: art, ethnic identity, and home rule politics in the Isle of Man, 1880–1918', *Journal of British Studies*, 39 (2000), 217–40.

30 I borrow this, via John Belchem, from the phrase 'we are King Orry's men still', in Thomas Henry Hall Caine, *The Little Manx Nation* (London, 1891), 46–9.

Volume 3 Abbreviations

ACA
The Annals of Connacht, M. Freeman (ed.) (Dublin 1944).
AFM
The Annals of the Kingdom of Ireland by the Four Masters, J. O'Donovan (ed.) (7 vols, Dublin 1848–51).
ALC
The Annals of Loch Cé, W.M. Hennessy (ed.), *Rolls Series*, 54 (2 vols, London 1871; facsimile Dublin 1939).
AI
The Annals of Innisfallen, S. Mac Airt (ed.) (Dublin 1951).
APS
The Acts of the Parliaments of Scotland, T. Thomson & C. Innes (eds) (12 vols, Edinburgh 1814–75).
AU
The Annals of Ulster (to A.D. 1131), S. Mac Airt & G. Mac Niocaill (eds), (Dublin 1983), and thereafter W.M. Hennessy and B. MacCarthy (eds) (4 vols, Dublin 1887–1901).
Anderson, *Scottish Annals*
Scottish Annals from English Chroniclers A.D.500 to 1286, A.O. Anderson (ed.) (Edinburgh 1908).
Anderson, *Early Sources*
Early Sources of Scottish History A.D. 500 to 1286, A.O. Anderson (ed.) (2 vols, Edinburgh 1922).
BAR
British Archaeological Reports, Oxford.
Bekker-Nielsen *et al.* (eds), *Eighth Viking Congress*
H. Bekker-Nielsen, P. Foote & O. Olsen (eds), *Proceedings of the Eighth Viking Congress, Århus, 24–31 August 1977* (Odense 1981).
B.L.
British Library, London.
Broderick, *CKMI*
G. Broderick (ed.), *Cronica Regum Mannie & Insularum. Chronicles of the Kings of Man and the Isles* (Douglas 1979; 2nd edn, 1995).
Broderick, *PNIM*
G. Broderick, *Placenames of the Isle of Man* (7 vols, Tübingen 1994–2005).
CDI
Calendar of Documents relating to Ireland (1171–1307), H.S. Sweetman (ed.) (5 vols, London 1875–86).
CDS
Calendar of Documents relating to Scotland preserved in Her Majesty's Public Record Office, London (1108–1509), J. Bain (ed.) (vols 1–4, London, 1881–88); G.G. Simpson and J.D. Galbraith (eds) (vol. 5, Edinburgh 1988).

ChR
Calendar of Charter Rolls (1226–1517), PRO (London 1903–1927).
CCR
Calendar of Close Rolls (1272–1509), PRO (London 1892–1963).
CCW
Calendar of Chancery Warrants (1230–1326), PRO (London 1927).
CFR
Calendar of Fine Rolls (1272–1413), PRO (London 1911–33).
CPR
Calendar of Patent Rolls (1216–1586), PRO (London 1894–2002).
CS
Chronicum Scotorum, W.M. Hennessy (ed.), *Rolls Series*, 46 (London 1866; repr. Wiesbaden, 1964).
Coucher Book of Furness
The Coucher Book of Furness Abbey, J.C. Atkinson & J. Brownbill (eds), 2 vols in 6 parts, Chetham Soc., new ser, 9, 11, 14, 74, 76 and 78, 1886–1919.
Davey (ed.), *Man and Environment*
P. Davey (ed.), *Man and the Environment in the Isle of Man*, BAR (British Series) 54 (Oxford 1978).
Duffy, 'Irishmen and Islesmen'
S. Duffy, 'Irishmen and Islesmen in the kingdoms of Dublin and Man, 1052–1171', *Ériu* 43 (1992), 93–133.
Duncan & Brown
A.A.M. Duncan & A.L. Brown, 'Argyll and the Isles in the Earlier Middle Ages', *Proceedings of the Society of Antiquaries of Scotland*, 90 (1956–7), 192–220.
EHR
English Historical Review.
ERS
Exchequer Rolls of Scotland (1326–1600), J. Stuart & G. Burnett (eds) (23 vols, Edinburgh 1878–1908).
Fell *et al.* (eds), *The Viking Age in the Isle of Man*
C. Fell, P. Foote, J. Graham-Campbell & R. Thomson (eds), *The Viking Age in the Isle of Man: Select Papers from the Ninth Viking Congress, Douglas, Isle of Man 1981* (London 1983).
Foedera
Foedera, Record Commission edn (3 vols, London 1816–30).
Johnsen, 'Payments from the Hebrides'
A.O. Johnsen, 'The payments from the Hebrides and the Isle of Man to the crown of Norway 1153–1263. Annual ferme or feudal casualty?', *SHR*, 48 (1969), 18–34.
JMM
Journal of the Manx Museum, 88 numbers, Douglas (1924–1980).
Kinvig, *Isle of Man*
R.H. Kinvig, *The Isle of Man. A Social, Cultural and Political History* (Liverpool 1975).
Kneen
J.J. Kneen, *The Place-Names of the Isle of Man with their Origin and History* (6

vols, Douglas 1925–8; repr. 1970, in one vol.).
Megaw, 'Norseman and native'
B. Megaw, 'Norseman and Native in the Kingdom of the Isles' *Scottish Studies*, 20 (1976), 19–20.
MNHL
Manx National Heritage Library, Douglas.
Moore, *Isle of Man*
A.W. Moore, *A History of the Isle of Man* (2 vols, London 1900).
NAI
National Archives of Ireland, Dublin.
NTSV
Norsk Tidsskrift for Sprogvidenskap.
Oliver, *Monumenta*
Monumenta De Insula Manniae, J.R. Oliver (ed.), Manx Society, 4, 7, 9 (Douglas 1860–2).
Ó Cuív, 'A poem in praise of Raghnall'
B.Ó. Cuív, 'A poem in praise of Raghnall, king of Man', *Éigse*, 8 (1955–57), 288–89.
PSAS
Proceedings of the Society of Antiquaries of Scotland.
PRO= TNA
Public Record Office, London.
Proceedings
Proceedings of the Isle of Man Natural History and Antiquarian Society.
Scotichronicon
Scotichronicon by Walter Bower in Latin and English, D.E.R. Watt *et al.* (eds) (9 vols, Aberdeen and Edinburgh, 1987–98).
Sellar, 'Hebridean sea kings'
W.D.H. Sellar, 'Hebridean sea kings: the successors of Somerled, 1164–1316', in *Alba: Celtic Scotland in the Medieval Era* (East Linton 2000), 187–218.
SHR
Scottish Historical Review.
SRO
Scottish Record Office, Edinburgh.
TNA The National Archive, London, formerly the PRO.
Wilson (ed.), *Register of St Bees*
J. Wilson (ed.), *The Register of the Priory of St. Bees*, Surtees Society (Durham & London 1915).

Bibliography: editions of primary sources and earlier printed texts

A Description of the Isle of Man by George Waldron (1731), W. Harrison (ed.), Manx Society, 11 (1865).

A History of the English Church and People by the Venerable Bede (731), L. Sherley-Price & R.E. Latham (eds) (Harmondsworth 1968).

A Scottish Chronicle Known as the Chronicle of Holyrood, Anderson M.O. (ed.) (Edinburgh 1938).

A short treatise of the Isle of Man, digested into six chapters, by James Chaloner, one of the commissioners under Lord Fairfax, for settling the affairs of the Isle of Man in 1652; and afterwards Governor of the island, from 1658 to 1660. Originally published in 1656, as an appendix to 'King's Vale Royal of England; or, the County Palatine of Chester, illustrated, J.G. Cumming (ed.), Manx Society, 10 (1864).

Acts of the Kings of the English by William of Malmesbury (1241), W. Stubbs (ed.), *Rolls Series* 90 (London 1887–9).

Acts of the Lords of the Isles, 1336–1493, J. & R.W. Munro (eds), *Scottish History Society*, 4:22, 1988.

Ágrip af Nóregskonunga sogum, Fagrskinna–Nóregs konunga tal, B. Einarsson (ed.), *Íslenzk Fornrit*, 29 (Reykjavik 1985).

Aided Con Roi, R.I. Best (ed.), *Ériu* 2, 1905, 20–31.

Altrom Tige Dá Medar, M.E. Dobbs (ed.), *Zeitschrift für Celtische Philologie* 18, 1930, 189–230; L. Duncan (ed.), *Ériu* 11, 1932, 184–225.

An Abstract of the Laws, Customs, and Ordinances of the Isle of Man by John Parr (1690), J. Gell (ed.), Manx Society, 12 (Douglas 1867).

An Account of the Isle of Man by William Sacheverell (1702), J.C. Cummings (ed.), Manx Society, I (Douglas 1859).

Anglicae historiae libri xxvi by Vergil Polydore (1534); *Three Books of Polydore Vergil's English History, Comprising the Reigns of Henry VI, Edward IV, and Richard III*, H. Ellis (ed.) (Camden Society, old ser 29, 1844).

Anglo-Scottish Relations 1174–1328: Some Selected Documents, E.L.G. Stones (ed.) (London 1965).

Annales Cambriae, J. ab Ithel (ed.), *Rolls Series*, 20 (London 1860).

Annales Furnesiensis: history and antiquities of Furness Abbey, T.A. Beck (ed.) (London 1844).

Betha Colaim Chille by Manus O'Donnell (1532), A. O'Kelleher & G. Schoepperl (eds) (Urbana, Illinois 1918).

Brenhinedd y Saesson, or the Kings of the Saxons, T. Jones (ed.), Board of Celtic Studies, University of Wales History & Law Series (Cardiff 1971).

Brennu-Njáls saga, E.O. Sveinsson (ed.), *Íslenzk Fornrit*,12 (Reykjavik 1954).

Britannia by William Camden (1588), R. Gough (ed.) (London 1806).

Brut y Tywysogyon; or The Chronicle of the Princes. Peniarth MS. 20 version, T. Jones (ed.), Board of Celtic Studies, University of Wales History & Law Series, 11 (Cardiff 1952).

Brut y Tywysogyon; or, The Chronicle of the Princes, Red Book of Hergest Version, T. Jones (ed.), Board of Celtic Studies, University of Wales History and Law Series, 16 (Cardiff 1955).

Calendar of Chancery Warrants (London 1927).

Calendar of the Close Rolls (London 1892–1963).

Calendar of Documents relating to Ireland, H.S. Sweetman (ed.) (London 1875–86).

Calendar of Documents relating to Scotland preserved in Her Majesty's Public record Office, London, 1–4, J. Bain (ed.) (London 1881–88); 5, G.G. Simpson & J.D. Galbraith (eds) (Edinburgh 1988).

Calendar of Entries in the Papal Registers relating to Great Britain and Ireland, Papal Letters, Vol. 1, A.D. 1198–1304, W.H. Bliss & J.A.Twemlow (eds) (London 1893, repr.1971).

Calendar of Entries in the Papal Registers relating to Great Britain and Ireland: Petitions, 1342–1419, W.H. Bliss (ed.) (London 1896).

Calendar of Entries in the Papal Registers relating to Great Britain and Ireland: Papal Letters III: 1342–1362, W.H. Bliss & C. Johnson (eds) (London 1897).

Calendar of Fine Rolls (London 1911–1962).

Calendar of entries in the Papal Registers relating to Great Britain and Ireland, xiii, *Papal Letters 1471–1484*, J.A. Twemlow (ed.) (London 1955).

Calendar of Papal Letters to Scotland of Clement VII of Avignon, 1378–1394, C. Burns (ed.), Scottish History Society, 4:12, 1976.

Calendar of Patent Rolls (London 1891–1916).

Calendar of recognizance rolls of the palatinate of Chester, part I, appendix to the *Thirty-Sixth Report of the Deputy Keeper of Public Records* (London 1875).

Calendar of State Papers, Domestic Series, of the Reigns of Edward VI, Mary, Elizabeth I and James I Preserved in the State Paper Department of Her Majesty's Public Record Office, R. Lemon & M.A.E. Green (eds) (London 1856–72).

Calendar of State Papers, Domestic Series, of the Reign of Charles I, 1625(–1649), Preserved in the State Paper Department of Her Majesty's Public Record Office, J. Bruce, W.D. Hamilton, & S.C. Lomas (eds) (London, 1858–97).

Calendar of State Papers and Manuscripts Relating to English Affairs, Existing in the Archives and Collections of Venice and in other Libraries in Northern Italy, 1527–1533, R.L. Brown (ed.) (London 1871).

Calendar of State Papers and Manuscripts Relating to English Affairs, Existing in the Archives and Collections of Venice and in other Libraries in Northern Italy, 1534–1554, R.L. Brown (ed.) (London 1873).

Cartulaire de l'ancienne Estaple de Bruges, L.G. van Severen (ed.) (Bruges 1904–8).

Chartularies of St Mary's Abbey, Dublin, J.T. Gilbert (ed.), *Rolls Series* (London 1882–3).

Chester Customs Accounts, 1301–1566, K.P. Wilson (ed.), Record Society of Lancashire & Cheshire, 111, 1969.

Chronica de Mailros, J. Stevenson (ed.) (Edinburgh 1835).

Chronica Monasterii Sancti Albani, H.T. Riley (ed.), *Roll Series* (London 1866).

Chronica Regum Manniae et Insularum, P.A. Munch (ed.) (Christiania 1860).

Chronicle of Man and the Sundreys, P. Munch (ed.), Manx Society (Douglas 1874).

Chronicles of Edward I and Edward II, W. Stubbs (ed.), *Rolls Series* (London 1882–3).

Chronicles of England, Scotland and Ireland by Raphael Holinshead (1557), J. Johnson (ed.) (London, 1807–8).
Chronicles of the Reigns of Stephen, Henry II, and Richard I, R. Howlett (ed.), *Rolls Series*, 82 (London 1884–9).
Chronicles of the Revolution, 1397–1400, C. Given-Wilson (ed.) (Manchester 1993).
Chronicon by Adam of Usk (c1421), E.M. Thompson (ed.) (London 1904).
Chronicon de Lanercost, J. Stevenson (ed.) (Edinburgh 1839).
Chronicon Galfridi le Baker de Swynebroke, E.M. Thompson (ed.) (Oxford 1889).
Chronicon Regum Manniae et Insularum: The Chronicle of Man and the Sudreys, D. Goss (ed.), The Manx Society, 22 (Douglas 1874).
Chronicum Scotorum, W.M. Hennessy (ed.), *Rolls Series*, 46 (London 1866; repr. Wiesbaden 1964).
Chronique by Adémar of Chabannes (c1028), J. Chavanon (ed.) (Paris 1897).
Chronique de la Traison et Mort de Richart Deux Roy Dengleterre, B. Williams (ed.) (London 1846).
Codex Frisianus (known as *Fríssbók*), C.R.Unger (ed.) (Christiania 1871).
Cóir Anmann, W. Stokes W. & Windisch E.(eds), *Irische Texte*, 3:2, 285–444 (Leipzig 1895).
Correspondence of Edward, Third Earl of Derby, T. Toller (ed.), Chetham Society, new ser., 19, 1890.
Cronica Regum Mannie et Insularum, G. Broderick (ed.) (Douglas 1979; 2nd edn, 1995).
Danakonunga sogur, B. Guðnason (ed.), *Íslenzk fornrit,* xxxv (Reykjavik 1982).
Danorum Regum Heroumque Historia, Books x–xvi, by Saxo Grammaticus (c1220), E. Christiansen (ed.), 1980–1, BAR int ser 84 (London 1980–1).
De Locis Sanctis by Adomnán (c690), B. Meehan (ed.) (Dublin repr. 1983).
De unione regnorum Britanniae tractatus by Sir Thomas Craig (c1605), C. S. Terry (ed.), Scottish History Society, 60, 1909.
Diplomatarium Norvegicum, C.A. Lange *et al.* (eds) (Christiania 1849–1995).
Documents illustrating the Overseas Trade of Bristol in the Sixteenth Century, J. Vanes (ed.) (Bristol 1979).
Documents Illustrative of the History of Scotland, J. Stevenson (ed.) (Edinburgh 1870).
Duanaire Finn, E. Mac Néill (ed.) (Dublin 1904).
Early Irish Myths and Sagas, G. Gantz (ed.) (New York 1981).
Early Scottish Charters prior to A.D. 1153, A.C. Lawrie (ed.) (Glasgow 1905).
Early Sources of Scottish History A.D. 500 to 1286, A.O. Anderson (ed.) (Edinburgh 1922).
Ecclesia Scoticana, D.E.R. Watt (ed.), *Series Episcoporum Ecclesiae Catholicae Occidentalis*, 6:1, 1994.
Eirspennill: AM 47 fol., F. Jónsson (ed.) (Christiania 1918).
English Historical Documents c. 500–1042, D. Whitelock (ed.) (London 1979).
Exactions from the Norwegian Church Province to the Apostolic Chamber and College of Cardinals 1311–1523 from entries in the Papal Archives, Storm G. (ed.) (Christiana 1897).
Exchequer Rolls of Scotland, J. Stuart & G. Burnett (eds) (Edinburgh 1878–1908).
Expugnatio Hibernica by Giraldus Cambrensis (1188), A.B. Scott & F.X. Martin (eds) (Dublin 1978).

Eyrbyggja saga, E.O. Sveinsson & M. Þórðarson M. (eds) (Reykjavík 1935).
Fasti Ecclesiae Scoticanae edii aevi ad annum 1638, D.E.R. Watt & A.L. Murray (eds) (Edinburgh 2003).
Fasti Ecclesiae Scoticanae medii aevi ad annum 1638: Second Draft, D.E.R.Watt (ed.) (St Andrews 1969).
Flateyjarbók, G. Vigfússon & C. Unger C. (eds) (Copenhagen 1860–8).
Foedera, T.Rymer (ed.) (London 1816–30).
Fragmentary Annals of Ireland, J.N. Radner (ed.) (Dublin 1978).
Gesta Hammaburgensis ecclesiae Pontificum by Adam of Bremen, B. Schmeidler (ed.) (Hanover 1917).
Gesta Regis Henrici Secundi by Benedict of Peterborough (c1192), W. Stubbs (ed.), *Rolls Series*, 49 (London 1867).
Giraldi Cambrensis Opera Omnia, J.S. Brewer *et a.l* (eds), *Rolls Series*, 21 (London 1861–91).
Ågrip af Nóregs konungasogum: A Twelfth-Century Synoptic History of the Kings of Norway, M.J. Driscoll (ed.) (London 1995).
Hákonar saga Hákonarsonar etter Sth. 8 fol., AM 325 viii 4° og AM 304 4°, M. Mundt (ed.), Norsk Historisk Kjeldeskrift-Institutt, *Norrøne tekster* 2 (Oslo 1977).
Handlist of the Acts of Alexander III, The Guardians, John, 1249–1296, G.G. Simpson (ed.) (Edinburgh 1960).
Heimskringla by Snorri Sturluson (c1235), E. Monson & A.H. Smith (eds) (Cambridge 1932; repr. New York, 1990); Aðalbjarnarson B. (ed.), *Íslenzk Fornrit* xxvi–xxviii (Reykjavik 1941–51); L.M. Hollander (ed.) (Austin 1964); S. Laing (ed.), Everyman, revised edn (London 1961–4).
Highland Papers, J.R.N. Macphail (ed.), Scottish History Society, 2nd ser, 5, 12, 20; 3rd ser, 22, 1914–34.
Historia Anglicana by Thomas Walsingham (c1422), H.T. Riley (ed.), *Rolls Series* (London, 1863–4).
Historia Ecclesiastica Gentis Anglorum by the Venerable Bede (731), C. Plummer (ed.) (Oxford 1896).
Historia Hiersolymitana by Albertus Aquensis (1121), *Recueil des Historiens des Croisades*, 4, 675–78 (Paris 1879).
Historia Norvegiae, I. Ekrem & L.B. Mortensen (eds) (Copenhagen 2003).
Historiae Dunelmensis Scriptores Tres, J. Raine (ed.), Surtees Society, 8, 1839.
Historians of the Church of York, J. Raine (ed.), *Rolls Series*, 71 (London 1879–94).
Historic and Municipal Documents of Ireland, AD 1172–1320, J.T. Gilbert (ed.), *Roll Series* (London 1870).
History and Topography of Ireland by Gerald of Wales (1188), J.J. O'Meara (ed.) (London 1985).
History of Gruffydd ap Cynan, A. Jones (ed.) (Manchester 1910).
History of Ireland by Jeoffrey Keating (c1634), P.S. Dinneen (ed.), Irish Texts Society, 7, 1908.
History of the Kings of Britain by Geoffrey of Monmouth (1138), L. Thorpe (ed.) (London 1966).
Hrafns saga Sveinbjarnarsonar, G.P. Helgadóttir (ed.) (Oxford 1987).
Icelandic Sagas, G. Vigfusson (ed.), *Rolls Series* (London 1887–94).

Immram Brain: Bran's journey to the land of women, S. Mac Mathúna (ed.) (Tübingen 1985).
Insulae Britannicae by Adam of Bremen (c1072), B. Schmeidler (ed.), *Gesta Hammaburgensis Ecclesiae Pontificum* (Hanover 1917).
Inventaire des archives de la ville de Bruges, L.G. van Severen (ed.) (Bruges 1871–2).
Islandske Annaler indtil 1578, G. Storm (ed.) (Christiania 1888).
Islendingabók, Landnámabók, J. Benediktsson (ed.), *Íslenzk Fornrit*, 1 (Reykjavik 1968).
Íslenzkir Annálar in *Sturlunga Saga including the Islendinga Saga of Lawman Sturla Thordsson and other works*, G. Vigfusson (ed.) (Oxford 1878).
Jacobean Union: Six Tracts of 1604, B.R.Galloway & B.P. Levack (eds), The Scottish History Society, 4:21, 1985.
Jóns saga helga, Biskupa sögur, J. Sigurðsson *et al.* (eds) (Copenhagen 1858–78).
King Arthur's Death: Morte Arthure, Le Morte Arthur, B. Stone (ed.) (London 1988).
Konge Speilet, R. Keyser *et al.* (eds) (Christiania 1848).
Konungs Skuggsjá, L. Holm-Olsen L. (ed.), 1983, *Norsk-Historisk Kjeldeskrift-Institutt, Norrøne tekster*, 1 (Oslo 1983).
L'histoire de la congrégation de Savigny by Claude Auvry, A. Laveille (ed.) (Paris 1896–8).
La Practica della mercatura by Francesco Balducci Pegolotti (1471), A. Evans (ed.) (Cambridge, Mass. 1936).
Landnámabók. Book of Settlements, H. Pálsson & P. Edwards (eds) (Winnipeg, 1972).
Le Liber Censuum de L'Eglise Romaine, P. Fabre & L. Duchesne (eds) (Rome 1889).
Le Morte d'Arthur by Sir Thomas Malory, J. Lawlor & J. Cowen (eds) (London 1960).
Lebor Gabála Érenn parts 1–4, R.A.S. Macalister (ed.) (Dublin 1938–41).
Legislation by Three of the Thirteen Stanleys, Kings of Man, W. Mackenzie (ed.) (Douglas 1860).
Lex Scripta, G. Jefferson (ed.) (Douglas & London 1819).
Liber Luciani de laude Cestrie, M.V. Taylor (ed.), Lancashire and Cheshire Record Society, 1912.
Life of Columba by Adomnán, A.O. & M.O. Anderson (eds) (Oxford 1991).
Manx Synodal Statutes, C.R. Cheney (ed.), *Cambridge Medieval Celtic Studies*, 7 & 8, 1983–4.
Méliador by J. Froissart & A. Longnon (eds), Société des Anciens Textes Français (Paris 1895–9).
Memoranda de Parliamento, F.W. Maitland (ed.), *Rolls Series*, 98 (London 1893).
Monachi Sancti Albani, Chronica Majora by Matthew Paris (c1257), H.R. Luard (ed.), *Rolls Series*, 57 (London 1872–83).
Monumenta de Insula Manniae: Or, a Collection of National Documents Relating to the Isle of Man, III, J.R. Oliver (ed.), Manx Society, IX (Douglas 1862).
Monumenta Germaniae Historica: Scriptores, G.H. Pertz (ed.) (Hanover 1844).
Morkinskinna, F. Jónsson (ed.), *Samfund til udgivelse af gammel nordisk litteratur*, 53 (Copenhagen 1932).
Oidheadh Chloinne hUisneach, C. Mac Giolla Léith (ed.) (London 1993).
Orkneyinga saga, F. Guðmundsson (ed.), *Íslenzk Fornrit*, 34 (Reykjavik 1965);
H. Pálsson & P. Edwards (eds) (London 1978; Penguin edition 1981).

Polychronicon by Randulph Higden (c 1357), C.J. Babington & L.R. Lumby (eds) (London 1865–86); J. Taylor (ed.) (Oxford 1966).

Regesta Norvegica 2, 1264–1300, N. Bjorgo & S. Bagge (eds) (Oslo 1978).

Regesta Regum Scottorum, I. The Acts of Malcolm IV, King of Scots 1153–1165, G.W.S. Barrow (ed.) (Edinburgh 1960).

Regesta Sodorensia, E. Gunnes (ed.), *Regesta Norvegica I 822–1263* (Kjeldeskrift-fondet 1989).

Reginaldi monachi Dunelmensis libellus de admirandis beati Cuthberti, J. Raine (ed.), Surtees Society, 1 (1835).

Register of St Bees, J. Wilson (ed.), Surtees Society, 126 (London 1915).

Registrum Magni Sigilli Regum Scotorum, J.M. Thomson (ed.) (Edinburgh & London 1882–1914).

Registrum Secreti Sigilli Regum Scotorum: The Register of the Privy Seal of Scotland, M. Livingstone *et al.* (eds) (Edinburgh 1902–82).

Rental of Orkney by Lord Henry Sinclair (1492), W.P.L. Thomson (ed.) (Orkney 1996).

Rettelser til Hákonar saga Hákonarsonar etter Sth. 8 fol., AM325 viii 4º og AM 304 4º [Corrections], J. Knirk (ed.), Norsk-Historisk Kjeldeskrift-Institutt, *Norrøne tekster*, 2 (Oslo 1980).

Rotuli Parliamentorum 1272–1326, J. Strachey (ed.) (London 1767–1832).

Rotuli Scotiae, D. Macpherson, Record Commission (London 1814–19).

Rotulorum Patentium et Clausorum Cancellarie Hiberniae Calendarium, E. Tresham (ed.) (Dublin 1828).

Royal and other Historical Letters illustrative of the Reign of Henry III, W.W. Shirley (ed.), *Rolls Series*, 27 (London 1882–6).

Saga Ólafs Tryggvasonar af Oddr Snorrason munk, M. Rindal (ed.) (Oslo 1997).

Sanas Cormaic, K. Meyer (ed.) (London 1913).

Saxonis Gesta Danorum, J. Olrik, H. Ræder & F. Blatt (eds) (Copenhagen 1931–57).

Scotichronicon by Walter Bower (c 1421), D.E.R. Watt (ed.) (Aberdeen & Edinburgh 1987–98).

Scotichronicon; Regesta Regum Scotorum. V. The Acts of Robert I, A.A.M. Duncan (ed.) (Edinburgh 1988).

Scottish Annals from English Chroniclers A.D.500 to 1286, A.O. Anderson (ed.) (London 1908); reprinted M. Anderson (ed.) (Stamford 1991).

Scottish Historical Documents, G. Donaldson (ed.) (Edinburgh 1970).

Select Cases in the Court of King's Bench, G.O. Sayles (ed.), Selden Society 55, 57, 58, 74, 76, 82, 88 (London 1936–71).

Silva Gadelica, S.H. O'Grady (ed.) (London 1892).

Skálholtsbók yngsta, A. Kjær & L. Holm-Olsen (eds) (Christiania 1910–86).

Statuta Capitulorum Generalium Ordinis Cisterciensis, J.-M. (ed.) (Louvain 1933).

Sverris saga, G. Indrebø (ed.), Den Norske Historisk Kildeskriftkommission (Oslo 1920).

Symeonis Monachi Opera Omnia, T. Arnold (ed.) (London 1882–5).

Taxatio Ecclesiastica Angliae et Walliae Auctoritate P Nicholai IV, circa A.D. 1291, T. Astle, S. Ayscough & J. Caley (eds) (London 1802).

The Acts of Malcolm IV King of Scots 1153–1165, G.W.S. Barrow G.W.S. (ed.), *Regesta*

Regum Scottorum I, 131 (Edinburgh 1961).
The Acts of the Parliaments of Scotland, T. Thomson & C. Innes (eds) (Edinburgh 1814–75).
The Adventures of Art Son of Conn, and the Courtship of Delbchaem, R.I. Best (ed.), *Ériu*, 1901, 149–73.
The Annals of Connacht, A.M. Freeman (ed.) (Dublin 1944).
The Annals of Innisfallen, S. Mac Airt (ed.) (Dublin 1951).
The Annals of Loch Cé, W.M. Hennessy (ed.), *Rolls Series*, 54 (London 1871, facsimile Dublin 1939).
The Annals of the Kingdom of Ireland by the Four Masters, J. O'Donovan (ed.) (Dublin 1848–51).
The Annals of Tigernach, W. Stokes (ed.), *Revue Celtique*, 16–18, 1895–7 (repr. Lampeter 1993).
The Annals of Ulster, W.M. Hennessy & B. MacCarthy (eds) (Dublin 1887–1901); to A.D. 1131, S. Mac Airt & G. Mac Niocaill (eds) (Dublin 1983).
The Book of Leinster, R.I. Best & M.A. O'Brien (eds) (Dublin 1954–83).
The Bruce by John Barbour (1376), A.A.M. Duncan (ed.) (Edinburgh, 1997).
The Chartulary or Register of the Abbey of St Werburgh, Chester, J. Tait (ed.), Chetham Society, new ser, 79, 1920.
The Chronicle of England by John Capgrave (c1464), F.C. Hingeston (ed.), *Rolls Series* 1 (London 1858).
The Chronicle of Lanercost, H. Maxwell (ed.) (Glasgow 1913).
The Chronicle of Melrose from the Cottonian Manuscript, Faustina B.IX in the British Museum, A.O. & M.O. Anderson & W.C. Dickinson (eds) (London 1936).
The Coucher Book of Furness Abbey, J. Brownbill (ed.), Chetham Society, 74, 76, 78 (Manchester 1915–19).
The Coucher Book of Furness Abbey, J.C. Atkinson (ed.), Chetham Society (new ser, 9, 11, 14) (Manchester 1886–8).
The Dean of Lismore's Book (1529), T. M'Lauchlan & W.F. Skene (eds) (Edinburgh 1862).
The Diplomatic Correspondence of Richard II, E. Perroy (ed.), Camden Society, 3rd ser, 48, 1933.
The Dublin Guild Merchant Roll, c.1190–1265, P. Connolly & G. Martin (eds) (Dublin 1992).
The Earliest Norwegian Laws, L.M. Larson (ed.) (New York 1935).
The Gesta Normannorum Ducum by William of Jumièges (c1070) and Robert of Torigni (1139), E. van Houts (ed.) (Oxford 1992).
The history of English affairs by William of Newburgh (c1198), Book 1, P.G. Walsh & M.J. Kennedy (eds) (Warminster 1988).
The History of the Church of York 1066–1127 by Hugh the Chantor (c1139), C. Johnson (ed.) (London 1961).
The King's Mirror, L.M. Larson (ed.) (New York 1917).
The legend of St Christina by William Paris (c1399), G.H. Gerould (ed.), *Modern Language Notes*, 29, 1914, 129–33.
The Life of Saint Werburge of Chester by Henry Bradshaw, C. Horstmann (ed.), Early English Text Society, old ser, 88, 1887.

The Orkneyinga Saga, A.B. Taylo (ed.) (Edinburgh 1938).

The Patrician Texts in the Book of Armagh, L. Bieler (ed.) (Dublin 1979).

The Peterborough Chronicle 1070–1154, C. Clark (ed.) (Oxford 1958).

The Register of Holm Cultram, F. Granger & W.G. Collingwood (eds), Cumberland and Westmorland Antiquarian and Archaeological Society, Record Series, 7 (1929).

The Saga of Hacon and a Fragment of the Saga of Magnus with Appendices, G.W. Dasent (ed.), *Icelandic Sagas*, iv, *Rolls Series* (London 1894).

The Song of Dermot and the Earl, G.H. Orpen (ed.) (Oxford 1892).

The Statutes of the Isle of Man, Volume 1, from A.D.1414 to A.D. 1824, J.F. Gill (ed.) (London 1883).

The Tax Book of the Cistercian Order, A.O. Johnsen & P. King P. (eds) (Oslo 1979).

The Tri Thruaighe na Scéalaigheacht part 2, E. O'Curry (ed.), 1863, *Atlantis* 4, 113–240.

The Turke and Gowin, J.W. Hales & F.J. Furnivall (eds), *Bishop Percy's Folio Manuscript: Ballads and Romances* (London 1867–8).

The Voyage of Bran, K. Meyer (ed.) (London 1895).

Theodrici Monachi Historia de Antiquitate Regum Norwagiensium, G. Storm (ed.), *Monumenta Historica Norvegiæ: Latinske kildeskrifter til Norges historie i middelalderen* (Christiania 1880).

Thesaurus Palaeohibernicus, W. Stokes & J. Strachan (Cambridge 1901–3; repr. Dublin, 1975).

Tochmarc Luaine ocus Aided Athairne, W. Stokes (ed.), *Revue Celtique*, 24, 1903, 270–87; L. Breatnach (ed.), *Celtica*, 13 (1980), 1–31.

Tromdámh Guaire, M. Joynt (ed) (Dublin 1941).

Vetera monumenta Hibernorum et Scotorum historiam illustrantia, A. Theiner (ed.) (Rome 1864).

Vita Germani episcopi Autissiodorensis by Constantius of Lyons (c480), W. Levison (ed.), *Monumenta Germania Historia Scriptores Rerum Merovingicarum*, 7 (Hannover 1920).

Vita Patricii by Jocelyn of Furness (c1185), *Acta Sanctorum*, 17 March, Société des Bollandistes (Antwerp 1668), 540–80.

Voyage au Purgatoire de Saint Patrice, A. Jeanroy & A. Vignaux (eds), *Texts Languedociens du Quinzième Siècle*, Bibliothèque Méridionale, 1st ser, 8 (Toulouse 1903).

Monro's Western Isles of Scotland and Genealogies of the Clans by Donald Munro (1549), R.W. Munro (ed.) (Edinburgh and London 1961).

Gesta Regum Anglorum by William of Malmesbury (c1120), W. Stubbs (ed.), *Willelmi Malmesbiriensis Monachi De Gestis Regum Anglorum Libri Quinque*, *Rolls Series* 90 (London 1887–9).

Ypodigma Neustriae by Thomas Walsingham (c1419), H.T. Riley (ed.), *Rolls Series*, 28 (London 1876).

Bibliography: books and articles

Allen M., 2001, 'The Volume of the English Currency, 1158–1470', *Economic History Review* 54:4, 595–611.

Andersen P.S., 1991, 'When was regular, annual taxation introduced in the Norse islands of Britain? A comparative study of assessment systems in North-Western Europe', *Scandinavian Journal of History*, 16, 73–83.

Anon, 'Document No 6', *JMM*, 2:27, No 27, 21.

Armit I, 1996, *The Archaeology of Skye and the Western Isles* (Edinburgh).

Ashley A., 1958, *The Church in the Isle of Man*, St Anthony's Hall Publications 13 (York & London).

Bagge S., 1987, *The Political Thought of the King's Mirror*, Medieval Scandinavia Supplements 3 (Odense).

Bannerman J.W.M., 1974, *Studies in the History of Dalriada* (Edinburgh).

Barnwell E.L., 1866, 'Church furniture in Malew Church, Isle of Man', *Archaeologia Cambrensis*, XII, No XLVIII, 472–76.

Barratt J.K., 1965, 'The Franciscan friary at Bymacan', *JMM*, 6:80, 209–13.

Barrell A.D.M., 1995, *The Papacy, Scotland and Northern England, 1342–1378* (Cambridge).

Barrett J. H., (ed.), 2003, *Contact, Continuity and Collapse. The Norse Colonization of the North Atlantic* (Turnhout).

Barrow G.W.S., 1973, *The Kingdom of the Scots* (London).

Barrow G.W.S., 1981, *Kingship and Unity: Scotland 1000–1306*, New History of Scotland, vol. 2 (London).

Barrow G.W.S., 1988, *Robert Bruce and the Community of the Realm of Scotland*, 3rd edn (Edinburgh).

Barrow G.W.S., 1988, 'Badenoch and Strathspey, 1130–1312: 1. secular and political', *Northern Scotland*, 8, 1–15.

Barrow G.W.S., 1992, *Scotland and its Neighbours in the Middle Ages* (London).

Bartlett R., 1994, *The Making of Europe: Conquest, Colonization and Cultural Change, 950–1350* (London).

Batey C. & Graham-Campbell J., 1988, *Vikings in Scotland. An Archaeological Survey* (Edinburgh).

Batey C.E., Jesch J. & Morris C.D. (eds), 1993, *Caithness, Orkney and the North Atlantic* (Edinburgh).

Baylé M., 1990, 'Reminiscences Anglo-Scandinaves dans la sculpture romaine de Normandie', *Anglo-Norman Studies*, 13, 35–40.

Bean J.M.W., 1954, 'The Percys' acquisition of Alnwick', *Archaeologia Aeliana*, 4:32, 309–319.

Bean J.M.W., 1959, 'Henry IV and the Percies', *History*, 44, 212–27.

Bekker-Nielsen H., Foote P. & Olsen O. (eds), 1981, *Proceedings of the Eighth Viking Congress* (Odense).

Belchem J., 2000, 'The Little Manx Nation: Art, Ethnic Identity, and Home Rule Politics in the Isle of Man, 1880–1918', *Journal of British Studies*, 39, 217–40.

Bennett M.J., 1983, *Community, Class and Careerism. Cheshire and Lancashire Society in the Age of Sir Gawain and the Green Knight* (Cambridge).

Bennett M.J., 1997, 'The historical background', in D. Brewer and J. Gibson (eds), *The Gawain-Poet. A Companion* (Woodbridge), 71–90.

Bennett M.J., 1999, *Richard II and the Revolution of 1399* (Stroud).

Bennett M. J., 1997, 'The historical background', in Brewer D. & Gibson J. (eds), *The Gawain-Poet. A Companion* (Woodbridge), 71–90.

Bennett M.J., 2004, 'Sir John Stanley of Lathom, c. 1351–1414', *The Oxford Dictionary of National Biography*, 52, 226–27.

Bernard J., (ed.), 1968, *Navires et gens de mer à Bordeaux vers 1400–vers 1550* (Paris).

Bersu G., 1949, 'A promontory fort on the shore of Ramsey Bay, Isle of Man', *Antiquaries Journal*, 29, 62–79.

Bersu G.,1967, 'Excavation of the Cashtal, Ballagawne, Garwick, 1941', *Proceedings*, 7, 88–119.

Bersu G. & Wilson D.M., 1966, *Three Viking Graves in the Isle of Man*, The Society for Medieval Archaeology Monograph Series: No. I (London).

Beuermann I., 2002, *Man amongst kings and bishops- What was the reason for Godred Olafsson's journey to Norway in 1152/53?* Centre for Viking and Medieval Studies, University of Oslo, Occasional Papers 4/2002.

Blackburn M. & Pagan H., 1986, 'A revised check-list of coin hoards from the British Isles, c. 500–1100', in M.A.S. Blackburn (ed.), *Anglo-Saxon Monetary History* (Leicester), 291–313.

Blackburn M., 1996, 'Hiberno-Norse and Irish Sea imitations of Cnut's Quatrefoil Type', *British Numismatic Journal*, 156, 1–20.

Blackburn M., 2001, 'Expansion and Control: Aspects of Anglo-Scandinavian Minting South of the Humber', in Graham-Campbell *et al.* (eds), *Vikings and the Danelaw* (Oxford), 125–42.

Boardman S., 1996, *The Early Stewart Kings: Robert II and Robert III 1371–1406* (East Linton).

Bois G., 1984, *The Crisis of Feudalism: Economy and Society in Eastern Normandy c.1300–1550* (Cambridge).

Boon G., 1986, *Welsh Hoards 1979–81* (Cardiff).

Booth P.H.W., 1981, *The Financial Administration of the Lordship and County of Chester*, Chetham Society.

Bornholdt Collins K., 2003, *Viking-Age Coin Finds from the Isle of Man: A Study of Coin Circulation, Production and Concepts of Wealth during the Viking Age* (PhD thesis, Cambridge University).

Bornholdt Collins K., forthcoming, *Manx Museum, Douglas: Anglo-Saxon, Hiberno-Scandinavian, Hiberno-Manx and other Coins to 1280*, Sylloge of Coins of the British Isles (Oxford).

Bridgeman G. T. O., 1888–90, *History of Wigan* (4 vols, Chetham Society, n.s. 15–18).

Broderick G., 1981–2, 'The baronial possessions of Bangor and Saul in Man', *Bulletin of the Ulster Place-name Society*, Ser 2, 4, 24–26.

Broderick G., 1994–2005, *Placenames of the Isle of Man*, 7 vols (Tübingen).

Brook G.L., 1963, *Selections from Lagamon's Brut* (Oxford).

Brooke D., 1994, *Wild Men and Holy places: St Ninian, Whithorn and the Medieval*

Realm of Galloway (Edinburgh).

Broun D., 1999, 'Anglo-French acculturation and the Irish element in Scottish identity', in *Britain and Ireland 900–1300* in B. Smith (ed.), *Insular Responses to Medieval European Change* (Cambridge), 135–53.

Bruce J.R., 1964, *The Friary Church of Bymacan: Notes on the Masonry and Construction*, unpublished MSS, MNHL MD 212, 6270.

Bruce J.R., 1968, *The Manx Archaeological Survey, Sixth Report 1966: keeils and burial grounds in the sheading of Rushen*, Manx Museum and National Trust (Douglas).

Buhot J., 1936, 'Le Abbaye Normande de Savigny', *Le Moyen Age*, 46, 1–19.

Bush H., 1828, *Bristol Town Duties* (Bristol).

Butler L.A.S., 1988, 'The Cistercian Abbey of St Mary of Rushen: Excavations 1978–79', *Journal of the British Archaeological Association*, 141, 60–104.

Butler L.A.S., 2002, 'The Cistercian Abbey of St Mary of Rushen, Isle of Man: Excavations on the East Range, 1988–89', *Journal of the British Archaeological Association*, 155, 168–94.

Byock J., 1988, *Medieval Iceland: Society, Sagas and Power* (Berkeley).

Byrne F.J., 1973, *Irish Kings and High-Kings* (London).

Caine T.H., 1891, *The Little Manx Nation* (London).

Cameron A., 1894, 'Book of Clanranald', *Reliquiae Celticae: Texts, Papers and Studies in Gaelic Literature and Philology*, in A. MacBain and J. Kennedy (eds), 2 vols (Inverness), ii, 153–57.

Cant R.G., 1894, 'Norse Influence in the Organisation of the Medieval Church in the Western Isles', *Northern Studies*, 21, 1–14.

Carney J., 1950, *Poems on the O'Reillys* (Dublin).

Carpenter D. M., 1988, 'The pilgrim from Catalonia/Aragon: Ramon de Perellós, 1397', in M. Haren and Y. de Pontfarcy (eds), *The Medieval Pilgrimage to St Patrick's Purgatory, Lough Derg and the European Tradition* (Enniskillen), 99–119.

Carus Wilson E.M., 1933, 'The Iceland trade', in E. Power & M.M. Postan (eds), *Studies in English Trade in the Fifteenth Century* (London), 155–82.

Caxton W., 1480, *The Cronicles of Englond ... Taken oute of Higden's Policronicon*, (Westminster).

Chadwick N.K., 1962, 'The Vikings and the western world', in *Proceedings of the International Congress of Celtic Studies...1959*, B. Ó Cuív (ed.) (Dublin), 13–42.

Challis C.E. (ed.), 1992, *A New History of the Royal Mint* (Cambridge).

Chaplais P., 1994, *Edward II's Adoptive Brother* (Oxford).

Charles-Edwards T.M., 1972, 'Kinship, status, and the origins of the hide', *Past and Present*, 56, 3–33.

Chibnall M. (ed.), 1969–80, *The Ecclesiastical History of Orderic Vitalis* (6 vols, Oxford).

Christansen R.T., 1931, *The Vikings and Viking Wars in Irish and Gaelic Tradition* (Oslo).

Clancy T.O. (ed.), 1998, *The Triumph Tree: Scotland's earliest poetry, 550–1350* (Edinburgh).

Clarke H.B., Ní Mhaonaigh N. & Ó Floinn R. (eds), 1998, *Ireland and Scandinavia in the Early Viking Age* (Dublin).

Clouston J.S., 1918–9, 'Two features of the Orkney Earldom', *SHR*, 16, 15–28.

Clouston J.S., 1927–8, 'The Battle of Tankerness', *Proceedings of the Orkney Antiquarian Society*, 6, 21–25.

Clouston J.S., 1932, *A History of Orkney* (Kirkwall).

Cokayne G.E., 1910–59, *The Complete Peerage*, revised by V. Gibbs *et al.*, 12 vols (London).

Constable G., 1996, *The Reformation of the Twelfth Century* (Cambridge).

Coppack G. & Johnson N.C. in preparation, 'The architectural fragments', in P.J. Davey (ed.), *Rushen Abbey, Ballasalla, Isle of Man: Second Archaeological Report*, Centre for Manx Studies.

Coppack G., 1998, *The White Monks: The Cistercian Order in Britain 1128–1540* (Stroud).

Coppack G., 2002, 'The planning of Cistercian monasteries in the later middle ages: the evidence from Fountains, Rievaulx, Sawley and Rushen', in J.G. Clark (ed.), *The Religious Orders in Pre-Reformation England* (Woodbridge), 208–9.

Cormack M., 1994, 'Saints and sinners: reflections on death in some Icelandic sagas', *Gripla*, 8, Rit Stofnunar Árna Magnússonar á Islandi, 187–218.

Cosgrove A. (ed.), 1982, *A New History of Ireland 11: Medieval Ireland 1169–1534* (Oxford).

Cowan E.J., 1982, 'Caithness in the Sagas', in *Caithness. A Cultural Crossroads*, J.R. Baldwin (ed.), Scottish Society for Northern Studies (Edinburgh), 27.

Cowan E.J., 1990, 'Norwegian Sunset – Scottish Dawn: Hakon IV and Alexander III, 1249–1286', in *Scotland in the Reign of Alexander III*, N.H.Reid (ed.) (Edinburgh), 103–131.

Cowan I.B., 1978, 'The Medieval Church in Argyll and the Isles', *Records of Scottish Church History Society*, XX, 15–29.

Cowan I.B. & Easson D.E., 1976, *Medieval Religious Houses, Scotland*, 2nd edn (London).

Coward B., 1983, *The Stanleys, Lords Stanley and Earls of Derby 1385–1672: The Origins, Wealth and Power of a Landowning Family* (Chetham Society, 3rd ser, 30).

Craigie W.A., 1897, 'Gaelic words and names in the Icelandic sagas', *Zeitschrift für Celtische Philologie*, 1, 439–54.

Crawford B.E., 1987, *Scandinavian Scotland* (Leicester).

Crawford B.E., 1991, 'Caithness', in *Series episcoporum ecclesiae catholicae occidentalis ab initio usque ad annum MCXCVIII*, 6:1, Ecclesia Scoticana, D. E. R. Watt (ed.) (Stuttgard), 29–31.

Crawford B.E., 1996, 'Bishops of Orkney in the eleventh and twelfth centuries: bibliography and bibliographical lists', *Innes Review*, 47, 1–13.

Crawford B.E., 1996, 'Holy Places in the British Isles. Some Parallels to Selja', in *Two Studies on the Middle Ages*, M.Rindal (ed.), KULT's Skrifterie, 66, 22.

Crawford B.E., 1998, 'St. Magnus and St. Rognvald, the Two Orkney Saints', *Records of the Scottish Church History Society*, 28, 23–38.

Crawford B.E., 2003, 'Orkney in the Middle Ages', in *The Orkney Book*, D. Omand (ed.) (Edinburgh), 64–80.

Crawford B.E., 2004, 'Harald Maddadson, earl of Caithness and earl of Orkney

(1133/4–1206) magnate', *New Dictionary of National Biography*, 101049351.
Crawford B.E. (ed.), 1995, *Scandinavian Settlement in Northern Britain* (Leicester).
Crawford B. forthcoming, 'The earls of Orkney and the Hebrides', in *Gall-Ghaidheil: the Western Isles in the Viking World*, M. MacLeod & C. Batey (eds).
Crellin M., 1969, 'An early manorial roll', *JMM*, 7:85, 98–9.
Crozier A., 1988, 'On the transparency of place-names in Ireland, England, and Sweden', *Ainm*, 3, 42–58.
Cubbon A.M., 1971, 'The medieval chapel of St Mary's, Castletown later the Castletown Grammar School', *Proceedings*, 7:3, 307–42.
Cubbon A.M., 1982, 'The Early Church in the Isle of Man', in S.M. Pearce (ed.), *The Early Church in Western Britain and Ireland*, BAR British Series 102, 257–82.
Cubbon A.M., 1982–4, 'Excavation of a medieval metalworking site, Braddan Vicarage 1966', *Proceedings*, 9, 197–237.
Cubbon A.M., 1980, 'The 1972 Kirk Michael Viking treasure trove. The hoard: its discovery, composition and general historical implications', *JMM*, 8:89, 5-ll.
Cubbon A.M., 2000, 'A remarkable decade of Manx coin hoards, 1972–1982', *Proceedings*, 11:1, 29–50.
Cubbon W., 1936, 'History of Rushen Abbey, Ballasalla, Isle of Man, to 1134', *Proceedings*, 4, 98–115.
Cuív B.Ó., 1955–57, 'A poem in praise of Raghnall, king of Man', *Éigse*, 8, 288–89.
Cunliffe B., 2001, *Facing the Ocean: The Atlantic and Its Peoples* (Oxford).
Curphey R.A., 1982, *Ancient Centres of Government on the Isle of Man* (Douglas).
Curphey R.A., 1984, 'Peel Castle - Summer Excursion: June 1979', *Proceedings*, 9, 59–94.
Davey P.J., 2000 'Identity and ethnicity: a ceramic case study from the Isle of Man', *Medieval Ceramics*, 24, 31–39.
Davey P.J., 2000, 'Medieval and later pottery from the Isle of Man', *Proceedings*, 11, 91–114.
Davey P.J. (ed.), 1977, *Medieval Pottery from Excavations in the north-west* (Liverpool).
Davey P.J. (ed.), 1978, *Man and Environment in the Isle of Man*, BAR, British Series 54 (Oxford).
Davey P.J. (ed.), 1999, *Rushen Abbey, Ballasalla, Isle of Man: second archaeological report*, Centre for Manx Studies Research Report 7 (Douglas).
Davey P.J. (ed.), 1999, *Recent Archaeological Research in the Isle of Man*, BAR, British Series 278 (Oxford).
Davey P.J. *et al*, 1995, *Kerrowdhoo, Bride, Isle of Man: fieldwork and excavations 1992–1994*, Centre for Manx Studies Research Report 4, Douglas,
Davey P.J., Freke D.J. & Higgins D.A., 1996, *Excavations in Castletown, Isle of Man, 1989–92*, (Liverpool).
Davey P.J. *et al.*, 2001, 'The curragh and other lowland wetlands of the Isle of Man', in M Atherden (ed.), *Wetlands in the landscape: archaeology, conservation, heritage*, Place, York, 12–40.
Davey P.J. & Finlayson D. (eds), 2002, *Mannin Revisited: Twelve Essays on Manx Culture and Environment* (Edinburgh).
Davey P.J. & Innes J.B., 2003, 'The Early Neolithic and the Manx Environment', in I.

Armit, E. Murphy, E. Nelis & D. Simpson (eds), *Neolithic Settlement in Ireland and Western Britain* (Oxford), 120–27.

Davey P.J. & Roscow J., 2010, *The Dissolution of Rushen Abbey*, Isle of Man Natural History and Antiquarian Society Monograph.

Davies E., 1956, 'Treens and quarterlands: a study of the land system of the Isle of Man', *The Proceedings of the Institute of British Geographers*, 22, 97–116.

Davies R.R., 1971, 'Richard II and the principality of Chester, 1397–9', in F.R.H. Du Boulay and C.M. Barron (eds), *The Reign of Richard II. Essays in Honour of May McKisack* (London), 256–79.

Davies R.R., 1980, *Domination and Conquest: the Experience of Ireland, Scotland and Wales 1100–1300* (Cambridge).

de hÓir É, 1972–3, 'The anglicisation of Irish place-names', *Onoma*, 17, 192–204.

Dickinson J.C. 1965, *History of Furness Abbey*, Ministry of Works Guide (London).

Dickinson J.R., 1991, *Aspects of the Isle of Man in the Seventeenth Century* (PhD thesis, Liverpool University).

Dickinson J.R., 1996, *The Lordship of Man under the Stanleys: Government and Economy in the Isle of Man, 1580–1704* (Chetham Society, 3rd ser, 41).

Dickinson W.C., 1977, *Scotland from the earliest Times to 1603*, 3rd edn, A.A.M. Duncan (ed.) (Oxford).

Diverres A.H., 1965, 'The geography of Britain in Froissart's *Méliador*', in *Medieval Miscellany presented to Eugène Vinaver by Pupils, Colleagues and Friends*, F. Whitehead, A.H. Diverres & F.E. Sutcliffe (eds) (Manchester), 97–112.

Dolley M., 1969, 'New light on the 1894 Douglas hoard', *JMM*, 7:85, 121–24.

Dolley M., 1975, 'The pattern of Viking-Age coin hoards from the Isle of Man', *Seaby's Coin and Medal Bulletin*, 296–302, 337–340.

Dolley M., 1975, 'Some preliminary observations on three Manx coin-hoards appearing to end with pennies of Edgar', *Spink and Son's Numismatic Circular*, 83, 146.

Dolley M., 1976, 'A Hiberno-Manx coinage of the eleventh century', *Numismatic Chronicle*, 136, 75–84.

Dolley M., 1976, *Some Irish Dimensions to Manx History* (Queen's University Belfast, New Lecture Series, No. 92).

Dolley M., 1980, 'The numismatic element of the hoard, and a possible historical context', *JMM*, 8:89, 11–20.

Dolley M., 1983, 'Toponymic surnames and the pattern of pre-1830 English immigration into the Isle of Man', *Nomina*, 7, 47–64.

Dolley R.H.M., 1980, 'Some insular(?) imitations from the 1030s of contemporary English pence of Cnut', *Spinks and Son's Numismatic Circular*, 88, 86.

Donkin R.A., 1978, *The Cistercians: studies in the geography of medieval England and Wales*, Pontifical Institute of Medieval Studies (Toronto).

Douch R., 1950, *The career, lands and family of William Montague, earl of Salisbury, 1330–1344* (MA thesis, London).

Dowden J., 1912, *The Bishops of Scotland: Being Notes on the Lives of all the Bishops, under each of the Sees, Prior to the Reformation* (Glasgow).

Du Boulay, F.R.H. & Barron, C. M. (eds), 1971, *The Reign of Richard II. Essays in Honour of May McKisack* (London).

Duby G., 1982, 'The culture of the knightly class, audience and patronage', in R.L. Benson & G. Constable (eds), *Renaissance and Renewal in the Twelfth Century* (Harvard, repr. Toronto, 1991).

Duffy S., 1991, 'The Bruce Brothers and the Irish Sea World, 1306–29', *Cambridge Medieval Celtic Studies*, 21, 55–86.

Duffy S., 1991, 'The 'Continuation' of Nicholas Trevet: a new source for the Bruce invasion', *Proceedings of the Royal Irish Academy*, 91, 303–15.

Duffy S., 1992, 'Irishmen and Islesmen in the kingdoms of Dublin and Man', 1052–1171, *Ériu*, 43, 93–133.

Duffy S., 1993, *Ireland and the Irish Sea Region, 1014–1318* (PhD thesis, University of Dublin).

Duffy S., 1995, 'The first Ulster plantation: John de Courcy and the men of Cumbria', in T. Barry *et al.* (eds), *Colony and Frontier in Medieval Ireland* (London).

Duffy S., 1999, 'John and Ireland: the origins of England's Irish problem', in S.D. Church (ed.), *King John: New Interpretations* (Woodbridge).

Dugdale D.S., 1998, *Manx Church Origins* (Llanerch).

Dugdale W., 1675, *The Baronage of England* (London).

Dumville D., 1997, *The Churches of North Britain in the First Viking-Age*, Fifth Whithorn Lecture (Whithorn).

Duncan A.A.M., 1975, *Scotland: The Making of the Kingdom* (Edinburgh).

Duncan A.A.M., 1988, *'Honi soit qui mal y pense:* David II and Edward III, 1346–52', *SHR*, 67, 113–41.

Duncan A.A.M. & Brown A.L., 1956–7, 'Argyll and the Isles in the earlier Middle Ages', *PSAS*, 90, 192–220.

Dunlop A.I., 1950, *The life and times of James Kennedy, Bishop of St. Andrews* (Edinburgh).

Durkacz V.E., 1983, *The Decline of the Celtic Languages: A Study of Linguistic and Cultural Conflict in Scotland, Wales and Ireland from the Reformation to the Twentieth Century* (Edinburgh).

Dyer C., 1989, *Standards of Living in the Later Middle Ages: social change in England c.1200–1520* (Cambridge).

Dyer C., 1997, 'Peasants and coins: the uses of money in the Middle Ages', *British Numismatic Journal*, 67, 30–47.

Easson A.R., 1986, *Systems of Land Assessment in Scotland before 1400* (PhD thesis, University of Edinburgh).

Ebel E., 1977, 'Kaufmann und Handel auf Island zur Sagazeit', *Hansische Geschichtsblätter*, 95,

1–26.

Ekwall, E., 1922, *The Place-Names of Lancashire* (Manchester).

Ervik Ø., 1993 *Kirkearkeologi og Kirkekunst. Studier tilegnet Sigrid og Håkon Christie* (Laksevåg).

Esty W., 1986, 'Estimation of the size of a coinage: a survey and comparison of methods', *Numismatic Chronicle*, 146, 185–215.

Etchingham C., 1999, *Church Organisation in Ireland, AD 650–1000* (Maynooth).

Etchingham C., 2001, 'North Wales, Ireland and the Isles: the Insular Viking Zone', *Peritia*, 14,145–87.

Evans D.S. (ed.), 1990, *A Mediaeval Prince of Wales: the Life of Gruffydd ap Cynan* (Lampeter).

Fell C., Foote P., Graham-Campbell J. & Thomson R. (eds), 1983 *The Viking Age in the Isle of Man*, (London).

Fellows-Jensen G., 1972, *Scandinavian Settlement Names in Yorkshire*, Navnestudier 11 (Copenhagen).

Fellows-Jensen G., 1983, 'Anthroponymical specifics in place-names in *-bý* in the British Isles', *Studia Anthroponymica Scandinavica*, 1, 44–60.

Fellows-Jensen G., 1983, 'Scandinavian settlement in the Isle of Man and Northwest England: the place-name evidence' , in Fell *et al* (eds), *The Viking Age in the Isle of Man* (London 1983), 37–452.

Fellows-Jensen G., 1985, *Scandinavian Settlement Names in the North-West*, Navnestudier, 25 (Copenhagen).

Fellows-Jensen G., 1992, 'Scandinavian place-names in the Irish Sea province', in J. Graham-Campbell (ed.), *Viking Treasure from the North West. The Cuerdale Hoard in its Context* (Liverpool), 31–42.

Fellows-Jensen G., 1993, 'Tingwall, Dingwall and Thingwall', *North-Western European Language Evolution*, 21/22, 53–67.

Fellows-Jensen G., 1996, 'Tingwall: the significance of the name', in D.J. Waugh (ed.), *Shetland's Northern Links: Language and History* (Edinburgh), 16–29.

Flanagan M.T., 1976–7, 'Hiberno-Papal Relations in the late twelfth century', *Archivum Hibernicum*, 34, 55–70.

Foote P.G. & Wilson D.M., 1970, *The Viking Achievement* (London).

Foote P.G, 'Jóns saga ens helga', in P. Pulsiano *et al.* (eds), *Medieval Scandinavia: An Encyclopedia* (New York & London), 345.

Fowler K., 1969, *The King's Lieutenant* (London).

Fox A. & Bornholdt Collins K., 2004, 'The 2003 "TT": A Viking-Age Silver Hoard from Glenfaba, Isle of Man', *Viking Heritage Magazine* 1, 3–5.

Fox C. & Dickens B. (eds), 1950, *The Early Christian Cultures of North-West Europe* (H>M> Chadwick Memorial Studies) (Cambridge).

Frame R., 1982, *English Lordship in Ireland, 1318–1361* (Oxford).

Frame, R., 1995, *Political Development of the British Isles 1100–1400* (Oxford & New York).

Fraser C.M., 1957, *A History of Antony Bek Bishop of Durham 1283–1311* (Oxford).

Frazer J., 1922, *The Golden Bough* (London).

Freeman E.A., 1882, *The Reign of William Rufus* (2 vols, revised edn, London).

Freke D., 1995, *The Peel Castle Dig* (Douglas).

Freke D. (ed.), 2002, *Excavations on St. Patrick's Isle, Peel, Isle of Man, 1982–88: Prehistoric, Viking, Medieval and Later* (Liverpool).

Fryde E.B. *et al.*, 1986, *Handbook of British Chronology*, 3rd edn (London).

Garrad L.S., 1964–72, 'Some thoughts on Manx woodland', *Proceedings*, 7, 668.

Gathorne-Hardy G.M., 1956, *A Royal Impostor* (Oslo).

Gelling M., 1970–1 'The place-names of the Isle of Man', *JMM*, 7:86, 130–39, 168–75.

Gelling M., 1978, 'Norse and Gaelic in Medieval Man; the place-name evidence', in T. Andersson & K.Sandred (eds), *The Vikings* (Uppsala), 107–18.

Gelling M., 1991, 'The place-names of the Isle of Man', in S. Ureland & G. Broderick (eds), *Language Contact in the British Isles. Proceedings of the Eighth International Symposium on Language Contact in Europe, Douglas, Isle of Man, 1988* (Tübingen), 141–55.

Gelling P.S., 1952, 'Excavation of a promontory fort at Port Grenaugh, Santon', *Proceedings*, 5, 307–15.

Gelling P.S., 1959, 'Excavation of a promontory fort at Cass ny Hawin, Malew, Isle of Man', *Proceedings*, 6, 28–38.

Gelling P.S., 1957, 'Excavation of a promontory fort at Scarlett, Castletown, Isle of Man', *Proceedings*, 5, 571–75.

Gelling P.S., 1963, 'Medieval Shielings in the Isle of Man', *Medieval Archaeology* 6–7, 156–72.

Gelling P.S., 1964, 'The Braaid site: a re-excavation of one of the structures', *JMM*, 6:80, 201–05.

Gemill E. & Mayhew N.J., 1995, *Changing Values in Medieval Scotland: a study of prices, money, and weights and measures* (Cambridge).

Gerould, G. H., 1914, 'The legend of St Christina, by William Paris', *Modern Language Notes*, 29, 129–33.

Gimpel J., 1976, *The Medieval Machine* (London).

Given-Wilson C., 1986, *The Royal Household and the King's Affinity: Service, Politics and Finance in England 1360–1413* (London).

Goodman A. & Gillespie J. (eds), 1999, *Richard II: The Art of Kingship*, (Oxford).

Göller E., 1907–11, *Die päpstliche Pönitentiare von ihrem Ursprung bis zu ihrer Umgestaltung unter Pius V* (Rome)._

Graham-Campbell J., 1975–6, 'The Viking-age silver and gold hoards of Scandinavian character from Scotland', *PSAS*, 107, 114–35.

Graham-Campbell J., 1976, 'The Viking-Age silver hoards of Ireland', in B. Almquist & D. Greene (eds), *Proceedings of the Seventh Viking Congress, Dublin 15–21 August 1973* (Dublin), 39–74.

Graham-Campbell J., 1987, 'From Scandinavia to the Irish Sea: Viking art reviewed', in M. Ryan, (ed.), *Ireland and Insular Art, A.D.500–1200* (Dublin), 144–53.

Graham-Campbell J., 1995, 'The Irish Sea Vikings: Raiders and Settlers', in T. Scott and P. Starkey (eds), *The Middle Ages in the North-West* (Oxford, 1995), 59–83.

Graham-Campbell J., 1995, *The Viking-Age Gold and Silver of Scotland (AD 850–1100)* (Edinburgh).

Graham-Campbell J. (ed.), 1992, *Viking Treasure from the North West. The Cuerdale Hoard in its Context* (Liverpool).

Grandsen A., 1974, *Historical Writing in England c. 550 to c. 1307* (London).

Grant A., 1992, 'The Otterburn war from the Scottish point of view', in A. Goodman & A. Tuck (eds), *War and Border Societies in the Middle Ages* (London), 30–64.

Grant A., 2000, 'The Province of Ross and the Kingdom of Alba, in E.J. Cowan and R.A. McDonald (eds), *Alba: Celtic Scotland in the Middle Ages* (East Linton).

Guilloreau L., 1909, 'Les fondations anglaises de l'abbaye de Savigny', *Revue Mabillon*, 5, 290–335.

Gwynn E. (ed.), 1913, *Poems from the Dindshenchas* (Dublin).

Hadley D. & Richards J. (eds), 2000, *Cultures in Contact. Scandinavian Settlement in England in the Ninth and Tenth Centuries* (Turnhout).

Halldórsson Ó., 1978, *Greenland in the Middle Ages* (in Swedish) (Reykjavik).

Halliwell-Phillips J.O. (ed.), 1850, *Palatine Anthology: A Collection of Poems and Ancient Ballads Relating to Lancashire and Cheshire* (London).

Hamilton J.S., 1988, *Piers Gaveston, Earl of Cornwall, 1307–1312* (Wayne State University).

Haren, M. & de Pontfarcy, Y. (eds), 1988, *The Medieval Pilgrimage to St Patrick's Purgatory, Lough Derg and the European Tradition* (Enniskillen).

Harrison W., 1879, *An account of the Diocese of Sodor and Man and St German's cathedral also a record of the bishops of Sodor and Man and a tabular statement of the rectors, vicars and chaplains in the seventeen prishes in said diocese with the date of their appointment and cause of vacancy*, Manx Society, 29 (Douglas).

Harrison W. (ed.), 1865, *A description of the Isle of Man: with some useful and entertaining reflections on the laws, customs, and manners of the inhabitants, by George Waldron, Gent., late of Queen's College, Oxon. Printed for the widow and orphans, MDCCXXX1*, Manx Society, 11 (Douglas).

Harrison W. (ed.), 1876–7, *A History of the Isle of Man written by William Blundell, Esq of Crosby, County Lancaster 1648–1656*, Manx Society, 25 & 27, (Douglas).

Harvey P.D.A., 1991, *Medieval Maps* (London).

Hatz G., 1974, *Handel und Verkehr zwischen dem Deutschen Reich und Schweden in der späten Wikingerzeit* (Lund).

Hayes L. & Jones D., 1990, 'Policy on the run: Henry II and Irish Sea diplomacy', *Journal of British Studies*, 29.

Hedeager L., 1994, 'Warrior economy and trading economy in Viking-Age Scandinavia', *The Journal of European Archaeology*, 2:1, 130–47.

Helle K. (ed.), 2003, *Cambridge History of Scandinavia 1. Prehistory to 1520* (Cambridge).

Henderson G., 1910, *The Norse Influence on Celtic Scotland* (Glasgow).

Herbert M., 1988, *Iona, Kells and Derry. The History and Hagiography of the Monastic Familia of Columba* (Oxford).

Higden R., 1865–86, *Polychronicon*, C. Babington & J.R.Lumby (eds), 9 vols, *Rolls Series*, 41 (London).

Hill B.D., 1968, *English Cistercian monasteries and their patrons in the twelfth century* (Chicago).

Holmes G., 1957, *Estates of the Higher Nobility in Fourteenth-Century England* (Cambridge).

Hudson B.T., 1979, 'The family of Harold Godwinson and the Irish Sea province', *Journal of the Royal Society of Antiquaries of Ireland*, 109, 92–100.

Hudson B.T., 1991, 'The destruction of Gruffydd ap Cynan', *Welsh History Review*, 15, 331–50.

Hudson B.T., 1991, 'The Viking and the Irishman', *Medium Ævum*, 60, 257–67.

Hudson B.T., 1994, *Kings of Celtic Scotland* (Westport & London).

Hudson B.T., 1994, 'Knútr and Viking Dublin', *Scandinavian Studies*, 66, 319–35.

Hudson B.T., 1994, 'William the Conqueror and Ireland', *Irish Historical Studies*, 29, 145–58.

Jackson K.H., 1951, 'Common Gaelic: the evolution of the Goedelic languages', *Proceedings of the British Academy*, 37, 71–97.

Jackson K.H., 1953, *Language and History in Early Britain* (Edinburgh).
Jackson K.H., 1972, *The Gaelic Notes in the Book of Deer* (Dublin).
Johnsen A.O., 1945, *Studier vedrørende Kardinal Nicolaus Brekespears legasjon til Norden* (Oslo).
Johnsen A.O., 1967, *On the Background for the Establishment of the Norwegian Church Province. Some new Viewpoints* (Oslo).
Johnsen A.O., 1969, 'The Payments from the Hebrides and the Isle of Man to the Crown of Norway 1153–1263. Annual ferme or feudal casualty?' *SHR*, 48, 18–34.
Johnson A.C.C., 1997, 'Archaeological sites and fossil landscapes in the Isle of Man', *Proceedings of the Isle of Man Hill-Land Seminar*, (Douglas) 53–55.
Johnson A.C.C., 1998, 'The Early Exploitation of the Upper Sulby Valley: a Field Survey', *Proceedings*, 10, 327–45.
Johnson A.C.C., 2000, 'A View from the Hills: Some Thoughts on the Reoccupation of the Promontory Forts and the Possible Origins of the Manx Homestead', *Proceedings*, 11:1, 51–66.
Johnson A.C.C., forthcoming, 'An Archaeological Investigation at Lag ny Keeilley'.
Johnson N.C., forthcoming, 'Rescue excavations at the IRIS site, Peel, 2000', in P.J. Davey (ed.) *Archaeological Research in the Isle of Man 1998–2000*, BAR, British Series.
Johnstone J., 1786, *Antiquitates Celto-normannicµ* (Copenhagen).
Jones G., 1991, 'Medieval settlement', in J. Manley, S. Grenter & F. Gale (eds), *The archaeology of Clwyd* (Mold).
Jones G.R.J., 1979, 'Multiple estates and early settlement', in P.H. Sawyer (ed.), *Early Medieval Settlement*, 2nd edn (London).
Jones M.K. & Underwood M.G., 1992, *The King's Mother: Lady Margaret Beaufort, Countess of Richmond and Derby* (Cambridge).
Jordan W.C., 1996, *The Great Famine: Northern Europe in the Early Fourteenth Century* (Princeton).
Kelly M., 2001, *A History of the Black Death in Ireland* (Stroud).
Kelly A., 1933–42, 'Echoes of Manx history in Somerset records', *Proceedings*, 4, 527–33.
Kenney J.F., 1929, *The Sources for the Early History of Ireland: Ecclesiastical, an introduction and guide* (New York; repr. Dublin 1997).
Kenny M., 1987, 'The geographical distribution of Irish Viking-Age hoards', *Proceedings of the Royal Irish Academy*, 87 C, 507–25.
Kermode P.M.C., 1907, *Manx Crosses* (London; reprinted Balgavies 1994).
Kermode P.M.C., 1910, 'S. Trinian's', *Proceedings*, 1, 332.
Kermode P.M.C. & Herdman W.A., 1914, *Manx Antiquities* (Liverpool).
Kinvig R.H., 1975, *The Isle of Man* (Liverpool).
Kneen J.J., 1925–8, *The Place-Names of the Isle of Man with their Origin and History*, 6 vols (Douglas; repr 1970 in one vol.).
Kneen J.J., 1927–32, 'Manx fairs and festivals', *Proceedings*, 3, 38–82.
Kneen J.J., 1936, 'Manx personal names and their romance', *Proceedings*, 4, 77–83.
Kruse S.E., 1988, 'Ingots and weight units in Viking Age silver hoards', *World Archaeology*, 20:2, 285–301.
Kunin D. & Phelpstead C. (eds), 2001, *A History of Norway*, Viking Society for

Northern Research Text Series XIII (London).
Langham A.F., 1994, *The Island of Lundy* (Stroud).
Lawson M.K., 1993, *Cnut* (London).
Legge M.D., 1948–9, 'Some Notes on the Roman de Fergus', *Transactions and Journal of Proceedings of the Dumfries and Galloway Natural History and Antiquarian Society*, 3:27, 163–71.
Lekai L.J., 1977, *The Cistercians, Ideals and Reality* (Kent, Ohio).
Lewis E.A., 1903, 'The development of industry and commerce in Wales during the Middle Ages', *Transactions of the Royal Historical Society*, new series, 17, 121–73.
Lewis E.A. (ed.), 1913, 'A contribution to the commercial history of medieval Wales', *Y Cymmrodor*, 24, 86–188.
Lewis J., 1982, *Sefton rural fringes survey* (Liverpool).
Lewis J.M. (ed.), 1992, *Peel Town: an archaeological and architectural assessment* (Douglas).
Lindsay J., 1839, *A View of the Coinage of Ireland* (Cork).
Lloyd T.H., 1977, *The English Wool Trade in the Middle Ages* (Cambridge).
Loomie A.J., 1963, 'An Armada pilot's survey of the English coastline, October 1597', *Mariner's Mirror*, 49, 288–300.
Lunt W.E., 1962, *Financial Relations of the Papacy with England 1327–1534* (Cambridge, Mass.).
Lustig R.I., 1979, 'The Treaty of Perth: a re-examination', *SHR*, 58, 35–52.
Lyons M.C., 1989, 'Weather, famine, pestilence and plague in Ireland, 900–1500', in E.M. Crawford (ed.), *Famine-The Irish Experience* (Edinburgh), 44–46.
MacCana P., 1980, *The Learned Tales of Medieval Ireland* (Dublin).
Macdonald C., 1950, *History of Argyll* (Glasgow).
Macdougall N., 1982, *James III: A Political Study* (Edinburgh).
Macgregor L.J. & Crawford B.E. (eds), 1987, *Ouncelands and Pennylands* (St Andrews).
Macinnes A.I., 1982, 'Scotland and the Manx connection: relationships of intermittent violence, 1266–1603', *Proceedings*, 8: 4, 362–77.
MacInnes J., 1972–4, 'West Highland sea power in the Middle Ages', *Transactions of the Gaelic Society of Inverness*, 48, 518–56.
MacInnes J., 1990–2, 'Clan sagas and historical legends', *Transactions of the Gaelic Society of Inverness*, 57, 377–94.
MacKay J.A., 1978, *The Pobjoy Encyclopaedia of Isle of Man Coins and Tokens*, 2nd edn (Sutton).
MacQuarrie, C., 2004, *The Biography of the Irish God of the Sea from the Voyage of Bran (700 AD) to Finnegan's Wake (1939): The Waves of Manannan* (Lewiston, New York).
MacQuarrie C, 2011,.'Recognizing Gods in Guises: Identity, Performance, and Performative Reading in O'Donnell's Kern', *Celtic Studies Association of North America Yearbook* 8–9, 147–56.
MacNeill E., 1916, 'Chapters of Hebridean history I: The Norse kingdom of the Hebrides', *The Scottish Review*, 39, 254–76.
Marcus G.J., 1956–7, 'Norse trade with Iceland', *Economic History Review*, 2:9, 408.
Marstrander C.J.S., 1932, 'Det Norske landnåm på Man', *Norsk Tidsskrift for*

Sprogvidenskap, 6, 40–386.
Marstrander C.J.S., 1934, 'Remarks on the place-names of the Isle of Man', *Norsk Tidsskrift for Sprogvidenskap*, 7, 287–334.
Marstrander C.J.S., 1937, 'Treen og Keeill', *Norsk Tidsskrift for Sprogvidenskap*, 8, 287–442.
Martin E. (ed.), 1872, *Fergus* (Halle).
Marstrander C.J. S., 1938, 'Om Tingsteder på Man', *Norsk Tidsskrift for Sprogvidenskap*, 10, 384–93.
Marwick H., 1934–5, 'Leidang in the West', *Proceedings of the Orkney Antiquarian Society*, 13, 15–29.
Marwick H., 1949, 'Naval defence in Norse Scotland', *SHR*, 28, 1–11.
McCance R.A. & Widdowson E.M., 1960, *The Composition of Foods* (London).
McCaughran M. & Appleby J. (eds), 1989, *The Irish Sea* (Belfast).
McCone K., 1990, *Pagan Past and Christian Present* (Maynooth).
McDiarmid M.P., 1971–2, 'Sir David Lindsay's Report of the Sack of Carrickfergus 1513', *Studies in Scottish Literature*, 9, 40–47.
McDonald A., 1995, 'Images of Hebridean lordship in the twelfth and thirteenth centuries: the seal of Raonall Mac Sorley', *SHR*, 74, 129–43.
McDonald R.A., 1995, 'Matrimonial politics and core-periphery interactions in twelfth- and early thirteenth-century Scotland', *Journal of Medieval History*, 21, 227–47.
McDonald R.A., 1997, *The Kingdom of the Isles: Scotland's Western Seaboard c. 1100–c.1336* (East Linton).
McDonald R.A., 1999, '"Treachery in the remotest territories of Scotland": northern resistance to the Canmore dynasty, 1130–1230', *Canadian Journal of History*, 33, 161–92.
McDonald R.A., 2003, *Outlaws of Medieval Scotland: Challenges to the Canmore Kings, 1058–1266* (East Linton).
McGladdery C., 1990, *James II* (Edinburgh).
McNamee C., 1997, *The Wars of the Bruces: Scotland, England and Ireland 1306–1328* (East Linton).
McUntire W.T., 1941, 'A Note on Grey Abbey and other religious foundations on Strangford Lough affiliated to the abbeys of Cumberland', *Cumberland and Westmoreland Antiquarian and Archaeological Society*, new ser, 41, 171–84.
Megaw B.R.S., 1957, 'The Scottish invasion of Man in 1456', *JMM*, 6:74, 23–24.
Megaw B.R.S., 1939, 'The barony of Bangor and Sabal in Kirk Patrick: remarkable survival of the Middle Ages', *JMM*, 4:60, 135–138, 135 and, 'The barony of Bangor and Sabal in Kirk Patrick: an account of its origin', *JMM*, 4:61, 159–60.
Megaw B.R.S., 1938–40, 'The Barony of Saint Trinian in Kirk Marown: a memorial to St Ninian of Galloway', *JMM*, 4:62, 175–7.
Megaw B.R.S., 1950, 'The Barony of St Trinian's in the Isle of Man', *Transactions of the Dumfriesshire and Galloway Natural History and Antiquarian Society*, 3rd ser, 27, 173–82.
Megaw B.R.S., 1959, 'The ship seals of the Isle of Man', *JMM*, 6:76, 76–80.
Megaw B., 1976, 'Norseman and Native in the Kingdom of the Isles', *Scottish Studies*, 20, 19–20.

Megaw B., 1976, 'Norseman and Native in the Kingdom of the Isles. A Re-assessment of the Manx evidence', in Davey (ed.), *Man and Environment*, 265–314.
Megaw E M, 1976, 'The cult of St Leonard and Manx medieval hospitals', *Journal of the Manx Museum*, 7:88, 225–31.
Mercier V., 1962, *The Irish Comic Tradition* (Oxford).
Metcalf D.M., 1977, 'A survey of numismatic research into the pennies of the first three Edwards', in N.J. Mayhew (ed.), *Edwardian Monetary Affairs (1279–1344)*, BAR 36 (Oxford), 1–31.
Metcalf D.M., 1986, 'Interpreting the alloy of the later Anglo-Saxon coinage', *British Numismatic Journal*, 56, 35–63, at p. 36.
Metcalf D.M., 1998, *An Atlas of Anglo-Saxon and Norman Coin Finds, c. 973–1086* (London).
Michell F., 1986, *Reading the Irish landscape* (Dublin).
Michell F. & Ryan M., 1997, *Reading the Irish landscape* (Dublin).
Monro J.H., 1978, 'Wool price schedules and the qualities of English wools in the later Middle Ages, *c*.1270–1499', *Textile History*, 9, 121, 160.
Moore A.W., 1891, *Folklore of the Isle of Man* (London).
Moore A.W., 1900, *A History of the Isle of Man* (London).
Moore A.W., 1906, 'The connexion between Scotland and Man', *SHR*, 3, 393–409.
Mossop H.R., 1970, *The Lincoln Mint c. 890–1279* (Newcastle upon Tyne).
Newman R., 1996, *The archaeology of Lancashire*, (Lancaster).
Nicholson R., 1965, *Edward III and the Scots* (Oxford).
Nicolaisen W.F.H., 1976, *Scottish Place-Names* (London).
Ó Cathasaigh T., 1977, *The Heroic Biography of Cormac mac Airt* (Dublin).
Ó Corráin D., 1971–3, 'The career of Diarmait mac Máel na mBó, king of Leinster', *Journal of the Old Wexford Society*, 3, 27–35; 4, 17–24.
Ó Corráin D., 1972, *Ireland before the Normans* (Dublin).
Ó Corráin D. & Maguire F., 1984, *Gaelic Personal Names* (Dublin).
Ó Cróinín D., 1995, *Early Medieval Ireland 400–1200* (London).
O'Grady S.H., 1892, *Silva Gadelica: A Collection of Tales in Irish, with Extracts Illustrating Persons and Places* (London).
Ó hÓgain D., 1991, *Myth, Legend and Romance: An Encyclopædia of the Irish Folk Tradition* (New York).
O'Neil B.H. StJ., 1946, *Castle Rushen, Isle of Man, an archaeological report for the Manx Government*, unpublished typescript (Douglas).
O'Neil B.H. StJ., 1951, 'Castle Rushen, Isle of Man', *Archaeologia*, 94, 1–26.
O'Rahilly T.F., 1932, *Irish Dialects Past and Present* (Dublin).
O'Rahilly T.F., 1950, '*Do-ním, déanaim*, "I proceed, go"',*Celtica*, 1, part 2, 318–21.
O'Rahilly T.F., 1976, *Early Irish History and Mythology* (Dublin).
Oram R., 2000, *The Lordship of Galloway* (Edinburgh).
Otway-Ruthven A.J., 1968, *A History of Medieval Ireland* (London).
Padel O.J., 1985, *Cornish Place-Name Elements*, English Place-Name Society, 56/57.
Page, R.I., 1983, 'The Manx Rune-stones', in Fell *et al.* (eds), *The Viking Age in the Isle of Man* (London 1983), 133–46.
Palmer J.J.N., 1972, *England, France and Christendom 1377–99* (London).
de Pange J., 1937, *Comment se fait un roi* (Paris).

Parker G., 2002, 'The Place of Tudor England in the Messianic Vision of Philip II', *Transactions of the Royal Historical Society*, 6:12, 167–221.

Parker Pearson M. *et al.*, 2004, *South Uist - Archaeology & History of a Hebridean Island* (Stroud).

Parry M.L., 1978, *Climatic Change, Agriculture and Settlement* (Folkestone).

Paul J. (ed.), 1904–14, *The Scots Peerage*, 9 vols (Edinburgh).

Phillips J.R.S., 1972, *Aymer de Valence, Earl of Pembroke 1307–24* (Oxford).

Platt C., 1995, *The Abbeys and Priories of Medieval England*, 2nd edn (London).

Poole R.L., 1911, 'The Scottish islands in the diocese of Sodor', *SHR*, 7, 258–63.

Power R., 1985, 'Magnus Barelegs' expeditions to the West', *SHR*, 65, 107–32.

Power R., 1994, 'The death of Magnus Barelegs', *SHR*, 73, 216–22.

Power R., 2000, 'Cursing the king: an Irish conversation in *Jóns saga helga*', *Saga-Book*, 25, 310–13.

Prestwich M., 1988, *Edward I* (London).

Price L., 1963, 'A note on the use of the word *Baile* in place-names', *Celtica*, 6, 119–26.

Quine G., 1990, *A Reconsideration of the Evidence of the Shieling in the Kingdom of Man and the Isles, with particular Reference to Man* (PhD thesis, University of Durham).

Quine J., 1899–1902, 'Rushen abbey', *Yn Lioar Manninagh*, III, 405.

Radcliffe W. & C., 1978, *Maughold and Ramsey Place-Names* (Ramsey).

Radcliffe W. & C., 1983, *Kirk Bride – a Miscellany* (Ramsey).

Ralegh Radford C.A., 2004, 'St Patrick's Isle, Peel: The Medieval Ecclesiastical Remains and Excavations of 1962', *Proceedings*, 11, 361–92.

Rawcliffe C., 2004, 'Stapleton, Sir Brian (*c*.1322–1394)', *Oxford Dictionary of National Biography* (Oxford).

Rees A. & B., 1961, *Celtic Heritage* (London).

Reid N., 1990, *Scotland in the Reign of Alexander III 1249–1286* (Edinburgh).

Reilley P., 1988, *Computer analysis of an Archaeological Landscape: Medieval Land Divisions in the Isle of Man*, BAR, British Series 190.

Reynolds S., 1977, *An Introduction to the History of English Medieval Towns* (Oxford).

Reynolds S., 1984, *Kingdoms and Communities in Western Europe 900–1300* (Oxford).

Rigby A., 1927, *Castle Rushen, a historical and descriptive account* (Douglas).

Rigold S.E., 1977, 'Small change in the light of medieval site-finds', in Mayhew N.J. (ed.), *Edwardian Monetary Affairs*, 59–80.

Ritchie R.L.G., 1954, *The Normans in Scotland* (Edinburgh).

Rivet A.L.F. & Smith C., 1979, *The Place-Names of Roman Britain* (London).

Rixson D., 1998, *The West Highland Galley* (Edinburgh).

Robinson V. & McCarroll D. (eds), 1990, *The Isle of Man: a Sense of Place* (Liverpool).

Rona G., 1956, *Kulturhistorisk Leksikon for Nordisk Middelalder* (Copenhagen 1956).

Roth B., 1909, 'The coins of the Danish kings of Ireland; Hiberno-Danish Series', *British Numismatic Journal* 6, 55–146.

Saul N.E, 1995, 'Richard II and the vocabulary of kingship', *EHR*, 90, 854–77.

Saul N., 1997, *Richard II* (London).

Sawyer B. & P., 1993, *Medieval Scandinavia: from Conversion to Reformation, c.800–1500* (London).

Sawyer P., (ed.), 1997, *The Oxford Illustrated History of the Vikings* (Oxford).

Sayles G.O., 1956–7, 'The siege of Carrickfergus Castle, 1315–16', *Irish Historical Studies*, 10, 94–100.

Sellar W.D.H., 1965, 'The origins and ancestry of Somerled', *SHR*, 45, 1–142.

Sellar W.D.H., 1971, 'Family Origins in Cowal and Knapdale', *Scottish Studies*, 15, 21–27.

Sellar W.D.H., 2000, 'Hebridean sea kings: the successors of Somerled, 1164–1316', in *Alba: Celtic Scotland in the Medieval Era*, (East Linton), 187–218.

Serjeant W.R., 1960–61, 'The Isle of Man and the Anglo-Scottish War, 1296–1328', *JMM*, 6:77, 126–28.

Simms K., 1987, *From Kings to Warlords. The Changing Political Structure of Gaelic Ireland in the Later Middle Ages* (Woodbridge).

Simms K., 1989, 'The Norman invasion and the Gaelic recovery', in R.F. Foster (ed.), *Oxford Illustrated History of Ireland* (Oxford).

Simpson G.G. (ed.), 1990, *Scotland and Scandinavia 800–1800* (Edinburgh).

Sims-Williams, P., 2011, Irish Influence on Medieval Welsh Literature (Oxford).

Skene W.F., 1886–90, *Celtic Scotland* (2nd ed., Edinburgh).

Skúlason S., 1938, 'Hafnarfjörður: Ein Beitrag zur Geschichte des Islandhandels', *Hansische Geschichtsblätter*, 63, 170–226.

Smit H.J. (ed.), *Bronnen tot de Geschiedenis van den Handel met Engeland, Schotland en Ierland, 1150–1485* (s'Gravenhage).

Smout C., 1960, 'The Foreign Trade of Dumfries and Kirkcudbright, 1672–1696', *Transactions of the Dumfriesshire and Galloway Natural History and Antiquarian Society*, 3:36, 36–47.

Smyth A.P., 1975–9, *Scandinavian York and Dublin: the History and Archaeology of Two Related Viking Kingdoms* (Dublin).

Spaan D., 1965, 'The place of Manannán mac Lir in Irish mythology', *Folklore*, 76, 177.

Spurgeon J., 1991, 'Mottes and moated sites', in J. Manley, S. Grenter & F. Gale (eds), *The archaeology of Clwyd* (Mold), 157–72.

Stacey R., 1993, *Road to Judgment: From Custom to Court in Medieval Ireland and Wales* (Pennsylvania).

Stalley R., 1987, *The Cistercian monasteries of Ireland* (London and New Haven).

Steer K. & Bannerman J., 1977, *Late Medieval Monumental Sculpture in the West Highlands* (Edinburgh).

Steinnes A., 1927, *Leidang og Landskyld*, Skrifter utgitt av Det Norske Videnskaps-Akademi i Oslo, 9 (Oslo).

Steinnes A., 1959, 'The "Huseby" System in Orkney', *SHR*, 38, 36–46.

Stell G., 1996, *Dumfries and Galloway* (Edinburgh).

Stenning E.H., 1935–37, 'Ancient structures uncovered at Derbyhaven May 1935', *Proceedings*, 4, 145–51.

Stevenson A., 1988, 'Trade with the south, 1070–1513', in M. Lynch, M. Spearman & G. Stell (eds), *The Scottish Medieval Town* (Edinburgh), 183–86.

Stewart I., 1964, 'An eighteenth-century Manx find of early Scottish sterlings', *The British Numismatic Journal*, 33, 48–56.

Stringer K.J., 1993, 'Periphery and Core in Thirteenth-Century Scotland: Alan son of Roland, Lord of Galloway and Constable of Scotland', in A. Grant & K.J. Stringer (eds), *Medieval Scotland: Crown, Lordship and Community. Essays Presented to G.W.S. Barrow* (Edinburgh), 82–112.

Stringer K.J., 1993, *The Reign of Stephen. Kingship, Warfare and Government in Twelfth-Century England*, Lancaster Pamphlets (London & New York).

Stringer K.J., 2000, 'Acts of lordship: the records of the lords of Galloway to 1234', in T. Brotherstone & D. Ditchburn (eds), *Freedom and Authority, Scotland c.1050–c.1650: Historical and Historiographical Essays presented to Grant G. Simpson*, (East Linton), 203–34.

Stringer K.J., 2003, *The reformed church in medieval Galloway and Cumbria: contrasts, connections and continuities. The Eleventh Whithorn lecture 14 September 2002* (Whithorn).

Stringer K.J. (ed.), 1985, *Essays on the Nobility of Medieval Scotland* (Edinburgh).

Sylvester D., 1958, *The historical atlas of Cheshire*, Cheshire Community Council, Chester.

Talbot T., c1890, *The Priory of Whithern (Candida Casa), and its lands and churches in Mann*, privately published (MML F22/17).

Taylor A.G., 1930, 'The monastic orders of Rushen abbey (Savignac and Cistercian)', *Proceedings*, 3, 250–57.

Taylor J., 1966, *The 'Universal chronicle' of Ranulph Higden* (Oxford).

Thirsk J. (ed.), 1967, *The Agrarian History of England and Wales* (Cambridge).

Thompson J.D.A., 1956, *Inventory of British Coin Hoards A.D.600–1500*, Royal Numismatic Society.

Thompson S., 1984, 'Why English nunneries had no history: a study of the problem of English nunneries founded after the conquest', in J.A. Nichols & L.T. Shank (eds), *Medieval religious women 1, Distant echoes*, Cistercian Publications (Kalamazoo), 131–49.

Thomson R.L., 1960–3, 'The Manx Traditionary Ballad', *Études Celtiques*, 9, 521–48; 10, 60–87.

Thomson, R.L., 1978, 'The interpretation of some Manx place-names', in Davey (ed.), *Man and Environment*, 319–25.

Thomson W.P.L., 2001, *The New History of Orkney* (Edinburgh).

Thomson W.P., 2002, 'Ouncelands and Pennylands in the West Highlands and Islands', *Northern Scotland*, 22, 27–43.

Thornton T., 1998, 'Scotland and the Isle of Man, *c.* 1400–1625: noble power and royal presumption in the northern Irish Sea province', *SHR*, 77, 1–30.

Thornton T., 1999, 'The Alleged French Raid on the Isle of Man, 1377', *Northern History*, 35, 208–13.

Thrupp S.L., 1957, 'A survey of the alien population of England in 1440', *Speculum*, 32, 270–72.

Thurneysen R., 1946, *A Grammar of Old Irish* (Dublin).

Todd J.H. (ed.), 1867, *Cogadh Gaedhel re Gallaibh*, *Rolls Series*, 48, (London).

Toll H., 1927, 'Konung Magnus Barfots välske riddare', *Norsk Historisk Tidsskrift*, 6:5, 174–81.

Tomlinson P.R. & Warhurst M. (eds), 1991, *The Archaeology of Merseyside (Journal*

of the Merseyside Archaeological Society), 7.
Tout T.F., 1923–35, *Chapters in the Administrative History of Medieval England*, 6 vols (Manchester).
Turner R.V., 1994, *King John* (London & New York).
Wagner H., 1981, 'Origins of pagan Irish religion', *Zeitshchrift für Celtische Philologie*, 38, 1–28.
Wait G.A., 1985, *Ritual and Religion in Iron Age Britain* (Oxford).
Walker K., 2000, 'The Widowhood of Alice Spencer, Countess Dowager of Derby, 1594–1636', *Transactions of the Historic Society of Lancashire and Cheshire*, 149, 1–17.
Warner R., 1975–6, 'Scottish silver arm-rings: an analysis of weights', *PSAS*, 107, 136–43.
Watson W.J., 1926, *The History of the Celtic Place-Names of Scotland* (Edinburgh).
Watt D.E.R., 1994, 'Bishops in the Isles before 1203: bibliography and biographical lists', *Innes Review*, 45, 99–119.
Webster G., Dolley R.H.M. & Dunning G.C., 1953, 'A Saxon treasure hoard found at Chester', *Antiquaries Journal*, 33, 26–29.
Webster B., 1975, *Scotland from the Eleventh Century to 1603* (New York).
White R.H. (ed.), 1986, *Peel Castle Excavation. Final Report I: The Half Moon Battery* (Peel).
Whitehead, F., Diverres A.H. & Sutcliffe, F.E. (eds), 1965, *Medieval Miscellany presented to Eugène Vinaver by Pupils, Colleagues and Friends*, (Manchester).
Williams D.G.E., 1996, *Land Assessment and Military Organisation in the Norse Settlements of Scotland, c. 900–1266 AD* (Ph.D. thesis, University of St Andrews).
Williams D.H., 1969, *The Welsh Cistercians* (Pontypool).
Wilson D.M., 1970–73, 'Manx memorial stones of the Viking period', *Saga-book*, 18, 2–7.
Wilson D.M., 1974, *The Viking Age in the Isle of Man: The Archaeological Evidence*, C.C. Rafn Lecture 3 (Odense).
Wilson D.M. (ed.), 1976, *The Archaeology of Anglo-Saxon England* (Cambridge).
Williams J.M., 1979, *The Stanley Family of Lathom and Knowsley, c. 1450–1504: A Political Study*, (MA thesis, University of Manchester).
Williams M. & de Rothschild J.A. (eds), 1925, *A Miscellany of Studies in Romance Languages and Literatures presented to Leon E.Kastner* (Cambridge).
Williams R., 1984, *The Lords of the Isles: The Clan Donald and the Early Kingdom of the Scots* (London).
Woods J., 1867, *A new atlas & gazetteer of the Isle of Man, consisting of seventeen highly-finished maps, compiled from original and authentic sources, describing the civil and ecclesiastical boundaries of each parish, and the boundaries of the several baronies, freeholds, and quarterlands, as well as the boundaries of the several farms as they are now held in possession* (London).
Woolf A., 2003, 'The Diocese of the Sudreyar', in S.Imsen, (ed.), *Ecclesia Nidrosiensis 1153–1537. Søkelys på Nidaroskirkens og Nidarosprovinsens historie*. Senter for Middelalderstudier. NTNU Skrifter nr.15 (Trondheim), 171–82.
Wright M.D., 1984, 'Excavation at Peel Castle, 1947', *Proceedings*, 11, 21–57.
Youd G., 1962, 'The common fields of Lancashire', *Transactions of the Historical*

Society of Lancashire and Cheshire, 113, 1–41.
Young G.V.C., 1980, *The History of the Isle of Man under the Norse* (Peel).

Index

Compiled by JOSHUA COPELAND

Printed and bound by CPI Group (UK) Ltd, Croydon, CR0 4YY

16/09/2026

14963468-0001